THE HEBREW BIBLE—
A SOCIO-LITERARY
INTRODUCTION

WITHDRAWN

NORMAN K. GOTTWALD

FORTRESS PRESS
PHILADELPHIA

The art on the cover and title pages is reproduced by Courtesy of the Trustees of the British Museum (124909; slab VI of XII slabs of the Conquest of Lachish by Sennacherib: an Assyrian taking Jews into exile).

Figure 1 (p. 476) originally appeared in S. H. Hooke, *In the Beginning,* Clarendon Bible, vol. 6 (London: Oxford University Press, 1947).

Library of Congress Cataloging in Publication Data

Gottwald, Norman K. (Norman Karol), 1926–
  The Hebrew Bible—a socio-literary introduction.

  Bibliography: p.
  Includes index.
  1. Bible. O.T.—Introductions. 2. Bible. O.T.—
History of Biblical events. 3. Jews—History—To 70 A.D.
I. Title.
BS1140.2.G59 1985   221.6   84–48719
ISBN 0–8006–0853–4
ISBN 0–8006–1853–X (pbk.)

1268I84   Printed in the United States of America   1–853

To all those in whose company I have learned
what I know of the Hebrew Bible

---

family and friends,
students and colleagues,
scholars and amateurs,
believers and doubters,
activists and quietists.

Contents

Contents

PART II

INTERTRIBAL CONFEDERACY: ISRAEL'S
REVOLUTIONARY BEGINNINGS

Contents

PART III
MONARCHY: ISRAEL'S COUNTERREVOLUTIONARY ESTABLISHMENT

Contents

PART IV
HOME RULE UNDER GREAT EMPIRES:
ISRAEL'S COLONIAL RECOVERY

Contents

Illustrations

TABLES

CHARTS

FIGURE

Abbreviations

AASOR	Annual of the American Schools of Oriental Research
AB	The Anchor Bible
AbrN	*Abr Nahrain*
AJSL	*American Journal of Semitic Languages and Literatures*
AKE	Norman K. Gottwald. *All the Kingdoms of the Earth: Israelite Prophecy and International Relations in the Ancient Near East.* New York: Harper & Row, 1964.
ALI	Yohanan Aharoni. *The Archaeology of the Land of Israel from the Beginnings to the End of the First Temple Period,* ed. Miriam Aharoni. Trans. A. F. Rainey. Philadelphia: Westminster Press, 1982.
AMB	The Amplified Bible
AnBib	Analecta Biblica
ANET	James B. Pritchard, ed. *Ancient Near Eastern Texts Relating to the Old Testament.* 3d ed. Princeton, N.J.: Princeton University Press, 1969.
APOT	R. H. Charles, ed. *The Apocrypha and Pseudepigrapha of the Old Testament in English.* 2 vols. Oxford: At the Clarendon Press, 1913.
ASTI	*Annual of the Swedish Theological Institute*
ASV	American Standard Version
ATANT	Abhandlungen zur Theologie des Alten und Neuen Testaments
AV	Authorized Version (= King James Version)
BA	*Biblical Archaeologist*

BAR	*Biblical Archaeologist Reader*
BARev	*Biblical Archaeology Review*
BASOR	*Bulletin of the American Schools of Oriental Research*
B.C.E.	Before the common era (= B.C.)
BHK	*Biblica Hebraica,* ed. R. Kittel.
BHS	*Biblica Hebraica Stuttgartensia,* ed. K. Ellinger and W. Rudolph.
Bib	*Biblica*
BL	Norman K. Gottwald, ed. *The Bible and Liberation: Political and Social Hermeneutics.* Rev. ed. Maryknoll, N.Y.: Orbis Books, 1983.
BSac	*Bibliotheca Sacra*
BTB	*Biblical Theology Bulletin*
BZAW	Beihefte zur *ZAW*
ca.	circa
CBQ	*Catholic Biblical Quarterly*
CBQMS	*CBQ* Monograph Series
C.E.	Of the common era (= A.D.)
CH	The Chronicler's History
CMHE	Frank M. Cross, Jr. *Canaanite Myth and Hebrew Epic.* Cambridge: Harvard University Press, 1973.
CNEB	Cambridge Commentary on the New English Bible
ConBOT	Coniectanea Biblica, Old Testament Series
CQR	*Church Quarterly Review*
CTM	*Concordia Theological Monthly*
CurTM	*Currents in Theology and Mission*
D	Deuteronomy, the Deuteronomic writer(s), or the Deuteronomist
DA	Paul D. Hanson. *The Dawn of Apocalyptic: The Historical and Sociological Roots of Jewish Apocalyptic Eschatology.* 2d ed. Philadelphia: Fortress Press, 1979.
DH	The Deuteronomistic History (Joshua through Kings) or the Deuteronomistic Historian(s)
E	The Elohist
EHI	Roland de Vaux. *The Early History of Israel.* Philadelphia: Westminster Press, 1978.
EJ	*Encyclopaedia Judaica*
EOTHR	Albrecht Alt. *Essays on Old Testament History and Religion.* Garden City, N.Y.: Doubleday & Co., 1968.
ET	*Expository Times*

ExB	The Expositor's Bible
FOTL	Rolf Knierim and Gene M. Tucker, eds. The Forms of the Old Testament Literature. Grand Rapids: Wm. B. Eerdmans, 1981–.
G	The common pool of united tribal traditions that J and E drew upon (from the German *Grundlage*, "foundation")
GBS	Guides to Biblical Scholarship
HeyJ	*Heythrop Journal*
HI	John Bright. *A History of Israel.* 3d ed. Philadelphia: Westminster Press, 1981.
HIOTT	Siegfried Herrmann. *A History of Israel in Old Testament Times.* Rev. ed. Philadelphia: Fortress Press, 1981.
HIR	Georg Fohrer. *History of Israelite Religion.* Nashville: Abingdon Press, 1972.
HPT	Martin Noth. *A History of Pentateuchal Traditions,* with introduction by Bernhard W. Anderson. Englewood Cliffs, N.J.: Prentice-Hall, 1972.
HSM	Harvard Semitic Monographs
HSS	Harvard Semitic Studies
HTR	*Harvard Theological Review*
HTS	Harvard Theological Studies
HUCA	*Hebrew Union College Annual*
IB	*The Interpreter's Bible*
ICC	The International Critical Commentary
IDB	*The Interpreter's Dictionary of the Bible*
IDBSup	*IDB* Supplementary Volume
IEJ	*Israel Exploration Journal*
IJH	John H. Hayes and J. Maxwell Miller, eds. *Israelite and Judaean History.* Philadelphia: Westminster Press, 1977.
Int	*Interpretation*
IOT	Georg Fohrer. *Introduction to the Old Testament.* Nashville and New York: Abingdon Press, 1968. Complete revision of original by Ernst Sellin.
IOTS	Brevard S. Childs. *Introduction to the Old Testament as Scripture.* Philadelphia: Fortress Press, 1979.
IR	Helmer Ringgren. *Israelite Religion.* Philadelphia: Fortress Press, 1966.
ITC	International Theological Commentary
J	The Yahwist
JAAR	*Journal of the American Academy of Religion*

JAARSup	*JAAR* Supplement
JANES	*Journal of the Ancient Near Eastern Society of Columbia University*
JAOS	*Journal of the American Oriental Society*
JB	The Jerusalem Bible
JBC	*The Jerome Biblical Commentary,* ed. R. Brown et al. 2 vols. in 1. Englewood Cliffs, N.J.: Prentice-Hall, 1968.
JBL	*Journal of Biblical Literature*
JBLMS	*JBL* Monograph Series
JCS	*Journal of Cuneiform Studies*
JETS	*Journal of the Evangelical Theological Society*
JJS	*Journal of Jewish Studies*
JLBBM	George W. E. Nickelsburg. *Jewish Literature Between the Bible and the Mishnah: A Historical and Literary Introduction.* Philadelphia: Fortress Press, 1981.
JNES	*Journal of Near Eastern Studies*
JNSL	*Journal of Northwest Semitic Languages*
JQR	*Jewish Quarterly Review*
JR	*Journal of Religion*
JSOT	*Journal for the Study of the Old Testament*
JSOTSup	*JSOT* Supplement Series
JSS	*Journal of Semitic Studies*
JTS	*Journal of Theological Studies*
KJV	King James Version (= Authorized Version)
LB	Yohanan Aharoni. *The Land of the Bible: A Historical Geography,* ed. Anson F. Rainey. Rev. ed. Philadelphia: Westminster Press, 1979.
LBP	The Living Bible Paraphrased
LTQ	*Lexington Theological Quarterly*
LXX	The Septuagint
MBA	Yohanan Aharoni and Michael Avi-Yonah. *The Macmillan Bible Atlas.* Rev. ed. New York: Macmillan Co., 1977.
MLB	The Modern Language Bible
MT	Masoretic Text of the Hebrew Bible
NAB	The New American Bible
NASB	The New American Standard Bible
NCBC	The New Century Bible Commentary
NEB	The New English Bible
NERT	Walter Beyerlin, ed. *Near Eastern Religious Texts Relating to the Old Testament.* Philadelphia: Westminster Press, 1978.

NICOT	The New International Commentary on the Old Testament
NIV	The New International Version
NJPS	The New Jewish Version
NKJV	The New King James Version
OBT	Overtures to Biblical Theology
OTFC	John H. Hayes, ed. *Old Testament Form Criticism.* San Antonio: Trinity University Press, 1974.
OTL	Old Testament Library
OTMS	Harold H. Rowley, ed. *The Old Testament and Modern Study: A Generation of Discovery and Research.* Oxford: At the Clarendon Press, 1951.
OTP	James H. Charlesworth, ed. *The Old Testament Pseudepigrapha, Vol. 1: Apocalyptic Literature and Testaments.* Garden City, N.Y.: Doubleday & Co., 1983.
OTS	*Oudtestamentische Studiën*
OTT	Gerhard von Rad. *Old Testament Theology.* 2 vols. New York: Harper & Row, 1962, 1965.
P	Priestly writing or Priestly writer(s)
PEQ	*Palestine Exploration Quarterly*
PTMS	Pittsburgh Theological Monograph Series
RAI	Theodorus C. Vriezen. *The Religion of Ancient Israel.* Philadelphia: Westminster Press, 1963.
RB	*Revue Biblique*
RevQ	*Revue de Qumran*
RSV	Revised Standard Version
RV	Revised Version
SAIW	James L. Crenshaw, ed. *Studies in Ancient Israelite Wisdom.* New York: Ktav Publishing, 1976.
SBA	Studies in Biblical Archaeology
SBLDS	Society of Biblical Literature Dissertation Series
SBLMS	Society of Biblical Literature Monograph Series
SBLSP	Society of Biblical Literature Seminar Papers
SBT	Studies in Biblical Theology
SC 1	Carl D. Evans, William W. Hallo, and John B. White, eds. *Scripture in Context: Essays on the Comparative Method.* PTMS 34. Pittsburgh: Pickwick Press, 1980.
SC 2	William W. Hallo, James C. Moyer, and Leo G. Purdue, eds. *Scripture in Context II. More Essays in Comparative Method.* Winona Lake, Ind.: Eisenbrauns, 1983.
SEÅ	*Svensk exegetisk årsbok*

SHANE	Studies in the History of the Ancient Near East
SJT	*Scottish Journal of Theology*
ST	*Studia theologica*
StudBT	*Studia Biblica et Theologica*
SWBAS	The Social World of Biblical Antiquity Series
TD	*Theology Digest*
TDH	Martin Noth. *The Deuteronomistic History.* JSOTSup 15. Sheffield: JSOT Press, 1981.
TEV	Today's English Version (Good News Bible)
THI	Martin Noth. *The History of Israel.* Rev. ed. New York: Harper & Brothers, 1960.
TI	George W. Anderson, ed. *Tradition and Interpretation: Essays by Members of the Society for Old Testament Study.* Oxford: At the Clarendon Press, 1979.
TOT	Otto Eissfeldt. *The Old Testament: An Introduction.* New York: Harper & Row, 1965.
TY	Norman K. Gottwald. *The Tribes of Yahweh: A Sociology of the Religion of Liberated Israel, 1250–1050 B.C.E.* Maryknoll, N.Y.: Orbis Books, 1979.
TZ	*Theologische Zeitschrift*
VE	*Vox Evangelica*
VT	*Vetus Testamentum*
VTSup	*VT* Supplements
WC	Westminster Commentaries
WHJP	Benjamin Mazar, ed. *World History of the Jewish People: First Series: Ancient Times.* Jerusalem: Jewish Historical Publications, 1970–.
YBFT	Peter F. Ellis. *The Yahwist. The Bible's First Theologian.* Notre Dame, Ind.: Fides Press, 1968.
ZAW	*Zeitschrift für die alttestamentliche Wissenschaft*

Note: For abbreviations of the Dead Sea Scrolls, see table 7.

Preface

The study of the Hebrew Bible is in ferment and undergoing rapid change. This book attempts to orient the reader to a critical understanding of the Hebrew Bible and to the current state of biblical studies as an intellectual and sociocultural practice. It underlines the expanding range of choices in methods of biblical study now available, a range far wider than at any time in the long history of biblical interpretation.

My approach intends to be in deliberate continuity with older historical-critical scholarship, but it engages with the profound shift and enrichment of biblical studies introduced by the new approaches that have gathered force and momentum only in the last two decades. By "A Socio-Literary Introduction," I wish to identify those literary and social scientific approaches to the Hebrew Bible which, in interaction with older critical methods, appear to be proving decisive for the changing directions of biblical studies.

Within newer literary criticism I take account of its several forms, namely, the Bible as literature, rhetorical and stylistic criticism, and structural analysis. Within social scientific criticism I attend to those aspects of anthropological and sociological method and theory that have been most crucial for biblical studies, and I also indicate their present yield in an enlarging understanding of biblical social organization and social history. Redaction criticism and various types of canonical criticism, which do not fall neatly within major new literary or social science paradigms, are shown also to be important contributors to the current multifaceted excitement of biblical studies.

This volume follows broadly the historical format of my earlier *A Light to the Nations: An Introduction to the Old Testament* (New York: Harper & Row, 1959). It differs from that work, however, not only in the far-reaching changes brought by the literary and social science perspectives, but also in its greater concentration on the exilic and postexilic periods. Neglect of the later biblical era can be seen as a peculiarly Christian, even specifically Protestant, bias uncritically reflected in the work of many non-Jewish biblical scholars. The increasingly ecumenical character of biblical scholarship has helped to correct the blind spots of any single tradition and thus to sharpen the tools we can now bring collegially to bear upon these texts.

This Introduction is organized in four parts. Part I sets forth contextual knowledge for approaching the Hebrew Bible: the history of its interpretation, the biblical world, and the literary history of the Hebrew Bible. Parts II–IV present the biblical literature in sequence according to its sociohistoric settings. A prologue to each of the last three parts discusses the sources of our knowledge for each period as it is examined.

A problem of organization arises when presenting biblical writings in approximate historical sequence, as in parts II–IV: where should one place biblical books or sources that have a long tradition history and reflect a growth in stages over centuries? When treating composite or slowly evolved biblical writings, two flexible working principles are followed in this volume: (1) when there is wide agreement about a writing's sociohistoric anchor points, the work is discussed as often as necessary at each relevant stage, as, for example, with the Priestly writer (§15.1; 17.1–2; 19.2.a; 19.4; 48; 49) and the Book of Isaiah (§37.2; 50.2; 50.4.a); (2) when, on the other hand, the sociohistoric settings of a writing are vague or highly disputed, it is presented only at its most securely fixed historical point. Thus, the composite Books of Amos and Micah, although containing much later material, are discussed only once and in their eighth-century contexts (§34.3; 37.1), and Daniel, although preserving older traditions, is treated solely in its second-century milieu (§55.2).

As appropriate, chapters are introduced by lists of relevant readings in the biblical text and are keyed to the collection of historical and textually oriented maps published in Yohanan Aharoni and Michael Avi-Yonah, *The Macmillan Bible Atlas*. The text itself is subdivided into numbered sections that are generously cross-referenced. Maps of the ancient Near East and of biblical Palestine at different historical periods have been provided as part openers and as adjuncts to the section on the political, cultural, and social history of the ancient Near East (§9).

Numerous tables and charts are supplied to enhance the comprehension of visually oriented readers. Among these is a table of ancient Near Eastern texts (table 1) keyed to James B. Pritchard, ed., *Ancient Near Eastern Texts Relating to the Old Testament,* and to Walter Beyerlin, ed., *Near Eastern Religious Texts Relating to the Old Testament.* The tabular numbers of the Near Eastern texts are referred to in the body of this book. Specific pages in Pritchard or Beyerlin are cited in the body of the text only when the reference is to limited pages within the broader pagination given in the table. A table of literary genres, forms, or types in the Hebrew Bible (table 8) is likewise cited by the tabular numbers at various points in the literary analysis.

A working bibliography is provided, consisting of two parts: (1) books and articles arranged according to the sections of the text; and (2) commentaries arranged according to the biblical books. The titles listed are confined to English.

The chronology adopted for the divided monarchy is that of Edwin R. Thiele, *The Mysterious Numbers of the Hebrew Kings,* 3d ed. (Grand Rapids: Zondervan, 1983). I chose this scheme not because it is unimpeachable, but because it seems to me, on balance, to be the most satisfactory solution of the chronological problems proposed to date.

For the benefit of those who do not know the Hebrew language, I have transliterated Hebrew terms approximately as they are pronounced, even though this entails some inconsistencies according to the customary systems of transliteration.

Last, I have consistently used the dating sigla of B.C.E. and C.E., in preference to the more usual B.C. ("before Christ") and A.D. (*anno Domini,* "in the year of the Lord"), because I feel that it is important for all students of these texts to make a mental break between our own religious stances and the conditions and beliefs of biblical times. This is a necessary break if we are to appreciate the Bible as more than a sectarian or dogmatic document that simply mirrors our own religious ideas.

Within the wide network of my indebtedness to others as expressed in the dedication, I single out the curiosity and imagination of my students who over three decades have helped me to deepen and clarify my understanding of the Hebrew Bible and to communicate that understanding concretely and appealingly. At a more technical level, close colleagues in various working groups of the American Academy of Religion and the Society of Biblical Literature have given timely support and challenge.

With respect to the book in hand, the staff at Fortress Press has encouraged the project and expedited its production with alacrity and skill.

Among them I particularly salute John A. Hollar who fanned the first sparks of my interest in writing this volume and whose advice and encouragement sustained me in the task. I am pleased to credit his direct and indirect imprint on many of the organizational and instructional features of this work.

NORMAN K. GOTTWALD
New York City
March 17, 1984

PART I

THE TEXT IN ITS CONTEXTS

THE ANCIENT NEAR EAST

BLACK SEA

C

MACEDONIA THRACE

Pontic Mts.

AEGEAN
SEA

GREECE

ANATOLIA (ASIA MINOR)

URAR

A

CRETE

Taurus Mts.

MESOPOTA

AS

CYPRUS

SYRIA

Euphrates R.

MEDITERRANEAN SEA

PALESTINE

LIBYA

LOWER
EGYPT

SINAI

ARABIA

Nile R.

RED
SEA

UPPER
EGYPT

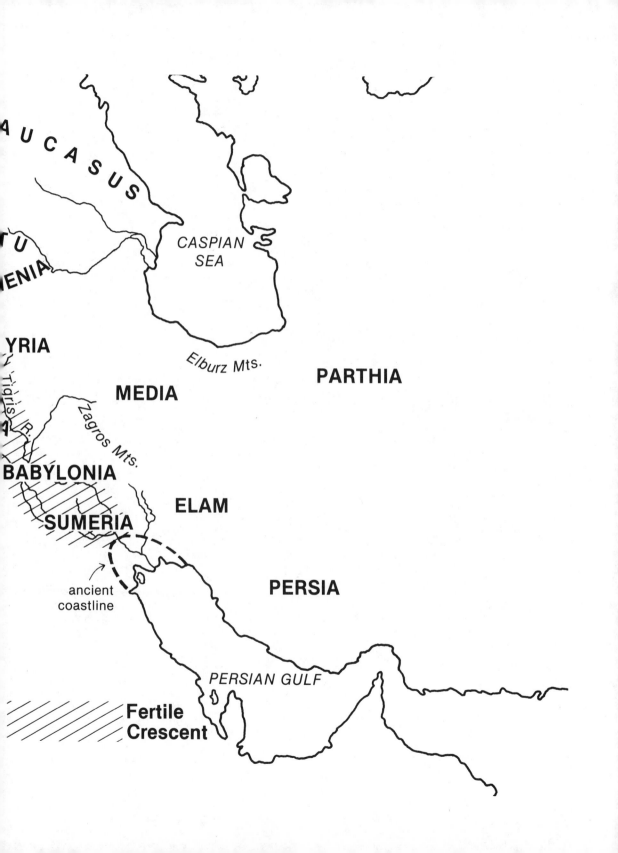

CHAPTER 1

Angles of Vision on the Hebrew Bible

The Hebrew Bible, known to Jews as the Tanak[1] and to Christians as the Old Testament, attracts and engages readers for many reasons. Among its many literary forms are vivid compact narratives and lively image-filled poems that readily catch the eye and ear. The story line recounts a conflict-charged political history, intertwined with more than a thousand years of ancient Near Eastern history. Its laws, stories, lists, prophetic speeches, and wisdom sayings touch on a host of social institutions and practices that change over the centuries. It presents the public words and deeds of figures such as Moses, David, and Jeremiah, who are often seen as examples of religious faith or of communal leadership. It teems with strong expressions of Israelite/Jewish[2] belief in the God whose special name was Yahweh, leading to a wide spectrum of religious and ethical concepts and practices closely connected with the social and political experience of the people. Finally, because the Hebrew Bible is sacred scripture for Jews and Christians to this day, and has gained a significant place in Western civilization, it beckons the reader to understand and consider its notions of deity and humanity, of historical process and social order, and of ethics and the good life.

1
A WEALTH OF METHODS IN BIBLICAL STUDIES

Any one of the mentioned points of engagement with the Hebrew Bible—and I have stated only the most prominent—constitutes a proper starting point for approaching the text, and necessarily carries with it distinct methods of analysis and interpretation. In earlier centuries, when the Bible was almost solely used to provide underpinning for Jewish and

1. TaNaK is an acronym from the first letters of the three divisions of the Hebrew Bible: Torah (Law or Pentateuch), Nevi'im (Prophets), and Kethuvim (Writings). Wherever "Bible" or "biblical" are used in this book, reference is to the Hebrew Bible, unless context makes clear that the Christian Bible, including the New Testament, is intended.

2. In current biblical studies, "Israel" and "Israelite" (distinguished from "Israeli," a citizen of the modern state of Israel) refer to the people in their early history down to or through the Babylonian exile, while "Jew" and "Jewish" refer to the people after their restoration to Palestine following exile. The term "Jew" comes from the Hebrew word $y^e h\bar{u}d\bar{i}$, "Judahite" ("Judean" in later Latinized form), that is, of the tribe or land or kingdom of Judah in preexilic usage. After the exile, the word $y^e h\bar{u}d\bar{i}$ referred mainly to Jews in an inclusive sense, wherever they lived, but on occasion was applied more restrictedly to Judahites/Judeans, that is, those Jews who lived in a restored Palestinian community in the land and former state of Judah. "Israel" is also used for the entire biblical period, especially in speaking of the people as a religious entity. "Hebrews," once used extensively to refer to the early Israelites, is now out of favor. The language of the Bible, a form of old Canaanite, is called "Hebrew." Thus, by "Hebrew Bible" we mean that the Jewish Scriptures were written in the Hebrew language.

Christian religious communities, there were decided limits on the ways the text was studied. In recent centuries, owing to the Renaissance, the Reformation, the Enlightenment, major social changes, and the steady expansion of scientific method over most areas of human experience, the Bible has been freed from an exclusively doctrinal (confessional) and church-centered (ecclesiastical) religious approach. It has now become approachable in scientific ways according to the many possibilities of inquiry that the various sciences have opened up.

"Scientific" is here intended in the broad sense of a systematic method of study necessary for the intelligible analysis and explanation of any subject matter. Science, in relation to biblical studies, includes not only natural, social, and psychological sciences, but also efforts at greater precision of method in the humanities, as in the study of language, literature, and history, and in the exercise of philosophy as a kind of overarching reflection on scientific methods and results as they relate to other kinds of knowledge.

It is typical of current study of the Hebrew Bible that more and more methods used in the human sciences, especially refinements in the humanities and the social sciences, have been employed in order to understand these ancient writings. As recently as two decades ago, there was a consensus among scholars about using a fairly limited number of critical methods for study of the Bible, but today the spectrum of methods employed in biblical studies has enlarged dramatically. Moreover, each of these methods is sufficiently self-contained and fundamental in its presuppositions and ways of working that the methods taken together do not suggest any single obvious picture or model (paradigm) of the nature and meaning of the Bible. How these different methods of biblical inquiry are to be related logically and procedurally has become a major intellectual challenge that will require a comprehensive frame of reference not readily at hand. At present there is probably no single biblical scholar who commands an in-depth grasp of all the methods now operative in biblical studies.

It is desirable that the serious student of the Hebrew Bible have some sense of the main phases in the development of methods in biblical studies. These stages can be described in chronological order because certain methods arose earlier than others and in various combinations held dominance among biblical interpreters until other methods joined or displaced them. The history of method in biblical studies has gathered complexity over the centuries, not only because of the accumulated details of scholarly names and theories, but because methods of biblical study, once they are developed, do not normally die out like extinct species. Sometimes they continue defiantly among interpreters who reject newer methods. Or, an old method, with minor or major alteration, persists within the new enlarged format of study.

There is wide recognition today that virtually all methods ever employed in biblical study have some reasonable basis for their use, so that the issue is now seldom seen as a matter of agreeing on what *one* method should replace the others but rather the question of how *various legitimate methods,* according to the purposes in view, should be joined so as to produce an overall grasp of the Hebrew Bible in its most fundamental aspects. For example, the initial literary interest of biblical scholars was to identify the sources used by the authors. Over the course of the last sixty years literary study has expanded to include oral tradition, typical forms (genres) and the settings in life where they were used, the final editing or redaction of a book, and the place of the single book within the whole collection of books (canon). Usually those who practice the newer literary methods do not deny that sources were often used by biblical authors, nor do they necessarily insist that it is pointless to inquire into those sources. The enlarged agenda of biblical literary critics suggests rather that determination of sources is only one among several valid questions about a biblical book and not the issue of all-consuming importance it was once thought to be. In short, the emergence of so many methods of biblical study for various purposes has tended to relativize and qualify the status of every method.

It is easy to be impatient with discussions of method. We want to get on to the "content" and the "meaning" of the Bible, often forgetful of the fact that we have no access to the content and meaning of the Bible apart from *some* method of study. All interpreters come to the text with assumptions, dispositions, and tools of analysis that lead them to single out aspects of the text and to arrange, emphasize, and interpret those aspects in meaningful patterns. Only by an awareness of method, as actually applied to the text, will we be able to see concretely why biblical interpreters have differed in their conclusions and to give a confident account of the basis and justification for our own methods.

2

THE CONFESSIONAL RELIGIOUS APPROACH
TO THE HEBREW BIBLE

The first stage in the study of the Hebrew Bible was basically religious in a confessional sense. Jews and Christians studied scripture to give understanding and shape to the practice of their religions. In both communities, until the last two centuries, there was a solid consensus about the religious role of the Bible. It was believed to be the divinely revealed foundation document of their faith. From the close of the first Christian century until the Jewish Enlightenment in the eighteenth and nineteenth centuries, orthodox Rabbinic Judaism interpreted the Tanak through the norms of the Oral Law or Talmud, and this "normalized" view of the Bible held sway among Jews without serious challenge (§10.2.c). From the late second Christian century until the Protestant Reformation in the sixteenth century, orthodox Catholic Christianity adopted a similar normalized interpretation of the Old Testament, as viewed by the New Testament and church dogma. Protestantism in its various branches soon fell into dogmatic interpretations of the Bible. Departures from the normative religious readings of the Hebrew Bible were a threat that might be tolerated, as in the case of mystics, or more often had to be expelled, as in the case of heretical sects. In our context the significance of the Protestant Reformation was that there now existed two major Christian ways—Catholic and Protestant—of confessing the religious meaning of Scripture, as well as several different forms of Protestant interpretation.

It is not as though a confessional religious understanding of the Hebrew Bible has ceased in our time. It is rather that *multiple* Jewish and Christian religious interpretations have emerged, and not simply along denominational lines within each religion but also along a spectrum from more literal to more symbolic interpretations and from more conservative to more liberal or radical interpretations. Moreover, there are now thriving formulations of an understanding of the Hebrew Bible that are "free-thinking"—humanist and secular in orientation. These approaches acknowledge the religious content of the Bible but interpret its truth claims and meanings in ways contradictory to the main bodies of Jews and Christians. This mushrooming variety of alternative options for understanding the Bible, both within and beyond the control of religious bodies, is one effect of the broad and penetrating social and intellectual forces that have accumulated in Western society over the last few hundred years.

All in all, the question intrudes itself: Why is it that people have such different, even contradictory, understandings of the religious meaning and value of the Bible? Of course people vary greatly in the degree to which they have been exposed to this variety of views about the Bible. Although the traditional confessional interpretations are no longer unchallenged, they are still powerfully advocated in many Jewish and Christian circles. It is common for faithful synagogue and church members to be surprised and shocked when they first seriously encounter other ways of viewing the Bible. The Bible has been internalized as a basic part of their religious instruction, so that when their unclouded "naive" grasp of the Bible confronts scientific methods of biblical study it often becomes a mind-stretching, value-questioning, and soul-searching experience.

3
THE HISTORICAL-CRITICAL APPROACH
TO THE HEBREW BIBLE

The second major phase in the study of the Hebrew Bible was adoption of the historical-critical method. Instead of taking the stated authorship and contents of documents at face value, this method tries to establish the actual origins of the text and to evaluate the probability that events it relates happened in the way described. Evidence for this critical inquiry derives from within the document and from a comparison with other documents from the same period or of the same type.

In the Renaissance, historical-critical method was applied to Greek, Roman, and other presumably ancient writings, including documents of the church. This method was slower in entering the sacred precincts of Scripture; the Protestant Reformation, however, by asserting the historical and theological superiority of the Bible over the church, indirectly encouraged the application of the secular historical-critical method to the biblical text. During the Enlightenment of the eighteenth century this method was unleashed on the Bible in full measure. Initially concentrated in Germany, the historical-critical study of the Bible rapidly spread over the entire educated Western world.

From the beginning this scientific way of studying the Bible made a place for itself within many sectors of the very Jewish and Christian religious communities that had traditionally interpreted the Hebrew Bible solely in a confessional religious manner. The stage was set for prolonged conflict, and for various kinds of accommodation, between religious and scientific methods of biblical study. For the moment we will turn our attention to how the Hebrew Bible appeared when analyzed and evaluated from the standpoint of historical-critical method.

3.1 The Bible as a Human Creation

In their choice of secular method to study the Hebrew Bible, historical critics were not denying the inherent religious character of the Bible, nor did they for the most part believe that the Bible lost its religious significance when studied critically. The basic presupposition of historical critics was that the religious aspect of life, however "supernatural" it claims to be in its orthodox Jewish and Christian versions, is similar to all other aspects of life in being historical and developmental. Religious ideas and practices arise, gain dominance, change, combine, mutually interact, decline, and die out. As with everything human, religious phenomena have a history.

In particular, historical critics believed that a careful study of the Hebrew Bible, using precisely the methods applied in the study of any literary product, would be able to uncover the actual origins and development of Israelite/Jewish religious ideas and practices which had long been hidden behind the compiled form of the Hebrew Bible interpreted as a unified supernatural story. The valid religious truth or "message" of the Hebrew Bible could only be brought to light when seen as the religion of a particular people at a particular time and place as expressed in these particular writings. Even though it might give disquiet to traditional views of the Bible in religious circles, historical critics regarded it as their intellectual obligation, even their religious duty, to inform believers and nonbelievers alike about the historical actuality of the origins of the Hebrew Bible and of the Israelite/Jewish faith.

3.2 Source Criticism and Form Criticism

Historical critics turned to the study of the Hebrew Bible as they would to the study of Homer, Thucydides, Dante, or Shakespeare, discovering as they went the peculiarities of the biblical literature. For one thing, the Bible proved to be a sizable collection of books from many hands with an inner history of development that had to be reconstructed from clues in the text and from analogies with similar types of literature. Authors of biblical books were frequently anonymous and explicit information for dating books was often meager.

A limited aspect of literary criticism as we now understand it, namely, source criticism, was employed to identify both fragmentary and extended sources within biblical books. For example, four literary sources were recognized as extending through two or more of the books in the first division of the Hebrew Bible (§13), and it was established that prophetic books not only contained the words of the original prophet named but many additions and revisions over time (§28). By the early twentieth century this source-critical project was expanded by so-called form criticism which aimed to isolate characteristic smaller units of tradition that were felt to be oral in their origin and highly conventional in their structure and language (§11.1.b). These smaller and larger sources, merged or strung together in the completed books of the Bible, were placed, insofar as possible, in their respective historical or typical settings.

We can illustrate the criteria and results of source criticism with reference to the Pentateuch by indicating the evidence for replacing Moses as its author with a theory of four later writers:

1. *Textual references to or implications about authorship.* Except when he speaks, Moses is referred to in the third person. Only certain parts of the text are explicitly said to have been written by Moses (e.g., Exod. 17:14; 24:4; 34:27–28; Num. 33:2). The implication is strong that the writer does not regard Moses as the author of extended books but only of some materials embedded in larger accounts.

2. *Language and style of the text.* Variations in vocabulary, often for the same persons, places, and things, appear regularly as "literary constants" in passages which display markedly different styles. For example, in places where the name *Yahweh* (RSV "Lord") is used, the mountain of the covenant is called *Sinai,* the original inhabitants of Palestine are *Canaanites,* and Moses' father-in-law is named *Reuel* or *Hobab.* In treating the same events, however, other passages employ *Elohim* for deity (RSV "God"), the covenant mountain is *Horeb,* the pre-Israelite people of Palestine are *Amorites,* and the father-in-law of Moses is called *Jethro.* Because these variations in vocabulary are so regularly joined with differences in style, concept, and historical viewpoint, they cannot be adequately explained as synonymous terms used by a single writer to relieve monotony or to make different emphases.

3. *Ethical and theological concepts in the text.* A spectrum of views appears within the Pentateuch concerning the imaging of deity, the remoteness or nearness of the divine, how Yahweh/Elohim communicates with humans, and what Yahweh/Elohim expects of them. These variant views are intimately correlated with the literary constants. For example, the "Yahweh-Sinai-Canaanites-Reuel/Hobab" sections vividly portray an actively intervening God who appears directly to people and expects childlike faith and devotion that will bless all nations (so-called J source; §13.1; 31.1), while the "Elohim-Horeb-Amorites-Jethro" sections show a more reserved deity who communicates by dreams and visions, and stresses the danger of apostasy from foreign nations and the extraordinary demands of religious loyalty (so-called E source; §13.2; 34.1). A third cluster of literary constants, primarily in Deuteronomy, derives ritual and social behavior from a prescribed lawbook given by the deity whose "name" abides with Israel at the Jerusalem temple cared for by Levites (so-called D, or expanded DH, source; §13.3; 22.2; 26; 37.3). Yet a fourth set of literary constants is committed to more elaborate ritual led by an Aaronid priesthood and pictures a lofty deity whose "glory" abides with Israel as

long as the people faithfully adhere to the proper ritual and moral law (so-called P source; §13.4; 17.1–2; 19.2.a; 49).

4. *Continuities and discontinuities in the text.* The stories and laws of Genesis-Deuteronomy do not read with smooth progression, but jar us with gaps and contradictions that do not indicate the point of view of a single composing mind. Some matters are simply unexplained (Where did Cain get his wife?). The line of action is often broken or obscure (How many times does Moses go up and down the mountain of Sinai/Horeb?). At times the same account gives contradictory information (How long did the flood last?). On occasion basically the same incident is repeated as though it happened two or more times (Did Abraham *twice* and Isaac *once* "pass off" their wives as their sisters?).

√5. *Historical standpoint of the text.* Offhand details in the text show the narrator to be speaking from a time later than Moses (e.g., references to Philistines, Israel's monarchy, domesticated camels, renamed cities, etc.). More significantly, the sources identified as above yield definite signs that they were written at points of differentiated sociopolitical and religious conditions and concerns in Israel's later experience: the J source implies an age of vigorous and self-confident national independence; the E source speaks from an era of innercommunal conflict and religious apostasy; the D/DH source arises at a time of national social, political, and religious reformation centered on the Jerusalem temple and tries to make the failure of that reform effort understandable; and the P source presupposes the loss of political independence and a studied reworking and reaffirmation of religious ritual and priestly control to provide communal security.

Furthermore, it became evident that the order in which the books were finally arranged in the Hebrew Bible was *not* the order in which the books had been written. Solutions to this chronological puzzle were made all the more complicated by the fact that single biblical books often contained materials from different time periods. This was the case with the Book of Isaiah, wherein large parts of chaps. 1—39 are oriented to the eighth century B.C.E.[3] (Isaiah of Jerusalem), whereas chaps. 40—66 are oriented to the sixth century B.C.E. (Isaiah of the Exile, eventually subdivided into Deutero-Isaiah, chaps. 40—55, and Trito-Isaiah, chaps. 56—66).

An arrangement of blocks of literary materials from the Hebrew Bible according to their approximate order of composition shows a very different

---

3. For an explanation of the use of the abbreviations B.C.E. (instead of B.C.) and C.E. (instead of A.D.) to identify dates in the biblical period, see the Preface to this book.

sequence than now appears in the traditional ordering of the books (chart 3). Even the traditional grouping of biblical books has varied among Jews, Catholics, and Protestants. It is obvious that the final compilers of the Hebrew Bible had additional criteria in mind for grouping books besides the date of composition. For example, the Book of Genesis, standing at the beginning of the Bible, did not reach its present form until after the Books of Deuteronomy through Kings had been composed during the late seventh and sixth centuries B.C.E. along with major portions of prophetic books such as Amos, Hosea, Isaiah, Micah, Jeremiah, and Ezekiel. On the other hand, although Genesis through Numbers was not brought to its present form until sometime during the fifth century B.C.E., those books contain a considerable number of narratives, poems, and laws written at least as early as the tenth and ninth centuries B.C.E.

3.3 Authorship of Biblical Books

The authorship of biblical writings received close scrutiny by historical critics. It was argued, on the basis of ancient literary practices and in terms of internal evidence, that many of the biblical claims to authorship were traditional assignments which are not to be taken strictly in terms of modern literary authorship. The biblical world was surprisingly devoid of personal pride in authorship and it knew nothing of copyright laws. When the Torah or Pentateuch is assigned to Moses, the Psalms to David, and wisdom books to Solomon, we should probably understand Moses as the prototype of lawgiver, David as the prototype of psalmist, and Solomon as the prototype of sage or wise man. On such an understanding, any or all laws, psalms, and wisdom sayings might be traditionally attributed to those figures as the true fountainheads of the tradition. This of course leaves open to inquiry whether in fact particular laws may reasonably be assigned to Moses, certain psalms to David, or some wisdom writings to Solomon. Historical criticism opens up the possibility that Davidic authorship of psalms and Solomonic authorship of wisdom may best be understood as royal sponsorship of psalms and wisdom in their role as kings responsible for court culture, without any necessary insistence that they were the actual writers.

It was also observed by historical critics that even when the core of a biblical book is correctly attributed to the named author, as for example Amos or Isaiah, numerous additions have been made by later hands, some by second- or third-generation disciples of the master (one thinks of the problem of distinguishing Socrates from Plato in the latter's dialogues) and others by literary editors (redactors). Critical assessment of the traditions of biblical authorship, first pursued by source criticism, later by form criticism and tradition (tradition-historical) criticism, and most recently by redaction (editorial) criticism (§5.2.a; 11.1; 13.5; 28) has shifted the emphasis from privately motivated and self-conscious "authors" in a modern sense to writers in a communal context and especially to the creative processes of tradition formation in the Israelite/Jewish community.

The oral and written molding and remolding of traditions is seen to be a crucible in which biblical literature was refined by abbreviating, expanding, combining, and elaborating units of tradition, often through many stages of development, until the final state of the Hebrew Bible was reached over a span of postexilic time from the sixth through the second centuries B.C.E. Sometimes this tradition-forming process has led to talk of "communal authorship," an expression that somewhat misleadingly points to the fact that many of the biblical writings drew upon immediate communal concerns and movements and became, if they were not from the start, the common property of groups who valued them and passed them along with creative additions and modifications.

3.4 Biblical History and Archaeology

The process of unraveling the literary structure of the Hebrew Bible and assigning its parts to a long historical trajectory has underlined the intimate connection between the Bible as a literary collection and the history of the Israelite/Jewish people from the Exodus to Maccabean times, somewhat over a thousand years in all. The biblical text itself relates a large part of that history, but does so selectively and unevenly. We know much more, for instance, about the united kingdom and parts of the divided kingdoms than we do about the earlier tribal period and the later exilic and postexilic periods. Also, one has to reckon with the reality that much of the biblical history is given a moralizing or theologizing twist, or is interpreted from the bias of a later standpoint in history.

Historical critics enlarged their task accordingly in order to recover as much additional information as they could, both about the history of the biblical communities and about the history of surrounding peoples with whom Israel was in frequent interaction. Historically enlightening records from Israel's neighbors, although rarely mentioning Israel, have the advantage of surviving in the form in which they were first written, without the kind of expansion and revision that biblical materials have undergone (§8.1; table 1; §10.1). Archaeological recovery of material and intellectual culture, including an ever-growing body of inscriptions and texts, has aided greatly in the task of cultural and historical reconstruction (§8.2).

It has become possible to plot the broad outlines of the growth of the biblical literary traditions against a historical scenario with spatial and temporal axes. The temporal axis stretches from the Middle Bronze Age (ca. 2100–1550 B.C.E.), as the most commonly accepted period for the biblical ancestors Abraham, Isaac, and Jacob (patriarchs), down to the Maccabean age in Palestine (167–63 B.C.E.), the age of the composition of Daniel and Esther, probably the last biblical books to be written. The spatial axis locates Israelite Canaan/Palestine at the center, with concentric geographical circles or spheres extending first to non-Israelite Palestine and Syria, then to Egypt and Mesopotamia (including Sumeria, Assyria, and Babylonia), and finally to Anatolia (Asia Minor), Iran (Media, Persia), Arabia, and the Eastern Mediterranean coastlands including Greece (§7.1).

4
INTERACTION BETWEEN RELIGIOUS AND HISTORICAL-CRITICAL APPROACHES TO BIBLICAL STUDIES

4.1 Collision and Accommodation of Conflicting Methods

It was previously noted that the historical-critical method of biblical studies early found its way into Jewish and Christian circles. For two hundred years now, two methods of biblical study have operated among Jews and Christians: the Bible approached as the revealed Word of God and the Bible approached as the human literary product of an ancient sociopolitical and religious community. Although greatly simplified, it can be said that historical-critical method has found readiest acceptance among educated clergy and laity and in the universities and theological faculties, and more rapidly among Protestants and Jews than among Catholics. To this day, however, there are large bodies of orthodox Jews and Christians who are actively hostile to the method, and many rank and file members of religious groups supposedly accepting of the method are poorly informed about it. Relatively few synagogues and churches regard it as an intrinsic part of their task to practice the method and instruct their members in it.

In any particular religious or academic institution, the religious or the historical approach to the Bible may push the other aside in practice, or rule it out of consideration on principle. Theories to justify some combination of the two methods, when suitable qualifications are made in one or both of them, have enjoyed some success, notably among liberal Jews and Protestants and increasingly among Roman Catholics over the last fifty years. Frequent among those who wish to join religious and historical-critical methods is the claim that the central religious ideas of the Bible and/or the significance of the synagogues and churches springing from biblical Israel are not invalidated by the fact that the Bible is a human document. God is viewed as having used the human processes in Israel's history to reveal religious truth and to preserve it in written records that continue to awaken faith in God even if they are not statements of a literal truth.

Some believers make peace with historical-critical method by applying it to carefully limited aspects of the Bible. They may, for instance, accept critical literary analysis, since they find it immaterial for faith whether Moses did or did not write the Torah, but they may insist that theological dimensions of the Bible, especially its views on creation, sin, and redemption, must be exempted from criticism since they are absolutely and eternally true. Or they may admit critical method in the form of textual criticism,[4] in order to establish the nearest possible approximation to the original Hebrew text. Or they may open the physical world view of the Bible to criticism, which they admit to be pre-scientific, while insisting that on all matters of history and religion the Bible is sacrosanct.

On the whole it seems fair to say that Jews and Christians have yet to work out ways of correlating the religious and historical approaches to the Hebrew Bible that can become an intrinsic and convincing part of the daily life and thought of believers. The relativizing humanistic implications of the historical-critical method clash with the practical belief in an unchanging, transcendent God. This unresolved tension, repeatedly bursting into open conflict, is a nagging source of disquiet in many religious bodies among those who want authoritative and secure mental and spiritual maps of the world. Literalistic biblical interpretation, misconstruing both the substance and emphasis of biblical teachings, sometimes accompanies socially reactionary thinking as people fear for the stability of their social world. A kind of domino reaction is felt to extend from doubt about the truth of the Bible through doubt about the reliability of the church to doubt about the security of the social order and even one's very self-identity. Nonwhite and poor white religious believers have understandable grounds to be suspicious of historical-critical biblical method as an intellectual version of the socioeconomic and political oppression they have suffered.

4. Textual criticism has often been called "lower criticism," since it is involved in the preliminary task of producing a secure Hebrew text on the basis of which historical-critical method, or "higher criticism," can do its work. Since the terms "lower" and "higher" are likely to imply judgments of worth or value, these designations are falling into disuse.

The climate of public philosophy and social theory in the West during the period of emergence of historical-critical method has not encouraged a new synthesis of the meaning of the Hebrew Bible that could go beyond the traditional religious interpretations, or at least offer a coherent alternative to them. In general, religion has suffered decline in its ability to inform and guide the public consciousness and behavior of people in the Western world, and particularly to challenge rampant racial, socioeconomic, and political domination and oppression. Philosophy has characteristically treated religion as a private persuasion to be admired and tolerated, or as an institutional construct or societal influence to be applauded, limited, or abolished.

4.2 Attempts at a Synthesis: Existentialism and Biblical Theology

We shall now look at some of the specifically churchly and theological efforts to synthesize religious and historical perspectives on the Bible. Between the two world wars a revival of Protestant Reformation theology in modern form, known as neo-orthodoxy—championed by Karl Barth—provided an attractive way to harmonize the results of historical-critical biblical study with a "high" view of biblical revelation. This theological synthesis was widespread in Europe and had a major impact in the United States from 1940 to 1960. In biblical studies it took the form of a "biblical theology" movement that forged the category of "history" into a bridge between the critical results of biblical scholarship and a notion of biblical faith as "revelation in history" or "the acts of God in history."

Somewhat similar influences were at work among Roman Catholic biblical scholars, encouraged by the liberalizing tendencies of the Vatican II Council in 1965, who discovered enlarged common ground with their Protestant and Jewish counterparts, to such an extent that from the content of particular studies on the Hebrew Bible it is now often impossible to know whether the scholar is Protestant, Catholic, or Jewish. This feature of recent biblical studies, a kind of trans-confessional community of biblical scholarship, has pushed forward on many levels of inquiry.

For some years it seemed that the religious and historical-critical methods in biblical studies might be on the way to a lasting synthesis, but the expected union failed. The biblical theology bridge between history and theology sagged and collapsed as it became clear that the Hebrew Bible, when viewed historically, contains several theologies and that in the end any theology or philosophy for integrating the interpretation of the whole Bible has to be provided by the modern interpreter.

Among the most influential modern schemes for reading off the meaning of the biblical text have been the existentialist philosophy of Jean-Paul Sartre and the phenomenological philosophy of Martin Heidegger. The biblical critic Rudolph Bultmann drew upon these philosophical frames to interpret the New Testament, and existentialist perspectives were likewise applied to the Hebrew Bible, though seldom in so rigorous a form, by scholars such as Gerhard von Rad. In contrast to the biblical theology movement which emphasized the religious meanings of particular historical events (exodus, conquest, exile, restoration) as revelations of God, the existentialist reading of the Bible saw the historical revelations of the Bible as models or paradigms of the human situation faced with crisis that offers an ever-emerging possibility of new beginnings through self-understanding and self-renewal. Von Rad had clung to a necessary historical core in the biblically recited "acts of God," as Bultmann insisted on the central reality of the death and resurrection of Jesus, but this core was not securely attached to probable historical events. Later existentialist biblical interpreters were often more consistent in regarding the biblical events and their interpretation as valuable but not indispensable occasions for self-understanding and self-renewal. Many of them retreated into highly abstract analyses of language as a mode of meaningful communication and self-definition that did not connect fruitfully with biblical and theological studies.

4.3 Breakdown of Consensus in Biblical Studies

In the late 1960s both "revelation in history" and "existential self-understanding" reached a point of diminishing returns as resources for biblical studies. Each seemed to be straining after an artificially constructed center of meaning in the Bible, or in the interpreter, which obstructed the way to an actual examination of the shape of the biblical text. The impulse to "relate" Bible and modern world, to "appropriate" the Bible for the concerns of people today, had issued in "harmonies" or fusions of history and religion that looked like special pleading and served to narrow the range of interest in the multiple facets of biblical texts.

Newer forms of religious thought, such as process theology and political theology, have made only tentative excursions into the biblical materials but not enough to produce master schemes or paradigms with the convincing power that biblical theology and existentialist interpretation expressed in their day. Indeed, the biblical conceptual framework of much political theology, including liberation theology stemming from Latin America, seems not to differ greatly from the biblical theology movement, although it reads the content and implications of "revelation in history" in a far more social and political manner.

By the opening of the 1970s, study of the Hebrew Bible was pervaded by a sense of dissatisfaction and disorientation. The older theological modes of confessional orthodoxy and liberalism had proven incapable of synthesizing the historical and religious meanings of the Bible, and the more recent excursions into biblical theology and existentialism had not been, in the end, any more satisfactory. Moreover, no other theological current commanded the necessary explanatory power to replace the previous inadequate formulations. This situation of receding theological involvement with the Hebrew Bible, after a long period of theological triumphalism in biblical studies, might have provided the occasion for the discipline, largely freed from the interference of discredited theological schemes, to pursue its own proper object through a study of the Bible in and of itself. In a sense this is what has occurred, but not as though the object and methods of study were perfectly clear.

With the relative shift away from theological domination of biblical studies, the drastic paradigm crisis surrounding the limitations of the historical-critical method has come fully to light. Theology can no longer be cited as the sole obstacle to an integral understanding of the Hebrew Bible. Theology aside, the Hebrew Bible is seen now as a different sort of object to different kinds of interpreters. What characterizes the present period in biblical studies, and makes it so difficult to typify in any simple way, is the explosion of several methodologies, each claiming to grasp an important neglected or downgraded feature—even the sole essential feature—of the structure and meaning of the Hebrew Bible. It is not clear to what extent these newer methods are mutually exclusive or potentially compatible, or possibly even complementary or necessary to one another. So rapid has been the expansion of these methods in small-scale studies that there has been little time or occasion to think through their implications for biblical studies as a whole.

5
EMERGENCE OF NEW LITERARY AND SOCIAL SCIENCE APPROACHES TO THE HEBREW BIBLE

5.1 Perceived Limits of Historical and Religious Approaches

The relation of the newer methods to the dominant methods of the past is complex and ambivalent. Most advocates of new methods seem to recognize that the confessional religious and the historical-critical methods of interpretation succeeded in identifying and clarifying important aspects of the biblical text. Misgivings and objections to the older methods center on their limitations and the tendency of their conflicting presuppositions to monopolize discussion about the meaning of the Hebrew Bible.

Clearly, historical-critical method has been able to illuminate the collected writings of the Hebrew Bible, rooted in the history of Israel, as expressions of a religious faith unfolding in communal settings and historical sequences over more than a thousand years. Whereas the confessional religious approach saw the religious aspect of the Bible as a divinely caused revelation, with few questions asked, historical-critical method, by specifying in detail how the writings are shaped and colored by the sharp religious perspectives of writers and editors, was able to interpret that same religious dimension of the Bible as a richly nuanced historical development. This achievement of historical-critical method provided a basis for many biblical interpreters to attempt a reconciliation between the historical and religious views of Scripture.

Nonetheless, even when the historical-critical method was expanded beyond source criticism to include oral tradition, form criticism, and tradition-historical criticism, its main focus continued to be the subordination of literary considerations to the reconstruction of history and religion. The result was that certain classic problems—such as the composition and historical anchorage of the various parts of complex books such as Deuteronomy and Isaiah—were repetitiously reworked without much benefit of new evidence or fresh angles of approach.

Just as the older confessional religious approach lost explanatory power when it gave dogmatic answers to historical questions, so the historical-critical method exposed its limits when it could only answer some historical questions adequately and when it was realized that new questions about the literary shape of the Bible and the social milieu of ancient Israel were beyond its competency. In short, religious and historical-critical schemes of biblical interpretation are widely perceived to have reached their limits on their own turf and to be inappropriate to clarifying major aspects of the Hebrew Bible that excite curiosity and imagination. On every hand one meets disappointment, restiveness, and a measure of resentment toward methods that promised so much but have insisted on exclusive billing long after they have made their best contributions. One may even speak of a widespread revolt against the tyranny of narrowly historical and religious methods of biblical study.

Yet we must state the shift from older to newer methods carefully, so as not to miss the notes of ambivalence and tentativeness in the present methodological situation. That the newer moods and thrusts in biblical studies threaten to abolish the older methods on principle is highly doubtful, even if a particular "new critic" should happen to think so. The present mood is not so much "See how wrong the old methods have been!" but rather, "See what valuable results the new methods can produce!" In any event, the latest trends are emphatically in the direction of freedom from the domination of history and religion and toward the opening up of methodological space to explore new avenues of access to the Hebrew Bible. It remains to be seen whether the older methods will be categorically outmoded, or are simply partial and problematic to the whole of what must be done to understand the Hebrew Bible. If it is now widely believed, however, that religion and history—at least as customarily formulated by confessional religious and historical-critical methods—are not sufficient paradigms for understanding the Hebrew Bible, the question insistently arises: What other methods are able to carry us forward to new understandings?

At least two major paradigms, or related sets of methods, have emerged in an attempt to get around the present impasse in the study of the Hebrew Bible. One is the paradigm of the Hebrew Bible as a literary production that creates its own fictive world of meaning and is to be understood first and foremost, if not exclusively, as a literary medium, that is, as words that conjure up their own imaginative reality. The other is the paradigm of the Hebrew Bible as a social document that reflects the history of changing social structures, functions, and roles in ancient Israel over a thousand years or so, and which provides an integral context in which the literary, historical, and religious features of the Israelite/Jewish people can be synoptically viewed and dynamically interconnected.

5.2 Newer Literary Methods

Within the new literary paradigm for approaching the Hebrew Bible there is substantial agreement that the text as it stands constitutes the proper object of study in that it offers a total, self-contained, literary meaning that need not depend upon analysis of sources, historical commentary, or normative religious interpretations. Biblical literary critics vary in how they make this point. Many allow that the older methods of study have value and may helpfully give context or nuance to literary study, but they express a nearly unanimous caution against predetermining literary study of the Bible with the old questions and modes of attack. For them literature is not, in the first instance, a means to something else, such as historical or religious understandings of the writers and their everyday world. Literature is a world all its own, in and of itself, biblical literature included. Thus, "Who wrote this book, or part of a book, from what sources, in what historical setting, and with what aims?" is for literary critics in the new mode a far less productive series of questions than "What is the distinct structure and style of this writing, or segment of writing, and what meaning does it project from within its own confines as a work of art or as a system of linguistic meanings?"

5.2.a The Bible as Literature and New Literary Criticism

One current in the literary paradigm derives from the so-called new literary criticism in secular literary studies, now some decades old, associated with literary critics such as Northrop Frye and I. A. Richards. This perspective stresses the distinctiveness of each literary product and seeks to analyze its peculiar conventions of genre, rhetorical devices, metaphor and irony, and the overall resulting unity and effects. This approach focuses in part on the stylistic devices and verbal formulations which tend to be of the sort that previously drew the attention of biblical form critics and tradition critics. New literary criticism, however, looks at the rhetorical texture of the work as a finished whole rather than viewing it along a chronological line of development from small units through larger cycles to the last stage of composition. In this sense the "Bible as literature" movement is closely related to rhetorical criticism, a spinoff from form criticism, that seeks to establish the literary individuality of texts by analyzing their arrangements of words, phrases, and images that structure firm beginnings and endings, sequences of action or argumentation, repetitions, points of focus and emphasis, and dynamic interconnections among the parts.

The approach to the Bible as literature has affinities also with redaction criticism, which developed as a sort of final stage in the evolution of historical-critical method. First applied to the New Testament, redaction criticism is now widely practiced by Old Testament scholars, for example, in the study of the Deuteronomistic History in Joshua through Kings (§13.3; 22.3; 26) and also in the prophetic books (§28; 34.3; 34.5; 37.5; 50.2). The aim of redaction criticism is to discern the hand of the final writer or editor (redactor) in single books, or in a series of books, by distinguishing how the final framing stage of composition has arranged earlier materials and added interpretive cues for the reader. In this way one can see how the entire composition was intended to be read, even though much of the content derived from earlier writers with differing points of view.

Overlapping in some aspects with redaction criticism, and sharing with the Bible as literature movement a concern for the finished state of the text, is a method that has generally been known as canonical criticism (§11.2.b; 48). Advocates of this approach are interested in how the biblical text was developed and interpreted as scripture. Some stress a "canonical process" at work in shaping the literary texts, even before there was a formal canon. Others, using redaction criticism, focus on the way that the editing of certain books and collections discloses a "canonical consciousness" by which books or collections of books were intended to be interpreted cross-referentially in the light of one another. Still others emphasize the final form or "canonical shape" of the Hebrew Bible as an authoritative religious document that may give us clues to new formulations of biblical theology. Canon contextual criticism has been proposed as a technical term to encompass these several types of study of the Hebrew Bible as scripture.

Careful distinctions are necessary among these various related types of criticism. Biblical literary critics of the new breed concur with redaction and canonical critics in trying to illumine how the entire composition of a biblical writing is to be read in its integrity. On the other hand, they leave aside the moot point of what shape parts or earlier editions of the work may have had before the finished book was produced, and it is no matter of interest to them to argue for or about the theological authority of the finished Hebrew Bible.

While touching significantly on the concerns of form criticism, tradition criticism, rhetorical criticism, redaction criticism, and canonical criticism, the new literary criticism of the Bible goes beyond any of these methods in its comprehensive search for clarity about the shape and interconnection of biblical literary conventions and genres. One result has been to see biblical literature less in the tragic mode (the hero defeated by self or others/the hero cast out of community) and more in the comic mode (the hero's aspirations fulfilled after trials/the hero incorporated in a new community) [§20.2; 29.3]. There is also an explicit interest in comparing and contrasting biblical literature with other literatures on the assumption that all individual texts comprise one vast corpus of literature and share similar creative properties which show patterned variations (§20.1–2).

5.2.b Structural Criticism

A second current in the new literary paradigm is known as structural criticism or structural exegesis. It differs from the Bible as literature movement in its assumptions about structural patterns that not only lie within particular writings but also in a sense "underlie" them (often called "deep structures"). These structures may be traced in groups or "sets" of similar texts, such as in parables or miracle narratives. There is a frequent interest in locating the primary functional elements in a story which appear in a fixed set of roles and schematized plots. Structuralism tends to see deep structures in terms of polar categories ("binary oppositions") rooted in basic mental structures that organize great ranges of human experience into such opposites as good/bad, nature/culture, man/woman, life/death, secular/profane, and having/not having (§20.3; 23.2).

It is important to observe that structuralism is a broad-ranging methodological approach to reality that has surfaced in many disciplines such as mathematics, logic, biology, psychology, linguistics, social sciences, and philosophy. A structure of whatever type—and they may range from numerical groups through organisms to literary texts and religious or philosophical concepts—may be understood as a closed or self-regulating system of transformations. The system is seen both as structured and in the process of structuring. Structural criticism entered biblical studies chiefly through linguistics and anthropology. Linguistic structuralism (deriving from F. de Saussure) distinguishes between language as capacity, or engendering potentiality, and the particular engendered words of any given speech-act or text. Anthropological structuralism (associated with C. Lévi-Strauss) stresses the analytic capacities of the human mind as expressed in myth making and systems of kinship classification.

One impression accompanying the inrush of structural criticism to biblical studies is that it has no regard whatsoever for the historical and social dimensions of texts. Lévi-Strauss's structuralism seems to make history and society into mere occasions for the universal deep structures to operate. It is becoming clear, however, that there are biblical structuralists of many persuasions and that they do not all agree in attitude toward the strictly nonliterary aspects of literary texts. Some biblical structuralists contend that, although the theoretical work of Lévi-Strauss and of A. J. Greimas is markedly antihistorical, their actual detailed analyses of texts, especially those by Greimas, contain many openings for the possible synthesis of literary structural and historical/social concerns.

A major problem with biblical structuralism to date is that, like its linguistic and anthropological progenitors, it uses technical jargon, which is particularly confusing because different vocabularies are used by different structuralists, according to which structuralist authority they prefer and in keeping with their own modifications for biblical interpretation. At present it is often difficult for structuralists to communicate with one another and to compare results, not to mention the problem in making their method known to nonstructuralist scholars. This is a difficulty analogous in many ways to the terminological disarray that has plagued form criticism and which has only recently been seriously grappled with by form critics. Before structuralism can be fully productive in biblical studies there will need to be further progress toward clarifying and standardizing technical terms and concepts, with a winnowing of the various forms and possibilities of structuralism to determine which offer the best payoff in analyzing biblical texts.

5.3 Social Science Methods

Within the social science paradigm there is broad concurrence that the biblical writings were rooted in interacting groups of people organized in social structures that controlled the chief aspects of public life, such as family, economy, government, law, war, ritual, and religious belief. Moreover, it is widely perceived that these units of social life, taken as a total network in flux, supply an indispensable context for grounding other aspects of biblical studies, including both the older and the newer methods of inquiry. The guiding question for social science approaches becomes, "What social structures and social processes are explicit or implicit in the biblical literature, in the scattered socioeconomic data it contains, in the overtly political history it recounts, and in the religious beliefs and practices it attests?"

But how new is social scientific study of the Hebrew Bible? Not entirely so, for earlier generations of biblical interpreters showed interest in social data, sometimes episodically in reference to legal texts or lists/summaries of political administration, and sometimes in terms of gross comparisons between Israelite society and other societies, notably the customs of pre-Islamic Arabs or the religious confederations of ancient Greeks. Most of these social probes have been oriented to solving literary and historical puzzles or have been hampered by undeveloped anthropological and sociological methods and models. The most sophisticated large-scale sociological analysis of ancient Israel from earlier scholarship, worked out by the sociologist Max Weber, is as problematic as it is brilliant, and it has scarcely been extended or rigorously tested in the sixty years since it was published.

5.3.a Social Reconstruction of Early Israel

In the early 1960s, a new hypothesis about the origins of Israel was advanced with the assistance of data and methods from the social sciences. It was contended that Israel originated, not as nomads invading or infiltrating from the desert, but largely as a coalition of peasants who had been resident in Palestine as subjects of the hierarchic city-states (§24.1.c;

24.2.c). At first largely dismissed as preposterous, this so-called revolt model of Israelite origins has gained credibility through more systematic examination of the internal biblical evidence and the external data from the ancient Near East, along with the aid of more controlled social scientific methods. The model entails a cautious comparative method for employing studies on social forms—such as nomadism, tribalism, peasant movements and revolutions, and imperial bureaucracies—in order to theorize about the early social history of Israel in a period when the texts are too fragmentary and revised to be able by themselves to give us a whole picture of the beginnings of Israel. Whether or not this model will prove adequate in the main, it is evident that an entirely new concern with social history and social system has entered biblical studies alongside the continuing concerns with political and religious history.

5.3.b Social Reconstruction of Prophecy and Apocalyptic

Sociological interest, at first concentrated on Israelite origins, has now spread to other segments of Israelite history and religion. Social scientific tools, notably studies on millenarian sects in the Third World and within the history of Christianity, have contributed to new interpretations of the bizarre symbolic systems of intertestamental apocalyptic thought, as in the biblical Book of Daniel, and to a social psychological understanding of the advocates of such views (§55). More recently, biblical prophecy is being reexamined sociologically after a fifty-year gap following Weber's "charismatic" explanation of the social character of prophecy (§28; 36.5; 37.5). Insights from studies of spirit possession and the function of inspired holy persons in simpler societies are being used to get a better comparative grasp of what is common and what is distinctive in Israelite and non-Israelite prophecy. Drawing from social psychology, role theory has been employed to illuminate aspects of prophetic performance and cognitive dissonance theory has been applied to the hermeneutics of reinterpreting failed prophetic predictions.

5.3.c Varieties of Social Scientific Criticism

Like the literary paradigm, the social science paradigm is represented by different methodological currents. Some inquiries are focused on institutional sectors of ancient Israelite social life, treating offices or role functions and administrative structures at the points where they appear as traces or outcroppings in biblical texts, often with attention to ancient Near Eastern parallels or wider-ranging comparisons from comparative anthropology or sociology. This line of work continues, in more sophisticated form, the inquiries of older scholars such as Albrecht Alt and William F. Albright.

Other approaches are broadening the field of comparison under the influence of studies in prehistory and anthropology, so that cautious analogies are proposed between ancient Israelite society and virtually any other society thought to exhibit similar features in some relevant regard, always allowing for different developmental and structural-functional contexts in the instances compared. Most of these comparative studies are deliberately constructed to guard against the mania for making superficial parallels that has swept over biblical studies from time to time in the past. There seems less dogmatism about whether similar societal features are borrowed or independently originated, both possibilities being left open from case to case. All in all, there is greater self-confidence in proposing hypotheses about Israelite society. Granted that important social data are lacking for ancient Israel, we can form testable models for conceiving the society that are necessary for interpreting the knowledge we do have and suggestive of additional research needed to refine or revise our tentative mappings of biblical society.

Some biblical social science critics are expanding their horizons toward a comprehensive account of Israelite society under the impetus of the macro-social (large-scale/global) theorists Karl Marx, Emile Durkheim, and Max Weber. Precisely how the methods and constructs of these social theorists are to be related in their own terms, and how they are to be applied to specific Israelite social conditions, is by no means agreed. The use of Marxian, Durkheimian, and Weberian tools in biblical sociology is often highly eclectic, but they hold increasing attraction because their perspectives are broad in that they view the components of society as multidimensional and interactive, giving rise to contradictions in society and the emergence of new sociohistorical syntheses. After a long period of reaction against the crude social evolutionary schemes of the nineteenth century, neo-evolutionary social theory is finding application to ancient Israel, allowing as it does for different rates of social change in different societies, for "leaps" in stages and retrograde developments, and for calculations of trends or tendencies in terms of probabilities instead of heavy-handed determinisms according to a supposed predestined inexorable march of history.

Finally, all of the above types of anthropological and sociological criticism are having a spillover effect on the task of exegesis (systematic interpretation) of texts, to the extent that one may now speak of sociological exegesis. Sociological exegesis tries to situate a biblical book or subsection in its proper social setting—taking into account the literary and historical relations between the parts and the whole. It further attempts to illuminate the text according to its explicit or implied social referents, in a manner similar to historical-critical method's clarification of the political and religious reference points of texts. Biblical texts differ greatly in the ease and method by which their social milieus and references can be ascertained. In general, laws and prophetic texts appear thus far to be more amenable to sociological exegesis than do imaginative narratives (sagas and legends) and wisdom sayings. Yet it is fair to say that some headway is being made in the sociological exegesis of texts composed of all the major types of biblical literature. It is evident that all adequate future exegesis of biblical texts will have to entail a social science dimension alongside the customary literary, historical, and religious dimensions.

Meanwhile, social scientific criticism has stimulated an interest among archaeologists to examine ancient Israelite remains with more explicit cultural and social questions by means of appropriate methods and strategies. This is a shift from the typical orientation of earlier decades when interest in the Hebrew Bible among archaeologists was largely religious and historical. Whereas formerly, for example, the dating of the destruction of Jericho, in correlation with Joshua chaps. 2—6, was a typical overweening archaeological issue, today many archaeologists are as much, or more, interested in learning how early Israelites lived materially and socially in small farming villages as they are in determining the dates and circumstantial details of biblical events, on which archaeology has at best only been able to throw limited light (§8.2; 24.1).

5.4 Common Ground in New Literary Criticism and Social Scientific Criticism

New literary and social science methods of biblical study share a common frustration with the limited achievements of the religious and historical-critical paradigms. Each of the newer approaches in its own way tries to shift the object of study in biblical studies so as to provide access to overlooked dimensions of the writings that are felt to be indispensable to a full understanding of the Hebrew Bible. The literary paradigm does this by shifting attention from religious systems and historical reconstructions to the Hebrew Bible as a literary world. While initially this limits the range of what is studied, it actually enlarges the data by opening up fictive literary worlds that exist by virtue of the original composition of the biblical books and their endurance into the present. The social science paradigm shifts attention from the history and religion by concentrating on the Hebrew

Bible as a residue of social worlds in which real people lived in social networks and fought out social struggles that were highly influential in the environment of the biblical writers, and which are attested in social data and allusions in biblical texts. This anthropological and sociological accent also seems at first to be a reduction of subject matter, but in fact it provides a wider milieu in which to locate and interconnect other kinds of interests in ancient Israel.

But do the newer literary and social science methods have anything more in common than a shared grievance with older methods of biblical inquiry? Indeed they do because common to both paradigms is a central concern with *structure:* the structure of the writings of the Hebrew Bible and the structure of the Israelite/Jewish society in which the Hebrew Bible was written and handed down. Exactly how these two structural enterprises are to be related to one another, and both to the continuing religious and historical-critical quests, is an unfolding challenge on the frontiers of biblical research.

For the moment, the chief stress lies on the sharp differences between the newer paradigms and the older paradigms, rather than on the relationship of the newer paradigms to one another. The literary critic of the Hebrew Bible seems often to be most clearly distinguished by disinterest either in the historical reconstruction of ancient Israel or in the coherence or validity of its religious claims, both of which appear immaterial to "literary truth." Similarly, the social scientific critic of the Hebrew Bible seems often to be most readily defined by an attempt to subsume or "reduce" political and religious history, including the religious truth claims of the texts, to instances or forms of social interaction. Much in the stance of literary and social scientific critics can be explained by their impatience with religious and historical monopolies on the Hebrew Bible which overlook the literary and social worlds and either grasp at a historical picture which is irretrievable or trivial, or else conjure up a religious system abstracted from the world of language and of social interaction.

How might literary structure and social structure be more exactly related? If, on the one hand, literary critics insist that social context has no bearing on texts and if, on the other hand, anthropological and sociological critics claim that texts are pure and simple projections of social life and consciousness, it is likely that points of contact between them will be minimal at best and hostile at worst. If structural criticism of texts presupposes a constantly structured and structuring human mind, however, sociological data will at least appear as instances of this unitary mind at work, parallel in a sense with literary instances of that mind. This outlook could provide a harmonizing of the two kinds of structures, as indeed Lévi-Strauss seems to presuppose for primitives, but it is a harmony that will not readily attract those social scientific critics who want to know why markedly different social structures have developed over time if a unitary human mind is in fact expressed in them all. On the other hand, language itself as the medium of literature is a social code and thus literature is a social expression. Although appealing, this pathway will not be too hastily followed by literary critics who want to linger over the question of why and how it is that literature creates its own special world and does not simply directly mirror its society. Exactly how does social reality inscribe itself in language and in literary creations? To date the theoretical lines for relating the two kinds of structure in biblical studies are only in a rudimentary stage of exploration (§23.2).

6
CREATIVE FERMENT IN CONTEMPORARY BIBLICAL STUDIES

6.1 A Common-sense Assessment of Options

A "common-sense" reflection on the history of angles of vision for approaching the Hebrew Bible, and on the methods appropriate to its study, might proceed somewhat as follows. Each of the paradigms we have examined points to an undisputed dimension of the Hebrew Bible as a collection of writings that teems with religious concepts and practices, discloses segments of an involved history, reflects and presupposes social structures and processes, and is itself an artful literary work.

The paradigm of the Hebrew Bible as a *religious testimony* has the advantage of having been the controlling conception by which the collection of writings was made as an authoritative body of texts, the canon, toward the end of the biblical period, as well as the advantage of being the chief way that millions of Jews and Christians view their Tanak or Old Testament. The disadvantage of this approach is that it blocks out of consideration much else of potential interest in the Bible, on the assumption that what is explicitly or traditionally religious is always of highest concern and importance, not to mention the growing lack of religious consensus in our culture on the basis of which biblical authority could be assured. Not to be overlooked also is the question of whether "religion" meant the same thing to biblical writers as it does to moderns, or whether it was viewed as prescriptive or authoritative in the same way throughout biblical times as it is for Jews and Christians today. These questions are also relevant to the type of canonical criticism that identifies the "meaning" or "intention" of the Bible with the final form of the text as it was judged to be authoritative (canonization) and which is taken to provide a theological hermeneutic (principle of interpretation) for modern Jewish and Christian readings of the Bible and its application to life.

The paradigm of the Hebrew Bible as a *historical witness* has the edge attained by an impressive scholarly accomplishment in reconstructing the main outlines of the development of Israelite literature, history, and religion. It is popular nowadays to deride historical-critical method in biblical studies, but very few of its detractors seem aware of the extent to which its basic procedures and its main conclusions form a part of their own outlook on the Bible. The disadvantage of this approach is that it treats the literature of the Hebrew Bible as instrumental to historical and religious interests and fails to contextualize political and religious history sufficiently in its wider social history. It is also true that historical critics have at times been too cocksure of their judgments and too given to belaboring literary and historical questions about which we lack the necessary information to offer more than an educated guess. Nonetheless, every method of biblical inquiry has had its overzealous enthusiasts whose very abuses in practice are called into question by the insistent strictures of the method itself.

The paradigm of the Hebrew Bible as a *literary world* has the advantage of concentration on the accessible form of the biblical text and does so with the valuable aid of a comparative body of related or contrasted literatures. By teaching us to observe rhetorical structures and devices in the text it prepares a way to enter the language world of the Hebrew Bible without the need to decide prematurely what is of significance in that world. It facilitates a zone of suspended judgment in approaching a literature that has been subject to unproductive controversy and prejudgment. The disadvantage of this approach is that it ignores the social and historical substrata or contexts out of which the literature arose, genre by genre, source by source, writing by writing, collection by collection, until it reached its end form. The literary world is real enough, as literary critics remind us, but its writers lived in an everyday world of their own and many of the topics and interests of biblical texts reflect the conditions and events of that everyday biblical world which it is folly to ignore if we want a well-rounded understanding of ancient Israel.

The paradigm of the Hebrew Bible as a product and reflection of the *social world* has the advantage of establishing the public and communal character of biblical texts as intelligible creations of a people working out their social conflicts and contradictions in changing systemic contexts. The social world of ancient Israel gives us a vital integral field, larger than but inclusive of its political and religious history, and likewise linked to a literary world, since both literature and society constitute "fictions" which are intimately if indirectly connected. The disadvantage of this approach is that it has to hypothesize structures and processes at points where textual information is insufficient to rule firmly for or against alternative hypotheses.

The social science paradigm is also capable of quite as much self-defeating dogmatism as the historical-critical and religious paradigms, and can lapse into a kind of pseudotheology. It is also evident that anthropological and sociological categories deal with the typical and thus provide "average" descriptions and general tendencies which by themselves may miss the momentary oddities and exceptions of historical figures and happenings. There remains, as we have noted, the issue of how the social world can be accommodated to the literary world, but this is not so much a defect either of the social science paradigm or of the literary paradigm as it is a promising question addressed to both methods.

6.2 A Preview of Biblical Studies to Come

It sounds commonplace to say that the advantages and disadvantages of the various paradigms of biblical studies are largely due to a required limitation of perspective and method in order to achieve clarity and coherence of results. Yet this truism has significant implications not often considered. Once a question about the Hebrew Bible or ancient Israel is framed in a certain way, the search for an answer gravitates toward one or another of the broad methodological channels we have described.

Consider, for example, the widely different methodological "plans of attack" customarily adopted to deal with such questions as these: Who wrote the Book of Proverbs and when? Are the stories of the patriarchs historically true? What happened to the Israelites during the exile? What is the structural meaning of the Book of Ruth? What sources were used in writing the Books of Samuel? What was the relation between state and tribes during the Israelite monarchy? Was the understanding of God held by Moses theologically correct? What authority does Pentateuchal law have for practicing Jews or Christians today? Quite different sorts of evidence and criteria are appropriate from question to question.

The point is that the range of questions an intelligent reader is likely to ask spill out beyond the province of any single paradigm.[5] Moreover, we

---

5. Indicative of the extent to which the several paradigms have entered "the toolbox" of scholars and even of religious workers is the fact that one elementary guide for first-time Bible readers by a French Catholic responsible for lay education speaks not only of the *religious* and *historical-critical* approaches but also introduces the *social science* approach—under the title of "materialist exegesis"—and the *new literary* approach, in the form of "structuralist analysis" (Etienne Charpentier, *How to Read the Old Testament* [New York: Crossroad, 1982], 11–13).

may discover that more than one paradigm is appropriate, even necessary, to answer a single question fully, particularly as we find our question changing shape and enlarging beyond its original, often rather naive, formulation. If it should become common practice to "cross over" and "move back and forth" from one paradigm to another, there arises the issue of how the relations among the paradigms are to be negotiated. By what rules do we leap from one to the other? When does one paradigm have precedence over another? How are we to bring together the results from two or more methods of inquiry to provide a synthesis that is more than an arbitrary pasting together of unrelated elements?

More important than pressing any particular way of negotiating the paradigms, however, is the awareness that we have entered a situation in biblical studies where interaction among an enlarged number of paradigms is potentially more complex, problematic, and exciting than ever before in the long history of interpretation of the Bible. The confessional religious paradigm is the end product of a two-thousand-year development and for two hundred years this initial paradigm has been in dialogue with the historical-critical paradigm. With the emergence of the new literary paradigm and the social science paradigm, the former two-party conversation is suddenly enlarged into at least a four-party conversation, or actually into a conversation with as many parties as there are articulate versions of each paradigm concerning one or another point in biblical studies.

Obviously there will have to be considerably more research, discussion, and debate among all self-aware participants before the outlines of the most recent stage of biblical studies will become clear enough to know how the paradigms will "shake out": whether one paradigm will eventually win out over the others, or whether they will continue in friendly or hostile competition, or whether there will emerge a kind of "paradigm of paradigms" (a higher-order model) that can encompass all previous methods and models in such a way that the valuable contribution of each is retained within a set of "transformations" that can communicate among all paradigms at a new level of integration.

In any event, the present introduction to the Hebrew Bible will observe various ways of relating, or separating, the paradigms, along with their noteworthy methods and results to date, but no attempt will be made to provide a higher-order "covering paradigm" for integrating all the paradigms into a single interpretive structure. In the Conclusion of this book, one way of collecting and mapping some of the major results of the various paradigms in terms of "trajectories" will be suggested and tentatively illustrated.

CHAPTER 2

The World of the Hebrew Bible

Consult Maps in *MBA*

nos. 1–23

7
PHYSICAL AND ECONOMIC GEOGRAPHY

The immediate land of the Bible—known as Canaan, Israel, or Palestine—bordered the eastern Mediterranean Sea. It was here, in an area not more than 150 miles from north to south and 75 miles from west to east, that most of the Hebrew Bible was written and most of the events it relates took place. Geographically and historically, however, this heartland of the Bible was merely a small part of a vast area known today as the Middle East and, in its early history, generally characterized as the ancient Near East. The ancient Near East embraced southwest Asia along with lesser sections of northeast Africa and southeast Europe, where three continental land masses met in contours shaped by large bodies of water. It is the whole of this ancient Near East that forms the proper horizons of biblical Israel.

7.1 The Ancient Near East

The region pertinent to an understanding of biblical geography reaches from west to east approximately two thousand miles from the Aegean coast of Turkey to the Hindu Kush mountains of Afghanistan. From north to south a nearly similar distance is spanned from the Caucasus Mountains between the Black and Caspian seas to the southwestern tip of the Arabian Peninsula. However, the ancient Near East did not consist of a large, undifferentiated square of land. The land mass of this region was penetrated, hedged about, and constricted by five large bodies of water: the Red, Mediterranean, Black, and Caspian seas, and the Persian Gulf. It was greatly differentiated internally by mountains, plateaus, deserts, and river valleys.

It is believed that the Near East acquired its geological structure when two vast blocks of hard rock, the Siberian shield to the north and the Afro-Arabian shield to the south, began to move toward one another. In the depression that lay between the shields (which eventually would contain the last four bodies of water named above) sediments from the shields were compressed and folded upward to create the mountains that run generally west to east across the entire northern section of the region. These mountains—including the Taurus and Pontic ranges of Turkey and the Zagros and Elburz ranges of Iran—form a double loop (like an elongated figure eight on its side). The two loops come together in the knot of Armenian mountains of eastern Turkey. Both loops enclose extensive plateaus (in Iran a desert) cut by lesser mountain ranges.

Moreover, the great pressure that folded up the northern mountains caused the southern rock shield to crack and break, opening rifts or faults along whose lines materials either rose to form block mountains or fell to form rift valleys. These block mountains and rift valleys extended roughly north to south from Syria and Palestine through the entire length of Arabia and Egypt and included a great rift valley in which the Red Sea eventually formed. Along crack lines in both the folded and block mountains, volcanic peaks arose and lava flows poured forth. During all this geological activity an immense area to the south and east of the major mountain-building was relatively undisturbed. This desert region, "the Arab Island," extended over the territory of present-day Iraq, Syria, Jordan, Saudi Arabia, and the smaller Persian Gulf states.

By neolithic and early historical times, the climate of the Near East had become rainfall-deficient. Rainfall was seasonal, coming during the winter in the northern sections affected by the cyclonic storms from Europe and during the summer in the far southern sections affected by the fringes of the monsoon rains from the tropics. This rainfall, concentrated in a relatively few days, was often torrential and accompanied by rapid evaporation, fast runoff, and heavy soil erosion. Great care had to be taken to harbor water and soil and to control flooding. As a general rule, higher elevations received heaviest precipitation, and mountain slopes facing the cloud-bearing rains were far wetter than slopes to the leeward (rain shadow effect). In the great interior region of Mesopotamia and the Arabian Peninsula, rainfall rapidly tapered off to amounts too slight to permit regular cultivation of the soil. A similar rainfall deficiency marked northeast Africa west of the Red Sea. In both regions true desert conditions prevailed. All in all, the ancient Near Eastern combination of geology and climate presented precarious conditions for human life. Yet it was in the Near East that two of the great cradles of civilization were located. How did this come about?

We first observe that along the southern slopes and piedmonts of the northern mountain ranges rainfall was fairly plentiful and climate more temperate than in deserts or mountains. Similarly hospitable conditions prevailed along the eastern Mediterranean coast, the Levant. From these areas come our earliest evidences of the neolithic revolution in plant and animal domestication and settled village life, evolving in a margin of land between the harsher high mountains and the water-deficient desert. In this favorable niche of the ancient Near Eastern environment, human life began to thrive and reach out toward further mastery of the natural world.

Neolithic and chalcolithic humans observed the great rivers that arose in the well-watered mountains and flowed across vast desert spaces, depositing rich alluvium along their course and creating great marshes at their mouths. Out of the northern ranges flowed the Tigris and Euphrates rivers, converging before entering the Persian Gulf. The Nile River sprang out of the Ethiopian mountains at the eastern edge of the Sahara Desert and threaded its way to the Mediterranean Sea. In spite of the great summer heat of these river valleys, the rich soils were inviting. To cultivate these alluvial soils dependably, however, it was necessary to capture and control the seasonal runoffs of the rivers. So ambitious a plan required satisfaction of two conditions: (1) development of adequate techniques for building canal and dike systems, and (2) coordination of the efforts of many people over great distances and spans of time. Technical requirements in the two valleys were somewhat different in that the Nile's rise and fall was regular and predictable in volume whereas the Tigris and Euphrates, especially the former, were subject to erratic flooding. Nevertheless, by about 3000 B.C.E. both river systems had been mastered by irrigation projects sufficient to promote intensive farming and a greater density of population.

In this manner history began along the great rivers, first in Sumeria and a little later in Egypt, as people who had been scattered in the piedmont regions of the Near East and North Africa were at last able to concentrate in larger communities in the irrigation-fertile river valleys. When we speak of "the dawn of history" we mean the beginning of a written record of human events and achievements, but we also mean the emergence of a more elaborate social organization which introduced authoritative leadership and administration to oversee the taming of the rivers and the cultivation of the fields, and to enforce certain allocations of the increased wealth that the new techniques and organization made possible. This form of social organization was the state, and with its development politics in the full sense of the word came into being.

From about 3000 B.C.E. onward, a succession of states dominated human social organization and wrote the majority of records in the ancient Near East down through biblical times. At first these states were confined to the river valleys, and usually the strongest states were based in these valleys, but in time the state form of human social organization spread to the mountain and plateau regions on the north and east of Mesopotamia, into Syria, Palestine, and southern Arabia, and along the upper reaches of the Nile south of Egypt. From time to time people from within or from outside these various Near Eastern states were able to overthrow the regimes in power and to replace them with their own forms of political organization, which generally meant yet another centralized state.

It is of significance for our study that Israel first appeared on the stage of history as just such a disturber of the existing order in ancient Canaan. The people who formed Israel were, however, opposed not simply to Canaanite states but to the state form of social organization as such, preferring to live in a looser tribal system. Later in this chapter we shall examine in brief the succession of states that dominated the ancient Near East (§9). In following chapters we shall examine the origins and fortunes of Israel's life as a rebellious latecomer to the world of contending Near Eastern states (§14; 24).

If one traces a line from the mouth of the Tigris-Euphrates rivers on the Persian Gulf northward along the course of the rivers, curving west to the Mediterranean Sea and then southward through Syria and Palestine as far as the Nile Delta of Egypt, this line will appear as an arc, half-moon, or crescent. The swath of land demarcated by this arc includes the largest concentrations of population, the most fertile agricultural areas, the most frequently traveled routes, the territories most fought over by armies, and the great majority of powerful states in the ancient Near East. This so-called Fertile Crescent designates the crucial zone of economic and political development in the ancient Near East. It embraces and connects the two great river valleys at either end along a route of easy access that avoids the hazards of desert and high mountain transport.

Within this great arc describing and connecting Egypt and Mesopotamia, the populace engaged in many economic activities. Easily the vast majority of people farmed, either in the irrigated valleys or in the rain-fed regions along the outer rim of the crescent in Mesopotamia and in the mountainous country of the Levant. Staple crops were grain, either emmer wheat or barley, flax for linen, olive, castor, sesame, or saffron oils, wine and beer, supplemented by fruits, pulses, and vegetables.

The primary animals for milk products, meat, wool, and hides were sheep, goats, cattle, and camels (after ca. 1200 B.C.E.). Asses, mules, and oxen were used for transport and farm work, and horses, at first for pulling chariots and later for cavalry, were introduced after 1750 B.C.E. Animals had long been domesticated in the neolithic communities of farmers. In time pastoral nomads specialized in grazing herds of sheep, goats, and eventually camels, over regions of semidesert, steppe, and mountains not normally cultivated. These nomads varied widely in their habits of residency and movement, but were usually in close and regular mutual relations with the more sedentary peoples. Past historians of the ancient Near East tended to vastly overstate the number and impact of nomads in their accounts of population movements and the conquest of states. Explanations of the origins of Israel have suffered greatly from this bias (§24.2.a).

The needs of farmers and pastoral nomads were largely met by their own labor, allowing for simple barter, so that a modest division of labor seems to have been practiced in the villages and encampments of the mass of the populace. It was otherwise in the great state administrative centers where the appetites of ruling classes sought satisfaction in the works of skilled artisans. Trade also began to flourish. It was common for states to trade in valuable resources and finished products such as precious metals, timber and stone for building, military equipment, exotic herbs and spices, jewelry, and decorative ceramics. A system of roads fanned out over the Fertile Crescent and branched northward into Anatolia, eastward into Iran toward India and China, and southward into Arabia. Maritime trade followed the Indian Ocean to East Africa and India, and the Mediterranean Sea to Greece, Italy, and North Africa.

Privileged corps of bureaucrats operated the great states and their smaller counterparts. They included administrators of taxes and royal estates, diplomats, military commanders, scribes to keep state records and to train new generations of bureaucrats, and priests who operated the state cults and often administered extensive temple holdings. Thus, alongside the centralized state in the ancient Near East there appeared social stratification. A small minority of government-favored people (from 1–5 percent of the total population) controlled most of the economic surplus. "Surplus" here refers to what is produced over and above the minimum required to keep the 95–99 percent of farmers, herders, and laborers alive and working. Professional soldiers formed the backbone of state armies, but for major campaigns the common people were often conscripted. The most menial work, including the monumental building projects, was often done by state slaves, although state slavery seems never to have reached the scale that it later did in Rome. It was also not infrequent for governments to compel legally free citizens to contribute uncompensated labor to state projects.

7.2 Palestine

Palestine was located along the arc between Mesopotamia and Egypt at a point where the Mediterranean Sea on the west and the Arabian desert on the east constricted the inhabited area into a narrow corridor ranging in width from about 35 miles in the north of the land to about 90 miles in the south.

The relief structure of the Palestine corridor, about 150 miles in length, extended northward for another 250 miles throughout Syria, forming a Syro-Palestinian corridor between the great bend of the Euphrates River and the Sinai Desert approach to Egypt. This structure is generally described as a series of four longitudinal zones, which proceed in order from the sea on the west to the desert on the east:

1. the coastal plain;
2. the western mountains or highlands (Cisjordan in Palestine);
3. the rift valley (the Jordan River and Dead Sea in Palestine);
4. the eastern mountains, highlands, or plateau (Transjordan in Palestine).

Although this is a useful initial description, the terrain is actually far more complicated than the customary division allows for.

For one thing the four zones do not continue unbroken or with the same prominence over the whole Syro-Palestinian corridor. For example, the coastal plain is interrupted in Palestine by Mt. Carmel and likewise at several points in Syria. The western highlands are only a tableland in the Negeb of southern Palestine, and Samaria and Galilee are separated from one another by the east-west valleys of Esdraelon and Jezreel that cut through the western highlands from the sea to the Jordan River. The rift valley is cut off from its counterpart in Lebanon by a tangle of mountains west of Mt. Hermon. The eastern highlands are often a tableland or plateau rather than a range of mountains or hills. In Palestine, because their western face is a steep scarp dropping into the rift valley, the eastern highlands look like mountains from Cisjordan, whereas from the eastern desert plateau they are far less prominent.

Furthermore, although the most obvious features of the Palestinian landscape run north and south, the underlying geological structure—which the north-south rift valley has obscured—is in fact on a tilted axis from north-northeast to south-southwest. Thus, the dome of the Gilead mountains east of the Jordan is actually an extension of the mountain mass of Judah west of the Jordan. In addition, hinge faults appeared at right angles to the main structural lines, creating depressions that were of importance for lateral movement from zone to zone. Some run from west to east (as in the Acco–Lake of Galilee–Bashan depression), while others orient northwest to southwest (as in the Sidon–Wadi Sirhan depression and in the Esdraelon Valley–Wadi Fariʿa depression).

The net effect of the complicated relief structure of Palestine is that the country consists of a fair number of markedly different subregions that did not easily communicate with one another. The trend toward local self-sufficiency in these regions made unification of the land, for whatever reason, a difficult task. In this respect, ancient Israel was much like ancient Greece. In both instances we observe a strong persisting sense of cultural

unity among a people torn by internal political divisiveness that corresponded in large measure to the pronounced regionalism of the land. The
nature of the initial Israelite social movement, the division into two kingdoms, the hostility between Jews and Samaritans, as well as many other
aspects of Israel's history, can only be understood on the ground plan of the
cantonal divisions of Palestine.

Like the greater part of the ancient Near East outside of Egypt and
Mesopotamia, Palestine lacked any great river that could be harnessed for
irrigation. Its people, crops, and herds were necessarily rain-fed. The vital
rains came off the Mediterranean from about mid-October to early April,
falling most abundantly in the north of the land and decreasing strikingly
toward the south. The north coast and the seaward slopes of the highlands
east and west of the rift valley received the fullest watering, while the
windward slopes of the highlands and the rift valley, lying in the rain
shadow, had far less rain. In addition, rainfall amounts were highly variable
from year to year as well as from region to region, and the spacing of the
rains so unpredictable that crops could fail from too much or too little rain
at crucial points in the growing season.

The soils in Palestine varied greatly in their suitability for cultivation. The
hard limestones in the hill country provided an excellent building stone and
decomposed into a rich permeable soil for farming. Much of the hill
country, however, was formed of chalk that cultivated very poorly but had
the advantage of wearing away rapidly so that roadways followed these
chalky deposits wherever possible. Some surfaces were totally unmanage-
able for agriculture: sandstone, frequent on the western edge of the Transjordan highlands and containing copper deposits; the salt-laden marls of the
Jordan Valley; and the basalt rock of eastern Galilee that had not yet
decomposed into soil as it had in parts of Bashan. Much of the coastal plain
was enriched by alluvial soil washed out of the western highlands, but sand
dunes impeded drainage and kept sizable parts of the plain out of cultivation. Some regions with rich alluvium were too marshy to cultivate, such as
the Plain of Sharon south of Mt. Carmel and the upper Jordan Valley in the
Huleh basin.

The result of this combination of relief, rainfall, and soil factors was that
the reliable farming areas of Palestine amounted to less than one-half of the
total land area. The reliable core farming regions of Palestine were approximately as follows:

1. the coastal plain north of Mt. Carmel (the Plain of Acco) and between the Plain
   of Sharon and Gaza to the south (the Philistine Plain), and including the lateral
   Esdraelon-Jezreel valleys;

2. the Cisjordan highlands for their whole length from Galilee to a point south of Hebron in a strip averaging perhaps twenty miles in width;
3. some points in the upper Jordan Valley north of Beth-shan;
4. the Transjordan highlands for their whole length from Bashan to Edom in a strip averaging perhaps ten miles in width.

A comparison of the western and eastern highlands as arable zones is instructive. Clearly, the Cisjordan highlands represented the larger and more productive agricultural region. The dependably arable zone in Transjordan was for the most part much narrower than in Cisjordan, but showed decided irregularities in shape. It bulged far inland in Bashan and Gilead but narrowed to a single string of villages along the high uplift of southern Edom which received adequate rain, while the lower Negeb to the immediate west was virtually arid. Noteworthy too is the generally greater variety of crops in the western highlands. For the most part Transjordan could not grow vines and olive trees, so that Gilead alone in the eastern highlands could duplicate the mix of grain, wine, and oil that was so familiar to the western highlands.

This does not mean of course that all the land outside of the reliable agricultural heartland was an economic wasteland. For one thing, sheep and goats could be grazed over the grasses that sprang up with the winter rains. Here and there springs created lush oases in otherwise arid regions, as at Jericho and En-Gedi in the rift valley. It was always possible to hazard plantings in marginal areas, if one was not wholly dependent on them; it is likely, for instance, that an appreciable barley harvest could have been gotten in the Beersheba basin on the average of every third year. Also, if good reason existed for inhabiting a desert frontier region, it was possible to dam and terrace wadi beds so that trapped runoff waters would support agriculture, as was the case during the Israelite monarchy in Jeshimon (the Wilderness of Judah) and in parts of the Negeb on into Nabatean, Roman, and Byzantine times.

Yet it was precisely in the securest farming lands of the Cisjordan and Transjordan highlands that the first Israelites lived as farmers and resident pastoralists. The territories of Judah, Benjamin, Ephraim, and Manasseh in the western highlands formed the heartland of ancient Israel. Here were located the cities of Hebron, Bethlehem, Jerusalem, Gibeon, Bethel, Shiloh, Shechem, Tirzah, and Samaria. Two major Israelite strongholds stood apart from this central base: Galilee to the north, separated by the Esdraelon-Jezreel valley corridor, and Gilead to the east, cut off by the deep rift valley. Possibly first colonized by Israelites from the Judah-Samaria highlands, Galilee and Gilead were always precariously held by

Israel and the regionalism of the land shows up in the suspicion and hostility often expressed back and forth among these regions—including pronounced tension between Judah and Samaria, even though they both held secure positions in the privileged western highland core. Only under David were the coastal plain, the rift valley, and most of Transjordan brought under Israel's control. Whenever the political power of Israel contracted, it was these secondary regions that were first lost. The hill country of southern Cisjordan, and the more vulnerable offshoots in Galilee and Gilead, remained the physical and economic base and the cultural and spiritual homeland of biblical Israel.

7.3 Subregions Important to Biblical Israel

Against the backdrop of the general features of Palestinian geography, we will now pinpoint the subregions that had the most significant bearing on Israel's experience.

7.3.a The Coastal Plain

For its entire length Palestine was flanked on the west by the Mediterranean Sea. Natural and political circumstances blocked Israel from developing toward the sea or adventuring on the sea. Israel neither fully settled the coastal plain nor became a maritime power. Why?

To begin with, the Palestine coast, with the exception of the Bay of Acco north of Mt. Carmel, was unrelieved by indentation and the development of harbors was frustrated by silting from the Nile Delta deposited all along the coast. As for settlement in the coastal plain, the intractable marshes of the Plain of Sharon inhibited occupation in its center and the Philistines held the desirable southern part of the plain where it fanned out to its greatest breadth. Even after David reduced the Philistines as a military threat, Israel appears to have accepted the continuing Philistine presence on the plain (§30.1–3). The far northern coast beyond Carmel was also contested land, frequently held by the Phoenicians.

The skilled exploiters of the Mediterranean were the Canaanites who lived along the narrow coastal plain in Syria and Lebanon. Ugarit and Byblos were major ports before being succeeded by Tyre and Sidon in early Israelite times. Under the name of Phoenicians, the merchants of Tyre and Sidon rapidly became the chief maritime power of the great inner sea (§30.4). Key factors in this Phoenician "opening to the sea" were availability of good harbors, lack of land for farming, and isolation from land trade being drawn toward inland Damascus.

Despite reports in the Bible that early Israelites operated ships, or more likely served on them, and that some of Israel's kings made valiant—if largely unsuccessful—efforts to develop a fleet through the Red Sea outlet to the Indian Ocean, Israel remained essentially landlocked. The chief significance of the coastal plain for Israel was that through it ran the trunk road from Egypt to Mesopotamia, bringing merchants, diplomats, and invading armies. Moreover, north of Mt. Carmel this coastal plain penetrated all the way across Palestine to the Jordan River by way of the valleys of Esdraelon and Jezreel, through which passed two branches of the trunk road as it turned inland toward Damascus. Here the level coastal terrain was drawn into the heart of Israel as a mixed blessing of fertile land, facilitated communication, and vulnerability to attack.

The major Philistine cities of the plain were (from south to north) Gaza, Ashkelon, Ashdod, Gath, and Ekron. During the monarchy, and even in postexilic times, there were Israelite settlements north of Philistia in such locations as Gibbethon, Jabneel, Gezer, Lod, Joppa, Tell Qasile (biblical name unknown), Aphek, Hepher, and Dor, and likewise north of Mt. Carmel in Nahalol, Aphek, Achshaph, Acco, and Achzib.

7.3.b The Hill Country of Judah

Judah comprised the southernmost extension of the western highlands. Its center was a high, rocky plateau averaging three thousand feet in altitude, fertile to the west of the water divide, but desolate to the east where the Wilderness of Judah or Jeshimon dropped toward the sheer cliffs overlooking the Dead Sea. The most important settlement in this wilderness was the oasis at En-Gedi on the Dead Sea. In the cliffs at the northwest end of the sea a sectarian community, keepers of the renowned Dead Sea Scrolls, lived in virtual isolation from ca. 100 B.C.E. to 70 C.E. (§10.2.b; 47).

The fertile western heights of Judah were protected by the rugged lower hills of the Shephelah ("lowlands" or "foothills"), which was separated from the steep scarp of the highlands by a narrow north-south moat valley. The Shephelah, much contested by Philistines and Judahites, contained the settlements of Tell Beit Mirsim (possibly Debir), Lachish, Mareshah, Keilah, Adullam, Socoh, Azekah, and Beth-shemesh. The Judean massif dropped away south of Hebron into the undulating Negeb, or southland, where the territory of Simeon, with its settlements of Beersheba, Kabzeel, Hormah, and Arad, was early incorporated into Judah. The approaches to Judah, heavily fortified during the monarchy, were thus decidedly defensible on all sides except the north (§33.2; 33.6).

In the fertile highlands of Judah lay the towns of Maon, Carmel, Ziph,

Adoraim, Hebron, Khirbet Rabud (probably Debir), Bethzur, Tekoa, Etam, Bethlehem, and Jerusalem. Throughout this area vineyards were the specialty crop, and wheat and barley were grown in quantity. Olives were planted but winter cold and decreased rain made them less plentiful the farther south one went into the highlands. The most fertile region of Judah was directly south of Jerusalem in the vicinity of Bethlehem and Etam. Sheep and goats were extensively bred over the whole area, and even pastured in the accessible parts of the Wilderness of Judah. The main road followed the north-south watershed line with the villages lying to either side on defensible sites.

7.3.c The Hill Country of Samaria

The central bulk of the western highlands was separated from Judah by the so-called Saddle of Benjamin. Here, just to the north of Jerusalem, the highlands dropped several hundred feet below their usual height. This was a major crossroads, offering the easiest access into the highlands, from the coast by way of the pass of Aijalon and from the rift valley via a road from Jericho. The buffer zone of Benjamin between Judah and Ephraim, containing the settlements of Gibeah, Ramah, Mizpah, and Gibeon, was often disputed by the northern and southern kingdoms of Israel and it always presented a problem for the adequate defense of nearby Jerusalem.

To the north the limestone dome of Ephraim stretched across the entire highlands, a tightly defended bastion of small villages well suited to olive and vineyard cultivation. Major towns were Bethel, Ophrah, Baal-hazor, Jeshanah, Shiloh, Zeredah, and Tappuah. Still farther north lay the territory of Manasseh where the central highlands split into two arms fanning out to embrace a large downfaulted basin in the center of which rose the peaks of Ebal and Gerizim, with the major crossroads city of Shechem situated between the two mountains. Other important settlements in Manasseh were Arumah, Janoah, Tirzah, Thebez, Bezek, Samaria, and Dothan. The basins were ideal for growing grains and the slopes abounded in vineyards and olive groves.

The interplay between geography and politics is complex in this region. The proximity of the valleys of Esdraelon and Jezreel to the north invited Manasseh to spread out into them, even though in the Bible these valleys are assigned to the lesser tribes of Issachar and Zebulun. It was thus mainly Manasseh that challenged the Canaanite hold on Ibleam, En-gannim, Taanach, Megiddo, and Jezreel in the transverse valleys. The spread of several sizable valleys within the hill country basins made for good internal communication, but the fact that Manasseh was not well defended against penetration from the coastal plain, from the valley of Esdraelon, or from the rift valley—plus the fact that for a long time the northern kingdom did not have a fully defensible capital city in this region (§33.2–3)—meant that natural conditions here did not favor political stability. The regions of Ephraim and Manasseh taken together (the so-called Joseph tribes) were eventually known as Samaria, after the fortified capital built by Omri, but the unity of this heartland of the northern kingdom was jeopardized by different geopolitical realities in the massif of Ephraim and in the open basins of Manasseh (§33.6).

Mt. Carmel was the farthest northwest extension of a thirty-mile-long ridge that angled out of the Samarian highlands and reached to the very edge of the sea. This ridge, although never attaining as much as two thousand feet, was forbiddingly steep and forested—thus unsettled—and served to split the coastal plain so that traffic was channeled through its narrow passes into the valleys of Esdraelon and Jezreel which thus became the central nexus of communication in the north of Palestine.

7.3.d The Hill Country of Galilee

Galilee resumed the north-south mountainous terrain, rising in two steps northward from the Esdraelon-Jezreel valleys. Lower Galilee was composed of shattered limestone and chalk hills, not exceeding two thousand feet, with many internally connecting downfaulted basins. Here lay the biblical settlements of Jabneel, Madon, Heleph, Gath-hepher, Japhia, Shimron, Rimmon, and Jotbah, amid slopes and basins well adapted to the favored Israelite mix of olives, vines, and grains. In the eastern section there was much basalt rock that extended to the Lake of Galilee in the rift valley. This region was crossed from southwest to northeast by the trunk road from the valley of Esdraelon which passed north of the Lake of Galilee.

Upper Galilee rose to three thousand feet and higher over a large area prominently uplifted along an east-west scarp that towered over Lower Galilee. At its foot ran a direct route from the Lake of Galilee to Acco on the coast. On the edges or within this rocky fastness lay Hazor, Merom, Kedesh, Beth-anath, Beth-shemesh, Yiron, and Kanah. The area possessed potentially good soil and excellent rainfall, but it is not known how extensively the early Israelites cleared its thicketed and forested expanses. The Bible itself says very little about this region, although there is archaeological evidence that a network of small farming villages, probably Israelite, did spread over parts of this region prior to the monarchy (§24.1.a).

7.3.e The Rift Valley

By and large, the rift valley was not conducive to settlement except at a few oasis sites such as Jericho and Beth-shan, or where the fresh streams from the Transjordan highlands emptied into the Jordan valley. The water of the Jordan River itself was too saline for agricultural use. The rift valley did afford convenient north-south travel, although roadways had to be carefully chosen because of the tributary wadis, the twisted marls, and the basalt outflows. The river, lined by a tamarisk jungle, cut a deep channel through the marly badlands from south of Beth-shan all the way to the Dead Sea, and thus could be crossed only at a few fording points.

The gargantuan rift valley, visible from many parts of the highlands, imparted a sense of grandeur and spaciousness—of being amid landscapes of immense heights, depths, and distances—to a land that more often drew attention to its miniaturized local environments. In spite of its precipitous drops and barren aspect, the rift valley did not create an impassable barrier to east-west movement. Where regions in the highlands on either side of the rift valley were similar, communication and a sense of joint community could be maintained—as was certainly the case between Manasseh in Cisjordan and Gilead in Transjordan.

7.3.f The Hill Country of Gilead

Located east of the rift valley, opposite Manasseh and Ephraim, Gilead rose in a great limestone dome that protected small village life and encouraged the typical mixed farming patterns of the Israelites. By contrast, the lands of Transjordan to the north and south of Gilead were less strategically secure and tended to be given primarily to one or another crop, grains being especially plentiful in Bashan to the north and Moab to the south. Gilead was split by the east-west course of Wadi Jabbok, but similar natural conditions on both sides of the deep wadi contributed to a feeling of unity in the entire region. Ramoth-gilead, Beth-arbel, Lo-debar, Jabesh-gilead, Penuel, Mahanaim, Jazer, and possibly Abel-meholah (but perhaps in Cisjordan) were located in the highlands, while Zarethan, Zaphon, and Succoth were situated at the edge of the rift valley where wadis issued out of the Gilead escarpment. Since in the Bible Gilead was assigned partly to the half-tribe of Manasseh and partly to Gad, with claims sometimes overlapping, it is arguable that Gilead was colonized by Israelites from Cisjordan. The rocky and forested regions of Gilead were a frequent place of retreat in times of political difficulty.

7.3.g Ammon, Moab, and Edom

Three plateau kingdoms in Transjordan had frequent, mostly hostile, contacts with Israel. Ammon, to the southeast of Gilead, was a mixed farming and shepherding state on the very edge of the desert. Moab, directly south of Gilead, was a grain-growing and sheep-raising tableland overlooking the Dead Sea from the east. Its heartland was between the Wadi Zered on the south and the Wadi Arnon on the north, but, when strong, Moab controlled the tableland northward to Heshbon and even to the fords of the Jordan opposite Jericho. Edom, south of Wadi Zered, rose on a long uplift over five thousand feet high, where the additional altitude assured it sufficient rainfall for limited agriculture along the plateau crest.

The second most important route in Palestine, the King's Highway, connecting with the Spice Route to south Arabia, ran from the head of the Gulf of Aqabah northward through Edom, Moab, and Ammon toward Damascus. It was heavily trafficked by merchant caravans that were obliged to pay tolls whenever the plateau kingdoms were strong enough to exact them. The Midianites built a trading empire in this region during the days of the Israelite judges, and the Nabatean Arabs did likewise from their impregnable rock city of Petra in Edom during Hellenistic and Roman times. Whenever an Israelite king aimed at dominion over Transjordan, it was imperative to gain control of the lucrative commerce along the King's Highway (§30.4; 33.3).

8
ARCHAEOLOGY: MATERIAL AND WRITTEN REMAINS

8.1 Archaeology of the Ancient Near East

The previous description of relief and climate in the ancient Near East and Palestine rests heavily on geology, geography, and meteorology. At the same time, even so simplified a description calls attention to how the relief and climate impacted and shaped the lives of ancient people, which necessarily calls into play our historical knowledge of the ancient Near East. Strictly speaking, historical knowledge is written knowledge. It is possible, however, to acquire knowledge of human life in the past by carefully examining material remains so that, in a sense, the ancient objects are made to tell us something about those who made and used them.

Archaeology is the recovery and systematic study of the material remains of the past, from which inferences are drawn about the culture, society, and history of the people who left the remains. Archaeologically relevant objects include foundations, walls, buildings, statues, cooking and ceremonial vessels, tools, weapons, jewelry and other ornaments, metals, cloth, pottery, and animal and human bones. If we are fortunate, among the recovered objects will be occasional written materials, which may range from crudely scratched letters and words to extended literary texts. The material objects, including the inscriptions and texts, must be studied in relation to one another, both at the sites where found and in connection with other related objects and writings, in order to build up a grid of knowledge about the underlying culture, society, and history. Archaeological reconstruction is a slow and laborious process, often misunderstood by the general public who hears only of this or that sensational discovery—already often misinterpreted or blown out of proportion by the popular press.

Fortunately we possess a growing wealth of knowledge about the ancient Near East sifted and correlated from archaeological excavations. Ancient Near Eastern cities tended to develop in successive levels of occupation on strategically chosen sites that tended to be used again and again rather than abandoned, even after destruction. The artificial mounds (or tells), contructed somewhat like a layer cake, that mark the ancient cities are excavated in horizontal sections, generally by cutting trenches into the mound so that the layers are exposed one above the other. The oldest occupations of the site will be found at the bottom of the mound and the most recent occupations at the top. The layered objects are dated primarily by a refined analysis of the evolution of pottery types, which in turn are dated in relation to inscriptional materials.

Excavations all over the ancient Near East, heavily concentrated in the Fertile Crescent, have uncovered ancient cities and libraries which allow us to write a political history of those times with some measure of accuracy and detail. Most of the evidence in writing is from state or temple texts in the archives of the major powers of Egypt, Sumeria, Akkad, Old Babylonia, Assyria, the Hittite Kingdom, Neo-Babylonia, and Persia. Here and there the records of smaller states scattered over the ancient Near East have survived, as from Mari on the middle Euphrates and Ugarit on the Syrian coast. Similar records survive within the Hebrew Bible and appear additionally in an array of written inscriptions, mostly fragmentary, from Israelite Palestine.

It is essential for the biblical interpreter to be aware of the astonishing range of ancient Near Eastern texts that have a bearing both on the history recounted or presupposed in the Hebrew Bible and on virtually the entire spectrum of biblical genres and topics. A sample of ancient Near Eastern texts is listed below in connection with appropriate biblical books (table 1; §10.1). The texts are identified by their linguistic and/or political provenance and are keyed to the pagination of the standard English translations for ready reference.

This linkage of biblical and nonbiblical literature is not intended to imply that there is any necessary direct literary dependence of one writing on the other. Nor does it suggest that the biblical and nonbiblical texts always correspond closely in matters of content and detail. It is rather to show that there was a vast fund of writings in the wider world which used literary forms very much like the forms of biblical literature and that dealt with the same or similar historical and thematic concerns. The table is meant to show that not only did Israel participate in a common *geographical* and *historical* world but also in a common *literary* and *religiocultural* world.

8.2 Archaeology of Palestine

Palestinian archaeology has typically expressed a double-barreled interest in illuminating the Bible and in clarifying the relation of Israel to the surrounding cultures. Organizations funded to conduct scientific excavations in Palestine have been at work for about a century, and many institutions of higher education have sponsored excavations. Because archaeological techniques began crudely and because some excavators have been untrained or unskilled, the results of the large volume of archaeological work to date are uneven and must be evaluated critically. There are now recognized professional and publishing forums where the methods and conclusions of archaeological research are critically assessed and refined in ongoing dialogue.

Excavations in Palestine have unearthed materials from the entire range of archaeological periods, beginning with the Mesolithic Age and extending on through the most recent Islamic period. The generally accepted designations for the archaeological periods and their dating (about which there is continuing dispute) are listed below, together with chronologically related biblical periods, either known or conjectured (table 2). It will be noted that the convention is to specify some periods—especially those applicable to biblical times—according to the most advanced metal in use, for example, copper (chalcolithic), bronze, or iron.

Palestine has probably been as extensively surveyed and excavated as any ancient country in the world. Yet less than twenty years ago, an archaeologist noted that out of some five thousand recorded antiquities sites and monuments in Palestine, roughly three sites in a hundred had been scien-

TABLE 1
Ancient Near Eastern Texts Related to the Hebrew Bible
by Theme, Literary Genre, or Historical Connection

Key to the coding of texts by their linguistic/cultural/political categories

Ak	= Akkadian	Hi	= Hittite
Ar	= Aramaic	Mb	= Moabite
As	= Assyrian	NB	= New Babylonian
Cn/Ph	= Canaanite/Phoenician	OB	= Old Babylonian
Eg	= Egyptian	Su	= Sumerian
Hb	= Hebrew		

	Linguistic Code	ANET*	NERT*
1. Genesis			
A. Babylonian Creation Epic	OB/NB(?)	60–72, 501–3	80–84
B. Babylonian New Year Festival	OB/NB(?)	331–34	
C. Enki and Ninhursag (Sumerian Paradise)	Su	37–40	85–86
D. Adapa Myth	OB	101–3	
E. Dumuzi and Enkimdu (Cain-Abel motif)	Su	41–42	
F. Sumerian King List	Su	265–66	87–89
G. Ziusudra Myth (Sumerian flood)	Su	42–44	89–90
H. Gilgamesh Epic (tablet XI: flood)	Ak	72–99, 503–7	93–97
I. Atrahasis Epic (Babylonian flood)	OB	104–6, 512–14	90–93
J. Story of Sinuhe	Eg	18–23	
K. Nuzi Tablets	OB	219–20	
L. Story of Two Brothers	Eg	23–25	
M. Tradition of Seven Lean Years	Eg	31–32	
2. Exodus-Deuteronomy			
A. Asiatics in Egyptian Household Service	Eg	553–54	
B. Legend of Birth of Sargon	Ak(?)	119	98–99
C. Hymn to Aton	Eg	369–71	16–19
D. Merneptah or Israel Stela	Eg	376–78	

---

*Translations:
ANET = Pritchard, *Ancient Near Eastern Texts Relating to the Old Testament*
NERT = Beyerlin, *Near Eastern Religious Texts Relating to the Old Testament*

The collection of extrabiblical texts is far fuller in *ANET* than in *NERT*, which often abbreviates as well. The latter does have the advantage of clearer introductions and notes for the student, especially with reference to proposed parallels with the Hebrew Bible. Both anthologies have indexes of biblical references but the connections cited are far from exhaustive and in some cases seem peripheral or even off-target.

TABLE 1 (continued)
Ancient Near Eastern Texts Related to the Hebrew Bible
by Theme, Literary Genre, or Historical Connection

		Linguistic Code	*ANET*	*NERT*
E.	Law Codes:			
	Ur-Nammu	Su	523–25	
	Lipit-Ishtar	Su	159–61	
	Eshnunna	OB	161–63	
	Hammurabi	OB	163–80	
	Middle Assyrian	As	180–88	
	Hittite	Hi	188–97	
	Neo-Babylonian	NB	197–98	
F.	Edict of Ammisaduqa	OB	526–28	
G.	Hittite Suzerain-Vassal Treaties	Hi	201–6, 529–30	
H.	Syrian and Assyrian Suzerain-Vassal Treaties	Ar, As	531–41, 659–61	129–31, 256–66
3.	Joshua-Judges			
A.	Execration of Asiatic Princes	Eg	328–29	
B.	Amarna Letters	Eg	483–90	
C.	Journey of Wen-Amon to Phoenicia	Eg	25–29	
D.	War Against the Sea Peoples	Eg	262–63	
E.	Baal and Anath	Cn/Ph	129–42	190–221
F.	Legend of King Keret	Cn/Ph	142–49	223–25
G.	Tale of Aqhat (Daniel)	Cn/Ph	149–55	225–26
4.	Samuel-Kings			
A.	Ahiram Inscription	Cn/Ph	661	
B.	Gezer Calendar	Hb	320	
C.	Story of Idrimi of Alalakh	As	557–58	
D.	Plague Prayers of Mursilis	Hi	394–96	169–74
E.	Moabite Stone	Mb	320–21	
F.	Zakir Stela	Ar	655–56	229–32
G.	Samarian Ostraca	Hb	321	
H.	Siloam Inscription	Hb	321	
I.	Arad Ostraca	Hb	568–69	253
J.	Assyrian Royal Annals	As	274–301	
K.	Neo-Babylonian Chronicles	NB	302–7, 563–64	
L.	Lachish Letters	Hb	321–22	

TABLE 1 (continued)
Ancient Near Eastern Texts Related to the Hebrew Bible
by Theme, Literary Genre, or Historical Connection

	Linguistic Code	*ANET*	*NERT*
5. Ezra-Nehemiah			
A. Babylonian Ration Tablets	NB	308	
B. Nabonidus Texts	NB	308–16, 560–63	
C. Cyrus Cylinder	NB	315–16	
D. Elephantine Papyri	Ar	491–92, 548–49	252–55
6. Prophetic Books			
A. Protests of the Eloquent Peasant	Eg	407–10	
B. Prophetic Sayings from Mari	OB		122–28
C. Assyrian Oracles of Salvation	As	449–50, 605	
D. Letter from the Time of Josiah	Hb	568	
7. Psalms			
A. Egyptian Hymns	Eg	365–81	39–43
B. Mesopotamian Hymns and Laments	Su, OB, As	383–92, 573–86	99–115
8. Proverbs			
A. Old Babylonian and Assyrian Proverbs	OB, As	425–27, 593–96	
B. Instructions of Amen-em-opet	Eg	421–24	49–62
C. Words of Ahiqar	Ar	427–30	
9. Job and Ecclesiastes			
A. Man and His God (Sumerian Job)	Su	589–91	140–42
B. "I Will Praise the Lord of Wisdom"	NB	434–37, 596–600	137–40
C. Dialogue About Human Misery (Babylonian Ecclesiastes, Babylonian Theodicy)	NB	438–40, 601–4	133–37
D. Pessimistic Dialogue Between Master and Servant	NB	437–38, 600–601	
E. A Satirical Letter	Eg	475–79	
F. Shurpu Texts ("Negative Confessions")	OB		131–32

54

TABLE 1 (continued)
Ancient Near Eastern Texts Related to the Hebrew Bible
by Theme, Literary Genre, or Historical Connection

	Linguistic Code	*ANET*	*NERT*
10. Lamentations			
A. Lamentation Over the Destruction of Ur	Su	455–63	116–18
B. Lamentation Over the Destruction of Sumer and Ur	Su	611–19	
11. Song of Songs			
A. Egyptian Love Songs	Eg	467–69	
B. Sumerian Love Song	Su	496	
12. Daniel			
"A Ruler Will Come . . ."	As	606–7	118–19

TABLE 2
Archaeological Periods in Biblical Palestine

Archaeological Periods	Biblical Periods
Mesolithic (Natufian) 8000–6000 B.C.E.	
Pre-Pottery Neolithic 6000–5000 B.C.E.	
Pottery Neolithic 5000–4000 B.C.E.	
Chalcolithic (Copper) 4000–3200 B.C.E.	
Esdraelon 3200–3000 B.C.E.	
Early Bronze (EB) 3000–2100 B.C.E.	
EB I 3000–2800 B.C.E.	
EB II 2800–2600 B.C.E.	
EB III 2600–2300 B.C.E.	
EB IV (or IIIb) 2300–2100 B.C.E.	
Middle Bronze (MB) 2100–1550 B.C.E.	
MB I (or EB-MB) 2100–1900 B.C.E.	Possible period of the patriarchs Abraham, Isaac, and Jacob (differently dated by various scholars in EB IV, MB, or LB) [see §16]
MB IIa 1900–1700 B.C.E.	
MB IIb 1700–1600 B.C.E.	
MB IIc 1600–1550 B.C.E.	

TABLE 2 (continued)
Archaeological Periods in Biblical Palestine

Archaeological Periods	*Biblical Periods*
Late Bronze (LB) 1550–1200 B.C.E.	
LB I 1550–1400 B.C.E.	Possible period of the patriarchs
LB IIa 1400–1300 B.C.E.	
LB IIb 1300–1200 B.C.E.	Moses and the exodus [see §18.1]
Iron I (Ir) or Early Iron (EI) 1200–900 B.C.E.	
Ir Ia 1200–1150 B.C.E.	Joshua
Ir Ib 1150–1025 B.C.E.	Judges of Israel
Ir Ic 1025–950 B.C.E.	Saul David Solomon
Ir Id 950–900 B.C.E.	Division of the kingdom
Iron II (Ir) or Middle Iron (MI) 900–600 B.C.E.	
Ir IIa 900–800 B.C.E.	
Ir IIb 800–700 B.C.E.	Fall of Israel (northern kingdom)
Ir IIc 700–600 B.C.E.	Reformation of Josiah
Iron III, Late Iron, or Persian 600–300 B.C.E.	Fall of Judah (southern kingdom) Exile to Babylonia Restoration of Judah Nehemiah and Ezra

TABLE 2 (continued)
Archaeological Periods in Biblical Palestine

Archaeological Periods	*Biblical Periods*
Hellenistic 300–63 B.C.E.	Maccabean Revolt Hasmonean Dynasty
Roman 63 B.C.E.–323 C.E.	Rise of Christianity First Jewish Revolt Second Jewish Revolt
Byzantine 323–636 C.E.	
Islamic 636 C.E.–	

tifically excavated, including small soundings and clearances, while roughly only one site in two hundred had been the scene of major archaeological work.[1] Even if we estimate that two or possibly three times that number of sites have by now been excavated in some fashion, an enormous number of sites remains to be attended to. In the meanwhile, additional sites keep coming to the attention of archaeologists.

The following table of major excavations in Palestine (table 3) is arranged according to the geographical divisions of the land discussed in §7.3. The biblical names of locations are stated when they are known with a high degree of certainty. In other cases still under dispute, the modern names of sites are given. A key is included to indicate remains at each site according to the archaeological periods represented (only a very few pre-Bronze sites are included. Iron I and II are treated together, and Iron III is called Persian). It is at once apparent that the coastal plain, Judah, and Samaria exhibit a larger concentration of important excavated sites during the biblical period than do Galilee, the rift valley, Gilead, and the plateau kingdoms of Ammon, Moab, and Edom. How much this is due to the actual distribution of total sites, or to the greater interest of excavators in digging in the biblical heartland territory, is difficult to judge. In some instances, in order to fill out the table for the less-excavated regions, minor excavations have been included.

Palestinian archaeology has commonly been called biblical archaeology, which appropriately emphasizes the consuming interests of past archaeologists in the bearing of archaeology on the literature and history of ancient Israel. These interests admirably supplemented the historical-critical aspect of biblical studies (§16.1; 24.1; 27; 39), and continue to have a vital place in the archaeology of Palestine. Paralleling the emergent methods of new literary criticism and social scientific criticism in biblical studies, however, is a growing interest in archaeology as an important contributor to the reconstruction of ancient Israelite life in its total cultural range, including its social history (§24.1). This accent, long significant in Native American (= American Indian) studies and in prehistoric archaeology, is at last receiving fuller attention in the archaeology of historical Palestine. The relation between the older and newer emphases is highlighted in the recent discussion as to whether the discipline should be called biblical archaeology or Palestinian archaeology.

Even during the long period when history and religion in relation to the biblical text dominated Palestinian archaeology, the process of excavating

---

1. Paul W. Lapp, "Palestine: Known but Mostly Unknown," *BA* 27 (1963): 121–34.

TABLE 3
Major Excavations in Biblical Palestine

Key to the coding of remains by archaeological periods (see table 2 for the dates of these periods)

M = Mesolithic (Natufian)	LB = Late Bronze
N = Neolithic, Pre-Pottery and Pottery	Ir = Iron I and II
C = Chalcolithic (Copper)	P = Persian or Iron III
EB = Early Bronze	H = Hellenistic
MB = Middle Bronze	

	M	N	C	EB	MB	LB	Ir	P	H
The coastal plain									
Acco					X	X	X	X	X
Aphek				X	X	X	X		
Ashdod					X	X	X	X	
Ashkelon					X	X			X
Dor						X	X		
Gezer			X	X	X	X	X	X	X
Joppa			X	X		X	X		X
Sharuhen					X	X	X		
Tell Abu Huwam						X	X	X	
Tell el-Ḥesi				X		X	X	X	X
Tell Nagila				X	X		X		
Tell Sheikh el-ʿAreini			X	X		X	X		
The hill country of Judah **(including Shephelah and Negeb)**									
Arad			X	X			X	X	X
Beersheba							X	X	X
Beth-shemesh				X	X	X			
Bethzur				X	X		X	X	X
En-gedi							X	X	X
Hebron				X	X	X			
Jerusalem			X			X	X	X	X
Khirbet Rabud			X	X	X	X			
Mareshah			X	X	X	X			
Ramat Raḥel							X	X	X
Tell ʿAitun						X	X		
Tell Beit Mirsim				X	X	X	X		

TABLE 3 (continued)
Major Excavations in Biblical Palestine

	M	N	C	EB	MB	LB	Ir	P	H
The hill country of Samaria (including Benjamin, valleys of Esdraelon/Jezreel)									
Ai				x			x		
Bethel						x	x	x	
Beth-shan			x	x	x	x	x		x
Dothan			x	x	x	x	x		x
Gibeah					x		x		x
Gibeon				x	x	x	x		
Megiddo				x	x	x	x		
Mizpah				x			x	x	x
Naḥal Oren, Mt. Carmel	x	x							
Samaria							x		x
Shechem			x		x	x	x	x	x
Shiloh					x		x		x
Taanach				x	x	x	x		
Tirzah			x	x	x	x	x		
The hill country of Galilee (including rift valley north of Beth-shan)									
Beth-yeraḥ				x				x	x
Dan				x	x	x	x	x	x
ʿEn Gev							x		
ʿEn Mallaha	x								
Hazor					x	x	x	x	
Khirbet Qedîsh (Kedesh Naphtali)				x		x			
The rift valley (south of Beth-shan)									
Jericho	x	x		x	x	x			
Khirbet Qumran									x
Telleilat Ghassul			x						
The hill country of Gilead									
Pella			x		x	x	x		
Ramoth-gilead							x		
Tell Deir ʿAlla					x	x	x		
Tell es-Saʿidiyeh							x	x	x

TABLE 3 (continued)
Major Excavations in Biblical Palestine

	M	N	C	EB	MB	LB	Ir	P	H
Ammon, Moab, and Edom									
Aroer				x	x	x	x		
Bab edh-Dhra				x					
Dibon				x	x	x	x		
Heshbon							x	x	x
Petra									x
Rabbath-ammon		x	x	x	x	x	x		x
Sela							x		

and recording inevitably produced an impressive range of information that advanced our knowledge of the physical, technological, economic, social, aesthetic, and intellectual life of the ancient inhabitants of Palestine. Nonetheless, partly because of the orientation of archaeologists primarily toward history and politics and partly because of the social class identity of those who left the most impressive remains, our archaeological information is mostly about life among the rulers and upper classes in the large administrative centers of the land. In that respect, Palestinian archaeology is as selective in its picture of ancient conditions of life as is Near Eastern archaeology as a whole. This means that we can visualize the layout and major architectural features of a Canaanite city in the Lower Bronze Age or of Jerusalem and Samaria during the Israelite kingdoms, but that we have far less information concerning the tribal period when Israel did not have a state structure of its own. In fact, the rural life of Israel over the entire biblical period is not well documented archaeologically. Considering that Israel's largest cities were never large by modern urban standards, and that probably close to 90 percent of the populace always lived in small towns and villages, it is obvious that we are far from having a well-rounded picture of the total material and spiritual culture of biblical Israel.

Given the impressive recent advances in archaeological techniques, current sociological curiosity about how all the strata of Israelite society lived has encouraged archaeologists to turn their refined methods to the challenging task of excavating small, unwalled, agricultural settlements in their total setting of fields, terraces, and water systems. In general, whatever the character of the excavation, there is growing sensitivity to the class indicators that may be reflected in the data. All of this is of great importance for many of the classical topics of biblical studies: the origins of Israel in a tribal social movement, the transition to the monarchy, the internal structure and external relations of the kingdoms of Israel and Judah, the circumstances of Israel's dispersion after the fall of both kingdoms, and the basic terms of Judah's restoration to Palestine.

Technology, long treated in a somewhat isolated and atomistic fashion in Palestinian archaeology, is drawing renewed attention in a more holistic framework. There is reason to believe that a conjunction of technological factors, some of them unknown or neglected in the past, made the Israelite domination of the highlands possible in the first place (§24.1.c). It is probable also that a fuller understanding of military and agricultural technology, in relation to state trade monopolies in the Israelite kingdoms and among their larger imperial neighbors, will aid us materially in understanding the socioeconomic, political, and religious strains and challenges within ancient Israel. Our rudimentary knowledge of the land tenure systems in biblical Israel may also be enlarged by the newer cultural and sociological emphases of archaeology (§30.5). In all these matters archaeology can be of immense help, provided that it has a large and sufficiently refined design concept to know what to look for and how to record what it sees for maximum use by all the specialists who contribute to biblical studies.

9
POLITICAL, CULTURAL, AND SOCIAL HISTORY OF THE ANCIENT NEAR EAST

The accumulating wealth of material and written remains from the ancient Near East has made it possible to write a coherent history of that region beginning shortly after 3000 B.C.E. As expected, given the centrality of the great irrigation valleys, the focal points of that ancient history were in the Nile Valley and in the middle and lower Tigris-Euphrates valleys. There were, however, important political centers in Anatolia, in the upper Tigris and Euphrates valleys, and in Iran that dominated international affairs in the ancient Near East for long periods.

An attempt at schematizing these political developments is presented in chart 1: in their chronological order (reading vertically) and in terms of the coexistence of states in different regions (reading horizontally). The various political regimes are arranged on vertical lines representing the major geographical regions of the ancient Near East. Reading from left to right on the chart, these lines follow the arc of the Fertile Crescent from Egypt in the west to Iran in the east. Three of these geographical regions—Anatolia, Iran, and Greece—lie outside the Fertile Crescent altogether, but from each of them came conquerors who dominated part or all of the Fertile Crescent: from Anatolia came the Hittites, from Iran the Persians, and from Greece the Macedonians.

Of all these regions, Egypt showed the firmest political continuity, doubtless due to isolation of the country by desert and sea. Yet there were periods of decline and contending dynasties, as well as major conquests from without by the Hyksos, Assyrians, Persians, and Macedonians. The Tigris-Euphrates valleys, open to entrance on all sides, experienced more frequent political changes and domination by regimes whose ruling classes came from outside the Fertile Crescent. In varying degrees, this appears to have been true of Akkadians, Guti, Elamites, Mitannians, Kassites, Medes, Persians, and Macedonians.

The original political core of Mesopotamia was in the southern Sumerian city-states. Later the center passed to Akkad and Babylon in the middle section of the valleys. Babylon remained an important capital or administrative center through Persian times. Meanwhile, Assyrian power emerged along the northern Tigris Valley and the Hittites and Mitannians held sway in the northern Euphrates region. The upper Euphrates adjoined Syria on the west, and over this whole area there appeared middle-sized kingdoms such as Mari and Ugarit. To their number must now be added Ebla in Syria whose rich archives have recently come to light. The sensational claims about Ebla's connection with the biblical patriarchs must be taken with healthy skepticism, pending publication of the texts, since those claims are similar to the mistakenly exaggerated claims made for the biblical relevance of earlier textual finds such as the archives of Mari and Ugarit.

The state form of political organization that facilitated irrigation agriculture spread rapidly over the whole ancient Near East. The smallest independent region usually had its king, bureaucracy, and army. Rivalry among these states, and turmoil of classes and claimants to the throne within them, became the normal course of affairs. Leaders or even entire regimes were periodically swept away. States facilitated trade with one another, carried on elaborate diplomacy, established alliances, and fought for supremacy. Every such state explained its origins and justified its existence and its practices by recourse to the declared will of divine beings. Everywhere religion served as an ideology to legitimate the existing social and political order.

Powerful states began to extend their rule far beyond their homelands, dominating larger and larger sections of the ancient Near East. Kingdoms thus became empires. The Akkadians and Old Babylonians had considerable success in imperial ventures, as did the revived Sumerian Ur III dynasty, but their control was limited mainly to the Tigris-Euphrates valleys. The Hittites of Anatolia penetrated from the north into upper Mesopotamia and Syria. Assyria eventually dominated the entire Fertile Crescent and held Egypt for a brief time. The Neo-Babylonians emulated the Assyrian success for a shorter period. The Persians, based in Iran, mastered the whole Fertile Crescent, Egypt and Anatolia included. The Macedonians, under Alexander, briefly possessed the entire Persian domain until, at their leader's death, it was divided among his generals—Ptolemy receiving Egypt and Seleucus possessing Syria, Anatolia, Mesopotamia, and Iran.

These ancient Near Eastern imperial adventures were of varying magnitude, cohesion, and durability. It was customary to subordinate conquered

CHART 1

Political Regimes of the Ancient Near East, 3000–63 B.C.E.

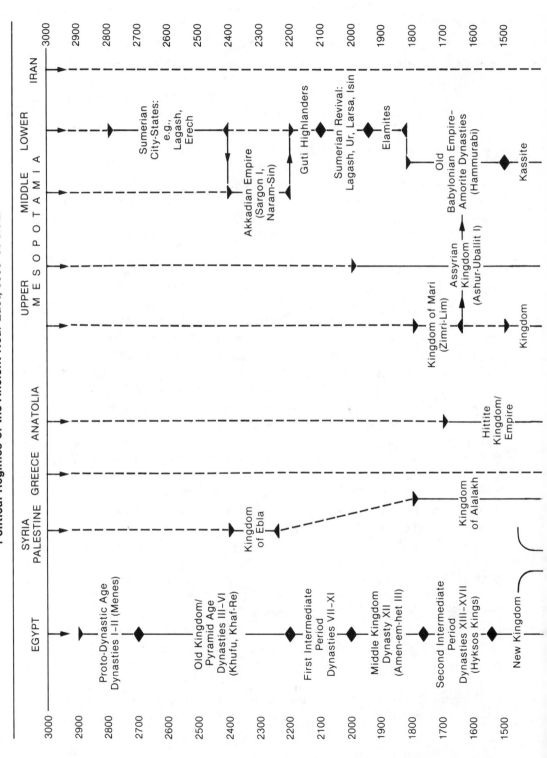

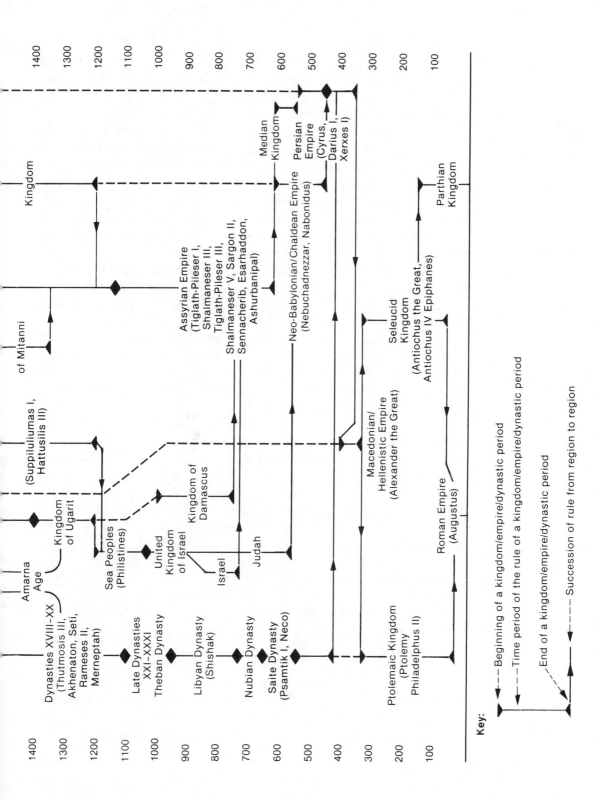

Key:

-------- Beginning of a kingdom/empire/dynastic period

-------- Time period of the rule of a kingdom/empire/dynastic period

-------- End of a kingdom/empire/dynastic period

-------- Succession of rule from region to region

states as vassals headed by local princes, thereby securing the subject states' military and economic assets on the side of the conqueror. To secure greater control and efficiency, the Assyrians began to turn many of their conquered territories into provinces headed by Assyrian officials. This practice was continued by the Neo-Babylonians, Persians, and Macedonians. After the brief flowering of Israel as a united kingdom under David and Solomon, its weakened divided branches were drawn increasingly into imperial diplomacy and warfare (§33; 36). The northern branch, Israel, fell to the Assyrians and the southern branch, Judah, was overthrown by the Neo-Babylonians. The return of Judahite exiles to Palestine was sponsored by the Persian Empire with the aim of securing its frontier with Egypt by means of a strong colony of loyal subjects (§44).

The imperial adventures of Egypt first surfaced under the Middle Kingdom when it penetrated up the Nile to Nubia and east of the Nile Delta into the Sinai Peninsula. The New Kingdom turned Egyptian ambitions toward the Fertile Crescent. For a time Egypt held Palestine and southern Syria (§24.1.c) while the Hittites controlled northern Syria. Egypt was engaged in repeated contests with Assyria and Neo-Babylonia, but apart from one brief foray into upper Mesopotamia, the land of the Nile was by now too weakened to do much more than aid and abet rebellions against Assyria and Neo-Babylonia among their subject states in Palestine. The little Palestinian states of Israel and Judah were often caught in this cross fire between imperial powers.

The political history of the ancient Near East is easier to picture in chart form than are the cultural and social histories. It is difficult enough to determine the characteristic features and boundaries of the cultures, but it is even more perplexing to judge the extent to which political and cultural boundaries in the ancient Near East were identical or divergent. It is generally agreed that a common core of culture, material and intellectual, runs through both the history of Egypt and of Mesopotamia, with Syria-Palestine developing local features that were heavily influenced from the older valley centers. The shape and flavor of these cultures come to expression in the abundance of ancient Near Eastern texts as sampled, for instance, in table 1.

In Egypt the continuity of language, arts, and mythology is evident. In Mesopotamia the oldest Sumerian city-states laid down a structure in style of writing, in the arts, and in mythic thought that carried through the whole of Mesopotamian history. But the peoples who entered into this heritage brought many additions and modifications. The cuneiform style of writing continued, but the Sumerian language was confined later to sacred texts, and the new languages were either Semitic for Akkadians, Old Babylonians, Assyrians, and Neo-Babylonians, or Indo-European for Hittites, Mitannians, and Persians, or, like the Sumerian language itself, unclassifiable in the case of the Elamites.

The political, cultural, and social histories of the ancient Near East, which scholars normally treat in isolation from one another, intersect when we try to visualize the actual continuities and discontinuities of daily life in relation to the clash and succession of political regimes. As noted above, the records we possess for the ancient Near East are primarily accounts written by ruling classes. In the past, changes in Mesopotamian and Syro-Palestinian regimes and cultures have usually been explained as the displacement or overrunning of populations by nomadic hordes from the desert or mountains. Of course there is little doubt that migration of peoples in the ancient Near East occurred frequently and that some of the politically and culturally expressed changes had to do with actual population movement. As an explanatory concept in this case, however, the notion of population displacement is extraordinarily weak and often ill fits the evidence (§24.2.a). For one thing it is naive to equate all migration with nomadism. Also, it is now clear that pastoral nomadism was never the major force in the ancient Near East that anthropologically uninformed scholars took it to be.

Nomadism aside, there are many difficulties with an undiscriminating appeal to population displacement. For one thing, a change of political regimes can occur in many ways, ranging from a small cabal that seizes power in a coup to a massive conquest from without. For another, the new regimes may differ greatly in the extent to which they use or replace old personnel, forms of administration, and intellectual culture. Even a change in official language cannot be unambiguously correlated with population change, inasmuch as what we may be examining is primarily the language of the political leadership and the social strata supporting the leadership. The language spoken by the majority of common people is another question. In upper Mesopotamia, for example, the Mitannian leadership of Indo-Europeans used one language and the mass of Hurrian subjects spoke another. For that matter, political leaders might use different languages in different contexts. The language of the conquering Assyrians, and of their historical records, was a form of the Semitic Akkadian or Old Babylonian tongue, but the Assyrians used Aramaic as the official language in the western part of their empire, and the Persians, who were Indo-European, fell heir to Aramaic as their imperial lingua franca. Therefore, at any given time and place, the language used in international politics, the language of a particular political leadership, and the language or languages of the populace at large might correspond or differ according to the influence of many historical, cultural, and social factors.

The deceptively simple surface of the political history of the ancient Near East passes over a depth and complexity of cultural and social dynamics that are a matter of great significance in ascertaining the origins of the biblical Israelites. The straight story line of the Hebrew Bible may be, and often is, read like the perfectly clear political account of self-contained events. But as soon as we look attentively at the literary forms in which Israel's early life is reported, we are immediately carried into the complex cultural and social world of ancient Palestine. It is a world in which Israel appears at a date that was well past the midpoint in the whole course of ancient Near Eastern history. The concept of Israelite pastoral nomads sweeping in from the desert to kill off all the Canaanites makes a dramatic picture, but it neither accords with the full evidence of the Hebrew Bible nor with our growing understanding of the ancient Near East.

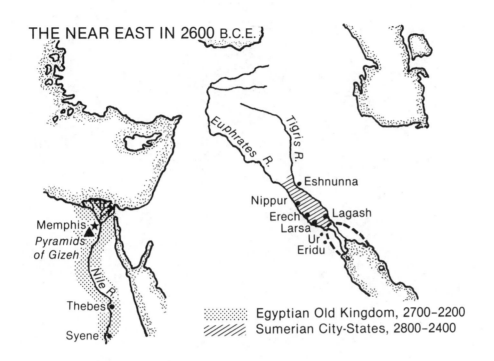

THE NEAR EAST IN 2600 B.C.E.

Euphrates R.
Tigris R.
• Eshnunna
Nippur
Erech • • Lagash
Larsa •
Ur •
Eridu

Memphis ★
Pyramids
of Gizeh

Nile R.

Thebes •

Syene •

Egyptian Old Kingdom, 2700–2200
Sumerian City-States, 2800–2400

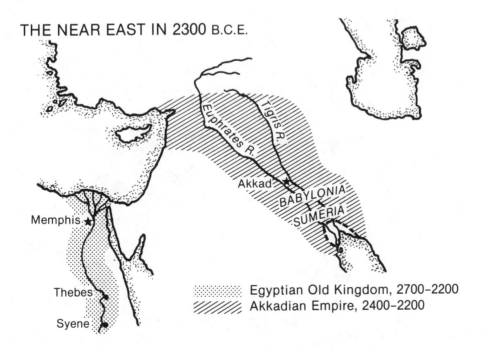

THE NEAR EAST IN 2300 B.C.E.

Euphrates R.
Tigris R.

Akkad ★
BABYLONIA
SUMERIA

Memphis ★

Thebes •

Syene •

Egyptian Old Kingdom, 2700–2200
Akkadian Empire, 2400–2200

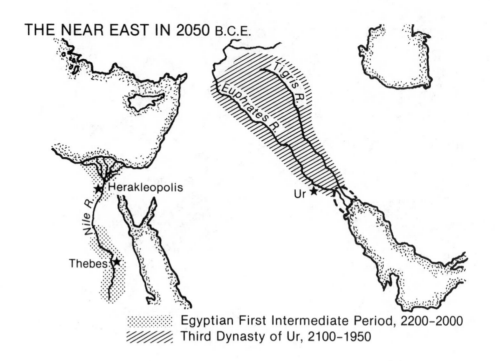

THE NEAR EAST IN 2050 B.C.E.

Herakleopolis

Thebes

Nile R.

Tigris R.

Euphrates R.

Ur

Egyptian First Intermediate Period, 2200–2000
Third Dynasty of Ur, 2100–1950

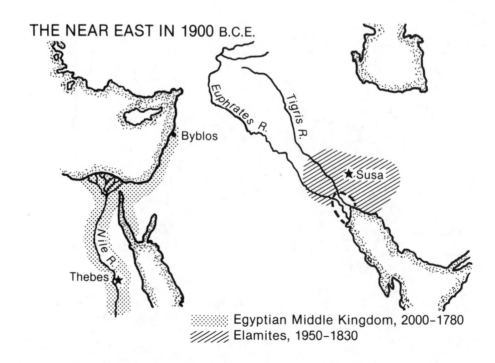

THE NEAR EAST IN 1900 B.C.E.

Byblos

Nile R.

Thebes

Euphrates R.

Tigris R.

Susa

Egyptian Middle Kingdom, 2000–1780
Elamites, 1950–1830

THE NEAR EAST IN 1700 B.C.E.

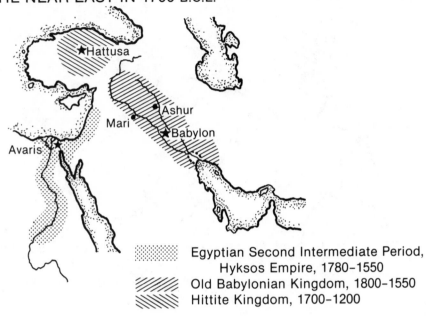

★Hattusa

Mari ● ●Ashur
★Babylon

Avaris

░░░░░ Egyptian Second Intermediate Period,
Hyksos Empire, 1780–1550
▨▨▨ Old Babylonian Kingdom, 1800–1550
▤▤▤ Hittite Kingdom, 1700–1200

THE NEAR EAST IN 1400 B.C.E.

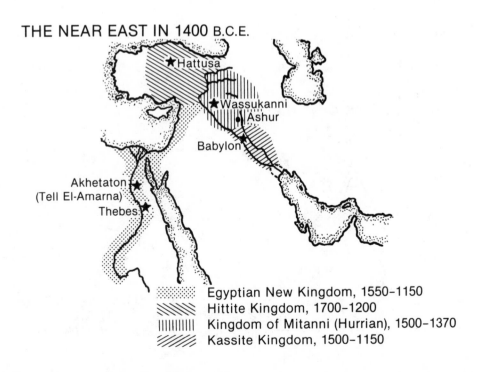

★Hattusa

★Wassukanni
●Ashur

Babylon

Akhetaton ★
(Tell El-Amarna)
Thebes ★

░░░░░ Egyptian New Kingdom, 1550–1150
▨▨▨ Hittite Kingdom, 1700–1200
||||||| Kingdom of Mitanni (Hurrian), 1500–1370
▨▨▨ Kassite Kingdom, 1500–1150

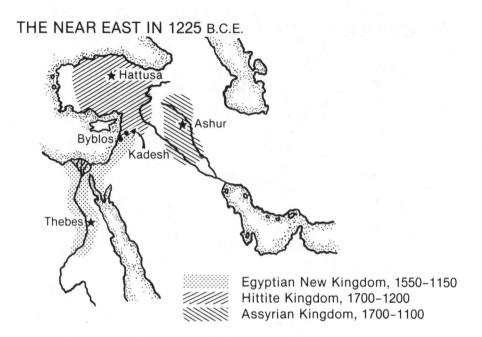

THE NEAR EAST IN 1225 B.C.E.

Hattusa
Ashur
Byblos
Kadesh
Thebes

Egyptian New Kingdom, 1550–1150
Hittite Kingdom, 1700–1200
Assyrian Kingdom, 1700–1100

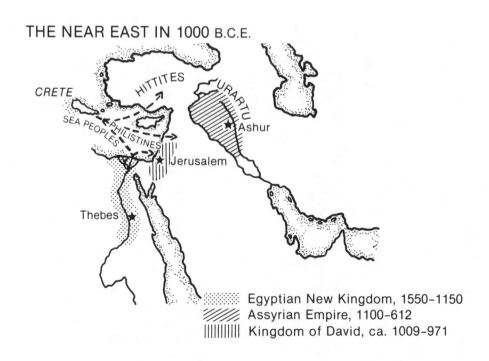

THE NEAR EAST IN 1000 B.C.E.

CRETE
HITTITES
URARTU
SEA PEOPLES
PHILISTINES
Ashur
Jerusalem
Thebes

Egyptian New Kingdom, 1550–1150
Assyrian Empire, 1100–612
Kingdom of David, ca. 1009–971

THE NEAR EAST IN 800 B.C.E.

Nineveh

Qarqar

Tigris R.

Euphrates R.

Bubastis

Nile R.

Libyan Dynasty of Egypt, 950–730
Assyrian Empire, 1100–612

THE NEAR EAST IN 660–605 B.C.E.

Carchemish

Haran ★Nineveh

★Ecbatana

Sais

Babylon ★

Thebes

Napata

Assyrian Empire, at Its Zenith, ca. 650
Saite Dynasty of Egypt, 663–525
Held by Egypt, 609–605
Median Empire, 612–550
Chaldean or Neo-Babylonian Empire, 612–539

THE NEAR EAST IN 580 B.C.E.

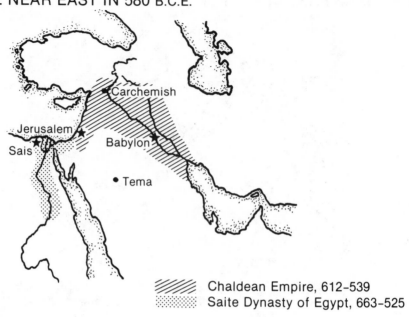

Carchemish

Jerusalem
Sais
Babylon

Tema

///// Chaldean Empire, 612–539
····· Saite Dynasty of Egypt, 663–525

THE NEAR EAST IN 500 B.C.E.

Sardis
Athens

Haran
Arbela
Damascus
Ecbatana

Babylon
Sais
Jerusalem
Susa
Empire extends
to Indus R. →

Memphis
Persepolis

Elephantine

····· Persian Empire at Its Zenith

THE NEAR EAST IN 334–323 B.C.E.

Battle of Granicus
334

Battle of Issus
333

Battle of Gaugamela
331

328

326

330/329

325

Indus R.

Pella

Tyre

Babylon
323

Alexandria
332

Ecbatana
330

Susa
331

Persepolis
324

▓ Macedonian Empire, 334–323
➤ Itinerary of Alexander and His Army

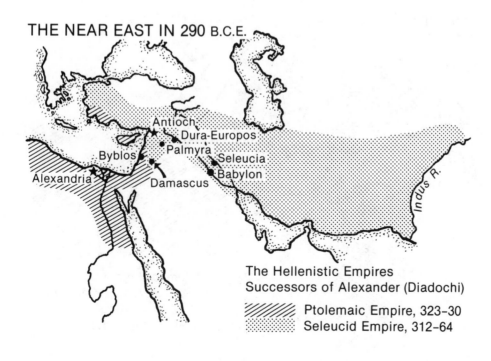

THE NEAR EAST IN 290 B.C.E.

Antioch

Dura-Europos

Byblos

Palmyra

Seleucia

Alexandria

Damascus

Babylon

Indus R.

The Hellenistic Empires
Successors of Alexander (Diadochi)

▨ Ptolemaic Empire, 323–30
▓ Seleucid Empire, 312–64

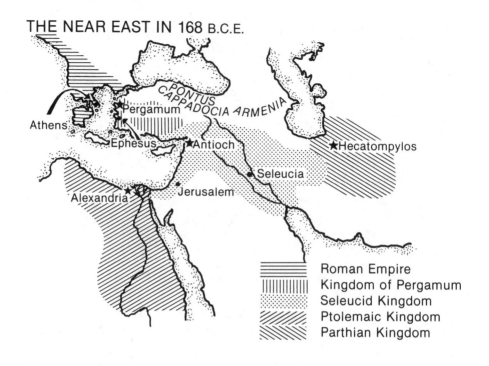

THE NEAR EAST IN 168 B.C.E.

PONTUS
CAPPADOCIA ARMENIA
Pergamum
Athens
Ephesus
★Hecatompylos
★Antioch
Seleucia
Alexandria
Jerusalem

|||||||||||| Roman Empire
|||||||||||| Kingdom of Pergamum
  Seleucid Kingdom
  Ptolemaic Kingdom
  Parthian Kingdom

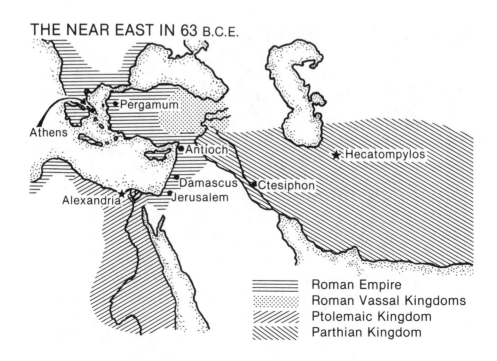

THE NEAR EAST IN 63 B.C.E.

Pergamum
Athens
Antioch
★Hecatompylos
Damascus   Ctesiphon
Alexandria Jerusalem

  Roman Empire
  Roman Vassal Kingdoms
  Ptolemaic Kingdom
  Parthian Kingdom

CHAPTER 3

The Literary History of the Hebrew Bible

10
RELATION OF THE HEBREW BIBLE TO
OTHER BODIES OF LITERATURE

An appropriate start for tracing the literary history of the Hebrew Bible is to situate its writings in relation to other closely related bodies of literature. The connections between these literatures can be viewed in terms of their temporal sequences, the languages in which they were written, their affinities and interdependence, and their transmission and translation histories. The following discussion of these related literatures is supplemented graphically by chart 2.

The *Hebrew Bible* itself was written between ca. 1200 and 125 B.C.E., largely in Hebrew but with brief passages in Aramaic. It has been continuously transmitted from antiquity to the present by religiously observant Jewish communities. For centuries it was passed down in handwritten copies until, after the invention of printing in 1480 C.E., it also became available in printed editions. From earliest times Christians also made use of the Hebrew Bible, but almost entirely in translation until the Renaissance and Reformation. In recent centuries, Protestant and Catholic scholars have devoted increasing attention to the original text of the Hebrew Bible.

10.1 Independent National Literatures:
The Ancient Near Eastern Texts

Beginning long before the first biblical writings, the peoples of the ancient Near East developed extensive literatures (note the specimens listed in table 1). These literatures from ancient Egypt, Mesopotamia, Iran, and Anatolia were written in the favored languages of the literate circles where they were composed. There are sizable bodies of texts in the Egyptian, Sumerian, Akkadian, Old Babylonian, Assyrian, Neo-Babylonian, Persian, Aramaic, and Hattic (Hittite) languages. These texts employ a striking variety of literary forms or types, so that the range of literary types in the Hebrew Bible (table 8) can be illustrated with plentiful examples from other national literatures contemporary with the Bible.

Unlike the Hebrew Bible, however, these extensive writings largely disappeared with the decline of the ancient Near East. Only selective quotations and summaries survived in later Greek and Iranian writings. From ca. 1800 C.E. onward, excavations in the ancient Near East have brought these submerged literatures of antiquity to light. Most of their languages have been deciphered and, as we have seen, the texts are accessible in modern translations. It is obvious that the Hebrew Bible and the ancient Near Eastern texts share a broad cultural heritage. Since Israel was a relatively small and insignificant historical force in the biblical era, its literature did not noticeably influence its neighbors. The literary dependence of Israel on the writings of its neighbors was immense in terms of common literary forms and themes, but the direct literary dependence of biblical texts on ancient Near Eastern texts is arguable only in a comparatively few instances (§54.2).

10.2 Jewish and Christian Literatures Dependent on the Hebrew Bible

The other literatures to be surveyed all arose after the Hebrew Bible was largely completed. Since these later literatures were written by Jews, or by Gentile Christians familiar with the Jewish heritage, they are totally aware of the Hebrew Bible and either continue along its lines of development or constitute commentary and interpretation of it.

10.2.a Apocrypha[1] and Pseudepigrapha[2]

The Apocrypha of the Hebrew Bible (chart 2) contains writings composed between ca. 200 B.C.E. and 100 C.E. Although widely used by Jews in that period, they did not become a part of the accepted Jewish canon of scripture (table 4A). Since these works were popular among Greek-speaking Jews in the Dispersion, they were venerated by the early Christians and became a part of the canon of Catholic Christianity as eventually confirmed by the Council of Trent in 1546 (table 4B, left col.). At the Reformation, Protestants denied the Apocrypha equal status with the Hebrew Bible (table 4B, right col.), but the major Protestant groups regarded its contents as useful for piety and instruction insofar as they did not contradict biblical teachings (table 5). Under the influence of the Protestant Reformation, the status of the Apocrypha in the major Eastern Orthodox churches has been

1. *Apocrypha* means literally "hidden things or writings," referring to these books being hidden or lost to view when they were rejected from the canon by Judaism and Protestantism. Technically, however, an *apocryphon* (sing.) is a book whose traditional author (e.g., an ancient such as Enoch or Moses) is said to have withheld the work from general circulation until the approaching end of time. In this sense, only 2 Esdras in the Apocrypha is an apocryphon. Catholics call the books of the Apocrypha "deuterocanonical," that is, the second set of canonical Old Testament books, since they have always been a part of Catholic scripture.
2. *Pseudepigrapha* means literally "false superscriptions, that is, false claims to authorship," which refers to the fact that many ancient authors, especially apocalyptic writers, claimed that their compositions were actually written much earlier by honored ancestors such as Abraham, Moses, or Isaiah. In this technical sense, many of the Pseudepigrapha are indeed pseudepigrapha, but many others are not. Even though the title is inaccurate in this respect, Pseudepigrapha is firmly established in scholarly and popular usage.

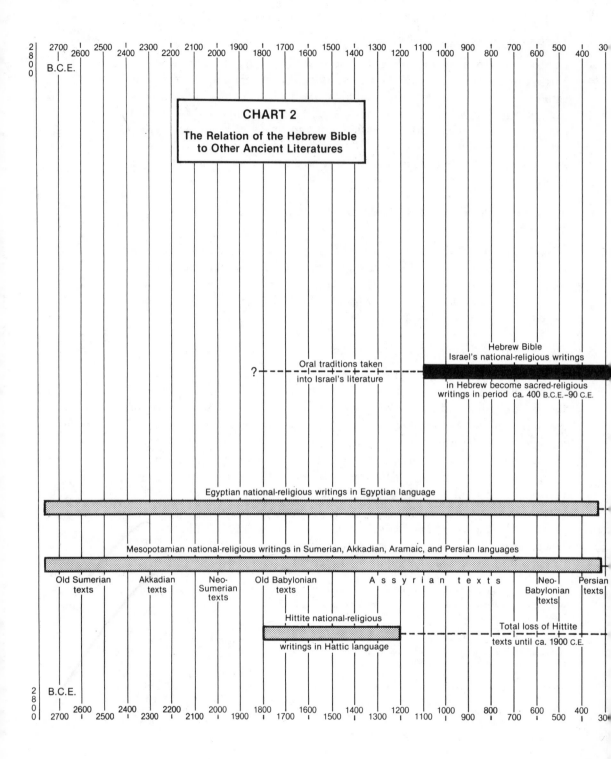

CHART 2

The Relation of the Hebrew Bible
to Other Ancient Literatures

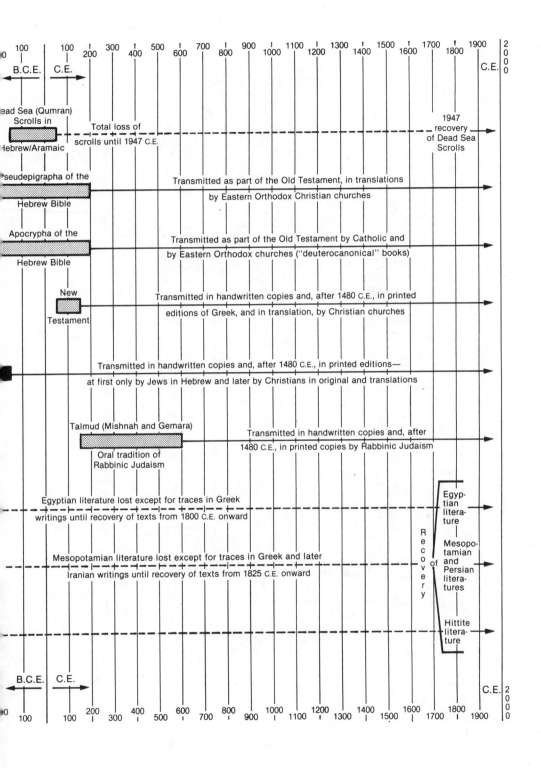

100 100 | 300 | 500 | 700 | 900 | 1100 | 1300 | 1500 | 1700 | 1900 2
0 200 400 600 800 1000 1200 1400 1600 1800 0
0
B.C.E. C.E. C.E. 0

ⁱead Sea (Qumran)
Scrolls in
Total loss of
scrolls until 1947 C.E.
1947
recovery
of Dead Sea
Scrolls
ꞁebrew/Aramaic

ᵖseudepigrapha of the
Transmitted as part of the Old Testament, in translations
by Eastern Orthodox Christian churches
Hebrew Bible

Apocrypha of the
Transmitted as part of the Old Testament by Catholic and
by Eastern Orthodox churches ("deuterocanonical" books)
Hebrew Bible

New
Transmitted in handwritten copies and, after 1480 C.E., in printed
editions of Greek, and in translation, by Christian churches
Testament

Transmitted in handwritten copies and, after 1480 C.E., in printed editions—
at first only by Jews in Hebrew and later by Christians in original and translations

Talmud (Mishnah and Gemara)
Transmitted in handwritten copies and, after
1480 C.E., in printed copies by Rabbinic Judaism
Oral tradition of
Rabbinic Judaism

Egyptian literature lost except for traces in Greek
writings until recovery of texts from 1800 C.E. onward
Egyp-
tian
litera-
ture

Mesopotamian literature lost except for traces in Greek and later
Iranian writings until recovery of texts from 1825 C.E. onward
R
e
c
o
v
e
r
y
of
Mesopo-
tamian
and
Persian
litera-
tures

Hittite
litera-
ture

B.C.E. C.E. C.E. 2
0
0
0
100 100 200 400 600 800 1000 1200 1400 1600 1800
100 100 300 500 700 900 1100 1300 1500 1700 1900

TABLE 4
The Canonical Books

A.
Jewish Canon of the Tanak

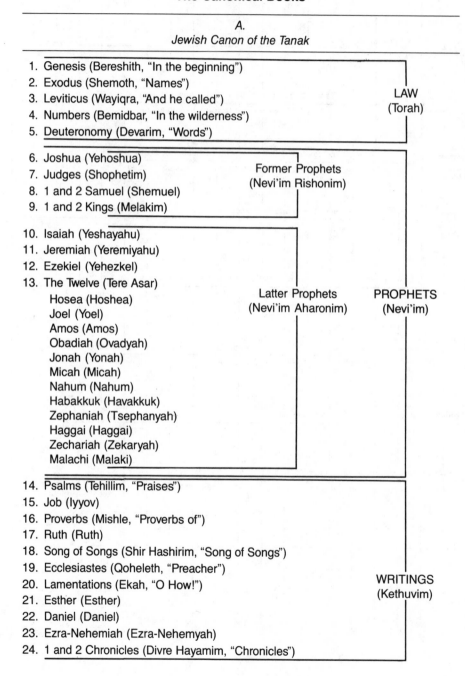

1. Genesis (Bereshith, "In the beginning")
2. Exodus (Shemoth, "Names")
3. Leviticus (Wayiqra, "And he called")
4. Numbers (Bemidbar, "In the wilderness")
5. Deuteronomy (Devarim, "Words")

LAW (Torah)

6. Joshua (Yehoshua)
7. Judges (Shophetim)
8. 1 and 2 Samuel (Shemuel)
9. 1 and 2 Kings (Melakim)

Former Prophets (Nevi'im Rishonim)

10. Isaiah (Yeshayahu)
11. Jeremiah (Yeremiyahu)
12. Ezekiel (Yehezkel)
13. The Twelve (Tere Asar)
    Hosea (Hoshea)
    Joel (Yoel)
    Amos (Amos)
    Obadiah (Ovadyah)
    Jonah (Yonah)
    Micah (Micah)
    Nahum (Nahum)
    Habakkuk (Havakkuk)
    Zephaniah (Tsephanyah)
    Haggai (Haggai)
    Zechariah (Zekaryah)
    Malachi (Malaki)

Latter Prophets (Nevi'im Aharonim)

PROPHETS (Nevi'im)

14. Psalms (Tehillim, "Praises")
15. Job (Iyyov)
16. Proverbs (Mishle, "Proverbs of")
17. Ruth (Ruth)
18. Song of Songs (Shir Hashirim, "Song of Songs")
19. Ecclesiastes (Qoheleth, "Preacher")
20. Lamentations (Ekah, "O How!")
21. Esther (Esther)
22. Daniel (Daniel)
23. Ezra-Nehemiah (Ezra-Nehemyah)
24. 1 and 2 Chronicles (Divre Hayamim, "Chronicles")

WRITINGS (Kethuvim)

84

TABLE 4 (continued)
The Canonical Books

B.

Roman Catholic Canon of the Old Testament	Protestant Canon of the Old Testament
1. Genesis	1. Genesis
2. Exodus	2. Exodus
3. Leviticus	3. Leviticus
4. Numbers	4. Numbers
5. Deuteronomy	5. Deuteronomy
6. Joshua	6. Joshua
7. Judges	7. Judges
8. Ruth	8. Ruth
9. 1 Samuel	9. 1 Samuel
10. 2 Samuel	10. 2 Samuel
11. 1 Kings	11. 1 Kings
12. 2 Kings	12. 2 Kings
13. 1 Chronicles	13. 1 Chronicles
14. 2 Chronicles	14. 2 Chronicles
15. Ezra	15. Ezra
16. Nehemiah	16. Nehemiah
17. Tobit———————————————	——In the Apocrypha
18. Judith———————————————	——In the Apocrypha
19. Esther (including Additions to Esther)———————	17. Esther ——In the Apocrypha
20. Job	18. Job
21. Psalms	19. Psalms
22. Proverbs	20. Proverbs
23. Ecclesiastes	21. Ecclesiastes
24. Song of Solomon = Song of Songs in Jewish canon	22. Song of Solomon
25. Wisdom of Solomon———————	——In the Apocrypha
26. Ecclesiasticus——————————— (Wisdom of Ben Sirach)	——In the Apocrypha
27. Isaiah	23. Isaiah
28. Jeremiah	24. Jeremiah
29. Lamentations	25. Lamentations
30. Baruch (including the——————— Letter of Jeremiah)	——In the Apocrypha
31. Ezekiel	26. Ezekiel

TABLE 4 (continued)
The Canonical Books

| B. (continued) | |
Roman Catholic Canon of the Old Testament	Protestant Canon of the Old Testament
32. Daniel (including Additions to Daniel: The Story of Susanna, The Song of the Young Men, The Story of Bel and the Dragon)	27. Daniel
	——In the Apocrypha
33. Hosea	28. Hosea
34. Joel	29. Joel
35. Amos	30. Amos
36. Obadiah	31. Obadiah
37. Jonah	32. Jonah
38. Micah	33. Micah
39. Nahum	34. Nahum
40. Habakkuk	35. Habakkuk
41. Zephaniah	36. Zephaniah
42. Haggai	37. Haggai
43. Zechariah	38. Zechariah
44. Malachi	39. Malachi
45. 1 Maccabees———	———In the Apocrypha
46. 2 Maccabees———	———In the Apocrypha

TABLE 5
Books of the Protestant Apocrypha to the Old Testament

*1. 1 Esdras (= Roman Catholic 3 Esdras or Greek Ezra)

*2. 2 Esdras (= Roman Catholic 4 Esdras or Ezra Apocalypse)

3. Tobit

4. Judith

5. The Additions to the Book of Esther

6. The Wisdom of Solomon

7. Ecclesiasticus, or the Wisdom of Jesus the Son of Sirach

8. Baruch

9. The Letter of Jeremiah

10. The Prayer of Azariah and the Song of the Three Young Men

11. Susanna

12. Bel and the Dragon

*13. The Prayer of Manasseh

14. 1 Maccabees

15. 2 Maccabees

*These three books are not canonical for Roman Catholics, but the first two do appear in some Vulgate translations. All the other books are part of the Roman Catholic canon and are called "deuterocanonical" in reference to the decision of the Council of Trent in 1546 which judged them to be canonical in the face of Protestant objections.

problematic. The Greek church confirmed acceptance of most of the Apocrypha at the Synod of Jerusalem in 1672 but there have been persistent misgivings about the decision. The Russian church, on the other hand, rejected the Apocrypha as scripture by the nineteenth century, but even so there has been some use of its writings in that body.

The Pseudepigrapha of the Hebrew Bible (chart 2) derives from the same period as the Apocrypha. The two collections are broadly similar in types and themes, except that the former is considerably larger and contains more apocalyptic writings similar to Daniel in the Hebrew Bible and 2 Esdras (= 4 Esdras) in the Apocrypha. The books of the Pseudepigrapha were not part of the Jewish or Catholic canons of scripture, but they were accepted in varying combinations among certain Eastern Christian bodies such as the Coptic, Ethiopic, and Syrian churches (table 6).

Apocrypha and Pseudepigrapha were written in Hebrew, Aramaic, and Greek. In the case of the Apocrypha, either the originals or translations in Greek (in one case Latin) survived by way of the Catholic canon, and in some instances the Semitic originals have been found in whole or in part. With the Pseudepigrapha, the textual and translation history is more confused. A majority of the Pseudepigrapha survived in the languages of the Eastern Orthodox Christian communities that preserved them, such as Ethiopic, Syriac, and Slavonic. Protestant Bibles are increasingly returning to the practice of including the Apocrypha in an appendix to translations of the Hebrew Bible. Critical editions of both bodies of literature in modern translation are available, but the exact boundaries of the Pseudepigrapha, drawn as its contents are from various Eastern Orthodox canons and other sources, are yet to be agreed upon.

10.2.b Dead Sea Scrolls

The Dead Sea Scrolls (chart 2), found in the library of a Jewish sectarian community, probably Essenes, include a wealth of biblical and nonbiblical documents, mostly fragmentary, written between 150 B.C.E. and 70 C.E. (table 7). The nonbiblical texts include already-known Apocrypha and Pseudepigrapha, but there are several writings known only from this source. The discovery of the biblical texts, older by many centuries than any other extant manuscripts, is of the highest importance for reconstructing the history of the development and transmission of the text of the Hebrew Bible (§11.3.a). The nonbiblical manuscripts provide vivid evidence that the outburst of literary production toward the close of the biblical era was not confined, as once thought, to Jews who lived outside Palestine but extended significantly into the Jewish homeland. Aside from a

TABLE 6
Jewish Books Among the Pseudepigrapha of the Old Testament Predating 70 C.E.*

Adam and Eve, Life of (or Apocalypse of Moses)

Aristeas, Letter of

2 (Syriac) Baruch

Elijah, Apocalypse of

1 (Ethiopic) Enoch

2 (Slavonic) Enoch

Isaiah, Ascension of

Job, Testament of

Jubilees

3 Maccabees

4 Maccabees

Moses, Testament of (Assumption of)

Lives of the Prophets

Sibylline Oracles

Psalms of Solomon

Testaments of the Twelve Patriarchs

*This list is composed of pseudepigrapha generally recognized to contain at least a core of Jewish material predating 70 C.E., although in many instances expanded or revised after that date by Jewish or Christian writers. All are translated in Charlesworth, *OTP*; the majority are also translated in Charles, *APOT*. Their literary and historical features are discussed in Nickelsburg, *JLBBM*.

TABLE 7
Important Documents Among the Dead Sea Scrolls*

1QapGen	Genesis Apocryphon from Qumran Cave 1
1QH	Hodayot (Thanksgiving Hymns) from Qumran Cave 1
1QIsa^a	First Copy of Isaiah from Qumran Cave 1
1QIsa^b	Second Copy of Isaiah from Qumran Cave 1
1QpHab	Pesher (commentary) on Habakkuk from Qumran Cave 1
1QM	Milhamah (War Scroll)
1QS	Serek hayyahad (Rule of the Community or Manual of Discipline)
1QSa	Appendix A (Rule of the Congregation) to 1QS
1QSb	Appendix B (Blessings) to 1QS
3Q15	Copper Scroll from Qumran Cave 3
4QFlor	Florilegium (Eschatological Midrashim) from Qumran Cave 4
4QMess ar	Aramaic "Messianic" Text from Qumran Cave 4
4QpNah	Pesher (commentary) on Nahum from Qumran Cave 4
4QPrNab	Prayer of Nabonidus from Qumran Cave 4
4QTest	Testimonia Text from Qumran Cave 4
4QTLevi	Testament of Levi from Qumran Cave 4
5QJN ar	Aramaic Description of the New Jerusalem from Qumran Cave 5
11QMelch	Melchizedek Text from Qumran Cave 11
11QPs^a	The Psalms Scroll from Qumran Cave 11
11QTemple	The Temple Scroll from Qumran Cave 11
11QtgJob	Targum of Job from Qumran Cave 11

*The commonly accepted abbreviations for the Dead Sea Scrolls, widely used in scholarly discussions of the texts, employ the system of listing first the assigned number of the cave where found, then Q for Qumran (to distinguish from other Dead Sea area sites where manuscripts have been found), and finally the name of the particular document. As necessary, small letters raised above the line denote different copies of the same document found in a single cave (e.g., 1QIsa^a and 1QIsa^b), and small letters on the line indicate appendices to a document (e.g., 1QSa and 1QSb).

few obscure references to these scrolls in late antiquity and early medieval times, the Dead Sea Scrolls dropped from view until they were rediscovered in caves near the sect's headquarters at Qumran in 1947 C.E. Critical editions of these scrolls are steadily being published in modern translations.

10.2.c New Testament and Talmud

These two important Christian and Jewish literary works are grouped together in this discussion because each in its own way provides a definitive conceptual structure for interpreting the Hebrew Bible that Christians and Jews jointly share but appropriate very differently. The early Christian community, at first a Jewish movement, had become a separate religious entity by the end of the first century C.E. Rabbinic Judaism, surviving the fall of Jerusalem in 70 C.E., rapidly standardized forms of ritual and biblical exegesis that had earlier been much more fluid and contested among Jews. While both religious communities adhered tenaciously to the Hebrew Bible, the authoritative New Testament and Talmud guaranteed that they would see the same texts through markedly different confessional lenses.

The first Christians were Jews who regarded the Hebrew Bible, whether in the original or in Greek translation, as their authoritative religious texts (§12.1.a). They did not need any other scripture for many decades. Their own writings set forth Jesus as the fulfillment of the religious anticipations of the Hebrew Bible. Even as they broke off from the Jewish community, Christians did not feel the need to conceive of their own writings as an addition to or a replacement for the Bible. Only as conflicts in the church over the nature of Christian faith and identity arose in the second century C.E. did it become urgent to assert that the Hebrew Bible was indeed scripture but that, in addition, a core of early Christian writings constituted a second equally authoritative division of scripture. Thus arose the designation *Old Testament* (or *Covenant)* for the Hebrew Bible and *New Testament* (or *Covenant)* for the sacred Christian literature (chart 2). Thereafter, the Hebrew Bible in Greek or Latin translation, supplemented by the Apocrypha, was combined with the New Testament to form the Bible of Catholic Christians. The Eastern Orthodox Christians concurred, except that they included further books of the Pseudepigraha.

The Talmud (i.e., "study/instruction") is the vast body of codified Oral Law that developed from ca. 250 B.C.E. to 550 C.E. (chart 2), on the basis of which rabbinic authorities definitively shaped the structure of Judaism after the fall of Jerusalem in 70 C.E. had effectively eliminated rival forms of Jewish religious life and thought. The roots of oral supplementation of the legal and cultic instructions of the Hebrew Bible probably reach back to a time not long after the restored Judahite community overtly adopted the Law (Genesis-Deuteronomy) as its charter document. The essence of these oral supplements or interpretations/reinterpretations was to elicit from the biblical text exact directives for current Jewish religious and ritual conduct (Halakah, i.e., "walking, guiding one's life"). Generations of interpreters, identified with the Pharisees from about 150 B.C.E., developed these oral laws which were codified about 180 C.E. in the Mishnah (i.e., "repetition/study"), written in Hebrew and composed of sixty-three tractates in six divisions. Aramaic commentary on the Mishnah continued to ca. 550 C.E. The Mishnah was combined with this Aramaic commentary, known as the Gemara (i.e., "completion"), to form the Talmud.

Meanwhile, pious interpretation/reinterpretation of nonlegal biblical texts developed alongside the legal and cultic reinterpretation of the traditions. By elaborating on the biblical stories and prophecies, Jewish faith and hope were encouraged (Haggadah, i.e., "narration"). The haggadic reflections found their way into Midrash (i.e., "exposition"), consisting of many commentaries on biblical books that were written from 150 to 1300 C.E. The midrash (pl., midrashim) as a literary form is of growing importance in biblical studies because some scholars argue that this mode of written reappropriation of an earlier valued text was already practiced in postexilic biblical books such as Chronicles and Daniel.

Because Rabbinic Judaism did not recognize a new historical revealer of God in the way that Christianity recognized Jesus, there was no impetus among Jews to extend the Hebrew Bible to include the Mishnah or the full Talmud. In fact, it was contended that Moses himself at Sinai had begun the process of giving explanatory oral laws alongside the written laws. The Talmud as codified Oral Law was conceived as the continuing living word of Moses, and therefore entirely consistent with the words of the Law in the Hebrew Bible. There was no occasion to refer to the Hebrew Bible as the Old Law and the Mishnah and/or Talmud as the New Law. Instead, the former received the simple descriptive name Tanak, calling attention to its threefold contents (chap. 1 n. 1), or it was simply called Torah, employing the name of the first division to refer to the whole.

11
HOW THE HEBREW BIBLE CAME TO BE

The printed copies of the Hebrew Bible used by readers today, either in the original language or in a modern translation, are the end product of a complex literary process reaching over more than three thousand years.

Historical-critical method has made it possible to reconstruct the growth of the Hebrew Bible in its main outlines and with considerable detail, although there remain gaps in information and major disputes about the groupings and sequences of the written traditions in the earliest phases of the history. Further manuscript finds, such as the Dead Sea Scrolls and the Aleppo Codex, together with refined methods in textual and canonical criticism, have greatly improved both the quantity and quality of our knowledge about the literary evolution of the Hebrew Bible.

The literary history of the Hebrew Bible is divisible into three partially overlapping phases:

1. The stage of *the formation of the separate literary units*, oral and written, that eventually became a part of the Hebrew Bible, from about 1200 B.C.E. to 100 B.C.E.

2. The stage of *the final formation of the Hebrew Bible* as an authoritative collection of writing in three parts (Law, Prophets, Writings), beginning ca. 400 B.C.E. with the Law as the kernel, later supplemented by the Prophets, and culminating ca. 90 C.E. with delimitation of the boundaries of the Writings.

3. The stage of *the preservation and transmission of the Hebrew Bible*, both in the original tongue and in translations into other languages, which involved two phases:

   a. The period when the finalization of the contents of the Hebrew Bible was still in process, ca. 400 B.C.E. to 90 C.E.

   b. The period when the Hebrew Bible had reached definitive form, from 90 C.E. to the present.

11.1 Formation of the Separate Literary Units

11.1.a Processes of Literary Composition

Israel did not begin as a book-oriented people, nor was its religion a book-based religion until toward the end of the biblical period. It may be confidently said that, with the exception of a few final redactors (editors) responsible for writing only a relatively small amount of the text, biblical writers had no awareness or intent of contributing to a great collection of writings that would form the authoritative basis of a religion.

Israel was primarily a sociohistorical entity, possessed of a distinctive religion, that produced over the centuries a rich literature addressed to immediate situations of communal need and crisis. These diverse writings took many literary shapes for a great variety of purposes. In short, no one mind foresaw and designed the scope and contents of the Hebrew Bible. To the contrary, the Hebrew Bible grew as the result of the combination of separate literary units that were progressively grouped together and treated as sacred literature under the pressure of events and circumstances in postexilic Judah. Of course Jews and Christians have claimed that *God* foresaw and designed the Hebrew Bible, but that is a value judgment made after the fact and not a description of the actual literary process as experienced by those who did most of the writing and collecting and editing.

Only a very few books in the Hebrew Bible may possibly be simple unities in the sense that they were composed by a single writer (Jonah and the Song of Songs might be such simple unities). The vast majority of biblical books, including all the largest ones, give plentiful indications that they are of composite authorship. In some cases this means that a single author has quoted from other sources, either as directly stated in the text or as inferred from internal evidence. Sometimes a work written basically as a unity may have had an oral prehistory (the Book of Ruth novella probably had an earlier oral saga form). In other cases originally separate literary units have been deliberately joined so that a freshly edited work has been produced. In still other instances a primary literary core has been supplemented with smaller insertions or blocks of material of a related literary or thematic nature.

All in all, the formation of the Hebrew Bible proceeded by adding together and splicing smaller compositions to form larger entities. The process varied from book to book, but often there were several stages in adding, rearranging, merging, and commenting editorially on the joined subcollections or on the supplemented core. The distance between the shape of the original core of a biblical book and its final form was frequently a span of centuries in which the growing work changed more than once in contents and structure.

Precisely because the biblical books by and large had long trajectories of growth, it is necessary to view their formation not only in terms of the successive phases of single books or bodies of tradition, but also as the simultaneous development of coexisting or parallel books and bodies of traditions. For example, while the early anonymous sources of Genesis-Numbers, known as J and E, were being written in the tenth and ninth centuries, cycles of stories and state and temple records that were eventually to be part of Joshua-Kings were also taking written shape. Likewise, when the first prophetic books emerged in the eighth and seventh centuries, collections of aphorisms that were to become part of Proverbs were already in writing. During the entire course of the preexilic history, psalms were composed that would finally be incorporated in the postexilic redaction of Psalms, and were very likely passed along in various subcollections until their inclusion in the finished book. It is obvious that many hands were at work in the manifold processes of literary formation which were intimately tied to the tides and fortunes of the social, political, and religious institutions of biblical Israel.

The metaphor of a large river system may help to visualize the composition of the books of the Hebrew Bible, individually and as a whole. The waters of a great river are the confluence of rivulets, brooks, streams, tributary rivers, and branches of the main river. When we see such a river near its mouth, we are impressed by its singular irresistible sweep toward the sea, and yet we know that the waters now concentrated in one channel are actually slowly collected from scattered runoff over the vast basin that the river drains. As the now-mighty river gathers its volume and effects as it flows, so the final unity of the Hebrew Bible arises through an additive process spread out over time and space. And just as part of the river's waters comes not from rainfall but from melted snow and ice, so too not all the words of the Hebrew Bible are of a single origin or form, for this vast collection includes words that were originally spoken and only written down secondarily, and its traditions came to expression in manifold literary genres.

11.1.b Oral Tradition and Literary Genres in the Composition Process

In tracing the formation of the Hebrew Bible we must be attentive to the powerful influence of oral tradition which, directly and indirectly, contributed far more to the literary structure than we are apt to realize because of our bookish orientation toward the text. In the course of trying to determine the authorship, date, and sources of biblical books, scholars gradually realized that much biblical literature had complex and deep-seated oral roots and that these could only be located and described by expanding the repertory of historical-critical methods to include form criticism. Form or genre criticism works on the widely demonstrated axiom that in the everyday culture of people there are relatively fixed forms of oral communication appropriate to particular settings in life.[3]

Oral forms may be as simple as the accepted formulas for exchanging greetings or for addressing people according to their different stations or roles in society. These oral forms ramify into all the spheres of life, particularly among preliterate peoples or in premodern societies, such as

---

3. Gerhard Lohfink (*The Bible: Now I Get It! A Form-Critical Handbook* [Garden City, N.Y.: Doubleday & Co., 1979]) skillfully introduces the student to form criticism by citing modern fixed forms of oral and written speech, such as letter, weather report, obituary, recipe, sermon, etc.

ancient Israel, where reading and writing tend to be restricted to certain groups and used for limited purposes. Among the common oral forms identified as underlying the biblical texts are the following: *narratives* that treat important ancestors or religious figures in an imaginative wonder-filled style that transcends everyday experience, and which may serve to explain the origins of geographical features, institutions, and customs; *hymns* and *thanksgiving songs* that celebrate victory in war or deliverance from famine, sickness, or oppression by attributing the turn of fortune to deity; *laments* that mourn the death of important persons or bewail public catastrophes; *laws* that regulate the communal behavior; *priestly regulations* that guide ritual practices; *prophetic sayings* that proclaim judgment or salvation to individuals or nations; *aphorisms* or *artistic proverbs* that distill wisdom drawn from wide experience.

These oral forms had characteristic structures and verbal formulas, treated a customary set of topics, and were recited in specific life settings. Probably many of the first written texts in Israel had been orally composed and recited before being committed to writing, as is likely the case with many of the ancestor stories in Genesis 12—50 and with verse compositions such as the Song of Deborah in Judges 5. Writing might occur in order to standardize the oral recitation of a form. Or it might occur when oral recitation was declining and there was a desire to preserve the specimens of a form before they disappeared altogether. Or the writer of an extended composition might choose to write an oral specimen into the body of the larger text because of its felt appropriateness to the context. Such apparently was the reason for the Deuteronomistic Historian, or an earlier compiler, to insert Judges 5 into a context that is otherwise prose. The transition from the tribal period of Israel's life to the monarchy witnessed the rise of a literary court culture alongside the old oral forms of tribal life. There was a sudden burst of literary activity as the earlier oral forms were taken up into writing and often arranged in larger compositions that had a distinctly literary character.

As long as oral forms were anchored to definite life situations they stayed within clear boundaries and kept their typical shapes. A lament, for instance, was restricted to some immediately experienced loss or suffering. Any particular oral lament, such as David's lament over the death of Saul and Jonathan in 2 Sam. 1:17–27, could be directly written down and preserved for posterity. The committing to writing of particular oral specimens, however, was far from the whole of the complicated interaction between oral tradition and literary types. The forms as forms, with their conventions of speech and conceptual structures, continued to exert a powerful influence on writers who imitated and modified them for purposes very different than their oral usages. Prophets, for example, employed laments to bewail the moral and religious state of the nation, or to anticipate its collective destruction, or even to mock and deride the high and mighty by celebrating their imminent deaths. Thus, in new literary contexts, the oral forms acquired new life settings and changed the particulars of form and content.

The relation of oral tradition and its forms to the literary composition of the Hebrew Bible is a complicated subject still being explored by biblical form critics and literary critics. Long after certain oral forms ceased to be widely used in everyday life, or were used in altered or diffused ways, a literary prophet like Isaiah of the Exile could employ an impressive array of oracles of salvation, hymns, trial speeches, and disputation speeches, plus other genres, to construct a studied work of powerful rhetorical force that was intended to be read, probably aloud, in order to inculcate specific religious attitudes and policies among the exiled Israelites (§50.2). The second-century writer of Daniel used narratives about Jews serving in foreign government that followed closely the pattern of ancient sagas about the deliverance of ancestors and pious leaders (§55.2). It is even likely that he drew upon and elaborated oral sagas about faithful Jews in Babylonian (Persian? Ptolemaic?) exile in order to counsel patience under persecution in his own Hellenistic Seleucid age.

In sum, to sketch adequately the formation of the biblical literature it is necessary to engage in two processes that are logically distinguishable and yet very closely interwoven in practice. The first task is to discern the overall compositional shape of a biblical writing ("what holds it together") and the second task is to isolate the intact or broken genre elements which contribute structural "building blocks" or rhetorical "mortar" to the finished text ("what makes it come apart"). In examining the ingredient genres of a biblical book or stratum, one is looking both for instances of preexistent oral or written units taken into the larger work *and* also for the way genre elements have functioned as models for fresh literary compositions. It is customary to work back and forth between the synthetic literary approach and the analytic form-critical approach in order to attain a progressive refinement of understanding about the genesis and completed shape of biblical writings.

Because the analysis of literary types or genres is not familiar to most readers of the Bible, and also because the classification of biblical materials by genres is not fully agreed upon by scholars nor are the genre names standardized,[4] it is advisable to present a fairly full list of the major literary types that have been identified in the Hebrew Bible (table 8). Classification and labeling of narrative and reportorial kinds of literary genres have been especially difficult to agree upon. The system in table 8 prefers the Old Norse term *saga* (no. 20) for brief imaginative stories of simple plot and few characters, set in a traditional past and lacking documentation, that recount the deeds of ancestors or leaders in overcoming great difficulties. Often such sagas have been called legends, but *legend* (no. 21) is best reserved for stories that focus on the religious qualities and gifts of the central figure and that aim to edify the reader. Sagas or legends may appear in chains or cycles, or a saga or legend may be elaborated by extending plot or lengthening speeches so as to create a *short story* or *novella* (no. 22). In the Bible, *myth* (no. 18) and *fairy tale* (no. 19) appear only as fragmentary pieces or motifs in other literary types, both because the sole God of Israel replaces other deities as actors and because the generality of time and place in myths and fairy tales is normally countered by the Israelite habit of specifying names and places in imaginative narratives. All of these narrative types are distinguishable from reportorial types (nos. 24–29) situated in recent times that report what they have to say with an everyday matter-of-factness and often with evidence of historical documentation.

Fifty-nine literary genres out of a much larger number, probably upward of two hundred—which one or another scholar has claimed to find represented in the biblical text—are listed in table 8. A certain measure of arbitrariness is involved in such lists, since, for example, the three kinds of lists under reportorial types (nos. 24–26) might be collapsed into a single type called "lists." Form critics often distinguish sagas that give explanations of origins (etiologies) according to whether they are geographical, ethnographic, or ritual etiologies, but it is disputed whether these etiologies constitute a separate genre or whether they are simply motifs that occasionally are attached to the saga type. Among the fifty-nine listed genres, some are clearly much more pervasive than others, especially in the extent to which they generate biblical materials at the literary level. To indicate something of this difference, twenty-one of the entries—which probably account for the great majority of genres in all categories of biblical writing—are marked with a dagger (†).

Under each of the broad categories of writings (historical-legal, psalmic,

---

4. A first step toward general agreement among scholars in the use of genre names has been taken by including a glossary in each volume of the projected 24-volume FOTL. When this form-critical commentary series is completed, the editors intend to revise all the glossaries and publish a single unified glossary as vol. 24 of the series.

TABLE 8
Literary Genres, Forms, or Types in the Hebrew Bible*

Literary Genres in the Historical and Legal Writings

Directive Literary Genres

   1. Formulas and Sayings of Everyday Life (Gen. 35:17; Ps. 2:7)

† 2. Rules of Conduct in Categorical Form = apodictic laws (Exod. 20:1–17; Lev. 18:7–12, 14–16)

† 3. Legal Maxims and Decisions = casuistic laws (Exod. 21:12–17; Deut. 22:6–8)

† 4. Treaties and Contracts Between Humans and with God (1 Kings 5:2–12; Gen. 23:16–17; Exod. 24:1–11; Josh. 24:1–27)

Requesting and Wishing Literary Genres

   5. Requests and Wishes (Gen. 47:15; 1 Sam. 10:24)

   6. Formulas of Salutation (Judges 6:12; 1 Sam. 25:6)

   7. Blessings and Curses (Num. 6:24–26; Josh. 6:26; Jer. 20:14–18; Psalm 41; Job 1:20; 3)

   8. Oaths (Num. 14:21; 1 Sam. 14:39; Amos 4:2; 6:8; 8:7; Job 31)

Proclaiming and Instructing Literary Genres

   9. Oracles (1 Sam. 23:2, 11; 2 Sam. 5:23–24; Ezek. 21:18–23)

 10. Judgments by ordeal (Num. 5:11–31; Josh. 7:14–21; Ps. 7:3–5)

†11. Cultic Regulations and Priestly Professional Lore (Numbers 15; Leviticus 11—15; Psalms 15; 24:3–6)

 12. Approvals (Deut. 1:14), Rejections (Gen. 34:7), Rebukes (2 Sam. 16:10)

Communicating Literary Genres

 13. Conversations (1 Sam. 24:8–22; 1 Kings 18:7–15)

†14. Formal Speeches (Deut. 20:5–8; Joshua 23; 2 Kings 18:17–35; 2 Chron. 13:4–12)

 15. Sermons (Deuteronomy 1—10; 28—31)

 16. Prayers (Judges 16:28; 1 Kings 8:15–53; 18:36–37)

 17. Letters (2 Sam. 11:15; 2 Kings 5:5–6; 10:2–3; Jer. 29:1–28)

Narrative Literary Genres

 18. Myths—only fragmentary examples within other genres (Gen. 6:1–4, marriage of divine beings to human women; Isa. 14:12–20, an arrogant divine being is cast into the underworld; Isa. 51:9–11, God destroys the sea monster Rahab = Egypt; Gen. 1:2, the watery chaotic "deep" from which God creates)

 19. Fairy Tales—only motifs within other literary genres (Gen. 39:7–20, a lewd woman seduces a young man; 1 Kings 3:16–28, a wise king decides an insoluble legal case; Job 1—2; 42:7–16, a pious man bears the divine test by great suffering without complaint)

---

*This table draws upon the classification and naming of literary genres in Fohrer, *IOT*; Eissfeldt, *TOT*; and Hayes, *OTFC*. The structure of the table is closest to Fohrer's analysis, but with additions and deletions in the genres and with differences in the illustrative biblical texts cited.

†Most frequently occurring genres.

TABLE 8 (continued)
Literary Genres, Forms, or Types in the Hebrew Bible

Literary Genres in the Historical and Legal Writings (continued)

---

†20. Sagas (Gen. 21:22–31; 32:25–33; Exod. 17:8–16; 32; Daniel 1—6)
Saga Chains or cycles (Gen. 12:4–9; 13—14; 18—19, Abraham and Lot cycle)
†21. Legends (1 Samuel 1—3; 1 Kings 17—19; 2 Kings 2:19–22; 13:20–21)
†22. Novellas (i.e., "little novels") or Expanded Sagas (Genesis 37; 39—48; 50; Jonah; Ruth)
23. Anecdotes (Judges 15:1—16:3; 1 Sam. 23:8–23)

Reportorial Literary Genres

†24. Lists of Persons and Groups (Genesis 10; Numbers 1; 26; 2 Sam. 8:16–18; 20:23–26; Ezra 2; Nehemiah 3)
†25. Lists of Places (Num. 33:1–49; Joshua 15—19; Micah 1:10–16)
26. Lists of Material Objects (Exod. 35:21–29; Isa. 3:18–23; Ezra 2:68–69)
†27. Annals and Chronicles (1 Kings 9:15–23; 14:25–28)
†28. Historical Narratives (Judges 9; 1 Samuel 11)
Historiography (2 Samuel 9—20; 1 Kings 1—2)
29. Biography (Neh. 1:1—7:5; 11:1–2; 12:27—13:31)
For other literary genres in historical-legal writings, see nos. 30, 32, 34–36, 38, 41–43, 45, 47, 49, 51, 52, 56, 57, 59.

Literary Genres in the Poetic Writings

Song Genres of Everyday Life

30. Work Songs (Num. 21:17–18)
31. Drinking Songs (Isa. 22:13; 56:12)
32. Taunts or Mocking Songs (Num. 21:27–30; Judges 5:28–30; Isa. 44:12–20; Ps. 137:7–9)
33. Love Songs (Song of Songs; Isa. 5:1–7; Ezekiel 16; 23)
†34. War and Victory Songs (Exod. 15:20–21; Josh. 10:12; Judges 5; 1 Sam. 18:6–7; Isa. 63:1–6; Psalms 20—21)
35. Dirges or Funeral Songs (2 Sam. 1:17–27; Amos 5:1–3; Isa. 14:4–21)

Literary Genres in the Psalms

†36. Hymnic Songs (Deut. 33:1–5, 26–29; Psalms 46—48; 78; 93; 96—99; 103; 105—6; Habakkuk 3; Job 6—7)
†37. Laments (Psalms 6; 22; 44; 69; 74; 137; Isa. 52:13—53:12; Job 3:17–19; 10:8–17)
38. Thanksgiving Songs (1 Sam. 2:1–10; Psalms 67; 107; 124; 136; Jonah 2:2–9)
39. Royal Songs (Psalms 2; 20; 44—45; 72; 101; 110; 132; 144; Isa. 9:2–7)
40. Wisdom and Didactic Poetry (Psalms 34; 37; 49; 73; 91; 111—12; Hosea 14:9)
For other literary genres in the Psalms, see nos. 1, 7, 10, 11, 32, 34, 41.

TABLE 8 (continued)
Literary Genres, Forms, or Types in the Hebrew Bible

Literary Genres in the Prophetic Writings

---

41. Solicited Oracles (1 Kings 14:5–16; 2 Kings 20:1; Pss. 20:6–8; 60:6–8; 85:9–10; 95:7–11; Jer. 37:17)
†42. Threats or Words of Judgment (2 Kings 1:3–4, 6, 15–16; Jer. 28:12–16; Amos 7:16–17)
†43. Promises or Words of Salvation (1 Kings 17:14; 2 Kings 3:16–19; Jer. 28:2–4; 32:14–15; Isa. 41:8–13)
44. Exhortations or Admonitions (Isa. 1:10–17; Jer. 7:1–15; 25:3–7; Amos 5:14)
45. Trial or Judicial Speeches (Isa. 41:1–5, 21–29; 50:1–3)
    Lawsuits (Deuteronomy 32; Isaiah 1; Jeremiah 2; Micah 6)
46. Disputation Speeches (Isa. 40:12–31; 49:14–26; Micah 2:6–11; Malachi 1—2; 3:6–15; Job 4—42:6)

Prophetic Reports

†47. Vision Reports (1 Kings 22:19–22; Amos 7:1–9; 8:1–3; Zech. 1:7—6:8; Daniel 7—12)
    Call Reports (Isaiah 6; Jeremiah 1; Ezekiel 1—3)
†48. Symbolic Action Reports (Hosea 1; 3; Isa. 7:3; 8:1–4; 20:1–6; Jer. 13:1–11; 32:1–15; Ezek. 12:1–20; 24)

Prophetic Narratives

†49. Legends (1 Kings 11:29–39; 14:1–18; Isa. 38:1–8; see also no. 21)
50. Biography (Jeremiah 26—28; 36—45)
    For other literary genres in prophetic writings, see nos. 7–9, 17, 18, 22, 25, 26, 31–40, 51, 53, 56, 58.

Literary Genres in the Wisdom Writings

---

51. Popular Proverbs (1 Sam. 24:14; Jer. 23:28; Ezek. 18:2; Zeph. 1:12)
52. Riddles (Judges 14:14; Prov. 1:6)
53. Numerical Sayings (Amos 1:3—2:8; Ps. 62:11; Job 5:19–22; Prov. 6:16–19; 30:15–16, 18–19, 21–31)
†54. Aphorisms or Proverbs as an Artistic Form (Proverbs 10—29; Eccles. 1:12–18; 2:1–11; 3:1–15)
55. Wisdom and Didactic Poetry (Job 18:5–21; 20:4–29; 28; Proverbs 1—9)
56. Parables (2 Sam. 12:1–4; Isa. 5:1–7; 28:27–29; Jonah)
57. Fables (Judges 9:8–15; 2 Kings 14:9; Prov. 30:24–31)
58. Allegories (Ezekiel 15—17:10; 19:1–14; Prov. 15:15–23; Eccles. 11:9—12:8)
59. Lists of Nouns or Onomastica (1 Kings 4:29–34; Job 28; 36:27—37:13; 38:4—39:30; 40:15—41:34)
    For other literary genres in wisdom writings, see nos. 7, 8, 18, 19, 36, 37, 46.

---

prophetic, and wisdom), the most prominent types are listed. At the end of each of these divisions, types that are less frequent in such writings are indicated by cross-reference numbers. Thus, religious song types appear not only in Psalms but in all four kinds of writings, and sagas and legends are not simply ingredient to narrative works but also appear in prophetic writings and even serve apocalyptic ends in Daniel. So, although types tend to cluster in one or another category of writing, they are very movable in that they can appear in changing combinations and varying literary contexts.

Once the major literary genres of the Hebrew Bible are in view, it is possible to represent the growth of the writings from the smallest literary units to the great literary compositions (chart 3). It will be seen that this graphic representation takes on the shape of a "literary river," with the smaller and more numerous units at the top of the chart, like rivulets, brooks, and streams, "flowing" into the larger compositions at the bottom of the chart, like tributary rivers and branches of the main river. An effort has also been made to show the preexisting genre elements that have been taken into biblical texts (marked by brackets) and the determinative shape of the books that variously subsume the genre elements (marked by parentheses). Even so, neither the literary composition history nor the oral and written aspects of the literary types could be shown in all their detail on the table and chart which aim chiefly to give an initial orientation to aspects of literary analysis that will be discussed in more detail in later chapters with reference to particular biblical books and bodies of tradition. In the Conclusion, we will see how the literary "streams of tradition," intermixed with social and theological developments, formed recognizable "trajectories" over long spans of biblical history.

11.2 Final Formation of the Hebrew Bible

The final formation of the biblical text entailed two developments: (1) the task of collecting and editing that rounded out the finished form of each of the three parts of the Bible, and (2) the investing of these collections with a definitive authority as the foundational documents for the community. The finished Hebrew Bible viewed as authoritative in this manner is generally called the *canon* (from a Greek word for "reed, measuring rod, standard") and the process by which valued writings became uniquely authoritative writings is called *canonization*.

11.2.a The Authoritative Collections

THE LAW

The first portion of the Hebrew Bible to reach completed form as a definitive collection was the Law, encompassing Genesis through Deuteronomy. It is probable that the demarcation of this unit was simultaneous with the decision of the postexilic Jewish community to make this document the written foundation of its developing style of religious faith and practice. This very likely occurred about 450–400 B.C.E. during the reforming activities of Ezra and Nehemiah (§10.3). Precise circumstances and motivations attending the elevation of the Law are poorly known, but a general reconstruction of the situation is possible.

The Jews who were restored by the Persians to Palestine following the exile were in a problematic position. As a community they were no longer politically independent but functioned as an administrative unit within the Persian Empire. They were accorded freedom in cultural and religious affairs and authority was divided locally between a high priest and a governor answerable to the Persians. Israel no longer had kings nor could it conduct foreign policy. Being an Israelite or Jew (chap. 1 n. 2) was no longer definable as membership in a fully independent political community on a par with other national states. Moreover, during the exile the Israelites had largely ceased to be Hebrew-speaking in daily life. They now spoke the Aramaic language they had adopted in Babylonia. Only those who cultivated Hebrew as a literary and liturgical language could read the traditional Israelite writings; otherwise, they would be understandable only if someone translated them into Aramaic (§12.1.c). All of these circumstances indicate limited options open to the Jewish community in comparison with preexilic times when, first as tribes and then as one or two independent states, Israel was a full and active participant in ancient Near Eastern affairs.

The clearest connecting feature that postexilic Jews had in common with their ancestors was their religion which had in fact grown stronger in exile. An effective way to define and solidify the restored community was to stress its religious continuity with Moses, the lawgiver, and with the patriarchs, judges, kings, priests, and prophets of preexilic and exilic Israel. This reaffirmation of the religious past was accomplished institutionally by rebuilding the temple and reestablishing its services of prayer and sacrifice, along with the festivals and rites that had helped to preserve Israelite identity during the exile. This same link with the past was affirmed literarily by carefully collecting and reading the ancestral writings that had managed to survive the exile.

By about 450 B.C.E., these ancestral writings included two major blocks of narratives that treated the history of Israel, although, as observed (§11.1.b), much of this "history" was in the imaginative form of sagas, legends, and novellas. In addition, there were prophetic books, psalms,

CHART 3
From the Small Oral/Literary Units to the Large Compositions and Collections

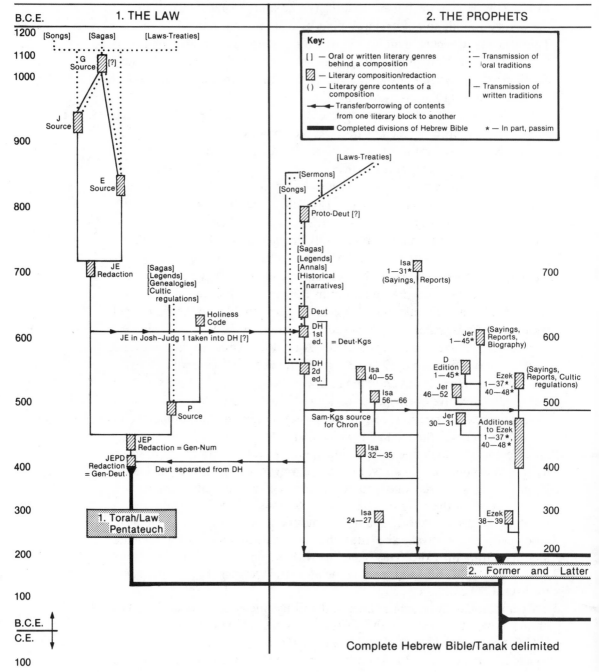

B.C.E.   **1. THE LAW**   **2. THE PROPHETS**

1200   [Songs]   [Sagas]   [Laws-Treaties]

Key:

[ ] — Oral or written literary genres behind a composition ⫶ — Transmission of oral traditions

▨ — Literary composition/redaction

( ) — Literary genre contents of a composition │ — Transmission of written traditions

◄─── Transfer/borrowing of contents from one literary block to another

▬▬ Completed divisions of Hebrew Bible   ★ — In part, passim

1. Torah/Law Pentateuch

2. Former and Latter

Complete Hebrew Bible/Tanak delimited

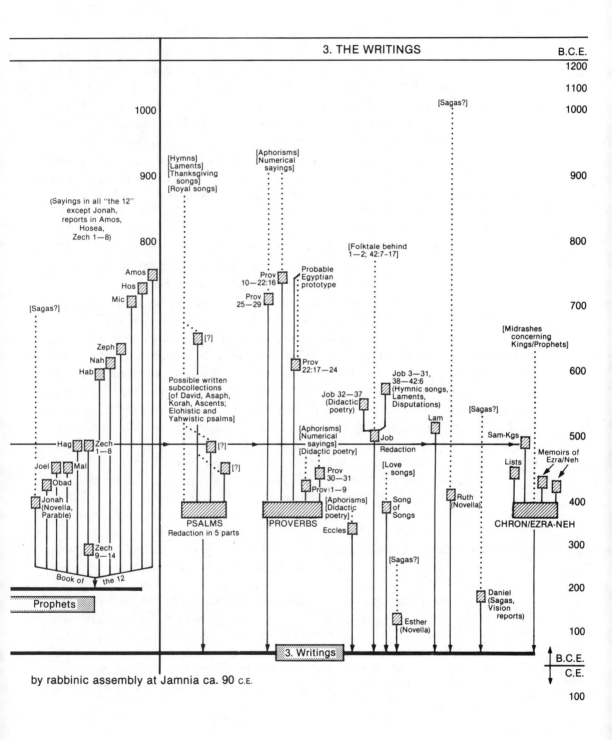

3. THE WRITINGS

B.C.E.

1200

1100

1000

[Sagas?]

1000

900

[Hymns]
[Laments]
[Thanksgiving songs]
[Royal songs]

[Aphorisms]
[Numerical sayings]

900

(Sayings in all "the 12" except Jonah, reports in Amos, Hosea, Zech 1—8)

800

[Folktale behind 1—2; 42:7-17]

800

[Sagas?]

Amos

Hos

Mic

700

Prov 10—22:16

Prov 25—29

Probable Egyptian prototype

[Midrashes concerning Kings/Prophets]

700

Zeph

Nah

Hab

[?]

Possible written subcollections [of David, Asaph, Korah, Ascents; Elohistic and Yahwistic psalms]

Prov 22:17—24

Job 3—31, 38—42:6 (Hymnic songs, Laments, Disputations)

600

Job 32—37 (Didactic poetry)

Lam

[Sagas?]

Hag

Zech 1—8

[?]

[Aphorisms]
[Numerical sayings]
[Didactic poetry]

Job

Redaction

Sam-Kgs

Memoirs of Ezra/Neh

500

Joel

Mal

Obad

Jonah (Novella, Parable)

[?]

Prov 30—31

Prov 1—9

[Aphorisms]
[Didactic poetry]

[Love songs]

Lists

400

Song of Songs

Ruth (Novella)

PSALMS
Redaction in 5 parts

PROVERBS

Eccles

CHRON/EZRA-NEH

Zech 9—14

300

[Sagas?]

Book of the 12

Prophets

200

Daniel (Sagas, Vision reports)

Esther (Novella)

100

3. Writings

B.C.E.
C.E.

by rabbinic assembly at Jamnia ca. 90 C.E.

100

wisdom collections, and independent short stories. The two great narrative blocks, Genesis through Numbers and Deuteronomy through Kings, were the equivalent of "national epics" in that they recounted the story of Israel's past down to the exile. All the other types of literature were more topical and episodic, lacking the panoramic sweep of the narrative blocks. Moreover, it was among those narrative chains that the instructions about worship and the daily conduct of life were preserved in the form of laws given by Moses. It was on the basis of these laws that the community was reconstructed in its cultural and religious dimensions, including the revival of the temple cult. In fact, so central was the prescriptive role of these laws that the entire collection Genesis through Deuteronomy came to be known as the Law of Moses.

But why were Genesis through *Deuteronomy* chosen? Why not Genesis through *Numbers*, corresponding to the first of the narrative blocks, or Genesis through *Kings*, representing a combination of both blocks? Probably two factors account for the inclusion of Deuteronomy in the Law and the exclusion of Joshua through Kings. The intent in elevating the Law was to make it the undisputed foundation document that every member of the restored Jewish community had to observe to be in good standing. With that aim, the relevant laws were not restricted to the preexisting Genesis through Numbers. Deuteronomy, which introduced the long historical work extending through Kings, also contained laws attributed to Moses. For the community's foundation document to give a complete text of the known laws of Moses it was necessary, therefore, to include at least the Book of Deuteronomy along with Genesis through Numbers.

The remaining Deuteronomistic books posed a problem, however. They told of the conquest of Canaan by Joshua, the settling of the tribes, the wars of the judges, the conquests of David, and the subsequent history of the divided kingdoms. These accounts were blatantly political and military. Since the restoration of Jews to Palestine was part of a Persian design to strengthen their empire, the assertive national independence expressed in Joshua through Kings was openly at odds with Persian imperial power and could even encourage Jewish nationalists to rebel against Persia. Since none of the vital laws was found there anyway, the politically dangerous content and tone of Joshua-Kings weighed decisively against its inclusion. It was decided to sever Deuteronomy from its position at the beginning of the Deuteronomistic History and attach it to the end of Genesis-Numbers, thereby forming the five books of Moses, known as the Law or Torah (§48).

THE PROPHETS

The decision to make Genesis-Deuteronomy the measure of faith and practice in the restored community did not mean that the other writings were lost or destroyed. They continued to be read and used in various contexts of public life or in private reading. The next stage in the collection of the Hebrew Bible is difficult to discern because we have almost no historical documentation from Palestine between 400 and 200 B.C.E. During this period the prophetic writings were rounded out. Probably all of the prophetic books existed in some form by 400 B.C.E., although additions were made in most of them during the next two centuries.

The severe restriction of Jewish national life in Palestine and the increasing sense that the golden age of religious revelation was in the past contributed to the decline of fresh prophecy. The prophets were of course highly venerated as past speakers for God who had assisted the people in weathering the difficult time of exile from their land. Now that the prophets were no longer alive, their writings constituted a virtually completed collection that logically supplemented the Law (§48). The collection of these prophetic books was arranged on two principles: size and chronological order. The longer Books of Isaiah, Jeremiah, and Ezekiel came first in proper temporal order. The much shorter remaining books, forming the so-called Book of the Twelve, were also grouped in what appears to have been an approximate chronological order, but perhaps also in some cases on the basis of catchwords near the beginning and end of books that linked them.

Curiously enough, however, the "prophetic" collection was not confined to gathering together the explicitly prophetic writings. The great bulk of the Deuteronomistic History, its introduction already removed to become the last book of the Law, was placed at the beginning of the prophetic collection. The narrative block, Joshua through Kings, was known as the Former Prophets, while the prophetic books proper, Isaiah through Malachi, were known as the Latter Prophets. The decision to give the Deuteronomistic History the recognition that it had missed acquiring in the fifth century as part of the Law was probably facilitated by a change in the political climate after the collapse of the Persian Empire. Apparently the Ptolemaic Hellenistic rulers of Palestine, who inherited the Jewish community of Palestine within their realm, were not as sensitive to ancient Jewish national independence as the Persians had been. Likewise, the temptations to Jews to misread Joshua-Kings as a stimulus to rebellion may by this time not have seemed a live danger to the Jewish leaders who did the collecting and accorded authority to the prophetic writings.

Prefacing the explicitly prophetic works with Joshua through Kings was sensible in that those books also told of prophets who did not write books (e.g., Nathan, Ahijah, Elijah, and Elisha) and they further provided historical setting for the prophets who did write books. By this time there also existed a third independent narrative account in Chronicles and Ezra-Nehemiah (§39; 51), dependent in part on Samuel-Kings, but carrying the story of Israel another 150 years beyond the Deuteronomistic History, that is, down to ca. 400 B.C.E. The Chronicler's work could also have been included appropriately in the Former Prophets, considering that it gave historical context for the Latter Prophets Haggai, Zechariah, and Malachi. Why the Chronicler's History was not included is uncertain. Perhaps, insofar as it focused on the postexilic age, it may not have been felt to be closely linked to the great age of prophecy which had been preexilic and exilic. Possibly also, the extensive repetition of parts of Samuel-Kings in Chronicles made it unacceptably redundant to the collectors.

THE WRITINGS

The remaining works that came to form the Hebrew Bible were grouped in a miscellaneous collection called "The Writings" (§51–55). They included (1) the Psalms, which had become the song book of the restored temple; (2) the wisdom writings of Job and Proverbs, which struggled with questions of human success and adversity in the light of the promises of Israel's religion; (3) five short compositions used at festivals, the short stories of Esther and Ruth, the dirges over the fall of Jerusalem in Lamentations, the love poetry of the Song of Songs, and the skeptical wisdom Book of Ecclesiastes; (4) the apocalyptic Book of Daniel; and (5) the just-mentioned historical works of Chronicles, Ezra, and Nehemiah.

It is far from apparent why the Writings were generally placed in the order listed above (there are frequent variations in Hebrew manuscripts). Perhaps Chronicles and Ezra-Nehemiah were placed *last* in order to form a balancing counterpart to the historical books Genesis through Kings at the beginning of the collected traditions. Interestingly, the chronological order of these concluding historical works was disrupted by putting Chronicles *after* Ezra-Nehemiah, presumably because Nehemiah ends on a rather dour note whereas Chronicles concludes with an upbeat reference to rebuilding the temple—a more suitable conclusion to the Hebrew Bible in its entirety.

Probably the latest compositions in the Writings were Daniel, written about 165 B.C.E. (§55.2), and the final redaction of Esther, perhaps as late as 125 B.C.E (§53.2). By this time there also existed a number of other Jewish books, in Hebrew, Aramaic, and Greek, which we have briefly characterized as the Apocrypha and Pseudepigrapha (§10.2.a), and the Dead Sea Scrolls (§10.2.b). This literature continued to appear, and even to intermingle in usage and regard with the Psalms, Proverbs, Job, the Festival Scrolls, Daniel, Chronicles, Ezra, and Nehemiah. It took another two centuries until in 90 C.E. the fixed boundaries of the Writings were agreed upon.

As far as we know, there was never any serious argument that additional books should be admitted to the Law or Prophets. But since the Writings were a miscellaneous assortment of texts that lacked the historical or thematic unity of the earlier Law and Prophets, it was not surprising that its contents were variously conceived by different Jewish groups. The different views of the scope of the Writings reflected serious partisan splits within Palestinian Judaism that deepened in the period between the Maccabean Wars, beginning 167 B.C.E. and ending with the War against Rome and the destruction of Jerusalem in 66–70 C.E. (§46–47).

It is evident from the numerous nonbiblical scrolls of the Dead Sea community that the production of religious books flourished in this age of domestic turmoil and foreign attack. Some of these books were the work of Dispersion Jews, especially those living in Alexandria, Egypt, where they were greatly influenced by the urbane cultural and intellectual climate of Hellenistic society. Particularly popular in Palestine were apocalyptic writings in the manner of Daniel (cf. the near-contemporary early parts of *1 Enoch* and the *Testament of Moses*) that attempted to read the chaotic events of the age within a symbolic framework of doomed earthly kingdoms giving way to the kingdom of God (§55.1). There also appeared historical books such as 1 and 2 Maccabees, wisdom compositions such as the Wisdom of Ben Sirach and the Wisdom of Solomon, and short stories such as Tobit and Judith. Some of these "extra" writings were actually intended as supplements to biblical texts. The Greek translations of Daniel and Esther have additions not found in the Hebrew.

As the biblical period came toward a close, there was a sudden literary explosion producing many candidates for a further collection of authoritative books. In principle, Jews might have gone on endlessly creating such authoritative collections of scripture. Why did the process stop with the Writings? And how was it decided which books, among the many contenders, would be allowed among the Writings? The turn of historical events aborted the scripture-building process by leaving one Jewish party in control and able to decide about the sacred books as it preferred. The circumstances of the Jewish revolt against Rome, beginning in 66 C.E., and the resulting destruction of Jerusalem in 70 C.E., effectively eliminated the leadership and programs of all the bitterly contending Jewish tendencies and parties, except for one. The Pharisees, champions of the Oral Law which was, in time, to become the Talmud (§10.2.c), were left to have the final say about which books would be included among the Writings and, more importantly, how the canon of the Hebrew Bible as a whole would be interpreted and how it would function within the emerging Rabbinic Jewish community.

11.2.b Factors in the Canonical Closure: From Ezra to the Rabbinic Assembly at Jamnia

Public religious usage of the biblical writings has ordinarily been stressed as the key factor leading to canonization. In a way it is hard to quarrel with this view, since unused books certainly do not get canonized, but it is not evident that this notion unaided really has much explanatory power. In one often-overlooked detail, however, the precise nature of the usage of biblical "books" is important.

It is often unrealized that the canon, at the time of its closure, was not an edition of the text but rather a judgment about the text's authority. The practice of binding loose pages together to form a book (codex) was first developed by Christians in the third and fourth centuries C.E. Prior to that time, all writings intended for lasting use were copied on cumbersome scrolls. One large-sized biblical book was about all that a scroll could hold and still be conveniently handled. Therefore, during the entire period we are discussing, there was absolutely no way that Jews could give expression to the canonical authority of the Bible by including all its contents on one scroll. What we mean by a canonical collection at that time is simply the bringing together in the synagogues and scribal schools of all the books regarded as of equal value and authority but as yet copied on separate scrolls. In this sense the role of institutional religious use of the canonical scrolls was critical. Canon was a recognized concept for ensuring the supervised preservation, transmission, and use of the books judged to be acceptable, while firmly excluding others, whatever their value in other respects.

Yet it is insufficient to talk about religious use of the biblical books in a generalized sense. It is necessary to examine particular uses by particular groups in the context of the unfolding sociohistorical experience of the Jewish people during the period of canonization. The struggle to determine which of the Israelite/Jewish writings were authoritative, and in what way they were authoritative, was a struggle for power among contending groups in the community. Very rarely has the canonization process of the Hebrew

Bible been studied in terms of the religious politics entailed, and admittedly such an inquiry is complicated by the uneven nature of our knowledge about the period 400 B.C.E.–90 C.E. Some of the basic developments in this period, however, may help us to understand the persisting forces that moved Jews steadily toward becoming a people of a very deliberately constructed Book, selectively composed from a much larger body of Jewish religious literature.

From the exile on, in spite of the successful restoration of a Judahite community in Palestine, there was a decided decline in the power of self-determination exercised by Jews. By comparison with the greater independence they had known in preexilic times, Jews were henceforth decisively limited by non-Jewish imperial powers. Much energy went into securing what autonomy they could from their political overlords, while resisting intrusions into their cultural and religious life and protecting their land from excessive economic depletion.

A large factor in this postexilic struggle was the exercise of class privilege within the Jewish community, since it was in the conquerors' interests to cultivate a local Jewish elite (§42). The leadership of the restored Judahite community, including Ezra and Nehemiah, were just such an elite (§44). So also were the Hellenized Jews who collaborated with the Seleucids at the time of the Maccabean Wars (§46), and the Sadducees who monopolized the high priesthood in Roman times. During the period of Jewish independence after the Maccabean Wars, the Hasmonean kings developed into an elite who sought to play power politics on a par with other Hellenistic kingdoms (§47).

Jewish elites operating under such imperial conditions were in an ambiguous position and were looked upon with ambivalence by their less-advantaged fellow Jews—with gratitude for the communal favors that the elite might extract from the empire, or the protection they might afford the community, but also with suspicion and hostility for the excessive share of privilege and wealth that they reserved for themselves. Since religion was of such pronounced importance to Jews, it is to be expected that elites and their critics would both try to summon religious support for their positions and programs. Decisions about holy books were thus not only decisions about religious matters but about who had controlling power in the life of the community (§48). The role of elites and non-elites, their succession and changing composition, requires much further study in tracing the late biblical sectarian battles in relation to the formation of the canon.

Along with the sense of a greatly diminished sphere for public Jewish life there went a sense of lost religious power. Since the religion of Israel had always been a communal matter that tended to find expression in the whole range of national life, whatever diminished the total life options of postexilic Jews also reduced their religious options. This mood found expression in the notion that God was more remote and not as active in Israel's behalf as in ancient days. The dictum gradually gained currency that religious revelation ended with Ezra about 400 B.C.E. All of the prophets were understood to have lived before Ezra. In the deliberations in 90 C.E. that concurred on the contents of the canon, one objective criterion for judging the authority of books was the conviction that all sacred texts must have been written no later than the time of Ezra. Canonical books that historical-critical study has shown to be later than 400 B.C.E. were admissible only because the traditional claims to authorship by Solomon or Daniel were taken literally.

The splitting of Israel's religious history into a past golden age and a present age of decline and limitation was combined with a countervailing determination to make the utmost of the religious options for self-expression that were available. Thus the restored temple assumed a singular communal importance that it had not had when it was one of a number of national monarchic institutions. Since the distinctive features of Jewish identity were rooted in the Law of Moses, the faithful observance of that document as the constitution of the restored community became central.

Focus on the text of the Law as a guide for the essential matters of communal life also served to stimulate interest in *all* the surviving literary traditions of Israel. The prophetic writings were collected and studied for lessons of history and as pointers to the still-unfinished future of the community (§48). The combining of the short prophetic writings into one "Book of the Twelve" was probably symbolic of a felt identity between the twelve tribes of ancient Israel and the community collecting the books. The Psalms were edited in five parts, probably on the model of the five books of the Law (§52.2). Wisdom writings, although saturated with notions common to the whole ancient Near Eastern wisdom tradition, were pointedly thematized around the Jewish Law as the supreme source of wisdom (§54).

In this situation of restricted possibilities and determined commitments, the period from 167 B.C.E. to 70 C.E. was riddled with threats and crises for Palestinian Judaism (§46–47). The Seleucid and Roman powers impinged on Palestine more drastically than had the Persian and Ptolemaic authorities. In the Maccabean Wars the religious identity of Jews as observers of the Law was nearly expunged. Moreover, these wars exposed deep internal divisions among the Jews of Palestine over how open they should be to Hellenistic culture and what were the religious limitations to be placed on the political institutions and behavior of Jews when they were independent, as occurred under the Hasmonean kings from 140 to 63 B.C.E.

Elites rose and fell, coalitions formed and fell apart, as religion, politics, and social class intermixed in changing patterns. The collapse of the Hasmonean kingdom and the entrance of Rome into Palestine, at first under native Herodian princes and then under Roman administrators, brought heavier taxation and harder economic conditions for a depressed peasant populace. Meanwhile, Jews living outside Palestine were subject to the allurements of Hellenistic culture, and the turning of the sect of Jewish Christians into a missionary religion among Gentiles and Dispersion Jews raised the danger of major attrition in the ranks of Jews.

In short, the process of canonizing scripture came to its culmination as one aspect of a larger response of the Jewish community under virtual siege conditions, endangered by Roman oppression and by Hellenistic culture, and torn within by competing programs for survival advanced by Sadducees, Essenes, Zealots, Jewish Christians, and Pharisees. When the Jewish uprising against Rome was suppressed, the Pharisees alone survived it as an effective force in the Jewish community. By default, as it were, their program of building grass-roots Jewish communities around the Law as interpreted by Oral Tradition stepped front and center. And it was they who met for consultations at Jamnia ca. 90 C.E. to put the finishing touches on the shape of the Hebrew Bible to be recognized as holy Scripture.

The dates for the first two stages of collecting and according authority to the Hebrew Bible, 400 and 200 B.C.E., are only approximations. We do not know of any formal pronouncements or even records of deliberations connected with those stages, unless Nehemiah 8 implies such, and not all scholars are agreed that the finished Law of Moses is there referred to. The one deliberation on canon that we know anything about took place in a rabbinic assembly or consultation in 90 C.E. at the small Palestinian coast town of Jamnia, serving in place of Jerusalem which the Romans had made out of bounds to Jews since 70 C.E. As part of a general program of consolidation of the community after the disastrous uprising, it was recognized that the Law and the Prophets and the Writings, as we now know them, carried sole scriptural authority. Reports of these deliberations in the Talmud tell of objections and reservations about Ezekiel (because of inconsistencies between his imaginary design of a new temple and the Law of Moses), Song of Songs (because of its explicit erotic poetry), Ecclesiastes (because of its bitterly despairing outlook on life), and Esther (because it was secular and endorsed the Feast of Purim which was not yet widely accepted in the Jewish community.)

In the end all objections were met, at least to the satisfaction of a majority of rabbinic scholars in the assembly. Using the aims and methods of rabbinic reinterpretation and harmonizing of inconsistencies in biblical writings, Ezekiel's discrepancies were explained away, Song of Songs was given a mystical reading so that it spoke of love of God for Israel, both the Song of Songs and Ecclesiastes were accepted as the work of Solomon, and Esther was approved because it had become a symbol of Jewish survival in the face of severe persecution. Nonetheless, Jamnia did not issue a formal edict. More than anything else, it placed a seal of approval upon the books that the rabbinic movement had already been using for some time, officially confirming that books infected by Hellenistic culture or distorted by eschatological fervor had gone the way of destruction and discredit along with the Sadducean, Essene, Jewish Christian, and Zealot proponents.

If we ask how the canonizers at Jamnia viewed the authority of the Hebrew Bible they affirmed, the place to look is in the way the Talmud and the Midrash exegete scripture in order to develop a system of highly motivated and well-ordered daily religious practice. The base of this system is halakhic observance of the Law, but it simultaneously provides for haggadic upbuilding of piety by free use of all the strictly nonlegal parts of the Bible (§10.2.c).

The Hebrew Bible was moving from being simply the story of a people and its God to becoming an oracle and guide book, a full-orbed resource for determining the will of God in every present situation. Yet it was not an oracle thought to answer indiscriminately any and all questions on all subjects. Its authority had chiefly to do with a form of quietistic religious politics appropriate to a people who had just emerged badly shaken from war and civil strife. The Hebrew Bible—at last clearly demarcated and viewed through the Oral Law—provided a discipline of religious practice in community and a strategy for coping with life in a hostile world. This communal life strategy was made operable in circumstances where Jews had conclusively lost all direct political power. A book-centered piety and practice became central to the religiocultural "enclave system" by which late biblical Jews forged their way of life.

11.3 Preservation and Transmission of the Hebrew Bible

The process of transmitting the Hebrew Bible began with the handing down of the separate literary units, and their ingredient subunits, after they first appeared in writing. This process extended through all the stages of the growth and stabilization of the text. It continued with the passing along of the stabilized text in manuscripts written by hand and published in printed editions—all the way down to the present moment. Broadly conceived, the transmission of the Hebrew Bible included translations into the native languages of Jews and Christians who either did not know Hebrew at all, or who understood it imperfectly, or who preferred a version of Scripture in their spoken tongue.

11.3.a The Transmission Process Extending to the Stabilization of the Consonantal Text, ca. 100 C.E.

All the original copies of the individual biblical writings, as well as their sources, have perished or eluded the excavators. It is probable that they were written on papyrus made from the sliced stem of a fibrous Egyptian plant. As the writings gained status, they were copied on more durable leather. When made from skins of high quality and prepared by special treatment, the leather was known as parchment or vellum. Throughout the entire period under consideration, the manuscripts—whether on papyrus or on leather—were in scroll form. The maximum suitable length of a scroll, beyond which it became unwieldy to unroll and reroll, was about twenty-five feet. A scroll of that size would accommodate one large biblical book, or two at most if the writing were very fine. It is plausibly proposed that the divisions of the books of the Law and Former Prophets reflect accommodation to scroll length, and that alongside the large prophetic books, each with its own scroll, all the smaller prophetic books were grouped together on a single scroll to form the Book of the Twelve.

Most, if not all, of the biblical documents were written in the Old Hebrew or Phoenician script which the preexilic Israelites had shared with the Canaanites and Phoenicians. After the exile, the Aramaic script influenced the writing of Hebrew in the direction of the Square Script that had fuller, block-shaped letters. Eventually this Square Script (also called Aramaic or Assyrian) became the standard form, although during the Maccabean age and the Wars against Rome in 66–70 C.E. and 132–35 C.E., the Old Hebrew Script was briefly revived in outbursts of nationalistic fervor.

Prior to 1947, our earliest Hebrew manuscript evidence was almost entirely confined to medieval manuscripts no earlier than the late ninth century C.E., with some fragments reaching back to the fifth century C.E. To be sure, a version of the Law in Old Hebrew Script had been preserved by the Samaritan community that had broken away from the main body of Jews in pre-Christian times. The manuscripts of this Samaritan Pentateuch, however, were as late as the Jewish medieval manuscripts and its departures from the official Jewish text (MT) were difficult to evaluate.

With the recovery of the Dead Sea Scrolls (§10.2.b) came a radical change in the state of our Hebrew manuscript evidence. In addition to one virtually complete copy of Isaiah (1QIsaᵃ) and a partial copy of the same prophet (1QIsaᵇ), the Dead Sea Scrolls included fragments of all biblical writings except Esther, as well as portions of biblical texts in commentaries and all or parts of forty-one biblical psalms in a collection that included apocryphal psalms (11QPsaᵃ). Some of the biblical fragments are dated to the third century B.C.E., possibly even to the fourth century, and the complete Isaiah scroll may date as early as 150 B.C.E.

Easily the most significant textual feature of the biblical manuscript finds at Qumran is the discovery that they represent a variety of family types or redactional traditions. The official standardized text of the Hebrew Bible that reached its pinnacle of development in the medieval Jewish Tiberian school of Palestine is called the Masoretic Text ("traditional text," or "text of the traditionists"). It is this text, abbreviated MT, that forms the basis of all modern printed editions and translations of the Hebrew Bible. Naturally scholars were curious to see how the Dead Sea biblical texts, a thousand years older, would compare with MT. What they found was that 1QIsaᵃ, along with other less-complete manuscripts, exhibited a text that was a clear forerunner of MT, differing mainly in spelling features and occasional grammatical forms. It was evident that the medieval Masoretes had preserved a manuscript tradition that ran back to pre-Christian times.

What greatly surprised scholars, however, was the simultaneous discovery of other biblical manuscripts at Qumran that did not fit a proto-Masoretic type. Some of these corresponded closely at points with the Samaritan Pentateuch readings. Others, notably fragments of Samuel and Jeremiah, showed a Hebrew text that accounted for previously unexplained differences between the Greek translation of the Hebrew Bible and MT. This Greek translation, called the Septuagint (§12.1.a), contained many deviations from MT. It was now obvious that some of these differences were due to the fact that—at least in certain biblical books—the Septuagint was faithfully translating a form of the Hebrew text that no one had known about until it came to light among the Dead Sea finds.

One way of viewing the fluidity of the Hebrew text traditions in this pre-Christian period is to think of three basic families of texts: (1) a proto-Masoretic family of texts that fed into the later MT; (2) a family of texts most fully represented in the Samaritan Pentateuch; and (3) a family of texts from which at least part of the Greek Septuagint was translated. Some scholars explain these three types of texts by geographical isolation, arguing that they were locally developed text types: the Samaritan Pentateuch group belonging to Palestine, the Septuagint group to Egypt, and the proto-Masoretic group to Babylon.

Other scholars have not been convinced by the local text hypothesis, but prefer to see the proto-Masoretic text as the work of fastidious scholars, while the other two types were popularized texts. It is also claimed that certain differences in family types may be accounted for by their incorporating different stages in the development of a biblical book. For example, the Septuagint-type Jeremiah text may have embodied a first edition of the prophetic book, while the proto-Masoretic Jeremiah text may have carried a second revised edition. Finally, there are those who are not inclined at all to see three distinct families of texts, but who recognize instead a plurality of redactional traditions. Nevertheless, all concede that the Hebrew text was still in a state of flux prior to the end of the first century C.E., with extensive variations in spelling and grammar and moderate variations in words and phrases and even in contents and order of materials.

Fluidity in the form of the biblical text corresponded to the indeterminacy of the scope of the biblical canon and to the variety of contending interpretations of scripture within the Jewish community. As we might expect, the stabilizing of the form of the text shows up in manuscript evidence close upon the heels of the closure of the canon by the rabbinic authorities who survived the fall of Jerusalem in 70 C.E.(§11.2.b). Biblical fragments, deposited in caves in the Dead Sea region (at Wadi Murabba'at and Naḥal Ḥever) during the Second Jewish Revolt of 132–35 C.E., clearly attest to this textual process. They consistently present a text that continues the standardizing tendencies of the proto-Masoretic Qumran texts and points forward toward the later MT. In fact, manuscripts of the Samaritan Pentateuch and Septuagint types have disappeared altogether.

In moving to consolidate the Jewish community after 70 C.E., the rabbinic leaders stabilized both the canon and the form of the text. The stabilization of the text consisted not in the preparation of a critical edition of the Hebrew Bible but in the selection of one of the existing text types as the official text. This official text was almost certainly not in the form of a single document, since the codex or book form that could have held the entire Hebrew Bible had probably not yet been adopted by Jews. Moreover, to stabilize the text at this time meant to stabilize a text composed only of consonants. Hebrew was a language written with twenty-two consonants, but without any vowels. The appropriate vowel sounds (apart from an occasional marking of a long vowel by a consonantal sign) were supplied by the reader, and, in an ancient sacred text, a tradition of proper vocalization kept alive among copyists and interpreters accompanied the text from generation to generation.

11.3.b The Transmission Process Extending to the Stabilization of the Vocalic Text, ca. 1200 C.E.

Once a consonantal text (MT) had been officially adopted, it was the task of the copyist-scholars to exercise utmost care in passing on the text.[5] A critical test of accuracy in preservation of the text occurred each time a copy was made to replace a worn-out scroll with a fresh scroll. By the fourth or fifth century C.E., the codex form was adopted by Jews, except for scrolls of the Law and Esther mandated for synagogue reading. The codex form greatly facilitated the transmission of the text since it was now possible to include the entire Hebrew Bible in one binding. Although it was Palestinian Jews who had led the reconsolidation of Judaism after 70 C.E., the authoritative effects of their reform spread to Jewish communities everywhere (§44) so that Babylonian Jews in particular were soon fully engaged in the faithful preservation of the official consonantal text as chosen by the Palestinian rabbinic authorities.

As the Talmud neared completion in the period 450–500 C.E., copyists and scholars of the text began to experiment with critical markings in manuscripts in order to indicate the proper vocalization of the text. This strategy must have arisen because of a fear that the proper pronunciation, and thus the correct sense of the text, was in danger of distortion. Hebrew was known then only as a literary and liturgical language, and the correct way to read a text must have come often into question or dispute the longer the vowel sounds were carried only in the oral tradition. Various graphic systems for indicating the vowels were worked out in Babylon and Palestine. The basic method was to specify vowels by placing dots and strokes above or below the consonants, so that the process was called "pointing the text" and the symbols were called "vowel points." The Babylonian and Palestinian systems placed vowel points above the consonants, but the later Tiberian system that supplanted them by about 900 C.E. located all vowels but one *below* the consonants. The vowel points were accompanied by accents that served as punctuation and as a guide for chanting the texts in synagogue services.

---

5. Ernst Würthwein (*The Text of the Old Testament. An Introduction to the Biblica Hebraica*, rev. ed. [Grand Rapids: Wm. B. Eerdmans, 1979], 12–35) describes the main features of the Masoretic Text, including the Masoretic notations, and illustrates with sample pages from manuscripts (pls. 17–25).

The consonantal text of the opening phrase of Genesis in Hebrew, reading from right to left, looks like this: בראשית ברא אלהים. In English it would be like a text that said "N TH BGNNNG GD CRTD." The same phrase in Hebrew with vowel points looks like this: בְּרֵאשִׁית בָּרָא אֱלֹהִים. This fuller script gives the equivalent in English of "IN THE BEGINNING GOD CREATED."

Besides the introduction of vowel points and accents, the copyist-scholars made critical observations of a grammatical and statistical nature, at first orally, and then on all four margins of the text and at the end of manuscripts. These notations were called the Masorah ("tradition") and the scholars responsible were called Masoretes. Actually the three basic tasks of textual transmission were designated by functional terms: Sopherim ("scribes/writers") wrote the consonantal text, Nakdanim ("pointers") added vowel points and accents, and Masoretes ("traditionists") supplied the marginal and final notes. In practice, all of these functions were frequently carried out by the same scholar. The first and third of these terms, however, were used more inclusively. Sopherim referred in Jewish tradition to the learned copyists, guardians, and interpreters of the Law who preceded the Masoretes in an unbroken chain back to Ezra. Masoretes came to refer to all the copyist-scholars who developed the vocalic pointing and the Masoretic notes and, as keepers of the biblical text, were conceived as successors and continuators of the Sopherim.

Included in the marginal and final Masorah was a great mass of technical information and instructions that served to alert copyists to the minutest details and peculiarities of the text so that they might be copied with unfailing accuracy. The Masoretic notes identified unusual spellings, words, and grammatical forms, and often took account of their frequency of occurrence and exact locations throughout the biblical text. Total numbers of letters, words, and verses in biblical books were computed. Middle verses and letters of books and of the three major divisions of the canon were specified. In order to crowd all this Masoretic data into the manuscript margins and endings (colophons), an elaborate but terse system of abbreviations was designed.

As for the internal divisions of the MT, spaces were left to mark paragraphs, a practice that reached back as far as some of the Dead Sea biblical manuscripts. In the Talmudic period the text was divided into sections for reading in a three-year Palestinian cycle and a one-year Babylonian cycle. Verses were often marked but not numbered. The present numbered chapter divisions are attributed to Stephen Langton, an English churchman, who inserted them in the Latin Vulgate in 1205 C.E. These were entered in a Hebrew Bible by a rabbi in 1330 C.E. in order to facilitate references to the text in matters of controversy with Christians. The numbering of the verses within chapters was first employed in a Hebrew Bible in 1571 C.E.

In the centuries that the Masoretes worked, they did everything conceivable to ensure a faithfully preserved text. Given the long period of fluid textual traditions before the consonantal and vocalic texts were stabilized, however, textual errors and alterations occurred that were taken up into MT. The Masoretes were aware of some of these difficulties. For example, they cite eighteen "emendations of the Sopherim" that were intended to eliminate or soften potentially blasphemous or offensive words or ideas in the biblical text. Scholars differ as to the accuracy of these claims, but there was sufficient midrashic treatment of scripture in late biblical times to lend credence to the candor of the Masoretes in pointing out previous pious alterations in the text that they were aware of. Furthermore, in numerous instances the Masoretes note that a word written in one way must be read in another way (*Qere-kethiv* readings). At times this seems to be the Masoretes' way of making "oral emendations" where the received text seemed ungrammatical, offensive, or irreligious. In other cases these oral substitutions apparently preserve textual variants which attest to the fact that alternative readings of the biblical text had not been entirely suppressed in spite of the strong drift toward stabilization of the text since 100 C.E.

The work of the Masoretes reached its apex in the Tiberian school of Palestine in the tenth century C.E. where the ben Asher and ben Naphtali Masoretic families were active. Conflicting practices of vowel pointing and Masoretic notation were more or less standardized at that time. The major accomplishment in this regard is attributed to the influential ben Asher family, whose work is represented in a codex of the prophets from 895 C.E. (Codex Cairensis); a codex of the entire Bible from 900–950 C.E., three-fourths of which has survived (Aleppo Codex); and a codex of the complete Bible from 1008 C.E. (Codex Leningradensis or MS B 19a). The Masoretic family of ben Naphtali, once thought to have been outright rivals of the ben Ashers, probably contributed measurably to this "Tiberian consensus," although it is not certain that we can identify manuscripts that are distinctively from ben Naphtali. While the great Tiberian manuscripts, such as the Aleppo Codex, were serious attempts to provide the whole Bible with a consistent vocalic system and Masorah, it cannot be said that any of them presents an entirely unified application of the principles of the ben Asher school. Nevertheless, it was the heritage of this Tiberian school of Masoretes that provided the basis for all printed editions of the Hebrew Bible to this day.

11.3.c Printed Editions of the Hebrew Bible

Printed editions of the Hebrew Bible—at first of parts of the text and then of the whole—began to appear from 1477 on. The Second Rabbinic Bible was edited by Jacob ben Chayyim and published by the Bomberg Press in Venice in 1524/25 C.E. Ben Chayyim's text became the basic received text (Textus Receptus) among Jews and Christians, and the foundation of all printed editions down to 1936. It was employed by the translators of the chief English versions, including the King James Version (KJV). Ben Chayyim used Tiberian manuscripts but he worked eclectically, drawing now from one and now from another manuscript and indiscriminately compiling Masoretic notes whose key to understanding escaped him. Moreover, his manuscripts were more recent than and inferior to the ben Asher texts of the tenth century C.E. Finally, he failed to indicate the principles on which his choices of textual readings and Masoretic notes were based.

With the growing understanding of the work of the Tiberian Masoretes, the weaknesses of ben Chayyim's eclectic text as a Textus Receptus have become evident. In 1936, the third edition of Rudolph Kittel's *Biblica Hebraica (BHK)* abandoned the ben Chayyim text and printed the ben Asher Codex Leningradensis of 1008 C.E. This codex has remained the basis of subsequent editions of Kittel's text and also of the more recent *Biblica Hebraica Stuttgartensia (BHS)*, edited by K. Elliger and W. Rudolph. Since the recovery of the tenth century C.E. Aleppo Codex, it has become the basis of the Hebrew University Bible Project which has published sample editions of Isaiah as a preliminary to a critical edition of the entire codex to be edited by M. Goshen-Gottstein and S. Talmon. The United Bible Societies Hebrew Old Testament Text Critical Project plans eventually to publish a successor to *BHK* and *BHS* that will retain Codex Leningradensis as its basis but provide a totally new critical apparatus.

12
TRANSLATIONS OF THE HEBREW BIBLE

12.1 Ancient Versions

12.1.a Greek Septuagint

The first and most significant of the early translations of the Hebrew Bible was made into Greek. It was known widely as the Septuagint ("seventy") because of the tradition in the *Letter of Aristeas* that seventy (actually seventy-two) scholars translated it in Alexandria, Egypt, at the invitation of Ptolemy II Philadelphus (285–246 B.C.E.). It is probable that the Septuagint, abbreviated LXX, owed its origin less to the initiative of Greek scholars than to the needs of the Greek-speaking Jewish population in Egypt (§45). The Law was translated into the vernacular Greek, known as *koine,* about 250 B.C.E., and the Prophets and other books were completed by ca. 75 B.C.E. The other books included many writings that did not become part of the Jewish canon in 90 C.E. but were accepted into the early Christian canon and assigned to the Apocrypha by Protestants (table 6). Many translators were involved, the Law being more uniform and literal in its rendering than the other books which are often paraphrased.

Impingement of Hellenistic culture on the Jews of the Dispersion is amply illustrated in the Septuagint. Yahweh, the Israelite name for God, was largely eliminated from the LXX, being replaced by Lord (in Greek, *kurios*). Figurative references to deity were often decoded, for instance, "hand of God" became "power of God," and "robe of God" became "glory of God." The Bible of the first Christians was largely the LXX. In fact, its extant codices are all Christian in origin, since the Jews renounced this Greek version during the rabbinic consolidation after 70 C.E. because it had been too adaptive to Hellenistic culture and had become the province of Christians. Most of the scriptural quotations in the New Testament are based on the Greek version rather than on the original Hebrew. The LXX is of great importance in textual criticism since it is the most ancient translation and, in conjunction with the Dead Sea Scrolls, affords us access to an ancient Hebrew text type that differed from the proto-Masoretic text.

12.1.b Other Greek Versions and Hexapla

In the early Christian centuries other Greek versions appeared. Aquila made an exceedingly literal Greek translation about 100 C.E. to replace the Septuagint among Jews. Theodotion and Symmachus provided freer and more idiomatic renderings into Greek later in the second century C.E., but it remains unclear whether they were Jewish or Christian versions. Theodotion and Symmachus are lost except for a few fragments in the *Hexapla* ("six columns"), a critical compilation of the Greek translations by the Christian scholar Origen ca. 230–40 C.E., which he arranged in columns alongside the Hebrew text accompanied by a Greek transliteration of the Hebrew. It is one of the great losses of antiquity that, except for fragments, the *Hexapla* has perished.

12.1.c Aramaic Targums

Palestinian, Babylonian, and Syrian Jews spoke Aramaic from the time of the exile. The Hebrew sacred books were read in synagogue services and, in addition, an interpreter *(meturgeman)* gave an Aramaic translation or paraphrase *(targum)*. What we call the Targum are the several written forms into which these oral renderings were cast beginning early in the Christian era. The Targums are characterized by free interpretations that do not hesitate to expand or alter the original Hebrew in order to expound a message. In the fifth century C.E., two Babylonian targums were standardized and made authoritative for general Jewish use: Targum Onkelos of the Law and Targum Jonathan of the Prophets.

12.1.d Old Syriac, Peshitta, and Syro-Hexapla

Syriac translations of the Hebrew Bible may have begun as early as the mid–first century C.E., possibly by Jewish converts in the Syrian kingdom of Adiabene or somewhat later by Christians who spread to the Syriac-speaking interior of Syria. The Old Syriac translations give strong indications of having been developed from or influenced by Aramaic Targums. A revision of these translations was the Peshitta ("simple version") which became the official Syriac Christian Old Testament but not without centuries of competition with other Syriac translations. In the seventh century C.E. a Syrian churchman prepared a literal Syriac translation that also reproduced the Septuagint column of Origen's *Hexapla*. Large parts of this Syro-Hexapla have survived and thus preserve a witness to Origen's LXX text and the text-critical symbols that Origen employed in his now-lost *Hexapla*. The extent of the Syriac versions' actual dependence on the original Hebrew is problematic, since the Targums and the LXX have had such extensive influence on them.

12.1.e Old Latin and Vulgate

Most of the earliest Christians were Greek-speaking. With the spread of the faith to the western part of the Roman Empire, Latin began to emerge as a church language. From about 200 C.E. we have evidence of the first translation of biblical books into Latin. Known as Old Latin, these translations were no more a unity than the Septuagint translations, in fact less so. We can account best for the roughness and stylistic shifts on the supposition that these early Latin renderings were independent efforts to supply the needs of local congregations.

So unsatisfactory was the Old Latin that in 382 C.E. Pope Damasus commissioned Jerome to produce an official Latin version. Jerome learned Hebrew and used it for his Old Testament translation. The resulting version was known as the Vulgate ("common version") which took centuries to supplant its Old Latin predecessors in some of the remoter areas such as northern Europe. In the end, the sonorous cadences of the Vulgate secured for it a firm place in the liturgy of the Catholic church. In reaction to the biblical orientation of the Protestant Reformation, the Catholic church asserted the sole sufficiency of the Vulgate and all other translations of the Bible were required to be based on it until 1943 when Catholic scholars were at last permitted to work from the original languages.

12.2 English Versions and Translations

Although the terms are often loosely used interchangeably, there is a difference between a version and a translation. A version is a translation authorized by some ecclesiastical or governmental body and normally involving a number of translators, whereas a translation is an unofficial rendering that may entail many translators but more often is the work of one or two persons. There is a tendency, however, even in scholarly writing, to speak of all ancient translations as versions and this convention tends to carry through the history of English Bibles up to the King James Version, even though many of the early English Bibles were expressly opposed by crown and church. Accordingly, this convention will be followed for the older translations, but in discussing English Bibles in the twentieth century care will be taken to note which are actually versions in the technical sense.[6]

12.2.a English Versions and Translations Through 1952

The early English versions, from the Anglo-Saxon through Wyclif, were all based on the Latin Vulgate. With the invention of printing and rediscovery of Greek and Hebrew occasioned by the Renaissance, William Tyndale produced the first English version to be based on the original languages, although his translation of the Hebrew Bible was confined chiefly to the Pentateuch (1529). Throughout the sixteenth century a series of versions appeared, all in some measure dependent on their predecessors, and yet each contributed to the tradition that finally mingled in the King James

6. Some authorities reserve "version" for an edition of the Bible that incorporates the language and style of a previous translation or version in the same language, while using "translation" for editions that proceed directly from Hebrew or Greek. This usage partially suits earlier centuries but fails to take into account that recently sponsored "versions," such as TEV and NIV (see table 9), proceed directly from the original languages and are thus fresh translations.

Version. Worthy of singling out are Coverdale's Bible (1535), "Matthew's" Bible (1537), the Great Bible (1539), and the Geneva Bible (1560). Pressure for uniformity in the English translations prompted James I to summon the Hampton Court Conference in 1604. More than fifty scholars working in committees produced the Authorized Version (AV) of 1611, commonly known as the King James Version. Coming in the midst of the Elizabethan age, when the English language had flowered, and capitalizing on the brilliant work of Tyndale and other preceding translators, the KJV was marked by an elegance and felicity of style. Its high literary level and retention of "quaint" biblical linguistic constructions meant that it was not really, as sometimes claimed, a Bible in the common speech of the day. The KJV gained its superior position only after long competition with other translations, particularly the Geneva Bible.

As changes in the English language accumulated and new manuscript and archaeological finds provided improved tools for textual criticism, it became absolutely clear that KJV had to be updated. The Revised Version (RV) was published in England in 1885 and an American English version was issued as the American Standard Version (ASV) in 1901. Both revisions set out to give literal constructions of the text, at times to the point of obscurity. They have been extensively used as study Bibles, but failed to replace KJV in general church use and for literary purposes.

In 1952 the complete Revised Standard Version (RSV) was published, having been mandated to revise the KJV-RV/ASV versions. The RSV was the work of American scholars who were able to use far more critically edited manuscripts than any of their predecessors, taking advantage of the work of Paul Kahle in uncovering the ben Asher text in a more accurate form than the printed editions of the Hebrew Bible following ben Chayyim's text had been able to do. The RSV was also far closer to the literary excellence of KJV than either AV or ASV, especially in familiar passages. The RSV quickly gained a wide following both in general church use and for serious study.

All the above versions were Protestant Bibles, although by 1973 an RSV Common Bible, including Apocrypha/deuterocanonical books, was approved for use by Catholic and Orthodox churches. Earlier the needs of Roman Catholics were met by the Douay-Rheims Version of 1609, translated from the Vulgate in slavishly literalistic fashion and revised for improvement of style by Challoner in 1759–63. Taking account of earlier translations under Jewish auspices in England and the U.S., as well as the Protestant English versions, the Jewish Publication Society of America published *The Holy Scriptures According to the Masoretic Text* in 1917.

Fairly literal and reproducing biblical archaisms, this Jewish translation drew heavily on interpretive traditions in the Talmud and the medieval Jewish commentaries.

Two idiomatic Protestant translations, still widely used, were those of James Moffatt, *The Holy Bible: A New Translation* (1926; final revision, 1935), decidedly British in tone, and its American counterpart, J. M. P. Smith (Old Testament section) and Edgar J. Goodspeed, *The Bible. An American Translation* (1931; Apocrypha added, 1939), known as the "Chicago Bible." *The Bible in Basic English* (1950), under the supervision of S. H. Hooke, employed a vocabulary limited to one thousand words to produce a translation of striking directness and simplicity.

12.2.b English Versions and Translations Since 1952

Since the publication of RSV in 1952, there has been an explosion of translations into the English language. The factors prompting this rapid growth of translation activity are multiple and include the following: demand for idiomatic popular translations, development of sophisticated linguistic and translation theories, need for translations suitable as study Bibles, popularization of manuscript and archaeological finds bearing on the Bible, and profitability of Bible sales for commercial publishing houses.

Bible translations tend to follow one or the other of two basic philosophies of translation, although with varying degrees of rigor and consistency. "Formal correspondence" translations, sometimes misleadingly called "literal," render the technical vocabulary, sentence structure, and imagery of the original Hebrew and Greek as closely as possible, even when the result is not natural English. "Dynamic equivalence" translations render the meaning of the original text into the most natural and fluent English idiom, sometimes called "meaning-for-meaning equivalence," thereby smoothing out peculiarities of biblical speech. Bible readers should be familiar with both kinds of translations (see notations on table 9).

The most influential among the new versions and translations of the Hebrew Bible (in all instances including the New Testament, except for NJPS) appear in table 9. It is clear that since 1952 the massive domination of the English Revised tradition, stretching from KJV through RV/ASV down to RSV, has been shaken if not altogether broken. A great range of biblical translations is now in use, frequently cutting across denominational lines and sometimes across theological lines. It is common nowadays to find Bible readers who regularly use two or more translations. The TEV and LBP have found wide favor for rapid popular reading of the text, while NEB, NAB, and JB are much prized as study Bibles, especially JB with its

TABLE 9
Versions and Translations of the Hebrew Bible Since 1952

	Style	Format	Notes	Use of MT
Protestant Versions				
1. NEB The New English Bible, 1970 (includes Apocrypha) Sponsored by the Protestant churches of Great Britain; a fresh translation	Dynamic equivalence Complex and elevated	Prose in paragraphs, poetry in lines	Textual	Extensive textual emendations
2. TEV Today's English Version (Good News Bible), 1976 Sponsored by the American Bible Society; a fresh translation	Dynamic equivalence Idiomatic, simple vocabulary and style	Prose in paragraphs, poetry in lines	Textual	Modest textual emendations
3. NIV New International Version, 1978 Sponsored by the New York International Bible Society; a fresh translation	Formal correspondence Dignified, literary	Prose in paragraphs, poetry in lines	Textual	Modest textual emendations
4. RSV[2] Revised Standard Version, 2d ed.	Formal correspondence	Projected for publication in late 1980s		
Protestant Translations				
5. MLB The Modern Language Bible. The New Berkeley Version in Modern English, rev. ed., 1969 An updating of the language of KJV; Gerrit Verkuyl, editor in chief	Formal correspondence Somewhat freer than RSV	Prose in paragraphs, poetry in lines	Explanatory	Few textual emendations
6. NASB New American Standard Bible, 1971 Sponsored by the Lockman Foundation; a revision of the American Standard Version of 1901	Formal correspondence Literal and somewhat stilted	Prose in verses, poetry in lines	Textual and explanatory	Few textual emendations

	Style	Format	Notes	Use of MT
7. NKJV The New King James Version, 1982 Sponsored by Thomas Nelson Publishers; a modernizing revision of dation	Formal correspondence Modernizes language, updates punctuation, breaks up long sentences	Prose in verses (paragraphs marked by boldface verse numbers), poetry in lines	Textual	All alternative readings placed in footnotes without recommendation
Roman Catholic Translations				
8. JB The Jerusalem Bible, 1966 (includes deuterocanonical books) Originally a fresh translation into French by scholars at the Ecole Biblique in Jerusalem; translated into English from French with reference to the original biblical languages	Cautious dynamic equivalence Generally forceful and idiomatic	Prose in paragraphs, poetry in lines	Numerous textual and explanatory	Extensive textual emendations
9. NAB The New American Bible, 1970 (includes deuterocanonical books) A fresh translation by scholars of the Catholic Biblical Association of America	Balances formal correspondence and dynamic equivalence Generally clear and straightforward	Prose in paragraphs, poetry in lines	Textual (in some editions) and explanatory	Extensive textual emendations
Jewish Version				
10. NJPS The New Jewish Version, 1982 Sponsored by the Jewish Publication Society of America; a fresh translation	Formal correspondence Contemporary, reads smoothly	Prose in paragraphs, poetry (sometimes lists) in lines	Textual and explanatory	Few textual emendations but many alternative readings

TABLE 9 (continued)
Versions and Translations of the Hebrew Bible Since 1952

	Style	Format	Notes	Use of MT
Paraphrases and Amplifications				
11. AMB The Amplified Bible, 1966 Sponsored by the Lockman foundation; Frances E. Siewert, editor in chief	A synthetic effort to clarify the text by adding synonyms, wordy and potentially confusing and misleading	Prose and poetry in verses	Textual and explanatory	Problematic
12. LBP The Living Bible Paraphrased, 1971 A paraphrase by Kenneth N. Taylor based on ASV and other translations and manuscripts not identified	Colloquial and paraphrastic with admitted interpretive biases	Prose and poetry in paragraphs	Textual	Problematic

remarkably full notes. Among Protestant conservatives NASB serves a similar study function. The NJPS and NKJV are sufficiently recent that it is more difficult to judge their reception. The fate of NJPS among Christian readers will be particularly interesting to watch, since the scholarly understanding of the Hebrew Bible is so indebted to Jewish tradition—in contrast to popular Christian ignorance of that reality. In general church usage, KJV and RSV still hold a prominent, and the latter perhaps a central, position; but NEB, TEV, and NIV are finding wide currency in church circles and appear to be gaining ground.

PART **II**

INTERTRIBAL CONFEDERACY:
ISRAEL'S REVOLUTIONARY BEGINNINGS

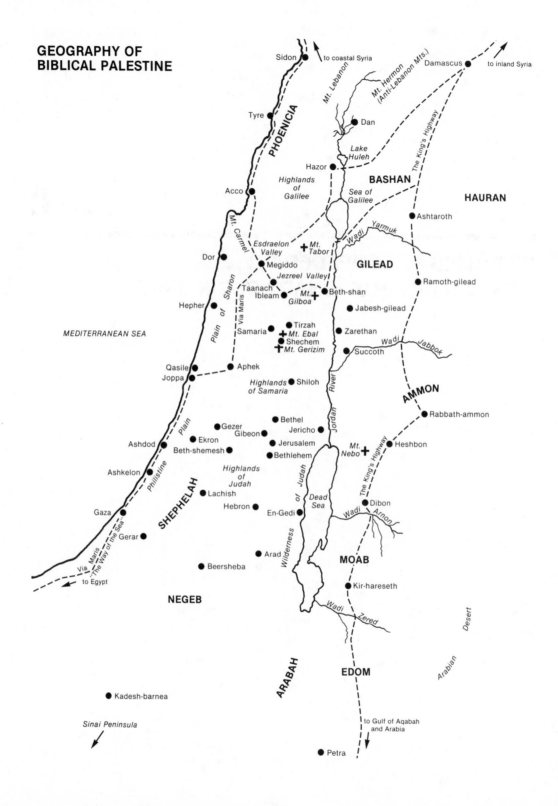

GEOGRAPHY OF BIBLICAL PALESTINE

Sidon · — to coastal Syria

Mt. Lebanon

Mt. Hermon (Anti-Lebanon Mts.)

Damascus · — to inland Syria

Tyre ·

PHOENICIA

Dan ·

Lake Huleh

Hazor ·

BASHAN

HAURAN

Acco ·

Highlands of Galilee

Sea of Galilee

Ashtaroth ·

Mt. Carmel

Esdraelon Valley

✝ *Mt. Tabor*

Dor ·

Megiddo ·

Jezreel Valley

GILEAD

Wadi Yarmuk

Plain of Sharon

Taanach
Ibleam ·

Mt. Gilboa ✝

· Beth-shan

Ramoth-gilead ·

The King's Highway

Hepher ·

Via Maris

Samaria ·

Tirzah ·
✝ *Mt. Ebal*
Shechem ·
✝ *Mt. Gerizim*

· Jabesh-gilead

· Zarethan

Succoth ·

Wadi Jabbok

MEDITERRANEAN SEA

Qasile ·
Joppa ·

· Aphek

Highlands of Samaria

· Shiloh

AMMON

Rabbath-ammon ·

Plain

· Bethel

Gezer ·
Gibeon ·

Jericho ·

Jordan River

Mt. Nebo ✝

Heshbon ·

Ashdod ·

· Ekron
Beth-shemesh ·

· Jerusalem

· Bethlehem

The King's Highway

Ashkelon ·

Philistine

Highlands of Judah

Lachish ·

of Judah

Dead Sea

· Dibon

Hebron ·

· En-Gedi

Wadi Armon

Gaza ·

SHEPHELAH

Wilderness

MOAB

Gerar ·

Via Maris "The Way of the Sea"

· Arad

· Beersheba

Kir-hareseth ·

— to Egypt

NEGEB

Wadi Zered

Arabian Desert

ARABAH

EDOM

· Kadesh-barnea

Sinai Peninsula

to Gulf of Aqabah and Arabia

· Petra

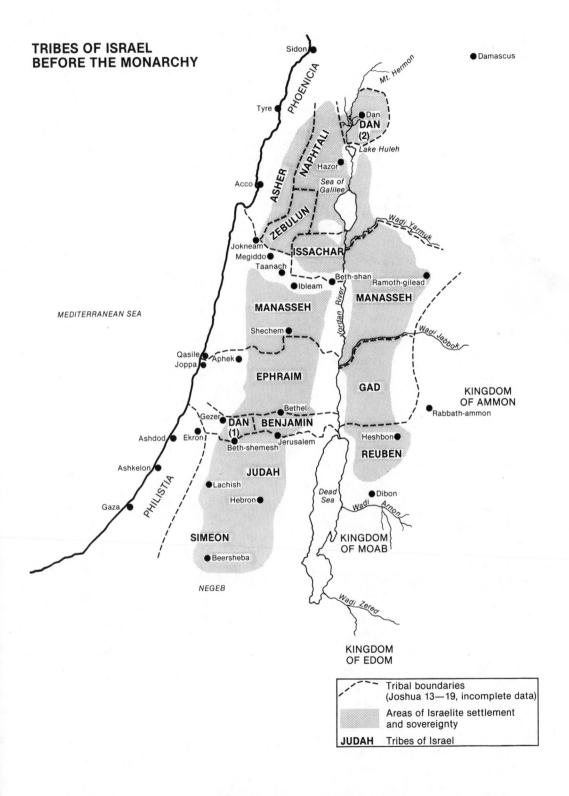

TRIBES OF ISRAEL
BEFORE THE MONARCHY

Sidon

●Damascus

PHOENICIA

Mt. Hermon

Tyre

Dan
DAN
(2)

Lake Huleh

Hazor

ASHER

NAPHTALI

Acco

Sea of Galilee

ZEBULUN

Jokneam
Megiddo

ISSACHAR

Wadi Yarmuk

Taanach

Beth-shan
Ramoth-gilead

Ibleam

MANASSEH

MANASSEH

MEDITERRANEAN SEA

Shechem

Wadi Jabbok

Qasile
Joppa ●Aphek

EPHRAIM

GAD

**KINGDOM
OF AMMON**

Bethel

Rabbath-ammon

Gezer
DAN
(1)
BENJAMIN

Ashdod
Ekron
Beth-shemesh
Jerusalem

Heshbon

REUBEN

Ashkelon

JUDAH

PHILISTIA

Lachish

Gaza

Hebron

Dead Sea

Dibon

Wadi Arnon

SIMEON

Beersheba

**KINGDOM
OF MOAB**

NEGEB

Wadi Zered

**KINGDOM
OF EDOM**

Jordan River

- - - Tribal boundaries
(Joshua 13—19, incomplete data)

Areas of Israelite settlement
and sovereignty

JUDAH Tribes of Israel

On the Sources for Israel's Premonarchic History

All preliminaries being over, we are about to embark on a reading of the Hebrew Bible. The aim of the body of this book (parts II–IV) is to facilitate a reading of the Hebrew Bible by placing its literature within the full history of Israel viewed in the context of all that we know about the ancient Near East at the time. This "full history" of the people of Israel will include material, cultural, social, political, and religious history.

In part II we shall examine the origins of Israel in the period before it became a national kingdom under Saul and David, ca. 1000 B.C.E. The emergence of Israel as a subject of history is assigned dates that range from as early as ca. 2200 B.C.E. to as late as ca. 1250–1150 B.C.E. In chap. 4 we shall see why there is as much as a one-thousand-year disagreement about Israel's date of origin.

Our biblical starting point will be the traditions of Genesis 12—50 about the ancestors of Israel. The traditions of Genesis 1—11 will be studied later (§31.1; 49) because these accounts of the beginnings of the world and of human history are part of a broad literary and conceptual heritage that Israel shared with its ancient Near Eastern neighbors. To understand the distinctive perspective of Israel on the origins of the world it is advisable to examine first the traditions about Israel's own beginnings.

Our chief source of information about Israel's early history is the Hebrew Bible itself. Although all the biblical books were completed after the exile, we have observed that they contain units of tradition and older continuous sources that derive from earlier stages of Israel's history. By probing these older—often orally rooted—traditions, it is possible to discern the basic outlines, and sometimes the rich details, of the history that lies behind and beneath the literature. To undertake historical reconstruction adequately, however, it is necessary to understand the distinctive shape of the literature relevant to each period of the history. Consequently, throughout parts II–IV, we shall be asking two fundamental questions:

1. How did the oral and literary traditions of the Hebrew Bible take shape and what is the sociohistorical understanding they provide or presuppose concerning each period in ancient Israel?

2. How does the sociohistorical picture of each period presented or implied in the Hebrew Bible enable us to comprehend Israel's place in its total ancient Near Eastern context?

Because the "historical value" of the biblical traditions is highly problematic, it will be essential in approaching each period of Israel's history to begin with an assessment of the literary sources.

13
THE GREAT TRADITIONISTS OF ANCIENT ISRAEL

Biblical data concerning Israel's earliest history are found in the Law and Former Prophets. Historical-critical study has identified four major literary hands at work in the growth of these traditions.

13.1 The Yahwist (J)

A connected story of Israel's beginnings from the creation of the world to at least the verge of Israel's entrance into Canaan was composed ca. 960–930 B.C.E., during the reign of Solomon, in the view of many scholars, although others date it later by as much as a century or more. This source can be identified, with a margin of variation in detailed analysis, in the Books of Genesis, Exodus, and Numbers. It is also possible that this same source told a story that continued through the conquest of Canaan and that some of its elements, much revised, can be detected in the Books of Joshua and Judges (§22.3).

We do not know the name of the writer. Apparently it was someone in governmental favor—if not actual government service—who provided a kind of "national epic" for the young kingdom of David and Solomon. This writer had a preference for calling the God of Israel by the proper name Yahweh. Thus, the unknown author is commonly called the Yahwist or J writer (J from the German spelling of Jahweh/Jahwist). The Yahwist wrote in Judah and stressed Judah's central role among the tribes. The literary symbol J therefore has a convenient double reference: first, to the preferred name of God (Yahweh) and, second, to the preferred tribe (Judah).

13.2 The Elohist (E)

After the disruption of the united monarchy, in the period 900–850 B.C.E., another writer told the early story of Israel (§34.1). It covered most of the same ground as J, beginning with the patriarchs and continuing either to the verge of Canaan (Genesis, Exodus, and Numbers), or possibly to the conquest itself (Joshua and perhaps Judges) [§22.3]. This writer deliberately chose the name Elohim for Israel's God in the period before Moses because of the belief that the name Yahweh was first given to Israel by Moses. Consequently, this anonymous writer is commonly called the Elohist or E writer. The author lived in northern Israel which by then was a part of an independent kingdom that retained the old name Israel (while the dynasty of David continued to rule over the kingdom of Judah in the south). The heartland of this northern kingdom consisted of the tribal territories of Manasseh and Ephraim and the entire realm was often simply called Ephraim. Just as J can represent Yahweh or Judah, so also E can represent Elohim or Ephraim.

How did the Elohist compare with the Yahwist? And why was a second story over the same historical ground deemed necessary? Beginning with Abraham, E treated all the major historical themes developed by J. Moreover, E developed the themes in literary types and with topical interests closely akin to J's. On the other hand, E frequently differed in vocabulary, style, mood, and emphasis, and a number of stories or tradition units appear in E that have no parallel in J. The Elohist put special emphasis on early Israel as a religiously and ethically obligated community in treaty (or covenant) with Yahweh. In the eyes of the E traditionists the covenant community of Israel was older and more fundamental than the political dynasty of David in Jerusalem or the more recently established northern kingdom. If the nearest affinities of J were with court circles in Jerusalem, the closest connections of E appear to have been prophetic circles of the sort that venerated Elijah and Elisha. In all events, the Elohist—less awed by governmental authority than the Yahwist—was fairly explicit in presenting criteria for defining Israel that transcended and criticized the current kingdoms of Judah and Israel. The E document was apparently intended as a conscious corrective to the J document.

13.3 The Deuteronomistic History (DH)

Circles of traditionists in the northern kingdom, beginning perhaps as early as the E writer, began to develop a style of instruction that impressed on people the significance of obedience to the covenant with Yahweh as expressed in old laws about social justice and religious fidelity. This style was highly sermonic and hortatory, and seems to have been cultivated in the periodic public assemblies for celebrating the renewal of the covenant between Yahweh and Israel. These covenant traditions showed a definite tension, and at times outright conflict, with the power politics of the Israelite monarchies. We speak of these traditionists as Deuteronomists, or in the singular as the Deuteronomist, designated D, because their work is most clearly exhibited in the Book of Deuteronomy (§37.3).

When the northern kingdom collapsed in 722 B.C.E., the Deuteronomic traditions were preserved by sympathizers in the south. A century later, in 622 B.C.E., the Deuteronomic tradition surfaced as the driving conceptual and documentary force in a major reform of the Kingdom of Judah launched by King Josiah. At the base of that reform were the laws now contained in Deuteronomy 12—26, set between a prologue and an epilogue of sermonic appeals for their observance. When Josiah's reform efforts failed, Deuteronomists brought together a great mass of traditions in order to interpret the course of the monarchies in Israel from the point of view of covenant loyalty and disobedience. These traditions appear in the present Books of Deuteronomy through Kings in what is called the Deuteronom*istic* History, symbolized as DH. During the Babylonian exile, the Deuteronomists undertook a second and final revision of their history.

The story told by the Deuteronomistic History began with a "review" or "second telling" of the law by Moses beyond Jordan just before his death. It then related the conquest of Canaan and the histories of the united and divided kingdoms, and ended in the midst of the exile, its last-recorded incident being datable to 561 B.C.E. The traditions were arranged by DH so that, after a lightning attack upon the land and a division of territories among the tribes (Book of Joshua), the separate tribes struggled to consolidate their holdings against resurgent Canaanites and other enemies (Book of Judges). In part III we shall be concerned with the largest part of DH which tells of the monarchies, and with Deuteronomy as the charter document of Josiah's reform. For the present assessment of the early history of Israel, however, our attention is drawn to Joshua and Judges.

In composing its version of the conquest of the land in Joshua and Judges, most scholars believe that DH drew on sources other than J and E. On narrowly literary grounds this is a tenable conclusion, since it is difficult to trace the vocabulary and style of J or E into Joshua and Judges. It is doubtful, however, that J and E stopped with the present ending of Numbers, since it leaves the Israelites short of possessing the land which both J and E anticipated throughout their narratives. It is likely, therefore, that DH, wanting to begin the history with solemn instructions and laws from Moses, decided to remove the old JE conquest traditions from their original setting and to rework them as part of a new composition. In the process DH tried to harmonize the conflicting traditions about total or partial victory by telling of an initial unified conquest under Joshua, followed by setbacks and protracted struggles to repossess the land under the judges (§22.2).

13.4 The Priestly Writer (P)

The last major contribution to the "national epic" now found in Genesis through Numbers was the work of a Priestly writer, symbolized as P, who wrote in the late exilic or early restoration period, ca. 550–450 B.C.E. (§49).

This writer was concerned with supplementing the old traditions with materials that would underscore the institutional and ritual constitution of Israel as a religious community uniquely separated from all other peoples (§19.2; 19.4). The P writer anchored the epic in a well-ordered account of creation and greatly developed the ritual features of Sabbath observance, circumcision, dietary provisions, treatment of diseases, and instructions on the priesthood and sacrifices. Most of the latter half of Exodus and the whole of Leviticus come from the P writer (§17). The narrative elements in P are minimal, but the milestones in the long history are strung together by means of lengthy genealogies and occasional chronological notations. There are old traditional elements in P, perhaps resting ultimately on oral sources, which throw valued light on the premonarchic period, but the preponderance of P is a testimony to the emergence of a strengthened Priestly tradition in late monarchic, exilic, and postexilic Israel.

13.5 The Redaction of JEP

In contrast to the Deuteronomistic History, which seems to have had a fairly rapid and homogeneous internal development in two editions, the combination of the separate J, E, and P documents was a slower process.

As long as the northern and southern kingdoms stood as rival Israelite kingdoms, the Yahwist and Elohist versions of the national epic were firm competitors. After the destruction of the northern kingdom in 722 B.C.E., the Elohist lost its home setting and a redactor in the southern kingdom joined the two documents, or, more correctly stated, supplemented J extensively with parts of E. For this reason, E is much less completely preserved than J. Because the two sets of traditions were joined, there are places, especially in the Book of Numbers, where it is not easy to disentangle them (§17.1). The effect of joining J and E was to affirm the national political tone of J but to permeate and leaven it with the religious and ethical qualifications of E. The date of this JE redaction fell within the period from 722 to 609 B.C.E.

The joining of combined JE with P was accomplished either by the P writer or by an independent editor. Scholars who stress the scarcity of narrative in P are inclined to view P as having directly incorporated JE in the course of composition, so that the writing of P in final form and the redaction of JE + P were in effect one process. Scholars who stress the ritual distance between JE and P doubt that P could have accepted the ritually "lax" JE materials, with the result that they incline toward an independent redactor for JE + P. In any case, the procedure followed in redacting JEP is fairly clear. The Priestly composition—with its genealogical, chronological, and ritual data—formed the framework into which JE traditions were inserted intermittently. Less frequently, JE and P materials were closely interwoven. The final editing, if done by someone other than P, apparently occurred not long after the composition of P. The effect of joining JE and P was to affirm the old JE political and religious tendencies, but at the same time to subordinate them to the overweening ritual concerns of the Priestly frame composition.

13.6 The Common Source of Yahwist and Elohist (G)

The far-ranging similarities of the two earliest continuous sources J and E strongly suggest that both derived from an older pool or fund of traditions, not only in particulars of story plots and characters, but also in a linking of the stories into episodic themes to form a narrative recital from the age of the patriarchs to the conquest of the land. This common pool of traditions is often called G (German *Grundlage*, "foundation"). This stock of thematically grouped traditions probably took shape in the cult, that is, formal worship assemblies, before the tribes of Israel opted for kings. The traditions were orally recited and transmitted in public ceremonies that renewed the covenant between Yahweh and Israel. Whether these tribal traditions had been written down at all before the extended compositions of J and E is not known. It would have been consistent with ancient practice, however, for the orally recited traditions to have been gradually committed to writing in order to supply an aid to memory or to establish a version that would limit oral expansions and alterations. J and E might have had access both to oral and written versions of the old cult traditions. In fact, some of the differences in J and E may be due to different versions of the traditions circulating in the southern and northern regions of Israel. In that event, G would not stand for a single standard version but would refer to a range of oral/written variants within broadly fixed parameters.

14
THE BEARING OF THE LITERARY
TRADITIONS ON THE
EARLY HISTORY OF ISRAEL

We have now described the main stages in the complex growth of the literary traditions in Genesis through Judges. Starting from oral units that were arranged according to leading themes in the cult of tribal Israel, these materials were later written into continuous sources that were finally revised or redacted to form the present biblical books. What are the implications of this literary growth for reconstructing the early history of Israel?

14.1 Nongovernmental and Oral Origins of the Traditions

It is clear that the traditions about premonarchic Israel derived from an essentially preliterary setting in communal life. Writing was certainly available to the Israelites of that period, but the crucial factor is that the spheres of life where writing was customarily practiced were *not* the spheres of early Israel's life. Writing throughout the ancient Near East was chiefly a politically oriented or enabled activity, sponsored and controlled by governmental authorities and their schools of professional scribes (§8.1; 9). Writing served to record administrative and ceremonial affairs of state, to regulate the orderly flow of high commerce, and to preserve religious texts that gave a rationale to state rule.

The united tribes of Israel arose, however, as a disturber of state interests and as an active opponent of Canaanite state authorities. Israel's first "literature" was "low literature," both in its origin among lower-class Canaanites and in its subject matter, that is, the worth and competence of a simple people to determine their own lives without the intervention of upper-class rulers (§24.1.c; 24.2.c). The early oral literature praised and recounted the deeds of the people and of their special God, Yahweh. The setting for the shaping of these traditions was in public assemblies for worship and covenant renewal. The rationale for this spoken literature was to validate and strengthen the intertribal movement of Israel. Only later, when Israel acquired kings, did the literary traditionists feel motivated to write connected accounts that validated Israel's own monarchy (J), or criticized the Israelite states (E and D), or sought a substitute for the lost Israelite states (P).

The preliterate people of Israel made use of precisely those literary types that belong characteristically to the pre-state life of a people. Among the literary types we have identified (§11.1.b; table 8), the following give us our primary information about Israel's early life:

Rules of conduct in categorical form (2)[1]
Legal maxims and decisions (3)
Treaties between Israel and Yahweh (4)
Blessings (7)
Sagas (20)
Legends (21)

---

1. The numbers in parentheses are keyed to the enumerated literary genres presented in table 8.

Novellas (22)
Anecdotes (23)
Lists (24–25)
Taunts (32)
War and victory songs (34)
Hymnic songs (36)
Thanksgiving songs (38)

These literary types were designedly instructional and celebrative, so that even the narratives were of a popular folk character that made no pretense of being carefully researched historical accounts. These narratives are "history-like" in the sense that they relate events of public moment, but they are not historiography in the strict sense. Traditions of this type can be used cautiously and indirectly to reconstruct history, especially cultural and social history, but they must be used critically, precisely as the historical-critical method of biblical study has correctly understood (§17; 22).

14.2 United Tribal Israel as the Subject of the Traditions

Within the preliterary phase of Israelite history, a distinction must be drawn between the period when the tribes of Israel gathered as a united people in Canaan and the preceding periods of the patriarchs and Moses. The oral traditions employed by J and E to compose their continuous sources were actually traditions developed strictly by the united tribes of Israel in Canaan (§24). Among the traditions of the united tribes were accounts of still-earlier ancestors (§15) and of the deliverer Moses (§17). Properly speaking, however, the patriarchs and Moses belong to the prehistory or protohistory of the united tribes of Israel. It is generally agreed that not even a majority of later Israelites took part in the deliverance from Egypt, and it is widely recognized that the stories of Abraham, Isaac, and Jacob speak of relatively small groups of people who were not yet a part of any great intertribal Israelite movement. The whole Israel who speaks of patriarchs and of Moses first existed in the land of Canaan about 1200 B.C.E. and not with any certainty before that time. The patriarchs and Moses of whom this united Israel speaks were figures of great importance to some groups who became Israelites and, in time, they were recognized as forefathers by all Israel. But the process of extending these traditions to the whole of Israel took time, and the ways in which the figures of the patriarchs and Moses were developed in the traditions of united Israel were the result of an interplay between how they had been remembered by segments of Israel and how they came to serve as ancestral or prototypical figures for the entire people (§15.4; 16.4; 18.2; 21).

14.3 Expansion and Elaboration of the History-like Themes of the Traditions

Within these early traditions a firm distinction must be drawn between the sequence of events as they were related from the patriarchs down to the judges, on the one hand, and the actual order in which events assumed importance and received attention in the process of tradition building in the cultic assemblies of tribal Israel, on the other hand. The sequence of history-like themes preserved in the final form of the Law and the Former Prophets is as follows for the premonarchic period:

Primal History: From Creation to Abraham
Patriarchs:
   Promise to Abraham
   Promise to Isaac
   Promise to Jacob
Descent Into Egypt: Joseph
Bondage and Deliverance from Egypt: Moses
  Guidance in the Wilderness: Moses (From Egypt to Sinai)
  Law and Covenant at Sinai/Horeb: Moses
  Guidance in the Wilderness: Moses (From Sinai to Moab)
Conquest of the Land: Joshua
Consolidation of Conquest: Judges

These history-like themes, however, did not appear full-blown at the beginning of the traditioning process; instead, they "snowballed" over decades of time within the living cult and later in the work of the great literary traditionists.

It is probable that the original core of tradition-telling in the cultic assemblies consisted of two basic themes (ca. 1200 B.C.E. [?]):

Bondage and Deliverance from Egypt: Moses
Conquest of the Land: Joshua

This core was expanded *externally* by prefacing it with additional history-like themes: first, about the patriarch Jacob (of the northern tribes), then about the patriarchs Abraham and Isaac (of the southern tribes), and further by an explanation of how the Israelites fell into Egyptian bondage (by ca. 1100 B.C.E. [?]):

Promise to Abraham
Promise to Isaac
Promise to Jacob
Descent Into Egypt: Joseph
Bondage and Deliverance from Egypt: Moses
Conquest of the Land: Joshua

The original core was also expanded *internally* by the insertion of new history-like themes at its center: the theme of Guidance in the Wilderness (to account for the survival of Israel in the Sinai, Negeb, and Transjordan on its way from Egypt to Canaan), and the theme of Law and Covenant at Sinai/Horeb (to give the longstanding public covenant-renewal ceremony a narrative position in the unfolding origin story of Israel). Interestingly, the Guidance in the Wilderness theme, probably of southern origin, was split open and the Law and Covenant theme, probably of northern origin, was sandwiched into it (by.1025 B.C.E. [?]):

Promise to Abraham
Promise to Isaac
Promise to Jacob
Descent Into Egypt: Joseph
Bondage and Deliverance from Egypt: Moses
Guidance in the Wilderness: Moses (From Egypt to Sinai)
Law and Covenant at Sinai/Horeb: Moses
Guidance in the Wilderness: Moses (From Sinai to Moab)
Conquest of Canaan: Joshua

This multiple-stage sacred tribal history of premonarchic Israel constituted the probable structure of G, the common pool of the united tribal traditions that J and E drew upon. One major addition and one important alteration of history-like themes occurred, however, in the later literary stage of the growth of the traditions. The Yahwist (J) added traditions from the creation of the world to Abraham, and the Deuteronomistic History (DH) rearranged the confusing traditions about the settlement of Canaan into two parts—the conquest of Canaan proper under Joshua and later setbacks and consolidation under the judges:

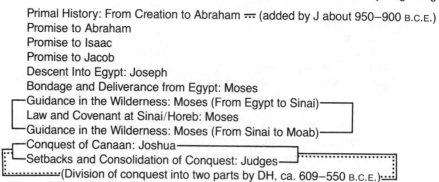

Primal History: From Creation to Abraham ⸺ (added by J about 950–900 B.C.E.)
Promise to Abraham
Promise to Isaac
Promise to Jacob
Descent Into Egypt: Joseph
Bondage and Deliverance from Egypt: Moses
   Guidance in the Wilderness: Moses (From Egypt to Sinai)
   Law and Covenant at Sinai/Horeb: Moses
   Guidance in the Wilderness: Moses (From Sinai to Moab)
   Conquest of Canaan: Joshua
   Setbacks and Consolidation of Conquest: Judges
   (Division of conquest into two parts by DH, ca. 609–550 B.C.E.)

14.4 Summary and Methodological Implications

Three major conclusions about the intent, locus, and thematic sequence of the traditions stand out as important for reconstructing Israel's early history:

1. *The intent of the traditions.* The traditions about premonarchic Israel were not documents intended to record historical information but rather sacral-oral "origin" or "charter" stories, poems, and laws intended for immediate instruction and celebration.

2. *The locus of the traditions.* The traditions come from and witness to united intertribal Israel, so that they tell us only secondarily, and at a considerable remove, about the groups and leaders of the earlier times of the patriarchs and Moses.

3. *The thematic sequence of the traditions.* The core of traditions about deliverance from Egypt and conquest of the land was expanded and embellished over decades and centuries, so that the eventual ordering and stressing of events resulted from a slow accumulation of tradition and *not* from a direct representation of events continuously reported by eyewitnesses.

Because the traditions do not yield a direct coherent history of early Israel, scholars understandably differ in the amount and type of historically relevant information they think can be derived from them. To date no nonbiblical information about the patriarchs and Moses has come to light,[2] so that the varying scholarly interpretations of those figures have depended largely on differing estimates of the historical reliability of the traditions (§16.1–3; 18.1–2). Even the course of the settlement of Canaan by Israel, attested in some fullness by archaeology, is envisioned differently by schol-

---

2. Concerning claims that patriarchs are named or directly illuminated by the Ebla texts, see chap. 4 n. 8.

ars according to the credence they give the traditions in Joshua and Judges
(§24.1).

Some biblical scholars, usually influenced by a confessional religious
regard for the Bible, tend to read the early traditions as straight history as
far as they go, recognizing at the same time that many gaps occur in the
biblical records. Other critics doubt that we can learn anything substantial
about Israel's history before the monarchy, preferring rather to focus their
attention on form criticism, tradition-historical criticism, source criticism,
and/or one or another mode of new literary criticism in order to illuminate
the skillfully elaborated architecture of the traditions. Yet others believe
that at least the broad processes and sequences by which Israel emerged, if
not all the geographical and historical detail, can be clarified from the
preliterary shape of the traditions. In short, given the "softness" of our
evidence about Israel's beginnings, there is as yet no single commanding
version of how Israel emerged into history. At most there are a number of
widely shared assumptions, differently emphasized and combined, on the
basis of which scholars organize the source materials into a range of partly
concurring and partly opposing versions of the premonarchic history of
Israel.

CHAPTER 4

Traditions About the Fathers and Mothers of Israel

Read the Biblical Text
Genesis 12—50

Consult Maps in *MBA*
nos. 24–42

15
THE SHAPE OF THE TRADITIONS IN
GENESIS 12—50

15.1 Distribution of the Tradition Units in J, E, and P

The traditions about the ancestors of united Israel appear in Gen. 11:27—50, and are recounted in three extended sources that cover much the same chronological and thematic ground. The Yahwist (J) and the Elohist (E) depended on an old oral—and perhaps partly written—pool of traditions, and the Priestly writer (P) drew upon JE, together with some independently derived oral or written traditions. The distinctive vocabulary, style, tone, and religious outlook of each of these traditionists can be appreciated by reading their versions of the patriarchal traditions as listed in table 10. When read separately, it is clear that J provides the most cohesive continuous account, since E appears largely as a redacted supplement to J, whereas P, in providing the final frame for Genesis, presupposes the incorporated JE document to provide the basic plot line (§49).

There is generally little disagreement about the identity of the P traditions. There is more dispute about the separation of J and E, particularly in passages where they have been closely woven together and where the most distinctive criteria of each are not represented. In the following representation of the sources in Gen. 11:27—50, approximately 730 verses are attributed to J, 336 verses to E, and 153 verses to P. This verse count includes the assignment of Genesis 14 and 49:2–28 to J, on the assumption that, whatever the peculiarity of their origin, they were probably taken into the Yahwist's account.

15.2 Analysis of the Tradition Units by Literary Genres

Form criticism indicates that by far the most frequent building block in these traditions is the literary type known as *saga.* Of the seventy-nine tradition units listed in table 10, sixty-three fall in this genre—forty-three being individual sagas and another twenty forming subunits of the Joseph *novella,* which was constructed by an internal expansion of the saga form into a highly developed plot with lengthy speeches. Each saga is a complete story, fairly brief (Genesis 24 is the longest example), with few characters, terse dialogue, frequent repetition, artful use of suspense, and great restraint in descriptions of scene and in analyses of the motivations and feelings of the actors.

In addition to saga and novella, there are other literary types that appear either independently developed alongside the sagas or as fragments or

TABLE 10

Tradition Units of Gen. 11:27—50 Distributed by Sources*

A. Yahwist (J) Traditions

ABRAHAM AND ISAAC

	1. Abram marries Sarai	11:28–30
	2. Call and journey of Abram to Canaan	12:1–4a, 6–9
	3. Abram and Sarai in Egypt	12:10–20; 13:1
	4. Abram and Lot separate	13:2–5, 7–11a, 13–18
	5. Abram's victory	14:1–24
	6. Yahweh's covenant with Abram	15:1–2, 4, 6–12, 17–21
	7. Birth of Ishmael/flight of Hagar	16:1b–2, 4–14
	8. Divine visitors to Abraham	18:1–21
	9. Abraham intercedes for Sodom	18:22–23
	10. Destruction of Sodom and Gomorrah	19:1–28, 30–38
	11. Birth of Isaac	21:1–2, 7
	12. Abraham passes Yahweh's test	22:14–18
	13. Descendants of Nahor	22:20–24
	14. Isaac marries Rebekah	24:1–67
	15. Descendants of Abraham by Keturah	25:1–6, 11b

(Bracket labeled **ABRAHAM-LOT SAGA CHAIN** encompasses items 2–11)

JACOB

	16. Birth of Esau and Jacob	25:21–26
	17. Esau surrenders his birthright	25:27–34
	18. Isaac and Rebekah in Gerar	26:1–11
	19. Treaty between Isaac and Abimelech	26:12–33
	20. Jacob steals Esau's blessing	27:1–45
	21. Jacob's dream at Bethel	28:10–11a, 13–16, 19
	22. Jacob marries Leah and Rachel	29:1–30
	23. The sons and daughter of Jacob	29:31–35; 30:4–5, 7–16, 21, 24
	24. Jacob gains wealth by trickery	30:25–43
	25. Jacob's flight and treaty with Laban	31:1–3, 17, 19a, 20–23, 25b, 27, 30a, 31, 36a, 38–40, 46–49, 51–53a
	26. Jacob prepares to meet Esau	32:3–11, 13a
	27. Jacob wrestles with God	32:22–32
	28. Jacob's reunion with Esau	33:1–3, 12–17
	29. Rape of Dinah/broken treaty with Shechem	34:1–31
	30. Reuben's incest	35:21–22a

(Brackets labeled **JACOB-ESAU SAGA CHAIN** encompassing items 16–28, and **JACOB-LABAN SAGA CHAIN** encompassing items 20–25)

---

*This distribution of the sources is based on a study of the biblical text and the proposed source divisions of Eissfeldt, *TOT*; Ellis, *YBFT*; and Noth, *HPT*. The listings under the Priestly traditions are not quite complete since some of P's brief notations are not included.

TABLE 10 (continued)
Tradition Units of Gen. 11:27—50 Distributed by Sources

A. Yahwist (J) Traditions (continued)

JOSEPH

	31. Joseph's dream	37:2b–21, 25–27, 28b
	32. Judah and Tamar	38:1–30
	33. Joseph's temptation and imprisonment	39:1–23
	34. The brothers' first visit to Egypt	42:4–5, 8–11a, 12, 26–28a, 38
	35. The brothers' second visit to Egypt	43:1–34
	36. Joseph tests his brothers	44:1–34
	37. Reconciliation of Joseph and his brothers	45:1, 4–5a, 16–28
	38. Jacob settles in Egypt	46:28–34; 47:1–4, 6b
	39. Joseph's agrarian policy	47:13–26
	40. Death of Jacob	47:29–31
	41. Blessing of Jacob on his sons	49:2–28
	42. Burial of Jacob	50:1–11, 14

NOVELLA OF JOSEPH AND HIS BROTHERS

B. Elohist (E) Traditions

ABRAHAM AND ISAAC

43. Yahweh's promise to Abram	15:3, 5, 13–16
44. Abraham and Sarah in Gerar	20:1–18
45. Birth of Isaac/banishment of Hagar	21:6, 8–21
46. Treaty between Abraham and Abimelech	21:22–34
47. Elohim tests Abraham	22:1–13, 19

JACOB

48. Jacob's dream at Bethel	28:11b, 12, 17–18, 20–22
49. The sons of Jacob	30:1–3, 6, 17–20, 22–23
50. Jacob's flight and treaty with Laban	31:2, 4–16, 19b, 24–25a, 26, 28–29, 30b, 32–35, 36b–37, 41–45, 50, 53b–55
51. Angels of Mahanaim	32:1–2
52. Jacob sends gifts to Esau	32:12, 13b–21
53. Jacob's reunion with Esau	33:4–11
54. Jacob purchases land at Shechem	33:18b–20
55. Jacob returns to Bethel	35:1–8, 14–15
56. Birth of Benjamin	35:16–20

TABLE 10 (continued)
Tradition Units of Gen. 11:27—50 Distributed by Sources

B. Elohist (E) Traditions (continued)

JOSEPH

57. Joseph's dream	37:22–24, 28a, 29–36
58. Joseph interprets prisoners' dreams	40:1–23
59. Joseph interprets Pharaoh's dream and attains high office	41:1–45, 47–57
60. The brothers' first trip to Egypt	42:1–3, 6–7, 11b, 13–25
61. Reconciliation of Joseph and his brothers	45:2–3, 5b–15
62. Jacob settles in Egypt	46:1–5
63. Jacob before Pharaoh	47:7–12
64. Jacob blesses Joseph's sons	48:1–2, 8–22
65. Joseph's forgiveness of his brothers	50:15–21
66. Death and embalmment of Joseph	50:22–26

(bracketed left label: NOVELLA OF JOSEPH AND HIS BROTHERS)

C. Priestly (P) Traditions

ABRAHAM

67. Abram journeys from Ur to Haran	11:27, 31–32
68. El Shaddai's covenant with Abram = Abraham	17:1–27
69. Abraham buys burial cave of Machpelah	23:1–20
70. Death and burial of Abraham	25:7–11a
71. Descendants of Ishmael	25:12–18

JACOB

72. Jacob sent to Aram to get a non-Hittite wife	26:34–35; 27:46—28:9
73. El Shaddai blesses Jacob	35:9–13
74. Descendants of Esau	36:1–14
75. Death and burial of Isaac	35:27–29
76. Chiefs and kings of Edom	36:15–42
77. Jacob's descendants settle in Egypt	46:6–27
78. Jacob blesses Joseph's sons	48:3–7
79. Death and burial of Jacob	49:29–33; 50:12–13

elements within a saga or other tradition unit. Two of these literary types serve as vehicles for introducing the role of deity in the unfolding account of the ancestors. The *treaty* or *covenant* form is independently represented in two versions of a covenant between God and Abraham (6 and 68), and elements of the same form appear in sagas that describe treaties between the ancestors and their neighbors or kin (19, 46, 50). *Blessings* or *promises of blessings,* conferred by God on the ancestors, recur in independent units (12, 41, 43, 73) and within sagas (2, 5, 20, 21, 64, and 78). *Lists* of persons or groups function to reveal the genealogical skeleton of the traditions, sometimes in concise separate units (13, 15, 71, 75, 76) and sometimes in a more diffused fashion as a feature within sagas (1, 5 [lists of kings], 23, 49). The *vision report* form may be attested in one covenant account (6) and in one saga (51). Abraham's intercession on behalf of Sodom (9) suggests the type of a *disputation speech.*

15.3 Composite Unity of the Traditions

The most fascinating and challenging literary feature of the ancestor traditions, as elsewhere in Israel's early written records, is the manner in which the individual units have been grouped and edited so as to produce complex and subtle literary effects. Some of the devices used for grouping, binding, and nuancing the traditions have been uncovered by source criticism, form criticism, and tradition-historical inquiry. Other devices have only recently come to light through the practice of the newer modes of literary criticism (§15.3.d). How these various devices are to be related to one another in the stages of the formation of the traditions and what they imply for the comprehensive interpretation of the traditions are still in a fluid state of exploration.

15.3.a Saga Cycles and Saga Chains

One of the most obvious larger groupings is the clustering of the traditions around prominent ancestors. Abraham and Jacob each formed magnets for the growth of cycles of traditions. By comparison, Isaac is a passive figure who tends to be submerged in the Abraham traditions, and Joseph, although elaborately treated in the novella, is actually thematically subordinate to the Jacob cycle of traditions. Within the *Abraham* and *Jacob cycles,* there are subgroupings. In addition to the *Joseph novella,* there are saga chains characterized by the relationship between an ancestor and one of his relatives: an *Abraham-Lot saga chain,* a *Jacob-Esau saga chain,* and a *Jacob-Laban saga chain.* The Jacob cycle is more complexly constructed than the Abraham cycle, as witnessed, for example, by the way that the

Jacob-Laban saga chain has been bracketed within the Jacob-Esau saga chain. This inclusion of one literary complex within another facilitates the plot by explaining Jacob's visit to Laban as a flight from Esau and his return to Canaan as a reunion with Esau. The Joseph novella, in itself a marvelous account of rivalry among brothers, serves the overall tradition structure admirably by accounting for the descent of Jacob and his family into Egypt and thus for the subsequent bondage of Israel in that land.

The positioning of the cycles and saga chains so that Abraham, Isaac, Jacob, and Jacob's twelve sons represent four successive generations in a single family provides the axis for the entire narrative complex. An unrelenting focus is sustained on this one biological line of descent that bears the divine blessing. The "family tree" potentiality of the traditions is held in check by brief reference to those who "branch off" from the main trunk and are immediately lost to the ongoing story: the Ammonites and Moabites through Abraham's nephew Lot; the Arameans through Abraham's brother Nahor; the Arabs through Ishmael and Abraham's wife, Keturah; and the Edomites through Esau. The central thread leads unerringly onward to Jacob's sons alone as the fathers of the twelve tribes of Israel.

15.3.b Itinerary and Chronology

Another means for articulating the separate traditions is the device of the itinerary. A considerable number of settlements and regions in and around Canaan are named in the traditions. It is argued that in many instances the separate tradition units originated at the places prominently named within them. In bringing the traditions together around the ancestors, a parallel or supplementary tendency arose to relate these many scattered places as points on the itinerary of a wandering ancestor. Abraham journeys from Ur and Haran to Canaan, thence to Egypt, returns to Canaan, settles at Mamre near Hebron, conducts a military campaign to the vicinity of Damascus, resides for a time in Gerar, prepares to sacrifice his son on Mt. Moriah, and gets his son a wife from among his kin living near Haran. Jacob flees via Bethel to the same kinfolk, returns by way of Gilead in Transjordan to Shechem and Bethel, and eventually follows his son Joseph into Egypt. The individual sagas either do not presuppose such movement or fail to conceive it as part of a larger design. By supplying itineraries linked closely to the divine directives and promises, the collectors of the traditions have imbued them with a sense of restlessness and inner urging that points forward toward the later themes of bondage and deliverance from Egypt, wilderness wandering, and conquest of Canaan. At the same time, many of the sites in the itineraries are locations for a revelation of

God to the ancestors or an occasion for sacrifice to God by the ancestors. In this manner the sacred places at Shechem, Bethel, Mamre-Hebron, Beersheba, Mt. Moriah and Salem (Jerusalem?), Beerlahairoi, Penuel, and Mahanaim are explained as having been established in the first instance by one of the ancestors. Form critics have referred to sagas of this sort as *etiologies* (i.e., origin accounts) of sacred sites, or as *foundation legends* in that they explain the founding of important sanctuaries.

Another binding feature in the traditions is the chronology provided by the Priestly writer. The old sagas are almost totally lacking in temporal indicators, beyond occasional references to day or night. Two sagas open with the phrase "after these things" (15:1; 22:1), and the Joseph novella has a number of time references, for example, "after two whole years" (41:1), and seven years of plenty and seven years of famine (41:53–54). The reference to "the days of" nine named kings (14:1) remains meaningless because none of the kings is certainly recognizable from any other source. The old sagas do make note of the advanced age of the ancestors (18:11; 24:1; 27:1). It was P, however, who supplied the total ages of the ancestors as a part of the comprehensive chronology with which he structured his work from Genesis through Numbers. Abraham lived for 175 years, Sarah for 127 years, Isaac for 180 years, Jacob for 147 years, and Joseph for 110 years. Although these are uncommonly long lives, they are vastly reduced from the ages attributed to pre-Abrahamic figures by P (e.g., Abraham's father Terah lived for 205 years, Noah for 950 years, and Methuselah for 987 years). Also, important events are dated by the age of an ancestor. Abraham was 86 at the birth of Ishmael, 99 when God covenanted with him, and 100 at the birth of Isaac. Esau was 40 when he married Judith and Basemath. Joseph was 30 when he entered Pharaoh's service. Jacob lived the last 17 years of his life in Egypt.

While the geographical and temporal indicators cited serve effectively to give unity to the mass of ancestor traditions, their value for situating the traditions historically is a much more problematic issue (§16.1).

15.3.c Motifs of Divine Promises to the Ancestors

Motifs of divine promise and present blessing are very subtly employed at key points in the traditions to impart a sense of continuity that links saga to saga and generation to generation. The traditions have been intensively studied by form critics with a view to unraveling the many types of divine blessings anticipated by promise or conferred in actuality. The most recurrent promises are of children and land. Sometimes the promise has to do with a single son, such as Isaac promised to Abraham, while in other contexts the promise is of many descendants. At points the promise of land has to do with the immediately needed land for cultivation and pasturage, while elsewhere the vast territory of the later Israelite kingdom is foreshadowed. In these varied promises we can see that both the immediate situation of the ancestors and their families and the later situation of Israel as a confederation of tribes or as a monarchy have become intertwined in the great body of traditions. In this respect the saga type as a means for telling national history in the form of a story about a prototypical individual and his family stands out sharply and becomes a critical factor in estimating the historical precision of such traditions (§15.4).

15.3.d Type-Scenes and Other Literary Features

Newer literary methods of biblical criticism have begun to work on the ancestor traditions from perspectives not limited to the older criticism's emphasis either on the oral stage of the sagas or on the work of the great JEP traditionists.

Working by analogy from Homer scholarship, one literary critic[1] has characterized the stylized treatment of conventional situations in the sagas as "type scenes," that is, typical episodes in the life of an ancestor hero that are composed of traditional elements which any particular storyteller may elaborate and vary within limits determined by skill and audience rapport. Among the stock type-scenes are the following:

1. Birth of an ancestor hero to his barren mother:[2]
   6, 7, 8, 11 (Isaac to Sarah); 23, 49, 56 (Jacob's sons to Rachel)
2. Encounter with the future betrothed at a well:
   14 (Abraham's servant finds Rebekah); 22 (Jacob finds Rachel)
3. The ancestor hero pretends that his wife is his sister:
   3 (Abraham and Sarah in Egypt); 44 (Abraham and Sarah at Gerar); 18 (Isaac and Rebekah at Gerar)
4. Rivalry between a barren, favored wife and a fertile co-wife or concubine:
   7, 45 (Sarah and Hagar); 23, 49 (Rachel and Leah)
5. Danger in the desert and discovery of a well:
   7, 45 (Hagar and Ishmael)
6. Treaty between an ancestor hero and a local king:
   5 (Abraham and Melchizedek); 46 (Abraham and Abimelech); 19 (Isaac and Abimelech)
7. Testament of the dying ancestor hero:
   20 (Isaac); 41, 64, 78 (Jacob)

1. Robert Alter, "Biblical Type-Scenes and the Uses of Convention," in *The Art of Biblical Narrative* (New York: Basic Books, 1981), 47–62.
2. The enumerated examples are keyed by number to the tradition units in table 10.

It should be emphasized that many of these same type-scenes, and others as well, recur in the later history-like themes of Exodus, Numbers, Joshua, and Judges. For example, the type-scene of the birth of an ancestor hero to his barren mother occurs with Samson in Judges 13, and the type-scene of encounter with the future betrothed at a well is applied to Moses in Exod. 2:15b–22.

Type-scene analysis touches directly on a feature that has long been recognized by biblical critics: often more or less the same story is told about different ancestors or about the same ancestor in different settings. The most striking instance is the threefold tale of "the ancestor's wife in danger" (cf. no. 3 in the list of type-scenes above). In fact, such literary doublets or triplets of a single basic story form one of the criteria used to distinguish sources. The tendency of scholars working with source and form criticism has been to try to reconstruct the original form of the story at the level of oral tradition. It may be, however, that there never was an "original" full story but only a traditional episode with conventional elements, and that it was a challenge to each storyteller or writer to fill out the episode and its conventions with fresh and appropriately varied content.

Source criticism in the past has tended to analyze vocabulary and style with little guidance from professional literary criticism. As a result, important rhetorical features were often missed or were described with such generalities (e.g., "terse, incisive style" vs. "labored, cumbersome style," etc.) that it was difficult to develop precise criteria that could break out of the web of circular reasoning in the discrimination of sources. Nowadays some progress has been made in refining descriptions of style and representation that may begin to provide more controlled ways of testing source hypotheses. For example, the recognized peculiarities of the Priestly (P) style of composition (§49.1) can be analyzed into such features as the use of "echo" from unit to unit (repetition of key words, phrases, or clauses), inverse correspondences in the structuring of elements of literary units (e.g., a b c/c' b' a', also called ring composition, chiasm, concentric inclusion, or palistrophe), and a fondness for panel writing in the sense of constructing incidents in succession that are similar in form and content. The covenant of God with Abraham in Genesis 17 evidences all three of these stylistic techniques of P. The "pedantry" or "monotony" that scholars have often noted in P is interestingly paralleled structurally in children's literature, which may suggest that the style of P was intended for instruction or catechesis.[3]

---

3. Sean E. McEvenue, *The Narrative Style of the Priestly Writer,* AnBib 50 (Rome: Biblical Institute Press, 1971).

Similarly, a careful stylistic analysis of the Hagar stories in J and E (table 10: nos. 7, 45) yields striking differences in the overall representations within the "doublets." The J story is told directly and vigorously with real dialogue in terse couplets, has the actors relating directly to one another but not to God, leaves all action in the hands of Sarai, and adds a divinely given theological perspective at the end. The E story is told subtly and indirectly, with exterior details and unrelated speeches, has the actors relating directly to God and not to one another, gives the decisive action to Abraham, and has God interacting at the human level, with miracles, at every step without rising to a climax.[4]

The art of representing human character in biblical narratives shows a scale of means, in ascending order of explicitness and certainty:

1. Report of actions;
2. Appearance, gestures, posture, and costume;
3. One character's comments on another;
4. Direct speech by the character;
5. Inward speech, summarized or quoted as interior dialogue;
6. Statements by the narrator about attitudes and intentions of the characters, either as flat assertions or explanations of motives.

Steps 1 and 2 on the scale present us with inference about character. Steps 3 and 4 offer different claims, sometimes conflicting, that have to be weighed. Step 5 moves us to relative certainty about character, while step 6 provides us the certainty of the narrator's judgment. It is characteristic of biblical narratives to disclose more fully the character of some actors than of others.[5] An analysis of ancestor traditions with respect to their application of the above scale of means in characterization would not only refine our understanding of the narrative art but might also provide an additional criterion for assessing the proposed source separation.

Interlocking stylistic and representational conventions of the sort just described, even though not often studied with such an intention, promise to advance source criticism beyond the limited frontiers it was able to reach mainly with the help of lists of isolated and disconnected words, phrases, and stylistic constructions taken to be more or less distinctive of one or another source.

Yet a further contribution of the newer literary criticism, particularly in its structuralist forms, is to focus on the effects that literary devices have on

4. Sean E. McEvenue, "A Comparison of Narrative Styles in the Hagar Stories," *Semeia* 3 (1975): 64–80.
5. Robert Alter, "Characterization and the Art of Reticence," in *The Art of Biblical Narrative*, 114–30.

the total composition, irrespective of how it may have reached its final state. In the older criticism, literary doublets and triplets were studied either as differentiating source phenomena or as pointers backward to the underlying oral form. It was generally assumed that the final redaction included duplicate accounts because they had become so highly prized that none could be sacrificed in favor of another for the sake of total coherence.

Rhetorical criticism and structuralism are more likely to consider how doublets or triplets function in the total composition, for example, how the threefold transformations of the type-scene "the ancestor's wife in danger" (table 10: nos. 3, 18, 44) operate in the whole of Genesis 12—50. One analysis of this sort traces two sets of transformations from 12:10–20 through 20:1–18 to 26:1–11. In one set of transformations it becomes clear that an ancestor gains wealth and progeny only as he does *not* expose his wife to an adulterous situation (by pretending or implying that she is not his wife). The other set of transformations shows different means by which a foreign king discovers that the woman he has taken, or was about to take, into his court is in fact the ancestor's wife: in one instance by an act of God (plagues), in a second instance by the word of God (in a dream), and in a third instance by personal observation (he sees Isaac fondling Rebekah). Seen in this way, the repetitions and novelties in the three enactments of one type-scene provide a progressive amplification of the concrete conditions under which the promises to the ancestors concerning children and land will be worked out in reality.[6]

It is obvious that the newer forms of literary criticism, although for the most part not directly concerned with the growth of the traditions, nevertheless are unearthing important new understandings that have far-ranging implications for the abiding questions about how the traditions grew into their present mammoth composite structure. These new literary insights are potentially applicable to any one or more of the hypothesized stages or junctures in the growth of the traditions:

1. The oral formation of the separate tradition units;
2. The oral formation of groups of tradition units around history-like themes in cult recitations;
3. The writing of the Yahwist (J) source;
4. The writing of the Elohist (E) source;
5. The redaction of JE;
6. The writing of the Priestly (P) source;
7. The redaction of JEP, whether by P or an independent editor.

6. Robert Polzin, " 'The Ancestress of Israel in Danger' in Danger," *Semeia* 3 (1975): 81–98.

Only as the emerging literary insights are applied across the whole range of the early traditions of Israel will it be possible to garner the full benefits of the newer studies for answering the continuing questions about the growth of the traditions.

15.4 Individual Family Traditions or Tribal Group Traditions?

A perplexing aspect of the ancestor traditions is the way they seem to vacillate between describing the actions of ancestors as individual family heads, on the one hand, and the actions of ancestors as symbolic heads of entire tribes, on the other hand. A person whose name, and often whose actions, represents a much larger group of people is known as an *eponym* ("to name after") and sagas about individuals in this collective role are called eponymous sagas. In Genesis 12—50, the eponymous function of the sagas emerges slowly but accumulates substance and overtones as the tradition sequences unfold. Virtually all of the Abraham sagas can be read as events in the life of a family head, except that the saga of the destruction of Sodom and Gomorrah ends with the announcement that Lot's two incestuous sons are named Moab and Ammonite (Ben-ammi), respectively fathers of Moabites and Ammonites "to this day" (19:37–38). We also observe that among the offspring of Nahor, Ishmael, and Abraham by Keturah are the names of various Aramean and Arab peoples (table 10: nos. 13, 15, 71).

As we reach the Jacob cycle of traditions, however, the eponymous dimension of the traditions becomes more explicit and insistent. Esau, brother of Jacob, is also openly identified as Edom, by use of a wordplay on the color "red," linking Esau's red hair and the red stew that he ate with the red sandstone that distinguishes the land of Edom (25:24–31; cf. 36:1–8). In a saga freighted with symbolic allusions (32:22–32), Jacob wrestles with "a man" who turns out to be "God (Elohim)" and who gives Jacob the new name of Israel (connected to the saga by the understanding that the name Israel means "he who has struggled [with] God [and men?]"; see v. 28). The capstone of the eponymous interpretation occurs with the birth of Jacob's sons (29:31—30:24; 35:16–20), whose names are identical with the later tribes of Israel (and in one instance Jacob's grandsons, Ephraim and Manasseh born to Joseph; 41:50–52; 48). Jacob's deathbed testimony to his "sons" is actually a chain of poetic blessings (and in some cases implicit curses or judgments) on the tribes conceived poetically under various plant and animal images. Dan is called "one of the tribes of Israel" (49:16).

The J writer brings the eponymous interpretation explicitly to light by following the poetic blessings with the summation: "All these are the twelve tribes of Israel" (49:28). Earlier, in 46:8–27, P prepares for this understanding by naming sixty-six "persons" who accompanied Jacob into Egypt, among whom are named not only his immediate sons (= tribes) but also grandchildren (= clans or subgroups within tribes), a point which becomes much clearer in fuller lists of the same type in Numbers 1 and 26. Also, the feigned treaty with Shechem in chap. 34 strongly echoes a situation in which large Israelite entities—certainly more than a handful of Jacob's sons— attempt a liaison with the city of Shechem that fails. Moreover, the account in chap. 38 of Judah and his Canaanite daughter-in-law Tamar seems to allude to the incorporation of Canaanite towns in the Judean shephelah into the tribe of Judah (Judah's sons Shelah, Perez, and Zerah are called "clans" in Num. 26:19–22, and Shelah's sons are elsewhere said to be the "fathers" of towns in the Judean shephelah: Lecah [Lachish?], Mareshah, Beth-ashbea, and Cozeba = Chezib, cf. 1 Chron. 4:21–22).

Fixing upon these pronouncedly eponymous aspects of the ancestor traditions, a number of past scholars attempted to understand the entirety of the traditions as more or less veiled tribal histories. Births were read as the origins of tribes and marriages were seen as the unions of two tribes. Aside from the difficulty that some of the names of individuals have no known identity as tribal groups (e.g., Abraham, Lot, Isaac, Laban, or even Jacob), it requires a very strained allegorical interpretation to carry through such a systematic collectivization of the traditions. It is far more likely that sagas about individuals and their families, identified as significant ancestors of Israel, have been given direct or indirect eponymous meanings, and have in turn given rise to tradition units that are eponymous at their core. Such at least seems to be the shape of the account of the birth of Jacob's sons, both in J and E, which shows signs of being one of the latest traditions to come to full flower in the common pool of oral materials. Nonetheless, even this unit has been accommodated in its plot to the conception of the ancestor Jacob and his individual sons.

With proper caution, the overtly eponymous features of Genesis 12—50 may be used to undertake a separation of those elements that are a retrojection of Israelite conditions in the time of the conquest of Canaan from those elements which reflect the pre-Israelite experience of subgroups that subsequently became a part of Israel. This is an inquiry extremely difficult to control, and will remain so until we acquire some clearer understanding of how saga as a literary type actually carries concentric individual/family and larger group/tribal-national meanings simultaneously or successively. To date it appears that no systematic study of this problem in biblical narratives, making use of comparative literary studies, has been undertaken.

16
SOCIOHISTORIC HORIZONS OF THE ANCESTOR TRADITIONS

Based as it was on a confessional religious approach to the Bible, the traditional interpretation of the stories about Abraham, Isaac, Jacob, and Joseph viewed them as straightforward historical reports. Historical-critical method took another tack by demonstrating that these ancestor traditions were not a historical work using documentation or eyewitness testimony (§11.1.b). The traditions were largely chains and cycles of sagas, and the literary type of the saga was recognized as an orally based form in which past persons, events, and typical experiences were imaginatively reworked into highly polished reflections of a later community's self-understanding. Far from documenting the ancestors as a modern historian would strive to do, the Israelite community reported as it did only to celebrate the ancestor heroes of their sagas as exemplary founders or precursors of a new socioreligious order.

Once the historical character of the ancestors fell into fundamental doubt, many biblical critics concluded that nothing historically substantial could be determined about them, since they were fabrications of a later community. In other words, the sagas about ancestors really told only of their descendants' history and viewpoint. Other critics, allowing for the saga form of narration and granting the undoubted retrojection of later Israelite thought and experience into the traditions, nonetheless tried to isolate valid historical elements in the traditions that could fix the approximate time and setting of the ancestors. Using extrabiblical texts and archaeological remains as external checkpoints, many scholars asserted that the ancestors of Israel could be placed either in the Middle Bronze I period (ca. 2100–1900 B.C.E., formerly included in the Early Bronze period), or in the Middle Bronze II period (1900–1550 B.C.E.), or in the early part of the Late Bronze period (1550–1200 B.C.E.). More recently this way of anchoring the ancestors in the historical world of the ancient Near East has been thrown into radical doubt.

An alternative option, still very undeveloped, tries to correlate the literary peculiarities of the traditions with the sociohistorical conditions of emerging Israel and especially with the pre-Israelite experience of the several previously separate groups that joined to form united Israel. On this view, the traditions of Genesis 12—50 hold far less promise for recovering the lost historical identities of individual ancestors and their families than they do for helping us to reconstruct how Israel took shape through the joining of preexisting groups that lived amid conditions and pressures of the sort attested in the sagas. In other words, the ancestor sagas tell not only of the self-understanding of later Israel but also something of the varied routes and complex processes by which that community came into being as a confederation of tribes.

16.1 Chronology and Archaeology

The biblical text supplies a skeleton of chronological information that can be pieced together from the DH and P sources. Solomon is said to have begun construction of the temple 480 years after the exodus (1 Kings 6:1; DH). A date in the period 967 to 958 B.C.E. for the laying of the temple cornerstone seems assured.[7] Reckoning backward, we arrive at a fifteenth-century date for the departure from Egypt, ca. 1447–1438 B.C.E. Exodus 12:40 (P) states that the stay in Egypt totaled 430 years (Gen. 15:13, from E, states 400 years), which would place the descent of Jacob into Egypt in the nineteenth century, ca. 1877–1868 B.C.E. When miscellaneous Priestly chronological notes are calculated (Gen. 47:9; 25:26; 21:5; 12:4) we reach a date of ca. 2092–2083 for Abraham's departure from Haran.

What should we make of this chronology? To begin with, it requires that we take at face value the excessively great ages of the ancestors (§15.3.b). Also, it is noted that the numbers given in the Samaritan Pentateuch and in the Septuagint frequently vary from those in the Masoretic Text. More seriously, to posit a fifteenth-century exodus flies in the face of the biblical picture of political conditions in Egypt at the time and also fails to explain why Israel was so little visible in Canaan in the period 1400–1250 B.C.E. In connection with the latter objection, it cannot be shown that the ʿapiru malcontents mentioned in the Amarna letters (table 1: 3B) as highly active in Canaan in 1425–1350 B.C.E. are to be equated with the Israel of the Books of Joshua and Judges.

With respect to the ancestors, there is simply nothing specific in the biblical traditions which can connect them with known history in or around Canaan in the period between 2092 and 1868 when, according to the biblical chronology, the ancestors were supposedly in Canaan. Some decades ago there was a flurry of excitement when King Amraphel of Shinar

7. The chronological system followed in this book (§25) dates the foundation of the temple to 967 B.C.E.

(Gen. 14:1) was identified with Hammurabi of Babylon, but this equation failed to stand up. Moreover, the then-preferred high date for the reign of Hammurabi (1848–1806) was subsequently shifted toward either of two later time spans (1792–1750 or 1728–1686). Likewise, the attempt to associate the rise of Joseph in Egyptian service with the coming of the Asiatic Hyksos to Egypt in the latter part of the eighteenth century is not persuasive on general grounds and, in any case, yields a date for the descent into Egypt more than a century later than the period of 1877–1868 posited by the biblical chronology. In short, the biblical traditional chronology of DH and P is not validated in any particular and actually contradicts the substance of biblical accounts, at least with respect to the exodus.

On the assumption that some traces of the manner of ancestral life reflected in Genesis 12—50 might appear in the material remains from Canaan, archaeology has been freely invoked to argue for one or another scheme for dating the patriarchs. Middle Bronze I (2100–1900 B.C.E., also called Intermediate Middle Bronze–Early Bronze), has appealed to many scholars as the patriarchal age because of its now richly attested nonurban culture. This interlude between periods of city-building in Canaan is often assumed to indicate an incursion of nomadic peoples presumably similar in life style to the ancestors of Israel. Contemporary documents from recently excavated Ebla in northern Syria are now claimed by some to strengthen the probability that Middle Bronze I was the fabled patriarchal age.[8]

Middle Bronze II (1900–1550 B.C.E.) is the preferred patriarchal era for other biblical specialists. An open-air sanctuary at Shechem, dating to ca. 1800 B.C.E., is associated with patriarchal worship at that site (Gen. 33:18–20), and the manner of Abraham's residence in a satellite village of Hebron is said to be paralleled in the layout of unwalled Givat Sharett close by Beth-shemesh (Gen. 13:18). Moreover, advocates of Middle Bronze II feel

---

8. Claims that the Ebla tablets either refer directly to the patriarchs or to Yahweh, or to other features of the patriarchal traditions, must await publication of the texts and further evaluation. While the publications of two of the excavators have begun to divulge the enormous historical and cultural importance of the finds, they disagree sharply over whether the texts refer to biblical traditions: Giovanni Pettinato, *The Archives of Ebla: An Empire Inscribed in Clay* (Garden City, N.Y.: Doubleday & Co., 1981), contends that they do, whereas Paolo Matthiae, *Ebla: An Empire Rediscovered* (Garden City, N.Y.: Doubleday & Co., 1981), dismisses such claims as "tales without foundation" (p. 11).

Summaries and preliminary assessments of the Ebla discoveries are reported in: Keith N. Schoville, *Biblical Archaeology in Focus* (Grand Rapids: Baker Book House, 1978), 242–46; Paul C. Maloney, "Assessing Ebla," *BARev* 4/1 (March 1978): 4–10; Edwin M. Yamauchi, "Unearthing Ebla's Ancient Secrets," *Christianity Today* (May 8, 1981): 18–21; Lawrence T. Geraty, "Update on Ebla," *Ministry* (January 1982): 24–27; and Hazel W. Perkin, "Tell Mardikh," in *The New International Dictionary of Biblical Archaeology*, ed. Edward M. Blaiklock and Roland K. Harrison (Grand Rapids: Zondervan, 1983), 440–42.

that a lowering of the patriarchal era by two or more centuries brings the ancestors into more satisfactory chronological connection with the widely accepted thirteenth-century date for the exodus.

All in all, however, archaeological buttressing of one or another date for the ancestors has not proven convincing. For one thing, the evidence is not consistently supportive of any scheme of dating. Neither of the important patriarchal sites of Beersheba and Shechem yields any sign of occupation in MB I; in fact, Beersheba appears not to have been built until ca. 1200. According to the biblical texts, the location of the early Israelite holy place at Shechem was probably not within the walled city where the cultic installation was found by excavators. Moreover, most of the archaeological assessment has proceeded on a vast overestimation of the role of pastoral nomadism in early Israel and on very dubious assumptions about how pastoral nomadic social organization can be "read" as present in material remains (§24.2.a).

Perhaps most critically, archaeology has been made to carry more of a burden than it can possibly bear in reaching historical conclusions. Only when solid historical elements can be established in the ancestor sagas— through independent historical evidence or through controlled comparative literary studies that demonstrate the historical particulars that sagas are prone to preserve—only then will archaeology be able to offer supplementary support or clarification to those elements. Failing to find inscriptional evidence relevant to the ancestors, the ambiguous material remains from archaeology can only combine with the ambiguous data from the sagas to produce ever more complex ambiguities.

In the attempt to correlate biblical text and archaeology in order to situate the ancestors historically, the operative line of reasoning goes as follows: *if* elements *a* and *b* in the sagas are taken to be historical, *then* elements *c* and *d* from archaeology tend to corroborate them. This is clearly a much shakier line of argument than either of the following alternatives: (1) *because* elements *a* and *b* in the sagas are known independently to be historical, *therefore* their historical worth is clarified or extended by elements *c* and *d* from archaeology, or (2) *because* elements *c* and *d* from archaeology are historically firm (e.g., inscriptional evidence), *therefore* the identical saga elements *c'* and *d'* and/or the related saga elements *a* and *b* are provided historical credibility. So far it does not appear that we possess either literary-historical or archaeological-historical data that enable us to reason securely in either of the latter two ways.

16.2 Political and Geographical Data

The relatively sparse political allusions and the more abundant geographical references in the ancestor traditions have been ransacked in a search for clues to the historical setting, or settings, of the ancestors. The results have been either vaguely inconclusive or blatantly contradictory. Historical contexts ranging over as much as eighteen hundred years have been seriously proposed as the periods when the ancestors lived or, if they were literary fictions, when they were created. The earliest positioning of the ancestors wants to make them contemporaries of the Ebla texts, ca. 2400–2000 B.C.E., and the latest would bring the existing textual representations of the ancestors into the sixth-century Judean exile. A brief survey of the political and geographical data shows why scholars vary so drastically in their historical situating of the ancestors, and why many scholars desist from any endeavor in that direction.

The fullest political information in these traditions appears to be found in Genesis 14 where Abraham defeats a coalition of four kings from afar who, in carrying out a punitive campaign against five rebellious vassal kings in the vicinity of the Dead Sea, arouse the ire of Abraham when they capture his nephew Lot. The regimes of the foreign kings are apparently in Mesopotamia and Anatolia. Elam is clearly named, and the other three states are probably conceived as Assyrian, Babylonian, and Hittite. Numerous historical identifications of these kings have been proposed with no reliable results. Especially dubious is the text's conception of Elam, based in southwestern Iran, exercising imperial control over part of Canaan. Moreover, there is no evidence that four kings from these distant regions ever formed a coalition against city-states in Canaan. The size of the coalitions is on such a large scale and the territory over which the campaign rages so extensive that the narrative gives the impression of deliberate "overkill." A widely held view is that Genesis 14 is a midrash (free interpretation) intended to show that Abraham, "the father of a multitude of nations" (cf. Gen. 17:5), was a fully participating equal of great kings—or, in fact, their superior, since with his 318 armed men he was able to defeat the united armies of four great kings. Possibly a much more modest military action, aimed at controlling commercial routes, underlies the inflated tradition. If so, we have no information for reconstuction and dating it. Melchizedek, king of Salem (Jerusalem?), who blesses Abraham after his victory (14:17–20), is otherwise unknown.

King Abimelech of Gerar, first deceived by Abraham and Isaac and later joined in treaties with them (Gen. 21:27; 26:26–31), is also not known from any other source. The identification of Abimelech as "king of the Philistines" (26:1; cf. 21:32, 34; 26:14, 15, 18) would not have been a historically accurate title until the Philistines colonized Canaan beginning about 1150 B.C.E. Genesis 36:15–42 is a compendium of lists about "chiefs" and "kings" of Edom, apparently joined by P, or the final redactor, to the lists of the descendants of Esau in 36:1–14. None of these Edomite leaders is independently attested and, even if we could place them historically, there is no reason to believe that these lists were connected with the patriarchal traditions until late monarchic times. The pharaoh who enlists Joseph in his service is anonymous, and the Egyptian names that appear in the novella are not familiar before the tenth century from Egyptian sources. The centralized agricultural policy reported in 47:13–26 probably best accords with Egyptian economic controls under the New Kingdom, but that embraces the long period from 1570 to 1085 B.C.E. At a number of points in Genesis 12—50 the designation of regions/peoples/political units by terms such as Amorite, Hittite, Horite = Hurrian, and Canaanite is not obviously different from similar usages in later periods and thus no particular time frame of Syro-Palestinian political history provides a clarifying context for the variously employed terms.

Do the regions and settlements named in the ancestor traditions point toward a specific historical context any more persuasively than the more limited political data? The place names tend to fall into two categories: (1) references to places in the mountainous heartland or in the northern Negeb of ancient Canaan where the ancestors resided; and (2) references to outlying areas of Canaan and the wider Near East with which the ancestors were in contact. These include regions from which the ancestors are said to have migrated (i.e., Ur, Haran) and with which they continued to communicate for purposes of intermarriage. Also referred to are regions where they withdraw for survival (Egypt) or which their descendants outside the main line of Abraham, Isaac, and Jacob eventually populate (e.g., the sons of Lot to Ammon and Moab, the sons of Abraham by Keturah to Arabia, and Esau and his sons to Edom). Further included are the regions of Transjordan and Sinai attacked by the five foreign kings (Genesis 14).

Two sources understand that Abraham immigrated to Canaan from an area around Haran in northern Mesopotamia, called Aram-naharaim (Aram Between the Rivers) by J and Paddan-aram (the Field of Aram) by P. The Priestly source (and maybe J) adds that, prior to coming to Haran, Abraham had lived in southern Mesopotamia at Ur. Support for the northern Mesopotamian origin of the ancestors of Israel is often cited in the fact that several of the relatives of Abraham possess names identical with known cities in that region: Terah, Nahor, Haran, and Serug. The specific connection of the first homeland of Abraham with places in Mesopotamia, however, belongs more to the framework of the traditions than to the contents of the sagas.

It is striking that the E source locates the homeland of Laban, not in far northern Mesopotamia, but just to the east or northeast of Transjordan. The fact that Ur is explained as a city of the Chaldeans would not have been a way of identifying that ancient Sumerian city until at least the tenth century and more likely in the eighth century when a strong Chaldean = Neo-Babylonian dynasty arose there. The designation of upper Mesopotamia as "Aram" depends on the rise to prominence of Aramean peoples which probably began by the fifteenth century but may not have led to the practice of naming regions as subdivisions of larger Aram (e.g., Aram-naharaim, Paddan-aram, Aram-damascus, Aram-zobah, etc.) until the eleventh century. Even the existence of northern Mesopotamian cities bearing patriarchal names is not as compelling evidence for MB II origins of the ancestors in that region as has often been claimed, since some of these names occur also in texts from much later centuries.

In short, a tendency toward systematizing the origins of the ancestors, and their relationships to other peoples, is noticeable in the literary stages of framing the traditions, especially in the work of the JE redactor and of P and/or the final redactor. It is far less clear that we can identify the beginnings of that process in the oral phase of the traditions, for which the generality of E's reference to the ancestors' homeland in "the land of the people of the east" (Gen. 29:1) may be more typical than the citing of place names.

The Palestinian locales of the ancestor sagas are concentrated in four areas: (1) in the Samarian highlands at Bethel and Shechem; (2) in Transjordanian Gilead at Penuel and Succoth; (3) in the Judahite highlands at Mamre-Hebron; and (4) in the Negeb of Judah at Gerar and Beersheba. Jacob is primarily associated with the first two groups of sites and Abraham-Isaac with the last two groups of sites. This concentration of the key patriarchal sites in precisely the areas where the Israelite tribes first appeared in strength at the end of the thirteenth century is significant. But to translate these geographical allusions into a prior historical setting for the individual ancestors is very precarious, not only because the biblical references are not clearly related on a single historical plane but also because the highland area of Canaan seems to have been politically undeveloped during most of the Bronze Age and consequently does not yield much textual information of any sort. Since the ancestor sagas developed orally and as literature over centuries of time, it is difficult to judge when, and with what historical understanding, the various place names were introduced to the traditions.

16.3 Customs and Laws

One of the most strongly asserted links in reconstructions of the patriarchal world in a Bronze Age setting has been the remarkable find of texts treating family law from Nuzi and adjacent locations in the upper Tigris Valley. These documents date from the fifteenth and fourteenth centuries B.C.E. and come from a Hurrian society situated some distance to the east of the supposed homeland of the patriarchs in Aram-naharaim (table 1: 1K).

A great range of customary legal practices evidenced in the Nuzi tablets have suggested close affinities with the marriage, family, and inheritance customs of the ancestors of Israel. Among the parallels between Nuzi and patriarchal family custom and law are the following:

1. A barren wife must provide her husband a slave girl through whom he may have children (Gen. 16:1–2; 30:9).
2. The status of the slave girl and her children is protected against the jealousy or arbitrariness of the wife or husband (21:9–14).
3. A husband could have the concurrent status of brother by adopting his wife from her natural brother (12:11–13; 20:2, 12; 26:7).
4. A person could sell a birthright to another (25:29–34).
5. A childless couple could adopt someone to provide for them who would in the end inherit their property, except that any subsequent naturally born son would automatically inherit in place of the adopted son (15:1–4).
6. The practice described in no. 5 was also applicable in cases where a son-in-law was adopted as one's son (31:1–2).
7. Possession of household gods (or *teraphim* in KJV) was a kind of title deed to inheritable property (31:34).
8. A deathbed testament, or blessing, by the head of a family could have the force of law (27:35–37; 48:8–22).

On the strength of these parallels it was widely concluded that Hurrian family law was observed over the whole of upper Mesopotamia and thus was known to the Israelite ancestors in Aram-naharaim, whence they brought it to Canaan. That most advocates dated Israel's ancestors some centuries earlier than the Nuzi records was not regarded as much of a difficulty since it was assumed that the same practices had been in vogue for a long time prior to being written down at Nuzi. Furthermore, it was alleged that these marriages and family customs, so peculiar in many respects, ceased to be observed in the ancient Near East by the end of the Bronze

Age. Therefore, the narrators of Genesis 12—50 must have had direct access to old Bronze Age customs since they could not possibly have been the free invention of J, E, or P. Also, it was felt that data from the Mari texts on the middle Euphrates, from ca. 1800 B.C.E., supplemented the fuller picture from Nuzi with respect to the notion of keeping family land intact in perpetuity. Moreover, Mari was also judged to demonstrate that the type of names borne by Israel's ancestors was a type restricted to the Bronze Age and most in evidence in northern Mesopotamia.

Despite the impressiveness of the argument from Hurrian and Amorite customs and laws, the weight of the evidence has been strongly challenged and extensively undermined by further study, including the publication of additional Hurrian texts. First, it is noticed that earlier interpreters tended to supply the Genesis sagas with missing elements in order to make the parallels with Nuzi closer than they actually were. For example, nothing is said about Laban adopting his son-in-law Jacob (31:1–2). Abraham's "explanation" of how Sarah really is his sister makes her a half sister and not an unrelated wife over whom he happens to have momentary adoptive-brother rights (20:12). Also, it is by no means evident that Abraham's reluctance to expel Hagar and Ishmael from his household is based on his familiarity with a custom or law that prohibits him (21:9–14).

Moreover, the Nuzi documents were often read to contain or imply provisions that would harmonize them with the biblical texts. For instance, although a man in Nuzi might receive his wife from a natural or adoptive brother who gave her away in marriage, it does not appear that the husband also took on the status of adoptive brother in place of the real or fictitious brother from whom he acquired his wife. It is also highly doubtful that possession of household gods was in itself a token of inheritance rights; they stood rather as symbols of the unity and integrity of the household. Finally, it is now believed that the Nuzi archives, although unique in the fullness of their representation of family law, are by no means peculiar to upper Mesopotamia in MB II and LB. Traces of similar laws have been detected in Old Babylonian and Assyrian laws, and the presence of the same or similar customs is cited in later centuries in the ancient Near East. The tendency, therefore, is to qualify sharply, or to deny totally, the claim that the Nuzi finds necessarily, or even probably, situate the ancestors of Israel in a Hurrian societal context in upper Mesopotamia in the period 2000–1400 B.C.E.

Another customary aspect of the Genesis traditions is the Egyptian coloration of the Joseph novella which reflects Egyptian loan words, court customs and titles, burial practices, etc. (cf. e.g., 40—41; 47:13–26; 50:26).

Many of these Egyptian elements are so general as to denote no particular historical period. Those that can be checked out against Egyptian data generally suggest that the Egyptian milieu reflected is more likely from the tenth century and later than from the Bronze Age. Moreover, two emphatic notices about Egyptian refusal to eat with Hebrews (Asiatics?) or to consort with shepherds (43:32; 46:34) find no support from Egyptian sources. It appears, then, that the most detailed Egyptian flavor in the Joseph novella is provided at the JE stage of written composition or later, and that it is not at all required that the oral storytellers or the writers of the Joseph traditions had any eyewitness knowledge of Egypt.

16.4 Social Struggles in the Ancestor Traditions

16.4.a The Uncertain Socioeconomic Niche of the Ancestors

We have noted difficulties in trying to fit the ancestors of Israel into any particular historical or social setting when pursued by the customary historical-critical methods. The fairly sparse chronological, political, and geographical data from the biblical text do not correlate and converge toward any definite setting. Nor does the external evidence from archaeological remains and from custom and law form any conclusive links with the biblical text. In short, the ancestors of Israel fit broadly into the whole sweep of Bronze and Iron Age Canaan and its environs, but without any more detailed reliable indication of date and without firm connections to political and social structures and events known from sources outside the Bible.

These obstacles to situating the ancestors of Israel have often been obscured by the assumption that references to their movements and manner of life indicate that the ancestors were pastoral nomads. In fact, the movements of the ancestors are largely explained as historically caused migrations for purposes of change of residence, religious pilgrimage, strife with outsiders, securing wives, escaping famine, and the like, rather than due to the regular seasonal movements of pastoral nomads. The references to the ancestors' forms of wealth include not only the flocks of sheep and goats typical of (though not exclusive to) pastoral nomads at the time, but also herds of cattle, wealth in metal, and cultivated land which suggest either sedentary farming and animal husbandry or commercial enterprise. Some interpreters have proposed that the patriarchs were merchants who moved their goods by donkey caravans, while others have suggested that they were independent transport contractors who worked for interstate merchants. The detail of Abraham as a commander of 318 armed men (14:13–16) hints at a military adventurer of the *'apiru* type (mentioned in the Amarna letters [table 1: 3B] and possibly echoed in the cognate biblical term *'ivri*, i.e., "Hebrew," v. 13) who served as a mercenary band leader for established city-states, and Isaac's relation to Abimelech can be understood similarly (26:1–33).

The ancestors are shown to reside in the vicinity of major population centers in the highlands and, insofar as they are "nomadic" at all, it appears that some members of their larger families/clans/bands took flocks into favorable seasonal pasturage while the rest of the group remained at home/headquarters (so-called transhumant pastoralism, cf. 37:12–17; 38:12–13, and possibly also 26:12–23). All in all, the socioeconomic traits of the ancestors are not delineated as clearly belonging to any one single type. This may mean either that the traditions reflect different occupational statuses because they refer to different groups or that changing conceptions of the occupational status of the ancestors came into play at different points in the process of gathering and editing the traditions about them.

There is also the challenge of sorting out defensibly which representations of ancestors are references to actual individuals and which are collective representations of tribes or of the whole people Israel. If it is judged that actual individual ancestors have been later turned into symbols of larger groups, how are the two kinds of references to be distinguished in the sagas? Some scholars resolve this problem by viewing Abraham as having been an individual while construing Jacob as a collective representation of Israel. It is not likely, however, that so neat a distinction can be drawn (§15.4). Frequently interpreters move back and forth between the individualizing and the symbolic lines of interpretation without making clear their basic principles of interpretation or how they apply them to *all* the ancestor traditions, and not merely to the more obvious eponymous texts. The result is considerable confusion because of lack of a more or less consistent method for sifting the sociohistoric indicators of individuals and their families from those of larger groups for whom the ancestors are eponyms.

Given such uncertainties, the soundest procedure for the moment is to recognize that the ancestor traditions entered the body of Israelite traditions in the tribal period. Granted that the J and E formulations of the traditions rest upon a fund of common oral traditions, the earliest firm sociohistoric anchor point for them is the situation of the confederation of Israelite tribes in Canaan before the rise of the kingdom. The traditions about ancestors become conceivable as the special legacies of different groups that joined to form Israel. It is noteworthy that the ancestors stand out as separate figures connected with different locales in Canaan. Only secondarily do they appear to have been linked by means of genealogies and itineraries.

It is plausible that Jacob was the ancestor hero of a group of northern Israelites in the regions of Ephraim and Manasseh, and that Abraham and Isaac were the ancestor heroes of groups of southern Israelites in the regions of the highlands of Judah and the northern Negeb. These originally separate ancestor figures were remembered in their communities through sagas featuring "type-scenes" (§15.3.d) that were affected by a tendency to view the life experiences of the ancestors as anticipations or "prophecies" of the later experiences of the entire groups who claimed descent from them (§15.4). Whereas the type-scene format for developing the sagas permeated all the ancestor traditions, the eponymous symbolizing process was applied more unevenly, with the result that Jacob appears much more fully presented as an eponym than does Abraham or Isaac.

Moreover, fairy tale or folklore motifs tended to be employed more frequently in connection with Jacob than with Abraham or Isaac. Jacob is portrayed in a variant on the motif of the wily trickster who first outwits his father and brother, and later does the same to his father-in-law. There are also noticeable traces of the motif of the ancestor's prodigious physical strength (a facet more fully developed in the case of Samson, Judges 13—16), since Jacob is able single-handedly to lift a well cover that normally required several men to move (29:2–3, 8, 10) and he is strong enough to wrestle all night with a preternatural figure who turns out to be God (32:22–32).

It appears further that Jacob was the first ancestor to be securely absorbed into the traditions of the Israelite tribal league, so that he became the immediate father of the people whose very name was Israel and whose sons bore the precise names of the twelve tribes. This primacy of Jacob in the traditions probably reflects the reality that the tribal confederation first formed in the northern area where Jacob sagas circulated. Abraham entered the ancestor corpus of united Israel later, probably already having incorporated Isaac as the ancestor of a Judahite subgroup. Being unable to dislodge Jacob as the immediate progenitor of Israel, Abraham was nonetheless accorded the honored position of the primal father of the people, the one who first ventured to Canaan and who became father of Isaac and grandfather of Jacob. In this way the separate experiences of ancestors dear to different segments of Israel were joined in one body of traditions which reflected the combined unity of the confederate tribes (§24.2.c). Eventually in some of the sagas there developed pronounced overtones of Abraham and Jacob as representatives of all Israel before deity, enduring a test of trust in God (22:1–14) or struggling tenaciously with God in an effort to secure blessing (32:22–32). Although we owe the present forms of these two sagas to E and J respectively, it is highly probable that the ancestors were already viewed as prototypes of Israelite piety in the intertribal cultic context.

16.4.b Concerns About Production, Reproduction, and Self-defense

If we begin from the relatively secure sociohistoric point of united tribal Israel remembering different segments of experience contributed by various of its member groups, there is one important line of inquiry that can be pursued: Can we determine the consuming interests and concerns of the groups who formulated and transmitted the ancestor traditions? Can we identify why it was in the interests of united Israel to combine the separate ancestor traditions in the form of all-Israelite traditions?

The concerns and interests of the ancestor traditions are primarily of two kinds: (1) the arduous struggle to secure a viable community as expressed in the need for offspring and productive land; and (2) the repeated defense of the community against outside pressures to absorb or destroy it. A majority of the type-scenes noted (§15.3.d) focus on the first struggle: how the ancestors are to get sons and to gain a secure hold on land. Yet, in the course of striving for children and land, the ancestors enter into complex relations of friction, conflict, asylum, and treaty with other peoples in Canaan and Egypt. The net sociohistoric profile of the ancestor traditions shows groups of people who are only marginally integrated into the economy, society, and politics of the highlands of Canaan. This marginality tends to be explained by the framework of the combined traditions with the notion that the ancestors were relative newcomers to Canaan. The naive assumption that they were also pastoral nomads has facilitated scholarly acquiescence in that notion. The contents of the sagas, however, tend to disclose that the ancestors were not well integrated into highland Canaan because they constituted small communities of people who did not want to integrate or submit to the prevailing social and political structures. This impression is all the more strengthened by other evidence concerning the circumstances of Israel's rise to power in Canaan (§24.1.c; 24.2.c).

One particularly intriguing aspect of the ancestor traditions is the prominence of the women within them. Sarah is a strong-willed equal of Abraham, capable of expelling her handmaid in a jealous fit (16:1–6) and not above laughing at the promise of a son in her old age (18:9–15). Hagar is sketched as a person able to risk her life and the life of her son in the wilderness (16:7–14; 21:15–21). Rebekah boldly addresses and ministers to Abraham's servant at the town well and she unhesitatingly agrees to go to Canaan as Isaac's wife (24:15–25, 55–58). Later Rebekah conspires to assist Jacob in outfoxing her weak and inept husband and helps her son to flee to Laban (27:5–17, 42–45). Rachel and Leah are fierce rivals for Jacob's affections (29:15–35; 30:1–24), and in their competition to bear sons they know how to bargain with one another (30:14–16). Both wives are stead-fastly loyal to Jacob when he flees from Laban with his questionably acquired goods (31:14–16), including the household gods which Rachel cleverly conceals (31:33–35). Tamar, daughter-in-law of Judah, cunningly adopts a harlot's ruse in order to father a son by Judah since he has unjustly denied her one of his sons for a levirate marriage (38:1–26).

A frequent approach of older scholars to the initiative taken by women (e.g., in naming their children) and to the supposed signs of matrilocality (e.g., Jacob lives for some time in his wives' home), was to suppose either that the "patriarchal" society was really matriarchal or at least that it attested to survivals of an earlier Semitic matriarchal society. The evidence for this hypothesis is extremely tenuous. It appears rather that the groups preserving the ancestor traditions were headed by males but possessed of very strong women who were regarded as forceful actors in the domestic sphere. Since the horizons of the sagas, apart from the tensions with outside groups, were largely domestic, the women have significant parts to play that are often essential to the unfolding of the saga plots. These women are as sharply etched characters as are the men. This habit of presenting well-developed active feminine characterizations extends on into later Isra-elite sagas (§21; 23.1), and in some measure into historical writing. It is possible that the regular inclusion of women in saga scenarios was one of the contributions to united Israel made by the groups that developed the ancestor traditions, for clearly we are dealing here with traditions that do not speak narrowly of the fathers of Israel but cast a wider net in telling of the fathers and mothers of Israel.

In sum, there appears to be some promise in locating the sociohistoric horizons of the ancestor sagas in the struggle for existence among small groups of people before they were able to combine into the intertribal confederation of Israel. In such a "social space" we should not expect to find political documentation about the ancestors. The great yearning for sons may very well reflect a situation of population decline in the Canaanite hill country, and the preoccupation with barren wives may indicate that sterility, whether because of deficient diet or disease, was a serious threat to the pre-Israelite residents of rural Canaan. The hunger for land, often romantically pictured as a nomadic trait, may be the search of marginated peoples for pasturage and arable fields not already monopolized by the city-states whose control they do not wish to submit to. Such hunger for "free space" was not the unique prerogative of pastoral nomads but belonged in general to rural villagers and marginated urban dwellers who, for one reason or another, dissented from the sovereignty of city-state and imperial apparatuses.

Once it is recognized that the several ancestors of Israel, and the complex traditions about them, have derived from different member groups within Israel, it may in fact be the case that they tell us indirectly—as the saga form always does—about several different socioeconomic strategies employed by the Canaanite highland populace to cope with their survival needs prior to the large-scale emergence of united Israel: strategies of farming and animal husbandry, strategies of transhumant pastoralism, strategies of mercenary soldiery, and strategies of commercial enterprise, either as merchants or as haulers of goods.

To propose the sociohistoric horizons of the ancestor traditions in this way is only to suggest relevant boundaries and possibilities for further inquiry. It leaves many questions unanswered and, in particular, it calls for carefully controlled assessments of the relation between the form and contents of sagas and the socioeconomic realities that underlie them. Since Icelandic and Teutonic sagas are often cited as examples for understanding Israelite sagas, it appears that a sociohistoric investigation of the foundations and contexts of northern European sagas would be highly instructive in providing comparative leverage for further examination of their Israelite counterparts. If scholars are to turn constructively to such an inquiry, however, they need first to be fully convinced of the generally negative results from trying to date the ancestors and they must simultaneously recognize that the historical locating of the ancestors is insoluble without a better understanding of the saga form itself. It simply is no longer sufficient merely to assert by fiat that this or that aspect of the ancestor sagas is "true history," or, on the contrary, to dismiss the sagas as sociohistorically worthless because they do not belong to the genre of historical writing.

This much is clear: historical-critical methods of research, coupled with archaeology, have reached an impasse in trying to contextualize the ancestors and the ancestor traditions. The presently emerging newer forms of literary criticism and of social scientific criticism are beginning to assess the possibilities that exist for establishing a description of the *social processes* by which groups of Canaanite people became united in Israel and, at the same time, a description of the *literary processes* (including oral literature) by which those groups expressed their deepest values and aims in the course of their struggles. To establish this social-literary interplay within the ancestor sagas as the central focus of inquiry is not to abandon history, but to conceptualize history on a plane to which the documented political history and the archaeological remains of the ancient Near East do not give direct access (§9).

CHAPTER 5

Traditions About Moses:
Exodus, Covenant, and Lawgiving

Read the Biblical Text
Exodus
Leviticus
Numbers

Consult Maps in *MBA*
nos. 43–53

17

THE SHAPE OF THE TRADITIONS IN EXODUS, LEVITICUS, AND NUMBERS

17.1 Distribution of the Tradition Units by Sources and Literary Genres

The traditions about Moses in the Books of Exodus, Leviticus, and Numbers are almost three times the length of the traditions about the patriarchs in Genesis 12—50. The greater bulk of the Moses traditions is not to be explained by an excessively complicated plot, for the main story is easily summarized. The offspring of Jacob in Egypt, now grown into large tribes, are oppressed by a new pharaoh. Moses demands their release in the name of Yahweh who afflicts the uncooperative Egyptians with a series of plagues. The Israelites go forth from Egypt, escape across a sea, and journey to a mountain where they behold an appearance of Yahweh, covenant with Yahweh, and receive Yahweh's laws. After apostasies, murmurings, and rebellions, both at Sinai and Kadesh, the people reach the verge of Canaan and partially settle in Transjordan. The great wealth of traditions, however, is marshaled around the basic plot in a profusion of embellishments and elaborations that include more or less complete subplots or type-scenes.

The sources J, E, and P, already isolated in the ancestor traditions (§15.1), continue into Exodus, Leviticus, and Numbers. There is, however, a radical shift in the relative proportions of the traditions assignable to each source. Therein lies much of the explanation for the complexity of the traditions. Whereas J accounted for 730 verses in the ancestor traditions, it is represented by only 435 verses in the Moses traditions. The E component decreases similarly from 336 verses to 188 verses. The dramatic difference is that P, with a mere 153 verses in Genesis 12—50, enlarges to 2444 verses in Exodus through Numbers: a fifteenfold increase! In addition, there is a body of *theophany, covenant,* and *law texts* in Exodus 19—24 and 32—34 which is clearly non-P but which cannot be assigned with confidence to J and E. The major reason for the inapplicability of the JE source divisions to the non-P Sinai traditions in Exodus 19—24, 32—34 is probably their derivation from liturgical program pieces in the covenant-renewal ceremonies and from a collection of customary law which have been joined and edited rather arbitrarily to fit their new narrative context. The Yahwist and Elohist may have had something to do with "writing up" part or all of these non-P Sinai texts, but the distinctive criteria of J and E do not appear with sufficient regularity in these chapters to make for critical consensus in assigning their different strands to the older pre-P sources.

Corresponding to the shift in the relative sizes of the three main sources is a distinct shift in literary types. In the ancestor traditions we noted that the great majority of the tradition units were sagas. This continues to be true of the diminished J and E sources in the Moses traditions, with the exception of a number of songs and oracles edited into J and E (table 11: nos. 21, 36, 43, 50, 52). *Sagas and poems* in J and E come to approximately 623 verses, to which may be added the 112 narratized verses of the non-P Sinai traditions and, generously estimated, about 364 narratized P verses. The total of narrative and song verses in Exodus through Numbers thus comes to approximately 1099 verses. By contrast, 1745 verses in P and 144 verses in the non-P Sinai traditions are devoted to *laws and regulations,* while another 333 P verses are *lists* concerned with tribal censuses, tribal arrangements for encampment and marching, land allotments and boundaries, and an itinerary of the people from Egypt to the plains of Moab. In all, 2222 verses in Exodus through Numbers are given to laws and lists, amounting to twice the quantity of sagas and poems recorded.

17.2 Complex Editing of the Moses Traditions

The saga clusters that carry the plot in the Moses traditions are concentrated in Exodus 1—24, 32—34, and resume more sporadically in Numbers 10—36. In the Exodus sagas, the people move out of Egyptian bondage and come to Sinai/Horeb for the revelation of Yahweh, the covenant making, and the lawgiving. In the Numbers sagas, the people move on from Sinai/Horeb to Kadesh and, after scouting Canaan, journey to its border in Transjordan. The mass of intervening traditions in P (Exodus 25—31, 35—40, the whole of Leviticus, and Numbers 1—9) consists of large groups or single units of religious laws given by Moses as an immense supplement to the mixture of non-P civil and religious laws presented more compactly in Exod. 20:22—23:19.

The non-P Sinai traditions are relatively brief and compact, but drastically and complexly edited. The lawgiving includes the so-called Ethical Decalogue (58)[1] and the Covenant Code (60) which have been sandwiched between an election proclamation (54) and a theophany (55–57) preceding and a theophany (62) and covenant-concluding ceremony (63) following.

---

1. The numbers in parentheses throughout this subsection are keyed to units or blocks of biblical traditions as enumerated in table 11.

TABLE 11
Tradition Units of Exodus, Leviticus, and Numbers
Distributed by Sources*

A. Yahwist (J) Traditions

PREPARATION OF MOSES

1. Oppression of Israel in Egypt	Exod.	1:8–12, 22
2. Birth of Moses		2:1–10
3. Moses flees to Midian		2:11–23a
4. Call of Moses and return to Egypt		3:2–4a, 5, 7–8, 16–22; 4:1–14, 19–20a, 22–23
5. Yahweh tries to kill Moses		4:24–26
6. Moses meets with Aaron and the people		4:27–31

PLAGUES

7. Moses requests freedom to worship in the wilderness/Pharaoh hardens oppression	5:1—6:1
8. Plague of water turned to blood	7:14–18, 20b, 21a, 23–24
9. Plague of frogs	7:25—8:4, 8–15
10. Plague of flies	8:20–32
11. Plague on cattle	9:1–7
12. Plague of hail	9:13–35
13. Plague of locusts	10:1–20
14. Plague of darkness	10:21–29
15. Announcement of final plague	11:1–8
16. Institution of Passover	12:21–23, 27b
17. Plague of death of the firstborn/ Pharaoh releases Israel	12:29–36

EXODUS/WILDERNESS TREK

18. Departure from Egypt	12:37–39; 13:20–22
19. Egyptians pursue the Israelites	14:5–7, 10–14
20. Israel crosses the sea	14:19b–20, 21b, 24–25, 27b, 30–31
21. Song at the sea	15:1–18
22. Israel at Marah and Elim	15:22–25a, 27
23. Provision of manna	16:4–5, 28–31, 35b–36
24. Water from the rock	17:2–7

[For possible J materials in Exodus 19—34, see subdivision C below in this table]

---

*See the note to table 10 for the basis of this source division.

A. Yahwist (J) Traditions (continued)	
25. Moses asks Hobab = Jethro to be Israel's desert guide	Num. 10:29–32
26. The portable ark	10:33–36
27. Scouts sent to Canaan	13:17b–20, 22–24, 27–33
28. Israel murmurs against Moses and Yahweh	14:1–4, 11–25
29. Unsuccessful attack on southern Canaan	14:39–45
30. Rebellion of Dathan and Abiram	16:1b, 2a, 12–15, 25–26, 27b–32a, 33–34
31. Edom refuses right of way to Israel	20:19–20, 22a
32. Battle of Hormah	21:1–3
33. Bronze serpent	21:4–9

PASSAGE THROUGH TRANSJORDAN

34. Israel's movements through Transjordan	21:10–20
35. Balak calls Balaam to curse Israel	22:3b–8, 13–19, 21–37, 39–40
36. Balaam's oracles	23:28; 24:2–25
37. Apostasy of Israel to Baal of Peor	25:1–5
38. Allotment of land in Transjordan	32:1, 16–19, 24, 33–42

B. Elohist (E) Traditions	

PREPARATION OF MOSES

39. Hebrew midwives	Exod. 1:15–21
40. Call of Moses/the name Yahweh	3:1, 4b, 6, 9–15
41. Moses returns to Egypt	4:15–18, 20b–21

EXODUS/WILDERNESS TREK

42. Israel departs Egypt with Joseph's bones	13:17–19
43. Song of Miriam	15:20–21
44. Victory over Amalekites	17:8–16
45. Reunion of Jethro and Moses/ appointment of Judges	18:1–27

[For possible E materials in Exodus 19—34, see subdivision C below in this table]

46. Israel's murmuring/Moses shares the Spirit with seventy Elders	Num. 11:1–35
47. Miriam's complaint and punishment	12:1–16
48. Water from the rock	20:1–13

B. Elohist (E) Traditions (continued)

PASSAGE THROUGH TRANSJORDAN

49. Edom refuses passage to Israel	Num. 20:14–18, 21
50. Victory over Sihon and Og	21:21–35
51. Balak calls Balaam to curse Israel	22:2–3a, 9–12, 20, 38
52. Balaam's oracles	22:41—23:27, 29–30;
	24:1

C. Sinai/Horeb Theophany, Covenant, and Law Traditions:
Composite JE and Special Source Materials

PREPARATION FOR COVENANT

53. Israel encamps at the mountain	Exod. 19:2b–3a
54. Election proclamation/covenant invitation	19:3b–6
55. Response of the people	19:7–9
56. Preparation of the people	19:10–15

THEOPHANY AND LAWGIVING

57. Theophany of Yahweh = Elohim	19:16–25; 20:18–21
58. The "Ethical" Decalogue	20:1–17
59. The fear of the people	20:18–21
60. The Covenant Code of laws	20:22—23:19
61. Instructions to possess Canaan	23:20–33
62. Theophany of Elohim (= Yahweh?)	
and meal	24:1–2, 9–11

COVENANT, APOSTASY, AND COVENANT RENEWAL

63. Sacrifice and covenant ceremony	24:3–8
64. Moses returns to the mountain	24:12–15
65. The golden calf	32:1–35
66. Assurance of Yahweh's presence	33:1–23
67. Covenant renewal	34:1–12, 27–28
68. The "Ritual" Decalogue	34:13–26

D. Priestly (P) Traditions

PREPARATION OF MOSES

69. Growth and oppression of Israel	Exod. 1:1–7, 13–14

TABLE 11 (continued)
Tradition Units of Exodus, Leviticus, and Numbers
Distributed by Sources

D. Priestly (P) Traditions (continued)

---

70. Israel's groaning	Exod.	2:23b–24
71. Call of Moses		6:2–13
72. House of Levi		6:14–27
73. Aaron as Moses' spokesman		6:28—7:7
74. Aaron's magic rod		7:8–13

PLAGUES

75. Plague of water turned to blood	7:19–20a, 21b, 22
76. Plague of frogs	8:5–7
77. Plague of gnats	8:16–19
78. Plague of boils	9:8–12
79. Pharaoh rejects Yahweh's wonders	11:9–10

PASSOVER, EXODUS, WILDERNESS TREK—EGYPT TO SINAI

80. Institution of Passover	12:1–20, 24–27a, 28
81. The exodus	12:40–42
82. Passover supplement	12:43–51
83. Israel crosses the sea	14:1–4, 8–9, 15–18, 21a,c, 22–23, 26, 27a, 28–29; 15:19
84. Quails and manna	16:1–3, 6–27, 32–35a
85. Israel's movements in the wilderness	17:1; 19:1–2a

RITUAL LAWS/TRIBAL ARRANGEMENTS AT SINAI

86. Cultic instructions	24:15—31:18
A. Introduction	24:15—25:9
B. Ark	25:10–22
C. Table	25:23–30
D. Lampstand	25:31–40
E. Tabernacle = tent of meeting	26:1–37
F. Altar and court	27:1–21
G. Priests' garments	28:1–43
H. Installation of priests	29:1–46
I. Altar of incense	30:1–10
J. Atonement tax	30:11–16
K. Water basin	30:17–21
L. Anointing oil	30:22–33
M. Incense	30:34–38
N. Artisans	31:1–11
O. Sabbath observance	31:12–17

D. Priestly (P) Traditions (continued)

87. Detailed execution of the cultic
    instructions in no. 86   Exod. 35:1—39:43
88. Erection of the tabernacle   40:1–38
89. Instructions about sacrifices   Lev.   1:1—7:38
    A. Burnt offerings   1:1–17
    B. Cereal offerings   2:1–16
    C. Peace offerings   3:1–17
    D. Sin offerings   4:1—5:13
    E. Guilt offerings   5:14—6:7
    F. Instructions to the priests   6:8—7:38
90. Consecration of the priests   8:1—10:20
    A. Installation of Aaron and his sons   8:1–36
    B. Aaron offers sacrifices   9:1–24
    C. Nadab and Abihu destroyed by "unholy" fire   10:1–20
91. Instructions on clean and unclean dietary
    and bodily conditions   11:1—15:32
    A. Clean and unclean animals   11:1–47
    B. Purification after childbirth   12:1–8
    C. Clean and unclean skin diseases   13:1–59
    D. Purification of a healed leper   14:1–54
    E. Unclean bodily discharges   15:1–32
92. Day of atonement ceremony   16:1–34
93. The Holiness Code of Laws (H)   17:1—26:46
    A. Proper slaughter of animals   17:1–16
    B. Forbidden sexual relations/marriages   18:1–18
    C. Assorted laws for a life of holiness   18:19—20:27
    D. Instructions to priests to preserve
       holiness   21:1—22:33
    E. Calendar of religious festivals   23:1–44
    F. Care of the tabernacle and equality
       before the laws of natives and
       sojourners   24:1–23
    G. Sabbatical year and jubilee year   25:1–55
    H. Consequences of obedience and
       disobedience to the laws   26:1–46
94. Religious votive gifts   27:1–34
95. Census of the tribes   Num.   1:1–54
96. Arrangement of the tribes in
    encampment   2:1–34

TABLE 11 (continued)

**Tradition Units of Exodus, Leviticus, and Numbers
Distributed by Sources**

D. Priestly (P) Traditions (continued)

---

97. Levites set apart as priests	Num.	3:1–51
98. Census of Levites		4:1–49
99. Instructions about judging a charge of adultery and Nazirite vows		5:1—6:21
100. A priestly blessing on Israel		6:22–27
101. Offerings from tribal leaders for the services of the tabernacle		7:1–89
102. Setting up the lampstand		8:1–4
103. Consecration of the Levites		8:5–26
104. Preparations for departure from Sinai		9:1—10:1

WILDERNESS TREK—SINAI TO MOAB

105. Israel on the march from Sinai toward Canaan	10:11–28
106. Scouts sent to Canaan	13:1–17a, 21, 25–26
107. Israel murmurs/refuses to enter Canaan and is condemned to perish in the wilderness	14:5–10, 26–38
108. Admonitions/warnings to observe the laws	15:1–41
109. Rebellion of Korah	16:1a, 2b–11, 16–24, 27a, 32b, 35–50
110. Duties of Aaronic priests and Levites	18:1–32
111. Water for impurity to remove defilement by a corpse	19:1–22
112. Death of Aaron on Mt. Hor	20:22b–29
113. Apostasy in Moab, Phinehas, the Aaronid priests	25:6–18
114. Second census of the tribes	26:1–65
115. Inheritance of property by women	27:1–11
116. Commissioning of Joshua	27:12–23
117. Schedule of offerings at appointed feasts	28:1—29:40
118. Fulfillment of vows	30:1–16
119. Holy war against Midianites	31:1–54
120. Allotment of land in Transjordan	32:2–15, 20–23, 25–32
121. Israel's itinerary from Egypt to Moab	33:1–49
122. Boundaries of the land to be allotted	34:1–29
123. Levitical cities and cities of refuge	35:1–34
124. Heiresses must marry within their tribes	36:1–13

Diverse sources are clearly distinguishable in the theophanic and covenant-making traditions of Exodus 19 and 24, but whether the sources are continuous between the two chapters is problematic. The covenant ceremony of 24:3–8, regarded by many scholars as E, provides one of the few connecting links in these chapters, since it refers back to the Decalogue as "the words of Yahweh" and to the Covenant Code as "the ordinances/customary laws" (v. 3) and envisions them both combined in "the book of the covenant" (v. 7).

At this point in Exodus begins the vast P excursus of instructions on building the tabernacle (86–88), offering sacrifices (89), consecrating the priesthood (90), clean and unclean dietary and bodily conditions (91), day of atonement ceremony (92), the so-called Holiness Code (93), and an assortment of laws, regulations, and lists that continue, intermixed with narratives, as the Israelites move on from Sinai to Kadesh and thence to Canaan.

A literary convention of repetition or reiteration, characteristic of folk and epic styles of narration, is especially evident in P's way of presenting the laws. A noteworthy instance occurs when the tabernacle is twice described in laborious detail—once as a set of instructions to Moses (Exodus 25—31) and a second time as the plans are executed and the tabernacle is assembled (Exodus 35—39). This reiteration of the tabernacle laws has afforded an editor the opportunity to try to bind together the disparate Sinai traditions. Between the two recitations of the tabernacle design chaps. 32—34, more properly related to Exodus 19—24, have been inserted. They tell of the Israelites' worship of the golden calf and their severe punishment. Moses in anger breaks the tables of the law, which according to 31:18 contained the verbose tabernacle instructions. When the tablets are reinscribed, however, they are said to contain the so-called Ritual Decalogue, regarded by many critics as J material, having mainly to do with sacrifices and feasts and entirely oblivious of the tabernacle and of the previous Decalogue in Exod. 20:1–17 (cf. 34:1, 4, 28). The P supplement of laws and regulations then resumes the account interrupted by chaps. 32—34 and continues uninterrupted to Numbers 10.

By means of such arbitrary and context-ignoring editorial maneuvers, the stay of Israel at Sinai/Horeb is made to accommodate differing sets of traditions about covenant and lawgiving, including sizable complexes of laws, that are juxtaposed or interlocked, both within the non-P Sinai traditions and between P and non-P traditions. The splicing of the golden calf incident and the remaking of the covenant into the P tabernacle laws has had a double effect: (1) on the one hand, it dovetails the P legal supplement (Exodus 25—31, 35—40; Leviticus; Numbers 1—9) with more narratized Sinai materials (Exodus 32—34), thereby asserting the necessary coexistence of two different types of traditions; and (2) on the other hand, by reporting the golden calf apostasy that causes Moses to smash the tablets, it provides an occasion to give yet another version of Sinai laws in 34:13-26 that varies not only from P but also from the non-P legal traditions in Exodus 20—23. The need to mass all these various traditions strategically at Sinai/Horeb has definitely taken precedence over any concern to present an intelligible narrative course of events.

In spite of all the effort to constellate Israel's law around the Sinai revelation, not quite all the supplemental P law managed to get—or to stay—connected to Sinai. Even after the Israelites moved on to Kadesh and thence to the Plains of Moab, they still receive legal instructions, although none of the post-Sinai units of law is nearly as lengthy as the Sinai-attached supplements. This disintegration of the symmetry of the Sinai lawgiving traditions may result from an editor trying to take into account independent traditions that connected lawgiving with Kadesh rather than Sinai. The result was an editorial compromise that placed *most* of the laws at Sinai but allowed *some* of the laws to trail along at Kadesh and the plains of Moab. The literary structure of Numbers 10—36 intersplices JE narratives and P laws to describe the movement from Sinai to Canaan.

Interestingly, the Book of Deuteronomy, yet another recitation of the laws of Moses, understands that Moses reviewed the Sinai/Horeb laws by reciting them once again (and perhaps adding to them? Cf. Deut. 29:1) in Moab beyond the Jordan River just before his death. Since the covenant texts of Exodus 19—24, 32—34, and of Deuteronomy contain many signs of having originated in periodic covenant-renewal ceremonies—observed more or less continuously from tribal times at least down to the exile—the confusing editorial practice of distributing laws not only to Sinai, but also to Kadesh and Moab, may be a literary attempt to assert the ever-renewed relevance of covenant and law that cannot be confined to any one time and place. Though given first at Sinai/Horeb, the covenant and law journey on with Israel through time and space.

In sum, we can say that onto the narrative frame of the themes about deliverance from Egypt, wilderness wandering, and theophany, covenant, and lawgiving at a sacred mountain, there has been grafted a large and complicated body of laws, some of them pre-P in origin, although the majority are sizable blocks and single units provided by P. It is on the strength of this profusion of laws connected with Sinai (and secondarily with Kadesh and Moab) that Genesis through Deuteronomy was eventually called Torah (= instruction/teaching/law [§11.2.a]). In actuality, the formal structure throughout Exodus, Leviticus, and Numbers, just as in Genesis, is a narrative structure, since all the laws are presented as laws given by Moses and relayed by him to Israel while the people camped at Sinai/Horeb (or later at Kadesh and in Moab). The laws and regulations have been so superficially narratized, however, that there is no longer a coherent saga chain or saga cycle account of what took place at Sinai and Kadesh. Later Israelite covenant and law concerns have overwhelmed the saga form and made it virtually impossible for historical-critical method to penetrate the thicket of traditions to ascertain what thirteenth-century events may underlie them.

18
HISTORICAL-CRITICAL APPROACHES TO THE MOSES TRADITIONS

18.1 The Egyptian Context

A primary approach of historical-critical method to the Moses traditions has been to attempt to contextualize them within our considerable wealth of knowledge about ancient Egypt. In fact, it is chiefly the weight of the Egyptian evidence that has inclined most scholars to prefer a thirteenth-century date for Israel's exodus from Egypt rather than the fifteenth-century date prescribed by the questionable biblical chronology (§16.1).

On initial examination, a fifteenth-century setting for the departure from Egypt seemed plausible, with Thutmosis III (ca. 1468–1436) as the likely pharaoh of the exodus. The Eighteenth Dynasty, which had expelled the Hyksos from Egypt, presumably had a great distaste for Asiatics and thus bore down heavily on their Hebrew slaves. Thus, both Joseph's favor with a Hyksos pharaoh and the subsequent Eighteenth Dynasty revulsion against Asiatic Israelites seemed to be appropriate correlations of the biblical and Egyptian evidence. Moreover, references in the Amarna letters to ʿapiru (= Hebrews) actively disrupting Canaanite city-states in the period ca. 1425–1350 were often explained as the activities of Israelites in their early attempts to conquer Canaan. Nevertheless, many scholars recognized that the Hyksos and ʿapiru data did not correlate in most respects with the biblical traditions. Joseph and his family neither appear as conquerors of Egypt or as cultural equals or kin of the ruling-class Egyptians. Likewise, the names, distributions, and tactics of the Amarna age ʿapiru do not correspond with the reports of Israelite conquest in Joshua and Judges.

Increasingly the circumstances depicted in the Moses traditions were judged to accord best with a thirteenth-century setting, with Rameses II (1290–1224) serving as the likely pharaoh of the exodus. The Israelites are shown as living and working in the vicinity of the Egyptian capital. In the fifteenth century the capital was far up the Nile at Thebes, whereas by the thirteenth century the Nineteenth Dynasty had established Avaris in the western delta, renamed Raamses, as its capital. Extensive building projects were launched to strengthen Raamses and surrounding cities as a base for Egyptian military campaigns into Canaan and Syria. The Israelites as forced laborers in the Delta store cities of Raamses and Pithom (Exod. 1:11) fit suitably into the known circumstances of the time but not into the fifteenth century. It has also been claimed that there was a dramatic increase of Asiatics in Egypt under the Nineteenth Dynasty and thus an increased drafting of Asiatic slave labor.

Opinion differs on whether the exodus occurred earlier or later in the thirteenth century, influenced in each case by the weight given to attending lines of evidence. Archaeological evidence of the destruction of some Canaanite cities ca. 1230–1200 and Pharaoh Merneptah's victory stela that speaks of defeating "Israel" in Canaan ca. 1220 may be construed to indicate that the Israelites who left Egypt were already in place within Canaan by the last quarter of the thirteenth century. If forty years of wandering in the wilderness are allowed them, they would have had to leave Egypt in the first third of the thirteenth century. It is far from demonstrated, however, that the destruction of Canaanite cities is attributable to exodus Israelites, or indeed to any Israelites, or that the Israel whom Merneptah attacked was composed of those who had recently been in Egypt.

Those who incline to place the exodus toward the end of the thirteenth century stress that a later date is mandated in order to give time for the Moabites and Edomites to be well established in Transjordan prior to Israel's encounters with them. Also, it is argued that the forty-year wandering is only a symbolic round number for a generation and thus the time in the wilderness might have been very much shorter. One scholar, impressed by the ancient testimony of the Song at the Sea, believes that the exodus took place under Rameses III (ca. 1176–1145), because not until the first half of the twelfth century were Philistines, Edomites, Moabites, and Canaanites coexistent in Canaan (Exod. 15:14–15).

Although a thirteenth-century date for the exodus contradicts the literal chronology of the later pentateuchal sources, it seems to accord best with the biblical data taken as a whole. In fact, the DH and P chronologies may rest upon an ancient scheme that reckoned one generation as forty years.

The 480 years of 1 Kings 6:1 in that case would stand for twelve generations which, more accurately calculated at twenty-five years per generation, would yield 300 years and thus a thirteenth-century exodus. Also, there are genealogical references in the Bible that tend to shorten the lapsed time between the descent into Egypt and the exodus (Num. 32:10 lists the grandson of Joseph as a contemporary of Moses) and between the exodus and the judges (Judges 18:30 has the grandson of Moses as the founder of a priestly line at Dan). Of course this evidence is qualified by a well-known tendency of genealogies to drop unimportant intervening generations.

In sum, historical-critical assessment of the Moses traditions against the backdrop of ancient Egypt has suggested a probable thirteenth-century setting for the exodus. The evidence is complexly woven and must take into account the whole chain of traditional events from the descent into Egypt to the settlement in Canaan. It is important to realize that this inquiry does not demonstrate when the exodus took place or even that it occurred at all. The reasoning involved assumes that there *is*—or posits that there *might be*—a historical core to the Moses traditions, but there is no biblical or extrabiblical evidence that has been able to establish fixed and reasonably certain historical correlations between the biblical text and external records. What we are given is the useful but hypothetical formulation: *if* some elements of the Moses traditions are taken to be historically attached, *then* they best fit into the Egyptian and Canaanite milieus *at this time* and *in this way*.

Cautions about the essentially undatable character of the Egyptian milieu of the exodus are appropriately sounded from time to time. Of late these cautions have taken on particular cogency with the burgeoning interest in new literary and sociological paradigms of biblical study which tend to accept the frustration of meager historical information more readily than historical-critical method. It is noted that the pharaohs are unnamed in the Joseph and Moses traditions, that Asiatics and even ʿapiru captives and slaves are referred to over several centuries in Egypt, that Egyptian names were given to people living in Canaan, and that even the store cities of Raamses and Pithom are mentioned down to as late as the fifth century. In other words, nothing in the biblical traditions points unequivocally to the thirteenth century, and only the thirteenth century, as the time of the exodus. Some go so far as to question that the Egyptian milieu of the Moses traditions is historically grounded, since it could very well be a deliberate literary creation by traditionists possessing a general familiarity with Egyptian life. That radical doubt raises the question: If Moses and at least some Israelites were never in Egypt, why has tradition claimed that they were?

18.2 Moses: Formative Influences and Leadership Roles

Moses is presented as a deliverer of his people from bondage who also led them through the first phases of their new life of freedom. All of our information about him comes from narrative literature of a history-like quality that stops short of being actual historiography. We shall focus later in this chapter on an assessment of the motifs and type-scenes (or traditional episodes) which structure and communicate the work and meaning of the man. For the moment we take note of attempts to look within the traditions for signs of a reliable outline of his career and how he might have been concretely rooted in his time and place.

From among the history-like accounts of Moses it is possible to extract a plot line that exhibits unity of action and causal connections. For example, his life could be described in capsule form as follows: Moses was born to Israelite parents in Egyptian slavery, and bore an Egyptian name, as did several other Israelites in the period (e.g., Hophni, Phinehas, Merari). After unsuccessful efforts to alleviate the affliction of his people in their slavery, he fled into Sinai/Midian, married into the priestly family of Jethro, and returned to lead his people out of Egypt. In the wilderness he struggled to organize the community by means of religious covenant and law, and he led them to the verge of Canaan where he died. This is not much information for reconstructing anyone's life, and critical analysts of the Moses tradition would question the strength of the evidence for a number of elements in this skeletal reconstruction.

The preceding sketch of the life of Moses, or any of a number of other possible versions, is actually no more than an abstraction from the rich saga-related account of Moses as the immediate hero through whom the invisible, ultimate divine hero Yahweh works. Every attempt to discern the historical Moses, like every attempt to locate the historical bondage and exodus of the people, inevitably requires a critical abstraction that has to struggle against the historiographic resistance of the saga form of literature. Nonetheless, historical-critical method has undertaken just such a struggle by vigorously exploring all imaginable possibilities, if only to be able to say that some reconstructions of the historical Moses are more probable than others. Unfortunately, the results of the inquiry, beyond the probability that a historical person does lie behind the traditions, have won no consensus among historians, because every posited "historical Moses" has relied upon questionable and arbitrary dependence on the traditions or has taken flight into unverifiable conjecture.

If we grant that an actual leader of some group that became a part of

Israel is referred to in these traditions, how might he be conceived in his historical environment? Of course, even in exploring some of the most favored ways of approaching that question, we are inevitably caught in a measure of circular reasoning because the very traditions we want to assess constitute the greater part of the evidence we have to work with. Granted this limitation, however, we may at least try to formulate hypotheses for which there is some possibility of external support.

One element in the traditions claims that Moses was brought up in the Egyptian court, and this may be lent some credence by the fact that his name, meaning "son," is Egyptian. Even if the specifically asserted court connection of Moses is an embellishment of saga, the tradition may point to his advantaged exposure to Egyptian culture and learning, giving him bicultural knowledge and facility as an Egyptian and as an Israelite. In this regard, the monotheistic religion of Pharaoh Akhenaton (ca. 1364–1347) is thought by some to have been an influence on the religious views of Moses. No indications of Moses' dependence on Akhenaton's reforms appear in the Bible or in Egyptian history. Given the reality that Akhenaton's religion was the sole worship of the sun and that it was mediated through his royal person, it was to all appearances markedly different from what tradition tells us about the religion of Moses. Of course, if Moses had some immersion in "high" Egyptian culture, it is conceivable that he knew of the religious reforms that had occurred in fourteenth-century Egypt. It is even imaginable that the Pharaoh's forceful advocacy of a new religion was a source of encouragement to Moses. In terms of the content or the sociopolitical structure of the two religions, however, there is no recognizable bridge between Atonism and the Yahwism attributed to Moses.

Another proposal is that Moses learned about the religion of Yahweh from the traditions of his own people. This notion has taken a number of different forms depending on one or another fancied occurrence of the name Yahweh outside the Bible. Recently, for example, it has been proposed that the Israelites were from that larger body of Asiatics identified in Egyptian texts as Shosu, often explained as "bedouins/nomads" but more correctly understood as "plunderers." Egyptian records from the fourteenth/thirteenth centuries contain references to "the Shosu land Yahweh," which seems to have been in central Syria (although some connect it with Edom). This place name, however, has no demonstrated connection with a deity, and thus carries no more attestation to a pre-Israelite belief in Yahweh than do Amorite personal names of the form *Yahwi-ilu* (which means not "Yahweh is God" but "the god creates/produces" or "may the god create/produce"). A similar reservation must be entered concerning the alleged occurrence of the shortened divine name "Ya" in proper names mentioned in the Ebla texts.

The most substantial notion of formative influence on Moses depends on a particular reading of the biblical evidence. It is contended that Moses derived his belief in Yahweh, along with many cultic and legal practices, from his Midianite father-in-law. Jethro is called "priest of Midian" and joins (presides at?) a feast with the Israelites as they celebrate the deliverance from Egypt (Exodus 18). Kenites/Rechabites, who appear to have been a subgroup of Midianites, lived among the Israelites in Canaan and were ardent devotees of Yahweh (Judges 1:16; 4:11; 1 Sam. 15:6–7; 2 Kings 10:15–27; Jer. 35:1–11). Some of the advocates of the so-called Kenite hypothesis of Yahwistic origins have contended that the voluntary adoption of a new deity by Moses and Israel contributed the element of radical ethical choice to Israelite religion, but, judging by other known group conversions to a new faith, this seems to be an arbitrary and excessive claim.

New support for the Midianite/Kenite origins of Yahwism has been claimed on the basis of the discovery of a shrine at copper mines in the Arabah, some distance north of the Gulf of Eilat in Midianite territory. When the mines were worked by Egyptians, the shrine was dedicated to the goddess Hathor. After about 1150, when the Egyptians abandoned the site, the Hathor cult symbols were discarded and a tent shrine was introduced in company with a gilded copper snake image. Possibly this points to Midianites who continued a type of worship employing a tent shrine (cf. the tabernacle or tent of meeting in Exodus and Numbers) and a bronze serpent (Num. 21:8–9; 2 Kings 24:8), cult regalia which they had already contributed to the Israelites under Moses. Of course the opposite explanation is not impossible, namely, that Moses introduced Yahwism to the Midianites.

Even if we posit that Moses was generally informed and equipped for his work by acculturation to Egypt and that he derived all or part of his religious beliefs and practices from Midianites, regrettably we are not able to make the most of such possibilities in the absence of an otherwise solid account of his life. Moreover, we do not know which elements of Egyptian culture might have influenced him most, nor do we have information about how Yahwism might have been practiced by the Midianites, other than the ambiguous Timna shrine remains.

In turning to the leadership roles credited to Moses, it is astonishing how numerous his functions are said to have been. He was negotiator with Pharaoh, miracle worker by a magical rod, logistics expert in leading the exodus and wilderness trek, covenant mediator between Yahweh and Israel, lawgiver to the community, military commander in chief against Amalek and Midian, appointer and installer of priests, judge of disputes among the people, and a prophet—indeed more than a prophet—in the directness of his communication with God. Kingship is the one function not assigned to Moses, yet as "all-purpose" leader he exercised comprehensive authority over the tribes analogous to the authority of a king over a monarchic state. His authority in various roles was sometimes shared or delegated for the occasion or in perpetuity, notably in the case of priestly office.

How Moses is to exercise supreme leadership, while distributing the workload and drawing others into positions of delegated authority, is an issue that runs through the traditions both as the sine qua non of Israel's birth and survival and as the source of continual unrest and bitter power struggles. A careful reading of the traditions about priesthood throughout the Bible makes it abundantly clear that rival priestly groups throughout Israel's history sought to trace their pedigrees back to a commissioning by Moses, Samuel, or David (§48). The exaltation of Aaron in the P traditions is underscored by the foolish endeavor of the Levite Korah and his co-conspirators to seize some of Aaron's authority (table 11: no. 109), and the high-risk obligations of Aaron's office are highlighted by the deaths of his sons Nadab and Abihu when they offer improper sacrifice (table 11: no. 90C). In J, E, and non-P Sinai traditions, however, Aaron lacks the sole priestly prerogative and is both severely chided for making the golden calf (table 11: no. 65) and less directly criticized for supporting Miriam's complaints against Moses (table 11: no. 47).

Besides the general murmuring and complaints of the people against Moses for deepening their oppression under Pharaoh and for leading them into a hostile wilderness, there are frequent open references and more guarded allusions to factionalism and uprisings in the community. The golden calf apostasy is put down by armed Levites. Miriam, with Aaron's complicity at least, objects to Moses' behavior in monopolizing leadership. Dathan and Abiram protest that Moses has made himself "a prince" over Israel (an incident intertwined with Korah's rebellion). All the scouts, except Joshua and Caleb, recoil from an attack on Canaan in spite of Moses' encouragement, but a little later attempt the attack after Moses has forbidden it. "The chiefs of the people" are implicated in an apostasy to Baal of Peor. Execution, plague, skin disease, and swallowing up by the underworld are fates reserved for the rebels in these instances. On the other hand, Moses accepts advice to spread the task of judging the people among a sizable staff of judges. On another occasion "the spirit of prophecy" which had rested peculiarly on Moses was shared with seventy elders in order to help him "bear the burden of the people," and the same spirit is magnanimously recognized by Moses in the case of two laggard elders who had ignored his earlier instructions.

No doubt many of the Moses traditions about his leadership are intended to legitimate certain offices and functions in later Israel. There is no reason, for example, to think that Israel knew of prophets in the community prior to the time of Samuel. The question as to whether Moses was himself a covenant mediator and lawgiver is complicated by the fact that the covenant and law traditions show clear evidence of rising from later Israelite assemblies called to renew the covenant and recite the law. There is a strong case to be made for the likelihood that an office of covenant mediator was occupied by cult personnel who took the role of reciting the covenant formulas and the law stipulations during the renewal ceremonies. Such a hypothesis helps to explain the hortatory and sermonic addresses that surround the laws in the Book of Deuteronomy (§37.3).

In the end, therefore, there is no consistently principled way of knowing which leadership roles, and which aspects of those roles, actually were performed by the real Moses, in contrast to those that have been attributed to him as a way of validating later Israelite forms of communal leadership. There obviously is a tremendous "overload" of leadership roles heaped on Moses, and yet it is well recognized that major leaders in tribal social organization often do exercise broad and fluid leadership powers. Likewise, the pervasive theme of obstinate rebellion against Moses was a convenient way to stigmatize various kinds of dissenters against subsequent Israelite leaders who invoked Moses' authority. On the other hand, it is not at all surprising that early Israel, venturing into new forms of social organization, should have been torn repeatedly by internal strife and rival leadership. It has been suggested plausibly, although without conclusive evidence, that Moses failed to enter Canaan because he was murdered in one of the uprisings against his command.

18.3 Unity of Action in Exodus and Wandering

On the assumption that the Moses traditions record a more or less unified and continuous movement of people from Egypt to Canaan, there have been many attempts to reconstruct the route of march and particularly to identify the exact locations of the crossing of the sea and the mountain of covenant making and lawgiving. Numbers 33 presents a complete itinerary of the people from Egypt to the verge of Canaan, attributable to the P source. It has been suggested that this was an ancient Israelite pilgrim route that shows how preexilic Israelites understood the terrain and the route of march. It can be just as readily understood, however, as a learned summary of scattered traditional data by a late compiler. Only the cities of Raamses and Pithom at the start of the journey, Kadesh and Ezion-geber in the wilderness, and Moabite sites at the end of the itinerary have been identified with any degree of certainty. The location of the critically important sea and mountain are simply unknown.

In the past there was a general consensus that the crossing of the sea occurred at the northern extremity of the Red Sea in the Gulf of Suez. Taking account of the fact that the Bible speaks of the "Sea of Reeds" (not Red Sea) and that the Gulf of Suez would have been a very exposed route for escaping from the Delta region, alternative crossing sites have been proposed. Some of these lie about midway between the Gulf of Suez and the Mediterranean Sea in the vicinity of Lake Timsah and the Bitter Lakes. Others are placed closer to the Mediterranean at Lake Menzaleh or Lake Sirbonis.

According to a tradition that goes back to the fifth Christian century, Mt. Sinai/Horeb has been identified as Jebel Musa in the southern Sinai Peninsula. It is an impressive upthrust of granite, the sort of place where the holy mountain "ought" to have been, but pilgrim piety has a fertile imagination and we have no way of knowing if the early Christian sense of the site rested on anything more solid than the impressiveness of the mountain. Historians who doubt that the sacred mountain could have been as distant as Jebel Musa is from the main wilderness encampment at Kadesh have argued for one or another of several less-spectacular mountains in northeast Sinai or in the Arabah. Still others, believing that the description of the theophany of Yahweh shows the mountain to have been volcanic and probably also within Midianite territory, have favored a location east of the Gulf of Aqabah. Independent verification of these various sitings of the mountain is unobtainable.

As to the events at the sea, historians frequently single out a J reference to the action of Yahweh who "drove the sea back by a strong east wind all night" (Exod. 14:21). This can be understood as a storm-driven and tide-related recession of coastal waters, allowing passage of the Israelites, followed by a sudden return of the waters that engulfed the Egyptians. A variant of this view proposes that the receding waters exposed sandbars that people on foot could cross but on which horses and chariots would become bogged. The J-based reconstructions are more "natural" than P's account of deep waters that were split to form a land bridge through the heart of the sea (Exod. 14:22). A third conception of what occurred at the sea infers from the poetic description of the Song at the Sea (Exod. 15:4–10) that the Egyptians pursued the Israelites in boats that capsized from a violent storm. In spite of intense efforts to reconstruct the crossing of the sea, our evidence is far too scanty to do more than guess as to how natural and historical elements were combined in the events that underlie the biblical traditions.

The dominant line of interpretation, beginning with later biblical writers, has identified the crossing of the sea as the nucleus of the exodus. There is, however, another tradition, perhaps more ancient, which speaks of the Israelites despoiling or plundering the Egyptians (Exod. 3:21–22; 11:2–3a; 12:35–36; Ps. 105:37). This tradition pictures the Israelites escaping from Egypt by stealth with spoil taken from their captors. As the text now stands, the plundering of the Egyptians is subordinated to the crossing of the sea. The breakdown of negotiations between Pharaoh and Moses in Exod. 10:28–29 (prior to the final plague), however, may once have provided the background for the secret flight of the Israelites, which in turn might better explain the frantic pursuit by the Egyptians. The incongruity of "asking" the Egyptians for treasures that are to be forcibly taken from them is probably an allusion to proper decorum toward superiors, introduced by the narrator with a wry and mocking sense of humor.

In other words, there may once have existed an independent alternative version of the *means* of exodus: not a sea crossing but a clandestine flight with stolen goods. Interpreters who insist that the sea crossing must rest on some actual experience, however irrecoverable to our view, not only overlook the option of a secret flight but also take little account of the possibility that the theme of the sea as a cosmic force of chaos and death may have been used to heighten the significance of the exodus. It has also been proposed that the experiences of more than one group of escapees from Egypt have been combined in the biblical traditions, in which case the secret flight and the crossing of the sea should be associated with two separate exoduses.

We have observed that the complex editing of the Moses traditions has greatly confused the unity of action that ever-so-tenuously holds together the immense body of traditions (§17.2). This is evident in trying to visualize the movement of the people in the wilderness and, in particular, in attempting to establish the relationship between Sinai and Kadesh. In the present form of the traditions, Israel goes from Egypt to the mountain at Sinai/Horeb, covenants and receives the law, and then moves on to Kadesh, from which Canaan is scouted and from which the final approach to the land via a Transjordanian detour is eventually undertaken. It is evident that the itinerary in the wilderness is presented in a very fragmentary and discrepant manner which the final editing does not succeed in overcoming. In fact, the traditions contain hints that Sinai and Kadesh were close together. Particularly striking is the fact that a series of incidents and themes *first* placed between Egypt and Sinai (Exodus 16—18) are *repeated* at Kadesh (Numbers 10—20):

1. Moses consults with Jethro (Exod. 18:13–27; Num. 10:29–32);
2. The people murmur against Yahweh and Moses (Exod. 16:1–12; 17:1–7; Num. 11:1–6; 14:1–3, 26–38; 16:41; 17:11);
3. Quails are provided for food (Exod. 16:13; Num. 11:31–35);
4. Water is provided from a rock at Meribah (Exod. 17:1–7; Num. 20:2–13).

It is thus completely clear that the great blocks of Sinai materials in Exodus 19 through Numbers 10 have intentionally disrupted the original unity of the sagas in Exodus 16—18 and Numbers 10—20. This in turn strongly implies that in an earlier stage of the traditions the sagas of Exodus 16—18 and Numbers 10—20 belonged to the same geographical horizon at Kadesh. The later insertion of the Sinai traditions has made it appear that Sinai was a great distance from Kadesh and has displaced some of the originally Kadesh-oriented traditions to points on the route from Egypt to Sinai. In short, the great cultic and theological significance attached to covenant making and lawgiving has been expressed structurally in the final state of the Moses traditions by sharply separating Sinai geographically from the rest of the wilderness sites, making it a mysteriously remote mountain.

Kadesh is identifiable as ʿAin el-Qudeirat, a copious spring permitting limited agriculture, located approximately fifty miles southwest of Beersheba on the southern fringe of Canaan. Two nearby springs, although less abundant, add to the available water supply (ʿAin Qoseimah and ʿAin Qedeis, the latter retaining the name of Kadesh). These together are capable of supporting several hundreds or thousands of people for an extended period of time. If there is any single discernible unity of action beneath the wilderness accounts, it is that the Israelites moved directly from Egypt to Kadesh (as reported in Judges 11:16). Any covenant making and lawgiving that occurred in the wilderness would thus have taken place at or near Kadesh. It has been suggested that the alternative name of En-mishpat ("well of judgment") for Kadesh, reported in Gen. 14:7, retains a memory of Moses' judgment of the people (Exod. 18:13–27), or possibly even of lawgiving at Kadesh rather than at a distant Sinai. The Meribah of Exod.

17:7, connected with Kadesh in Num. 20:1, 13, is more explicitly called Meribath-kadesh by Ezekiel (47:19; 48:28).

Consequently, one way of resolving the problem of the unity of action behind the Moses traditions is to suppose that all the wilderness events took place at or near Kadesh, including the covenant making and lawgiving that was later transferred to far-off Sinai. An alternative way of perceiving the underlying events is to detach the nuclear theme of the exodus from the Kadesh traditions altogether and to presuppose that the Kadesh traditions originally had nothing to do with Israelites who had been in Egypt but rather with a different group of Israelites who went on to enter Canaan from the south rather than through Transjordan. In this way the experiences of at least two groups (a Sinai group and a Kadesh group) are discernible behind the enforced unity of the wilderness traditions as edited. This hypothesis raises the question of how one or both of the Sinai and Kadesh groups were related to Israelites who escaped from Egypt, whether by a crossing of the sea or by secretive flight.

It is likely that such analysis and speculation will appear to many Bible readers as hairsplitting or nit-picking. It certainly is true that none of the historical-critical reconstructions of the actual unity of action beneath the compiled traditions is conclusive or complete. The primary point is that the critical reconstructions are inconclusive and incomplete precisely because the biblical traditions are inconclusive and incomplete on the historical plane. If any serious effort is made to visualize concretely the sequences of events alluded to in the Moses traditions, then a speculative reconstruction is inescapable. In the biblical traditions we can only observe how Israelites at various later points in time conceived the course of events and in what locales they placed them. Each of those later perspectives has been incorporated in a literary complex that demands to be historically decomposed and recomposed. Because the biblical evidence is historically so fragmentary and indirect, and because the extrabiblical sources of information are so general that they do not engage the biblical traditions head-on, historical inquiry must rest content with a very incomplete picture that can only be filled in if further extrabiblical evidence comes to light.

19
RELIGION OF MOSES AND THE EXODUS-WILDERNESS ISRAELITES

The effort to ascertain the religious concepts and practices of the actors in the Moses traditions runs up against the same problem faced by all historical-critical research into this early horizon of Israel's experience. The essential problem is to isolate the religious elements that are credible within the imperfectly known historical context of Moses from the religious elements that later traditionists have intermixed in their retelling, rewriting, and reediting of the traditions. Realistically, we have to settle for an approximation to the religion of the historical Moses. Since there are so many indeterminate factors in the recovery of the historical circumstances attending the work of Moses and the exodus-wilderness group or groups, the reconstruction of their religious faith must be similarly tentative and open-ended. Instead of thinking that we are delving into the original historical core of the religion of Moses and his people, we are wiser to accept that we are sketching how the religion of Moses was remembered and conveyed in traditions that arose among the intertribal Israelites in Canaan during the generations after his death.

19.1 Covenant

Israelite tradition identifies Moses as the one who first brought the whole people into covenant with Yahweh, as distinguished from the anticipatory covenants made earlier with the individual ancestors Abraham, Isaac, and Jacob. "Covenant" is an awkward and somewhat misleading term for the Hebrew word *b^{e}rīth* which refers to a formal, solemn, and binding agreement between parties in which there are obligations to do certain acts, or to refrain from doing them, and there are promises or threats of consequences that will follow on fulfillment or breach of the obligations. The English word "covenant" is now so archaic, or used in such specialized legal or sentimental contexts, as to be very inadequate. Yet no other term fully grasps the meaning, although aspects of *b^{e}rīth* are better captured by terms such as "agreement," "arrangement," "compact," "contract," "commitment," "treaty," "alliance," "obligation," "bond," and "relationship."

Many biblical covenants are arrangements between two persons, between a person and a group, or between groups. Other biblical covenants are arrangements between a person or a group, notably the entire people Israel, and God. When humans and the deity are said to "covenant" a figure or metaphor from social life is used to explain and to mandate behavior conceived as divinely given and freely accepted by the community. As long as we understand "covenant" to mean an ordered relationship between God and people that is two-sided, though not necessarily even-handed in the involvements and obligations of both parties, it is a useful term to employ.

Interestingly, the Moses traditions themselves are not heavily charged with direct covenant references. The non-P Sinai materials speak of a covenant between Israel and Yahweh mediated by Moses, first in an anticipatory election proclamation (Exod. 19:5) and again in two tradition units that describe covenant-making incidents at the mountain (24:7–8; 34:10, 27–28). A third unit widely construed as covenant making in content does not use directly covenantal language (24:1–2, 9–11), and is seen by some critics as simply a theophany. Indeed, those who claim a Deuteronomistic revision of the non-P Sinai units sometimes deny that there are any pre-D references to covenant in the Sinai texts which they tend to read as theophanies throughout. Identifiable J and E traditions do not refer to the covenant, except for J's "ark of the covenant" (Num. 10:33; 14:44). All of the germane P uses of *berîth* occur in the Holiness Code, a block of laws generally taken to be an independent source incorporated by P (see table 11: no. 93; Lev. 26:9, 15, 25, 44, 45). It is possible that P's term *'ēdûth*, usually translated "testimony" and frequent in the phrase "ark of the testimony," may actually have the force of "covenant" or "covenant obligation(s)" (e.g., in Exod. 25:21–22; 31:18). In the sweep of Deuteronomistic History from Deuteronomy through Kings, the covenant is frequently mentioned and often explicitly connected with Moses in key reports of covenantal infidelities and reaffirmations.

The weight of this testimony seems to put the tradition of Moses as covenant mediator into some doubt, especially given the fact that so many biblical recitations of exodus, wandering, and entrance into the land omit any reference to covenant and law. There is, however, another way of viewing the literary evidence. If the argument is accepted that the matrix for the history-like traditions of the ancestors, exodus, wandering, and conquest of the land was the covenant-making and law-reciting assembly of Israelite tribes, it is obvious that covenant concepts and mechanisms existed in Israel not long after the reputed lifetime of Moses. The virtual restriction of covenant rhetoric in Exodus through Numbers to Exodus 19—24, 32—34 is a literary result of a secondary transformation of covenant ritual formulas into a narrated episode at the sacred mountain in the wilderness, a transformation that probably had already occurred by the time that J and E wrote. It thus seems reasonable to say that Israelites within a generation or two after Moses were celebrating a covenant with Yahweh that they believed originally stemmed from their forefathers who came out of Egypt.

This constitutes fairly strong testimony in favor of the covenant as deriving in some way from the Mosaic period, although the narratized form of that covenant in Exodus 19—24, 32—34, composed of diverse and severely edited texts from ritual ceremonies, appears to have arisen in the common pool of pre-JE materials later than all the other major narratized traditions about Moses, the exodus, and the wanderings. That P does not make much explicit reference to covenant at Sinai is not a serious objection, since the P laws and regulations were arbitrarily spliced into Exodus 19—24, 32—34 by the overlap of Exodus 25—31 with the apparent purpose of asserting that the P laws depended on the prior covenant.

One of the difficulties that has bedeviled a full understanding of the covenant in early Israel has been the persisting tendency to see the covenant solely in religious terms. One source of this tendency is the growing theologizing of covenant and law in the D and P sources. Another source of difficulty is later Jewish and Christian obsessions with covenant and law, under whose spell we are still inclined to read all parts of the Hebrew Bible. Insofar as covenant was a way of symbolizing the ground and origin of the proper ordering of Israel's communal life, the covenant was a total religiopolitical reality. Israel formulated its self-definition as a people and its basic social institutions by means of the concept and ritual practice of a covenant with deity. It would be a misjudgment of the prominent religious component in the covenant to suppose that this meant all Israel's communal needs were cared for supernaturally without reference to sociopolitical practice by the people.

In fact, the religious covenant was also a way of binding together the tribes so that they could effectively subordinate their separate interests to the common project of winning their collective freedom and security from Canaanite city-states that tried to subject them to state domination. That the covenant mechanism associated the religious sovereignty of Yahweh with the historical sovereignty of the people is clear from the prohibitions against making treaties (i.e., covenants) with the Canaanite ruling classes and adopting their religious practices (Exod. 23:32; 34:12, 15). If a historical thread actually runs backward from the intertribal covenant of the free tribes in Canaan to Moses as a covenant-making leader of some of the peoples who later became part of the tribal confederacy of Israel in Canaan, one of its strongest strands was probably a political affirmation of Israelite self-determination. The line of continuity would then run from Moses' covenant to create a minicommunity free of Egyptian control to the multitribal covenant in Canaan to create a greatly enlarged community free of Canaanite city-state control.

In the last quarter of a century a theory about the origin of the covenant has developed that both argues for the origin of the covenant with Moses and for its explicit political derivation and significance. The theory is that the instrument adopted by Israel to formalize its relation to the god Yahweh was the ancient Near Eastern international suzerain-vassal treaty concluded between an imperial overlord and a subject ruler. The majority of the texts of suzerain-vassal treaties are fourteenth and thirteenth century Hittite texts, but Aramean and Neo-Assyrian texts of similar form are known down to the seventh century (table 1: nos. 2G and 2H). The chief elements of the suzerainty treaty form, which either occur typically in the treaty texts or are inferred from references in other texts, are listed in table 12 along with biblical passages that have been claimed to exhibit these formal elements.

The assumption is that Israel conceived of its relation to Yahweh as that of subject peoples to a world king and that they expressed this relationship in the concepts and formulas of the suzerainty treaty. It was once thought that this treaty form died out totally after the thirteenth century so that it could be argued that Moses *must* have been the deviser of the covenant form so directly based on a treaty form. Now that it is apparent that the treaty form continued into later centuries among other states beyond the Hittite Empire, it is appropriate to make the more modest claim that Moses *could* have known of the treaty form when he developed the covenant. But it is also possible that the treaty form only influenced Israel's views of covenant at a later date in its history.

The key issue is really whether the suzerainty treaty form is evidenced in biblical texts and, particularly, whether the earliest covenant texts show dependence on it. There is wide agreement that the treaty model was influential on the Deuteronomic versions of the covenant dating from the eighth/seventh centuries (§37.3), since in many respects they show familiarity with Neo-Assyrian diplomatic conventions and treaty forms, notably in the elaborate development of the curses. But whether the *full* treaty form lies behind the *older* pre-D covenant texts is warmly disputed. Aside from Deuteronomy, the major elements of the treaty form are not solidly represented in any single text but have to be culled from several texts.

Those who deny the treaty form in Exodus covenant traditions claim that the theophany replaces the historical prologue there and they cogently note that curses and blessings are absent. It is insisted that the rites of covenant making in Exodus are ceremonies of union confirming alliance on fraternal or kinship grounds and that teaching and admonition predominate over strictly contractual-legal aspects. Advocates of treaty-form influence on the Mosaic covenant admit that the treaty schema in biblical texts has been altered, that in fact the Hebrew Bible contains no formal text of a covenant. Instead, we are given formulas taken from covenant rituals that have been more or less narratized as events at Sinai/Horeb. It is asserted, however,

TABLE 12
Structural Elements of the Suzerainty Treaty Form*

1. Preamble or title of the author/superior party to the treaty
   (Exod. 20:2a; Deut. 5:6a; Josh. 24:2a)

2. Historical prologue or antecedent history of relations between the treaty partners
   (Exod. 20:2b; Deuteronomy 1—3, 5:6b; Josh. 24:2b–13)

3. Stipulations stating the obligations imposed upon the vassal or inferior party to the treaty
   (Exod. 20:3–17; Deut. 5:7–21; 12—26; Josh. 24:14)

4. Provision for deposit of the treaty text in a temple and periodic public reading
   (Exod. 25:21; 40:20; Deut. 10:5; 27:2–3; 31:10–11)

5. Lists of gods (or elements of nature/people) as witnesses to the treaty
   (Josh. 24:22, 27; Isa. 1:2; Micah 6:1–2)

6. Curses and blessings invoked for disobedience/obedience to the treaty stipulations
   (Deuteronomy 27—28)

7. Oath by which the vassal pledges obedience to the treaty
   (Exod. 24:3; Josh. 24:24)

8. Solemn ceremony for formalizing the treaty
   (Exod. 24:3–8)

9. Procedure for initiating sanctions against a rebel vassal
   (Hosea 4:1–10; Isa. 3:13–15)

*The elements of the suzerainty treaty form and the biblical covenant citations are drawn chiefly from K. Baltzer, D. J. McCarthy, G. E. Mendenhall, and P. A. Riemann (see bibliography to §19.1).

that these formulas more closely correspond to the typical concepts and language of the suzerainty treaty form than they do to any other ancient Near Eastern forms of agreement. Moreover, the adoption by Moses of the treaty form is viewed as a highly effective way to assert that in the new community of equal families/clans (later tribes) of Israel there were to be no human overlords but simply a sovereign god who legitimated the familial/clan-based (later tribal) social organization of the covenanting people.

19.2 Covenant Stipulations: "Laws"

Among the various covenantal stipulations of obligation in the early biblical traditions are there any that are likely to have derived from the historical Moses? The stipulations or "laws" are of different sorts and present different problems in understanding and dating them.

19.2.a Priestly Instructions and Regulations

It is overwhelmingly clear that the style and emphases of these stipulations represent a late exilic and early postexilic priestly community that was striving to establish the legitimacy of its leadership in a restored Judahite community (§49). The P stipulations of Exodus, Leviticus, and Numbers cannot have come directly from the time of Moses. For one thing, Aaron and his family are given an eminence among the priests that contradicts his more limited role in the JE traditions and that corresponds temporally with the elevation of the Aaronic priests in Ezekiel (§50.1), and in Chronicles, Ezra, and Nehemiah (§51). Also, the tabernacle in the wilderness is conceived as a movable prefabricated half-sized version of Solomon's temple (§30.4). There are, however, elements in P which are older than the source as a whole and which may go back at least to tribal times, if not to Moses, in their nuclear form: (1) socioeconomic and ritual laws in the Holiness Code (table 11: nos. 93C and 93G); (2) census data that may refer to old army musters (table 11: 95 and 113); (3) some details concerning the tabernacle that may accurately reflect an ancient tent shrine (table 11: 86E; §19.4).

19.2.b Collections of Customary Socioeconomic and Religious Laws

The so-called law codes of Exod. 20:22—23:19 and of Deuteronomy 12—26 are compilations of case law precedents for specific aspects of civil and religious life. They imply development from customary usage, but they have been edited to include attached explanations and motivations for obeying the laws. The so-called Covenant Code of Exod. 20:22—23:19 was probably compiled in its present form in ninth-century northern Israel and the Deuteronomic Code of Deuteronomy 12—26 as arranged dates from seventh-century Judah (§37.3). It is obvious, nonetheless, that many of the provisions of these precedent codes legislate for conditions of life that originated before the monarchy. The difficulty in connecting them with Moses is that they presuppose a sedentary village life and an agricultural cultus that would hardly have been operative among the Israelites in the wilderness.

19.2.c Terse Lists of Prohibitions: The Ten Commandments

There are two lists of pithy prohibitions in Exod. 20:1–17 and in Exod. 34:11–26 that occupy pivotal points in the theophany and covenant texts. The first of these is repeated, with minor variations, in Deut. 5:6–21. The lists of Exodus 34 and Deuteronomy 5 are called "ten commandments" in the biblical text (cf. Exod. 34:27 and Deut. 4:13; 10:4) and that title, or the equivalent Latin term "Decalogue," has traditionally been applied to the list of Exodus 20/Deuteronomy 5. Biblical scholars often distinguish the Exodus 20/Deuteronomy 5 list from the Exodus 34 list on the basis of content by referring to the former as the Ethical Decalogue and the latter as the Ritual Decalogue.

The basis for precisely *ten* commandments as the summation of ethical or ritual requirements was probably to facilitate memory by associating each prohibition with one of the ten fingers. Actually Exodus 34 has *twelve* commandments, and is, therefore, often called a Dodecalogue. It appears that two of its twelve commandments are intrusive and that the original was probably composed of only ten members. Other decalogues have been proposed in Lev. 18:6–18 and 20:2–16, and Deut. 27:15–26 contains twelve ritual curses that may once have been ten in number. Elsewhere in the Bible are lists of the ethical traits of the worshiper acceptable to Yahweh (e.g., Ezek. 18:5–9 and Ps. 24:2–5) which appear to presuppose the decalogue structure, although not the exact content of the extant decalogues.

Characteristic of the decalogue form is that it is composed of brief negative commands or prohibitions, without any provision of punishment for violating them. Two of the commands in the Ethical Decalogue are positively formulated, as are half of the commands in the Ritual Decalogue, but it is likely that in their original form all the decalogue stipulations were negatively formulated. Also, the core prohibitions in the Ethical Decalogue have been considerably expanded by explanations and motivations. Disentangled from these additions, the ten brief and grammatically complete prohibitions are widely attributed to Moses. Judgments about the age of the Ethical Decalogue depend primarily on two factors: (1) whether the degree of generality in the list is to be understood as preceding or following the formulation of the more specific stipulations in the law codes; and (2) whether the socioeconomic and religious conditions presupposed in the prohibitions are consistent with probable conditions during the lifetime of Moses. The application of these criteria is in turn affected by exactly how the particular meaning of ambiguous prohibitions is to be construed. The prohibitions of the Ethical Decalogue, together with some of the disputed lines of interpretation, are set forth in table 13.

It is evident that these pithy prohibitions are far from clear in specifying the exact conduct they exclude from the community. It is reasonably certain that many modern interpretations of the jurisdictional force of the Decalogue did *not* apply in ancient Israel. The prohibitions did not treat swearing in common speech, did not regard a married man who had sex with an unmarried woman as adulterous, did not forbid capital punishment, killing in war, or abortion, and did not validate the right to hold unlimited amounts of property. All these are "revisionist" interpretations which can only be argued for as extensions of the "principles" or "spirit" of the Decalogue instead of mandates laid down in the Decalogue.

The assumption that the prohibitions presuppose the village life of Israel in Canaan is qualified considerably once the secondary expansions of the short form of the prohibitions are removed. Moreover, if some Israelites spent years at Kadesh before entering Canaan, it is likely that they practiced limited agriculture at its oases. Too little is known of the origin or early significance of Sabbath observance to judge conclusively whether it could have been a central practice for Moses. It is possible to construe all the prohibitions as consistent with the conditions of Israelite life in Moses' lifetime. Whether the Decalogue actually goes back to Moses depends of course on the closely related issue of whether Moses mediated a covenant between Yahweh and the people. Some who favor the treaty form of the Mosaic covenant view the Decalogue as a policy statement of the spheres of life claimed by the sovereign deity, concerning which more detailed stipulations were to be provided in the various case laws. Acknowledgment of Yahweh's sovereignty in these domains of life would be prerequisites for membership in the cultic and civil community of Israel.

In any case, it is probable that the Decalogue belongs to a relatively early period of Israel's life, probably within the premonarchic age. Had it been constructed as a late summary or abstraction from the existing case laws, one might have expected it to be more explicit and precise about the exact meaning of the prohibitions.

TABLE 13
Prohibitions of the Ethical Decalogue

1. *Prohibition of the worship of any god other than Yahweh,* either in the sense that no other god may be worshiped at a cultic site devoted to Yahweh or in the sense that there is to be no recognition of any other god as having a claim upon Israelites (Exod. 20:3; Deut. 5:7; cf. Exod. 22:20)

2. *Prohibition of making images of gods/God,* either to represent Yahweh or to represent any other god, or in both senses (Exod. 20:4; Deut. 5:8; cf. Exod. 20:23)

3. *Prohibition of misuse of the name of Yahweh,* either in the sense of oaths undertaken lightly, unnecessarily, or dishonestly, or in the sense of magical use of the name to curse or call up evil spirits to do harm to others unjustly (Exod. 20:7; Deut. 5:11)

4. *Prohibition of work on the seventh or Sabbath day* (Exod. 20:8; Deut. 5:12)

5. *Prohibition of cursing one's parents,* either in the sense of youths who dishonor parents who still have guidance over them or in the sense of mature adults dishonoring or failing to care for their older parents (Exod. 20:12; Deut. 5:16)

6. *Prohibition of murder of another Israelite,* either homicide with malice or in the sense that the murderer or perpetrator of a capital crime may not be executed without proper judicial procedure, or both (Exod. 20:13; Deut. 5:17)

7. *Prohibition of adultery,* either embracing a variety of prohibited sexual liaisons, as in Lev. 18:6–18, or referring to sexual union with a married or affianced woman (Exod. 20:14; Deut. 5:18)

8. *Prohibition of stealing property/person(?),* either in the sense of stealing all kinds of personal possessions or in the sense of stealing, that is, kidnapping, a person, which was a common source for the slave trade in antiquity (Exod. 20:15; Deut. 5:19; cf. Exod. 21:16)

9. *Prohibition of accusing another Israelite falsely,* either as plaintiff in a suit or as a witness, or both (Exod. 20:16; Deut. 5:20)

10. *Prohibition of lusting after/seizing another Israelite's house/household members,* either in the sense of condemning the inner desire or greed to take property or persons belonging to another or in the sense of willfully seizing property to be distinguished from the seizure of persons in no. 8 (Exod. 20:17; Deut. 5:21)

19.3 The Divine Name

The plain truth is that no one knows the meaning of the divine name Yahweh. The P source explicitly says that the deity known to the ancestors as El Shaddai (God Almighty in many translations) became known to Moses by the name of Yahweh (Exod. 6:2). The E source prior to the revelation to Moses agrees with P in consistently avoiding the use of the name Yahweh. The J source, on the contrary, declares that Yahweh was worshiped by that name in preflood antiquity (Gen. 4:26).

The Elohist and Priestly sources seem closest to historical reality in stressing that a radically fresh understanding of deity appeared with Moses, an understanding that was taken up into the intertribal confederacy of Israel in Canaan when it adopted Yahweh as its god. On the other hand, the Yahwist source, underscoring the continuity of Yahweh's work from pre-Mosaic through Mosaic times, may also indirectly preserve a historical memory about the pre-Israelite worship of Yahweh. On the basis of the analysis of personal or place names at Mari, Ugarit, and Ebla, and in Egyptian references to the Shosu, claims have been made from time to time that Yahweh was worshiped in the ancient Near East in pre-Mosaic times. None of these alleged pre-Mosaic cults of Yahweh has proven convincing. We have seen that if a god Yahweh was known before the time of Moses, it was most likely among the Midianites (§18.2), but unfortunately we do not possess a shred of evidence as to how the Midianites might have interpreted the meaning of the divine name.

The one and only explanation of the divine name in the Hebrew Bible appears in the E source (Exod. 3:14–15), and this "explanation" has prompted a host of interpretations. When asked about the divine identity, Elohim says to Moses, "'*ehyeh 'asher 'ehyeh* . . . Say this to the Israelites, '*'ehyeh* has sent me to you,'" which is then enlarged so as to connect *'ehyeh* = Yahweh with Elohim unqualified and with the Elohim of each of Israel's ancestors: "Yahweh, the Elohim of your fathers, the Elohim of Abraham, the Elohim of Isaac, and the Elohim of Jacob, has sent me to you."

Exodus 3:14 regards the divine name as formed from the Hebrew verb *hyh*, "to be." If this verb is understood in the simple stem, *'ehyeh* means "I will be," or "I am," and Yahweh is understood to mean "he will be," or "he (always) is." Because biblical Hebrew lacks the kind of tense distinctions made in other languages, it is uncertain whether the allusion is to present or future. The Septuagint translation renders *'ehyeh* into "I am the One who (eternally) is." This metaphysical twist has accorded well with later Jewish and Christian theological affirmations of an absolute and unchangeable god. It is highly questionable, however, that the Elohist understood the divine name in this way, or that Moses would have so understood it. Pointing to a more active, operational sense of "to be" in surrounding E contexts ("But I will be with you" [Exod. 3:12], and "I will be with your mouth and with his mouth" [Exod. 4:15]), some interpreters prefer the meaning "he who is present, accompanies, helps."

If the verb is understood in the causative stem, 'ehyeh conveys the meaning "I cause to be" or "I bring about what comes into existence." This has often been construed as implying a general notion of creation, of a sort not strongly evident in Israel before the time of the monarchy. The causation implied, however, may be focused on the production of novel realities in the sociohistorical life of Israel: Yahweh is the bringer of a people out of bondage and into autonomous intertribal security. One theory, which also attempts to explain the connection between the older divine name El/Elohim and the newer divine name Yahweh, suggests that the proper name Yahweh sprang from an original epithet for El, in something like the form "El who creates (yahwī) the hosts."[2] For Israel this would have meant "hosts" in a double sense: the armed hosts of heaven (natural elements such as stars, sun and moon, rain, hail, wind, and personifications of the divine agency such as the angel or messenger of Yahweh) and the armed hosts of earth (the citizen army of Israel). In time, according to this hypothesis, the causative verb yahwī was separated to form an independent and distinctive, even preferred, name for Israel's god, although El, in the form Elohim, continued as an appropriate alternative name. This is an attractive theory but for the moment it lacks conclusive verification.

Other interpreters caution that, although E takes Yahweh to derive from hyh, in fact the consonants of Yahweh presuppose the verbal root hwh. This, in their view, is only one of a large number of popular but erroneous etymologies of names that appear commonly in the J and E sources. On the assumption that the actual verb behind Yahweh is hwh, a connection is sometimes made with the Arabic hwy, "to blow, to fell, or to knock down." Yahweh would thus mean "he who blows or fells," that is, a storm-god. Another understanding of the Arabic hwy interprets Yahweh as "he who acts passionately/compassionately." A further suggestion cites a Ugaritic root hwt in proposing that Yahweh meant "he who speaks." From a Phoenician inscription in Anatolia it has been argued that Yahweh meant "sustainer, maintainer, establisher." It is not certain, however, that hwh need

2. Frank M. Cross, *CMHE*, 65–71.

have a different meaning than *hyh,* since in a few instances (although admittedly in later biblical times) there are usages of *hwh* that unmistakably mean "to be."

Still other scholars are inclined to believe that all derivations of the divine name from a verbal form are mistaken, and that, probably in the short form of Yah or Yahu, the name was simply an emotional shout or cultic cry with something like the sense of "He" or "O That One." The short form Yah occurs twenty-five times in the Hebrew Bible and the forms Ya, Yo, and Yahu appear frequently in biblical proper names and extrabiblical inscriptions. The attestations to the longer form, Yahweh, however, go back as far as the premonarchic Song of Deborah and the ninth-century extrabiblical Moabite Stone. At present there does not seem to be any firm historical or etymological argument for regarding one form or another as having unmistakable precedence.

Despite exhaustive studies, there is no way to uncover precisely what the name Yahweh meant to Moses or to the circle of tradition that gave this name to the tribal confederacy of Israel in Canaan. To know the exact meaning of the name might give us important clues to the source of Israel's faith, but if the name already had a prehistory it cannot be taken for granted that Moses or the first Israelites would have attached any special significance to the name per se. The etymology of Exod. 3:14 is not only a rationalization of the name but also a circumlocution, since it is deliberately vague and cryptic, perhaps thereby insisting on the reticence and mystery of Israel's God.

19.4 Cultic Rites and Objects

The final redaction of the Torah, decisively influenced by the Priestly viewpoint, assumed that the worship practices of the postexilic community had been received from Moses and had continued unchanged over the centuries. Once it is recognized that in fact the cult of ancient Israel underwent development over time, the question arises: Is it possible to determine the actual worship forms of Moses, or at least of the first Israelites who developed the Moses traditions?

The P source gives an elaborate description of animal and cereal sacrifices, presided over by an Aaronic priesthood with Levitical assistants, and conducted at a movable shrine (tabernacle) housing a wooden chest (ark) which stood at the center of the Israelite wilderness camp. Each of these elements requires separate assessment to determine to what degree the P writer reflects ancient traditions.

The portable wooden chest, or ark, and the portable shrine, or tent of meeting (= tabernacle), are mentioned in the JE Moses traditions, but never together. The ark was a wooden chest that appears to have represented the presence of Yahweh in the form of a pedestal or throne for the imageless deity. It is also conceived as a repository for tablets containing the Decalogue. It had a function to accompany the Israelites in battle, serving as a palladium, that is, a sacred object with the power to safeguard those who possessed it. P's conception that the ark was overlaid with a cover of gold ("the mercy seat") to which were attached winged guardian figures (the cherubim), seems to have been a retrojection into the wilderness of adornments first given the ark when it was installed in Solomon's temple.

The tent of meeting as mentioned in E, where it is a small oracle shrine in contrast to P's mini-temple for sacrifice, is congruent with a simple desert shrine in tent form. Both among pre-Islamic and Islamic Arabs such shrines, usually carried on camelback, are well attested. In pre-Islamic times, the shrine, holding the tribe's stone idols, was carried in combat and consulted for oracles. In Islamic times, the shrine took two forms: one that continued the old desert tribal shrine without the idols, and the other consisting of a tent containing a copy of the Koran that led caravans of pilgrims to Mecca. The range of functions associated with Arab shrines and with the Israelite ark and tent are not directly equatable, but the general functional parallels are instructive. It is evident that the use of portable cultic objects of the ark/tent type is consistent with conditions of migratory life and with monotheistic religious claims.

All in all, the evidence for the ark as a Mosaic element in Yahwism is somewhat stronger than the evidence for the tent, in the sense that the ark can be traced at points in early Israelite history while the whereabouts of the desert tent after the entrance into Canaan, or even its actual existence, is more obscure. Noting the persistent separation of ark and tent in pre-P traditions, some scholars have argued that the ark and tent derived from separate groups and were never associated in the cult. There is reason to keep ark and tent together, however, in spite of the fragmentary and confused textual traditions. An ark would have necessitated the sort of shelter a tent would provide, and a tent shrine would have invited some symbol of deity, so that, with images excluded, the simple chest as a throne base of the deity would have served that function well.

The sacrificial system according to P included the following types of offerings:

1. Animal offerings entirely consumed on the altar (whole burnt offerings or holocausts);
2. Animal offerings partly burnt and partly consumed by priests and worshipers (peace or communion offerings);

3. Animal offerings to atone for intentional and unintentional sins of laity and priests, which the guilty parties could not consume (sin and guilt/reparation offerings);
4. Grain offerings, sometimes presented separately and sometimes accompanying animal sacrifices (cereal offerings);
5. Offerings of incense or of aromatic mixtures of spices (incense offerings);
6. A display of loaves of bread on a table in the tabernacle, eaten weekly by the priests (showbread, i.e., "bread laid out on display," or bread of the presence).

Narrated references to whole burnt offerings and peace offerings go back to earliest times in Israel. On the other hand, sin and guilt offerings are not certainly mentioned earlier than Ezekiel and P (§49). Because P's description and explanation of the sin and guilt offerings are far from clear, this may be a sign that the P writer is attempting to codify older practices without fully grasping their former meanings. In any case, sin and guilt offerings did not have the major significance in early Israel that P attached to them. Also, throughout the pre-P references to sacrifice, there is no evidence that Aaronid priests had a monopoly on sacrifice in contradistinction to the whole body of Levites. Moreover, a number of ancient biblical references indicate that lay folk were entirely competent to offer sacrifice.

When comparison is made between Israelite sacrifice and the sacrifices of other Near Eastern people, it is apparent that the closest connections are to be found between Canaanite and Israelite forms of sacrifice, especially in the prominence given to whole burnt offerings and peace offerings. In the importance assigned to the blood in certain sacrifices, however, Israelite practices stand closest to Arab practices. It has been conjectured that the oldest form of Israelite sacrifice was that of the Passover lamb with its blood rites and that, once in Canaan, the Israelites expanded their sacrificial repertory to include typically Canaanite agricultural rites. This assumes, of course, that all or most of the Israelites came from Egypt and the desert, a questionable hypothesis to be further assessed (§24.1.a).

A much-debated issue concerns the incidence and obligatoriness of human sacrifice in ancient Canaan and within Israel proper. It is clearly stated that Jephthah sacrificed his daughter (Judges 11:30–40) and that, in the late monarchy, the kings Ahaz and Manasseh sacrificed their sons by fire (2 Kings 16:3; 21:6). Ancient cultic stipulations to give all the firstborn to Yahweh (Exod. 22:28–29), or to allow firstborn children to be ransomed while firstborn animals were to be sacrificed (Exod. 34:19–20), are construed by some interpreters to mean that human sacrifice was a mandated feature of the earliest Yahwism, later tempered by animal substitutions. In that context, the near-sacrifice of Isaac by Abraham is seen as a polemic against widely accepted human sacrifice (Gen. 22:1–14).

Evidence on human sacrifice from the immediate Canaanite environment of Israel is blurred. Archaeological recovery of the skeletal remains of children may attest to so-called foundation sacrifices, that is, interring sacrificed children in the foundations of new buildings in order to gain divine favor (cf. 1 Kings 16:34). Some, if not all, of these skeletal remains may simply point to a high infant mortality rate, however. Inscriptions and historical reports from Phoenicia and its colonies in Carthage and Malta, from the seventh through the fourth centuries, speak more tellingly of child sacrifice in time of national crisis.[3] Outbursts of this sort of human sacrifice in a national emergency occurred in ninth-century Moab (2 Kings 3:27) and in eighth- to seventh-century Judah (cf. the references to Ahaz and Manasseh above).

In sum, it is unlikely that either Canaanite or Israelite religion directly legislated or normally required human sacrifice. The notion, however, that all life belonged to the deity and that even human life could be efficaciously "returned" to deity in order to resolve an extreme crisis seems to have hovered in the background waiting to be activated in times of desperation. Only on the basis of such a lingering assumption could Abraham's willingness to sacrifice Isaac have been regarded as plausible rather than demented, and only in this way could the relatively few biblical instances of human sacrifice have been carried through in the confidence that more was to be gained than lost in the cruel undertaking.

As for the Israelite festivals, they are presented essentially as a cycle of agricultural feasts geared to the rhythms of harvest in Canaan: an early spring wheat harvest (Passover), a late spring barley harvest (Weeks, later called Pentecost), and an early fall harvest of grapes (Ingathering or Booths). The day of atonement in P, like the sin and guilt offerings, is not attested in early Israel. It is probable that this sequence of festivals, together with the types of sacrifice, was developed in Canaan. On the other hand, the Passover contains not only an agricultural component (unleavened bread) but a pastoral component as well (a sacrificed lamb with blood rites). Many interpreters believe that the pastoral Passover derived from Moses and was later conflated with a wheat harvest festival at the same time of year. This hypothesis is usually connected with problematic assumptions about the exodus Israelites as pastoral nomads.

The prohibition against Israel making images or idols, either of Yahweh or of other gods, appears to have been an ancient one. It is impossible to

---

3. Lawrence E. Stager and Samuel R. Wolff, "Child Sacrifices at Carthage—Religious Rite or Population Control?" *BARev* 10/1 (January/February 1984): 30–51.

reconstruct the exact force and scope of the prohibition. It may have been meant to set up barriers against copying or borrowing from other religions or entering alliances with their practitioners. A further purpose may have been to stress the invisibility of Israel's God whose presence and activity could not be contained or manipulated. If ark and tent go back to Israel's beginnings, however, it is evident that prohibition of images did not exclude all symbols of deity nor did it rule out concrete forms for human worship and communication with Yahweh. Under the influence of later Jewish and Christian theologies, the prohibition of images has been excessively "spiritualized" and "theologized." It is more appropriate to the evidence not to overstate or to speculate too freely about the original significance of this ancient prohibition.

20
NEWER LITERARY APPROACHES TO
THE MOSES TRADITIONS

20.1 Folk Tale Plot-motifs and Traditional Episodes

One line of literary approach to the Moses traditions has attempted to apply the categories of folk tale analysis to the biblical narratives. For example, starting off from Stith Thompson's comprehensive index of folk tale motifs, one study narrows down from his *motif* ("the smallest element in a tale having power to persist in the tradition") to *plot-motif* ("a plot element which moves the story forward a step") and to *traditional episode* ("a series of events in the story [that] taken together forms a more or less set part of the tale").[4]

This is recognized as a precarious fledgling enterprise since ancient Near Eastern and biblical folk tale types and motifs have never been classified, largely because the materials available are very limited in comparison with European and other folk literatures that offer hundreds of examples of each type and usually many instances of each motif. Nonetheless, it is argued that motif and episode analysis can help to clarify the plots of biblical tales and can also bring out the values and emphases peculiar to biblical tale-tellers and hearers.

Five plot-motifs in the Moses traditions are identified and discussed:

1. The persecuted baby (Exod. 2:1–10; cf. the endangered children in Genesis 21 and 22);
2. The bloody bridegroom (Exod. 4:24–26);

4. Dorothy Irvin, "The Joseph and Moses Narratives [Parts 3–4]," in *IJH*, 180–209.

3. The inanimate animal (Exod. 4:1–5; 7:8–12);
4. The obedient water which disappears or moves (Exodus 14; cf. Josh. 3:7—4:7; 2 Kings 2:6–14) or appears (Exod. 17:5–6; Num. 20:7–13) at command;
5. The plagues (Exodus 7—11).

For each of these plot-motifs, from one to five instances from ancient Near Eastern texts are supplied and the special twists of emphasis or context in the biblical plot-motif are highlighted. In the instance of the bloody bridegroom it is claimed that only a knowledge of the Egyptian counterpart enables us to see that the point of the puzzling story is deception of a bloodthirsty deity in that Yahweh is led to believe that Moses has been circumcised when Zipporah circumcises their son and applies blood from the lad's foreskin to the "feet," that is, genitals, of Moses.

Typically the plot-motifs have very different imports in their ancient Near Eastern and biblical uses. In the extrabiblical environment they often concern the escapades of the gods, sometimes cater to the whims of royalty, and occasionally have a moral application. The Israelite plot-motifs tend to focus on the political imperative of releasing the Israelites from bondage, which includes its own "prophetic morality" of a community-yet-to-be, and thus a morality that could have no authority for the Egyptians. Even the grotesque bridegroom of blood plot-motif serves to underline the vital importance of circumcision as a collective marker for male Israelites.

The traditional episode cited in the Moses narratives is that of "sending the savior." Three Sumero-Babylonian, one Hittite, and one Ugaritic example of "sending the savior" are compared with Exodus 3—4 and three later formulations in Isaiah 6, Ezekiel 1—2, and Job 1—2. An organically linked set of elements unfolds as a predictable pattern lying behind the many examples, no one of which contains all the elements. The full series of elements, together with references for those that occur in Exodus 3—4, are as follows:

1. The problem described;
2. The meeting of the divine assembly;
3. The problem presented: Exod. 3:7, 9;
4. The solution proposed: Exod. 3:8;
5. The question, "Who will go?";
6. The hero is called: Exod. 3:11;
7. The hero demurs: Exod. 3:11; 4:10;
(8.) The hero is assured: Exod. 3:12; 4:11–13; or
(9.) Another hero is called: Exod. 4:14–16;
10. The hero stipulates a reward;

(11.) Wonders are worked for or by the hero as a trial of strength;
or
(12.) Wonders are worked as part of his reassurance;
or
(13.) Wonders are worked as part of his instructions: Exod. 4:1–9;
14. Instructions (and weapons) are given: Exod. 4:15–17, 21;
15. The hero departs: Exod. 4:18–20;
16. The conflict: ⎫
17. The outcome: ⎬ Exod. 4:29–31; 5ff.

An examination of the plot-motifs and traditional episodes is helpful in differentiating the stock conventions employed by biblical narrators. In fact, the traditional episode is very close to what another literary critic, looking mainly at the ancestor traditions, has called type-scenes (see §15.3.d above). There are, however, such a relatively small number of biblical and extrabiblical examples in each category, and such great plasticity in the way the plot-motifs and episodes are treated, that one is not sure how sound a footing the comparative study rests on. By conceiving the sending of Moses in an episodic linkage of scenes and images of the divine council, the enemy as chaos to be overcome, the demurrer of the elected savior, the efficacy of wonders in the conduct of the mission, etc., the stylized story elements are brought into prominence for further study.

Whether the prophetic and wisdom citations are actually instances of the sending of the savior episode is questionable, since the final success of the prophet-savior is not recounted (is it rather a sending of a messenger episode?), and the Joban instance has no savior in view but rather an accusing Satan who is defeated when Job "redeems," as it were, his own piety by faithfulness. One interesting observation flowing from this comparative folk tale approach is the analyst's conclusion that, unlike the ancient Near Eastern versions, the biblical sending of a savior episode sees the established forces of order as the oppressive enemy to be overthrown which "might almost characterize OT theology, with its dedication to the success of the unpromising and its hymn to upheaval (see 1 Sam. 2:1–10)."[5]

Suggestive as this folk tale analytic method is, it is still far from a fully controlled method, and will doubtless remain somewhat impressionistic until there is a thorough comprehensive study of all available ancient Near Eastern and biblical texts, which ought to be carried out in relation to motifs, plot-motifs, and traditional episodes in European and other folk literatures.

5. Ibid., 202.

20.2 Biblical "Comedy"

Another new literary approach, applying a distinction between comedy and tragedy made by literary critic Northrop Frye, compares Exodus 1—15 as comedy with Euripides' *The Bacchae* as tragedy, and concludes that the two works use similar literary conventions to opposite ends.[6] Both Exodus 1—15 and *The Bacchae* tell stories of how strange and little-known gods (Yahweh/Dionysus) authenticate their claims to godhood by unleashing their divine power against proud and stubborn unbelievers (Pharaoh/Pentheus, king of Thebes). The heart of both works is a contest between deity and the unbeliever, Yahweh of course working through the mediation of Moses whereas Dionysus assumes a human incognito. Pharaoh and Pentheus function as examples of the *alazon,* or boaster, who claims more knowledge and power than he actually has, and Moses and Dionysus are examples of the *eiron,* or dissembler, who pretends to know less than he actually knows in order to lead the *alazon* to destruction.

The result in Exodus 1—15 is a comedy because the hero Moses is incorporated into the new community of liberated Israelites, while the result in *The Bacchae* is a tragedy because the hero Pentheus is cut off by death from his position of leadership in Thebes. Throughout Exodus 1—15, the lines between righteous Yahweh/Moses and evil Pharaoh are clearly drawn so that the reader's sympathy is entirely on the side of the former. By contrast, in *The Bacchae* the virtues and vices of Dionysus and Pentheus are so modulated in their interaction that the reader remains highly ambivalent toward both figures to the very end. Irony is everywhere present in *The Bacchae,* but sharply excluded from Exodus 1—15.

By blocking out commonalities and contrasts with another piece of literature, the study is useful in posing questions about the larger design and intent of Exodus 1—15. By calling attention to the *agon,* the contest or ordeal between Moses and Pharaoh in their protracted negotiations punctuated by plagues, the conflictual element of the biblical story is highlighted. Interestingly, it has been argued that Exodus 1—15 is a legend that owes its composite dramatic form to recitation/reading in a Passover ritual where the crucial contest between Moses and Pharaoh was declaimed and perhaps enacted in "cultic glorification."[7]

This comparative study of the Greek and Israelite works does not, however, take sufficient account of their differences in literary genre and in

6. David Robertson, "Comedy and Tragedy: Exodus 1—15 and the Bacchae," in *The Old Testament and the Literary Critic,* GBS (Philadelphia: Fortress Press, 1977), 16–32.
7. Johannes Pedersen, *Israel. Its Life and Culture,* vols. III–IV (London: Oxford University Press; Copenhagen: Povl Branner, 1940), 728–37.

sociohistoric setting. The "tragedy" of *The Bacchae* is a staged drama by a single playwright aimed at provoking reflection on the positive and negative vitalities of the Dionysian mystery religion, whereas the "comedy" of Exodus 1—15 is an agglomeration of anonymous traditions growing out of the public cult and aimed at the periodic celebration of the foundations of the Israelite community. The Greek drama is coterminous with the events it creates, while the Israelite saga sequences are later reflections on earlier happenings no longer reconstructable as history and/or as symbolic allusions to similar kinds of deliverances from external oppressors which later Israelites experienced in Canaan. Euripides, as an outsider to the Dionysian cult, offers wise and purposely contradictory observations on religious trends within the established Greek community, while the tellers/writers of Exodus, firmly rooted in the Yahweh cult, project the foundation or charter story of a people still struggling to establish themselves securely as an independent society. In short, genre and sociohistoric distinctions will have to be taken more adequately into account before comparative literary studies of this sweeping order can make their fullest contributions to biblical studies.

20.3 Structural Narrative Programs and Isotopies

A reading of Numbers 11—12 along the lines of the narrative models of A. J. Greimas has been proposed by a structural critic.[8] The main program of the narrative is analyzed as follows: *Yahweh* is the "sender/giver" of *the promised land* as "object" to *the people of Israel* as "receiver." *Moses* is the "subject/protagonist" who facilitates the action with *provisions* of quail, manna, and elders conceived as "helper." Under this program, movement toward Canaan is positive and delay in the desert is negative, but movement can occur only if certain conditions are met by the people. The rebellions of the people are counterprograms, to which Yahweh responds with blocking measures or counter-counterprograms.

The meaning-effects of the text are gathered under two "isotopies," or broad semantic categories: (1) the people of Israel as a hierarchy of unmixed entities consists of a top to bottom ranking of Moses, Aaron, people, Miriam, and rabble; (2) the communication of knowledge about the main program comes from Yahweh who acts through natural elements and through Moses to overcome the people's deception by maximizing their

8. David Jobling, *The Sense of Biblical Narrative. Three Structural Analyses in the Old Testament (1 Samuel 13—31; Numbers 11—12; 1 Kings 17—18.* JSOTSup 7 (Sheffield: JSOT Press, 1978), 26–62. For a simplified presentation and explanation of Greimas's structural "actantial model," see chap. 1 n. 5.

awareness. These isotopies or meaningful themes are worked out in the text through a series of codes or systems of classification: geographical and temporal codes, political-hierarchical code, topographical codes (tent, camp, outside the camp), and alimentary (food) code.

The method is controlled and fruitful in its manner of bringing out complex structures in the narrative, although there is as yet no agreement among structural critics as to how appropriate the method is for analyzing heavily edited narrative texts in contrast to oral myths. As applied to Numbers 11—12, room is left for engagement with historical-critical and social scientific methods of criticism. It is also recognized that more and more units of the biblical traditions will have to be analyzed structurally before the full import of the results in any one section are evident. An interesting potential spinoff of structural criticism is broached when this structural exegete claims that the perceptive narrative observations of pre- or noncritical biblical commentaries (often confessional religious in presuppositions and tone), especially in rabbinic literature, can be newly assessed with the controls of structural method.

20.4 Concluding Assessment

The three reported instances of newer literary approaches to the Moses traditions vary greatly in their levels and methods of analysis—to such an extent that the results are not simply combinable nor can they be directly linked with historical-critical or social scientific methods. Each study, following a different method from the others, throws some light on the literary conventions within the Bible, permitting, even compelling, us to see the stylizations of structure, language, and semantic units that are so intricately interwoven in the text. The first two studies attempt comparisons with extrabiblical literature, while the third study confines itself to innerbiblical connections. None of the studies embraces more than fifteen chapters in the Moses traditions. Of the three studies, the structural exegesis is most explicit about the method followed, what it purports to do and what it does not attempt to do or cannot yet do, and it is the most tightly argued. The more such precision about method can be developed in all literary studies and the more texts that can be analyzed by means of the various literary options, the sooner it should be possible to consider how the literary methods relate to one another and what compelling considerations they present for historical-critical and social scientific methods.

21
SOCIOHISTORIC HORIZONS OF
THE MOSES TRADITIONS

We found the ancestor traditions resistant to placement in any firm single historical frame of reference (§16.1–3). Preserving diverse memories of groups that became part of Israel, their clearest sociohistoric horizon lies in the effort of united Israel in Canaan to develop a synthesized account of its origins (§16.4).

The Moses traditions certainly have a more compact origin than the ancestor traditions, in the sense that they point to a movement in the thirteenth century of a group (possibly groups) of state slaves from Egypt to Canaan. Through the link with the ancestor traditions and on the basis of Egyptian historical texts, the escapees from Egypt are conceivable as former residents of Canaan, probably including war captives as well as voluntary migrants. Their leader Moses, who organized the slave uprising and flight but died before entering Canaan, bore an Egyptian name, intermarried with Midianites of the Sinai region, was of Levitical descent and identified as the grandfather of a priest of Dan in the time of the judges (Judges 18:30).

21.1 The Moses Group as a Pre-Israelite Entity

The socioreligious element in the traditions most often judged to be authentic for that period is the introduction of a new deity under the name of Yahweh and of a cult that may have included an ark and/or tent and some form of sacrifice (§19.4). To this horizon may also belong a covenant instrument for linking the exslaves to one another and to Yahweh, and very likely also basic provisions for the internal ordering of the community such as those set forth in the short form of the Decalogue (§19.2.c).

On the other hand, it is evident that the fullest statement and elaboration of the cult, laws, and regulations belong to the sociohistoric horizon of priestly practice at Jerusalem many centuries later during the late monarchy, exile, and Judahite restoration (§49). Even the covenant and law complex of non-P traditions in Exodus 19—24, 32—34 bears the marks of formulation in covenant-renewal practices among the Israelites after they were established in Canaan during the tribal and early monarchic periods, and Deuteronomy reflects covenant-renewal rites at a somewhat later stage in the monarchy. Likewise, the rich traditional portraiture of Moses and Israel in the desert, especially concerning the "offices" of Moses and the rebellions of the people, appear to have been shaped under the pressure of sharp leadership struggles in the larger intertribal confederation of united Israel.

It is important to identify the differences between the Moses Israelites and the later Israelites in Canaan. For one thing, the very name Israel (with reference to the divine name El/Elohim), rather than Israyah (with reference to the divine name Yahweh), was probably first adopted by the community in Canaan. Second, the Moses group was not yet a people engaged in intensive farming on its own home ground and defending itself against adjacent city-states, as was to be the case with Israel in Canaan. From the limited evidence available, the Moses group appears to have been composed of a mixture of stockbreeders (sheep, goats, and, more dubiously, cattle), small gardeners, and fishermen, who were forced by the harsh imposition of state slavery in Egypt into migratory habits for survival. Third, the Moses group, generally estimated to have been no more than a few hundred or thousand in number, were as yet not the large conglomerate of federated peoples from varied historical and cultural experiences who were eventually to form larger Israel. Whatever the diversity of their origins, the Moses group had experienced a recent common oppression in Egypt. In the desert they formed a small sovereign group in which leadership could be asserted and contested in face-to-face relationships. Once the Moses group entered Canaan and joined with other peoples to form the confederation of Israel, the earlier distinguishing traits of the group were merged with the cultural norms and historical experiences pooled by the whole body of Israel and the group's distinctive socioreligious organization was restructured in the design of a vastly expanded and elaborated social system of tribes in mutual aid.

21.2 Socioreligious Strategies Connecting the Moses Group and Later Israel

This way of viewing the relationship between the exodus-wandering forerunners of Israel and the whole people of Israel in Canaan immediately poses the question: Why was it in the interests of the confederacy of Israel to concentrate so much attention on the fortunes of what had been in fact only *one* among many groups who became part of Israel?

One answer to the question is that the key leadership in the formation of united Israel in Canaan seems to have come from the Levitical Moses group, as did also the crucial revelation and cult of Yahweh. Given the political decentralization of tribal times, it is hardly sufficient to explain the centrality of the Moses traditions as a forceful imposition of a minority heritage upon a submissive majority of Israelites. The early adoption of

Yahwism by the militarily powerful tribes of Ephraim and Manasseh (perhaps belonging to the Moses group?) probably was a persuasive factor. The full dimensions of the socioreligious attraction of the Moses traditions for the confederacy of Israel, however, has to be explained with reference to lines of connection drawn between the *critical problems* faced by the Moses group and by later Israel and with reference to the lines of connection between the *socioreligious strategies* for coping with those problems developed respectively by the earlier migratory and later sedentary communities. It is to be noted that the desert community was migratory and not pastoral nomadic in terms of its longstanding sociocultural identity.

Among the significant lines of connection between Israel-in-embryo in the wilderness and Israel-in-florescence in the land are the following:

1. A people oppressed by kings unites to escape from physical and mental bondage to the oppressor;
2. A people freed from an imposed social order unites and experiments to create a tribal/intertribal community of mutually supported equals;
3. A people whose leaders had been imposed now struggles to create necessary leadership in the absence of coercive state power;
4. A people in a very precarious economic situation labors to provision itself both as it migrates and as it cultivates its own land;
5. A people threatened by disease and plague, and perhaps underpopulation, struggles to reproduce and preserve itself by adequate hygienic measures;
6. A people without precedents for the public activity of women—discovering that women have been active and necessary participants in the fight against external oppression—now struggles to determine what the roles of women will be in their own autonomous society.

In each of the spheres cited, the experience of the Moses group and its legacy of Yahwism was regarded as prototypical of the challenges Israel faced in its amplified existence in Canaan. This suggests that when Israelites read in the Moses traditions about bondage in Egypt and deliverance from Pharaoh they perceived these themes as "covering paradigms" for any and all such experiences that the various member segments of the confederacy had undergone. What happened to the Moses group in Egypt became thereby an "umbrella metaphor" for what happened when other Israelites fought with Egyptians in Canaan (as recounted in the Merneptah stela [table 1: 2D]), or with various Canaanite city-states, or with Midianites and Moabites, or with Philistines (as the heirs of Egyptian sovereignty over Canaan). This means also that, as the Israelite confederacy took shape, it perceived that the work of Moses in forming a desert community almost "from scratch" was analogous to what it faced in the even more complicated and ambitious task of forming many tribes into a confederacy.

Similar analogies must have been seen between the exodus-wandering community and the community grounded in Canaan in all the spheres named above: in the determination of leadership forms and personnel, in the successful production of basic life necessities, in the maintenance of public health, and in the securing of a fuller place for women in their new society. These socioeconomic and religiopolitical themes that span the two Israels and come to expression in the Moses traditions are charter themes of the new community, "paradigms of Israel's root condition as a people," as it were. It is possible that a fuller structural analysis of the isotopies, or big semantic themes, in the Moses traditions may permit literary data to illuminate more fully the sociohistoric stance and preoccupations of early Israel (§20.3).

Probably the most problematic of the lines of connection cited is that of the role of women. As in the ancestor traditions (§16.4), women frequently occupy key positions as *facilitators* and *celebrants* of Israel's deliverance from oppression in the Moses traditions: Hebrew midwives frustrate Pharaoh's genocidal plans, Pharaoh's daughter saves the infant Moses, Zipporah averts Yahweh's wrath against Moses by circumcising her son, Miriam dances and sings with "all the women." At the same time women are a threat, either to external apostasy or to internal leadership: a Cushite wife of Moses (is this Zipporah or another woman?) arouses the ire of Miriam and Aaron, a sexual liaison of an Israelite man with a Midianite woman is severely condemned (and related to plague), and Miriam is "defrocked" of her leadership functions when she challenges Moses' monopoly on authority. These latter involvements of women are clearly connected with the boundaries and cohesion of the community and with matters of public health, and it may be that the Miriam incident reflects a move for greater power by women within the confederacy which was suppressed. The full meaning of the place given to women in the traditions is far from clear because of our limited knowledge of the actual status of women in early Israel. Intensive research on the neglected history of women in early Israel is greatly needed, for the present state of the traditions may mask an aborted movement for fuller feminine participation in society.

Finally, the current debate over the adequacy of the suzerainty treaty form as a model for the early Israelite covenant (§19.1) can be constructively furthered by comparing the sociopolitical organization implicit in the treaty form with the socioreligious organization of early Israel. In three respects the treaty model does not appear closely analogous to Israel's self-formation and self-understanding. First, Israel understood itself to be a new people without a prehistory *as a people*, even though it speaks volubly of a prehistory in the family experiences of Abraham, Isaac, and Jacob. By contrast, a suzerainty treaty was always enacted between the heads of two already-existing states, so that the treaty did not create the vassal state but only obligated it to a new sovereign. Second, Israel understood itself as internally constituted by its covenant with Yahweh and not only externally demarcated and obligated. By contrast, a suzerainty treaty controlled only the foreign policy of a vassal state, entering into its internal affairs only so far as to ensure the continuity of leadership within the vassal state; otherwise, the vassal state pursued its own administrative structures, laws, policies, and customs. Third, Israel saw itself as the sole people in such an explicit knowing relationship with Yahweh. By contrast, the suzerainty treaty was not restricted to a single vassal state, with the result that any particular overlord might be in treaty with two or more vassals at the same time.

It is possible of course that Israel, in employing the treaty model, made significant modifications in concept and practice, to the extent even that it served as a sort of "anti-model" that Israel pointedly altered. Or, we may be led to conclude that the treaty model was only a partial or peripheral factor in shaping the earliest covenant notions and instruments of Israel, probably only becoming significant in the later Deuteronomic concept of covenant. In any case, it will henceforth be necessary to take sociohistoric base factors into account in assessing the combination of derivation and innovation reflected in Israel's covenant practice and thought.

CHAPTER 6

Traditions About Intertribal Israel's Rise to Power in Canaan

Read the Biblical Text
Joshua
Judges

Consult Maps in *MBA*
nos. 54–82

22
THE SHAPE OF THE TRADITIONS IN
JOSHUA AND JUDGES

22.1 Contents and Literary Genres

Our information about the rising presence of Israel in Canaan during the period ca. 1200–1000 B.C.E. is largely derived from the Books of Joshua and Judges. The first of these books relates how Joshua, successor to Moses, led the united tribes of Israel in the conquest of sizable parts of the western hill country of Canaan and how the conquered (and yet-to-be-conquered) lands were divided among the tribes. The second of these books relates the successes and failures of individual tribes in displacing Canaanite rule, goes on to tell of the exploits of military leaders and the rule of civilian leaders (variously called "deliverers" and "judges"), and concludes with stories of the relocation of the tribe of Dan and of a civil war between Benjamin and the rest of Israel.

There is a wealth of tradition units representing a spectrum of literary types intricately arranged and interpreted. It is widely agreed that Joshua and Judges constitute parts of one immense composition beginning with Deuteronomy and extending on through Samuel and Kings. This work is known as the Deuteronomistic History (§13.3). It is furthermore recognized that a deliberate and comprehensive editorial point of view has been imposed on the extremely diverse traditions of Joshua and Judges by the compositional and editorial hand of the Deuteronomistic compiler/author. Any adequate understanding of these books, and of the historical events and social processes they attest, requires balanced attention both to the forms and contents of the separate traditions and to the editorial perspectives that shape the diverse traditions into an uneasy multifaceted unity. Before examining the distinctive authorial stance of DH in Joshua and Judges, we shall attend to the major divisions in the books, an outline of their contents, the primary literary types, and the major difficulties standing in the way of coherent interpretation (table 14).

22.1.a Joshua 1—12

In Joshua 1—12 the dominant literary form is a chain of *sagas* which relate events in the Israelite occupation of Canaan. In several of the sagas prominent objects (standing stones; heaps of stones; a ruined city; large stones against the mouth of a cave) and the separate status of certain groups in Israel (Rahab and her family; the Gibeonites) are traced to events at the conquest. The objects and statuses cited are said to be in existence "to this

TABLE 14
Major Divisions of Joshua-Judges

A. Joshua 1—12: Israel's Conquest of Cisjordan Under Joshua's Leadership

1. Preparation for conquest: 1
2. Spying out Jericho; treaty with Rahab: 2
3. Crossing of the Jordan River: 3—4
4. Israel at Gilgal: circumcision; Passover; theophany: 5
5. Conquest of Jericho; rescue of Rahab: 6
6. Achan's theft; defeat at Ai; Achan's punishment: 7
7. Conquest of Ai: 8:1—29
8. Altar and reading of the Law at Mt. Ebal and Mt. Gerizim: 8:30–35
9. Treaty with the Gibeonites: 9
10. Battle at Gibeon/Beth-horon; conquests to the south: 10
11. Battle at Merom; conquests in the north: 11:1–15
12. Summaries of conquests and list of defeated kings: 11:16—12:24

B. Joshua 13—22: Allotments of Land to Tribes and to Public Institutions by Joshua

13. Preparation for land allotments: 13:1–7
14. "Flashback" to allotments of land to Reuben, Gad, and half-Manasseh by Moses in Transjordan: 13:8–33
15. Land allotments to Caleb, Judah, Ephraim, and half-Manasseh in Cisjordan: 14—17
16. Land allotments to Benjamin, Simeon, Zebulun, Issachar, Asher, Naphtali, Dan, and to Joshua in Cisjordan: 18—19
17. Designation of six cities of refuge for legal asylum: 20
18. Designation of forty-eight cities for the priestly Levites, and brief summary of conquest-settlement: 21
19. Dispute of Transjordanian and Cisjordanian tribes over an altar built by the former at the Jordan River: 22

C. Joshua 23—24: Two Farewell Addresses of Joshua

20. Joshua warns Israel against apostasy from Yahweh and consequent annihilation/ expulsion from the land: 23
21. Joshua recites saving deeds of Yahweh and brings tribes into treaty with Yahweh; Joshua's death recorded: 24

TABLE 14 (continued)
Major Divisions of Joshua-Judges

D. Judges 1:1—2:5: Piecemeal and Incomplete Conquests of Land
by Individual Tribes After Death of Joshua

---

22. Judah, Simeon, Othniel, Kenites, and Caleb take the southland: 1:1–20
23. Benjamin fails to take Jerusalem: 1:21
24. House of Joseph takes Bethel, but its member tribes Manasseh and Ephraim fail to drive out Canaanites: 1:22–29
25. Zebulun fails to drive out Canaanites: 1:30
26. Asher fails to drive out Canaanites: 1:31–32
27. Naphtali fails to drive out Canaanites: 1:33
28. Dan fails to drive out Amorites but Ephraim conquers the Amorites: 1:34–35
29. Messenger of Yahweh announces: because of Israel's treaties with Canaanites, Yahweh will not drive out the Canaanites whose religion will "snare" Israel: 2:1–5

E. Judges 2:6—3:6: Interpretive Introduction to the Era of Judges

---

30. Joshua's death retold; a new generation arises who do not know Yahweh: 2:6–10
31. Theological introduction: Yahweh raises judges to deliver sinful and unrepentant Israel: 2:11–19
32. Theological introduction: Yahweh will not drive out Canaanites who will "test" Israel's obedience to Yahweh and "train" Israel in war: 2:20—3:6

F. Judges 3:7—16:31: Narratives and Annals of "Judges/Deliverers"
in Military Roles (= M) or in Civil Roles (= C)

---

33. Othniel of Judah (M): 3:7–11
34. Ehud of Benjamin (M): 3:12–30
35. Shamgar (M): 3:31
36. Deborah of Ephraim (C and M[?]) and Barak of Naphtali (M): 4—5
37. Gideon of Manasseh (M): 6—8
38. Abimelech of Manasseh/Shechem, an illegitimate king: 9
39. Tola of Issachar (C): 10:1–2
40. Jair of Gilead (C): 10:3–5
41. Jephthah of Gilead (M): 10:6—12:6; (C): 12:7
42. Ibzan of Judah or Zebulun (C): 12:8–10
43. Elon of Zebulun (C): 12:11–12
44. Abdon of Ephraim (C): 12:13–15
45. Samson of Dan (M): 13—16

TABLE 14 (continued)
Major Divisions of Joshua-Judges

G. Judges 17—21: Two Narrative Supplements

46. Resettlement of the tribe of Dan and foundation of a sanctuary with a kidnapped Levite as its priest: 17—18

47. Crime and punishment of the tribe of Benjamin for the rape-murder of a Levite's concubine; measures to save Benjamin from annihilation: 19—21

day" (4:9; 5:9; 6:25; 7:26; 8:28–29; 9:27; 10:28), as viewed from the time of an undated narrator. Stories containing an explanatory motif of this sort are often called "etiological [origin] sagas." It was once thought that the sagas were largely created ad hoc to satisfy popular curiosity about the origins of the places, objects, people, customs, or rituals in question. It is now more widely proposed that etiological motifs tended to be attached secondarily to stories already in existence, more or less altering the older sagas in details of form and content. For example, an old saga about a treaty between Gibeonites and Israel appears to have been drastically obscured by the inclusion of an etiological motif. Other sagas, such as the Rahab story, seem to have been less disturbed by an etiological element. Attempts to reconstruct the supposed pre-etiological form of the sagas have, however, lacked convincing criteria.

A significant etiological factor not directly acknowledged in the text is evident in the sagas of Josh. 2:1—8:29 that focus on the initial penetration of the Israelites across the Jordan River and their early conquests at Jericho and Ai. The core of these stories (probably 2; 3:1—5:1; 6) was decisively shaped by a ritual enactment of the crossing of the river and the circling of the ruined (= "captured") city of Jericho. This ritual, attached to the Gilgal sanctuary nearby, involved a procession of priests and laity carrying the sacred ark.

On analysis, it is clear that most of the sagas in Joshua 2—11, in contrast to the comprehensive DH introduction and summaries, are restricted to the locale of the tribe of Benjamin. The exceptions are the spectacular defeats of coalitions of Canaanite kings at Gibeon/Beth-horon in the south-central highlands (chap. 10) and at Merom in the far north (chap. 11). The first battle opened the way to the conquest of Judah to the south and the second battle freed Galilee for Israelite settlement. Interestingly, nothing is said about battles in Samaria, the territories of Manasseh and Ephraim, even though Joshua is identified as an Ephraimite. In fact, the DH image of Joshua as leader of united Israel in a total conquest of the land is thrown into radical doubt by the restricted scope of this saga collection.

22.1.b Joshua 13—24

In Joshua 13—24 the primary literary form is a series of *lists* which contain inventories of the territorial holdings of the tribes of Israel. Some of the lists are *boundary inventories* that describe the borders of tribes as running through, along, or around settlements and natural features such as rivers, mountains, passes, stones, etc. Other lists are *city inventories* that detail the settlements belonging to tribes, or to the landless Levites, or designated as cities of refuge to facilitate legal process. Sometimes the city lists are embellished by *regional inventories* that either identify regions by name or describe geographical horizons by means of the formula "from (place name) to (place name)."

A noticeable feature of these allotment inventories is that the boundaries, cities, or regions of no single tribe are given in their entirety. Benjamin and Judah come nearest to being completely catalogued. The western boundary and western settlements of Benjamin seem to be missing, however, and Judah lacks a list of cities for the central region between Jerusalem and Bethzur. The city lists for the southernmost tribes are fullest, while none at all survives for Ephraim. Boundaries are given in part for all tribes except Simeon and Dan. Some borders between tribes are detailed twice, and occasionally a missing border can be supplied from the border descriptions of an adjacent tribe.

Distributed among the allotment lists, according to their tribal connection, are *annals* telling of battles, seizures or occupations of cities and regions, and failures to expel Canaanites. The subject in each of the annals is a single tribe and not the united Israel of the sagas in chaps. 1—12. The annals are usually brief and written in a terse report style giving the impression of minutes or annotations. Significantly, these annals have exact or near parallels in Judges 1 where a large block of annals is concentrated.

Just as the Priestly regulations of Exodus, Leviticus, and Numbers were narratized by events at Sinai and during the wilderness wandering, so the boundary and city inventories of Joshua 13—21 are narratized as land grants to the tribes after the conquest of Canaan. There are internal inconsistencies in this narratization. Joshua 14:1–5 reports that Joshua, the priest Eleazar, and the tribal heads, gathered at Gilgal, distributed land to nine and one-half tribes in Cisjordan. Joshua 18:1–10 reports that Joshua alone, located at Shiloh, distributed land to seven tribes in Cisjordan following a land survey required because Judah, Ephraim, and half-tribe Manasseh had monopolized the choicest land. Moreover, 14:5 and 19:49 imply a form of the tradition in which the allotment of the land was determined by the people at large rather than by Joshua.

This section of Joshua also contains a saga about a serious dispute over whether the Transjordan tribes were properly observing the cult of Yahweh (22:7–34). It is often said that the book closes with two "farewell addresses" by Joshua. In fact, only chap. 23 is a farewell address, whereas chap. 24 is a narrative (a narratized liturgy?) of an assembly of tribes at Shechem over which Joshua presided. Joshua opens the assembly with a recital of the saving deeds of Yahweh and follows up with a call for the gathered tribes to enter into covenant/treaty with Yahweh. After suitable solemnities, the compact with Yahweh is concluded. The final verses describe the death and burial of Joshua, the continuing adherence to Yahweh of "the elders who outlived Joshua," the reburial of the bones of Joseph brought from Egypt, and the death and burial of Eleazar.

22.1.c Judges 1:1—2:5

The opening of the Book of Judges is composed of a string of *annals* that tell of the military-political struggles of individual tribes (or at most two tribes collaborating) to gain control over the western hill country. Judges 1:1–21 recounts successes by Judah, with minor appended qualifications, whereas 1:22–36, after relating an early success by the house of Jacob at Bethel, dwells heavily on the weaknesses of the northern tribes in failing to dislodge large numbers of Canaanites, although these negatively oriented annals have in view the eventual dominion of Israel over the north achieved by David. The section closes with a stern rebuff by the messenger of Yahweh who announces that because of Israel's disobedience not all the Canaanites will be expelled from the land (2:1–5).

Since identical or similar annals about Israel's struggles for dominion appear as isolated units or incorporated into fuller accounts at the end of Numbers, throughout Joshua, and at the end of Judges, it is probable that there once existed a stock or fund of reports that recorded separate tribal victories, settlements, and necessary accommodations with Canaanites. Judges 1 represents a limited selection from this parent body of *dominion annals*. These annals are significant for the glimpses they provide into the ebb and flow of Israel's protracted struggles to gain dominance from region to region within Canaan. They strongly challenge the oversimplified view of a rapid conquest by united Israel set forth in Joshua 1—12 and presupposed by division of conquered Canaan among the tribes in 13—21. It is perfectly clear, however, that this arbitrary selection of dominion annals in Judges 1 is not itself a coherent historical survey of the conquest but rather a collage of materials put together in present form in order to magnify Judah, denigrate the northern tribes, and justify the judgment of the author of Judges 2:1–5 concerning the covenant disloyalty of Israel as a whole.

22.1.d Judges 2:6—3:6

What amounts to a second introduction to Judges is launched by a restatement of the death and burial of Joshua (Judges 2:8–9 = Josh. 24:29–30) and the inauguration of the era of the Judges as "another generation [after the death of the elders who outlived Joshua, cf. Judges 2:7, 10a with

Josh. 24:31] who did not know Yahweh or the work which he had done for Israel" (Judges 2:10b). The body of the introduction is a two-stage moral and theological *discourse* by the DH narrator. The first section of the discourse dwells on the apostasy of Israel from Yahweh, the divine anger in giving Israel over to oppressors, and the divine mercy in raising up "judges" to deliver them periodically, even though the Israelites persist in deepening their apostasy (2:11–19). The second section of the discourse emphasizes that Yahweh will leave Canaanites in the land in order "to test" Israel's obedience and in order "to train" Israelites in war (2:20—3:6)

22.1.e Judges 3:7—16:31

The main body of the Book of Judges consists of traditions about measures of self-defense taken by various sectors of Israel against Canaanite, Moabite, Ammonite, Midianite, and Philistine oppressors. Characteristically only a few tribes are involved in each military action, but as many as six tribes collaborated in one crucial victory over the Canaanites, while four others are condemned as violators of their religiopolitical duty (5:12–18). The *saga* literary form predominates with vivid narratives of military victories achieved by Ehud, Deborah and Barak, Gideon, and Jephthah at the head of Israelite forces, and by Samson in a series of single-handed skirmishes and reprisals. One saga, so circumstantial as to be called history by some scholars, concerns Abimelech, son of Gideon, who aspired illicitly to be king over a mixed realm of Israelites and Canaanites and met a deserved early death (chap. 9).

Explicit etiological motifs appear in some of the sagas (6:24; 10:4; 15:19; and elsewhere in Judges at 1:21, 26; 18:12). The cult played an immediate hand in providing the life context for the composition of the Song of Deborah which celebrates Yahweh's victory through Israel over the Canaanites. The hymn makes rich use of the language of theophany to underscore how Yahweh combined the forces of nature with the fighting zeal of Israel to defeat the enemy.

The Israelite cult is visible in other ways, either through the cultic activities of actors in the sagas or through the influence of cultic models on the literary form of the sagas. Jephthah is said to have made a rash vow to sacrifice whichever person first greeted him upon returning victorious from battle. For this irrevocable vow he was compelled to sacrifice his daughter. Some commentators view the story as an improvisation to provide an etiology for an annually observed four-day mourning by the daughters of Israel on the mountains (11:37–40; probably a Canaanite festival?). The call of Gideon (6:11–24) and the announcement of the birth of Samson

(13:2–25) are framed as theophanies by the messenger of Yahweh and each entails animal sacrifice. The call of Gideon, including his diffidence and need for reassurance, is typical of other biblical calls or summons to vocation, especially in prophetic literature (cf. the "traditional episode" of "sending the Savior" [or "sending the messenger"?], §20.1). The announcement of the birth of Samson corresponds to the type-scene of the birth of an ancestor hero to his barren mother (§15.3.d). The identification of Samson as a Nazirite, who does not drink wine and allows his hair to grow, is probably a secondary element in the saga with the point of giving the unsavory hero a more religious aura.

Amid the wealth of sagas are two series of *annotated annals* which give a roster of Israelite leaders who "judged" Israel (10:1–5; 12:7–15). The annals provide data about their places of origin and burial, their families and wealth, and the lengths of their terms in office. Nothing at all is said, however, about what the leaders actually did when they "judged" Israel. The Song of Deborah mentioned above (chap. 5) is a *hymn* or *song of triumph* memorializing a victory that is also treated in saga form (chap. 4). A *fable* concerning trees, embedded in the Abimelech story (9:7–15), passes severe judgment on those who aspire to kingship. Samson propounds an insoluble *riddle* that is marred by his wife giving away the answer (14:14, 18).

Sagas, annotated annals, and hymns are joined together by a framework that carries through the program of moral and theological evaluation of the era already starkly announced in the introduction of 2:6—3:6. The framework of the first episode, the "judgeship" of Othniel, appears in full exemplary form (3:7–11). Thereafter episodes are introduced and rounded off by less complete framing formulas. At two points, where the Gideon and Jephthah episodes are introduced (6:7–10; 10:6–16), the framework enlarges into discourse that elaborates and extends the evaluative interpretations of the book's introduction. Here occurs the only reference in the book to Israelite confession and repentance (10:10, 15–16).

Traditionally the Israelite leaders described in the book have been called "judges." Unfortunately the term gives an erroneous impression of the Hebrew terminology employed and also a false sense of certainty as to what the functions of these leaders actually were. It is striking that only in the DH introduction (2:16–19) are these leaders called "judges." Othniel (3:9) and Ehud (3:15) are called "deliverers" in the frameworks to their episodes. The frameworks for the first leader, Othniel (3:10), and for the last leader, Samson (15:20; 16:31), employ a verb form to report that these men "judged Israel." Within the sagas themselves only Deborah is said to have been "judging Israel," reference being made to her making "judgment" in cases brought to her as she sat under a palm tree (4:4–5). But it is not clear that her summons to Barak to raise an army was an aspect of her judging, since it is more likely that her title as "prophetess" was most germane to the warfare she stirred up. DH pictures the later Samuel as a circuit judge administering justice in parts of Benjamin (1 Sam. 7:15–17), but at the same time Samuel is said to have "judged" Israel by intercessory prayer, offering sacrifice, and possibly even by leading in battle (1 Sam. 7:5–14).

In short, the Israelite leaders told about in the sagas are overwhelmingly military deliverers, only Deborah among them being involved in the administration of justice. On the other hand, the leaders cited in the annotated annals are consistently said to have "judged" Israel, although they are never called "judges." These so-called minor judges (distinguishable from the major judges of the sagas) are, however, never said to have been military commanders and their concrete duties are never specified. The fact that Jephthah appears both as a minor judge (12:7) and as a major judge (10:17—12:6) may provide an important clue to the book's obscure and confusing ways of reporting on the leaders of Israel in this period.

The source of the difficulty seems to be that DH tried to standardize terminology for the leaders of Israel in the premonarchic era and, in doing so, misconstrued the slim evidence available. Noticing that the old annotated annals stated that the leaders named "judged Israel," DH assumed that they bore the title of "judges." Noticing further that Jephthah, one of those named in the annals, was simultaneously a military leader, DH took the additional step of conceiving Jephthah as "judge" in his military role. It was then an easy extension to regard all the military leaders in this era as "judges" (2:16–19). Such seems to have been the origin of the generalizing use of the term in the book's introduction which influenced the Septuagint's choice of Judges as the title for the book. In a later section we shall attempt to specify the various functions of leadership in Israel during this period (§24.2.c), even though it may be impossible to know exactly what titles of office were used in premonarchic times.

22.1.f Judges 17—21

Two lengthy sagas flesh out the Book of Judges. Compositionally they lack the customary DH framework concerning judges, but they are flagged by editorial notes as belonging to the general period (18:1; 19:1; 21:25). Unlike the other episodes in the book, with the mentioned exception of the Abimelech saga, there is no foreign oppressor in sight and thus no Israelite military deliverer. The sagas are similar in that they treat the fortunes of two tribes, Dan and Benjamin, in conflict with fellow Israelites, feature Levite priests as central figures, and allude to important sanctuaries (Laish = Dan in the first story and Bethel, Mizpah, and Shiloh in the second story). The saga of Micah and the Danites (17—18) tells of the migration of Dan from the shephelah of Judah to the headwaters of the Jordan River and of the tribe's brazen kidnapping of a Levitical priest who has served the Ephraimite Micah. The saga of the crime and punishment of Benjamin (19—21) recounts first the near-extermination of Benjamin by the other tribes to avenge the rape-murder of a Levite's concubine at the hands of citizens of Gibeah. The story goes on to relate how wives were found for the surviving Benjaminites to ensure that the tribe would not become extinct.

22.2 Joshua-Judges and the Deuteronomistic History

DH conceives the history of Israel from Moses to the exile as encompassing four phases: the era of Moses and lawgiving (Deuteronomy); the era of Joshua and the conquest (Joshua); the era of the Judges and Israelite apostasy and oppression (Judges–1 Samuel 7); and the era of the monarchy from Saul to the fall of Judah (1 Samuel 8–2 Kings). Representations and evaluations of these eras are formulated in relation to how the Law given to Israel through Moses (Deuteronomy 12—26) was implemented or violated in the course of the history. Deuteronomy serves as the programmatic pacesetter for what follows in Joshua through Kings. It is generally accepted that Deut. 1:1—4:40 and much, if not all, of Deuteronomy 29—34 were DH introduction and conclusion intended to transform Deuteronomy itself into a grand introduction to the entire DH composition. Motifs set forth in Deuteronomy recur and are elaborated in the following books.

It is characteristic of the DH author-compiler to supply the major historical periods with interpretive passages in the form of introductory and summary surveys, speeches, and prayers, often placed in the mouths of principal characters. These interpretive inserts periodize and nuance the enclosed older materials and link the four historical periods according to the moral-theological program established in Deuteronomy.

The structure and motifs of DH for the first three eras (we shall examine the fourth period, the monarchy, in part III) may be grasped by a careful reading of the programmatic texts presented in table 15.

The relations between the three eras treated in Deuteronomy through 1 Samuel 7 may be summarized as follows:

1. The *era of Moses* constituted the people of Israel in a covenant

TABLE 15
Programmatic Texts in DH: Deuteronomy–1 Samuel

I. *Era of Moses and Lawgiving*

  A. *Introductory Speech of Moses* (Deut. 1:1—4:40)

    Summary of events from Horeb to Plains of Moab

    Joshua will lead Israel in conquest (1:34–40; 3:18–29)

    Obedience to the Law sanctioned positively by long life in the land and disobedience to the Law sanctioned negatively by expulsion from the land

  B. *Summary Speech of Moses* (Deut. 31:1–29; 32:44–47)

    Moses announces his impending death

    Joshua summoned and commissioned to lead Israel into the land

    Moses gives the Law and a song of reproach to the people as "witnesses" against their anticipated apostasy

    Obedience and disobedience to the Law sanctioned positively and negatively

II. *Era of Joshua and Conquest*

  A. *Speech of Yahweh to Joshua* (Josh. 1:1–9) and *Introductory Speech of Joshua* (Josh. 1:10–18)

    Joshua commanded to lead the people decisively and courageously into the land

    Yahweh will be with Joshua as he was with Moses

    Obedience to the Law sanctioned with promises of success in taking the land

    All Israel will find "rest" in the land after the Transjordanian tribes help the Cisjordanian tribes to complete the conquest

    The people promise to obey Joshua, the living interpreter of Yahweh's commands, just as they obeyed Moses

  B. *Summary Speech of Joshua* (Joshua 23)

    Joshua announces his impending death

    Yahweh has fought for Israel and provided secure allotments of land in Canaan

    Obedience to the Law by not mixing with the remaining nations (through intermarriage or adopting their religions) is sanctioned positively with a promise to drive out the remaining nations

    Disobedience to the Law by mixing with the nations sanctioned negatively with a threat of Israel's expulsion from the land

  C. *Other DH Interpretive Passages*

    Josh. 8:30–35: at Mts. Ebal/Gerizim (Shechem) Joshua builds an altar, writes the Law on standing stones, and reads the Law to the people in fulfillment of Moses' command in Deut. 27:1–8

    Josh. 11:15–23: Summary of Joshua's conquests in carrying out the command of Yahweh through Moses, extending to the vicinity of Mt. Hermon (far short of the Euphrates River specified by Moses in Deut. 1:7)

TABLE 15 (continued)
Programmatic Texts in DH: Deuteronomy–1 Samuel

Josh. 13:1–7: Joshua instructed to allot the conquered land to the Cisjordan tribes, and is promised that the remaining land will be possessed as far as the "entrance of Hamath" (farther north than Mt. Hermon but not as far as the Euphrates River)

Josh. 21:43—22:6: Summary of Yahweh's gift of the land to the people who, having overcome all enemies, find "rest" in the fulfillment of all the promises of Yahweh. Joshua returns the Transjordan tribes to their lands with an injunction to observe the Law

III. *Era of the Judges, Apostasy and Oppression*

   A. *Introductory Discourse on the Judges* (2:6—3:6)

     A new generation does not know Yahweh or his work for Israel (repeats elements of Josh. 24:29–31)

     Apostasy of Israel brings enemy oppression which Yahweh mercifully alleviates from time to time by raising up "judges" who deliver Israel, even though the people deepen their apostasy

     Yahweh refuses to drive out the remaining nations, leaving them in order "to test" Israel's obedience to the Law and "to teach" them the hard lessons of war

   B. *Summary Speech of Samuel* (1 Samuel 12)

     Recapitulation of foreign oppression in the era of the Judges and of the confession and repentance of Israel issuing in deliverance by Jerubbaal = Gideon, Bedan (perhaps a mistake for Barak), Jephthah, and Samuel (cf. 1 Sam. 7:15—8:3 for Samuel as the last "judge")

     Israel confesses the further sin of asking for a king

     If people and king obey the Law, Israel will continue as God's people, but if they disobey, they will be "swept away"

   C. *Other DH Interpretive Passages*

     Judges 2:1–5: An angelic judgment speech condemns Israel to live henceforth with the Canaanites as "adversaries" and their gods as "a snare" since Israel has "made treaty" with them, for which the people lament and sacrifice

     Judges 6:7–10: A prophetic judgment speech indicts Israel for worshiping Amorite = Canaanite gods in spite of Yahweh's deliverance of the people and his express command to avoid pagan worship

     Judges 10:6–16: A divine judgment speech rejects an initial confession of apostasy by Israel; only when the people match confession with a renunciation of foreign gods does Yahweh (reluctantly?) take up their cause

relationship with Yahweh which was to be lived out by obedience to the Law and to the revelations given through Moses, the covenant-law interpreter. The disobedience of the people prevented them from an immediate entrance into the land and condemned them to a forty-year wandering in the wilderness. Moses himself, rebellious against Yahweh, was prohibited from entering the land.

2. The *era of Joshua* represented the completion of the program to conquer the land that had been frustrated by the sins of the people and of Moses. Joshua is the bona fide successor to Moses as the covenant-law interpreter and as the military commander. Joshua and his generation are largely faithful to the commands of Yahweh, for all actual or potential infractions of the Law are punished or avoided before the whole people is endangered. The land was conquered and settled in Joshua's lifetime, as far north as Mt. Hermon. Joshua promises, however, that the remaining land, as far as the entrance of Hamath, will be taken if the people remain faithful to Yahweh (still not as far as the Euphrates River of Moses' original promise).

3. The *era of the Judges* is stamped by a turning of Israel to wholesale apostasy, for which Israel is repeatedly given into the hands of oppressing nations. When Israel cries out to Yahweh, he repeatedly raises "judges" to deliver the people, who nonetheless persist in apostasy and even deepen their waywardness. Although Yahweh continues to deliver his people in their extremities, he also resolves not to drive out the remaining nations, including the Philistines and those peoples located between Mt. Hermon and the entrance to Hamath (in short, the sweeping promise of Moses to Joshua and the people is cancelled). The reason given for the suspension of the program to expel the remaining nations is that they will now serve "to test" Israel's fidelity to the Law and "to teach" them the bitter lessons of warfare brought on by apostasy.

The implication of the DH discourse in Judges 2:6—3:6 is that both the seductive "other gods" and the enemy "plunderers" of Israel are from the ranks of the remaining nations. The identities and territorial bases of all the oppressors in the stories of the judges fit this format except for Jabin of Hazor (Judges 4:2, cf. 1 Samuel 12:9) who is positioned in upper Galilee in a region that Joshua supposedly had already captured (Josh. 11:1–14). Two interpretive passages give another impression, however: that the seductive foreign gods are the gods of the Canaanites/Amorites among whom Israel dwells and who have therefore not been totally annihilated or expelled (Judges 2:1–5; 6:7–10). In fact, 2:1–5, following upon an account of Israelites living immediately among Canaanites (Judges 1), explicitly identifies those who will not henceforth be expelled as local Canaanites with whom Israel has compromised by treaty relationships. Even the concluding verses of the DH introductory discourse (3:5–6) state that Israel was thus condemned to live among local pagans whom Deut. 7:1–5 had targeted for destruction immediately upon entering Canaan.

These tensions within the highly moral-theological perspective of DH, revolving around fidelity/infidelity to the Law and to the authorized covenant-law interpreter, raise the question of the place of national guilt and repentance in the prosecution of the conquest. All the frames of DH, whether or not they concede foreign influences and enemies within the already-conquered territories, jointly pay service to the view that Israel's success or failure in taking and keeping the land is *ultimately* dependent on Israel's adherence to or deviation from the Law. What is striking, however, is that this transparent hinge condition for Israel's success is not at all apparent in the old stories of the judges that are related with little or no DH editing. Particularly noticeable is the way that the angelic judgment speech of 2:1–5 culminates the story of limited conquests and enforced accommodations with local Canaanites in chap. 1. This judgment speech assumes that the Israelites *refused* to conquer all the Canaanites because of compromise. It is clear, however, that the old materials of Judges 1 presuppose that Israelites were *militarily incapable* of dislodging all the Canaanites and had to accept temporary enforced accommodations with them which were reversible only much later when Israel subjected them to forced labor (under David and Solomon).

Uneasiness about how closely Israel's settlement in Canaan was actually conditioned by law observance/non-observance extends into the DH frames themselves. There is in truth much less reference in the DH frames to Israelite repentance than has often been assumed. The introductory discourse pointedly maintains that the Israelites "did not listen to their judges; . . . they soon turned aside from the way in which their fathers walked, . . . whenever the judge died, they turned back and behaved worse than their fathers" (Judges 2:17, 19). The references to "soon turned aside" and "turned back" may be read to presuppose at least a formal adherence to Yahwism at times during the leadership of the judges, but this appears to be no more than grudging compliance and then only briefly after Yahweh has dramatically granted them deliverance through each new judge. In several of the story frames, it is observed that "Israel cried to Yahweh" for deliverance, but this resort in crisis is very dubiously interpreted as containing implicit repentance.

Only in the expanded frame preceding the Jephthah story is the people's cry a confession of sin (10:10). In this instance Yahweh's judgment speech does not accept the validity of their superficial confession. It is only when the foreign gods are actually set aside (10:16) that Yahweh acknowledges apparent repentance (even here Yahweh's response may be irritable impatience, §23.2). In 2:1–5 the angelic judgment speech leads to the people's contrition and offering of sacrifice, but too late it seems to spare the judgment. The prophetic judgment speech of 6:7–10 could have no other satisfactory response than repentance of Israel, but it is not forthcoming.

Some interpreters distribute the frames lacking or containing repentance to different editions of DH, or to pre-DH or post-DH editors, but the literary and conceptual criteria for this solution are not convincing. DH contains a built-in ambivalence and ambiguity about how law observance, and attendant guilt and repentance, actually affected the course of history under the judges and, by implication, under Joshua as well (§23.2). First Samuel 12:10, closing out the era of the Judges, alludes to the people's cry as embracing confession and pledged return to Yahweh, but the whole speech of Samuel is heavy with a sense of Israel's fickleness and persisting proneness to sin. All in all, DH perceives the contrition and repentance of Israel with respect to its violation of covenant law as either nonexistent or, when expressed, woefully superficial, belated, and ephemeral.

A final consideration in the DH framing of Joshua and Judges is the relation between the all-Israelite perspective of DH and the actual, more-limited subjects of the tradition units compiled by DH. A review of the framing surveys and speeches indicates that DH thinks of all Israel acting collectively as a national entity under Moses, Joshua, and the judges. The filler traditions vary greatly, however, in their formal and actual correspondence to this master assumption.

The conquest sagas within *Joshua 1—12* assume the form of stories about the whole of Israel conquering the land. The actual land conquered, however, is chiefly in Benjamin, with thrusts into Judah and Galilee, which taken together cannot account for all the military campaigning required to take the territory attributed to Joshua's conquests.

The boundary, city, and regional inventories of *Joshua 13—19,* on the other hand, are formally constructed as lists of individual tribal holdings which necessarily have to be described singularly. Combined, even though none of them is complete, the lists do treat all the tribes conceived to be a part of the intertribal system. Whatever their ultimate source(s), these dockets aimed to picture the land holdings of all Israel at some point in its history.

The assembly at Shechem in *Joshua 24* is pictured as a gathering of all the tribes where they are presented by Joshua with the choice of reaffirming loyalty to Yahweh or opting either for old tribal gods or Canaanite gods. The people reaffirm their covenant with Yahweh. The structure of the assembly, however, strongly suggests that this text is a transformed account of negotiations between a core Yahwistic group and previously non-Yahwistic groups who for the first time become Yahwists and join the Israelite movement. This interpretation is supported by the oddity of the "free" religious choice offered, by Joshua's "house" (house of Joseph, i.e., Ephraim and possibly Manasseh) as convinced Yahwists over against the other tribes, and by Joshua's curious attempts to dissuade the other tribes from covenanting with Yahweh lest they be later punished for their shallow commitment.

The annals concentrated in *Judges 1*, and paralleled by scattered annals in Joshua, are accounts of the military-political struggles of individual tribes to gain control of regions of Canaan. Unlike the sagas of Joshua 1—12, they derive their unity solely from the conception that the Israelite tribes consulted together about coordinating their several strategies for possessing their territories rather than from any unity of action, since the tribes must one by one make their own way in conquering and ousting the Canaanites.

The individual stories of *Judges 3:7—21:25* display a complicated texture with respect to the unity and diversity of Israel. All the stories with military judges are localized in particular regions and identify the tribal origins of the military leaders or other chief actors, as well as those tribes that joined with them to do battle. The entirety of Israel is never pictured in action together: at most six tribes are said to have fought with Deborah and Barak, while four others are condemned for failing to participate (Judges 5:12–18). The same tribal discreteness appears in the story of Micah and the Danites (17—18). It seems also that the unspecified references to "Israel/ites" in Judges 9:22, 55 have no more than the Israelite populace of Manasseh in mind since it was there that Abimelech tried to develop a dual monarchy involving the Canaanite city of Shechem and Israelites in its vicinity. Only in the concluding story of the crime and punishment of Benjamin is all Israel massed for action, first in military reprisal against Benjamin and then in recuperative operations to gain wives for the surviving Benjaminites. In its concept of united Israel, Judges 19—21 is the one story in the book on a plane with the stories of Joshua. Nonetheless, by means of numerous allusions, all the judges stories presuppose that the discrete tribes named are functional parts of a larger religiopolitical and cultural whole known as Israel.

The brief notations about "minor judges" in *Judges 10:1–5; 12:7–15,* which report that they "judged Israel," are commonly understood to refer to an office with an all-Israelite jurisdiction. This is not necessarily the conclusion to be drawn since in each instance their locales are restricted to a single tribe, or at most two tribes.

22.3 Pre-Deuteronomistic Sources in Joshua-Judges

We have seen that DH had available a number of bodies of tradition for the shaping of Joshua-Judges. These were worked into a continuous account, possibly in two major stages represented by a late preexilic first edition of DH and an exilic revision of DH which are most evident in the Books of Kings. Having characterized the shape of the tradition complexes (§22.1), and having observed the main tendencies and emphases of DH (§22.2), we will now indicate leading theories about the growth of the pre-DH traditions and the possible stages of their inclusion in DH.

The sagas about a united conquest under Joshua (Joshua 1—12) are grounded in localized accounts of the occupation of its territory by the tribe of Benjamin. Whatever actual settlement history underlies the account, it took its early form in a cultic ceremony of the procession of the ark across the Jordan and around Jericho. This Benjaminite account became the skeleton for developing narratives that fleshed out the last of the old history-like themes of Israel's early traditions (§14.3). The centralized cult that shaped this narrative sequence was north Israelite and its original content was exclusively that of the Joseph tribes in central Canaan.

This core sequence of conquests in the south-central highlands has been expanded by accounts of conquests in the foothills of Judah and around Hebron (10:16–43) and in northern Galilee (11:1–14). It was probably at this stage that Joshua, the Ephraimite leader, was introduced to the sagas as the leader of all Israel. These expansions are best explained as attempts to extend the original core of the conquest traditions so as to include references to later Judahite and Galilean converts to united Israel in order to lend greater credence to the claim that a united conquest of all Israel was here reported under Joshua as Moses' successor. Because the notion of all Israel in conquest is so decisive in these sagas it is probable that this stamp of unity was put upon the sagas in the premonarchic cult and that the sagas formed a part of the basic pool of old materials available to J and E. It is likely that DH received the sagas by way of E. Alternatively, the collection of sagas was formed independent of E and came directly as a separate entity to the attention of DH.

The localized settlement or dominion annals (Judges 1 and parallels in Joshua) were summaries of individual tribal occupations of land derived from the divergent subhistories of the several member groups of Israel. There was a common element in all the actions recounted both in the sagas and in the annals: a socially and politically insurgent people had carved out a living space in a broad movement of insurgency against the Canaanite city-states. There were, however, idiosyncratic features in the acquisitions of land and power by each tribe, and these differences were glossed over in the centralized account of Joshua 1—12 so strongly shaped by Benjaminite-Josephite experience. The summaries and anecdotes about distinctive tribal subhistories, unable to penetrate the centralized account of Joshua 1—12, nonetheless survived in the traditions of the separate tribes.

The annals now concentrated in Judges 1 appear to have been a selection from a larger body of traditions, as attested by direct parallels and similarly constructed additional examples in Joshua and at the end of Judges (§22.1.c). Whether they were gathered together in premonarchic times as a total "counterprogram" to the united conquest scenario of Joshua 1—12 is uncertain. Since the lists of tribal holdings in Joshua 13—19 are probably from administrative dockets of David's kingdom (see discussion of Joshua 13—23 below), it is plausible to look also to sociopolitical conditions in the time of David as the occasion for the first definite collection of the dominion annals.

By describing how each of the tribes had acquired territory and slowly gained political ascendency over Canaanites who resisted them, the combined annals formed a memorial, or set of public minutes, concerning the contributions of the individual tribes to the formation of the confederacy and the monarchy. They thus constituted a "statement of accounts" to the central government of David, compiled in order to limit the regime's exercise of power over the tribes. As such they were a reminder of the historical-territorial reality on the basis of which the tribal elders negotiated a treaty with David as the king of all Israel (2 Sam. 5:1–5).

The present form of Judges 1, however, is far from being such a complete statement of accounts. It is a highly slanted condensation that throws the successful conquests of Judah into sharp contrast with the circumscribed achievements of the northern tribes. It may be that an earlier form of Judges 1 presented the J writer's version of the conquest, as many scholars have contended. On the other hand, the editing of Judges 1 as it now stands has been closely conformed to the angelic judgment speech of 2:1–5 so that Judges 1:1—2:5 provides a second introduction to the book, supplementing the introduction of 2:6—3:6. The J substratum of Judges 1 may have reached a DH reviser who undertook to edit it with the bias of the angelic judgment speech, more or less in line with the other judgment speeches in the framework of Judges (cf. 6:7–10; 10:6–16).

In an attempt to identify the life settings of the tribal allotment lists (Joshua 13—19), scholars have noted a basic distinction between the boundary inventories and the city inventories. The city lists are taken to be administrative in intent and monarchic in date and variously placed from the reign of David to the reign of Josiah. The boundary delineations, by contrast, are widely thought to reflect the actual divisions of the tribes in the intertribal covenant community prior to the monarchy. It is more probable, however, that the originals—both of the boundary inventories and of the city inventories—belonged together as part of the archives of internal administration of the late Davidic–early Solomonic kingdom, in the period after David subdued the Philistines and remaining Canaanites but before Solomon reorganized the administration of his kingdom on an overtly nontribal basis (§30.4). It should be stressed that the present lists are poorly preserved torsos of the original complete archives, having suffered much in transmission and redaction. Their value for determining the original settlement patterns of early Israel is limited to the unevenly detailed view they give of how the tribes were distributed in the land at the dawn of the monarchy.

It is problematic whether the inventories have deeper roots in the premonarchic confederacy. Possibly an old nucleus of the city inventories consisted of clan rosters of the intertribal militia which, insofar as clans were identified with villages, laid the foundation for administrative city lists under David. There does not appear to have been any corresponding setting for an old nucleus of boundary inventories in the confederacy, considering that periodic reapportionment of lands in old Israel occurred within tribes rather than between tribes.

Consequently, a firm beginning for the boundary inventories, as for the city inventories, is best assigned to the rise of the monarchy, when the tribal regions that formed the socioeconomic components of premonarchic Israel were transformed into administrative districts in David's kingdom, particularly for purposes of taxation and the muster of manpower for public labor projects and military service. The "tribes," newly delineated as territorial entities, became the framework for consolidating previously Canaanite and Philistine areas and populations into the Israelite state. The "boundaries," which had once existed between tribes simply as the points where the people of one tribe lived adjacent to the people of another tribe, now became political designators for marking off the internal administrative divisions of the centralized state apparatus.

Although it is relatively easy to recognize the nine-and-one-half-tribe scheme and the seven-tribe scheme by which the allotment traditions of Joshua 13—19 were organized (table 14: B; §22.1.b), as well as their imperfect harmonization in 19:51, it has not proved possible to reconstruct a convincing tradition history of the overall growth of the enclosed traditions prior to their adoption by DH. There appears to have been a tendency in the traditions to move from tribes as collective self-alloters of land to the involvement of Joshua and then Eleazar and tribal heads in the process. Likewise, the once-unnamed site of the allotment is later identified as either Gilgal or Shiloh. The tension between Gilgal and Shiloh, even though secondarily introduced, draws attention to the prominence of the former site in Joshua 1—12 and of the latter site in Judges 21 and 1 Samuel 1—4, and may thus have served DH as a bridging device.

We can best account for the lamentable condition of the allotment descriptions on the theory that once they were no longer administratively employed after Solomon's reorganization of the kingdom, they fell into disuse. Only later did learned collectors gather them with an eye to including them in the traditions about the original division of the land among the united tribes under Joshua. Whether J and/or E were among these learned collectors is uncertain. If J included them, they stood prior to the dominion annals of Judges 1 and described the areas which each tribe claimed but which then had to be taken individually by force. If E included a version, it would have followed the unified conquest. It is probable that contradictory traditions as to whether the land allotments preceded or followed conquest contributed to the complications in the traditions at the close of Joshua and the opening of Judges. P-type terminology in 14:1–5 and 18:1–10 does not seem sufficient ground to claim the insertion of the allotment lists by P, or even a retouching by P.

As for the traditions in Judges, it is now widely hypothesized that 3:12—9:55 was composed as a collection of deliverer stories that told of the deliverers Ehud, Deborah and Barak, and Gideon, and ended with the figure of Abimelech, the upstart king, as an "anti-deliverer." Abimelech was joined to the sequence by a secondary identification of his father, Jerubbaal, with Gideon. The northern locales of the stories, the polemic against kings, and the elevation of the "prophetess" Deborah, suggest an origin in northern prophetic circles, perhaps in the late ninth century, although the stories and song of triumph probably derived from pre-monarchic times. An initial DH revision prefixed the sequence with Othniel, to provide a judge from Judah and to set forth the full form of the moral-theological framework that was used less completely to frame the remaining stories, and Jephthah and Samson narratives were appended. A further DH reworking provided the introductory survey over the whole period of judges and supplied chronological notes intended to correlate with 1 Kings 6:1. At the same time the annotated annals about leaders who "judged" Israel were inserted immediately before and after the Jephthah episode in order to juxtapose the double appearance of Jephthah both in an annal and in a narrative. A further Samson tradition was added and the schema of the "judges" as military figures, announced in the introduction, was extended through Eli and Samuel to the brink of the monarchy.

This leaves the problem of the double introduction to Judges and the appendix in chaps. 17—21 which lacks judges and the customary DH framework. A favored argument has been to view the dominion annals of Judges 1 as the introduction to the pre-DH Book of Judges. DH, finding the introduction objectionable because it belied a unified conquest, removed the dominion annals and substituted the survey of 2:6—3:6 as the sole introduction. A final editor reinserted the dominion annals, thereby creating a twofold introduction, and at the same time reinstated the "scandalous stories" of chaps. 17—21 which DH had also purged from its version.

An alternative suggestion is that the double introduction of Judges is related to the double conclusion of Joshua. It is likely that at one stage in the DH composition, Joshua 23 ended the traditions about Joshua and the history moved directly to the introductory survey of the judges in Judges 2:6—3:6 which also relates the death of Joshua. At a later stage a DH redactor, intent on underscoring Israel's apostasy, decided to bracket Judges with the fragmentary dominion annals at the beginning and the morally scandalous stories at the conclusion. At the same time the long DH history was being broken into distinct "books" on separate scrolls. The phrase "after the death of Joshua" was prefixed to the dominion annals at Judges 1:1 to correspond to "after the death of Moses" in Josh. 1:1. Joshua's assembly at Shechem was inserted at Joshua 24 to provide a double-barreled message of warning against apostasy just as the opening of Judges now supplied a double-barreled warning with its two introductions.

The full notice of Joshua's death and burial, which served a "run-on" literary function when the reader moved directly from Joshua 23 to Judges 2:6–10, was now awkwardly separated from the end of Joshua by Judges 1:1—2:5. The solution was to insert the notice of Joshua's death and burial at the close of Joshua 24 and also to leave the old notice to the same effect in Judges 2:6–9. This resumptive literary technique, qualified by a different ordering of elements in the two death notices, served to launch the era of the Judges as a period of sharp decline from the heights achieved by Joshua. It is problematic whether the editor who "overloaded" the end of one book and the beginning of the other, and who provided the restructured death notices, had any awareness that in ostensibly magnifying Joshua he was introducing in Judges 1 clear evidence that Joshua had not accomplished all the conquests attributed to him and that his guise as leader of united Israel was in fact a convenient fiction. That DH *deliberately* structured such discrepancies as an aspect of its moral-theological views is now claimed by one structuralist critic (§23.2).

23
NEWER LITERARY APPROACHES TO JOSHUA AND JUDGES

23.1 New Literary Studies of Deborah and Samson Traditions

The Song of Deborah has long been recognized as an artful specimen of ancient Israelite poetry (§52.1). Older literary studies of Hebrew poetics focused on scanning meter and characterizing the ways in which Hebrew poetic lines formed two "parallel members" that echoed, contrasted, or advanced the imagery and thought. Newer literary criticism attends to a wider range of poetic features within an overall structure and has benefited by the recovery of extensive examples of old Canaanite poetry which indicate that, in the poetic tradition on which Israel drew, meter was often mixed within a single poem and parallel poetic lines were often three in number, especially at points of emphasis or climax, and that outright repetition of terms and phrases—intermixed with artful variations—were typical of these verse compositions.

Recent literary studies of the Song of Deborah look for the wider rhythms within the poem, encompassing imagery and metaphors, sentence structure as a means of emphasis, the manner of opening and closing stanzas, and the sequence of ideas making use of anticipation, retardation, and irony. One study emphasizes a general compositional style known as parataxsis which involves words, clauses, images, and scenes placed side by side without connectives to coordinate the parts.[1] This creates a subtle, implicit, indirect unity below the surface. The lack of conspicuous links invites, even demands, that listeners/readers of the poem use their imaginations to make connections and fill gaps.

---

1. Alan J. Hauser, "Judges 5: Parataxsis in Hebrew Poetry," *JBL* 99 (1980): 23–41.

Parataxsis is seen as especially suited to the presentation of action. The song's staccato motifs of the cosmic power of Yahweh, the watery chaos unleashed on the enemy, the hammering hooves of the fleeing Canaanite horses, the desperate flight of Sisera on foot, and the sharply contrasted women ("daring Jael" and "self-deluding Canaanite ladies") produce a "multi-layeredness of characters, events, and scenes" whose meanings and relations must be synthesized in the mind of the audience. Such studies have increased respect for the received biblical text, since apparent irregularities may be an aspect of the literary art. At the same time, a caution is placed beside efforts to use the poem for historical reconstruction of events in the light of the highly artful arrangement of elements for literary impact.

Interestingly, the battle celebrated in the Song of Deborah is also treated in a prose narrative, which permits us two different literary outlooks on the same event. An analysis of the narrative structure and technique of Judges 4:4–22 has uncovered a story developed in four episodes with rapid scene shifts marked by circumstantial clauses.[2] Each episode has a scene-setting tableau, an initiating action, a speech, and a response, but the elements are varied in their proportions of speech and narration and in their compression or retardation of action so as to build tension and excitement toward the brief and stunning culmination of the story.

Although the surface of the story concerns the victory of Deborah and Barak over Sisera, the underlying structure concerns the culturally unexpected power of the women Deborah and Jael over against the culturally presumed power of the men Barak and Sisera. All the narrative elements are marshaled to "spring" the surprise of Sisera dying at the hands of Jael, which both finalizes the enemy's humiliation and snatches from Barak's hand the honor of killing his defeated Canaanite opponent. It can thus be seen why v. 11 is placed "out of context" so early in the story, since it serves as an anticipatory tableau to prepare for Jael's appearance without giving away either her name or her astonishing role.

Two conclusions follow from this close study of Judges 4. It appears that not only the poetic account of the battle but also the prose account are shaped by interests very different from historical reportage.[3] The fundamental interest of the story is to dramatize how Yahweh has given Israel

2. D. F. Murray, "Narrative Structure and Technique in the Deborah and Barak Story," VTSup 30 (1979): 155–89.

3. For another reading of Judges 4—5 that warns against "historicizing" harmonizations of the two accounts, see Baruch Halpern, "Doctrine by Misadventure Between the Israelite Source and the Biblical Historian," in *The Poet and the Historian,* ed. Richard E. Friedman, HSS 26 (Chico, Calif.: Scholars Press, 1983), 46–49.

power over Canaanite warriors through women rather than through men. In that event, the story cannot be trusted to throw direct light on the actual circumstances of the battle viewed as a whole. For example, that Jael's tent and Sisera's headquarters at Harosheth-ha-goiim are placed in apparent close proximity is less a dependable historical detail than a literary compression of geography in order to tighten the action and to maximize the ironic ineffectuality both of Sisera and Barak.

Such literary studies caution against treating Judges 4 and 5 as though they are eyewitness accounts that can be conflated to create a finished "historical" picture. Furthermore, if Judges 4 is the carefully crafted literary work it appears to be, formed to deliver a striking "feminist" message, it may be questioned if it was a hero saga straight out of folk tradition. It is also problematic whether the feminist bias of the story fits the presumed emphases of the pre-DH "book of deliverers" to which it is often assigned. The presence both in the story and the song of the feminist irony of Jael's role raises the issue of the connection between the two compositions and their place in the design of DH. Why has the feminist irony been deepened in the story and why the interest of DH in such a story, whatever its source?

Rhetorical-critical study of the Samson stories has similarly focused on narrative structure and technique of great intricacy.[4] Judges 13 is a ring composition concerning Samson's birth, framed by promise and fulfillment. It skillfully stresses the importance of his mother by redirecting attention away from the father and showing her to be more perceptive about Samson's divine destiny than is her husband. The birth story of Judges 13 balances the death story of Judges 16, both chapters being constructed around a fourfold asking and answering discourse. Thematic symmetry is traceable in the two clusters of Samson adventure stories in chaps. 14—15 and 16. In each of these cycles Samson sees a woman, is persuaded by a woman to reveal a secret, is bound and given captive to the Philistines as a result of his liaison with a woman, and in extremity calls on Yahweh and is answered.

The two cycles are knit by Samson seeking vindication (15:7; 16:28), by ironic wordplays on "calling/naming" (15:18–19; 16:25, 28), and by the opaqueness of Samson and others in "not knowing" Yahweh's activity in events (14:4; 15:11; 16:9, 20; cf. also 13:16, 21). The same two cycles are joined by ring composition, the first opening (13:25—14:2) and the second closing (16:31) with a "going down" from and a "coming up" to Samson's

---

4. J. Cheryl Exum, "Promise and Fulfillment: Narrative Art in Judges 13," *JBL* 99 (1980): 43–59; idem, "Aspects of Symmetry and Balance in the Samson Saga," *JSOT* 19 (1981): 3–29.

home "between Zorah and Eshtaol." It is conjectured that the twofold DH formula in 15:20 and 16:31, prompting the notion that chap. 16 is a secondary addition to the Samson cycle, is possibly DH's way of calling attention to the thematic symmetry of the two groups of stories.

A tighter structural design of correspondences is proposed between chaps. 14 and 15. Each chapter may be seen as composed of four episodes, the first three brief and the fourth as long as the first three combined. In the first set of episodes Samson converses with parent(s). In the second set of episodes animals are used to show Samson's prowess. In the third set of episodes the consequences of Samson's deeds with the animals are visited on his parents and on his wife and father-in-law, but to different ends (a gift to the former and death to the latter). In the fourth set of episodes the Philistines employ intimidation to secure third-party help in gaining advantage over Samson, in which two-party conversations feature upbraiding and retort, and in which riddle and wordplay are employed.

Each chapter is articulated by the motifs of coming and going, of telling and not telling, and of doing evil through retaliation. The fourth episode in chap. 15 (vv. 9–19) makes an emphatic theological point through the juxtaposition of Samson's power in killing a thousand Philistines with an ass's jawbone and his vulnerability to death by thirst. Although still self-centered, Samson admits his dependence on Yahweh for military deliverance and for physical survival. Each of these dependencies is marked by a place-name etiology. The site of the slaughter becomes Ramath-lehi ("Hill of the Jawbone," 15:17) and the site of the water supply becomes En-hakkore ("Spring of the Caller," 15:19).

The recognition of literary artistry that has woven thematic and structural frames interlocking and nesting within one another raises the question of how such authorial design intersects, if at all, with historical interests in disclosing the course of border warfare between Israelites and Philistines. Furthermore, the relation of this literary design to the various stages of the composition of Judges is sharply posed. Are such patterns to be connected with the old sagas, with an intermediary stage of collecting and editing, or with DH? Even though the Samson stories contain no distinctively Deuteronomistic vocabulary or style, is it possible that their internal literary shaping is after all DH's work? And, in any case, how do the Samson literary patterns fit into the larger DH structure?

23.2 Structuralist Studies

Two recent structuralist studies, one on Numbers 32 and Joshua 22 and the other on Joshua and Judges within DH, offer tantalizing possibilities for relating new literary analyses to source critical and sociohistorical concerns.

The shorter study starts off from the structural similarities between A. J. Greimas's literary analyses of the structures of narratives and anthropological and social scientific analyses of the structures of early Israelite society as practiced by N. K. Gottwald.[5] The parallel methods invite collaboration, which will become possible and attractive as literary structuralists extend their work on biblical texts and admit to the social scientific horizon attending all texts and as social scientific structuralists learn more sophisticated literary-critical methods. What both types of structuralists still lack is "theory about how social or psychological reality becomes 'inscribed' in literary texts."[6]

To explore the grounds for a meeting between biblical literary and social scientific structuralists, the study selects a central sociohistorical question about Israelite origins that might be testable through a structuralist textual study: Did Israel originate through the immigration of groups of outsiders or through a revolt of indigenous Canaanites (§24.1.b–c)? Since the immigration theory assumes major movement of Israelites from Transjordan into Cisjordan, the structural critic decides to study two texts, Numbers 32 and Joshua 22, that show how the early narratives of Israel viewed the idea of Israelites living east of the Jordan.

One aspect of this structuralist analysis is to examine the stories in terms of three major semantic themes or "isotopies": (1) the unity of Israel; (2) Israel's land; and (3) women and children and the coming generation(s). The study concludes that Transjordan is viewed as ambiguous and problematic Israelite territory. It has some sort of precedence, but it poses a sense of danger, and the relationship of the main body of Israelites to the Transjordanians calls for a formalized relationship that is precarious to secure and maintain. Within this "touchy" outlook, Transjordanian Manasseh (north of the Jabbok River) is viewed as more fully Israelite than Reuben and Gad (south of the Jabbok). Transjordanian women are a threat, but this is best overcome by marrying them.

The bearing of these structuralist findings on the central question of immigration vs. revolt models is felt to be "obscure." Indeed, the study does not indicate precisely how various attitudes toward Transjordanian Israelites would strengthen or weaken either immigration or revolt theories. In the course of the study, however, two other sociological connections are probed. Theory about conflict resolution by avoidance, conquest, and procedural resolution (including reconciliation, compromise by bargaining, and award by arbitration) is applied to the narrated conflicts between

---

5. David Jobling, " 'The Jordan a Boundary': A Reading of Numbers 32 and Joshua 22," SBLSP 19 (1980): 183–207.

6. Ibid., 185.

Cisjordanians and Transjordanians. Numbers 32 and Josh. 22:1–8 reveal compromise, whereas Josh. 22:9–34, while purporting to show compromise, contains unintegrated elements of award and reconciliation. Moses, as the Cisjordanian leader, appears authoritarian, whereas the Transjordanians are confident of compromise in the first story but rather manipulative and tricky in the second story.

More briefly, theories about daughters, local women, and concubines appearing in genealogies serving as eponyms of dependent, peripheral, foreign, inferior, or indigenous population elements are cited to suggest that the insecurity over how to deal with Transjordanian women is an expression of sociopolitical tension and conflict. In fact, at a deep level Cisjordan and Transjordan may be coded "male" and "female," thus delivering the message that Transjordan by its peripheral status and its devious fighting style is a troublesome threat to the dominance of the Israelites west of the Jordan from whose perspective the stories are told.

While this study about Transjordan is modest in its results, it is promising for its programmatic formulation of possible collaboration between literary and social scientific structuralist approaches and offers some suggestive first steps toward a method of correlation.

The larger-scale structuralist study sets out ambitiously to grasp the literary composition of the entirety of DH by a structuralist/formalist analysis of the relation between reported speech (addresses of God, Moses, prophets, etc.) and reporting speech (DH's direct utterances as a narrator).[7] To date the study has included Deuteronomy, Joshua, and Judges. Relying principally on Russian structuralists/formalists such as M. Bakhtin and B. Uspensky, DH is seen as the kind of literary work whose many "voices" are orchestrated by an "implied author." The voices are of two kinds: mixtures of reported and reporting speech on the expression plane of the text and distinguishably different systems of viewing the world on the ideological plane of the text. The ideological perspective of the implied author, in this case the final author-compiler (DH), shows up in the way the utterances of narrator and characters in the text are interwoven so that the contending ideological voices are finally "resolved" by the dominance of one voice over another.

In Deuteronomy the discourse is largely the reported speech of Moses within a terse framework of reporting speech by the narrator. In Joshua through Kings, the ratio of the two kinds of speech is dramatically reversed:

---

7. Robert Polzin, *Moses and the Deuteronomist. A Literary Study of the Deuteronomic History* (New York: Seabury Press, 1980).

reported speech is carried within a very much larger body of reporting narratives. On the expression plane of the text, the voice of Moses is at first distinguishable from the voice of God, then the speech of Moses merges with the speech of God, and, after the death of Moses, the words of Moses merge with the words of the DH narrator. In this way DH becomes the authoritative interpreter of divine speech past and present, with the privilege of interpreting and applying the divine words of Deuteronomy to explain the whole course of Israel's history to the exile. On the ideological plane, two primary voices are heard: the voice of authoritarian dogmatism which claims finality and completeness for the Mosaic law of Deuteronomy, and the voice of critical traditionalism which, by transferring the authority of God and Moses to DH, insists on the necessity and validity of interpreting, applying, and even modifying the Mosaic law according to new circumstances. Standing in dialectical tension are the unconditionality of covenant and the insistence of retributive justice should the covenant be violated. Divine justice and mercy operate in an exceedingly complex combination, so that the history of Israel goes forward but not according to the strict constructions of the Mosaic law posited by authoritarian dogmatism.

The voices set forth in Deuteronomy also come to expression in Joshua and Judges. Joshua is composed of narratives that show how both God and Joshua critically interpret the Mosaic law, along with fresh commands of God and outbursts of divine wrath, in keeping with unfolding circumstances that entail modifications of the Law unacceptable to authoritarian dogmatism. These critical interpretations take three forms: (1) direct reinterpretations of the divine words in terms of their intent (Josh. 4:3, 6–7, 21, 24; 5:2b, 9b); (2) indirect reinterpretations of the divine words in the light of events caused by disobedience (6:17–19; 7:11–12, 25); and (3) suspensions or limited fulfillments of divine commands (6:17; 8:2). The divine commands concerning holy war and mandated destruction of the Canaanites are greatly stressed, but in a dialectical manner. By counterposing speech about how the Canaanites *must be* and *were* destroyed against speech about how Canaanites *remained* in the land and were even *accepted* into Israel, DH weaves an ironic exposition on the problematic of carrying out God's commands.

It is noteworthy that throughout Joshua special attention is devoted to "exceptional outsiders," that is, groups of Canaanites and Israelites who do not belong to the primary core of "authentic" Israel: Rahab, Gibeonites, women, children, resident aliens, Levites, Transjordanian tribes, Caleb, daughters of Zelophehad, and even the exempted animals of Ai. The result is that, not only are many Canaanites unconquered, so that the full extent of the promised land is not taken, but numbers of weak and alien people are taken into Israel and given protective status. "As the narrative describes Israel-the-community settling within Israel-the-land, it never ceases to emphasize how much of the 'outside', both communally and territorially is 'inside' Israel."[8] This featuring of outsiders in Israel makes them into types of sinning and forgiven Israel at large. It is an aspect of the ideology of critical traditionalism which stresses that Israel will take the land, not because of special merit, but because of the wickedness of the nations already there (Deut. 9:4–5). Just as Israel does not deserve to take the land but does so, so Rahab and Gibeonites who deserve to perish are nonetheless brought under the protection of the covenant.

Judges carries forward the ideological impulse of DH by assembling stories in a framework that exposes Israel's utter desertion of God through religious apostasy and intermarriage with Canaanites. The debasement of Israel is so extreme that the whole people, according to the authoritarian dogmatism of one voice in Deuteronomy, ought by all rights to have been cast off by God. Yet God in mercy continually delivers Israel even though there is no repentance (in response to the one expression of Israelite repentance, 10:16 is taken to read "[Yahweh] grew annoyed with the troubled efforts of Israel"). In Judges retributive justice either stands apart from the divine commands of Mosaic Yahwism, as when Abimelech's fratricide is avenged by "God" (not Yahweh), or is grotesquely parodied when Samson goes to his ruin in a wild cycle of retaliatory actions involving the Philistines, or when the entire tribe of Benjamin is nearly extirpated to avenge a rape-murder and then immediately replenished by unmerited aggressions against Jabesh-gilead and Shiloh. In this manner the stories of Judges are assembled and framed not only to undermine authoritarian dogmatism but also to throw into question the handy applicability of critical traditionalism to history, since the religious and moral stances of the chief actors have so little to do with whether they prosper or fail. A pall of ignorance and ambiguity falls over the text, purposely conjured by DH in order to show how difficult it is to interpret Israel's history by any strict univocal reading of the divine law.

This initial structuralist analysis of Joshua and Judges teems with insights and imperatives for further inquiry. Since it touches on all the passages treated more microscopically in many shorter new literary studies (§23.1), it is of interest to observe the frequent points of agreement or convergence among literary critics concerning the significance of features customarily

8. Ibid., 145.

passed over by older critics. The decision to focus methodologically on literary structure clearly pays off, not only in single passages but in extended sources and whole books. This broad-ranging structuralist reading suggests live possibilities for relating literary structural exegesis to other forms of biblical criticism.

This sophisticated display of literary structure in Joshua and Judges prompts immediate dialogue with longstanding issues of literary history. If the contending ideological voices of DH are approximately as described, and if they have left such noticeable imprint on many details of reported and reporting speech, the intimation of a large role for DH in the composition of the enclosed traditions might be investigated by identifying how far the ideological voices actually penetrate into particular tradition units (where they once were thought to appear only in the frames) and by determining in detail the ways in which these voices are expressed by distinctive compositional features. The result might be either to reveal that DH was a much more original author than usually supposed, or that the pre-DH sources were more ironically ideological than previously recognized, or both may prove to be the case.

The role of "exceptional outsiders" in Joshua (also continued into Judges) raises the fascinating question of whether this ideological construct goes back to an actual sociohistoric horizon where Israel was in fact created out of disparate peoples, Canaanites included. Heretofore, the surface composition of Joshua and Judges, with its sharp polarity between Israelites and Canaanites, has obscured the irony that structural analysis now brings out: the deep ambiguity toward non-Israelites who again and again hold their ground against Israel or are actually taken up into Israel. Striking in this structural rendering is that DH comes off not as a clumsy editor who stupidly, or perhaps bound by tradition, selected stories of partial conquest that badly undermined his expressed belief in total conquest. Instead, DH appears more like an astute author-compiler who deliberately mixed a profusion of data and interpretations about partial and total conquests in order to show the ambiguous success of Israel in the land as a combination of mixed peoples, many of whom did not fit the profile of later nationalistic orthodoxy. Indeed, the inclusion of the "scandalous" annals and stories of Judges 1 and 17—21 may well be a supreme instance of the DH ideology of suspicion toward too-neat historical interpretations. In any case, the current rethinking of Joshua and Judges as sources for the reconstruction of the origins of Israel (§24) is clearly facilitated from a literary angle by this trenchant structural analysis.

24
SOCIOHISTORIC HORIZONS OF
JOSHUA AND JUDGES

24.1 Hypotheses About Israel's Rise to Power

The fundamental question of the origins of Israel may be posed in the following manner: How did Israel come into control of Canaan? Three primary explanatory models, accented in various ways, have been proposed.[9] It has been argued that Israel seized Canaan in a massive, unified military conquest. Alternatively, it has been contended that Israel occupied Canaan by peaceful infiltration, treaty making, and natural population growth. Finally, it has been recently claimed that Israel was a sector of the native Canaanite populace that revolted against the city-state overlords and upper classes and established its own sociopolitical and religious alternative order.

24.1.a The Conquest Model

The model of an Israelite military conquest of Canaan derives from the scenario of a united twelve-tribe invasion and seizure of the land under the direction of Joshua as reported in Joshua 1—12.[10] A straightforward reading of the biblical text envisions a series of lightning attacks that defeat armies, overthrow cities, and annihilate or expel the Canaanite populace en masse. The attackers are a people, escaped from slavery in Egypt, who have crossed the Sinai wilderness, traveled north through Transjordan, and launched their assault across the Jordan River from east to west. Attacking in the center around Jericho, Ai, and Gibeon, they then fan out to the south and to the north to bring the whole land into subjection. After overwhelming victory, they are able to divide and settle the land unhindered. This basic account is presupposed in other parts of the Hebrew Bible, and the sharp demarcation between Israelites and Canaanites as mortal antagonists, almost "natural enemies," seems to accord with this conception of two national and religious entities struggling over control of territory.

Archaeology has been enlisted to support the conquest model. Two types of evidence are cited: (1) widespread destruction of Canaanite cities in the

9. For a concise review, see George W. Ramsey, *The Quest for the Historical Israel* (Atlanta: John Knox Press, 1981), 65–98. The work of Chaney (n. 12 below), while opting for one model, subjects all of them to a careful critique.

10. G. Ernest Wright, *Biblical Archaeology,* rev. ed. (Philadelphia: Westminster Press, 1962), 69–85; idem, "Introduction to Joshua," in *Joshua* by Robert G. Boling, AB (Garden City, N.Y.: Doubleday & Co., 1982), 1–88 (written in 1973 and published posthumously).

approximate period when Israel is believed to have entered the land (ca. 1230–1175 B.C.E.); (2) a new and uniform type of occupation at some of the destroyed cities that is most logically associated with Israelites.

A series of excavated mounds, identified as particular biblical sites with a high degree of probability, show evidence of having been extensively or totally destroyed during the late thirteenth and early twelfth centuries. Five of the nine destroyed cities listed below are reported to have been taken by Joshua or the house of Joseph. Moreover, some cities which are omitted from the accounts of the conquest—or are specifically said *not* to have been conquered by Joshua—have, on excavation, shown no signs of destruction in this period. The most frequently cited locations for these two classes of evidence are listed in table 16, in each case cited in geographical order from north to south. (Consult table 3 for the range of archaeological periods represented at each site.)

All in all, supporters of the conquest model find major corroboration of the biblical account in the archaeological evidence about the cities conquered by Joshua and the cities not taken by him. Obviously, of course, the evidence about cities undestroyed in the period cuts somewhat against the grain of any literal acceptance of a total conquest theory, and is the first of many signs that the conquest theory is highly problematic.

Another kind of archaeological evidence, less dramatic and slower in accumulating, is given increasing credence. That is the evidence of the type and distribution of occupation in the layers following the late thirteenth and early twelfth century destructions. So far the reported evidence is concentrated at four sites: Hazor, Succoth, Bethel, and Debir (and possibly also at Gezer and Beth-shemesh). In each instance, following virtually complete destruction, unfortified and architecturally simple, even crude, settlements appear. It is claimed that these remains point to a culturally less-advanced population living in temporary encampments or in poorly constructed houses without fortifications. Assuming the new residents to have been the destroyers of the Late Bronze cities on whose ruins they settled, it is tempting to see them as the technically impoverished "seminomadic" Israelites.

To these settlements springing up on destroyed sites may also be added settlements on previously unoccupied sites or at places where there had been long breaks in occupation during the Late Bronze Age (table 17). The Iron I pottery at all these sites shows continuity with the pottery from the simple encampments at Hazor and Succoth and from the crude buildings at Bethel and Debir.

When the whole body of biblical and archaeological data is examined, the

TABLE 16
Archaeological Evidence on Destruction of Cities
in Late Bronze/Iron I Canaan

1. *Canaanite Cities Destroyed in the Late Thirteenth and Early Twelfth Centuries*

   *Hazor (Tell el-Qedaḥ)

   Meggido (Tell el-Mutesellim)

   Succoth (Tell Deir ʿAllā)

   †Bethel (Beitîn)

   Beth-shemesh (Tell er-Rumeileh)

   Ashdod (Esdûd)

   *Lachish (Tell ed-Duweir)

   *Eglon (Tell el-Ḥesî)

   *Debir/Kiriath Sepher (Khirbet Rabud or Tell Beit Mirsim)

2. *Canaanite Cities Not Destroyed in the Late Thirteenth and Early Twelfth Centuries*

   Beth-shan (Tell el-Ḥuṣn)

   Taanach (Tell Taʿannak)

   Shechem (Tell Balâṭah)

   Gibeon (el-Jîb)

   Gezer (Tell Jezer)

   Jerusalem (el-Quds)

*Conquered by Joshua.
†Conquered by house of Joseph.

TABLE 17
Archaeological Evidence on New Settlements
in Late Bronze/Iron I Canaan

1. *New Settlements on Previously Unoccupied Sites in the Late Thirteenth and Twelfth Centuries*

        Dor (Khirbet el-Burj)

        ʿIzbet Ṣarṭah (biblical site unknown)

        Tell Radanna (biblical Beeroth or Ataroth-[adar]?)

        Gibeah (Tell el Fûl)

        Giloh (biblical site unknown)

        Tell ʿÊṭûn (biblical site unknown)

        Beersheba (Tell es-Saba´)

2. *New Settlements on Long Deserted Sites in the Twelfth and Eleventh Centuries*

        Shiloh (Khirbet Seilûn)

        Ai (et-Tell)

        Mizpah (Tell en-Naṣbeh)

        Bethzur (Khirbet eṭ-Ṭubeiqah)

        Tell Masos (biblical Hormah?)

case for the conquest model of Israelite origins in Canaan is sharply reduced if not undermined beyond repair. In the biblical traditions there is a striking incongruity between the conception of total conquest expressed in the framework of Joshua and the stories and annals marshaled to illustrate the claim. The stories of Joshua 1—12 tell about military action in no more than three tribal areas: mainly in Benjamin, with thrusts into Judah and Naphtali. A list of thirty-one defeated kings who ruled over cities throughout the land shows only that all these kings were defeated, not necessarily that their cities were captured or destroyed (Josh. 12:7–24). In fact, the list includes cities which, after Joshua's death, were either first taken by tribes acting on their own or remained unconquered until the time of David. One suspects that this list of kings did not, in its original form, purport to tell of captured cities but rather of overthrown rulers; and that, when it later was understood as an inventory of captured cities, it was expanded so as to attribute the victories to the archetypal conqueror Joshua.

Discrepancies between claimed total conquest by united Israel and reported limited conquests by individual tribes have been unnoticed or evaded in part because, with the exception of Josh. 13:1–6a (dealing mostly with extra-Palestinian territories), the "negative" or limited conquest reports have placed outside of the Joshua conquest narratives proper and included either in the tribal boundary and city lists of Joshua 13—19 or in Judges 1. This has made it possible for interpreters either to avoid the contradictions or to rationalize that Joshua did conquer all or most of the land, but that after his death Israelite power waned, Canaanites staged a comeback, and the various tribes had to reconquer lost territories.

Given all the equivocations in the biblical data, most contemporary proponents of the conquest model have developed sharply modified versions of the hypothesis. What they now tend to say is that Joshua led a group of tribes (probably not all twelve of them) in a concerted attack that broke the resistance of the Canaanites in three swift campaigns: one in the center of the land at Jericho-Ai-Gibeon; a second in the Judean shephelah and highlands against Makkedah, Libnah, Lachish, Eglon, Hebron, and Debir (or at least some of those sites), and a third in Galilee against Hazor. These attacks are estimated to have loosened Canaanite sovereignty over the mountainous regions of Galilee, Samaria, and Judah and left the Israelites free to consolidate and extend their holdings without serious opposition.

Many proponents of the conquest model also concede that the absence of reports about military blows in the central regions of Ephraim and Manasseh, coupled with the assembly summoned by Joshua at Shechem

(Joshua 24), probably show that the center of the land was linked to Israel by peaceful entente (perhaps similar to the Gibeonite treaty) or by an amalgamation of the entering tribes with ethnically related peoples (*'apiru?*). There is also a willingness to grant that certain conquests achieved by individual tribes or clans in the wake of the initial military strikes have been erroneously attributed to Joshua in the course of consolidating and simplifying the traditions.

In curtailing the scope of the conquest model, its essential features become strained and dubious. Joshua as the unifying conqueror is not sharply characterized, appearing rather as an editorially introduced "bridge figure" to join the disparate narratives under the impression of a massive initial Israelite conquest. If his Ephraimite origin is correctly remembered, it is striking that no specifically Ephraimite or Manassite conquests are recorded under his leadership, although the battle at the pass of Beth-horon in Joshua 10 may be so construed. Moreover, an overlooked Israelite victory over royal armies in the vicinity of Shechem, poetically recalled in Ps. 68:11–14, may also have been led by Joshua. It is frequently contended that the assembly of tribes he gathered at Shechem was more truly Joshua's historical work than the various battles claimed for him.

How is the archaeological evidence for total conquest to be evaluated? It turns out that there is as much—and maybe more—to be said *against* using the archaeological results to support the conquest model as there is in its favor. To begin with, there is the gaping hole in the Joshua accounts created by the negative archaeological results from Jericho, Ai, and Gibeon. If Jericho stood at all in the late thirteenth century, it was no more than a small unwalled settlement, or at most a fort. Ai was not occupied at the time and had not been for centuries. If the actual conquest of Bethel has been confused with nearby Ai, we would still have two versions of how Bethel was taken and they do not agree in essentials (Josh. 8:1–29; Judges 1:22–26). No Late Bronze remains have been located at Gibeon (other than some tomb pottery from the fourteenth and possibly early thirteenth centuries), raising questions about Israel's purported treaty with the Gibeonites. Also, while the evidence from Hazor suits Joshua 11 well, it also creates problems in Judges 4 where Hazor is still in the hands of a king Jabin.

Such difficulties point up the necessity of cross-examining the archaeological data amassed to support the conquest model. There are three pertinent questions to be asked:

1. *Do we really know that it was the Israelites who conquered all the cities found destroyed in the late thirteenth and early twelfth centuries?* The con-

querors of the Canaanite cities did not leave any written or material record of their identities, so there is no evidence to tell us outright that they were Philistines, Egyptians, rival Canaanites or Canaanites in revolt, Israelites, or seminomadic raiders. Probably the least likely among the possible destroyers are the Philistines. It is extremely doubtful that they came into Palestine in any force before 1150 B.C.E. Prior to that they appear as select mercenaries of the Egyptians. But the Egyptians themselves are more probable candidates for at least some of the destructions.

The pharaohs of the Nineteenth Dynasty sought to reassert dominion over Syria-Palestine after a century of decline in their Asiatic empire. Although the itineraries of cities conquered by Seti I, Rameses II, and Merneptah tend to concentrate on the coastal regions and in the valleys, it is probable that Merneptah (or an earlier pharaoh) had a garrison at Nephtoah near Jerusalem, and Merneptah claims to have conquered Gezer and to have "destroyed Israel" (ca. 1230–1220 B.C.E. [table 1: 2D]). With the exception of Bethel and Debir, the destroyed cities in question were either in the valleys or in the lowlands on the edge of the highlands, within easy reach of Egyptian forces operating along the coastal road.

Similar openness must be maintained to the possibility of destruction caused by intercity strife or by open revolt within cities. The Amarna letters show that Canaanite cities were attacking one another in the fourteenth century, and the response of Jerusalem and its allies to Gibeon's treaty with Israel (Josh. 10:1–5) indicates that the same was true in the late thirteenth century. Judges 9:26–49 reports what terrible destruction could be inflicted on a city such as Shechem torn by civil strife, a reality earlier alluded to in some of the Amarna letters (table 1: 1K). It has been claimed that the total destruction of Canaanite cities could not have been caused by revolting Canaanites because they would have wished to preserve the cities for themselves after they had ousted the old rulers. But considering the destructive aftermath of the uprising against Abimelech, that does not seem a cogent argument.

To be sure, rebels might prefer a minimum of destruction, but they also were committed to inflict the destruction necessary to eliminate oppressive rulers. In addition, since the fortified cities were military, economic, and political nerve centers of hierarchic institutions, any revolt that was anti-hierarchic in intent might have deliberately aimed at smashing the urban centers rather than taking them over. The proposal that Canaanites may have destroyed one another's cities, or that the cities may have been ruined in civil wars and revolts, appears entirely consonant with the archaeological evidence.

2. *How do these late thirteenth and early twelfth century destructions and new settlements compare in number, quality, and distribution with destructions and resettlements of the same or similar cities in earlier and later periods?* Archaeologists have tended to address specific historical questions arising from the biblical text. They have been less interested in making a refined inventory of the frequency and types of destruction and settlement over regions of Canaan during long spans of time. A typology of destructions may admittedly be difficult to construct since techniques of military destruction, except where new types of fortification and siege warfare appear, do not change with anything like the discernible changes in pottery types.

Apparently the period in question did not see any marked technological changes in siege warfare between the arrival of the Hyksos in the eighteenth century and the penetration of the west by Assyrians in the ninth century. Indeed, it probably should be asked whether all the destructions by fire identified archaeologically were *necessarily* caused by military attack (cities do accidentally burn!). By contrast, a more refined archaeological interpretation of the modes of settlement, urban and rural, seems nearer of attainment. Area surveys and studies, such as those conducted around Ai and in upper Galilee, have been helpful in this regard, and the quickened attention to unwalled rural settlements has begun to enlarge the picture of life among "average" Israelites. The results so far, however, do not register unequivocally in favor of conquest as the means by which Israel took Canaan.

3. *If it was Israelites who destroyed some or all of these cities, what is there in the material evidence to show that they were destroyed in a coordinated campaign by united Yahwist Israelites?* Nothing whatsoever shows that the cities were conquered in a coordinated campaign or series of campaigns. Any combination of Israelite, Egyptian, Canaanite, or other attackers, could have conquered these cities over the fifty-year span involved. Or, they could have been ruined by Israelites operating as separate tribal entities or in combinations of two or more tribes. On the other hand, the general reconstruction of a culture intervening between extensive decline and destruction of Canaanite cities in the highlands and foothills, and the somewhat later arrival of a materially different Philistine culture, does bear considerable weight. But precisely what weight?

It is demonstrable that a culturally distinct network of settlements spread over mountainous Cisjordan from the late thirteenth century onward. Since it can hardly have been Philistine, and since it clearly was not Egyptian, it is entirely plausible to regard these settlements as broadly "Israelite." The decisive rub comes in giving specificity to this intervening culture in terms that correlate with the biblical text. There simply is no one-to-one correspondence between "Israelite" as understood from the material cultural evidence and "Israelite" as projected by the centralized biblical scheme of united Israel under Joshua.

"Israelite" in the material cultural sense does not mean twelve-tribe Israel taking Canaan by storm. It does not even imply that the material cultural remains belonged in all cases to groups who were at the time members of a Yahwistic league of tribes. "Israelite" in the material cultural sense supported by archaeology might well allow that its bearers were still proto-Israelites, or some combination of rebellious Canaanite peoples and incoming Yahwists from which "Israel" in its centralized biblical sense was only beginning to take form. These and perhaps yet other meanings of "Israelite" are admissible in archaeological terms. The archaeological typology of the period creates significant preliminary cultural material parameters that prove to be as complex and ambiguous as the biblical parameters themselves.

24.1.b The Immigration Model

Another view of how Israel entered Canaan began to gain advocacy as critical study of the Hebrew Bible succeeded in laying bare the units of biblical tradition and exposing their fragmented and contradictory character, at first in a literary-critical analysis of Judges 1 and then in intensive form-critical and tradition-historical investigations of the entire range of "conquest" traditions.[11] The immigration model theorized a long, complicated process of peaceful infiltration, uneven amalgamation with local peoples, and a final military-political triumph achieved only by Israel in the time of David. The DH vision of a total conquest by united Israel is judged to be a retrospective idealizing view developed *after* this protracted struggle for Canaan was won under the monarchy. By contrast, amid the older separate tradition units enclosed by DH can be seen traces of an originally peaceful occupation of the land, and even of outright intermarriage and treaty making with the Canaanite inhabitants. For example, it was noted that the patriarchs lived for the most part in harmony with the resident population, that Canaanite cities became Israelite clans in Manasseh (Josh. 12:17, 24; 17:2–3), and that Judah intermarried openly with Canaanites (Genesis 38).

11. Martin Noth, *THI*, 68–84; Manfred Weippert, "Canaan, Conquest and Settlement of," IDBSup, 125–30.

The cultural and religious separation between Canaanites and Israelites was construed as initially a difference between resident peoples and pastoral nomads and, in some cases, the difference between politically established people and social drifters described in the Amarna letters as *'apiru*, a term that is cognate with the biblical word "Hebrew(s)." Only slowly did these tensions push the parties into total ethnic and religious opposition.

On the one hand, stress is laid on the normalcy of bedouin penetration into settled areas, at first in seasonal movements entailing reciprocal agreements between herdsmen and farmers, and later in settlement on unoccupied land or seizure of land by force of arms. The earliest Israelites are often conceived as seasonal or seminomads who only slowly became numerous and coordinated enough to threaten the Canaanites. One form of the model conceived the Israelites as entering empty spaces between the widely scattered highland Canaanite cities. There the Israelites fell outside the jurisdiction of the city-states and developed for some time without significant contact with their agricultural and urban neighbors. Other immigration theorists see more contact and treaty relations between the two parties, even measurable intermixing of the two populations, as the Israelites more and more abandoned pastoral nomadic life and took up farming.

On the other hand, continuity is often underlined between at least some Israelites and the *'apiru* peoples who appear as social outcasts and outlaws throughout the ancient Near East, and whose presence in Canaan is documented from the late fifteenth century through the early thirteenth century. Sometimes the *'apiru* attacked the established authorities, but in Canaan they also appear as mercenaries. If the *'apiru* of the Amarna letters had gained control of parts of Canaan, thirteenth-century Israelites need not have employed force on entering the land because they would have been welcomed by their *'apiru* relatives. The prominence of Shechem, as a city that collaborated with *'apiru* in the Amarna age and served as an assembly point for early Israel, is frequently construed in terms of *'apiru*-Israelite collaboration. Unrecognized inconsistencies in the sociological analysis of early Israel often arise at this juncture when pastoral nomadic and *'apiru* data are uncritically harmonized.

One of the cardinal features of the immigration model has been its stress on uncoordinated movements of Israelites (or potential Israelites) into Canaan from different directions and at different times. An early wave, often thought to include tribes that later were displaced and declined in importance, such as Reuben, Simeon, Levi, and Gad, is generally assigned to the central western highlands. It is argued that, if the exodus from Egypt is historical—immigrationists are inclined to be skeptical on this point—

only a fraction of the eventual roster of Israelite tribes was involved in it. The penetration of the tribes of Benjamin, Ephraim, and Manasseh across the Jordan in the vicinity of Jericho-Gilgal later became the nucleus of the Joshua 1—12 stories of total conquest.

Another infiltration of Israelites moved northward from the Negeb, possibly the same group connected with Kadesh in the wilderness traditions, contributing to the formation of Judah. Colonization of Transjordan by Israelites moving eastward across the Jordan after settling in the western highlands is also claimed. The Galilee tribes are generally assumed to have entered the region in yet other migrations. The prehistory of Issachar is sometimes seen in a fourteenth-century Amarna letter that refers to corvée laborers on royal estates at Shunem, and a late thirteenth-century Egyptian reference to "a chief of Asher" is often read as an Israelite tribal identification.

When the immigration model first arose it was assumed that the twelve-tribe system in Israel was a late development during the monarchy. Subsequently it was argued that the twelve-tribe system was the early socioreligious framework by which the otherwise disparate tribes organized themselves in Canaan. On this view, the religion of Yahweh was the official cult of a new tribal league called Israel. The adequacy of this theory will be examined (§24.2.b).

By regarding the premonarchic tribal league as the life setting of the early traditions of Israel, it was possible to explain their mixed and fragmentary nature. The traditions were analyzed as an amalgam of materials drawn from the several members of the league and worked up in cultic recitations as enlargements of a series of basic history-like themes that give the foundation story of united Israel as the object of Yahweh's saving acts (§14.3). The present form of Joshua and Judges lends the stories a façade of national unity; however, when their contents are traced far enough back in the tradition-making process they reveal the conditions of separate tribes in their own locales prior to the unification in a religiously strong but politically loose league.

Advocates of the immigration model have tended either to ignore or to discount the historical value of archaeological evidence for illuminating the specifics of Israelite origins. They point, for example, to the shifting and now largely negative conclusions of archaeologists on such sites as Jericho and Ai. They believe that it was methodologically mistaken in the first place to think that, given the sparseness of solid historical records, archaeology could underpin the historicity of traditional biblical accounts that are so clearly partial, disconnected, and schematic. While immigrationists credit general sociocultural value to archaeological work, they stress its muteness for historical reconstruction in a situation where written remains, other than the legendary biblical texts, are so minimal.

24.1.c The Social Revolution Model

In the last two decades, a revolt model has emerged with the controversial proposal that we can adequately account for what the Bible tells us of Israel's emergence in Canaan on the theory that Israel was composed in large part of native Canaanites who revolted against their overlords and joined forces with a nuclear group of invaders and/or infiltrators from the desert (the exodus Israelites). This model draws on key elements from the conquest and immigration models, rearranging and nuancing them to form a fundamentally new conception of Israel's rise to power.[12]

In common with the conquest model, revolt theorists acknowledge an important dimension of armed conflict in Israel's emergence from the start, and they are inclined to see the exodus Israelites, with their faith in the militant delivering God Yahweh, as the final catalyst that clinched a long-brewing social revolution among depressed and marginated Canaanites. In keeping with the immigration model, revolt theorists urge that the formation of Israel was a coalition of many groups with separate prehistories and cultural backgrounds who contributed to the potpourri of traditions underlying the surface unity both in Genesis-Numbers and in Deuteronomy-Judges. Thus, like the immigration view, the revolt hypothesis rejects the notion of Canaanites and Israelites as monolithic ethnic blocs and seeks to trace the subtleties in the shift from Canaanites as city-state underlings to Canaanites as tribal Israelites. Also, while an exodus ingredient in the Israelite movement is generally granted as the "spark" that provided high morale and coordination, it was Canaanites who provided the "tinder" of human forces in motion for the revolutionary conflagration.

For some centuries Canaan had been dominated by city-states with hierarchies of aristocratic warriors and bureaucrats who took over the agricultural surplus of the villages where the majority of the populace lived and primary production was based. This tributary mode of production (often called the Asiatic mode of production) laid on the mass of peasants and herdsmen heavy burdens of taxation in kind, forced labor, and military

---

12. George E. Mendenhall, *The Tenth Generation. The Origins of the Biblical Tradition* (Baltimore: Johns Hopkins University Press, 1973); Norman K. Gottwald, *TY;* Marvin L. Chaney, "Ancient Palestinian Peasant Movements and the Formation of Premonarchic Israel," in *Palestine in Transition: The Emergence of Ancient Israel,* ed. David N. Freedman and David F. Graf, SWBAS 2 (Sheffield: Almond Press, 1983), 39–90.

service. Indebted peasants, deprived of independent means of subsistence, were recruited as cultivators of large estates or reduced to the status of tenant farmers. A large percentage of the communal productive energy and resources went into warfare and the luxuried life of the ruling classes that included lavish religious displays. Local Canaanite kings and elites passed on some of this communal product in tribute to the Egyptian imperial overlords when compelled to do so.

Various sectors of the Canaanite populace struggled against this social burden in different ways. The peasant majority resisted surrender of their produce and labor to the state as they were able, sometimes throwing their support to an enemy attacker or to a rebel faction within their city-state in the hope that new leadership might be less oppressive. Or they might attempt to retreat to highland or steppe regions where they would be less vulnerable to state power. Pastoral nomads had an advantage in their seasonal movements which made it somewhat more difficult for the state to control them and allowed them a measure of maneuver to throw their support to one state or another. 'Apiru social outsiders turned to robbery or mercenary service, which gave them leverage in the infighting among city-states, and sometimes, like the peasants, they retreated to mountain redoubts.

During the fourteenth and thirteenth centuries, as warfare among the city-states increased and as population apparently declined (for reasons unknown at present), restive peasants, pastoral nomads, 'apiru, and other disaffected elements, were drawn toward closer cooperation, even alliances, in order to fend off the control of the city-states. In time, probably with the arrival of the exodus Israelites, the religion of Yahweh became the socioreligious ideology and organizational framework that won over these rebellious peoples and helped to forge them into an effective revolutionary movement that expelled the tributary mode of production from the highlands and substituted a system of free peasant agriculture within a loose tribal design.

The early formulation of the revolt model tended to overstate the polarization of the total Canaanite populace for or against revolution and also to conceive the revolution as sudden, cataclysmic, and conclusive. Subsequent elaborations of the model have stressed that rebellious and potentially revolutionary forces had been at work in Canaan for decades, at first divided from one another by city-state and regional boundaries and by socioeconomic types (separate strategies by peasants, pastoral nomads, 'apiru, and other less clearly differentiated sectors such as the Shosu mentioned in Egyptian texts, ca. 1500–1150 B.C.E.). Slowly coalescing, first in an El-worshiping union, they finally became a greatly expanded Yahweh-worshiping coalition.

The Israelite revolution could only succeed by struggle on many fronts: by undermining the fundamental peasant base of the city-states, by countering the city-state religiopolitical propaganda with superior egalitarian Yahwist propaganda, and by driving a wedge into the loyalty of the governing apparatus so that elements of the bureaucracy and army could be split off, recruited, or neutralized. A long process of militarizing the peasantry, equipping them for self-sufficient marginal agriculture in the highlands, and training them in the cementing symbolic traditions of the new culture and religion was needed to forge the elements of victory. Even so, the social revolution of early Israel was arduous and protracted and did not culminate until the early rule of David, by which time hierarchic tendencies were resurgent within Israel.

As normally happens in a social revolution, the Canaanite populace responded to the uprising with varying degrees and kinds of support or opposition. There are instances of the formation of Israel out of Canaanite "converts," for example, subjects of the Amorite Sihon (Num. 21:27b–30), Rahab and her group at Jericho (Joshua 2; 6:22–25), an informer and his group at Bethel/Luz (Judges 1:22–26), and Adullamites and other urban groups in the Judean foothills (Genesis 38). There are other cases of Canaanite "neutrals" who observed nonintervention in the internal affairs of Israel and noncooperation in hostile actions against Israel initiated by other Canaanites, for example, Shechem and other cities in Manasseh (Gen. 48:22; Joshua 24; Judges 9), cities in upper Galilee (Joshua 11), and Jerusalem (Gen. 14:18–20; Josh. 10:1–5; 15:63; Judges 1:1–8, 21; 19:10–15). Lastly, there are examples of Canaanite "allies" under the protection of Israel who gave support to Israel while maintaining a separate status within the Israelite movement, for example, Gibeon and the other Hurrian cities in Benjamin (Joshua 9—10; 2 Sam. 4:1–3; 21:1–14), Meroz (Judges 5:23), Succoth and Penuel (Judges 8:4–17), and Kenites/Rechabites (Judges 1:16; 4:11; 1 Sam. 15:6–7; 30:29). These shifting and nuanced alignments are typical of revolutionary situations which involve vacillating "middle forces" who only reluctantly are driven toward one side or the other in the conflict.

Moreover, whole Israelite tribes give evidence of having been composites of local Canaanites, and possibly even of Philistines. The assembly at Shechem (Joshua 24) makes sense as a ritual incorporation of part of the Canaanite populace, purged of their oppressing kings, newly tribalized, who throw off the Baal religion and/or their own clan gods surviving from earlier spheres of group experience, and accept Yahweh of the Israelites who has helped them in their victories. The emergence of Judah as a composite of many southern groups, including absorption of Canaanites, would also make sense on such a model.

Moreover, Issachar, described as one who "bowed his shoulder to bear, and became a slave at forced labor" (Gen. 49:15), may well refer to the vulnerable position of underclasses in the Valley of Jezreel and their forced subservience as estate laborers to the nearby city-states of Beth-shan, Taanach, and Megiddo, until they grew strong enough to throw off their oppressors. It is not difficult to see Issachar as a "tribe" formed out of Canaanite serfs who threw off their masters with the aid of already-free Israelite tribes to their north in Galilee and to their south in Samaria. It has also been proposed that the tribe of Dan derived from the Sea Peoples known from Greek and Egyptian sources as the Denen or Danuna, who settled first on the Palestinian coast north of the Philistines before their conversion to Yahwism and eventual migration to the headwaters of the Jordan.

Thus the stock opposition Israelite vs. Canaanite can be seen to have undergone a conceptual shift over time. As soon as the Canaanite lower classes converted and left the city-state structure with its official Baal religion, they were no longer self-identified or viewed by others as Canaanites. The term Canaanite came to refer to city-state hierarchical structure, with its concomitant religious ideology of Baalism, that continued in the cities of the plains and tended to creep back into Israel as revolutionary fervor abated. This "reinvasion" of Canaanite institutions and ideology into the Israelite sphere was abetted by David when he incorporated whole Canaanite city-states into his empire which had never been a part of the Yahwistic religious and sociopolitical revolutionary process.

In time, as Israel gained primary identity as a national state with its own distinctive cult, Canaanite and Israelite were used as labels for two fixed national domains and peoples who presumably had always had entirely separate histories, with religious differences especially emphasized as the chief criterion of separation between them. As a pejorative expression of what early Israel actually opposed and overthrew, "Canaanite(s)" originally referred to a hierarchic and tributary socioeconomic and political system peopled by kings, administrators, armies, monopoly merchants, exploitative landlords and overseers, priests, and deities. Israel had countered and overcome this system by winning over many Canaanites to its own ideas, armed struggle, and social organization.

The revolt model deals more flexibly with archaeological evidence of destruction levels in Canaanite cities than the immigration and conquest models have tended to do, although so far it is not apparent how archaeology might validate or invalidate the revolutionary hypothesis. Destruction of cities by any of several agencies could easily fit within the theory. Some cities may have been destroyed by invading Israelites from Egypt or elsewhere. Others may have been destroyed by revolting Canaanite underclasses, either before or after they converted to Israel. Some may have been attacked by Egyptians in punitive operations to quell the spreading disorder. Still others may have suffered attacks from neighboring cities trying to take territory, acquire, plunder, overthrow a rival ruler, or establish hegemony.

Moreover, the typological evidence for a distinctive early Iron Age culture in highland Canaan seems to accord well with the hypothesis of a tribalizing confederacy of collaborative lower-class Canaanites and exodus refugees who took over the name Israel that had been adopted by an earlier El-worshiping union. The fact that new kiln techniques appear with Iron I may suggest that potters who served the elites were killed off or driven out with their overlords, so that the exodus and native rebels had to develop their own means of pottery making. For the most part they followed familiar Late Bronze ceramic shapes, although new forms appear and there are differences in color preferences. The markedly lower incidence of imported wares reflects no doubt the decline in luxury trade accompanying the radical shift from the Canaanite tributary system to the Israelite egalitarian social system. Likewise, discrepancies and gaps between archaeological and biblical data, as in the cases of Jericho and Ai, are no difficulty for the revolt model on principle since it shares with the immigration model the belief that the traditions of early Israel were frequently compressed, inflated, transposed, and conflated in the process of slow accumulation toward their finished status as a literary etiology of united Israel.

24.2 Hypotheses About Israel's Tribal Social Organization

The debate over models of Israel's rise to power in Canaan is in reality a much larger conflict over the proper understanding of Israel as a social system. This conflict has not fully surfaced in biblical studies because of biblical scholarship's backwardness in adopting a sociological approach to early Israel. The need for methodological clarity on the issue of Israel's social constitution is by now so urgent that further significant progress even on the historical front is impeded by the anemic state of social inquiry. For the issue at stake is not simply the territorial-historical problem of how Israel took its land (e.g., the segments of Israel involved, the regions controlled, the methods of occupation, the sequence of seizures and setbacks, etc.). Behind these concerns lurk the complementary questions: What was this formation of people called Israel that took control over the hill country and whose social system took form as it came to power? What were the shared goals and bonding structures of Israel's social system in comparison with those of other social systems from which it emerged and against which it was counterposed? Up to now biblical studies have grappled with models of the settlement in Canaan and with models of the production and development of literary traditions, but there has been no adequate linkage of these forms of inquiry within a larger analytic model of the social system operative simultaneously in the twin processes of land taking and tradition making.

24.2.a The Pastoral Nomadic Model

Efforts by both conquest and immigration theorists to understand the origins of Israel have been saddled with naive assumptions about Israelites as pastoral nomads who invaded or infiltrated Canaan from the desert. These presuppositions must be radically reassessed.[13]

Pastoral nomadism is a socioeconomic mode of life based on intensive domestication of livestock that requires movement in a seasonal cycle dictated by the need for pasturage and water. Without a doubt, pastoral nomadism existed in the biblical world. Unfortunately, biblical interpreters have acquired and clung to hopelessly exaggerated and outmoded conceptions of the place of pastoral nomadism in social evolution, the numbers of pastoral nomads, their self-sufficiency and isolation from settled peoples, their role as presumed originators of major historical, social, and cultural changes, and the supposed socioeconomic and cultural equivalence of village tribalism and pastoral nomadism.

Data from prehistory and anthropology have clarified the secondary and limited development of pastoral nomadism out of a prior mixture of agriculture and animal husbandry in settled areas. Humans first entered the river valleys of Mesopotamia, not from the Arabian Desert, but from the Anatolian and Iranian hills and grasslands (§7.1). Under specific economic and political conditions, goats, sheep, and asses (already domesticated in farming communities) were grazed in large herds on the marginal desert steppes. In modern times no more than 10 percent of the total Middle East

---

13. Manfred Weippert in *The Settlement of the Israelite Tribes in Palestine* (SBT, 2d ser., 21 [London: SCM Press, 1971], 102–26) reaffirms pastoral nomadic origins for Israel; Gottwald (*TY*, 435–63) rejects the nomadic hypothesis; see also Chaney, "Ancient Palestinian Peasant Movements," 41–44.

populace has been composed of pastoral nomads, and there appear to be no ecological or technological factors that would have enlarged that percentage in biblical times. In fact, before the advent of camel and horse nomadism, permitting deeper penetration of the Arabian Desert (from the twelfth century on), the number of nomads was probably far fewer.

The degree of self-sufficiency and isolation of pastoral nomads varies markedly and has usually been grossly exaggerated by biblical exegetes and historians. In some cases the same community has pastoral nomadic and farming segments; in other cases a whole people alternates pastoral nomadism with crop cultivation in half-year cycles. A gamut of complex relations between pastoral nomads and settled peoples ranges from virtually complete merger, except for the feature of the periodic trek with the herds, to frequent or stated periodic contacts between them for the exchange of goods and mutual services (e.g., grazing rights over field stubble in return for fertilization of the fields by animal manure). These contacts are more often friendly than hostile, although not invariably. On occasion pastoral nomads try to build commercial empires by controlling trade routes and imposing tribute, as was the case with the Midianites in Sinai and Transjordan in the eleventh century and with the Nabateans in the same region in Greco-Roman times.

Historical reconstructions of the ancient Near East, and of Israel in particular, have been distorted by a "pan-nomadic" hypothesis that posits the Arabian Desert as an inexhaustible source of population influxes, military conquests, dynastic changes, cultural departures, and religious innovations. Migrations due to uprooting by natural and historical circumstances have been repeatedly equated unjustifiably with nomadism as regular movement in the exercise of a socioeconomic mode of life. Amorites, for example, have been carelessly subsumed under the broad heading of "pastoral nomads," and with no grounds have been assigned an origin in the Arabian Desert. Amorites at Mari, who were indeed pastoral nomads of a sort, were integrated into village communities and their restiveness and conflict with the state was not due to their invading or infiltrating from the desert to seize land but rather to their rural-based resistance to the drafting and taxing powers of the state.

In socioeconomic terms, typical elements of rural life and key features of tribal organization have been gratuitously identified as exclusively pastoral nomadic traits. The great majority of cited pastoral nomadic indicators have no such exclusive diagnostic value. Asses were used as favorite riding animals and reliable beasts of burden throughout the settled zone, and sheep and goats were kept regularly by settled peoples. Tents were used by merchants, armies, and royal hunting parties, and by farmers for guarding and harvesting distant fields or where building materials were scarce. On the other hand, nomads often lived not in tents but in grass or wood huts, mud houses, windscreens, or caves.

There is likewise a regular litany of tribal social practices in Israel that are indiscriminately attributed to "democratic" or "egalitarian" pastoral nomadic origins: blood revenge and hospitality, brotherly covenants, solicitude for strangers, orphans, and widows, levirate marriage and right of asylum, as well as warfare by ambush, feigned flight, single combat, and destruction of captives and booty, to name but a few. In truth, every one of these traits, and sometimes all of them together, can be found throughout a range of tribal, and even statist, social organizations in which not a single pastoral nomad is present.

Nonetheless, a careful reading of the biblical texts suggests that a component of pastoral nomadism did exist in early Israel alongside the more dominant socioeconomic modes of life. Two forms of transhumant pastoral nomadism were practiced by members of settled communities in early Israel: (1) winter treks into the steppes lying south and east of Canaan, and (2) spring/summer treks into the better-watered uplands of Canaan. Owing to the close proximity of steppe and cultivated zone in Canaan, as well as the fluctuating line between them governed by erratic rainfall, agricultural and pastoral nomadic modes of life were closely juxtaposed and interwoven. Many pastoral nomads were part-time or seasonal, and there were farmers who took to pastoral nomadism and returned to farming as economic and political circumstances prompted.

Migration is not ipso facto pastoral nomadism, a distinction regularly overlooked by those who automatically assume that the biblical patriarchs were pastoral nomads (§16.4). A similar judgment is normally made concerning the exodus Israelites in the wilderness. The movement of Israelites out of Egypt and across the wilderness, however, fails to satisfy the appropriate criteria of the pastoral nomadic trek. The departure from Egypt was flight, expulsion, or armed escape—not a seasonal herding trek. The mass of migrants are pictured as unfamiliar with desert terrain and survival requirements. Animals and people perish. Only the intervention of Jethro, a Midianite familiar with the environment, saves the disoriented fugitives. They settle for an extended period around the oases at Kadesh where agriculture was probably practiced. The diet of fish and vegetables that they recall in Egypt was hardly pastoral nomadic fare. In every way the desert is presented as an alien place.

Did land-hungry Israelite pastoral nomads conquer Canaan? Once the assertion of the pastoral nomadic identity of patriarchs and exodus Israelites is set aside as counterindicated, the remaining evidence is precarious in the extreme. The tribalism of early Israel is in no way a phenomenon restricted to pastoral nomads. The practice of holy war, notably the ritual destruction of captives and booty repeatedly cited as a pastoral nomadic institution par excellence, is paralleled among tribes of agriculturalists and even more extensively among state-organized peoples. The logical move, following the exposure of the pastoral nomadic mirage, is to look for the origins of Israel in the land of Canaan itself, for it is not to be forgotten that even those who came out of Egypt are represented as once having lived in the land of Canaan.

24.2.b The Religious League Model (Amphictyony)

Common both to conquest and immigration theorists, as well as to some revolt theorists, has been the notion of early Israel as a twelve-tribe religious league. The assumptions and applications of this hypothesis, while by no means entirely baseless, have been almost as damaging for achieving a holistic view of Israelite social organization as has been the pastoral nomadic hypothesis.[14]

In this interpretation, Israel was a confederacy of exactly twelve tribes organized around the cult of Yahweh celebrated at a central shrine in analogy with the sacral leagues of Greek, Old Latin, and Etruscan city-states. This classical religiopolitical institution, best attested by the Apollo league at Delphi, was known to the Greeks as an *amphictyony*, generally derived from a term meaning "inhabitants of the neighboring district" or "dwellers around [a common sanctuary]." The Israelite religious confederacy construed as an amphictyony was believed to have possessed a central shrine, a council with tribal delegates and law-proclaiming officials, and to have consisted of twelve members—on the still-undemonstrated assumption that each tribe cared for the upkeep of the central sanctuary for one month of the year. The central shrine in Israel was located at Shechem at the beginning and at Shiloh by the late eleventh century; in between it seems to have been at Bethel and Gilgal, and perhaps at Gibeon.

The most prevalent reconstruction of the growth of the amphictyony posited an original six-member amphictyony in northern Israel, composed of Reuben, Simeon, Levi, Judah, Zebulun, and Issachar (so-called Leah

14. For a concise presentation of the amphictyonic hypothesis, see Noth, *THI*, 85–109. For rebuttals of the hypothesis which still recognize a social organizational unity to premonarchic Israel, see C. H. J. de Geus, *The Tribes of Israel* (Amsterdam: Van Gorcum, 1976) and Gottwald, *TY*, 345–86.

tribes). After the entrance of the exodus tribes into Canaan, the amphic-tyony was expanded to twelve members, adding Joseph, Benjamin, Dan, Naphtali, Gad, and Asher (so-called Rachel and concubine tribes). Within a short time Levi became a priestly tribe and was dropped from the tribal enumeration, but the roster of twelve members was maintained by dividing Joseph into the two tribes of Ephraim and Manasseh. It was also supposed that Judah was itself formed out of an older six-member amphictyony at Hebron composed of Judahites, Simeonites, Othnielites, Calebites, Jerahmeelites, and Kenites.

The religious league model recognized that the tribes named in the amphictyonic roster bore an official status that did not accurately reflect the historical decline of some tribes (e.g., Reuben, Simeon, Gad) nor always correspond to the common names for population entities (e.g., Machir and Gilead occur in the Song of Deborah in place of Manasseh and Gad). Thus, the amphictyonic tribal lists do not quite correspond to any specific histor-ical situation in premonarchic Israel but reflect rather a historical process that made adjustments in the membership of the league to retain archaic features and to accommodate new tribal developments.

In spite of the ingenuities of this theory, it is much more likely that Israel did not become a precisely twelve-member confederacy until the verge of the monarchy and that the tribal roster *omitting* Levi and including Ephraim and Manasseh is a list of the tribal entities used by David as administrative divisions of his kingdom (cf. §22.1.b), while the tribal roster *including* Levi and Joseph is a later programmatic "all-Israelite" statement formulated after Solomon reorganized the kingdom and ceased to use David's system of administration by tribal divisions. The Song of Deborah implies strongly that at one point Israel consisted of only ten tribes, two of them with names that did not survive in the later tribal nomenclature.

This amphictyonic theory, which did much to explain the function of covenant and law within a basically pre-state form of social organization, has been criticized both in its detailed reconstruction and in its adequacy for explaining the total scope of Israelite society. The theory begins from a real enough fact: the undoubted association of Israelite tribes in a common religious institutional and ideological framework in premonarchic times. Finding a broadly analogous situation in ancient Greece and Italy, the model transfers the detailed features of the Mediterranean amphictyony into the Israelite setting. References to twelve units in Israel, and to twelve (or six) units among some of Israel's neighbors, become proof of an amphic-tyonic form of association. Important cultic centers become official central shrines. "Princes/tribal heads" (*n^{e}sī'īm*) become delegates to the amphictyonic council and minor "judges" *(shōpheṭīm)* become proclaimers and interpreters of amphictyonic law. In all these cases, however, doubtful interpretations of the Greek and Italian amphictyonies are made and the biblical texts are gleaned far too arbitrarily to recover the Israelite "amphictyony."

In the extensive critiques and defenses of the amphictyonic theory, little attention has been paid to a comparison of how the Greek amphictyony and the Israelite tribal league functioned in their respective social systems. The comparable and singular traits of the two institutions may be represented as in table 18.

Surveying this trait typology, it is clear that the comparability of the two associational forms holds good on only two very general points: the formal likeness of associated autonomous political units and the formal likeness of primary definition of the association in terms of a common religious cult. When these formal similarities at a high level of abstraction are qualified by all the features present in one of the league forms but absent in the other, however, we note that the Greek amphictyony and the Israelite confederacy entailed different confederating elements arranged in different ways in relation to the overall Greek and Israelite social systems. The Israelite confederacy comprehended the whole of society, whereas the Greek amphictyony was only one of several circumscribed league arrangements within a much larger society. Moreover, the Israelite confederacy was a consciously contrived "substitute state" opposed to surrounding city-state organization, indeed a veritable "anti-state," whereas the Greek amphictyony was a limited arm of autonomous city-states to achieve certain purposes.

Failure to note that amphictyony and confederacy operated at different levels of organization and with different notions of the proper mode of social organization has had the effect of drastically overstating the role of religion in Israelite society, and in this sense actually confirming the old confessional religious approach to the Hebrew Bible. The amphictyony in Greece was a basically cultic institution that served sociopolitical and cultural ends, but no one believes that Greek society came into existence merely by a religious impulse and program. By contrast, Israel as an "amphictyony" is seen to be solely or largely a religious creation centered on faith in and worship of Yahweh.

In the process, the reality of Israel's material cultural and sociopolitical life is ignored, downplayed, or treated as an "ideal" spinoff from the religious foundation. Religion as symbolic ordering of meaning and as

TABLE 18
Comparison of Greek Amphictyony and Israelite Confederacy

Comparable Traits of the Greek Amphictyony and
the Israelite confederacy:

Each was an association of autonomous political units

Each supported a common religious cult as the basis of membership in the association

Traits of the Greek Amphictyony Lacking in
the Israelite Confederacy

A single (sometimes dual) shrine and cult was the distinctive form of association

Membership in the common cult permitted any number of other cultic and political commitments by the league members

An amphictyonic council composed of delegates appointed by each member unit was responsible for the upkeep and protection of the central shrine

Amphictyonic members were city-states and not tribes in the period providing most of our information

Traits of the Israelite Confederacy Lacking in
the Greek Amphictyony

The confederacy functioned as the primary legal community

The confederacy coordinated the national military organization

The confederacy was committed to a single national deity whose cult was observed at many shrines

The confederate organization was a national societal organization encompassing and subsuming all members and subgroups of the society, so that other political commitments by member units were prohibited or severely circumscribed

Trait Claimed for Amphictyonic Organization but
Undemonstrated Either in the Greek Amphictyony
or in Its Supposed Israelite Counterpart

The obligatoriness of precisely six or twelve members in order to maintain the amphictyonic cult in monthly rotation has yet to be proved

cultic action functioned meaningfully in the Israelite confederacy in close connection with legal and military instrumentalities and forms of social bonding for communities of peasants who took charge of their own agricultural surplus and physical energies against the grain of Canaanite hierarchy that sought to exploit peasant surpluses and energies as their tributary right. However we conceive the early religious confederacy of Israel, it must be understood as the religious dimension of a fundamental program of communal self-determination in all aspects of the common life.

Unfortunately, most critiques of the amphictyonic design have concluded that no intertribal league whatsoever existed in premonarchic Israel, only discrete tribal groupings with a more or less common form of religious affiliation who only randomly cooperated. On the contrary, the amphictyonic theory is not mistaken because it claimed an all-Israelite confederacy but because it misconceived its inner structure, modes of operation, and social scope. Thus, while the assumption of early Israelite pastoral nomadism was largely erroneous, the assumption of an early Israelite amphictyony, though erroneous in its form and therefore to be rejected, correctly pointed to the central importance of intertribal organization among the first Israelites. Only on the theory of far-ranging affiliation and cooperation among the tribes is it possible to understand how they mounted and sustained their successful social and religious revolutionary movement.

24.2.c The Socioreligious Retribalization Model

Prevailing models of Israel as an invading or immigrating seminomadic and/or ʿapiru people of a distinct ethnic type who formed a league almost exclusively devoted to religious matters have fundamentally failed to provide a plausible account of Israelite beginnings (§24.1.a–b). More convincing is the hypothesis that Israel burst into history as an ethnically and socioeconomically mixed coalition composed of a majority of tribally organized peasants (80 percent or more of the populace), along with lesser numbers of pastoral nomads, mercenaries and freebooters, assorted craftsmen, and renegade priests. These sectors of the indigenous populace joined in a combined sociopolitical and religious revolution against the imperial and hierarchic tribute-imposing structures of Egyptian-dominated Canaan (§24.1.c).[15]

Early Israelites were primarily engaged in intensive rain- and spring-

---

15. George E. Mendenhall, "Social Organization in Early Israel," in *Magnalia Dei: The Mighty Acts of God. Essays on the Bible and Archaeology in Memory of G. Ernest Wright*, ed. F. M. Cross et al. (Garden City, N.Y.: Doubleday & Co., 1976), 132–51; Gottwald, *TY,* 464–587, 650–63; Chaney, "Ancient Palestinian Peasant Movements," 48–83.

irrigated agriculture, supplemented by stockbreeding and simple hand-crafts. Within the momentum of the Israelite movement, diverse segments of the Canaanite underclasses, previously divided and at odds in their struggles, gathered in the hill country and united in free agriculture based on regional mixes of grains, wine, oil, fruits, and vegetables. They possessed small bovine herds and larger sheep and goat herds, a fraction of which were tended by seasonal movements into the steppes or uplands.

Therefore, Israelite tribal organization must be accounted for not by the imaginary extension of pastoral nomadism into Canaan, but by the organized resurgence of suppressed rural and village independence against the drafting and taxing powers of the tributary state system exercised by the Egyptian Empire, Canaanite city-states, Midianites who attempted a commercial empire in eleventh-century Transjordan, the nascent national states of Ammon, Moab, and Edom, and the Philistine military oligarchy. Family and village networks of self-help and mutual aid were revived and extended to larger social groupings, gaining strength and experience in proportion as the military and political dominion of the city-states was expelled from the hill country.

The egalitarian project of early Israel was a risky venture in "retribalization." Its success was facilitated by a timely conjuncture of technological developments exploited by the peasant movement: introduction of metal farming tools, waterproof cisterns and small-scale irrigation systems, and rock terracing on the steep slopes and in wadi bottoms. In order to establish themselves securely, the renegade Israelites needed to gather enough people, well-enough fed and housed and skilled enough in the new methods of upland agriculture, to be able to extend mutual aid to one another, to absorb and encourage newcomers, and finally to defend themselves collectively against efforts of the politically declining city-states to reestablish their control, as well as to counter attacks from other hierarchic foes attempting to step into the vacuum left by the weakened Canaanites.

The socioeconomic relations of Israelites were egalitarian in the sense that the entire populace was assured of approximately equal access to resources by means of their organization into extended families, protective associations of families (sometimes called "clans," but not to be construed as exogamous clans that mandate marriage outside the group), and tribes, federated as an intertribal community called "Israel," "Israelites," or "tribes/people of Israel/Yahweh." The "vertical" residential groups arranged regionally as largely self-contained productive units were crosscut and bonded by "horizontal" associations or sodalities among which were aspects of mutual aid and military mustering in the protective associations, the citizen army, the ritual congregation, the Levite priests (landless and distributed among the tribes as instructional cadres), and probably also the Kenites/Rechabites (understood as itinerant metalworkers).

The basic unit of material production and reproduction was the extended family, which consumed or bartered what it produced. The larger groupings of protective associations and other sodalities, tribes, and intertribal confederacy operated in various autonomous or combined ways to provide mutual aid, external defense, and a religious ideology of covenanted or treaty-linked equals. Tribal leadership was heavily male-oriented, although women as a whole—relative to Canaanite class society—benefited from their participation as members of the tribal production and defense systems. We have noted how surprisingly large and positive a place women occupied in the early traditions of Israel (§16.4; 21).

The defining feature of politics in old Israel was that political functions were diffused throughout the social structure or focused in temporary ad hoc role assignments. Primary leadership fell to tribal functionaries. Elders applied customary laws to cases requiring adjudication and made consensus decisions for war and peace. Priests taught the instructions of the deity as they related to societal norms and priorities as well as to the narrower sphere of ritual. Military leaders emerged to command forces from one or more of the tribes in defense of Israel's free zone of settlement. There may have been a priestly or lay figure who played the mediator role of Moses in the covenant-renewal ceremonies, a kind of prototype of the later DH law interpreter (§18.2). There were regular means of consultation among the tribes, whether or not that included a council of the confederacy.

We have seen how confusing a spectrum of leadership functions is depicted in Judges, complicated by the DH habit of viewing disparate roles as the work of "judges" (§22.1.e). No interpretation of the office(s) of judge in early Israel has convincingly unraveled the textual difficulties. Some think that the minor judges of the annotated reports were all-Israelite officials of the confederacy. Others see them as local figures. The sharp line between civilian and military judges is denied by others who point out that Jephthah was a military leader who gained the top post of leadership in Gilead. Max Weber's delineation of the judges as classic "charismatic" types, inspired leaders in crisis who are self-authenticating, has obscured the extent to which they appear within the fabric of traditional leadership roles, somewhat in the manner of "the big man" role in observed tribal societies.

Some of the supposedly freewheeling "charismatic" judges begin their "judging" either on the basis of a traditionally sanctioned office they already hold (Ehud as head of a delegation carrying tribute to Moab,

Deborah as a prophetess to whom Israelites come "for judgment") or on the basis of a direct charge by those occupying traditionally sanctioned offices (Barak is summoned by Deborah, Jephthah is appointed by the elders of Gilead after shrewd negotiations). In all events, the multiple leadership functions in early Israel lay outside the realm of state power and bureaucratic credentials. Where powerful local leaders parlayed wealth and influence in a move toward chiefdom or petty kingship (Gideon and Abimelech), they were fiercely resisted. Power lay widely distributed in the hands of many groups so that a leveling process worked against ambitious power seekers.

In the socioeconomic spheres similar efforts were made to ensure the self-sustaining integrity of the household productive units. Many laws and stories allude to or describe some of these measures. Land was to be held continuously within extended families and never sold for speculation. It was obligatory to extend aid to other Israelites in need and no interest was permitted on such emergency loans. Strict limits were placed on contract servitude. Special provisions for the socially vulnerable (widows, orphans, strangers) were insisted on. An even-handed judicial system was highly prized.

The retribalization model of early Israel's social system as a correlate of the revolt model of Israel's rise to power supplies a connecting link between the religious thrust of Yahwism and the socioeconomic and political realities of Canaan, a link which neither the pastoral nomadic nor the amphictyonic models—either in their conquest or immigration forms—could offer, other than in the most abstract ways. It proposes a combined social and religious revolution as the key to explaining the phenomenal rise of Yahwism, its indigenous roots and power to adapt, its cultural pervasiveness, and its astonishing growth and integrating inclusiveness. It suggests that the socioeconomic and political conditions in Canaan were ripe for just such a movement as Yahwism and that Yahwism must be understood as an indigenous movement specifically addressed to the life circumstances of underclass or marginal Canaanites.

The revolutionary retribalization hypothesis also furnishes a plausible sociopolitical matrix for the "snowballing" proliferation of Israelite literary traditions. The basic themes, subthemes, stories, and poems of the old traditions were symbolic deposits of the sorts of experience that these early generations of Yahwists lived through, whether as longtime residents of Canaan or as returnees from Egyptian captivity (§24.1.c). The Canaanite "insiders," in overthrowing or escaping their rulers had, like the "outsiders" from Egypt, overthrown their "pharaoh" and had been delivered in their own "exodus." The retribalizing matrix goes a long way toward clarifying why and how the polished and condensed main themes of the tradition gathered to themselves such an astonishing array of elaborating materials. Converted Canaanite peoples contributed their experiences in literary form to lend support to the sovereign unity of Israel and to praise their covenant overlord Yahweh. The religious traditions were alive and multifaceted because they symbolically enshrined the manifold convergent social and political experiences of these early Yahwists (§14).

Israel entered history as a people fully active in creating and sustaining their lives in all respects. The name "Israel" referred not merely to a religious community but to a sovereign retribalizing society concerned with fundamental issues of survival and the good life. The covenant linkage on the religious plane was at the same moment a set of covenant linkages on the socioeconomic, political, and cultural planes (§19.1). The literary traditions of this covenanted people show continuities of theme running from patriarchs through Moses and on to the conquest of the land that reflect critical problems in making revolution and the constant search for strategies to deepen and secure the revolution (§16.4; 21). The insistence on Israel's part that it was a new people without a customary prehistory, that it was first constituted from within as a covenant people of Yahweh, and that it was the sole people in its environment to have such an explicit knowing relationship with Yahweh (§21) is an understandable symbolic assertiveness rooted in the eruptive distinctiveness of this revolutionary retribalizing movement of Canaanites-become-Israelites.

PART III

MONARCHY: ISRAEL'S COUNTERREVOLUTIONARY ESTABLISHMENT

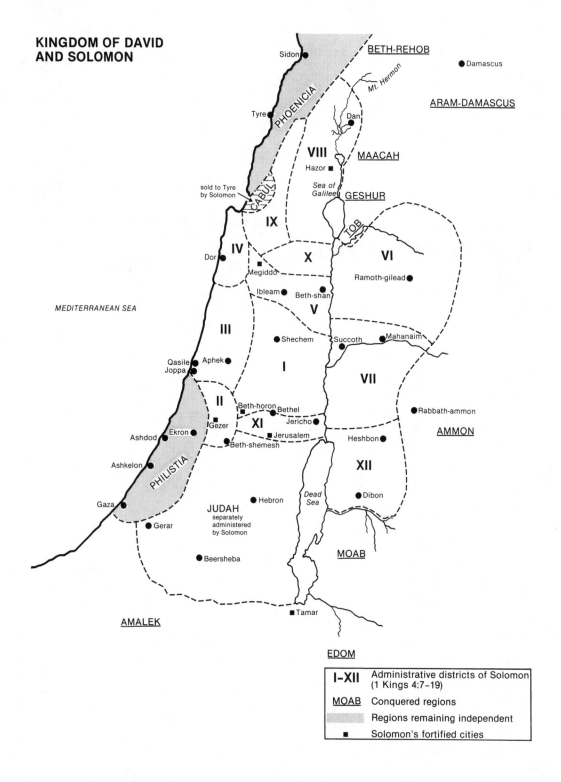

KINGDOM OF DAVID
AND SOLOMON

BETH-REHOB

● Damascus

Sidon

● Damascus

ARAM-DAMASCUS

Mt. Hermon

PHOENICIA

Tyre

Dan

VIII

MAACAH

Hazor ■

sold to Tyre
by Solomon

CABUL

Sea of
Galilee

GESHUR

IX

TOB

Dor ●

IV

X

VI

Megiddo ■

Ramoth-gilead ●

MEDITERRANEAN SEA

Ibleam ●

Beth-shan

V

III

Shechem ●

Succoth

Mahanaim ●

Qasile ●
Joppa ●

Aphek ●

I

VII

II

Beth-horon ■ Bethel ●

● Rabbath-ammon

Ashdod ●

Ekron ●

Gezer ■

XI

Jericho ●

Jerusalem ●

Heshbon ●

AMMON

Ashkelon ●

Beth-shemesh ●

PHILISTIA

XII

Gaza ●

● Hebron

Dead
Sea

Dibon ●

● Gerar

JUDAH
separately
administered
by Solomon

MOAB

● Beersheba

AMALEK

■ Tamar

EDOM

I–XII	Administrative districts of Solomon (1 Kings 4:7–19)
MOAB	Conquered regions
	Regions remaining independent
■	Solomon's fortified cities

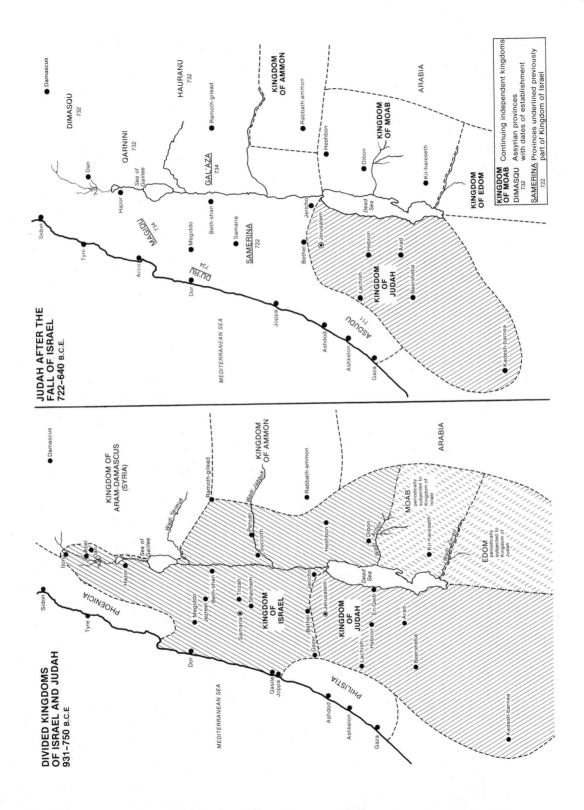

JUDAH AFTER THE FALL OF ISRAEL
722–640 B.C.E.

Damascus

DIMASQU
732

QARNINI
732

HAURANU
732

Dan

Sea of Galilee

Hazor

Ramoth-gilead

GAL'AZA
734

KINGDOM OF AMMON

MAGIDU
734

Megiddo

Beth-shan

Rabbath-ammon

Heshbon

Samaria

SAMERINA
722

Sidon

Tyre

Acco

DU.RU
734

Dor

Dibon

KINGDOM OF MOAB

Bethel

Jerusalem

Jericho

Dead Sea

Kir-hareseth

MEDITERRANEAN SEA

Joppa

Hebron

Arad

KINGDOM OF JUDAH

Lachish

Beersheba

ASDUDU
711

Ashdod

Ashkelon

Gaza

ARABIA

KINGDOM OF EDOM

Kadesh-barnea

	Continuing independent kingdoms
KINGDOM OF MOAB	
DIMASQU 732	Assyrian provinces with dates of establishment
SAMERINA 722	Provinces underlined previously part of Kingdom of Israel

DIVIDED KINGDOMS OF ISRAEL AND JUDAH
931–750 B.C.E

Damascus

KINGDOM OF ARAM-DAMASCUS (SYRIA)

Ijon

Abel

Dan

Sea of Galilee

Hazor

Wadi Yarmuk

Ramoth-gilead

KINGDOM OF AMMON

Wadi Jabbok

Penuel

Succoth

Rabbath-ammon

Heshbon

PHOENICIA

Sidon

Tyre

Dor

Megiddo

Jezreel

Beth-shan

Tirzah

Shechem

Samaria

KINGDOM OF ISRAEL

Bethel

Gezer

Jericho

Jerusalem

Dead Sea

Dibon

Wadi Arnon

MOAB
periodically subjected to Kingdom of Israel

Kir-hareseth

Wadi Zered

EDOM
periodically subjected to Kingdom of Judah

MEDITERRANEAN SEA

Qasile

Joppa

KINGDOM OF JUDAH

Lachish

Hebron

En-Gedi

Arad

Beersheba

PHILISTIA

Ashdod

Ashkelon

Gaza

ARABIA

Kadesh-barnea

On the Sources for Israel's Monarchic History

The monarchy of ancient Israel spanned four centuries, twice the length of the intertribal era. The first three kings of Israel ruled over a united kingdom. David and Solomon are said to have reigned forty years each (2 Sam. 5:4; 1 Kings 11:42), but these may be round numbers to express long and full reigns. In a disturbed text (1 Sam. 13:1), their predecessor Saul is said to have reigned for two years; possibly a further number has dropped out and the actual reign of Saul was something like twelve or twenty-two years. At most the united monarchy lasted about one century, beginning ca. 1020 B.C.E., and possibly for a much shorter period.

With the death of Solomon the monarchy was fatally ruptured. The dynasty of David continued to control Judah and a fluctuating area of Benjamin. All the other tribes withdrew to form their own monarchy, which carried the comprehensive national name "Israel" in contrast to the retention of the tribal name "Judah" for the southern kingdom. The two kingdoms ran parallel for 212 years, until the fall of Israel to Assyria in 722 B.C.E. Judah survived another 136 years before succumbing to Neo-Babylonia in 586 B.C.E.

In what follows, I will first treat the united monarchy (chap. 7). Then I will follow the northern kingdom through its history, with reference also to the less well documented southern kingdom during the same span of time (chap. 8). Finally, I will trace the history of the southern kingdom during the time it stood alone (chap. 9). Important biblical writings that derive at core or in whole from the monarchic age will be discussed in their sociohistoric contexts: the great traditionists J and E, the law document of Deuteronomy, and the prophetic writings of Amos, Hosea, Micah, Isaiah of Jerusalem, Jeremiah, and others. All of these works constitute sources for understanding the monarchic era, although they vary greatly in the explicitness and range of their references to external contexts since they represent differing sorts of literature.

After discussion of the vexed chronology of the divided kingdoms, we shall provide orientation to the direct historical sources for the monarchy contained in the DH Books of Samuel and Kings and in the separate work of Chronicles. We shall also take note of archaeological information on the period. Finally, we shall briefly examine the nature of the literary forms in the prophetic books since they are an unfamiliar type of literature that modern readers often find puzzling and unyielding to interpretation.

25
CHRONOLOGY OF THE DIVIDED KINGDOMS

The dating of the rulers of the divided kingdoms is under dispute. In pre-Roman antiquity there was no absolute chronology. The Christian system of dating did not develop until the sixth century C.E. Judaism had no generally agreed upon absolute chronology until the Middle Ages when the supposed date of creation was chosen as the year 1 (3760 B.C.E. according to the Christian calendar). Dates in pre-Roman times were expressed in terms of the years of the reigns of kings or by designating each year with the name of a high official. The years might be further distinguished by memorable events such as military campaigns, building operations, or eclipses. Sometimes the reigns of kings in different countries were synchronized in order to correlate their respective histories. This was the procedure followed by DH in reporting on the kings of Israel and Judah.

Each of the northern kings (Israel) is introduced with a notice of the date of accession expressed as the year of the contemporary southern king, a statement of length of reign, and a judgment on the king passed according to DH standards. For the southern kings (Judah), these details are supplemented by the age of the monarch at accession and the name of the queen mother. During the period when the two kingdoms ran parallel, the accounts are interwoven by switching back and forth according to the following pattern: after a king's reign is recounted in *either* of the two states, all rulers in the *other* state who came to power before his death are introduced and discussed. As soon as a king is reached whose death fell later than the last ruler already treated in the other state, the story line reverts to the next monarch in succession in the other state. The result is a "staggered" development of the kingdoms' histories in which events are not always described in strict chronological order.

The reigns of biblical kings can be correlated to the reigns of Assyrian and Neo-Babylonian kings who in turn can be dated absolutely by astronomical observations. The difficulty is that the biblical numbers either contain inaccuracies or were reached by methods of calculating that shifted over time. Scholars reach conclusions that vary by as much as ten years at the beginning of the divided kingdoms and narrow to a difference of one or two years toward the end of Judahite rule. These disputed reckonings result from different judgments about the operation of several key variables: (1) which of two sets of differing numbers in MT and LXX is to be preferred; (2) whether the new year began in the fall or in the spring; (3) whether the year in which a king took the throne was counted as his first regnal year or simply as an accession year to be omitted from the total figure for his reign; (4) whether co-regencies (simultaneous sharing of office by successive kings) were credited to the reigns of both kings; and (5) whether lengths of reign ever took into account rival claims to the throne. The chronology of the divided kingdoms followed in this book succeeds in adhering closely to the numbers in biblical MT by arguing that various systems of reckoning were used at different times in the two kingdoms according to discernible patterns.[1]

26
DH AS A SOURCE FOR MONARCHIC HISTORY

After a brief overview of the Deuteronomistic History (§13.3), we analyzed and evaluated the traditions and composition process of the author-compiler of Joshua and Judges in presenting the conquest of the land and the era of the Judges (§22.1–2). In Samuel and Kings, DH goes on to tell the story of the monarchy over its entire course, giving us by far our fullest source on the biblical monarchies (table 19).

The presence of the DH hand in Samuel-Kings stands out at once in the persistence of anticipatory and summary surveys, speeches, and prayers of the sort displayed in Deuteronomy through Judges (table 15). These passages function to divide the monarchy into critical phases and to highlight the explanations that DH advances for the ups and downs—and eventual failure—of Israel's experiments with kingship. The first of these passages (1 Samuel 12), carries the double task of closing out the era of the Judges and previewing the era of the Kings.

Within the framework of these pivotal interpretive passages, DH has enclosed materials from many sources:

1. independent cycles of traditions about Samuel, Saul, David, and Solomon;
2. administrative documents from the united monarchy;
3. excerpts from the royal archives ("chronicles") of the divided kingdoms;
4. excerpts from the Jerusalem temple archives;
5. cycles of prophetic tales.

We shall look at some of these sources in detail in chaps. 7–9. For the moment, it is to be noted that the enclosed DH materials contain information of great historical value but that this information is both unevenly distributed over the monarchy and stamped with DH's strongly biased interpretation.

In addition to the interpretive link passages cited above, DH used two

---

1. The chronological system adopted is that of Edwin R. Thiele, *The Mysterious Numbers of the Hebrew Kings,* 3d ed. (Grand Rapids: Wm. B. Eerdmans, 1983), and followed by Simon J. DeVries, "Chronology of the OT," in *IDB* 1: 580–99; idem, "Chronology, OT," in IDBSup, 161–66. For a condensed account of Thiele's chronology, see E. R. Thiele, *A Chronology of the Hebrew Kings* (Grand Rapids: Zondervan, 1977). The other chronological system widely employed among North American biblical scholars is that of William F. Albright ("The Chronology of the Divided Monarchy of Israel," *BASOR* 100 [1945]: 16–22), followed by John Bright, *HI.*

TABLE 19
Programmatic Texts in DH: Samuel-Kings

1. Speech of Samuel (1 Samuel 12): The fateful choice of monarchy

Recapitulation of oppression, repentance, and deliverance under the judges

Israel confesses the sin of asking for a king

If people and king obey the Law, Israel will continue as Yahweh's people; if they disobey the Law, they will be "swept away"

2. Speech of Nathan and prayer of David (2 Samuel 7):
   The promise of a "house" for David and
   a "house" for Yahweh

Yahweh gives David "rest" from all his enemies and Israel has peace and security unknown under the judges

Yahweh will build a "house" (dynasty) for David, and David's son will build a "house" (temple) for Yahweh

The dynasty of David will last forever, although a particular wicked king in the dynasty may be chastised

3. Blessing and prayer of Solomon (1 Kings 8:14–61):
   The temple ("house") dedicated as a lasting focus
   for Law observance

Solomon has fulfilled the promise of Yahweh that David's son will build the temple

Solomon prays for fulfillment of Yahweh's promise that David's dynasty shall last forever

Whenever individual Israelites or the whole people sin, they will turn to the temple, repent, and pray for deliverance, including preservation in any possible future exile from the land

All the promises of Yahweh to Moses have been fulfilled, Israel has "rest," and is urged to continue to observe the Law

4. Discourse (2 Kings 17:7–23):
   Rationale for the fall of the
   northern kingdom (Israel)

Jeroboam, first king of Israel, sinned and set a pattern habitually followed by later kings of the north

Israel has fallen and its people exiled because they turned to the religious apostasies of other nations and their own wicked kings

TABLE 19 (continued)
Programmatic Texts in DH: Samuel-Kings

In spite of repeated warnings by prophets, Israel stubbornly adhered to its apostasies

Judah also began to practice the same apostasies as Israel

5. Discourse and speech of prophets (2 Kings 21:2–16):
   Rationale for the fall of the
   southern kingdom (Judah)

Manasseh, king of Judah, introduced idolatry to Jerusalem and seduced Judah into more evil than the Canaanites had committed

Manasseh also "shed very much innocent blood"

Prophets announce that Judah, like Israel, is soon to be "measured" and "cast off" in judgment

compositional devices that further bind together the disparate traditions: (1) a synchronization of the rulers of the divided kingdoms (§25), with opening and concluding formulas surrounding reports about the reigns of the kings which vary greatly in length and detail. As with the judges formulas, these kings formulas function to give continuity to the succession of leaders; and (2) a schema of prediction and fulfillment for specifying how the words of Yahweh shaped events, serving in particular to draw prophets directly into the mainstream of historical action, since it is they who characteristically announce changes of dynasty in the north, major reform in the south, and the eventual doom of both kingdoms.

There is ample reason to believe that DH appeared in two editions, the first during the late reign of Josiah, the reforming king of Judah (622–609 B.C.E.), and the second in the exile after 561 B.C.E. (the date of the last incident in 2 Kings). The formula "to this day" is often used so as to imply that Judah is still an independent state (1 Kings 8:8; 9:21; 10:12; 2 Kings 8:22), and the easy availability of the great range and mix of sources employed is best accounted for by a Jerusalem milieu. The most compelling argument for two editions lies, however, in the tension in DH between threatened national doom and anticipated national survival or restoration, which is most reasonably explained if DH was a work first addressed to a declining but reforming Judahite state and only secondarily to groups of stateless Jews after the fall of Judah.

The main thrust of DH is to show how the monarchy, united and divided, stands under the obligation of obedience to the Law of Moses. Since that Law was repeatedly violated, the northern kingdom perished and the southern kingdom now faces the same dire judgment (first edition). Jeroboam, founder of the northern kingdom, although legitimated by a Yahweh prophet, turned to idolatry. Thereafter the dynasties of Baasha, Omri, and Jehu followed in his footsteps, in spite of numerous prophetic interventions and warnings.

In contrast to "the sin of Jeroboam" stood the promise of Yahweh to his faithful servant David which holds out the prospect that Judah will be spared the terrible fate of Israel. "For the sake of David" the sins of southern kings are viewed as less fatal than the sins of northern kings, and several southern rulers are given high marks for their piety: Asa, Jehoshaphat, Joash, Hezekiah, and Josiah. The last two kings named are reported to have carried out major cultic reforms which correspond closely to the program of DH urged in Deuteronomy (2 Kings 18:3–7; cf. 2 Chronicles 30; 2 Kings 22:8—23:25). Hezekiah and Josiah are praised as preeminent kings (greater than David?), just as Moses was the preeminent prophet (2 Kings 18:5; 23:25; cf. Deut. 34:10).

It is likely that the bulk of DH was composed as a propaganda work for Josiah's reformation of the cult and his political program to restore the empire of David in the wake of Assyria's sudden decline and retreat from northern Israel. In DH's mind, the fall of the north had been richly deserved. The south could escape the same fate only by backing Josiah's reform, while northern Israelites still in the land could be incorporated into the Neo-Davidic reign as Josiah extended his political power northward to recover the collapsing Assyrian provinces for Judah. It was a critical moment in which DH marshaled the Mosaic and Davidic traditions, carefully subordinating the eternal promise to David to the conditional promises of Mosaic Law, and reviewed the whole history of the monarchy toward the end of aiding and abetting a chancy but hopeful reform effort.

As events turned out, the reform did not stick, Judah collapsed at the hands of a major new world power, the Neo-Babylonians, and its leadership was taken into Babylonian captivity. With this catastrophic turn of events, DH was expanded to recount the sorry end of Judah (2 Kings 23:26— 25:30), and significant ideological revisions were made to explain why it was that Josiah's laudable reformation had failed (second edition). The basic explanation of the fall of Judah was that the sins of Manasseh, a predecessor of Josiah, had been so gross that they outweighed all the good efforts of Josiah which only succeeded in postponing the end (2 Kings 21:2–15; 22:15–20; 23:25b–27).

Was all hope in the promises of Yahweh and the future of Israel now lost? Far from it. The very fact of the updating of events into the exile, including the relatively favorable conditions of detention for King Jehoiachin in Babylon, indicates that the DH revision meant to explain the fall of both kingdoms so as to prepare the stateless Judahites, at home and in exile, for continuing adherence to their religiocultural identity. It was Yahweh who had brought about this abysmal state of affairs because Israel and Judah alike had failed to observe the Law of Moses. The promise to David had not been able to stem the consequences of gross abuses of the Law by kings and people. Nonetheless, Israelites survived who, like the DH reviser, still believed in Yahweh.

To round out DH as a document serviceable for conquered and dispersed Jews, forewarnings of the exile were introduced into many parts of the original DH composition (Deut. 4:27–31*; 28:36–37, 63–68; 29:27–28; 30:1–10*/**; Josh. 23:11–13, 15–16; 1 Sam. 12:25; 1 Kings 8:46–53*; 9:6– 9; 2 Kings 17:19; 20:17–19). Three of these exilic inserts (*) speak of

Israelites repenting and returning to Yahweh, while one of them (**) explicitly promises a return to the land. It is sometimes suggested that the favored treatment of the deported king of Judah mentioned at the end of DH was a restrained pointer to one possible way that Judah might recover, that is, through a Neo-Babylonian decision to reinstate Jehoiachin in Jerusalem at the head of a revived vassal state (2 Kings 25:27–30).

The positing of two settings for the present DH—one a reformed state context and the other a forlorn stateless context—brings considerable intelligibility to the mixed messages of doom and hope that sound throughout the work. It is interesting to speculate on the possible connection of this view of DH's literary history to the structuralist analysis of DH so far carried through Judges (§23.2). The two structurally identified "voices" of authoritarian dogmatism and critical traditionalism appear to be at play differently in the DH Josianic and exilic contexts. It might be concluded that in the Josianic edition of DH the voice of dogmatic authoritarianism stood at the forefront through its insistence that the Law of Moses must be observed, or the state would collapse, and furthermore that the needed reforms could be made. In the DH exilic revision, however, dogmatic authoritarianism, straining to explain matters by overweighing Josiah's faithfulness with Manasseh's sins, is itself outweighed by the stark reality of surviving Judahites who still listen to the words of Yahweh through the authoritative interpreter DH. This chastened audience, by returning to Yahweh, will be given another chance as a recognizable people of God, protected by their captors (1 Kings 8:46–53), even favored by them (1 Kings 25:27–30), and maybe eventually reempowered in their land (Deut. 30:1–10).

There may also be connections with analyses of Deuteronomy's supposed "humanism," including a "demythologizing" or "secularizing" of sacral traditions, which shows affinities to the wisdom sayings of Proverbs (§54.2). Certainly these proverbs reflect pronounced tensions between an "authoritarian dogmatic" insistence on immediacy of punishment and reward and a "critical traditional" flexibility and openness, even skepticism, about how closely virtue and vice govern the conditions of life, especially in politics.

Finally, the Books of Chronicles provide limited additional information on the monarchy (§51). Written between 525 and 375 B.C.E.—depending on whether the Books of Ezra and Nehemiah belong to the same work—Chronicles repeat large parts of Samuel and Kings to which they add some fresh information and much additional interpretation. Chronicles cite many sources on the kings and prophets, but the outcome is a religiously edifying work that must be used cautiously for reconstructing history. At some points, however, Chronicles preserve reliable details of genealogies, topography, and political administration that help to flesh out the skeletal information in Samuel-Kings. For example, two items in Chronicles, lacking in DH, are accepted by some interpreters as historically credible: Jehoshaphat's judicial reform by which he established lower courts in the fortified cities of Judah and a court of appeals in Jerusalem (2 Chron. 19:5–11) and the claim that Manasseh was summoned to Babylon to give account of his loyalty to his Assyrian overlord (2 Chron. 33:10–13).

Certain of the Psalms (§52.2) and older sections of Proverbs (§54.2) are evidently preexilic in setting, although both finished books are manifestly of postexilic date. There is some value in the indirect picture of the monarchic cult shown in these early psalms and also in the reflections of life among middle-level echelons of government bureaucrats indicated as the context for many of the oldest proverbs.

27

ARCHAEOLOGY AS A SOURCE FOR
MONARCHIC HISTORY

In recent years there has been a measurable enlargement of archaeological information on the monarchic period, with some corrections of earlier interpretations of architectural remains. Solomonic casemate walls (double walls with intervening rooms) and monumental city gates have appeared at Megiddo, Hazor, and Gezer (1 Kings 9:15–17), and also a ceremonial palace at Megiddo. A supposed Solomonic fortified copper smelter at Tell el-Kheleifeh on the Gulf of Aqabah is now recognized to have been a storehouse and granary, perhaps from the later monarchy. In fact, it is now doubtful that the copper mines of the southern Arabah were worked at all by Solomon. Nothing of Solomon's lavish building program in Jerusalem has been certainly identified because of later severe disturbances and rebuildings.

The northern kingdom is well represented by Jeroboam I's city gate and sanctuary at Dan, the Omri-Ahab capital city splendidly laid out on a hill at Samaria, and Omri-Ahab structures at Megiddo, including an offsets/insets type of wall and a stable complex, formerly thought to be Solomon's, which some now interpret as storage rooms or granaries. Water tunnels for assuring the city supply during siege have been found at Megiddo and Hazor.

The southern kingdom has yielded ample evidence of Sennacherib's destruction of Lachish at the end of the eighth century. Our understanding of Judahite military defenses and political administration is enhanced by the excavation of well-fortified sites at Beersheba and Arad in the Negeb. There is evidence of an increase in population and productivity throughout Judah in the late eighth and seventh centuries. It now seems clear that under Hezekiah Jerusalem's walls were extended to enclose the western hill. Weights, measures, seals, silver hordes, and stamped jar handles indicate a growth and standardization in trade and probably a more systematically planned national economy administered from Jerusalem. Although the interpretation is tentative, archaeological comparisons of ninth/eighth-century Israel and eighth/seventh-century Judah seem to suggest that greater prosperity was distributed throughout the countryside in Judah than in Israel.

In addition to the sanctuary at Dan, Yahwistic sanctuaries at Lachish and Arad have been uncovered, and Beersheba may have had a sanctuary, judging by a horned altar found there, similar to one at Dan (1 Kings 1:50). Archaeological demonstration of Judahite Yahwist sanctuaries outside of Jerusalem in monarchic times corroborates the historical-critical view that the Deuteronomic confinement of worship to Jerusalem did not take place until at least the time of Hezekiah and probably not with full effect until Josiah. The Arad sanctuary, located on the southern border of Judah, has been interpreted as a border shrine, in analogy with Jeroboam's shrines at Dan and Bethel. The excavator interpreted the physical evidence from the Arad sanctuary to mean that sacrifices ceased there at the end of the eighth century (Hezekiah's reform) and that the sanctuary was destroyed late in the seventh century (Josiah's reform).

It should also be added that a fair number of objects and inscriptions have thrown a little more light on the still-obscure origins and sociopolitical structures of the Philistines, Ammonites, and Syrian Arameans whose fortunes were closely intertwined with the Israelite monarchy.

Of particular value for illuminating monarchic history are inscriptions and texts from the period (cf. table 1: 4). A number of these are official records of foreign states concerning their military and diplomatic relations with united Israel or the divided kingdoms. Pharaoh Shishak (ca. 940–915) relates his military campaign into Palestine against Rehoboam of Judah and Jeroboam I of Israel. Particularly valuable are the annals of Assyrian kings, from Shalmaneser III (858–824) through Ashurbanipal (668–633), which recount military and administrative encounters with the western part of the empire, including Israel and Judah, over a period of two hundred years (table 1: 4J). The Neo-Babylonian Chronicles from the reign of Nebuchadnezzar (605–562) help to clarify the last years of independent Judah (table 1: 4K).

From Palestine proper have come a modest but growing number of inscriptions, including the long-known Gezer calendar, Moabite stone, Samarian ostraca, Siloam tunnel inscription, and Lachish letters, to which may now be added ostraca from Arad, Beersheba, Hazor, Tell Qasile, and Yavneh-yam (table 1: 6D), as well as tomb inscriptions from Khirbet el-Qom and Siloam, a papyrus from Wadi Murabba'at, and a Nimrud votive plaque.

The sum total of material and written remains accumulates impressively, although the lapsed time among archaeologists in publishing, interpreting, and synthesizing the finds—and among biblical scholars in appropriating them—appears to be as much as a decade or more.

28
FORMS AND SETTINGS OF PROPHETIC SPEECH

Several prophetic books provide significant broadly historical information on the monarchy, especially on socioeconomic life: chiefly Amos and Hosea for the northern kingdom, and Micah, Isaiah, and Jeremiah for the southern kingdom. The nature and value of that information can only be appreciated by grasping the peculiar literary character of prophetic books which do not have any ready analogies in modern literary culture.

There is abundant evidence that all the preexilic prophets were first speakers of relatively short, usually poetic, messages which they and their followers later committed to writing (on oral forms, cf. §11.1.b). These speeches drew upon conventional "fixed forms," even when those forms were modified or broken for special effects or to expand the range and subtlety of prophetic messages (on literary types in the prophets, cf. table 8: nos. 41–50). Prophetic books also contain narrative sections that include superscriptions to a whole book, time and place indicators for particular prophetic words, reports of commissioning to a prophetic vocation, visions, symbolic actions, conflicts among prophets, and incidents of acceptance or rejection of prophetic words by various audiences.

On the assumption that biblical prophecy had one primary locus of institutional origin, many attempts have been made to locate the central prophetic literary genre and its life setting, but the results have been inconclusive and problematic.[2]

2. For a terse and lucid analysis of prophetic speech forms and their disputed life settings, see Gene M. Tucker, "Prophetic Speech," *Int* 32 (1978): 31–45. Fuller accounts appear in Claus Westermann, *Basic Forms of Prophetic Speech* (Philadelphia: Westminster Press, 1967), and W. Eugene March, "Prophecy," in *OTFC*, 141–77.

One major approach has been to see the origin of prophetic speech in the *cultic oracle,* a divine communication solicited by devotees of the cult and delivered by authorized cult personnel. That many prophetic speeches represent Yahweh speaking in the first person, with the phrases "says Yahweh" or "oracle of Yahweh" attached, broadly accords with this understanding. Evidence is also cited that some, many, or all prophets served regularly—or had formerly served—in the official cult connected with shrines. On the other hand, many prophetic speeches are not direct words of God, their "oracles" were for the most part not asked for, and the content of their messages often directly challenged the presuppositions and typical messages of the official cult. Also, the opinion that the direct "threat" given in the divine words was rationalized and explained by a "reproach" after a period of secondary prophetic reflection on the threat, does not correspond with the way that judgments and their reasons or motivations flow together in prophetic speech.

Another approach to the roots of prophetic speech and ideology starts off from the formulations of *lawsuits* brought by Yahweh against Israel or the nations, which appear in prophetic books, sometimes in association with disputation speeches or debates. It is proposed that the institutional context of prophetic speech was located in juridical procedures. The prophets are seen as messengers of Yahweh the divine judge, delivering his verdict of guilt and sentence of punishment on a wayward covenant people. Valuable as a general metaphor for aspects of prophecy, it is difficult to reconstruct a plausible institutional origin in line with this theory. A setting for a covenant lawsuit in the civil courts of Israel seems out of the question, and the cultic lawsuit ceremony sometimes hypothesized would itself be a metaphorical construction transplanted from the legal into the symbolic religious sphere. There simply was no jurisdictional body competent to "try" a legal charge brought by Yahweh against the whole people or its collective leadership.

It is likely that interpreters make a mistake in trying to move so directly from given speech forms to particular institutional contexts. The great variety of prophetic forms of speech suggest a deliberate drawing on traditions and practices from many spheres of institutional life, including religious cult, law courts, military practice, political administration, scribal procedures, etc.—without any necessary implication that prophets served in these institutions (although it is not to be ruled out that from time to time prophets filled functional roles in one or another of these institutional subsystems).

By the time of Amos at any rate, whose word launched the first complete prophetic book, prophecy seems to have been well on the way to creating its own institutional matrix. It was achieving formalization and broad public recognition as a kind of "regularized criticism" of the established order. One of the developing prophetic institutional habits was to draw extensively on a wide range of preexisting speech forms in a daringly imitative manner to establish rapport and authority with audiences, while simultaneously freely transforming and mixing the speech forms in order to deliver arresting messages that cut to the core of popular and official presuppositions about the religious foundations of national life. It remains likely that in some way this prophetic movement took its rise from within cultic institutions (with their asserted monopoly over the voice of Yahweh), but it soon achieved enough institutional and ideological independence to stand on its own—both in communication and at odds with the older established sectors of society.

The literary history of prophetic books is an unavoidable but complicated issue for biblical interpretation. Speeches and narrative reports from a named prophet, such as Amos or Isaiah, formed the nucleus of the book bearing the prophet's name. In time, the words of other prophets or of commentators in the tradition of the original prophet were added to the nucleus. The grouping of the prophetic traditions according to various organizing principles—whether by original prophet, later followers, or final editor (redactor)—has become a subject of much inquiry by redaction criticism. Instances of at least four kinds of guiding principles in redaction have been proposed in one or another prophetic book or subcollection: (1) redaction by collecting originally separate oracles which are expanded and regrouped during the growth of the book; (2) redaction by a more deliberate process of placing one layer of material over another, rewriting and linking traditions so as to bring out a specific point of view that opposes or goes beyond the earlier layer of traditions; (3) redaction by artfully arranging elements or specimens of old genres to form what becomes either a new genre or a highly complex instance of a recognizably older genre; (4) redaction by using a small "seed unit" of tradition to introduce a following series of larger units that develop the germ ideas and echo the structure of the "seed unit" in expanded form.[3]

Finally, there is a set of sociopolitical questions about how the prophets were located in their social matrix and what stance they took toward other social actors and the social system itself. These issues are closely related to the authority of the prophets and the sources of prophetic "inspiration" and

3. These forms of prophetic redaction are described and illustrated by W. Eugene March, "Redaction Criticism and the Formation of Prophetic Books," SBLSP 11 (1977): 87–101.

"revelation." Former social interpretations of prophecy tended to be *psycho*social and to maximize the role of prophets as "lone critics" of society in the style of "great men who make history" or their obverse, "isolated intellectuals who feel left out of public decisions." A broader application of social scientific methods to prophecy suggests that the prophets were intimately a part of their society even as their stances toward its current directions were highly oppositional.[4]

Studies of shamanism and spirit possession among "holy men/women" or divine-human "intermediaries" have noted innumerable forms of inspiration and authority that are variously connected to traditional social institutions and roles. All these "prophets"—understood as exceptional spirit-guided people not dismissed by their society as mad—possess clear social meanings and values in their own contexts. A basic question is whether they are a part of the "central" socially empowered establishment or part of "peripheral" socially devalued and marginated groups. Obviously "central" and "peripheral" social locations tend to be relative and shifting as societies and "prophets" change. In many respects Israelite prophets appear to have been mixtures of "central" and "peripheral" types, the great prophets of later tradition being largely "peripheral" during the monarchy but surprisingly "central" in the exile once their interpretations of events were accepted as vindicated.

Studies of nativist, revitalization, and millennial movements have stressed the role of religious leaders or "prophets" in movements of broad social import, spurred by a sense of social deprivation. This social deprivation need not be total impoverishment or exclusion from power, since *any* keenly felt strategic deprivation can suffice to set the prophetically led protest movement on its way. Cognitive dissonance theory from social psychology and relative deprivation theory from historical anthropology have been instructive on this point (§55.1). The overtly religious motives and language of the prophetic leaders are entangled with social aims that may or may not have been recognized by them and their followers.

The explicit involvement of Israelite prophets in the social and political conflicts of the monarchy are rather obvious on the surface of the biblical text, but the detailed social dynamics require reconstruction. This process of social class and conflict analysis in prophecy, as throughout the Hebrew

---

4. Burke O. Long, "Prophetic Authority as Social Reality," in *Canon and Authority. Essays in Old Testament Religion and Theology,* ed. George W. Coats and Burke O. Long (Philadelphia: Fortress Press, 1977), 3–20; Robert R. Wilson, *Prophecy and Society in Ancient Israel* (Philadelphia: Fortress Press, 1980); David L. Petersen, *The Roles of Israel's Prophets,* JSOTSup 17 (Sheffield: JSOT Press, 1981).

Bible, has been obstructed and sidetracked by biblical scholars who lack a sense of the forms and complexities of class struggle. The fact, for example, that some prophets seem to have come from relatively privileged backgrounds does not in any way disqualify them from having held critical or radical sociopolitical views at odds with others of the same background, nor does it exclude them from involvement in organized or spontaneous actions directed to change social policies and structures (§37.5; 50.2; 50.4a).

For reconstructing the sociohistoric horizons of monarchy, the implications of the origin and shape of prophetic writings and of the sociopolitical matrix of prophetic functions may be summed up as follows:

1. The prophetic writings form "occasional" literature in the sense that they usually supply brief *vignettes or slices of public life* that lack extensive exposition or directly noted connections with other prophetic passages or with sociohistoric conditions. These writings, like much of Hebrew poetry, are often formed by parataxsis (§23.1), presenting a succession of *unintegrated vivid details* and *strong judgments* that must be mulled over and interconnected by reader and historian in order to relate them to a whole fabric of sociohistoric circumstance.

2. Since the original prophet's words are fused together with additional words from later prophets and commentators, the materials in any particular prophetic book are likely to reflect *sociohistoric settings widely separated over time.* Therefore, it is not enough, for example, to know the setting of Amos in the mid–eighth century to understand the Book of Amos, since in the final form of the book there are additions from late seventh-century Josianic and sixth-century exilic settings (§34.3). In the case of the Book of Isaiah, in addition to the late eighth-century milieu of the original prophet, there are major blocks of traditions from Josianic-Deuteronomic, exilic, and postexilic settings (§37.2; 50.2; 50.4; 55.2).

3. Just as the prophetic references to their own sociohistorical settings are fragmentary and indirect, requiring careful reconstruction by controlled hypothesis, so the prophetic references to broader *contemporary groups in sociopolitical conflict*—and *the place of prophets in those conflicts*—are fragmentary and indirect. They require careful inquiry in relation to all available narrative texts (as in DH and Chronicles), extrabiblical material remains, inscriptions, and records, and known processes of conflict in comparable social settings laid bare by social scientific study. It is no longer permissible in biblical studies to neglect the immersion of prophets in sociopolitical conflict on the basis of arguments that we lack such information or that prophets were so totally "religious" that they had no determinable secular intentions, functions, or meanings.

CHAPTER 7

Traditions About the United Kingdom

Read the Biblical Text
1 and 2 Samuel
1 Kings 1—11

Genesis 2—11

Psalms 2, 46, 48, 110
Proverbs 25

Consult Maps in *MBA*
nos. 83–115

29
THE SHAPE OF THE TRADITIONS
IN 1 AND 2 SAMUEL AND 1 KINGS 1—11

29.1 Source Statistics

The status of our sources for a knowledgable reconstruction of the united monarchy of Israel can be formulated statistically in terms of the amount and kind of coverage devoted to its three rulers and to Samuel, who prepares Israel for the transition to monarchy. Using biblical verses as the unit of computation, the materials in DH can be divided between two kinds of traditions (see table 20): (1) *annalistic political-historical documentation,* the kind of "hard" data on political administration, military affairs, foreign policy, economic activities, building operations, and religious measures that form the skeleton of historical writing; and (2) *miscellaneous literary traditions* in the form of sagas or legends, novellas, prophetic narratives, temple narratives, and poems, the kind of "soft" literary productions that touch political history less directly, tending rather to reflect aesthetic and cultural interests and to express the impressions made by historical leaders or movements on subgroups within the community.

The division between these two types of material is not hard and fast. They often appear side by side in DH and are sometimes mixed together in the same literary unit. There are instances where annals are expanded into imaginative narrative and other cases where the more literary works contain elements of political history within a framework stressing different concerns. Still, the basic differences are clear and an approximate distribution of the DH materials on this basis serves to point up some of the problems in writing a history of monarchic Israel.

The first thing to be noted about these statistics is the sparseness of the sources. In the RSV double-column translation of the Bible, there is an average of twenty-two verses per page in Samuel-Kings. This means that for the united monarchy the entirety of our DH sources (plus relevant documentation from Chronicles) is contained within *80 pages* of biblical text. A second observation is the underrepresentation of Saul, with a little less than *10 pages* (slightly more than 17 pages if we include verses where he is subordinated to David). By contrast David is given almost *54 pages* and Solomon almost *16½ pages.* A third feature is the imbalance between political-historical documentation and miscellaneous traditions. Of the 80-page total, only 13.5 pages or 18 percent set forth the hard-core information needed to write history. Especially striking is the fact that Saul is documented by *less than ½ page* of directly political-historical data, and

TABLE 20
Distribution of DH Verses to Kings of the United Monarchy
in 1 and 2 Samuel and 1 Kings 1—11

(Precursor) King	Political-historical Documentation	Miscellaneous Literary Traditions
(Samuel)	9	129 + (115)*
Saul	6	207 + (165)†
David	97 + (33)‡	1053
Solomon	162	199
Total	274 + (33)	1588

*Verses in which Samuel is subordinated to a primary interest either in Saul or in David.

†Verses in which Saul is subordinated to a primary interest in David.

‡Verses from Chronicles that supply annalistic data supplementing DH data.

Samuel by *less than ⅓ page,* by comparison with David's nearly *6 pages* and Solomon's more than *7 pages.* These figures are a rough reflection of the relative scarcity of direct sources on the monarchy and, in particular, they register the extreme difficulty historians have in gaining a properly detailed and proportioned picture of the roles of Samuel and Saul in the rise of the monarchy.

29.2 Older Literary Critical Studies

In discerning and assessing the sources for the early monarchy, historical critics were impressed by the concentration and relative fullness of materials with respect to a few basic themes: (1) how Saul came to be the first king; (2) how kingship was transferred from Saul to David; (3) how Solomon, among David's several sons, succeeded his father to the throne; (4) how the temple was built; and (5) how Solomon attained and displayed his wisdom. An intense focus on the personal relationships among the leading figures in the history was, however, not accompanied by substantial clarification of the wider sociopolitical and religiocultural conditions and factors that prompted and shaped the monarchy.

Early on it was seen that the accounts fell into thematic blocks with varying degrees of internal cohesion and problematic connections.

1. One block treated a cluster of family and public affairs in the court of King David and culminated in the choice of Solomon as his successor (2 Samuel 9—20; 1 Kings 1—2). This work, dubbed the "Court History" or "Succession Narrative," was taken to be a tightly composed and superb piece of historical writing.

2. A segment relating the rise to power of David, in tandem with the decline of Saul (1 Samuel 16—2 Samuel 5), was judged to contain more disparate units, including many doublets: David's introduction to Saul's court (1 Sam. 16:14–23; 17:55–58), David's flight to Achish of Gath (1 Sam. 21:10–15; 27:1–4), David's sparing of the life of Saul (1 Sam. 24:3–22; 26:5–25), and the death of Saul (1 Sam. 31:1–7; 2 Sam. 1:1–10), etc.

3. A section describing how Saul was elected and then rejected as king (1 Samuel 8—15) was seen to divide into two sources, one promonarchic (1 Sam. 9:1—10:16; 11:1–11; 13:1—14:46) and the other antimonarchic (1 Samuel 8; 10:17–27; 12; 15). Some analysts treated chap. 11 as a second promonarchic source. The promonarchic traditions were viewed as "early," nearly contemporary with Saul's installation as king, while the antimonarchic traditions were considered a "late" expression of resentment toward royal oppression under Solomon.

Several shorter blocks of tradition were identified in Samuel.

1. The Samuel birth and "call" stories (1 Samuel 1—3) were recognized to justify the replacement of the Elide priests of Shiloh with the line of Zadok of Jerusalem later installed by David (1 Sam. 2:27–36; cf. 2 Sam. 15:24–37; 20:25; 1 Kings 1:22–

39; 2:26—27). It was further noted that the birth story originally concerned Saul and not Samuel, since the wordplay on Samuel's name uses the verb from which Saul's name is formed ("he is lent/granted [Saul!] to Yahweh," 1 Sam. 1:28).

2. The story of the fortunes of the ark after its capture by the Philistines (1 Sam. 4:1—7:2) was perceived to link with the account of David's transfer of the ark to Jerusalem (2 Samuel 6) and sometimes with the following Nathan oracle on dynasty and temple (2 Samuel 7), the whole forming a kind of etiology of the cult establishment at Jerusalem.

3. An inset of material showing Samuel in various guises as a military and civil "judge" (7:3–17) was estimated to contain some old data much worked over and confused by the DH conception of Samuel as "the last judge."

4. An appendix of miscellaneous David traditions (2 Samuel 21—24), separating the body of the Court History in 1 Samuel 9—20 from its climax in 1 Kings 1—2 was often compared to a similar block of interruptive materials in Judges 17—21 (§22.1.f). The awkward position of the appendix was sometimes attributed to a later decision to transfer the end of the Court History to 1 Kings 1—2 as an appropriate opener for the Books of Kings.

The account of the reign of Solomon (1 Kings 3—11) was assessed as an eclectic mix of detailed description of the temple, administrative lists, reports of diplomatic relations, legends about the wise king, and heavy doses of DH ideology. A source reference by DH to "the book of the acts of Solomon" that told of the deeds and wisdom of the king (1 Kings 11:41) was puzzling, since temple, administrative, and diplomatic data were more likely to have come directly from temple and state archives than from a source that included wisdom sagas and sayings. In any case it was observed that 1 Kings 3—11 was organized so that Solomon's external political difficulties with Edom and Damascus (1 Kings 11:14–25) and his internal conflicts with northern Israelites (1 Kings 11:26–40) were placed at the end of his otherwise halcyon reign and bluntly blamed on religious corruption owing to the influence of his foreign wives (1 Kings 11:1–13).

As was noted in citing key interpretive passages in Samuel and 1 Kings (table 19), DH intruded strongly ideological passages here and there in the text. Because these DH interventions were confined to a few obvious points, scholars turned to other options to explain the continuity of the materials prior to the work of DH. Starting off from signs of parallel short sources, as in 1 Samuel 8—15, and of twice-told incidents, efforts were made to trace the pentateuchal sources J and E from Joshua and Judges into Samuel and Kings. The Yahwist was judged to have included the promonarchic segment of Saul's election as king and the vividly written Court History, while the Elohist was assigned materials in 1 Samuel 1—15 that exalt Samuel's leadership over all Israel and denigrate Saul. Some analyses carried the J source through the Solomonic traditions to the division of the monarchy. Based as they were on meager evidence and differing in criteria and results, these source analyses have won few adherents. In the meantime literary analysis has turned in other directions.

29.3 Newer Literary Critical Studies

The impact of new forms of biblical literary criticism has been felt in fresh assessments of the separate literary blocks in terms of their literary genres, frequently illuminated by similar ancient Near Eastern traditions. In addition, there is a strong move toward identifying a basic pre-DH ordering of the shorter blocks that does not depend on the dubious analysis into J and E sources. This new wave of work on the recognized segments within Samuel and their interconnections carries sizable implications for historical uses of these sources in studying the early monarchy.

The *ark narrative* has been treated as an instance of an ancient Near Eastern genre: a report of the capture in battle and the subsequent return of a people's god(s).[1] Victors sometimes displayed captured gods in their temples as trophies and signs of the impotence of the defeated nation. On occasion the divine images were returned in a show of magnanimity that further underscored the humiliation of the defeated worshipers. The genre shaping Israel's ark narrative is cast from the perspective of the defeated people who locate the reason for their defeat and for the capture of the god(s) in some national sin that has greatly displeased the deity. In time, however, the still-powerful captured god bests his captors and forces them to release the image(s) which are returned home in triumph. Moral: the angry deity has caused and controlled the humiliating events in order to teach his people a lesson. Given the applicability of the genre, Israel's ark narrative probably once included some part of 1 Samuel 2 to explain the capture of the ark by the gross sins of the Elide priests. The temporal location of the story would have been prior to David's sound defeat of the Philistines, for after that turn of events such a story was no longer needed to bolster Israel's morale. As eventually incorporated in 1 Samuel, the ark narrative was framed by chaps. 2 and 7 in order to magnify Samuel, but 2 Samuel 6, wherein David brings the ark to Jerusalem, is from another hand since it has the different purpose of chronicling the achievements of David.

Frequently *an old cycle of Saul stories* is posited in which Samuel played little or no part and in which ideological contention over the merits and

---

1. Patrick D. Miller, Jr., and J. J. M. Roberts, *The Hand of the Lord. A Reassessment of the 'Ark Narrative' of 1 Samuel,* The Johns Hopkins Near Eastern Studies (Baltimore: Johns Hopkins University Press, 1977).

demerits of kingship was not involved.[2] It is variously identified in accounts of the birth of Saul, his recovery of his father's lost asses, his victories over Ammonites and Philistines, and his decline and death. A cycle of this sort implies affinities with cycles about military deliverers in Judges. One study notes that the often observed "tragic" characterization of Saul, unbiblical in tone but recognizably Greek, may be related to the foreign motifs of the dead as effective beings, heroic suicide, mutilation of a fallen enemy, and honorable burial by cremation (in 1 Samuel 28; 31). These features suggest that the author of the Saul cycle was someone familiar with practices and literary traditions of Greeks and Hittites, plausible enough when one recalls that Philistines and Hittites were part of the Jerusalem court in David's time.

The *story of David's rise to power* has been compared with a special genre of Hittite historiography, best represented in the thirteenth-century *Apology of Hattusilis III*.[3] The Hittite apology is composed for a king who has usurped the throne in order to defend or justify his assumption of the kingship. It shares with David's apology several themes: early military successes as a trusted commander of his royal predecessor, popularity and support among the people, skill and restraint in waging the struggle that led without any design on his part to accession to the throne, complete blamelessness in all his dealings with his predecessor, and the special favor of deity as the reason for his rise to the throne. One study notes the special twist provided by the role of Saul's son Jonathan. David cannot simply take the kingdom; Saul must give it to him, but this Saul cannot do. Jonathan, Saul's rightful successor, can, however, voluntarily waive his right to the throne in favor of David—and he does just that!

It is noted that David's apology responds defensively and effectively to charges that David tried to advance himself in royal service at Saul's expense, that he was a deliberate deserter from the court of Saul, that he was a self-serving outlaw leader, that he was a mercenary collaborator with the Philistines and thus a traitor to his people, and that he was implicated in Saul's death and in the deaths of Saul's general, Abner, and Saul's heir, Ishbaal. Setting aside the few DH embellishments, this older defense of David's legitimacy as king does not show a developed royal theology of the dynastic type (unlike 2 Samuel 7). The document was probably written in

2. J. Maxwell Miller, "Saul's Rise to Power: Some Observations concerning 1 Sam. 9:1–10:16; 10:26–11:15 and 13:2–14:46," *CBQ* 36 (1974): 157–74; W. Lee Humphreys, "The Rise and Fall of King Saul: A Study of an Ancient Stratum in 1 Samuel," *JSOT* 18 (1980): 74–90.

3. P. Kyle McCarter, Jr., "The History of David's Rise," in *I Samuel*, AB 8 (Garden City, N.Y.: Doubleday & Co., 1980), 27–30.

Jerusalem and addressed to northerners during David's reign when his right to rule over the north was in question (2 Sam. 16:4–14; 20:1–22) or shortly after the division into two kingdoms when Judah still hoped to be able to lure the northern kingdom back into the Davidic fold (§33.1).

The search for an intermediate link between these separate tradition blocks and the final DH has led critics to postulate a "Prophetic History" that brought together all the segments of tradition in 1 Samuel 1 through 2 Samuel 5, so that DH needed only to introduce a few interpretive passages and expansions to link the work to the preceding judges and to the following kings.[4] The pervasive tendency of this pre-DH Book of Samuel was to elevate prophetic leadership over royal leadership. Kings are viewed with suspicion but tolerated as long as they remain subject to the election and guidance of prophets. Samuel is accordingly viewed as a prophetic king-maker who chooses and later rejects the recalcitrant Saul, only to designate David in his place.

The old Saul cycle of stories was broken up, his birth tradition worked into a story of Samuel's birth, his judgelike military accomplishments tempered by his refusal to take directions from Samuel, and his rejection and death firmly mandated by Yahweh through the prophet Samuel. The ark story was framed so as to vindicate Samuel's leadership as an obedient deliverer, a foil to the disobedient Elide priests and the rebellious Saul. The apology of David fits conveniently into the purpose of the alleged Prophetic History since it showed a divinely blessed David unfalteringly ascending to power while Saul, bereft of Yahweh, slipped to his doom.

The posited date for the Prophetic History was during or shortly after the fall of Israel in 722 B.C.E. and its presumed setting was within a northern prophetic circle critical of the monarchy in the manner of Hosea. The sympathy expressed for the Davidic dynasty means that the writer of the Prophetic History looked to the continuing kingdom of Judah as a context where the monarchic abuses of the annihilated northern kingdom could be corrected by subordinating kingship to prophecy. The legislation of Deuteronomy to eradicate the detrimental effects of evil kings (Deut. 17:14–20) and to purge Canaanites from the land (Deuteronomy 20) has marked connections with 1 Samuel 8 and 15. Since traditions lying behind Deuteronomy are believed to have originated in the north and to have passed into Judah after the debacle of 722 B.C.E., it is appropriate to speak of the Prophetic History as "proto-Deuteronomic," and it is possible that this

---

4. Bruce C. Birch, *The Rise of the Israelite Monarchy: The Growth and Development of 1 Samuel 7–15,* SBLDS 27 (Missoula, Mont.: Scholars Press, 1976); McCarter, "David's Rise," 18–23.

work, along with a core of Deuteronomic laws, was influential in Hezekiah's cultic reforms (§36.1).

For a long time the estimation of *the Court History of David* as a wonderfully constructed historical writing by an eyewitness to the events provided the linchpin for understanding the reign of David.[5] Bit by bit, however, it has become a locus of dispute as to its actual genre and what expectations a reader might reasonably bring to it. Three major new interpretations have been offered following from weaknesses exposed in the work's credibility as history, such as extensive use of private conversations and scenes that could scarcely have had eyewitnesses, scant treatment of public or political aspects of David's life, and an overweening concern with the character and personal motives of a few main actors.

One new line of interpretation, assuming a number of shapes, envisions the document as political propaganda.[6] The dominant form of the theory sees an attempt in it to justify and legitimate Solomon's succession to the throne of David by demonstrating how all the rival brothers were eliminated and how, in the end, Solomon was the prince-designate of his father. Picking up on features portraying David and Solomon in a negative light, an opposing position finds the propaganda to be anti-Davidic and anti-Solomonic. Others have argued that an originally anti-Davidic/anti-Solomonic text was later redacted to produce a pro-Solomonic final edition.

A second hypothesis categorizes the Court "History" as narrative wisdom writing, comparable to the Joseph novella, with the educational or didactic aim of inculcating virtues such as friendship, loyalty, patience, humility, and judicious speech.[7] As a "royal novel" from Solomonic scribal circles, its matrix was the new bureaucracy where Egyptian state administrative practices and wisdom writings influenced court tastes and encouraged sophisticated self-protective ethics among public officials and "civil servants."

Yet a third approach to the Court "History" finds the historiographic, political propagandist, and wisdom genre arguments weak in their reliance on the uncritical assumption that the document is an eyewitness account from the time of Solomon. In fact, it contains many alerting indicators that

---

5. Gerhard von Rad, "The Beginnings of Historical Writing in Ancient Israel," in *The Problem of the Hexateuch and Other Essays* (Edinburgh and London: Oliver & Boyd, 1965), 166–204 (orig. German ed., 1944). Adulation of this "historical masterpiece" reached a peak with Robert H. Pfeiffer and William G. Pollard, *The Hebrew Iliad. The History of the Rise of Israel under Saul and David* (New York: Harper & Brothers, 1957), still useful for Pfeiffer's brisk and colorful translation of the Hebrew text.

6. R. N. Whybray, *The Succession Narrative*, SBT, 2d ser., 9 (London: SCM Press, 1968), 50–55.

7. Ibid., 56–116.

the intended audience was not familiar with circumstances and customs in Davidic-Solomonic times. The work is rather best typified as a story, traditionally or conventionally told, devised as a work of art and serious entertainment.[8] The story's humanizing and universalizing treatment of the main characters is developed by the theme of David's "giving and grasping" in the interplay and conflict of family and political interests and forces.

Among traditional elements are motifs such as *David's love-hate relation to "the sons of Zeruiah"* (Joab and Abishai; 1 Sam. 26:6–12; 2 Sam. 3:30, 39; 16:5–13; 19:16–23; 22:15–17), *the judgment-eliciting parable* (2 Sam. 12:1–15; 14:1–24), *the woman who brings death to two men* (Rizpah to Abner and Ishbaal [= Ishbosheth], 2 Sam. 3:6–11, 26–27; 4:5–8, Bathsheba to Uriah and her illegitimate child, 2 Sam. 11:2—12:23; Tamar to Amnon and Absalom, 2 Sam. 13:1–33; 18:9–15; Abishag to Adonijah and Joab, 1 Kings 2:13–25, 28–35), *the woman who hides spies* (2 Sam. 17:17–20; cf. Joshua 2), *the sending and arrival of two messengers* (2 Sam. 18:19–33; cf. 1 Kings 1:42–43; 2 Kings 9:17–20), and *the letter commanding the death of its carrier* (2 Sam. 11:14–25, the only biblical example of a frequent folklore motif).

In addition, there are stock segments of narrative dealing with plot or description (cf. "type-scenes," §15.3.d) which appear in different stories in complex patterns of verbal similarity and variation, among them being *the gift of provisions* (1 Sam. 25:18; 2 Sam. 16:1), *the battle report* (1 Sam. 4:10, 17; 31:1; 2 Sam. 1:4; 2:17; 18:6–7), and *the news of defeat* (1 Sam. 4:12–17; 2 Sam. 1:2–4, interlocking with the preceding battle report). The stock segments in particular suggest that the stories originated in or were influenced by oral tradition. Historical matters may be related in this David story, but they are clearly incidental to the function of entertainment.

29.4 Implications of Literary Analysis for Historical Use of the Sources

The bearing of recent literary analysis on the historical use of early monarchic sources introduces sober caution, if not outright warning. Although there once was a "pro-Saul" source of some scope, it has been gravely disrupted and overlaid by the Prophetic History. Little remains of a recognizably historical Samuel apart from his function as a prophetic type vis-à-vis kings. Even though the dates of composition for the ark narrative and the David apology are now pushed to earlier times than once thought,

---

8. David M. Gunn, *The Story of King David. Genre and Interpretation,* JSOTSup 6 (Sheffield: JSOT Press, 1978), chap. 3.

their very genres mark them as highly biased and limited by "tunnel vision." The ark narrative is a formulaic way of putting the best face possible on a terrible defeat of Israel by the Philistines, while the apology of David is designedly one-sided and simply cannot be expected to tell Saul's side of the story, nor faulted for not doing what the literary genre automatically excludes. Even the formerly highly valued Court History has fallen from its privileged pedestal as historiography and is greatly qualified as an immediate reflection of Davidic conditions.

In short, our examination of the sources according to recent literary analyses bears out the initial impression of the statistical survey: the political historical core of textual data on the early monarchy gives us a narrow historiographic base, although around that core swirls a considerable body of literature, formed from a number of once-independent blocks, that gives us fascinating selective readings of limited aspects of the history of the times filtered by the lenses of genre and ideology.

30
THE RISE AND TRIUMPH OF
MONARCHY IN ISRAEL

30.1 External and Internal Factors

The most commonly recognized factor in the rise of kingship in Israel has been the centralized military threat of the Philistines who gained a solid hold on the southern coastal plain after 1150 B.C.E. and by 1050 B.C.E. were posing a serious threat to the mountainous heartland of Israel. The Philistines had the advantage of oligarchic leadership, unlike the divisive Canaanite city-states, and their iron weaponry and mobile strike force made them effective fighters in the hill country. This highly unified military threat called forth a countervailing unified military defense on Israel's part.

Israel's intertribal movement toward social equality was incomplete at the dawn of the monarchy, frustrated on the one hand by "converts" to its cause who did not fully implement its measures of socioeconomic leveling and sharing and on the other hand by the accrual of prosperity and influence to certain regions and families, particularly in Manasseh, Ephraim, Benjamin, and Judah. There are reports of priestly abuses by Eli's sons (1 Sam. 2:12–17) and of bribery and perversion of justice among Samuel's sons (1 Sam. 8:1–3). That David could gather several hundred distressed and indebted followers during his period of social banditry (1 Sam. 22:1–2) suggests that imbalances in wealth and lapses in the tribal mutual aid system had been developing for some time. The struggles between the houses of

Saul and David probably embodied efforts to monopolize leadership by coalitions of prosperous families and priesthoods in the two strongest areas of Israel.

30.2 Saul

The only certain functions of Saul as the first "king" of Israel were military, although he doubtless also had a role in cultic activities. Saul's major achievement was to drive back the Philistines for a season from the central hill country (how long this "breathing spell" lasted hinges on the indeterminable length of his reign [see p. 294]). He is also credited with victories over the Ammonites, as well as over Edomites, Moabites, Amalekites, and Arameans of Zobah (1 Sam. 14:47–48). In the end, he died in a crushing defeat by the Philistines, during a time when Israelite energies were badly divided in a dispute between Saul and one of his underlings, David.

Saul operated with a corps of seasoned Benjaminite warriors, to which the levies of other tribes were added as needed. He had a headquarters rather than a capital in the usual sense. There is no sign that he set up a state apparatus for taxing or conscripting manpower or for exacting tribute from conquered peoples. In what appear to be the most ancient segments of the Saul traditions he is called *nāgīd*, "prince/commander," rather than *melek*, "king." Saul seems to have exercised central military leadership "for the duration" of the Philistine emergency, which in his case turned out to be "for life." The actual powers exercised make him appear more an intertribal military "chieftain" than a "king" in the usual ancient Near Eastern sense. On the other hand, it was early assumed that one of his sons should succeed him in office, so that a dynastic tendency—if not an outright dynastic legitimation by the tribes—arose at least by the time of his death. This dynastic presumption was a useful vehicle for powerful northern forces to insist on keeping the chieftainship/kingship in their hands rather than relinquish it to a southerner.

30.3 David

David emerged in the service of Saul, fled from the king when a split opened up between them, and, after Saul's death, returned to Judah to become its *nāgīd*. For more than seven years there was a contest between Saulide forces in the north and Davidic forces in the south to determine which should rule over all Israel. David prevailed when the tribal elders of the north, without a worthy son of Saul to rally around, joined the Judahites in a treaty with David as king of all Israel. There is a difference of interpretation as to whether David was king over a single political entity Israel, or whether he joined the kingdoms of Israel and Judah in a personal union, mediated by his rule from the independently captured Canaanite city-state of Jerusalem.

David decisively defeated the Philistines, restricting them to the coastal plain, and moved to establish a state apparatus with its administrative center at Jerusalem. He assured a Yahwistic significance for Jerusalem by bringing the ark of the confederacy to a tent shrine at the capital city (§19.4) and by appointing Abiathar and Zadok as state priests, who may have represented respectively the old Israelite and new Canaanite components of the territorial state of Israel.

Apparently shortly after crushing the Philistines, David entered into foreign wars in Transjordan against Ammon, Moab, and Edom and against Aramean states northward into Syria, establishing hegemony as far as the Euphrates River (cf. the originally promised limits of the promised land in DH as announced by Moses and Joshua, §22.2). These territories were laid under tribute, some ruled by vassal kings and others by governors. David's successes were achieved during a political vacuum in the ancient Near East when no other sizable powers were contesting for control of the Syro-Palestinian corridor. Although he made some use of chariotry, David's military strategy and tactics were based on highly mobile infantry. Internally, he was able to put down rebellions against his rule by northerners and by his own son Absalom.

David is properly called "king" in several regards. He ruled over a territorial state that embraced Canaanites who had not been a part of the old intertribal confederacy. He took the initiative in fighting offensive wars that extended Israelite domination over Transjordanian and Syrian states. He assembled the basic elements of a state administration. In all these respects he was fully a king. It appears, however, that he conducted a modest building program, raised his military levies by tribal mechanisms, and found it unnecessary to tax his Israelite-Canaanite subjects since the state revenues required were drawn from foreign tribute.

30.4 Solomon

Solomon became successor to David after a bitter dynastic fight in which he had to forcibly suppress a powerful faction that backed his rival brother Adonijah. Opening his reign with an "iron fist" may have helped to stabilize his control in Judah and emboldened him to launch an ambitious program of political economy calculated to increase the wealth of his kingdom dramatically. His basic resources were the agricultural surpluses of peasants, which he supplemented by income from trade through tolls on caravans in transit and through shrewd commercial deals such as "arms sales" of Anatolian horses and Egyptian chariots to other states.

In order to secure his booming economic empire, he reached for military superiority by building massive fortifications and equipping large chariot forces. With his newfound wealth he built lavishly in Jerusalem, including a temple constructed on Phoenician lines and a palace for himself that exceeded the temple in size. The temple is generally understood to have been a tripartite fortresslike structure with two free-standing pillars at the entrance and provision for sacrificial rites at an open-air altar in the forecourt.[9] For a time Solomon relied on the old tribal administrative districts of his father, but before long he tightened administration by redistricting his kingdom and appointing officials in each of the new districts, thereby centralizing the command structure. By this new system he provisioned his court with sumptuous food and the temple with lavish sacrifices supplied from districts of roughly equal economic clout (the tribes had been unequal in size and productivity) and also hoped to control or neutralize the dangerously powerful northern tribes. Furthermore, to accomplish his construction of fortifications and to expedite his beautification of Jerusalem architecturally he forced his subjects into corvée labor gangs.

The economic surge that began so bravely ran into grave difficulties. Forced economic development pushed Solomon into policies that were mutually contradictory and issued in diminishing returns. In order to create a privileged upper class of economic nonproducers, he had to draw on expanding agricultural and commercial surpluses. He could only gather such forced wealth if he had a strong military establishment, which was itself exorbitantly costly, so that his resources were spread thinner and thinner. In order to build, Solomon needed timber and metals from abroad, for which he had mainly agricultural products to offer. In effect, the king commanded the laboring people to do tasks that contradicted one another: Stay on the land and produce more crops for export! Leave the land and serve in the army and build the cities! Taxation and corvée angered the populace and by the end of Solomon's reign one of his labor overseers in the north, Jeroboam, was organizing resistance and had to flee to Egypt, later

9. W. F. Stinespring ("Temple, Jerusalem," in *IDB* 4: 534–60) includes illustrated ground plans, drawings, and models, all of which are necessarily hypothetical reconstructions, with an update on comparative archaeological data in Jean Ouellette, "Temple of Solomon," in IDBSup, 872–74. Carol L. Meyers, "The Elusive Temple," *BA* 5 (1982): 33–41, emphasizes considerable changes over time in the structure and furnishings of the Solomonic temple due to economic, political, and religious factors.

to return as the first king of northern Israel. The vital monopoly on trade in the international corridor was jeopardized when Edom and Aram-damascus revolted. Saddled with a growing deficit, Solomon agreed to give away twenty cities in Asher to Phoenicia in return for precious metal.

Clearly Solomon was successful in securing a luxuried and privileged life for a small upper class in government and trade. Economic advantage to the common people was marginal at best. Over the years whatever improvements in productivity occurred were vulnerable to siphoning off for the benefit of the already-bloated rich. Insofar as this familiar model of the hierarchic city-state was totally contrary to the simplicities of previous Israelite social organization, it fueled intense resentment and grievance, and eroded the morale of the people. The overextended and unevenly "modernized" Solomonic economy left the gaudy empire vulnerable to an eventual conqueror or, as proved first to be the case, to the rebellion of his own subjects.

30.5 Major Enduring Structural Effects of the Monarchy

The combined work of David and Solomon moved Israel a long distance from "chieftainship" to "hierarchic kingship" along a trajectory that catapulted Israel into the forefront of ancient Near Eastern states, facilitated by the lack of any major contender for power at the time. The Solomonic bubble burst at his death when the empire split into two weaker core states after losing most of its extra-Palestinian territories. These weakened states eventually collided with the imperial designs of more powerful states (§33.5; 36.1; 36.4–5). Nonetheless, the forms of state rule launched by David and maximized by Solomon set patterns that were continued in both kingdoms. It is likely that the later northern rulers Omri, Ahab, and Jeroboam II (§33.3–4), as well as the southern rulers Uzziah and Josiah (§36.3), presided for periods over empires that approached the affluence and security of Solomon's domain. We shall comment on four structural changes that had enduring interlocking consequences.

1. *Political Centralization.* Israel had now become a state (and later would become two states) with taxing and conscripting powers and a monopoly of force over and above its people. To carry out these powers there were standing armies and empowered bureaucrats. These powers reached into the fields and villages to take crops and to conscript peasants for social purposes decided by a small minority in the royal court rather than by tribal elders sifting the mind of the people for a consensus.

2. *Social Stratification.* The monopoly of power in the new state was the monopoly of particular social groups. The state policy of deliberately

transferring wealth from the mass of productive people to a parasitic nonproductive class spawned not only a stratum of government officials but also strata of enterprising merchants and landlords who, by government grants and monopolies, gained affluence and status. These yawning social divisions were replicated and solidified from generation to generation, putting severe strains upon the old economic and legal structures of Israel.

3. *Shifts in Land Tenure.* In the intertribal confederacy land had been held in perpetuity by extended families and could not be sold out of the family; protective associations of families guarded the patrimony of each household (§24.2.c). As entrepreneurial wealth accumulated through taxes, plunder, and trade, the upper class looked for "investment opportunities." It is likely that much of this thirst could be satisfied, for a time, by purchases of land and extensions of loans at interest within the administrative urban centers and among the Canaanite regions of Israel unpracticed in old Israelite law. In time, however, the acquisitive drive began to encroach on tribal institutions and ways of life. It is doubtful that the old restraints on self-aggrandizement were ever formally repealed by state law or edict. Probably they were worn down by legal loopholes and circumventions of custom, with bribery at hand as a final recourse. Gradually loans at interest were extended to needy Israelites and their property mortgaged; many of them ended up as tenant farmers, debt servants, or landless wage laborers. Tribal economic security and tribal religious identity were undermined, and the social unity and political trust of the people in their leaders put in radical doubt.

4. *Domestic Repercussions of Foreign Trade, Diplomacy, and War.* To be a state in the Syro-Palestinian corridor meant to be caught up in an international web of trade, diplomacy, and war. Under David and Solomon, Israel was amazingly successful in that political-military game. For brief periods during the divided monarchies similar successes fell to Israel and Judah. And for fairly extended periods friction among the states was minor or at least manageable. When one of the Israelite states grew aggressive or a foreign power intruded on them, however, a "meat grinder" process of attrition tended to be set in motion.

For minor powers with relatively small populations and limited economic resources, frequently subject to drought, changes of course in foreign policy could have immediate, sometimes cataclysmic effects. The efforts required for these small states to secure favorable trade exchanges, to mount wars against neighbors, to absorb and turn back invasions, and to pay tribute and indemnities to imperial powers were quickly felt in the impoverished and demoralized lives of the common people and in the factional struggles among leaders. Native Israelite elites, when endangered by foreign attackers or exploiters, were inclined to lay heavier economic and ideological exactions on their people. Just when a closing of ranks for "national unity" against Damascus, Assyria, or Neo-Babylonia seemed urgent to top leaders, the contradictory real interests of people came to the fore and the lengthening social divisions among them were aggravated by what amounted to a war of attrition against ordinary Israelites who bore the brunt of their leaders' vaulting ambitions.

31
LITERARY CULTURE, RELIGIOUS CULT, AND IDEOLOGY

31.1 The Yahwist (J)

We have briefly characterized the J source of the Pentateuch (§13.1) and listed its contents in Genesis 12—50 (table 10) and in Exodus-Numbers (table 11) as well as noted the possibility that J survives in conquest traditions such as Judges 1 (§22.3). For a full picture of the hypothetical Yahwist document one must include the appropriate passages in *Genesis 2—11* (table 21).

The Yahwist fashioned a work of epic proportions that combines simplicity and grandeur. Single traditions and clusters of traditions, vividly shaped at an oral stage of composition, are joined in a great literary sweep of artfully arranged units and thematic emphases. Compactness of plot and pungency of style lend the narratives a wonderful transparency. Economy of expression and emotional restraint hold the story line in taut relief and mounting suspense. The Yahwist theologizes less by formal religious statement than by the linking of the stories and by the more or less direct way that the deity participates in or influences the action. A studied naiveté makes it difficult to summarize the exact religious tenor of the work.

The J writer has an ample distinctive vocabulary: "to know" as a euphemism for sexual intercourse; "to call upon the name of Yahweh" for worship of the deity; "to bless" as the beneficent action of deity toward humans and other creatures; "to find favor or grace" in the sense of "to please someone"; "according to these things," that is, "in this way, after this manner" (a common narrative transition); Canaanites for the inhabitants of Palestine (Amorites in E); Hobab or Reuel for the father-in-law of Moses (Jethro in E); Sinai for the holy mountain (as in P, but Horeb in E); Israel for the third patriarch (Jacob in E). Also, J favors the formal "my lord/your servant" for "you/I" in the address of inferiors to superiors; has a liking for

TABLE 21
Yahwist (J) Traditions in Genesis 2—11

Creation of earth and the first human pair	2:4b—3:24
Cain and Abel	4:1–16
Genealogy of Cain (Kenites)	4:17–26
Genealogical fragment of Noah	5:29
Divine beings copulate with women to produce giants on earth	6:1–4
Destruction of Earth by flood	
Introduction: Divine decision to destroy	6:5–8
Body: Execution of the flood	7:1–5, 7–10, 12, 16b–17, 22–23 8:2b–3a, 6–7a, 8–12, 13b
Conclusion: Divine renunciation of ecological destruction	8:20–22
Noah's curse of Canaan (Ham?) and blessing on Shem and Japheth	9:18–27
Table of nations	10:8–19, 21, 24–30
Tower of Babel	11:1–9
Genealogy of Terah	11:28–30

coupling two verbs to emphasize a single action, for example, "look and behold"; and delights in the wordplay on *'adāmāh*, "ground/soil" and *'ādām*, "human being" (one taken from the ground). Other preferred expressions are "to hasten," "it may be," "there was none left," and "behold now."

The Yahwist also displays a wide-ranging interest in etiologies, especially reveling in popular etymologies of the names of persons and places, often cast in the form of puns: Eve, "the mother of all living" (*ḥawwāh*, "Eve," resembles *ḥay*, "living," Gen. 3:20); Babel, where the tongues were confused (Babylonian *babel/bab'ilu*, "gate of God," resembles Hebrew *bālal*, "to confuse," Gen. 11:9); Edom, the other name for Esau (*'edōm*, "Edom," resembles *'ādōm*, "red," presumably for the color of the rock characteristic of the country, Gen. 25:30); Israel, "he who strives with God" (after his wrestling with God, replacing the old name Jacob, "supplanter" or "heel-grabber," who grasped precedence over his twin brother, ▓▓. 25:26; 32:27); Marah, "bitterness" (because of the acrid waters, Exod. 15:23). These fanciful associations of similar sounds and condensed word pictures are unreliable as actual etymologies, but they are wonderfully evocative of popular play with language.

Compared to later Pentateuchal sources, which are more restrictedly "religious" in their concerns, J shows a far-ranging interest in the wider sociocultural and political situation of Israel, connecting the stories of the ancestors of Israel with traditions about the earliest pre-Israelites, reaching as far back as the traditional original human pair. The Yahwist relates the deeds of the ancestors of Israel with gusto, even when their behavior is questionable or blatantly reprehensible; there is no flinching at the lie of Abraham (Gen. 12:10–20), the deceit and conniving of Jacob against Esau and Laban (Genesis 27; 30:25—31:1), Simeon and Levi's ruse in murdering the Shechemites (Genesis 34), or Moses' rashness in killing the Egyptian overseer (Exod. 2:11–15). While such behavior is not overtly commended, it is recounted by J, unlike P who seldom reveals such weaknesses in Israelite leaders. Moreover, J recounts these human blemishes without the rationalization or toning down typical of E.

Moreover, the Yahwist retains old traditions that are curiously unassimilated to the main thrust of his narrative. The story of divine beings who copulate with women, thereby spawning giants in the earth, is a baldly mythological fragment (Gen. 6:1–4). By serving as a partial explanation for the misconduct that triggered the flood, this fragment weakens any impression that the story of Adam and Eve is a programmatic account of the origin of all human wrongdoing. The story of Jacob's struggle at the Jabbok River with a powerful night demon, who turns out to be the deity, is related without embarrassment toward its animistic undertone (Gen. 32:24–32). The "bridegroom of blood" story, in which Yahweh inexplicably accosts Moses but is appeased when Zipporah circumcises their son (Exod. 4:24–26), lacks meaningful context and may have derived from an independent explanation of the origin of circumcision as a protectionary rite to ward off malicious deities.

The Yahwist stratum in the Pentateuch projects an intensely realistic conception or dramatization of God, shot through with descriptions of deity in terms of human physical features (anthropomorphisms) and human feelings (anthropopathisms). Without abashment, the Yahwist pictures God strolling in the garden in the cool of the day (Gen. 3:8), sealing the door of Noah's ark (Gen. 7:15c), visiting and dining with Abraham before his tent (Gen. 18:1–22), reconnoitering Sodom and Gomorrah to see if their sin is as perverse as rumored (Gen. 18:21), and taking off or clogging the Egyptian chariot wheels (Exod. 14:25). Yahweh is alluded to in well-nigh corporeal terms. Even as a human being cannot be conceived by J except as a body-soul unity, there being no disembodied human "soul," so God—while no mere human—is talked about in bodily and affective language. Yahweh is evidently not all-knowing, but shows an experimental openness toward creation, abandoning one line of action for another as advisable. On more than one occasion the deity is perturbed by the ways of humanity and is taxed to find new methods for coping with them.

On the other hand, the Yahwist does not seem to make literalistic univocal assertions about deity. Much of the naive conceptualization probably rests in the oral saga roots of the material. The Yahwist may in fact be playfully ringing changes on this older, robust, even touchingly comic, portrait of God as a forceful "folk" expression of divine presence and agency in the world. Yahweh is "high god," not confused with nature spirits, but an overarching root metaphor of a living reality to be pictured necessarily in human imagery.

The Yahwist thus became the first Israelite writer to give extended graphic literary expression to a "personal" and "transcendent" mode of conceiving deity that has prevailed in popular Judaism and Christianity ever since.[10] On the whole, Yahweh is experienced as personal but not as mere creature, as the parent of all creatures without being sentimental, as respectful of human freedom without being impotent, as moral without being

---

10. Dale Patrick (*The Rendering of God in the Old Testament,* OBT 10 [Philadelphia: Fortress Press, 1981]) develops the biblical depiction of deity as a dramatis persona and notes of Genesis 1—11 that "here at the beginning . . . the style and tone of biblical God-language is set" (15).

moralistic, and as strong-purposed without being dictatorial. Nonetheless, one must be extremely cautious in giving a profile of J's "doctrine of God," since the stories vary markedly in the words, actions, and attributes assigned to deity and contain virtually no direct theological reflection. Yahweh even alters his style of relating to humans according to the era of history recounted. For example, in Genesis 2—11, Yahweh displays a streak of capriciousness and fierce jealousy that takes preemptive action to protect heavenly prerogatives against the curiosity and ambition of humans (the so-called Promethean motif).

The J story of creation treats questions of human powers and limits in a form intelligible to the simplest mind, yet tantalizing to the wisest. The sociocultural viewpoint is that of a Palestinian peasant, for 'ādām, "the human being," is none other than the cultivator of the 'adāmāh, "the ground/soil." Life depends on the fickle dews and rains rather than on the irrigation waters of the great river valleys. Chaos is waterless waste. The human being, created prior to plants and animals, is shaped from the dust as "a living being," a body-spirit totality.

The idyllic garden is called Eden (cognate of Babylonian *edinu*, "plain/desert," translated by LXX as *paradeisos*, English "paradise"). The formal features of this story are presumably north Canaanite (Ezek. 28:12–19 gives an alternative version of the myth, possibly preserved in Phoenician form). Certain elements in the story do not cohere smoothly: the antiquarian interest in the network of rivers and in the precious metals (Gen. 2:10–14), and especially the anomalous tree of life (2:9b). The presence of two trees in the garden is ignored by Yahweh and the human pair until the end of the story (3:22); the reader wonders why the man and woman did not eat of the tree of life immediately after tasting of the tree of the knowledge of good and evil, thereby assuring themselves everlasting life.

The story does not permit any simplistic equation of work or sexuality with "sin" and its "punishment." The human being already works before disobeying Yahweh, and the man and woman share bodily union before their defiance of Yahweh. It is more precisely *miserliness* of the soil and *pain* of childbirth that are the baleful consequences of breaking Yahweh's prohibition. In fact the story has little technical theological language: "fall," "sin," "disobedience," "punishment," "freedom" are not words that occur in it at all. With respect to the relation of the sexes, the narrative strongly implies that prior to 2:21 Adam is asexual (or bisexual?), that is, the inclusive human being, who only becomes specifically "man" when "woman" is simultaneously created through dividing this single hermaphroditic human into its respective sexual "halves."

Coequality of man and woman is expressed, and in many respects the woman is shown as more intelligent and resourceful than the man. The imposition of man's "rule" over woman (3:16) is presented as a lapsed condition that is reprehensible and might be overcome through a restored relation of the human pair with Yahweh. Nevertheless, later Jewish and Christian exegesis has tended to read the story through male chauvinist eyes that blame woman disproportionately for the disobedience, even associating the eating of the fruit with sexuality itself and playing on the misogynist theme of "woman as temptress."

This elusive "fall" story may have been more combed for meaning than any other passage in the Hebrew Bible. Surprisingly, however, the exegetical and theological tradition that has labored over its meaning was very slow in developing. The story's lack of internal theological interpretation discouraged any clear appeal to it by later parts of the Hebrew Bible. The first speculation occurs in postbiblical Judaism (2 Esdras) and in early Christianity (Paul), tracing a connection between the sin of the first human pair and the subsequent sin of all humans, and Christian orthodoxy later developed a metaphor into the ironclad doctrine of original sin.

What the discourse of the story means in its own terms remains elusive. For instance, the import of the tree of the knowledge of good and evil has been endlessly discussed. It is probable that the Yahwist was not thinking mainly of moral judgment but of the knowledge of good and evil destinies, of the secrets of the divine knowledge and power, which can never be the unequivocal possession of humans, but which humans can and will strive after and "tap into" both creatively and destructively. The agency of discord between Yahweh and the humans and between the man and the woman is personified in the serpent who is not diabolical and malicious so much as shrewd and crafty. He is certainly not equated with Satan, a much later figure in Israelite thought (§54.3). The psychologized presentation of temptation is penetrating and provocative. Temptation appears as the lure of novel experience and expanded wisdom which sows doubt about received judgments and restrictions, appeals powerfully to the senses, and arouses self-confident ambition and thirst for knowledge and control.

The main tenor of the story in the overall context of J, and even more so in the context of the entire Hebrew Bible, has been perceived as the legitimation of Yahweh's behavior and the guilt of the human rebels. The story, however, has inner dynamics that resist this theological reduction, for it contains a strong undercurrent that at least tacitly commends the human pair for gaining knowledge, without which history outside the garden could never have begun. It is to be noted that Yahweh lies, or at least equivocates, when he says that "on the day that you eat of it [the forbidden fruit] you shall die," and the serpent exploits this divine "bluff" by claiming "you will not die ... your eyes will be opened and you will be like God." In large measure, the serpent was right: instead of immediate death, human eyes are opened to knowledge that both empowers and debilitates, leading to a constant struggle between life and death. But Yahweh was also correct in that guilt, social division, and death would overbalance the gains of knowledge unless Yahweh took further steps to rectify the flawed course of human history.

The unresolved inner divisions of the story have been exposed in a recent structuralist analysis following Greimas's actantial model (§20.3).[11] Yahweh is shown to be functioning in the deep structure of the story in such a way as to occupy three roles which are expressly conflicted. *Yahweh* is the initial "sender/giver" of *the human cultivator* (Adam) as "object" to *the whole created earth* as "receiver," in order to till its waiting soil. This promised narrative program, however, raises a fundamental suspicion of the deity as a deceptive giver, a folkloric villain, since he in fact withholds the human cultivator from the whole earth by keeping him as a personal attendant within the garden. The narrative program can only be carried out by *Yahweh* appearing in a second role as "helper" when he creates the serpent and a man-woman pair out of the undifferentiated human being. The serpent, by tempting, and the human pair, by succumbing to temptation, together become the "subjects/protagonists" who facilitate the blocked transfer of the human being as cultivator of the soil to the outside world. In the process, however, *Yahweh* must take on a third role as "opponent" who punishes the man in such a way that he enters the outside world as a greatly impaired cultivator since the soil will now produce poor yields.

This fascinating and controversial structural reading gives a narratized parallel to the theological enigmas that have built up around the story. Yahweh's conflicted roles of sender, helper, and opponent are ways of alluding to the unresolved problems about divine justice and power and about human freedom which are posed by the prohibition and the punishment for its violation. It can be said that we have a theological puzzle because we have a narrative program in which Yahweh appears to have put himself and the human pair in a "no-win" situation hedged by a "double bind." Message *one* reads: "Don't eat the fruit! Stay here in the garden! But of course then you will not 'know' and human life in the real world will never begin!" Message *two* reads: "Do eat the fruit! Gain knowledge and

11. David Jobling, "The Myth Semantics of Genesis 2:4b—3:24," *Semeia* 18 (1980): 41–49.

start living in the historical world! But of course then you will live a frustrated and limited life lacking the social harmony and physical abundance of the garden!" The pre-J tradition at this point may have been so weighted with the plight of Israel's hard-pressed peasantry in its struggle to cultivate the soil and bear children that the Yahwist's more optimistic outlook simply failed to find a satisfying resolution for the contradictory elements.

Beginning with the analysis of the Yahwist by G. von Rad,[12] there has been great stress on the architectural design of the traditions as arranged and linked by this inventive compiler-author. In the case of Genesis 1—11, the effect is to underscore the step-by-step deterioration of the human situation. There is an increase of sin and suffering that parallels the increase of human knowledge and skill in the episodic movement from the garden, through the Cain and Abel and flood stories, to the Tower of Babel. The inventiveness of humans does not gain unalloyed blessing but leads to social discord and violence. Yahweh intervenes to expel the first human pair from the garden, to punish the first murderer with homeless wandering over the earth, to expunge all people except for Noah and his family, and to scatter humans widely over the earth in separate language communities so that they will have difficulty cooperating in evil.

At the same time there is another line of development interwoven with the first. Yahweh mitigates each punitive intervention with "mercy" in the sense that Yahweh assures that human life will go forward toward new opportunities and possibilities. Yahweh's gracious mitigations of punishment are as follows: the deity clothes the first human pair with skins, puts a mark on Cain so that he will not be murdered, spares Noah from death in the flood, and, after the collapse of the Tower of Babel project, opens a new phase of history by calling forth Abraham as the father of the Israelites-to-come.

The spread of human sin issues in a catastrophic flood which nearly undoes creation altogether. Here the Yahwist is explicitly dependent on Mesopotamian traditions which we now know in three main versions: (1) a Sumerian version where the counterpart of Noah is Ziusudra (table 1: 1G); (2) an older Babylonian version with the hero Atrahasis (table 1: 1I); and (3) a somewhat later Babylonian version contained in the longer Gilgamesh Epic in which Utnapishtim survives the flood (table 1: 1H). Most likely, J was familiar with the third version of the flood and possibly also with the

---

12. Gerhard von Rad, *Genesis: A Commentary,* OTL (Philadelphia: Westminster Press, 1961); idem, *OTT,* 1: 48–56, 136–65.

second (P's acquaintance with the Atrahasis version is more explicit [§49]). As for attempts to demonstrate an ancient "universal flood" lying behind these traditions, there simply is no geological evidence that the entire Tigris-Euphrates region was ever inundated at once, much less the inhabited world.[13] It is possible that "flood" in these myths is a metaphor for military invasion and political collapse.[14] Nor is there any basis for crediting recent claims to have recovered remains of the ark on Mt. Ararat.[15] Many of the same formal elements appear in the Mesopotamian and biblical flood stories, although the J and P flood accounts express the divine action in much more reflective moral and theological categories by underscoring human sin and divine judgment and mercy. Nonetheless, the seed features of the Israelite flood traditions are all present in the older prototypes.

The J story of the flood is interwoven intricately with the P account but the vocabularies, styles, and conceptions of the two are so different that they can be readily separated.[16] In J, there is no account of the building of the ark (perhaps dropped in favor of P's detailed description) and Noah enters it with little advance notice and no explanation of why the flood is coming. In P, Noah is taken fully into God's confidence and is "theologically informed" about what will happen and why. In J, the flood, fed by rain, lasts for 40 days and recedes in two (possibly three) 7-day periods. In P the flood, caused by water breaking into the cosmos from the oceans below the earth and above the firmament, lasts for 150 days and takes another 220 days to recede. Interestingly, J remarks on clean and unclean animals in the ark (seven pairs of the former to every pair of the latter) and has Noah sacrifice after the flood, whereas P is silent on both points since in his view the sacrificial cult and the distinction between clean and unclean foods did not begin until the revelation to Moses.

Early phases of historical-critical study stressed the work of J as a collector and editor of old stories and poems, whose small units and oral tradition roots were subsequently studied intensively by form criticism (§11.1.b; 15.2). Around the mid–twentieth century, under the impetus of von Rad, the position gained currency that the Yahwist was an original writer, "Israel's first theologian," who shaped the ancient materials to stress the judging and saving activity of Israel's God over the span of time from creation to the conquest of Canaan (with various opinions on whether J

13. Andre Parrot, *The Flood and Noah's Ark* (London: SCM Press, 1955).
14. Thorkild Jacobsen, "The Eridu Genesis," *JBL* 100 (1981): 526–27.
15. Lloyd R. Bailey, *Where Is Noah's Ark?* (Nashville: Abingdon Press, 1978).
16. Norman C. Habel, *Literary Criticism of the Old Testament*, GBS (Philadelphia: Fortress Press, 1971), 18–64.

ended with Numbers or continued into Joshua and possibly beyond). The Yahwist is now widely dated to the Solomonic "enlightenment," more or less contemporary with the Court History of David, and expressive of a robust confidence that providence rules in the sometimes clouded acts and motives of human beings.

Recent studies have tended to view J as an etiology of the Davidic monarchy toward which the promises to the patriarchs are said to point (e.g., Gen. 15:17–19), and sometimes as a measured warning to the Davidic dynasty concerning its subservience to divine purposes and judgments that transcend any particular Israelite institution. The discerned decoded message: Beware of excessive human, even kingly, pride! If the early monarchy provided the cultural and technical literary conditions for writing the J document, the extent of its intended reference to the monarchy, either in endorsement or caution, is much more difficult to ascertain.

Although a Solomonic, or slightly later, date for J is presently favored by most scholars, attacks on this position from various directions warrant a rethinking of the consensus. Some would shift the date for J either into the seventh century, because of its presumed affinities with prophetic and Deuteronomic thought, or into the sixth century, because of a positive view of foreign nations and prominence accorded Abraham shared by J and some exilic writings. A more radical view holds that it is impossible to detect a single theological perspective in so-called J materials which are in fact composed of separate tradition complexes in Genesis, Exodus, and Numbers. It is noted, for example, that the J patriarchal promises announce a son, many descendants, and land, but they do not refer to a king or dynasty explicitly.

While these counterproposals have yet to be taken into account fully, it appears that the political geography of J fits most appropriately into the tenth-to-ninth-century horizon. On the other hand, it is probable that a supposed programmatic theological unity in the Yahwist has been overstated, and it should also be recognized that some elements in J may derive from the eighth or seventh centuries. Older literary source divisions of J into two or more strands reflected the lack of simple unity in the work. Nowadays the issue of the precarious unity of J resurfaces in redaction-critical efforts, as yet in their infancy, to establish the scope and sociohistoric setting of intentional redaction that may reveal two or more "editions" of J, or possibly one primary edition with later supplements.

31.2 Psalms and Wisdom

The present Book of Psalms (§52.2) and the wisdom writings (§54) are manifestly postexilic in their existing shapes. It is evident, however, that songs and wisdom writings were very ancient literary types in the Israelite milieu. The centralized cultic and court institutions introduced by David and Solomon provided opportune settings for psalmic and wisdom literature to be cultivated by royal officials. This royal sponsorship of psalmody and wisdom was expressed in the traditions of David as psalmist and Solomon as sage. The headings to the Psalms claiming Davidic authorship are late and unreliable, as are also the attribution of wisdom books, such as Proverbs, Ecclesiastes, and Song of Songs, to Solomon. Certain psalms (such as the royal psalms of Psalms 2; 18; 20—21; 45; 72; 101; 110; 132) and some proverbs (among the collections in Prov. 10:1—31:31), however, reveal preexilic monarchic references and codes of conduct typical of high court officials. Although it is impossible to attach them firmly to one reign or another (but cf. "men of Hezekiah" in Prov. 25:1), much less to the age of David and Solomon, these royal-oriented psalm and wisdom texts are very instructive about the general ethos and culture of the upper-class circles who prospered under the centralized institutions of kingship. Acquiring leisure and skill to cultivate a pragmatic intellectual culture, the "wise" mixed the symbolic concreteness of Yahwism with more aesthetic and cosmopolitan concerns.

31.3 David and Zion Traditions

We have called attention to a key DH interpretive passage in 2 Samuel 7 that grants the promise of an "everlasting" dynasty to David (table 19: no. 2). The language and concepts of this Davidic promise are far older than DH (and in tension with DH's overall outlook), as is evident in older psalms (e.g., Psalms 89; 132) and in eighth-century prophecies (Isa. 9:6–7; 11:1–5; Micah 5:2–5).

It is now common to distinguish a Davidic covenant of a promissory type from a Mosaic covenant of an obligatory type (§19.1), each as it were contesting the same ideological-institutional ground: either the national life is unequivocally assured by Yahweh (Davidic covenant) or problematically conditional on proven loyalty to Yahweh (Mosaic covenant). Others view the two concepts as operative in different spheres, either harmonistically (*if* the nation is faithful and endures, *this* is the dynasty that will rule in it) or formally unrelated (*granted* that the nation exists in which there are various possible candidates and claimants for royal office, *this* dynasty alone will rule because of entitlement by divine promise). The promise to David has been shown to resemble the ancient Near Eastern genre of a "royal grant" by a king to a faithful servant, as in the decree of Hattusilis, the Hittite monarch, to his chief scribe, Mittannamuwa.[17] The motif of disciplining the

17. Moshe Weinfeld, "Covenant, Davidic," in IDBSup, 190.

grantee, or his successors, as "wayward sons" is consistent with the irrevocable grant. A similar unconditional premise in promises to the patriarchs
has often been underscored and the covenant with Abraham is frequently
viewed as a typological foreshadowing of the Covenant with David (Genesis
15).

Other interpreters believe that the pervasiveness of a Davidic covenant
notion has been overstated; in fact, the term "covenant" is rather infrequent in these promissory royal texts. They claim that the dynastic promise
was only one of a number of motifs of royal theology which included
traditions about Zion (= Jerusalem) as the unshakeable earthly abode of
Yahweh. The Zion traditions, in part drawn from Canaanite cosmological
and mythological notions and possibly derived from pre-Davidic Jerusalem,
included motifs of the divine mountain, the river of paradise, the divine
conquest of chaos as the basis of creation, the defeat of the nations, and the
pilgrimage of chastened nations to Zion. By means of David's choice of
Jerusalem as his capital, these motifs mingled in complex ways within the
royal cult and the literature of psalms and prophets. The nature of the
monarchic cult in Jerusalem, how it conceived and celebrated kingship—
and particularly the role of the king in it—has been much debated in
relation to similarities and differences between Israelite and Canaanite/
ancient Near Eastern concepts of the king vis-à-vis deity.

Whatever the exact delineations of genres and motifs concerning kingship
at Jerusalem, it is clear that various positive religious evaluations of the
office within Judah were developed, no doubt beginning with Davidic-
Solomonic times. In one way or another the Judahite kings were judged to
be (1) in a distinctive filial relation to Yahweh; (2) intermediaries between
Yahweh and the people; (3) exemplars of piety and obedience to Yahweh;
and (4) executors of Yahweh's justice domestically and among the nations.
From these roots sprang the later "messianism" associated with the Davidic
dynasty.

David and Zion traditions were henceforth to retain a crucial place in
Israelite self-reflection. For some, they were unequivocal supports for
resting unqualified hopes of security in the triumphal Israelite state or
Jewish restored community. For others, they were ambiguous symbols of
hope that required tempering in the larger context of Mosaic and prophetic
sociotheological judgment. Many of the social organizational, cultic, and
ideological conflicts that we will trace in following chapters were focused on
how the disputants read the "promises" of Yahweh about David and Zion.

CHAPTER 8

Traditions About the Northern Kingdom

Read the Biblical Text
1 Kings 12—2 Kings 17
Amos
Hosea

Consult Maps in *MBA*
nos. 116–51

32
THE SHAPE OF THE TRADITIONS IN
1 KINGS 12—2 KINGS 17

32.1 Source Statistics

Our DH sources on the independent northern kingdom of Israel and the parallel kings (and one queen) of southern Judah, extending over 209 years, are composed of the two kinds of traditions identified for the united monarchy (table 22): annalistic political-historical documentation and miscellaneous literary traditions (§29.1).

As with the united monarchy, we encounter sparseness of sources and unequal distributions of verses by types of sources. Annalistic political-historical documentation from DH for the total of thirty-one rulers in both kingdoms over two hundred years (140 vv.) is less than the same sort of documentation for Solomon (162 vv.) who ruled a maximum of forty years. Annalistic material on David (97 vv.) exceeds that of the eleven kings in his dynasty who followed Solomon (63 vv.), plus the alien queen, Athaliah. Political documentation for Judah is happily assisted by some data from Chronicles (68 vv.), but Chronicles ignores the "apostate" northern kings. Another way to state the thinness of coverage for the divided kingdoms is to note that, including DH and Chronicles, there is an average of *1* annalistic verse for each year of the kingdoms from 931 to 722 B.C.E. as against *3.73* annalistic verses for each year of the reign of David and Solomon (calculated at eighty years).

Especially striking are the meager data on kings otherwise judged to have been of major political importance: Jeroboam I (10 vv.), Omri (5 vv.), Ahab (4 vv.), Jehu (2 vv.), Jeroboam II (2 vv.), in Israel, and Jehoshaphat (4 vv. DH; 10 vv. Chron) and Uzziah (3 vv. DH; 10 vv. Chron) in Judah. In the DH formulas on each of the kings (Athaliah, who usurped the Judahite throne for six years, is denied the royal formula), mention is constantly made of the chronicles of the kings of Israel and Judah, evidently the source for the annalistic comments of DH. These official records of the two kingdoms were patchily and arbitrarily excerpted by DH.

32.2 Prophetic Narratives

The accounts of the northern kings are expanded by miscellaneous literary traditions, the great majority being stories about prophets (occasionally only the message of the prophet) which selectively illuminate aspects of the reigns of certain kings:

TABLE 22
Distribution of DH Verses to Rulers of Israel and Judah
in 1 Kings 12—2 Kings 17

Israel			Judah		
Ruler	Political-Historical Documentation	Miscellaneous Literary Traditions	Ruler	Political-Historical Documentation	Miscellaneous Literary Traditions
Jeroboam I 931/930–910/909	10	67	Rehoboam 931/930–913	5 + (22)*	
Nadab 910/909–909/908	2		Abijah (Abijam) 913–911/910	0 + (4)*	
Baasha 909/908–886/885	11	5	Asa 911/910– 870/869	10 + (8)*	
Elah 886/885–885/884	2				
Zimri 885/884	8				
Omri 880–874/873	5				
Ahab 874/873–853	4	201†	Jehoshaphat 870/869–848	4 + (10)*	58
Ahaziah 853–852	2	16	J(eh)oram 848–841	4 + (5)*	
J(eh)oram 852–841	3	204†	Ahaziah 841	4	6
Jehu 841–814/813	2	65	Athaliah 841–835	2	20
J(eh)oahaz 814/813–798	5		J(eh)oash 835–796	2 + (2)*	33

*Verses from Chronicles that supply annalistic data supplementing DH data.
†Enumeration includes prophetic stories in which no king appears or the king is unnamed.

TABLE 22 (continued)
Distribution of DH Verses to Rulers of Israel and Judah
in 1 Kings 12—2 Kings 17

	Israel			*Judah*	
Ruler	*Political-Historical Documentation*	*Miscellaneous Literary Traditions*	*Ruler*	*Political-Historical Documentation*	*Miscellaneous Literary Traditions*
J(eh)oash 798–782/781	3	8	Amaziah 796–767	12	
Jeroboam II 782/781–753	2	3	Uzziah (Azariah) 767–740/739	3 + (10)*	
Zechariah 753–752	1				
Shallum 752	1				
Menahem 752–742/741	4				
Pekahiah 742/741–740/739	1		Jotham 740/739–732/731	2 + (3)*	
Pekah 740/739–732/731	5				
Hoshea 732/731–723/722	6		Ahaz 732/731–716/715	15 + (4)*	117
Total	77	569		63 + (68)*	234

1. *Ahijah of Shiloh* in the reign of Jeroboam I:
   1 Kings 11:26–40; 14:1–17
2. *Jehu ben Hanani* in the reign of Baasha:
   1 Kings 16:1–4
3. *Elijah the Tishbite* in the reigns of Ahab and Ahaziah:
   1 Kings 17—2 Kings 2:12
4. *Micaiah ben Imlah* in the reign of Ahab:
   1 Kings 22:1–36
5. *Elisha ben Shaphat* in the reigns of Jehoram, Jehu, Jehoahaz, and Jehoash:
   1 Kings 19:19–21; 2 Kings 2—10; 13:14–21
6. *Jonah ben Amittai* in the reign of Jeroboam II:
   2 Kings 14:25–27

There are also stories of anonymous prophets in the reigns of Jeroboam I (1 Kings 13) and of Ahab (1 Kings 20).

Many of the prophetic stories carry overt military-political content that focuses on changes of dynasty, sieges and battles, and confrontations between kings and prophets. Each of the dynasties of Jeroboam I, Baasha, and Jehu is shown to have been endorsed by prophets. The account of Jehu's purge of the Omri dynasty, triggered by Elisha, is full and vivid, but concerning his twenty-eight-year rule over Israel we have not a shred of biblical information identified as such (§33.4). The Elijah, Micaiah, and Elisha prophetic inserts for the reigns of Ahab (201 vv.) and Jehoram (204 vv.) are particularly extensive but historically confusing (§34.2). Since many of the kings in these prophetic stories are not named, it cannot be taken for granted that Ahab and Jehoram are the royal subjects in all cases, merely on the strength of the DH placement of the stories which may, after all, have had the aim of diverting criticism away from Jehu's dynasty. Many interpreters are of the view that some or all of the prophetic traditions assigned to the reign of Jehoram, last ruler of the Omri dynasty, and even some assigned to Ahab, actually belong to the following Jehu dynasty.

The prophetic narratives as a whole disclose varying supportive and critical stances of prophets toward kings, and vice versa, but it is not always clear how to transpose the moral-theological judgments of the prophetic stories and messages into the terms of military and political policies in the conduct of state. Thus there is a sense in which the excerpted chronicles of the two kingdoms and the prophetic narratives move on two different levels of narration and interpretation which often fail to meet at a point of common discourse.

The form and style of the prophetic stories show many affinities with the sagas of Genesis through Numbers (table 8: nos. 20–21; §15.2; 17.1), and some of them are "legends" in the technical sense of celebrating the wonderful powers of a prophet, notably in the case of Elisha. The stories appear to have been shaped and passed on (written down?) in circles or "schools" of prophets of the sort described in the Elisha stories.

32.3 Other Sources: Prophetic Books and the Elohist

All of the prophets discussed above are presented by DH in narratives told *about* them, within which some of their brief messages are enclosed. The first books actually written *by* prophets are those of Amos and Hosea in the mid–eighth century. In these specifically prophetic books the relation of narrative and speech is reversed: collections of prophetic words enclose brief narrative passages. The information that can be gleaned from Amos and Hosea concerning the history of Israel in its last decades is minimal as far as clear references to specific events are concerned. But both writings are of high value in disclosing aspects of the socioeconomic, political, and religious life at firsthand, even though their choice and development of topics is obviously strongly colored by their critical outlooks.

Finally, it is to this period in Israel's history that the Elohist is to be assigned (§34.1), presenting a northern version of the ancient history-like traditions which the Yahwist rendered in a southern version. The E source shows many affinities of thought with the Elijah-Elisha traditions and with the prophet Hosea (§34.4). It is most likely to be dated in the late Omri or early Jehu dynasties.

33
HISTORY OF THE NORTHERN KINGDOM
AND ITS RELATIONS WITH JUDAH (931–722 B.C.E.)

33.1 The Schism (931 B.C.E.)

The immediate cause of the breakup of the united kingdom was the oppressive economic and political policies of Solomon (§30.4). Revolt broke out among the labor battalions of Ephraim led by Jeroboam who became the first king of the north. The larger background of this political split was the long rivalry between Judah and Ephraim-Manassah-Benjamin as the two major power centers in the old confederacy. Interestingly, the withdrawal of the north from David's dynasty went largely uncontested. Apparently the two kingdoms were so exhausted after the Solomonic debacle that neither could force its will on the other.

33.2 Jeroboam and Baasha Dynasties (931–884 B.C.E.)

The basic structures of dynastic kingship seem to have been adopted in the new northern kingdom, although perhaps not all at once and in any case tempered by the absence of immediate imperial ambitions and programs. There were difficulties in settling on a suitable capital (Shechem, Penuel, and Tirzah are mentioned). The main data on Jeroboam I concern his replacement of the Jerusalem temple cult with sanctuaries at Dan and Bethel where he introduced "golden calf" worship. The calves were probably symbolic throne supports for Yahweh and no more "idolatrous" than the cosmic imagery in Solomon's temple (including ark with winged cherubim and a large water basin supported by twelve bronze oxen). Jeroboam installed his own priests after expelling the Davidic-Solomonic Levites, and he observed a new schedule of festivals. These religious measures were intended to give his kingdom total religious independence from Judah, just as he had asserted total political separation.

Details concerning the internal administration of Israel are lacking. Jeroboam would have required at least modest taxes, but a limited building program may have forestalled the need to reintroduce corvée. Since the first monarch of the north "inherited" Solomon's military and administrative structures in his territory, the extent to which they were dismantled, revised, or dropped will have depended greatly on how strongly the disaffected peasants, whom Jeroboam rode to power, were able to exert political pressure on him.

A destructive military campaign by Pharaoh Shishak of Egypt in the fifth year of Jeroboam and Rehoboam seriously depleted both kingdoms and further prevented a clear military victory of either Israel or Judah over the other. Baasha's rule witnessed the beginning of Israel's wars with the now-independent Arameans of Damascus, a seesaw struggle which went on intermittently throughout the ninth century. The sons of Jeroboam and Baasha both reigned briefly until overthrown by military coups.

Judah's most urgent immediate problem, after the withdrawal of the northern tribes, was to secure its position defensively. Rehoboam busied himself constructing a chain of fortresses to protect his kingdom. The location of Jerusalem so close to the northern border was the occasion for protracted border warfare between the two Israelite states. Under Asa, Judah succeeded in pushing its border to a point about nine miles north of Jerusalem which henceforth provided a buffer zone for defense of the Judean capital.

33.3 Omri Dynasty (880–841 B.C.E.)

Omri was the product of a military coup, but to gain the throne he had to prevail in a four-year civil war against "half of the people" who followed Tibni. The reasons for this deep and prolonged division and strife can only be speculated, but it is possible that the Tibni faction pressed for a limited monarchy while the Omri faction, headed by a professional soldier possibly of foreign origin (a Canaanite without Israelite grass-roots tribal upbringing?), favored a more centralized monarchy. On becoming king, Omri launched an ambitious "Davidic-Solomonic" type of reign by establishing an opulent new capital at Samaria and developing military and trade alliances with Phoenicia, Damascus, and Judah. He and his son Ahab were eminently successful in raising Israel's status in international politics. Ahab was able to contribute the largest contingent of chariots (two thousand we are told by the Assyrian annals) to a coalition of Syrian states that fought Shalmaneser III at Qarqar in 853 B.C.E. (table 2: 4J; see *ANET*, 278–79).

It was during Omri's dynasty that the first sustained prophetic opposition to Israel's kings is reported. Elijah and Elisha mounted harassing criticisms that focused on the penetration of Baal worship into Ahab's court by way of the king's marriage to a Phoenician princess, Jezebel (§34.2). How far this worship penetrated among the masses of Israelites is problematic, but the very espousal of Baal and Yahweh worship side by side in the royal court was in itself abhorrent to these exclusive Yahwists. Also, we begin to hear of socioeconomic abuses that included the expropriation of free Israelites' property. A severe drought compounded matters by adding to an impoverishment of the people that had doubtless been set in motion by Omri's grand plans to upgrade Israel as a military and political power. All this suggests that the preceding Jeroboam and Baasha dynasties may have soft-pedaled demands on their people by comparison with the Omrids who had to increase taxation and corvée to implement their ambitions.

The burgeoning Omrids made peace with Judah and were able to call upon Judahite forces to assist them in military campaigns against Damascus and Moab. The good relations were sealed by the marriage of the Judahite Jehoram to the daughter (or sister) of Ahab, Athaliah. Judah continued to hold sway over Edom. Jehoshaphat is said to have reorganized the administration of justice in Judah with a new court system centralized from Jerusalem.

33.4 Jehu Dynasty (841–752 B.C.E.)

Jehu came to power in a military coup sparked by the prophetic support of Elisha. He stamped out the practices of Baal religion in court circles and ruthlessly killed all representatives and influential supporters of the Omri dynasty. Since his sword did not spare Phoenician and Judahite royalty, his regime was quickly isolated from friendly ties with neighboring states. Early in his reign he hastened to submit to the Assyrian king Shalmaneser III and paid heavy tribute. The Assyrians soon withdrew from the west as a major force and the Jehu dynasty became embroiled in wars with Damascus that went very badly for Israel until the opening of the eighth century when Assyrian pressure on Damascus freed Israel for a major revival of power.

If the prophetic program of Elijah-Elisha was to restore exclusive Yahweh worship, to avoid all foreign alliances because they entailed recognition of foreign gods, and to maintain old practices and institutions of socioeconomic equality, the prophetic forces must have been disappointed in Jehu. He did extirpate Baal worship in Israel (at least for the moment) and he did break off the foreign ties established by the Omrids. On the other hand, he immediately submitted to Assyria, which meant the formal acknowledgment of Assyrian gods, and there is no evidence that he had either the will or the political means to improve the socioeconomic conditions of the common people. Political power, social privilege, and landed and commercial wealth passed from Omrid hands but apparently remained in a narrow circle that did not include the vast majority of the landed populace.

When Jehu's purge of the Omrids also swept away the Judahite king Ahaziah, his mother, Athaliah, seized the throne and attempted to extirpate the line of David. Successful for a few years, the Baal-worshiping queen was overthrown and replaced by a young Davidide, Jehoash, who had been hidden from Athaliah's knowledge. Under Jehoash a restoration of the temple at Jerusalem included a sounder administration of temple finances.

With Damascus and Assyria both weakened in the first half of the eighth century, first Jehoash and then Jeroboam II were able to reign over a peaceful and increasingly prosperous Israel, while a period of similar accomplishment was enjoyed by Judah under Amaziah and Uzziah. Agriculture and trade flourished. From the Book of Amos we learn, however, that the prosperity and national confidence were experienced chiefly at the summit of the society whereas the majority of peasants were in dire straits (§34.3). No doubt taxation and corvée played a role, but the particular focus of Amos is on the massive shift in land tenure from traditionally guaranteed family holdings to privately amassed estates taken over by debt foreclosures on impoverished farmers. In short, as in Solomon's united kingdom, the "wonders" of eighth-century Israel were concentrated in a privileged class who rose to their advantages by the systematic deprivation and disempowerment of the peasant majority.

33.5 Collapse of the Northern Kingdom (752–722 B.C.E.)

Solomon's nemesis had been internal revolt; the nemesis of the northern state proved to be a suddenly renascent Assyria that launched wave on wave of imperial attacks into Syria-Palestine. Assassination of Zechariah ended the Jehu dynasty and the kingdom began to come apart. Menahem tried to secure his place on the throne by making an enormous payment to Assyria which he raised by a tax on tens of thousands of Israelite landholders, but this did not prevent, and probably helped to spur, an anti-Assyrian reaction led by Pekah, who formed an anti-Assyrian alliance with Rezon (biblical Rezin) of Damascus. Israel and Damascus pressured Ahaz of Judah to join them, which provoked the so-called Syro-Ephraimite War between Israel and Judah.

Ahaz appealed to Assyria and the pressure on Judah was lifted when Assyria attacked Damascus and Israel and turned most of the northern kingdom into directly governed Assyrian provinces. This left a greatly reduced Israelite state restricted to the mountains of Samaria. A final rebellion against Assyria by Hoshea led to the siege and capture of Samaria, deportation of its upper classes, and an end to the independent Kingdom of Israel when Samaria was made into an Assyrian province. The climate of desperation and civil strife that pervaded the last three decades of Israel's independence is forcefully communicated in the embittered words of the prophet Hosea (§34.4).

33.6 Patterns of Development in the Two Kingdoms

Generalizations about the course of development in the two kingdoms are hampered by the sketchy and uneven sources. To all outward appearances, Judah was a far more stable kingdom than Israel. With the exception of Athaliah's brief usurpation, the Davidic dynasty remained in succession. On the average, Judahite royalty reigned longer than Israelite royalty: during the two hundred years of the Kingdom of Israel, there were twelve Davidic rulers in the south and nineteen northern rulers distributed through five dynasties (counting Menahem-Pekahiah as a dynasty). The acid test of course was that Judah survived whereas Israel came to an end.

The relative "weakness" or "strength" of the two kingdoms has been estimated and accounted for in various ways. One explanation is that Judah adhered to a "dynastic principle" of leadership, whereas Israel under Jeroboam I and Baasha—and again after the Jehu dynasty—tried to operate with the old "charismatic principle" of leadership. The "charismatic" mode of operation supposedly required that each new king be designated by religious choice, presumably through prophets, and acclaimed by the people. Thus each change of rule offered the potential for turbulence. While the Prophetic History in 1 Samuel 8—15 seems to imply such a charismatic program (§29.3), it is not likely that it was ever undertaken as a recognized scheme of government. A new king might benefit from prophetic support and popular acclamation, but everywhere in our sources it seems assumed that an able king will found a dynasty. Thus, the instabilities in the northern kingdom do not seem to have arisen from the institutional obligation to chose each ruler *de novo*.[1]

A more probable explanation of northern turbulence is geopolitical. Judah was a geographically compact area, separated from other regions, and offering a minimum of attraction to foreign conquerors. By contrast, the northern tribes were sprawled over a large territory in three mountain massifs and in the valleys and plains around them. It was both a more difficult territory for any centralized government to rule and more open and inviting to foreign powers who eyed its strategic communication routes and its rich grain crops. There was, therefore, a certain necessity for Israel to enter into relations with other powers that Judah might more easily avoid, and at the same time regional factionalism was more severe in the north, especially between Samaria and Transjordan. For a king to succeed in Israel he probably had to balance and satisfy a far-wider range of vested interests than any southern king. The practical result was that the more homogeneous leading families in Judah could close ranks in support of one royal lineage more readily than the diversified leading families of the north who tended to "fight out" their different interests by backing different candidates for king and withholding support from rulers who displeased them.

It is also not to be overlooked that Judah retained a tremendous asset by being the home ground of the illustrious dynasty of David and Solomon, in spite of its great loss in the schism. Any alternative claimant for leadership, as Athaliah was briefly, would face comparison with the proven record of David and Solomon. By contrast, the northern kingdom had to start "from scratch" so to speak. It inherited Davidic-Solomonic precedents and structures, but it had to make its own way in staying independent of Judah, in

1. The interpretation here follows Giorgio Buccellati, *Cities and Nations of Ancient Syria. An Essay on Political Institutions with Special Reference to the Israelite Kingdoms,* Studi Semitici 26 (Rome: Instituto di Studi del Vicino Oriente, 1967), and Baruch Halpern, *The Constitution of the Monarchy in Israel,* HSM 25 (Chico, Calif.: Scholars Press, 1981) against Albrecht Alt, "The Monarchy in the Kingdoms of Israel and Judah," in *EOTHR,* 313–35 (orig. pub., 1951).

unifying its separate regions and contending factions, and in coping with foreign incursions that did not so directly impact the Davidic state until two centuries later. As for Judah's survival after Israel's collapse, the objective situation was that Israel stood "next in line" as the target of Assyria's westward expansion. If anything served to spare Judah in the short run, it was Ahaz's decision to cooperate with Assyria and not join the Israelite-Damascus axis of rebels.

An even more concrete political organizational factor seems to have worked very much to Judah's advantage. From the time of Asa, Judahite monarchs began the practice of forming co-regencies. An incumbent king would designate his successor and involve him in practical affairs of state as "co-ruler." This both assured the exact line of succession and trained the next king for his eventual sole exercise of office. The chronology used in this study (§25) recognizes the following Judahite co-regencies:

Asa and his son Jehoshaphat	873/872–870/869
Jehoshaphat and his son Jehoram	853–848
Amaziah and his son Uzziah	792/791–767
Uzziah and his son Jotham	750–740/739
Jotham and his son Ahaz	735–732/731
Hezekiah and his son Manasseh	697/696–687/686

In contrast, there seems to have been only one co-regency in Israel, which smoothed the transition from Jehoash to his son Jeroboam II (793/792–782/781). Why the Omri and Jehu dynasties took so long to hit upon co-regency as an instrument for dynastic stability is not known.

34
LITERARY CULTURE, RELIGION, AND PROPHETIC CRITIQUE

34.1 The Elohist (E)

The E source has been briefly characterized (§13.2), its contents listed in Genesis 12—50 (table 10) and in Exodus-Numbers (table 11). It has also been observed that E probably survives in conquest traditions such as Joshua 1—12 (§22.3). It remains to elaborate E's literary features, leading motifs, basic perspective, and setting in life.

The vocabulary of E is set off clearly from J and P at many points of variance: Amorites for the inhabitants of the land (Canaanites in J); Jacob for the third patriarch (Israel in J); Horeb for the holy mountain (Sinai in J and P); Jethro for Moses' father-in-law (Hobab or Reuel in J); the temporal use of "after these things" in narration, for example, "after the aforementioned events" (in J, "after this manner"). "The River" designates the Euphrates; *ba'al* is used of a man as "master" or "husband"; "to give" is frequently employed with the sense of "to allow, give leave." Stylistically the Elohist has a fondness for repetitions, especially in direct address: "Abraham, Abraham!" (Gen. 22:11) and "Moses, Moses!" (Exod. 3:4). "Here I am!" is a favored expression on the lips of one replying to a divine or human superior.

The Elohist's moral and religious consciousness is given explicit articulation in a series of accents and emphases that distinguish his work from the Yahwist. The moral imperfections of the ancestors of Israel, which J did not hesitate to tell straight out, are glossed over or explained as appropriate in context. Abraham's lie is mitigated by the notation that Sarah was after all his half sister, thus presumably a permissible marriage partner, or at the very least Abraham was technically truthful (Gen. 20:12). The callous expulsion of Hagar from Abraham's household is explained as a direct divine command (Gen. 21:11–13 [§15.3.d]). Jacob's theft of Laban's flocks is attributed to the blessing of God (Gen. 31:4–12), while the mutual skulduggery of nephew and uncle is attributed solely to Laban.

The ritual interest is more pronounced in E than in J. In the latter, the various altars raised at open-air sanctuaries are memorial in nature and never described as places of sacrifice, while in E these altars are explicitly used for offerings. Among the abundant instances of ritual practice are the call of Abraham to sacrifice his son (Gen. 22:1–2), Jacob pouring oil on the stone pillar at Bethel (Gen. 28:18), and his vow of a tenth of his future gain to God (Gen. 28:20–22). One of the reasons for regarding non-P material in Exodus 19—24 as at least taken over by E, if not actually written by E, is the occurrence of many ritual features: Moses consecrates the people at Horeb by a washing of garments and by abstinence from sexual intercourse (Exod. 19:10–11a, 14–15); the covenant is sealed with animal blood thrown against the altar and on the people (Exod. 24:6, 8); the apostate Israelites manufacture a golden calf image for their god (Exodus 32).

Over all, the Elohist tends to draw moral conclusions and to admonish readers more freely than the Yahwist. There is more explicit teaching, but the "lessons" of history are not overly disruptive of the narrative for they are often skillfully introduced on the lips of chief participants in the story. Joseph, for example, warmly attests to the providential purposes of God when he consoles his brothers (Gen. 45:7; 50:20), while the deity elusively "explains" the new divine name Yahweh in answer to Moses' puzzlement (Exod. 3:13–15). The Elohist has also shaped the throat-catching story of the narrowly averted sacrifice of Isaac by his father Abraham (Gen. 22:1–

13, 19). This story of the "binding" of Isaac (the Akidah of later Jewish tradition) derives its extraordinary power from notions of human sacrifice as ultimate devotion, notions which were more or less operative in Israel's environment and continued to lurk in Israel's consciousness and occasional overt behavior (§19.4).

The Elohist emphasizes the status of Israel as a religious community in the sense that the total national life of Israel is grounded in faithful adherence to Yahweh through a purified cult and obedience to the fundamental laws traditionally connected with Moses. Although it cannot be firmly concluded by literary criteria, it is widely thought that the earliest form of the laws, the so-called Covenant Code (Exod. 20:22—23:19), was preserved in the E source (§19.2.b), probably after it was compiled in an effort to stem the socioeconomic and cultic abuses under the Omri dynasty. In some respects E retains more aspects of the premonarchic pool of tradition than does J (§13.6). This "antique quality" in E reflects the origins of Yahwism in northern Israel among the Joseph tribes. In E there simply is not the same focus on land and state that there is in J. The impetus to return to the deepest foundations of community, and thus not to be restricted or misled by hierarchic state structures (whether Davidic or north Israelite), is strongly articulated in E by means of a firm confidence in the whole people as recipients of Yahweh's judgment and grace.

There is a dedicated hortatory or "preaching" flavor in the style and motifs of E. The danger of apostasy is frequently sounded forth in company with a call to repentance and obedience. The models of leadership are prophetlike figures who embody faithfulness: Abraham, Joseph, and Moses. There is a stress on the proper "fearful" approach to God in observing correct cult forms and in noting the various ways that Yahweh communicates with humans in rituals, dreams, visions, and through divinely sent messengers. This explains the emphasis upon the "form" of God which is dangerous to behold without the most careful preparation and forethought. The aim of all this "cultic theology" is changed public life. In spite of the majesty and wrath of Yahweh, the God of Israel is incredibly patient, constantly inviting the people to turn and renew itself.

Although some scholars have denied any single source "E," preferring to view its contents as so many separate additions to J, the style and motifs of these old non-J traditions, connected as they are with literary doublets, argue that there was a continuous source.[2] It appears that E was severely

2. Alan W. Jenks, *The Elohist and North Israelite Traditions*, SBLMS 22 (Missoula, Mont.: Scholars Press, 1977), chaps. 1–2.

reduced in scope when it was "cut and trimmed" in the process of making a JE redaction of Genesis-Numbers (and of Joshua-Judges?). The joining of J and E occurred in Judah after the fall of Israel in 722 B.C.E. in a milieu where other bodies of north Israelite traditions (Elijah-Elisha stories, Prophetic History of the origins of the monarchy, and core of materials in Deuteronomy) were salvaged from the political ruin of the north and entered into the stream of southern literary and religious culture. Because the JE redaction project was controlled by southerners, J was employed as the ground plan of the redaction and E materials were used to supplement J.

The date and life setting of E are difficult to determine with exactitude. It could have been written at any time between Jeroboam I and the late Jehu dynasty. Since it does not allude directly to historical events at the time of its writing, its setting must be estimated on the basis of broad probabilities. E presupposes a dire situation of religious apostasy so great as to threaten the continuation of the nation. The Omri dynasty would satisfy that situation admirably, but hardly exclusively, considering that the stories of Elijah-Elisha and the words of Amos suggest that the Jehu dynasty failed to live up to its initial prospect of restoring the religious and social rectitude of Israel.

Because E keeps its distance from state structures, it is not likely that it was written in court circles as often hypothesized for its southern counterpart J. There were, however, other nongovernmental tradition contexts in the north that fairly closely approximated the motifs and language of E, namely, the prophetic circles responsible for Elijah-Elisha stories and the Book of Hosea, and probably also for the Prophetic History of the beginnings of monarchy (not that these originated from any single prophetic circle). On the other hand, the old covenant and law traditions behind Deuteronomy appear also to have come from the north, and it may have been in covenant-renewal contexts, among Yahwistically committed landed families and priests or Levites, that E originated, which might explain its interest in retelling the old history of Israel in terms of a more urgent sense of crisis in Israel's current self-understanding than J wished to portray.[3]

34.2 Elijah and Elisha

The Elijah-Elisha stories are a rich reservoir of popular stories about conflicts over military and political policies between prophets and kings, and also of "marvel" or "problem resolution" stories that tell how prophets

---

3. Ibid., chaps. 3–4.

met the basic life needs of common folk who were suffering under government abuse and famine.

They are dubbed "popular" stories because of the apparent powerful impression that the prophets made on a sector of the north Israelite populace. Yet not just anyone "impressed" by these prophets would have told such stories. The point is not that they indiscriminately did marvels, but that they did their wonders by the power of Yahweh against Baal and his followers and on behalf of Yahweh believers in dire need. The bearers of these stories must have been active propagators of Yahweh allegiance and consistent opponents of Baal, who suffered from famine, sickness, poverty, and expropriation of their land, and in whose minds the capacity of the Omri dynasty—and perhaps also of the Jehu dynasty—to reliably prosecute the necessary cult and social praxis was in growing doubt.

These thematic concerns were concretized by a community that is pictured in the conventicles of prophets led by Elisha and who were in touch with supporters in the wider society, including personnel in royal service such as Obadiah (1 Kings 18:3–4) and Jehu (2 Kings 9:1–3), and even Syrian officials such as Naaman (1 Kings 5) and the kings Ben-hadad and Hazael (2 Kings 8:7–15). The Elisha stories have to do with scarcity of food, shelter, and tools, both among prophetic communities and the rural populace at large. The elaborated legend of 2 Kings 4:11–37; 8:1–6 implies that the prophetic miracles were performed on behalf of weak and endangered members of prophetic groups and their supporters in cases where no juridical relief from king or law courts was forthcoming. The Elijah-Elisha stories may even be conceivable as a fund of stories intended to advocate the cause of defrauded and wronged Yahwists who, abandoned or even victimized by Israelite officials, were repeatedly brought to the attention of the established leadership by prophetic intervention (perhaps somewhat along the line of the Egyptian story of The Protests of the Eloquent Peasant [table 1: 6A]).

From this angle the bearers of the Elijah-Elisha stories look like religious formations at the lower fringes of society that functioned as rescue stations and advocacy groups. The underside of Israelite life, away from the "history-making" royal court, was filling up with more and more people pushed out of the old protective tribal structures by political centralization and social stratification. It was probably such groups that helped to fuel the sentiments for dynastic change and religious reform, but whose ideas seemed too simplistic or extreme to gain decisive force in government— even when one of their own kind, Jehu, finally "made it" to the throne.

34.3 Amos

The nine chapters of the Book of Amos present a stunning array of judgment speeches, visions, hymnic doxologies, admonitions, laments, one brief narrative, and a concluding burst of promises of salvation. The work divides into clearly distinguishable sections. Oracles against Damascus, Gaza, Tyre, Edom, Ammon, Moab, Judah, and Israel form a closely constructed series, each introduced by the formula "for three transgressions of x, and for four, I [Yahweh] will not revoke it [i.e., the punishment or anger of Yahweh]" (chaps. 1—2). A collection of judgment speeches against the northern kingdom, including woe oracles and a mocking play on priestly instruction, is punctuated by the formula "Hear this word!" (chaps. 3—6). A sequence of vision reports about impending judgment on the land is interrupted both by a narrative report of the prophet's encounter with the priest Amaziah and by further judgment speeches (chaps. 7:1—9:6). The book concludes with a threat of total destruction which is softened by assurance to righteous individuals and expanded into a promise of national restoration (9:7–15).

There is a sharp distinction in the book between speech of God in the first person in about twenty oracles ("commission-bound messenger speech") and speech of the prophet in the third person in about twelve oracles ("free witness speech"). The former is framed by the formulas "thus Yahweh has said" and "utterance of Yahweh." Sometimes divine speech and prophetic speech are mixed in the same unit. There has been extensive inquiry into the life settings of the forms of speech used by the prophet and much speculation as to whether the sources of the speech coincide with the institutional setting of the prophet and thus reveal the role he played in society.

There is considerable evidence that the round of foreign oracles in chaps. 1—2 was modeled on a liturgy, attested in the Egyptian Execration Texts, (table 1: 3A), in which curses were spoken against foreign enemies and against categories of domestic sinners.[4] It may well be that such a liturgy was practiced in the Israelite cult and that Amos drew upon its presuppositions and language to structure his oracle format. That this also argues for Amos himself having been a cultic prophet is more doubtful, particularly since the crowning piece in his "liturgy" is an expanded judgment speech not against particular Israelite sinners but against the entire superstructure of the Israelite state and society. It has been argued, partly on an assumed

4. Aage Bentzen, "The Ritual Background of Amos 1:2—2:16," *OTS* 8 (1950): 85–99.

evolution of prophetic outlook within the vision reports, that Amos began as a cult prophet who was radicalized to the point that he broke with the cult and called down destruction on the very institution he had formerly served.

The hymnic language of the doxologies (4:13; 5:8–9; 9:5–6) is likewise cited as evidence that Amos was a cult prophet. Now that we are aware of the pervasiveness of hymnic speech outside the cult, even in wisdom literature, this is a weak argument. The main point in employing the doxologies, which have been carefully placed in each case at the climax of an attack on the cult, is to deprive the cultic establishment of pretensions to "untouchable sanctity" by affirmation of Yahweh's cosmic transcendence. This is done ironically by turning the cult-originated hymnic language against the cult.[5]

On the other hand, several features of the prophet's speech have been connected with wisdom tradition: the graded numerical saying ("for three transgressions, . . . and for four"), woe cries, and didactic assertions of cause-effect relations based on empirical observation (e.g., 3:3–8). The wisdom indebtedness of Amos in this instance is probably not to the wisdom cultivated in the royal court but to the so-called clan wisdom of the older residual tribal organization of Israel in its village matrix that the monarchy overlaid, severely threatened, but had neither the will nor means to replace (§24.2.c). To have been a "sage" in that context would have meant being a local leader practiced in giving counsel and in passing judgment in the trial of peers. The reported activity of Amos as a shepherd and part-time agricultural worker from Tekoa provided him a milieu to imbibe deeply of the old tribal mores and socioethical presuppositions.[6] It is striking that for the most part his speech about God's judgment on Israel is not dressed in cultic language but in the language of struggle against a harsh natural environment that he knew at firsthand as herder-farmer from one of the marginal cultivated zones of Judah.

The status of Amos in relation to other prophetic functionaries has been hotly debated without much profit, mainly because the evidence available does not really conform to our questions. When Amos makes his famous disclaimer in 7:14, does he mean that he had not been a prophet or member of a prophetic group *until* Yahweh called him, but now he is one ("I *was* no prophet . . .")? Or does he mean that he is not a prophet *even now*

---

5. James L. Crenshaw, *Hymnic Affirmations of Divine Justice: The Doxologies of Amos and Related Texts in the Old Testament*, SBLDS 24 (Missoula, Mont.: Scholars Press, 1975), 39–46.
6. Hans Walter Wolff, *Amos the Prophet: The Man and His Background* (Philadelphia: Fortress Press, 1973).

that Yahweh has called him to speak the divine message ("I *am* no prophet...")? And what is to be made of the apparent non sequitur that, while Amaziah rebukes Amos as a "seer" *(ḥōzeh)*, Amos replies by denying that he is a "prophet" *(nāvī')?* It is by no means evident that this exchange of barbs tells us anything about the relation of Amos to other prophets in his day, for his remark seems focused on the one concern of making clear to Amaziah that he has a direct call to speak for Yahweh and therefore he cannot be dissuaded by any conventional understandings of prophets and seers that the priest may have. In that event, Amos was simply saying, "I am not like those 'prophets' who will say or do whatever they are paid or threatened to say and do!"

Redaction criticism has rendered a more complicated picture of the growth of the book than was once imagined. Source criticism (old-style literary criticism) has usually attributed the great bulk of the book to Amos, excepting only the oracles against Tyre, Edom, and Judah, the promises of salvation in 9:8b–15, and sometimes the doxologies. Recent redaction-critical studies assign as much as half or more of the work to later reworkings and supplements.

The fullest redactional study to date posits six stages in the development of the book, of which the first three fall within the eighth century: (1) the original collection of words of Amos in 3—6 may be the work of the prophet himself; (2) at a second stage the prophet's oracles against the nations and the vision reports were placed as beginning and conclusion of the older collection of judgment speeches; (3) an "old school of Amos" redacted the foregoing, inserting the Amaziah incident among the vision reports and adding admonitions; (4) in the time of Josiah, a Bethel exposition inserted the doxologies and enlarged on Amos's critique of Bethel and the cult in connection with Josiah's destruction of the altar at that city (2 Kings 23:15); (5) a Deuteronomistic redaction in the exile added the oracles against Tyre, Edom, and Judah and filled out references to older salvation history; (6) postexilic salvation eschatology was appended to the book to mitigate its somber negativity.[7]

Another redactional study of the Book of Amos simplifies the stages: (1) the words of judgment by Amos on Israel's ruling class in the mid–eighth century ("Amos A"); (2) a reinterpretation and expansion urging repentance on Judah and remnants of Israel in the midst of the hopeful reforms of Josiah in the last third of the seventh century ("Amos B"); (3) a reinterpretation and expansion for Judahite exiles or recent returnees to

7. Hans Walter Wolff, *Joel and Amos,* Hermeneia (Philadelphia: Fortress Press, 1977), 106–13.

Palestine once both kingdoms had fallen ("Amos C").[8] The point is well made that we only know about the original Amos as he is reported to us by interested successors. Fortunately they left sizable sections of his words intact. Prominent in this three-step redactional hypothesis is a fuller use of sociological criteria than any other redactional inquiry has attempted. An effort is made to differentiate among those social structures which Amos condemned, those which Josiah sought to reform, and those which the exilic/early postexilic redactor hoped to resuscitate in restoration Palestine.

In spite of many differences of judgment in detail, both of the cited redactional studies agree that the forceful words of the prophet have passed along in a complex transmission and editing process, the successive stages of redaction serving as nuclei for periodic societywide critical reflections in the manner of the eighth-century Amos. If the later reflections were more hopeful, that had to do with the seventh-century expectations aroused by Josiah's reforms (§36.3) and with the sixth-century challenge to reconstruct the community after Judah as a state had joined Israel in oblivion (§43). These redactional hypotheses, certain to be debated, have been particularly helpful in separating out the categorical and conditional modes of speech in the Book of Amos, making it plain that the initial harsh words of unmitigated punishment in Amos were plausibly tempered by admonition among the Josianic redactors, precisely because they believed that the warnings of Amos could help the Deuteronomic reform leaders prevent the catastrophe that had overtaken the unheeding northern kingdom.

The prophet whose work lies at the core of the book attacked the patriotic and pious conservative reaction that had gained currency among the upper classes during the prosperous reign of Jeroboam II (§33.4). The greedy upper classes, with governmental and juridical connivance, were systematically expropriating the land of commoners so that they could heap up wealth and display it gaudily in a lavish "conspicuous consumption" economy. Hatred of other nations, military swaggering, and religious rhetoric were generously employed to persuade people to accept their miserable lot because it was, after all, "the best of all possible societies."

Much of the monopolized wealth was poured into spectacles of sacrificial and liturgical worship at splendidly refurbished sanctuaries. Amos savagely attacked the overheated religious fervor as a fraudulent and despicable "cover" or "mask" for the leaders' gross selfishness and practical atheism. Or, as one commentator remarks, "It may cause surprise that the people,

8. Robert B. Coote, *Amos Among the Prophets: Composition and Theology* (Philadelphia: Fortress Press, 1981).

according to Amos' judgment, are doing too much rather than too little for Yahweh."[9] Amos announced that the Kingdom of Israel would be overthrown by an enemy power, probably Assyria, and its leaders deported, which would be "the end" (cf. 8:1–3) of an arrogant misplaced confidence in Yahweh as the justifier of the oppression of the little people.

From what sources did Amos draw the moral and intellectual energy single-handedly to proclaim the total rejection of Israel by Yahweh? First and foremost must have been his overwhelming encounter with God. He was completely confident in his commission to deliver God-given messages. Yet precisely this "calling" was grounded in the wholeness of his personhood in a particular community and tradition. Which elements of that tradition were ignited by the call of God? There is no single certain answer to that question.

It has been proposed that Amos drew upon a conditional covenant tradition of the sort articulated in Deuteronomy, and possibly less directly in Hosea, but there are no explicit signs of this in his language; he does not even refer to Israel's "covenant" with Yahweh. The exodus is referred to in 2:10 and 9:7, and probably also in 3:2, where the unique "knowing" of Israel by God seems to be a kind of special election tradition, from which the prophet concludes a special responsibility on Israel. In this connection, the particulars of Israel's responsibility are nowhere given, as would have been the case had Amos cited the infraction of particular laws as the basis for judgment. It has also been suggested that Amos drew on an El theology, influenced by Canaanite thought, to underpin his belief that Yahweh was universal lord of the nations. Also, some have thought that wisdom's cosmic universalism affected the prophet.

If we pay heed to the crushing of the poor as the central sin Amos condemns and to the way he pictures divine activity through rhetorical questions and figures of speech from the natural and social world of rural Palestine, we can make an informed estimate of what weighed most in his thinking. He knew at firsthand about the murderous oppression of the poor; not only did he detest that oppression, but he knew that it was diametrically opposed to Yahweh's wishes. How did he know this? He knew it from the traditions in narrative and law shaped by the old tribal life of Israel and presently enshrined in the practice of mutual help and discharge of justice in local courts (§24.2.c). The substance of the socioethical laws of Israel was known to him, even if he had never seen written laws (§19.2.b). These laws were more or less faithfully practiced before his eyes in villages

9. Wolff, *Joel and Amos,* 104.

like Tekoa, as they were grotesquely ignored and overriden in the governing circles of Israel by the very people who were loudest in their praise of Yahweh. Thus, the living integrity of village life based on traditional Yahwism and an astounding immediate experience of God provided both the structure of his critical analysis and the ground of his undeterred passion.

The immediate consequences of such forthright criticism are hinted at: rejected as a carpetbagger, Amos was probably expelled from Israel and sent back to his native Judah (7:10–17). But that was not the end of matters. It was not long before the Jehu dynasty collapsed and Israel started on its downward slide to political oblivion. It was observed that the once-preposterous threats of Amos accorded well with what eventually happened (§33.5). As sympathetic associates of Elijah and Elisha had preserved stories about them, so the impressed followers of Amos preserved his words—and reshaped and added to them as new situations dictated. More than this, the example of Amos, and even the specifics of his thought, stirred other voices with the result that a virile tradition of critical prophecy breaks forth and continues unbroken for three hundred years.

34.4 Hosea

The prophet Hosea was active in the northern kingdom in the final decades of the decline of Israel following the death of Jeroboam II, and it is possible that he outlived the fall of Samaria in 722 (§33.5). The smug self-confidence of the upper classes whom Amos had addressed some years earlier had noticeably faded in the face of social and political adversities. Amid demoralization and lack of direction, Hosea encounters a generation of "leaders" bent on protecting their own narrow interests by seizing every advantage at the expense of others. Yahweh has become for them the awarder and guarantor of personal advantages. The line between Yahwism and Baalism has worn thin.

The Book of Hosea divides into two unequal parts: (1) *Chaps. 1—3.* Narratives and sayings about the prophet's marriage and offspring, memorabilia of a sort, including a third-person account in chap. 1 and a third-person account in chap. 3 which enclose assorted sayings in chap. 2 that use the husband-wife pairing as an extended metaphor for the tie between Yahweh and Israel; (2) *Chaps. 4—14.* Judgment and tempered salvation speeches which berate the cultic and political sins of Israel and hold forth the hope of renewal only after national destruction and purgation. The text of these passionate reports and speeches is in a poor state, the meaning of many words, phrases, and whole lines hanging in doubt.[10] The delimitation of the literary units is far more difficult than in Amos because almost no oracle formulas are given as markers for the units. The poor composition or transmission of the text is not easy to explain, especially since most of the work seems to have been written down by the prophet or at his dictation, or by gathered recollections in a circle of followers within a generation or so of the prophet's death. It is possible that the turmoil at the fall of the northern kingdom damaged the original text, or parts of it, before it could be transferred to safekeeping in Judah.

One reconstruction of the composition of the book sees it as the result of combining three collections that were more or less simultaneously developed.[11] The first complex (chaps. 1—3) gathered around Hosea's own text in 2:2–15; 3:1–5, which a disciple supplemented with later sayings of the prophet and a narrative about Hosea's marriage and the birth of his children. The second complex (chaps. 4:1—11:11), opening and closing with two of the very few formulaic markers in the book ("Hear the word of Yahweh, O people of Israel," 4:1; "says Yahweh," 11:11), consisted of transcripts of the public preaching of Hosea and of private communications to his followers. The third complex (chaps. 11:12—14:9), also of mixed public and private communications, is distinguishable by several stylistic peculiarities and may have had liturgical usage (cf. 12:6). All three complexes move from accusation and judgment to promise of salvation, and all three show marked linguistic and conceptual affinities with Deuteronomic thought (§37.3). References to Judah are mostly secondary applications of the words of Hosea, either making the southern kingdom the target of judgment or promising it salvation. Since these references are brief, and usually cryptic, it is not easy to say during which periods of Judahite history they were inserted in the text.

The prophet worked up a marriage metaphor for the relation between Yahweh and Israel (chaps. 1—3), as well as a father-son metaphor (11:1–7). Actually these are but two of the more prominent specimens of a rich stock of metaphors and similes drawn from agriculture, animal life, and family relations. Yahweh is also described as a physician, a fowler, a lion, a leopard, a bereaved she-bear, dew, a luxuriant tree, pus (or moth?), and rottenness. Israel is seen as a sick person, a herd, a flighty dove, a trained

10. Francis I. Andersen and David N. Freedman, *Hosea,* AB 24 (Garden City, N.Y.: Doubleday & Co., 1980), 57–76, analyze the peculiar textual and literary qualities of the book with sensitivity and acumen.

11. Hans Walter Wolff, *Hosea,* Hermeneia (Philadelphia: Fortress Press, 1974), xxix–xxxii.

but balky heifer, a wandering wild ass, a grapevine and grapes, wine of Lebanon, an early fig, a lily, a woman in labor, an unborn son, an over-baked cake, a slack bow, early morning mist and dew, and blown chaff.

The tradition complex in chaps. 1—3 tells of the prophet's marriage by divine command to a woman, Gomer, who proved unfaithful, but whom he is in the process of winning back. Yahweh too is attempting a like "re-espousal" with faithless Israel. Whether this was an actual marriage experience in Hosea's life (in contrast to an allegory) and, if so, what its circumstances were, or indeed if the woman in chap. 3 is Gomer or another, are much disputed by interpreters.[12] Previous romanticized readings of Hosea's relationship with Gomer tend to be dismissed nowadays because they were speculative and prone to disregard the context of Hosea's mode of instruction by "shock method."

It is possible, some believe probable, that the woman named was a cult prostitute and in that case the image bore a double punch, inasmuch as the prophet was a searing critic of Baal worship, which had undermined Yahwism from within to the point that Yahweh was worshiped as though he were a Baal figure who could be magically manipulated. For the prophet deliberately to marry a Baal cult prostitute would be "asking for trouble." That the prophet makes use of this real or imagined marriage to convey a socioreligious message is dramatized by the symbolic names bespeaking judgment that he gave to the children born of the union: a son Jezreel, for the valley where Jehu's dynasty began and will end (1:4–5), a daughter Loruhammah, for the "unpitied" condition of Israel (1:6), and a second son Lo-ʿammi, "not my people," as an epithet for the bastard Israel (1:8–9).

Our understanding of the connections between Yahwism and Baalism in this period may be substantially improved by as-yet-unpublished inscriptions and drawings from Kuntillat ʿAjrud in northern Sinai. Recovered from a shrine of the ninth/eighth centuries, the evidence seems to show that Yahweh was worshiped there either as Baal, or in tandem with Baal, and that Yahweh had a consort called "his Asherah."[13] Thus, in spite of Jehu's supposed extirpation of Baalism in the north a century before (§33.4), it appears that a thoroughgoing syncretism had so fused the elements of Yahwism and Baalism that Hosea could describe the resulting cultic and sociopolitical situation as one of "no knowledge" (4:1–3; 5:3–4; 8:1–3).

12. Andersen and Freedman, *Hosea*, 115–309, explore at length the possible connections between the marriage metaphor, literarily and conceptually, and its rootage in the prophet's family life.

13. Preliminary reports of the Kuntillat ʿAjrud finds appear in Zeev Meshel and Carol Meyers, "The Name of God in the Wilderness of Zin," *BA* 39 (1976): 6–10, and Zeev Meshel, "Did Yahweh Have a Consort?" *BARev* 5/2 (1979): 24–35.

The prophet lays responsibility for this betrayal of old Yahwism at the door of shortsighted and self-serving leaders, especially priests, prophets, kings, and officials (4:4–6; 5:1–2; 8:4–5). Over against the enervating confusion of the times Hosea sets the justice of God as an offended struggling love that is both poignant and terrible. Cryptic remarks in 9:7–9 indicate that the prophet was barred from speaking publicly because he aroused bitter hatred, perhaps even that he was excluded from festivals in which he normally took part as a priest or cultic prophet. His self-chosen metaphor of "watchman" of Ephraim is later taken up and expanded by Ezekiel (3:16–21; 33:1–20) [§50.1].

It is sometimes said that Hosea did not condemn the socioeconomic wrongs that aroused Amos's ire. This is not the case. There are enough allusions to make it plain that Hosea also knew and opposed the internal maldistribution of wealth and depression of the lower classes. The Hebrew term *mishpāṭ* occurs both in the sense of "judgment" (5:1, 11; 10:4) and "justice" (2:19; 12:6) and even in a play on both meanings (6:5). The crimes listed in 4:1 by a series of nouns, that is, false swearing, stealing, and murder, were all involved in the debt foreclosures, land-grabbing, and court corruption pinpointed by Amos. In 10:4 the figure of judgment springing up like poisonous weeds in the furrows of fields suggests that the oaths and agreements condemned had to do with land transactions or loans to debtor farmers. Especially striking is the use of Genesis traditions about Jacob as a sharpster who cheated his brother in order to epitomize the northern kingdom as a land of economic greed and plunder (12:8–9). Finally, the climactic "true confession" of Israel in 14:1–3 states that "in you [Yahweh] the orphan finds mercy," a code phrase for the socioeconomic program of tribal Israel for protecting the weak.

It is the political situation of Israel that is particularly assessed by Hosea. Internecine strife among political factions (7:5–7) and between Israel and Judah (5:8–12) has rent the land. "The days of Gibeah" (9:9; 10:9) most likely refers to Saul's choice as king and intimates a long history of royal infamy most recently issuing in a spate of assassinations and an erosion of territory as the Assyrians incorporated more than two-thirds of the kingdom into directly governed provinces of the empire (§33.5). Alliances with Egypt and Assyria are futile since Yahweh will neutralize the strength of the ally or allow it to turn on Israel. In the meantime, the heavy drain in tribute (10:6) and in exports to allies (12:1) will deplete the economy. The envisioned decline of agriculture seems as much or more the result of such foreign exactions as of drought or neglect of cultivation or damage to crops due to civil strife and war.

With Amos, Hosea foresees military conquest and deportation of the leadership. He goes beyond Amos in talking about the conditions of the exile as a return to the wilderness in which the integrity of the people as a community will be retained in spite of terrible suffering. Drawing on the salvation traditions of the exodus, wilderness wanderings, and conquest, Hosea views the future "wilderness state" in a twofold way: as a time of punishment or enforced sociopolitical and religious regression and as a period of probation in which a renewal of national life can begin (cf. the analogy between the wife's probationary status and Israel's impending "many days" without the normal public institutions, 3:3–4). The geographical location of this "wilderness" is beside the point. Hosea does not literally see Israel once again in the desert of Sinai, or in the plains of Jericho, or in the valley of Achor. He speaks typologically. The expected exile from the land and return to wilderness are identical occurrences seen from two points of view: from the standpoint of contemporary history (punishment and hoped-for purgation by deportation) and from the standpoint of salvation history (punishment and hoped-for purgation by wandering in the wilderness or among the nations).[14]

Earlier interpreters were inclined to assume that Hosea, like Amos, held out no hope for Israel whatsoever and that all promissory passages in the book must be from later hands. There are, however, a number of reasons for believing that it was in keeping with the prophet's outlook to anticipate that after the total political destruction of Israel—and only *after*—repentance and renewal of genuine faith in Yahweh would lead to a new communal life, even though of a virtually unpredictable character as far as its cultic and sociopolitical forms were concerned.

Because Hosea saw Yahweh as grieving "husband" and "father," he understood that God was in a struggle to win the people by a love that would not forego justice. Also, the rapid disintegration of Israel after the death of Jeroboam so sharply validated Amos's warnings that Hosea was pushed to ask: After the fall of Israel, what follows? There is also the very real possibility that he lived to see the fall of Samaria and had to cope with the disoriented condition of the poorer classes of Israelites who were not deported by the Assyrians, who for the most part had been the victims of the Israelite ruling class, and who now had to find a new life under the Assyrian conquerors and alongside foreigners settled by the victors on Israelite territory (cf. 2 Kings 17:25–41).

In short, the kind of modestly hopeful "eschatological" thinking that we

14. Norman K. Gottwald, *AKE*, 132–35.

meet in Hosea, the belief that *necessary destruction of false structures* will release *new possibilities of communal life,* began to emerge in the prophetic communities from Hosea's time onward as a way "to learn from history" and to be ready for making new kinds of history instead of surrendering oneself to traditionless despair and unsocial self-aggrandizement.

CHAPTER 9

Traditions About the Southern Kingdom

Read the Biblical Text
2 Kings 18—25

Micah
Isaiah 1—39

Deuteronomy

Nahum
Zephaniah
Habakkuk
Jeremiah

Consult Maps in *MBA*
nos. 152–64

35
THE SHAPE OF THE TRADITIONS IN
2 KINGS 18—25

35.1 Source Statistics

The last segment of the history of Judah as an independent state continues to depend upon the DH sources, supplemented by Chronicles, once again broadly separable into sources that yield political-historical data excerpted from the royal archives and literary traditions in the form of prophetic narratives (table 23).

The final 136 years of the Kingdom of Judah are reported in 96 annalistic verses, DH and Chronicles combined, which means that the average year is treated by a little more than 0.7 of a verse. With the miscellaneous literary traditions added (130 verses), there are 1.66 verses for each year. In spite of this narrow DH/Chronicles source base, the data are concentrated in such a way, and enough other kinds of sources are available, to give a much fuller comprehension of the period than appears from the text of 2 Kings.

35.2 The Spectrum of Sources

For Hezekiah, Manasseh, and Josiah by far the chief interest both of the annals and the miscellaneous supplements is in their religious measures focused on the temple: Hezekiah and Josiah as reformers of the temple cult and Manasseh as profaner of the temple cult. There are some terse references to defensive and offensive military activities of Hezekiah and Manasseh and to Hezekiah's payment of tribute to Sennacherib. A detention of Manasseh by the Assyrians is referred to, perhaps to resecure his loyalty as a vassal. Josiah's death in battle against Neco of Egypt is briefly told. Military and political details concerning the last three kings of Judah in their vassal relations to Egypt and Neo-Babylonia are recounted, culminating in the revolts of Jehoiakim and Zedekiah and two attacks on Jerusalem, deportations of leaders of Judah, and, in the last instance, in the destruction of Jerusalem.

Prophetic narratives featuring Isaiah appear in 2 Kings 18:17—20:21 and are found practically verbatim in Isaiah 36—39. Most interpreters are of the view that the narratives, though derived from prophetic circles, were first taken up by DH and subsequently introduced, with minor changes, as an appendix to a collection of Isaiah's words (but prior to the addition of Isaiah 40—66 which comes from exilic and postexilic prophets). Huldah, a prophetess, appears in the narrative of Josiah's reforms but her presence is

TABLE 23
Distribution of DH Verses to Kings of Judah in 2 Kings 18—25

King	Political-Historical Documentation	Miscellaneous Literary Traditions
Hezekiah 716/715–687/686	8 + (9)*	82
Manasseh 687/686–643/642	4 + (6)*	12
Amon 643/642–641/640	2	
Josiah 641/640–609	13 + (10)*	36
Jehoahaz (Shallum) 609	3	
Jehoiakim (Eliakim) 609–598	4 + (1)*	
Jehoiachin 598–597	14	
Zedekiah (Mattaniah) 597–586	22	
Total	70 + (26)	130

*Verses from Chronicles that supply annalistic data supplementing DH data.

integral to a temple narrative, since it seems that she is a member of the temple staff.

The description of the last years of Judah in 2 Kings 24:18—25:21, 27–30 has been drawn into Jer. 52:1–27, 31–34 as an appendix to the prophet's words (analogous to the placement of Isaiah 36—39). On the other hand, Jer. 52:28–30 provides data on the Judahite deportees not in DH, and Jer. 40:7—41:18 is a fuller version of Gedaliah's administration summarized in 2 Kings 25:22–26. In none of these historical materials shared by Jeremiah and 2 Kings is there any mention of the prophet himself, however. The Manasseh tradition in 2 Kings 21:2–15, one of the key insertions of the exilic reviser of DH (table 19: no. 5), seems to reflect an underlying temple narrative and possibly some notations from annals. Huldah's speech, also redacted in the exile, probably belonged to the Josiah temple narrative.

Our understanding of the reign of Hezekiah is enhanced by speeches and one report in the Book of Isaiah (§37.2), and the reigns of Jehoiakim, Jehoiachin, and Zedekiah are illuminated by words of Jeremiah and sizable prophetic narratives about Jeremiah (§37.5). There are, in addition, the annals of the Assyrian kings (table 1: 4J; see *ANET,* 286–88) and the Neo-Babylonian Chronicles (table 1: 4K; see *ANET,* 303–5, 563–64), which fill out aspects of the suzerain-vassal diplomatic and military connections with Judah. Archaeological data on the last years of Judah are relatively full, including military letters from Lachish and Arad (table 1: 4I, 4L) and stamped jar handles and seals that bear on political administration.

In short, several categories of evidence converge to provide a fuller clarification of the history of Judah in this period than we possess for any other period of the divided kingdoms. The most serious gap is the long reign of Manasseh for which we have slim annalistic data and no certain prophetic sources, although Zephaniah probably reflects conditions at the end of Manasseh's rule before Josiah launched his reforms (§37.4).

36
HISTORY OF THE SOUTHERN KINGDOM
(722–586 B.C.E.)

36.1 Ahaz and Hezekiah (722–686 B.C.E.)

Having courted Assyria's favor to escape the menacing alliance between Israel and Damascus, Ahaz continued as a compliant vassal of Assyria. In an about-face, Hezekiah ascended the throne with hopes and plans for escaping Assyrian domination. He seems to have been initially cooperative with Ashdod in a revolt against Assyria in 713–712 B.C.E., although he submitted before suffering serious consequences. In 705 B.C.E., Hezekiah wholeheartedly joined in a coordinated revolt involving Sidon, Ashkelon, and Ekron in Syro-Palestine, and the Chaldeans in Babylonia. The king of Judah made elaborate military preparations, but the general revolt unraveled and Hezekiah suffered the decimation of the Judahite countryside before he submitted and paid tribute. Unlike other rebellious vassals, however, Hezekiah was left in his vassal kingship. This much the Assyrian annals and the biblical text agree on (table 1: 4J; see *ANET,* 287–88).

The prophetic narrative states that "the messenger of Yahweh" laid waste the Assyrian army, Sennacherib went home, and Jerusalem was spared (Isa. 37:36–37). Some interpreters have seen a plague in this reference to a wholesale slaughter, while others have suggested that news of disorders elsewhere in the empire induced Sennacherib to lift the siege prematurely. Why the siege was in force at all if Hezekiah had indeed paid the tribute is not explained in this theory, unless Sennacherib demanded an increase in tribute that Hezekiah balked at.

In order to make sense of the discrepancies, a two-invasion hypothesis is favored by some: (1) an invasion of 701 B.C.E. in which Hezekiah was forced to submit and pay tribute, and (2) an otherwise-unknown second invasion by Sennacherib, probably about 688 B.C.E., in which the Assyrians failed to take Jerusalem. The accounts of the two invasions are claimed to have been confusedly interwoven in 2 Kings as though only one attack occurred. This expedient of two invasions is improbable. It is far more likely that the miraculous delivery elements in Isaiah 36—39 (§37.2) are due to an ex post facto effort to understand what was a logical Assyrian policy of combined severity and leniency for a southern Palestinian vassal state in the late eighth century: to keep a rebellious but now chastened local vassal on the throne after demilitarizing and looting his land apart from the capital city.

The religious measures of Hezekiah were an aspect of his nationalistic anti-Assyrian program. He purified the temple cult of Assyrian and local non-Yahwist elements and probably attempted to close down the centers of popular worship outside Jerusalem (the so-called high places). His summons of northern Israelites to observe Passover in Jerusalem, using the northern calendar, was a practical embodiment of his wish to be regarded as the legitimate ruler of all Israelites, now that the northern kingdom was demolished. For the moment he could not challenge Assyrian control of the north, but he could lay the groundwork for that eventuality.

36.2 Manasseh (687/686–643/642 B.C.E.)

Manasseh's reign of fifty-five years (counting his ten-year co-regency with Ahaz) was the longest of any monarch in either kingdom, but it is poorly documented. The DH exilic revision attributes the fall of Judah to this king's dreadful apostasies and to his spilling of "very much innocent blood" (2 Kings 21:16). It looks as though Manasseh ruled as a loyal, even ardent, Assyrian vassal, at least for much of his time in office. Recent studies of Assyrian imperial policy reveal that the Assyrians did not force their religious cults upon subjects as once supposed. In that event, Manasseh may have been an enthusiastic vassal for whom collaboration with Assyria represented a modish cultural cosmopolitanism and in this respect he may have reflected the stance of a sizable group of upper-class Judahites who welcomed the spread of foreign influence within Judahite society. Civil strife may have broken out, with repression and murder of Yahweh partisans, perhaps driving prophets into hiding or silence.

The claim that Manasseh was carried captive to Babylon, and then returned to power by his Assyrian overlord, is difficult to evaluate (2 Chron. 33:10–13). The Assyrian annals report him as a reliable vassal who paid tribute and supplied auxiliary troops for imperial campaigns. A lapse in his loyalty to Assyria is connected by some historians with various uprisings known to have taken place against Esarhaddon and Ashurbanipal. Manasseh's deportation to Babylon (and not, as expected, to Assyria) is sometimes explained by his participation in an insurrection by Ashurbanipal's brother at Babylon, which was put down in 648 B.C.E. The leniency shown by the Assyrian overlord to Manasseh would accord with the known similar treatment of other rebels at a juncture where Assyria, facing difficulties on many fronts, opted for reconciliation wherever possible. Because of the difficulty of integrating the captivity of Manasseh into the biblical picture of his pro-Assyrian stance and the silence of the Assyrian records, a majority of scholars view the Chronicler's report as a fanciful concoction to show that Manasseh was after all punished for his evil ways and to foreshadow the later Babylonian exile.

36.3 Josiah (641/640–609 B.C.E.)

Manasseh's successor was soon assassinated, apparently by an anti-Assyrian faction in the court, who may have had in mind replacing the Davidic dynasty. Instead, they were murdered by "the people of the land" who put the Davidic Josiah on the throne. This elusive group, which appears on several occasions as the initiator of political change in Judah, seems always to have worked for the continuation of the Davidic line. Considering that the policies of Davidic monarchs shifted over time, however, it is difficult to denote their ideological or policy stance or even to know if "the people of the land" formed a constant institutional element in Judahite society, such as a national council, influential aristocrats, free citizens and property owners, landless poor, non-Jerusalemites, or whatever.

Josiah's reign coincided with the decline and demise of the Assyrian Empire. He was able to further the program of national purification and expansion that Hezekiah had tentatively begun. DH connects the king's reforms with the discovery of the lawbook in the temple, undoubtedly some form of the laws in Deuteronomy. Chronicles, on the other hand, pictures the reforms as having begun prior to the finding of the lawbook. It is widely thought that DH has telescoped several stages in the reform efforts which can be reconstructed as a succession of widening moves: (1) purification of the Jerusalem temple, (2) purification of outlying Judean holy places, (3) discovery/public presentation of the lawbook and a decision to centralize all worship at Jerusalem by closing outlying shrines, and (4) extension of purification and centralization to all the newly controlled territories in the coastal plain and northward into Samaria, and perhaps also into Gilead and Galilee.

This sequence fits the probability that initially it was easier to implement Deuteronomic demands for temple purification than Deuteronomic prescriptions for cult centralization. Also, reform by stages posits a widening course of action that accompanied the progressive disintegration of Assyrian rule over coastal and northern regions which Josiah was enabled to enter and claim step by step.[1]

The Deuteronomistic History concentrates almost exclusively on the religious reforms, whereas the lawbook of Deuteronomy prescribes a range of socioeconomic and political administrative measures integral to the reform movement (§37.3). We do not know if, or how, these noncultic aspects of the reform were implemented, other than the testimony of Jeremiah that Josiah's record for social justice was far better than that of his successor Jehoiakim (Jer. 22:13–19). In any event, just as Josiah was about to reap the full harvest of his program, shortly after the fall of the last stronghold of Assyrian power at Haran in North Syria, Josiah was killed in battle in 609 B.C.E. Egypt under Pharaoh Neco was campaigning through Canaan in order to bolster the remnants of the Assyrian army so as to

---

1. Stages and aspects of the reformation are discussed by Bustenay Oded, "Josiah and the Deuteronomic Reformation," in *IJH*, 458–69.

secure eventual Egyptian sovereignty over the international corridor against the Neo-Babylonian challengers. Josiah challenged Neco at Megiddo and lost his life.

36.4 Jehoiakim, Jehoiachin, and Zedekiah (609–586 B.C.E.)

Egypt immediately claimed Judah as a dependency and put Jehoiakim on the throne as vassal. Subsequently, when Neo-Babylonia drove Egypt out of Canaan, Jehoiakim shifted his allegiance to Nebuchadnezzar II, but then revolted at the first opportunity. In a retaliatory campaign, Nebuchadnezzar captured Jerusalem and deported his son Jehoiachin (perhaps after his father's assassination?), along with a sizable group of government officials. Zedekiah was installed as a vassal regent, Jehoiachin retaining the status of king in the eyes of the Neo-Babylonians and most Judahites. After more anti-Babylonian machination, relying on promised Egyptian support that fizzled, another revolt by Judah was crushed—this time with the baleful result of the destruction of Jerusalem and its temple, further deportations of leaders, and the cessation of the independent Kingdom of Judah.

The Neo-Babylonians chose a Judahite official, Gedaliah, to serve as governor of the province of Judah, residing at Mizpah some eight miles north of the ruins of Jerusalem. Shortly, however, Gedaliah and many of his staff were murdered by an aspirant to the Judahite throne and many of those who had joined in Gedaliah's regime fled to Egypt out of fear of Neo-Babylonian reprisals.

36.5 The End of Israelite Efforts at Political Independence

The account of the history of Judah from Hezekiah to Zedekiah has attained an "iconic," even "canonical," form, interpreted and embellished by DH and the prophets. It appears as the fatal consequence of religious apostasy and an oppressive social order. It is difficult to assess the events soberly and concretely in terms of the range of options open to the people and leaders of Judah and the constellation of factors at work in one direction or another.

Narrow limits hedged the path of any hierarchic state in the ancient Near East, especially a small one facing imperial powers. In the midst of the political power plays of the time, there lay a troublesome contradiction in the interplay between national self-assertion and national subservience. Self-assertion, entailing revolt against foreign imperialists, invited reprisal and destruction, and the danger of political extinction. On the other hand, acquiescence led to the diminution of the distinctive national culture and religion, if not because of foreign demand or overt pressure, nevertheless through the fascination and advantage of the ways of a superior power in the eyes of aspiring Israelite and Judahite elites.

If the continuation and cultivation of Israelite identity and national self-determination was the goal, then it is difficult to say that any other course of *state* foreign policy would have led to securer results. It was a precarious position for any self-determining state to be located in the strategic corridor between Assyria/Neo-Babylonia and Egypt. When the problem is formulated within the terms of the hierarchic state system, we can perhaps say that Judah did as well, perhaps much better, than other small states at the time.

The reality was, however, that in their historic pasts Israel and Judah had known another kind of social organizational experience which informed their peoples and came to expression in the Yahwism of the Elohist, DH, and the prophets. Israel had once been a *tribally organized confederacy* with approximate equality for all its members (§24.2.c). That confederacy had neither the power nor the will to enter into international politics in the way that rival states did. Under David, Israel crossed over into the institutional and symbolic terrain of the state and never voluntarily returned from it (§30.3–5).

Recollections and surviving aspects of the tribal social organization nonetheless had their effect within the monarchic culture and religion and set off far-reaching political reverberations. Only in terms of the tribal social organizational base can E, DH, and the prophets, together with the social constituencies they represented, be at all understood. In their indirect religious symbolic way, these "critical traditionalists" were reminding Israel that the charter of Israel's existence had been social equality and that, by endangering social equality to become a state, the basis of Israelite strength and its difference from other ancient Near Eastern peoples were jeopardized.

Especially in the radical prophets we encounter an implicit political theory that tended to pose the thorny problematic of being both a *state* and a *community* capable of serving the vital interests of all the Israelite people. Social equality and sociopolitical hierarchy did not readily mix, and it was the former that steadily lost ground to the latter. The human costs of waging war and engaging in hierarchic politics were so enormous that Israel as "winner," or merely as "survivor," stood to be an overall "loser" in all those vital social interests that had brought it into existence in the first place. Stated starkly, some prophets concluded that it would be just as well, and possibly more fruitful in the long run, for Israel and Judah to be subject to foreign oppressors than for the Israelite people to be crushed and disheartened by native Israelite oppressors.

The dilemma was intense and the struggle in and for the mind of the people desperate, bitter, sometimes savage. This radical egalitarian tendency in prophecy, extending a similar line of interpretation in E and DH, could be dismissed as a naive hunger for the good old days and a wistful dispirited opting out of the present. There were high stakes: Israel and Judah might perish if they tried "to stop the world and get off." Nonetheless, the insistent sociopolitical outlook of some prophets, and those for whom they spoke, pressed on toward that dangerous "self-fulfilling"/"self-annihilating" end: whatever security Israel can attain, and that is worth attaining, lies in the realization of its fundamental need and mandate for social equality. Accordingly, it is better to hew to a program of national social equality, against the tide of ancient Near Eastern political organization, and trust to Yahweh's future than to go forward under the cause of national security which systematically eviscerates the very social equality which is the substance and raison d'être of Israelite national culture.

When, like Israel before it, Judah fell, the debacle could be read in either of two ways: we did not elevate national security to a high enough priority, *or* we did not ensure the social equality that would have truly united and strengthened us. But of course what had happened under the monarchy could never again be "replayed" with the variables controlled one way and another to prove satisfactorily who was right.[2] There could only be another time or times when similar variables might come into play and new decisions would have to be made—provided of course that there were any Israelites and Judahites who survived the collapse of the kingdoms as a self-conscious tradition-bearing group.

37
LITERARY CULTURE, RELIGION, AND
PROPHETIC CRITIQUE

37.1 Micah

For so small a work, the Book of Micah contains an amazing range of literary genres and varied concepts in four (or six?) groupings that have

---

2. That the reasons for the fall of Judah are still a matter of dispute is evident, for example, in Morris Silver, *Prophets and Markets. The Political Economy of Ancient Israel* (Hingham, Mass.: Kluwer-Nijhoff, 1982), 213–51, who argues that monarchic economic development benefited almost everyone in the society and that the reform programs of Deuteronomists and prophets depressed the expanding economy and brought ruin to Judah. Interestingly, Silver's economic analysis virtually ignores the taxing function of the state and the effects of warfare and political vassalage.

been complexly edited. Only the materials in chaps. 1—3 can be confidently connected with the named prophet, Micah of Moresheth (1:1; probably Moresheth-gath of 1:14). This Micah was a contemporary of Isaiah who was active in the approximate period 725–701. He came from a small town in the Judean foothills, but spoke his condemnations directly to the leaders in Jerusalem. His biting indictments of socioeconomic injustice are similar to those of Amos, who was also from small-town Judah. The prophet knows at firsthand about the expulsion of small landholders from their traditional means of livelihood, dishonest business practices, venal priests and prophets, and a royal regime that connives in the oppression of the poor.

In 3:8 the prophet expresses an unbounded confidence that he is filled with power and justice to expose the public sins that are destroying the nation. This self-conscious empowerment may be related to the surprising fact that only one—or at most two—of his oracles contains direct speech of Yahweh; in all other instances Micah boldly relays Yahweh's indictments and punishments in his own words.

Starting off with an attack on the urban centers of Samaria and Jerusalem as the institutional nerve centers for the robbery and murder of defenseless small-town people (1:2–7), Micah turns to an account of an invasion of the land that passes through the Judean foothills near his own home town and reaches to the gate of Jerusalem (1:8–15; is it the invasion of Sennacherib in 701?). Chapters 2—3 are devoted to precise scathing attacks on the political and religious leaders responsible for the deterioration of the old tribal order of communal equity. He is merciless in his descriptions of the violations of person and property which the rich and powerful have perpetrated on their vulnerable fellow Judahites. All this culminates in the announcement that the city of Jerusalem and its temple will be flattened, never to be built again (3:12).

The present Book of Micah is constructed on a twofold redactional scheme of judgment-salvation (ABAB pattern), or possibly a threefold scheme (ABABAB pattern). Most commentators discern the former:[3]

Judgment	*Salvation*
1—3	4—5
6:1—7:7	7:8–20

It is to be observed, however, that 2:12–13 looks like a salvation oracle, so that a threefold pattern can be made out:[4]

3. James L. Mays, *Micah. A Commentary,* OTL (Philadelphia: Westminster Press, 1976), 21–33.
4. John T. Willis, "The Structure of the Book of Micah," *SEÅ* 34 (1969): 5–42.

Judgment	Salvation
1:1—2:11	2:12–13
3	4—5
6:1—7:7	7:8–20

The latter arrangement, on the other hand, breaks into the homogeneous Micah judgment speeches, and it is possible that 2:12–13 is after all a judgment prophecy about Yahweh leading his people *into* exile and not, as commonly understood, back *from* exile.[5]

Although he was a prophet dead set against urban Zion, Micah ironically has become the lodestone for attracting blocks of salvation oracles which point toward the redemption of the holy city as the center for a purified people of Israel and as an assembly point for the nations. This means that the words of a prophet whose firm rootage was in tribal Yahwism are now in the sharpest contradiction to Zion and Davidic traditions that fill out his book (§31.3; 52.3). In addition to the fact that the oracles about the rebuilt and glorified Zion are fundamentally out of step with Micah's outlook in chaps. 1—3, it is reported that the memory of Micah's prophecy of the destruction of Jerusalem was happily recollected by elders in the time of Jeremiah who were able to cite it as a precedent in defense of Jeremiah's similar audacious prophecies (Jer. 26:16–19). This almost certainly means that as late as the end of the seventh century there were no salvation oracles as yet connected with the Micah tradition, for if there had been, the appeal to Micah as a vindication of Jeremiah would have been greatly weakened if not entirely invalidated.

The panels of salvation and further judgment oracles that follow after Micah's prophecies in chaps. 1—3 are very intricately redacted by means of catchwords and chiastic or ring arrangement of the units. Indeed, what has been called "the breathtaking shift" from the utterly leveled temple site in 3:12 to the exalted temple mount that attracts nations in 4:1 is achieved by means of the catchword "the mountain of the house" which occurs in both verses. The "swords to plowshares" oracle of 4:1–4 is identical with Isa. 2:1–4 and is generally nowadays attributed to a third source from which the redactors of Isaiah and Micah have separately drawn. Among other familiar oracles are the prophecy of a ruler who will come forth from Bethlehem Ephrathah (5:2–4) and the torah on acceptable worship which reflects the design of priestly and especially wisdom instruction and which concludes with the celebrated epitome of prophetic religion:

5. Mays, *Micah*, 73–76.

He has showed you, O man, what is good;
and what does Yahweh require of you
but to do justice, and to love mercy
and to walk humbly with your God?
(6:8)

The final chapter has no genres within it that are characteristically prophetic, consisting rather of laments, trust songs, oracles of salvation, and praise songs that have been joined as a liturgy to extol the salvation of Zion and its redeemed people. This and other sections of the non-Micah expansions may have been used liturgically in exilic and postexilic contexts.

37.2 Isaiah of Jerusalem

A contemporary of Micah and Hosea, Isaiah was a Judahite prophet active at several crisis points between 740/739 and 701. In the former year he was called to prophesy by a stunning vision of Yahweh, the Holy One of Israel, "high and lifted up" above sinful Israel, while "the whole earth is full of his glory" (chap. 6). Isaiah's commission was to announce the unmitigated destruction of the twin kingdoms Israel and Judah. He lived to see the fall of the northern kingdom to Assyria in 722 and the supine vassalage of the southern kingdom to the same world power: at first by Judah's choice in 732 and later against its will in 701.

The basis of the announced destruction of the twin kingdoms was their rulers' rampant violation of the rights of the common people and their headlong rush to amass quick wealth and political power at any cost (1:12–17; 3:13–15; 5:1–7, 8–10). These leaders carried "blood guilt" for their crimes (1:15; 5:7). Gross disregard of the fundamental requirements of Yahweh as known in the received traditions of Israel made both states vulnerable to attack and annihilation by Assyria, their *external* fate being directly linked with their *internal* abandonment of the Yahwistic charter of social justice and equality. Because Isaiah saw little or no prospect of a change of heart among the leaders and thus no meaningful reforms, he announced total national destruction.

To be sure, Isaiah is often credited with belief in a saving remnant that would survive the debacle and form a new community. Indeed, he may have struck such a note, but always ambiguously, hinting at a modest contingent hope at best. As with Hosea (§34.4), he insisted that any hopeful future could only be realized after the total collapse of the existing perverse national structures.

Precise determination of the theological perspectives and political judgments of the prophet is complicated by the way his book has been edited so that everywhere his own words are mixed with later prophetic words that grew up as a carry-over of his influential outlook into later generations. These expansions and additions in an "Isaianic stream of tradition" are often credited to "disciples" who formed self-perpetuating groups which are somewhat loosely called "schools." In general, a minimal note of hope—contingent on repentance—was picked up and developed by interpreters in following centuries and the core of the prophet's collected works was supplemented by extensive traditions of salvation appropriate to later sociohistoric settings. The most notable of these is chaps. 40—66 which come from sixth-century exilic and postexilic prophets (§50.2; 50.4).

Isaiah's resources in Israel's traditions are eccentric compared to Amos and Hosea. He did not appeal to the Mosaic exodus-settlement or Sinai traditions, although his understanding of the content of what constituted proper Israelite norms of behavior was broadly congruent with the content of those dominant traditions. Instead, Isaiah cited images and norms concerning Zion as a city of righteousness and Davidic rulers as executors of peace and justice in the community. Some interpreters have concluded that the Zion traditions which Isaiah drew upon were pre-Israelite beliefs in a sacrosanct Jerusalem whose security against all outsiders was ultimately assured (§31.3), thus explaining how the prophet could relent and announce salvation for the city, after he had declared its destruction during Judah's revolt against Sennacherib in 705–701. This line of interpretation, however, calls the self-consistency and public credibility of the prophet into serious question. To the contrary, recent advances in redaction criticism of the Book of Isaiah tend to identify the words of Isaiah as consistently and soberly judgmental. At the same time it is understandable how his deep faith in Yahweh's justice over all nations could have given rise to surges of hope among those who looked at later historical situations through the lenses of his writings.

Although still much disputed, it is likely that Isaiah penned 9:2–7 as an imitation of a coronation psalm which celebrates the righteous deeds of a Davidic king, a text probably directed to Hezekiah at his accession to the throne.[6] Like so many of Isaiah's words, it was a deliberately ambivalent statement, both announcing the claim and possibility of royal righteousness and ironically exposing the hollowness of the claim and the frustration of its realization in the person of contemporary Judahite monarchs. In short, to Isaiah's way of thinking the Davidic traditions contained all the ethical and theological standards and political orientations necessary for the leaders of

6. R. B. Y. Scott, "Isaiah," in *IB* 5: 231–32.

Judah to pull back from their willful plunge toward destruction—but they would not "believe"! It was virtually inevitable that later traditionists, seeing the positive portrait of kingship in 9:2–7 but missing Isaiah's subtle irony, would read and elaborate it as an unequivocal promise.

Toward the beginning of his prophetic project, Isaiah had to deal with the pro-Assyrian king Ahaz (§36.1). In the face of pressure for the king either to join Israel and Syria in an alliance against Assyria or to ally with Assyria on favorable terms, Isaiah insisted on Judahite noninvolvement in international politics: neither to *submit* to Assyria nor to join in an *attack* on Assyria. This counsel, also attested in several other Israelite prophets, has often been understood as a narrowly religious judgment (since alliances required formally acknowledging the allies' deities) or as a wildly utopian view (since Yahweh will spare Judah without human effort). In fact, the prophet appears to have believed that what was religiously requisite was also politically practical. His conception of action in the world was what has been called "theopolitical."[7] Since Yahweh is lord of the world of nations, what is right for Judah to do will also be in the best national interests and will lead to the total welfare of the people.

Isaiah understood "what is right" for Judah to consist of a vigorous pursuit of domestic social justice coupled with neutrality in foreign affairs. Ahaz proceeded on his own course by submitting to Assyria, ignoring the warnings of the prophet set forth in the ironic names of three sons: Shear-jashub ("A Remnant Shall Return," 7:3), Immanuel ("God with Us," 7:14), and Maher-shalal-hashbaz ("Speeds the Spoil, Hastens the Prey," 8:1). The first and third of these sons were unmistakably Isaiah's children, and the context strongly argues that the second, Immanuel, was also the prophet's child.[8]

The irony of the prophet in pointing to the radically different courses of events that would be set in motion depending on the king's choice is starkly underscored by the double-edged meanings carried by each of the symbolic names with their explosive potentiality for threat or promise. Shear-jashub may mean that no one but a few survivors will be left if Ahaz pursues his alliance politics, or it may mean that a faithful remnant will rebuild Judah if the king is wise enough to believe in Yahweh and stay politically neutral. Immanuel may mean that God is with us to destroy us if we invite Assyria into southern Palestine, or it may mean that God is with us to save us if we avoid getting mixed up with Assyria or with Israel and Syria. Maher-shalal-

7. Martin Buber, *The Prophetic Faith* (New York: Macmillan Co., 1949), 67, 135.
8. Norman K. Gottwald, "Immanuel as the Prophet's Son," *VT* 8 (1958): 36–47.

hashbaz may mean that if Judah joins Israel and Syria against Assyria, the superior power will hurry on to destroy Judah after it has easily disposed of the other allies, or it may mean that a neutral Judah will be delivered of any threat from Israel and Syria because their rebellion against Assyria will utterly fail.

The ironic and subtle play of Isaiah's mind is everywhere at work with cunning images that expose the way the leaders of Israel and Judah become entrapped and boxed in by their own clever plans which repeatedly backfire because they are insubstantial and run straight against the grain of Yahweh's way of working in the world. Assyria, the "razor" hired by Ahaz to shave Israel and Syria, will in the end slash its smug Judahite client (7:20), and faith in Yahweh, the national "rock" of Israel, will be a foundation stone for some to build on and an obstacle of stumbling which will trip and overthrow many others (8:14–15; 28:16).

Because Ahaz was impervious to Isaiah's counsel, the prophet appears to have withdrawn for a time from public life and to have committed the incidents of that period to writing in what has been called his Memoirs or Testimony, or Book of Signs (6:1—8:18). In this way, Isaiah, although rebuffed, was fully "on record." With the coming of Hezekiah (§36.1) to the throne in 716/715, Isaiah may have had a somewhat more favorable hearing, at least for a period. He seems to have had some effect in limiting Hezekiah's participation in an anti-Assyrian revolt led by Ashdod in 713–711 (chap. 20). It is possible also that, along with other factors such as the recent fall of the northern kingdom, Isaiah was influential in moving Hezekiah toward reforms. The Deuteronomistic History speaks of these measures as cultic reforms (2 Kings 18:4), but whether Hezekiah also paid heed to the call of proto-Deuteronomy and of Isaiah for social justice in the land is not known. Failing the rectification of the plight of the impoverished and defrauded peasantry, Isaiah would not have found cultic improvements a substantial remedy of national ills (1:12–17; 22:12–14; 29:13–14).

By 705, with the death of the Assyrian king Sargon, Hezekiah became a ringleader in a major revolt of Syro-Palestinian states against Assyria that was backed by Egypt. We have seen the unhappy outcome of that venture for Judah, thereafter greatly reduced in territory and under heavier tribute. One strand of thought in the Book of Isaiah shows the prophet holding unswervingly to an announcement of doom throughout the revolt of Hezekiah and the decimation of Judah until only Jerusalem was left unmolested and Hezekiah had to surrender (22:1–4; 29:1–4; 30:1–5; 31:1–3). Another strand, both in narratives (chaps. 36—39, derived from 2 Kings 18—20) and in speeches of salvation (10:16–19; 14:24–27; 17:12–14; 29:5–

8; 31:5 + 8–9), pictures Isaiah declaring a reprieve and imminent deliverance of Jerusalem coupled with the destruction of Assyria (§36.1).

This contradiction has been explained in different ways. One view is that Isaiah simply changed his mind as the siege of Jerusalem wore on and switched from a message of doom to one of salvation. Others, who favor the two-invasion hypothesis, see Isaiah as a staunch prophet of doom in the 701 invasion but, concluding that it was time for Assyria to be punished, had evolved into a prophet of Jerusalem's salvation by the time of the supposed second invasion about thirteen years later. Since the Book of Isaiah is a compilation and redaction of material over a long tradition history, it is far more plausible to attribute the salvation "relapse" connected with 701 to postdeliverance Isaianic traditionists who were impressed by the historical fact that Jerusalem proper had not been destroyed and who retrojected this marvel into the prophecies of the master.[9]

It is obvious that later Isaianic traditionists played upon the many facets of Isaiah's fertile mind and modes of expression. The many-sidedness of Isaiah was a function of his dialectic way of thinking that often saw two or more aspects of a situation volatilely combined and recombined in a zigzag course of events. His ever-moving way of viewing the same decisions, events, and processes provoked a constant unsettling of appearances. Motives, confidences, plans, expectations, and beliefs alike turn into their unexpected opposites.[10] The "speech" and "deeds" of Yahweh in this world are distressingly "strange and alien" (28:11, 21). Accordingly, the international perspective of the prophet held all the ancient Near Eastern nations under scrutiny as accountable before the judgments of Yahweh.

On the one hand, the nations were used by Yahweh as punitive instruments against Israel and Judah ("Ah, Assyria, the rod of my anger, the staff of my fury!" 10:5). On the other hand, as free agents the nations exceed their assigned or permitted role as chastisers of others and engage in prideful excesses which Yahweh will in turn recompense ("Shall the ax vaunt itself over him who hews with it?" 10:15). Thus, 10:5–15 shows clearly that Isaiah expected Assyria to receive its own well-earned judgment—but in good time, *after* Judah's punishment at the hands of Assyria. The idea that Isaiah preached the deliverance of Jerusalem in 701 because he became a lightheaded patriot at the last moment erroneously implies that he had once been a lightheaded critic. If, as seems certain, his an-

9. Roland E. Clements, *Isaiah and the Deliverance of Jerusalem*, JSOTSup 13 (Sheffield: JSOT Press, 1980).
10. For an analysis of the Isaianic dialectic between what people intend and hope, especially in politics, and what they actually achieve, see Gottwald, *AKE*, 147–208.

nouncements of judgment on nations were dialectically thought through in a consistent fashion, then it would have made no sense at all for him to anticipate the breaking of Yahweh's "rod" Assyria *before* Judah had received the thorough thrashing that constituted the central political content of the prophet's message.

The collection and arrangement of the prophet's words together with expansions and supplements from other hands, which issued in the extant Book of Isaiah, was an exceedingly complex redaction process that is just beginning to be understood. The Book of Isaiah divides as follows:

1. *Isaiah 1—12.* Grouped around the centrally positioned Memoirs (6:1—8:18) are oracles of judgment from Isaiah against Israel and Judah, mainly the latter, stemming from his early career (chaps. 2—5; 8:19—10:33), among which are sprinkled later additions. The whole is prefaced by a summation of the prophet's message in chap. 1, which also serves as the introduction to the entire book. Chapters 11—12 are assorted oracles of salvation, culminating in a hymn of salvation.

2. *Isaiah 13—27.* A collection of prophecies against named foreign nations (13—23), a majority of which may be from Isaiah himself, leads on to the announcement and celebration of a general judgment on the nations en masse and the accompanying promise of a "final deliverance" for Jerusalem/Judah = Israel/Jacob (chaps. 24—27). This latter section has been dubbed "The Apocalypse of Isaiah." While lacking the fully developed literary form of an apocalypse, its heightened eschatology shares a number of concepts with later apocalypses (§55).

3. *Isaiah 28—35.* Oracles of judgment from Isaiah against Judah, and one against Israel that heads the collection, derive largely from the later career of the prophet in 705–701 (chaps. 28—31). There follow prophecies about the coming righteous king (chaps. 32—33) and a celebration of judgment on the nations and deliverance for Zion in a style closely linked to chaps. 40—66 (chaps. 34—35).

4. *Isaiah 36—39.* A narrative about the crisis of Sennacherib's dire threat to Jerusalem in 701 has been excerpted from 2 Kings 18—19 with the intent of documenting the prophet's promise of divine protection as a factor in the survival of the city and as a way of bridging the gap between 1—35 and 40—66 (§35.2).

5. *Isaiah 40—66.* Oracles of redemption for the Judahite exiles have been composed in a rhetorically vibrant and elevated style. On the basis of content and historical background this section is usually subdivided into chaps. 40—55 (§50.2) presupposing the last years of exile (ca. 550–539) and

chaps. 56—66 (§50.4) presupposing a return to Judah and a difficult struggle to reconstitute the Palestinian Jewish community (ca. 538–500).

The words of Isaiah of Jerusalem to his people, and especially to their leaders, are thus concentrated in chaps. 2—10 and 28—31. Each of these collections has been punctuated and concluded by later words of salvation. Words of Isaiah against the nations in 13—23 have been supplemented and concluded with later words of judgment and salvation. The result is that the first three major divisions of the book start off with judgment and rise to a crescendo of salvation. By contrast, chaps. 40—66 project salvation as their dominant message and tone, within which reminders of former judgment and of impending judgment on sinful individuals and groups are incorporated. The entirety of 40—66 has been linked to 1—39 by the common focus on Zion/Jerusalem as the center of a sociopolitically righteous and cultically faithful community which Israel's God works to perfect against the backdrop of other nations whom he likewise controls. In terms of historical settings, the book spans more than two centuries: the context of 1—39 is basically judgment on Israel and Judah by means of Assyria (eighth/seventh centuries) [§33.6; 36.1], while the context of 40—66 is basically redemption for Judah by means of the Persians after decades of punishing subjection at the hands of the Neo-Babylonians (sixth century) [§43].

Earlier literary and form-critical analyses of the book tended to conclude that the prophet's original words in 1—39 had been expanded and supplemented in a somewhat random manner, and that 40—66 were attached to Isaiah's writings rather arbitrarily, perhaps for so mechanical a reason as to fill out the scroll on which 1—35 was written. Recent studies of the growth and redaction of traditions within the book suggest a more purposeful process that occurred at particular historical-critical junctures and that spanned two or more of the subdivisions. Certain redactional strategies are identifiable even though there remains uncertainty about how these strategies were related temporally and conceptually.

The redactional maneuvers within the Book of Isaiah are complex, versatile, and pervasive. Chapters 40—66, for example, have been joined to 1—35 by the narrative seam of 36—39 in which Hezekiah's negotiations with a precursor of the later imperialist Neo-Babylonians "sets up" the Babylonian exile as the proper context for 40—66. There are words and motifs that recur, functioning adroitly as "clamps" to hold together the once-separate subdivisions and as "signals" that encourage a back-and-forth and part-to-whole reading of the completed work.

Zion and Babylon are two such recurrent redactional binders. Zion, punished and/or redeemed, appears prominently in each of the major subdivisions, notably in the openings and conclusions. Babylon is cited at the beginning and end of the oracles against foreign nations, sometimes in the form of a reassignment to Babylon of oracles originally directed against an earlier nation such as Assyria (14:3–20; 23:13). The diverse salvation prophecies and hymns that culminate the first three subdivisions (in 11—12, 24—27, and 34—35) show marked stylistic and thematic connections with 40—66, thereby anticipating the ecstatic tone and expectation that pervades 40—66. Chapter 1 (with its own superscription; cf. 1:1; 2:1) is both a compendium of the message of eighth-century Isaiah and a foretaste of the purgative redemption of Jerusalem spelled out over the course of the whole book. There are striking links in vocabulary and motifs between chaps. 1 and 65—66, strongly pointing to a redactional inclusio for the finished book.

One recently proposed redactional stage in the composition of the book goes a long way toward explaining why early oracles of Isaiah in chaps. 2—10 appear to be in such topical and chronological disarray.[11] This proposal accounts for the confusing shift in many passages from Yahweh *using* Assyria to judge Israel and Judah to Yahweh *judging* Assyria in such an abrupt fashion that the threatened initial judgment against Judah is weakened or altogether negated.

It has long been recognized, on the basis of the refrain "for all this his anger is not turned away and his hand is stretched out still," that 5:25–30 definitely belongs with a group of invective threats in 9:8–21. Similarly, the woe oracle of 10:1–4 belongs with a group of woe oracles in 5:8–24. Why this dislocation of materials should have occurred has, until now, never been satisfactorily explained. It is now argued that an extensive "Assyria redaction" of Isaiah's oracles—reaching across chaps. 2—32 (although not including all the present contents)—concretized the prophet's general warning against Assyrian pride into a specific announcement of imminent judgment. This redaction is connected with the Josianic period in the seventh century when Assyria was declining and it was felt appropriate to "cash in" overtly on Isaiah's prospect of an eventual punishment for Assyria.

11. The hypothesis about an "Assyria-redaction" of Isaiah's speeches in the era of Josiah advanced by Hermann Barth (*Die Jesaja-Worte in der Josiazeit. Israel und Assur als Thema einer Neuinterpretation der Jesajaüberlieferung* [Neukirchen-Vluyn: Neukirchener Verlag, 1977]) is followed with minor modifications by Roland E. Clements, *Isaiah 1–39*, NCBC (Grand Rapids: Wm. B. Eerdmans, 1980), 2–8.

As a part of this redaction, for example, it is proposed that the two sequences of invective threats and woe oracles by Isaiah were each broken apart and arranged chiastically around Isaiah's Memoirs as follows:

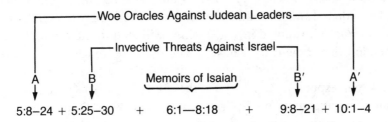

The effect of this redaction was to frame the concrete incidents of Isaiah's encounter with Ahaz by means of "inner brackets" that reminded of the fall of Israel and "outer brackets" that warned Judah in a cogent reactualization of the words of eighth-century Isaiah for the benefit of seventh-century Judahite readers. Other instances of redactional displacements of older oracles within the early chapters of the book have been proposed as measures to bind the previously separate chaps. 2—4 to what follows: 5:15–16 once was joined to 2:6–21, and 3:13–15 was once associated with 5:1–7. This same "Assyria redaction" is credited with pointed assertions of Assyria's impending downfall by means of additions to Isaiah's words, either joined with the prophet's text or standing as complete units (e.g., 10:16–19; 14:24–27; 30:27–33; 31:5, 8b–9; 31:1–5, 15–20). It has also been noted that this redaction's expectation of a divine destruction of Assyria, "without human hands," corresponds to the narrative account of the angel of Yahweh who is said to have killed 185,000 of Sennacherib's warriors in 701 (37:36–38).

No doubt the grounds of evidence for this Assyria redaction, as well as its exact scope and tendency, will be much debated, but it has already commanded serious attention. The particular power of the hypothesis lies in its capacity to explain some of the literary disorder in the book and to elucidate how Isaiah, the uncompromising preacher of judgment on Jerusalem, came to be pictured incongruously as the preacher of an instant doom on Assyria that would spare Jerusalem before it had tasted the threatened judgment. In this instance we see that redaction criticism can contribute measurably not only to our understanding of how the text was given its present shape but also to our grasp of the sociohistoric settings and theological readings of events at various points in the trajectory of the growth of Isaianic traditions.

In some cases, the same subunits in the Book of Isaiah have been analyzed both by redaction-critical and rhetorical-critical methods. Isaiah 28 is one such subunit. Redactionally, it is argued that the chapter was built from two "seed" oracles (vv. 7b–13a and 14–17a, 18–19) in which the prophet indicted Judah's leaders for uncomprehendingly rejecting previous words of Yahweh (quoted in v. 12) which will lead to their equally uncomprehended punishment by Yahweh. These "seed" oracles were expanded and vv. 1–4 were prefaced as the first in a series of larger sectional "woe" oracles (corresponding to 29:1, 15; 30:1; 31:1; 33:1). This redactional move meant that judgments on Ephraim and Judah were thematically linked, leaving an ambiguity in vv. 7–13 as to whether they refer backward to Ephraim or forward to Judah. The so-called parable of the farmer in vv. 22–29 rounds out the chapter by pointing to the possibility of intelligible human and divine activity in spite of the senseless behavior of Ephraim and Judah. An addition in vv. 5–6 radically alters the imagery of vv. 1–4 so that the "crown" is no longer Ephraim but Yahweh.[12]

Rhetorically, Isaiah 28 is shown to be amazingly dense with mixed metaphors and terse similes that convey an ominous, even terrifying impression, while the structure of the speech is rich in chiastic arrangements, at times involving smaller chiasms within larger chiasms.[13] Pursued independently, the redactional and rhetorical inquiries emerge with some broad agreements on the overall structure and meaning of Isaiah 28. Because the redactional approach accents how the passage was formed and the rhetorical approach stresses how diction, syntax, and rhetorical devices effect meaning, it is difficult to compare the results directly or even to determine precisely the extent and grounds of disagreement.

Broadly speaking, the combined effect of redactional and rhetorical studies on the same subunit in the Book of Isaiah is to expose an intricate texture of Isaianic speech that has grown by an innertextual "layering" process. The surface structure of brilliant tangled imagery, juxtaposed and interlocking motifs, speech units constructed out of key words from widely scattered contexts, and chiastic arrangements that "nest" inside one another—all this seems to have been "built up" in a process over time analogous to geological layering or to organic growth from seeds.

Isaiah of Jerusalem seems to have worked with a range of complex

---

12. David L. Petersen, "Isaiah 28, A Redaction Critical Study," SBLSP 17 (1979): 101–22.
13. J. Cheryl Exum, "Isaiah 28–32: A Literary Approach," SBLSP 17 (1979): 123–51 = " 'Whom Will He Teach Knowledge?': A Literary Approach to Isaiah 28," in *Art and Meaning: Rhetoric in Biblical Literature*, ed. D. J. A. Clines et al., JSOTSup 19 (Sheffield: JSOT Press, 1982), 108–39.

historical and theological topics that he attacked in a dialectical style, rich in figurative and multivalent language,[14] which tended to set the tone for those who elaborated on his work. The recognized wisdom elements in this prophet accord with his aim of forcing his contemporaries to think long and hard, to look at what was happening around them in a comprehensive way, and to act at a level that cut through superficial appearances. To call Isaiah "aristocratic" in a social class sense, as has sometimes been done, is to infer more than we know, but if we mean by that term "noble" or "elevated" in thought and style of expression it is a permissible characterization of his penchant to put every concrete situation into a large and principled context and to expose the deep logic in the surface surprises of events and to do so in colorful and memorable speech.

37.3 Deuteronomy

We have so far considered the Book of Deuteronomy mainly as the programmatic preface to the Deuteronomistic History (§13.2; 22.2). Prior to its final "bookish" function, however, Deuteronomy was shaped by a long organic growth of its traditions out of covenant-renewal ceremonies and recitations of the law, and some form of its laws, contained in chaps. 12—26, 28, eventually emerged as the platform for Josiah's reformation (§36.3).

The prose of Deuteronomy, both in the framework (1—11 and 29—34) and in the hortatory expansions of the laws, is written in a highly rhetorical style marked by long verbose sentences built from stereotyped phrases and linked by subordinate clauses (unlike the usual paratactic syntax of Hebrew (§23.1). This peculiar style communicates a distinctive cluster of concepts that gives the book an obvious unity. On analysis, however, Deuteronomy shows abundant signs of a long process of growth, by means of the expansion and supplementation of texts in the process of cultic recitation and in the redaction process as Deuteronomy was prefaced to DH.

The structure of the materials in Deuteronomy is the structure of a covenant-making or covenant-renewing ceremony, and in this respect it corresponds to the basic arrangement of the Sinai traditions in Exodus 19—24 (table 11: C). In both cases the stages in the growth of the traditions, as cultic or didactic texts were grouped and editorially accommodated to one another, are not easily determined.[15] In Deuteronomy, the covenant se-

---

14. Intricate poetic similes in Isaiah 29—31 are examined by Exum, "Of Broken Pots, Fluttering Birds, and Visions in the Night: Extended Simile and Poetic Technique in Isaiah," *CBQ* 43 (1981): 331–52.

15. Norbert Lohfink, "Deuteronomy," in IDBSup, 229–32.

quence is apparent in a historical résumé of the Sinai events (1—11), a recital of the laws (12:1—26:15), a proclamation of the establishment of covenant (26:16–19), and a recital of blessings and curses (27—28), with appended exhortations, poems, and narratives that adapt the document to its function as an introduction for Joshua–2 Kings (29—34). It has been suggested that the arrangement of the laws follows the divisions of the Decalogue (Deut. 5:6–21) [§19.2.c] in that the laws of chaps. 12—18 refer to "the privileges of Yahweh" analogous to 5:6–15, while the laws of chaps. 19—26 concern murder, family, neighbors, and court procedure in correspondence with 5:16–21.

DH reports that Josiah followed the instructions of a lawbook when he enforced centralization of worship at Jerusalem and celebrated Passover at the temple rather than in private homes, as also when he prohibited astral worship, sacred poles and pillars, cult prostitution, immolation of children, magic, and divination (2 Kings 23:4–14, 21–24). All of these reforms are explicitly legislated in Deuteronomy. Moreover, when it is said that the Levites from the banned centers of worship were *not* admitted into the Jerusalem temple service (2 Kings 23:9), it reads like an apology for the failure to carry out the incorporation of the country Levites at Jerusalem as directed by Deut. 18:6–8. In fact, Deuteronomy itself legislates triennial tithes to support Levites who are socially deprived now that the country sanctuaries are closed (14:28–29).

In Deuteronomy "priests" and "Levites" are interchangeable terms and all Levitical priests possess legitimacy of office; however, they may practice henceforth only at the Jerusalem temple. Since the central sanctuary in Deuteronomy is explicitly connected with Shechem in blessings/curses passages (11:26–32; 27), it is probable that the old cultic materials of Deuteronomy first developed in the north before the fall of Israel and, carried over into Judah, were subsequently transposed into a validation of sole worship at Jerusalem. Since the *Levitical priests* occupy so prominent a place in Deuteronomy, it is logical to assume that, as leaders in the covenant-renewal and law-recitation ceremonies, it was also they who were the bearers of the traditions and the shapers of the final form of Deuteronomy.[16] More recently, however, the occurrence of wisdom language and legal constructs that relate to neo-Assyrian diplomacy and treaty texts (table 1: 2H) has prompted the notion that the Deuteronomic traditionists were court officials, probably scribes.[17] Correspondence between the so-

16. Gerhard von Rad, *Studies in Deuteronomy,* SBT, 1st ser., 9 (London: SCM Press, 1953), 60–69.

17. Moshe Weinfeld, *Deuteronomy and the Deuteronomic School* (Oxford: At the Clarendon Press, 1972).

cioeconomic provisions of the laws and the prophetic critique have also favored an origin of Deuteronomy in prophetic circles.

It is possible to formulate a conception of Deuteronomy's development that takes the various influences into account. The cultic covenant-law provenance of Deuteronomy is the necessary foundation for any hypothesis. It was, however, only as this covenant-law stream of tradition entered into the royal establishments of Hezekiah and Josiah that it became a visible and effective part of national religious life in Judah. In that context, the Levitical priests at Jerusalem and the court officials (so prominent in Josiah's reforms, 2 Kings 22:3–4, 8–14) were no doubt collaborators in effecting reforms and in shaping the text of Deuteronomy. Thus, wisdom and Neo-Assyrian treaty language played a role in the conceptualizing of the covenant (§19.1) and in the didactic form of the book. Simultaneously, the preaching of the eighth-century prophets, Amos and Hosea in the north and Micah and Isaiah in the south, had sensitized priests and government officials to the urgencies of socioeconomic justice which also found strong expression in the laws of Deuteronomy.

When Deuteronomy is viewed as the end stage of a long process of covenant making and law recitation by a priesthood affected by prophets and collaborating with court officials, its "finding" in the temple in Josiah's reign need no longer be explained as a "pious fraud" to validate Mosaic authorship. The Deuteronomic partisans, like the prophets, had been driven underground during Manasseh's syncretizing reign (§36.2). The resurfacing of these Yahwists with their long-refined tradition meant the "reestablishment" and further prosecution by Josiah of reforms that Hezekiah had begun (§36.1; 36.3).

It is obvious that the reform program had far-reaching sociopolitical impact. In terms of the old north-south divisions, by adapting traditional northern covenant-law practices and concepts, the Davidic dynasty of Josiah was able to present itself as the true guarantor of Israelite interests north and south. Josiah's recovery of northern territories abandoned by the Assyrians was ideologically legitimated by Deuteronomy. Likewise, the intensification of Jerusalem's control over the countryside of Judah was enabled by reforming fiscal affairs so that the flow of revenues no longer passed through rural priests and elders but came directly to Jerusalem.[18] The increase in pilgrims to Jerusalem as a result of cult centralization was also certain to cause the capital city to prosper.

It is disputed whether in fact the old northern Deuteronomic tradition

18. W. Eugene Claburn, "The Fiscal Basis of Josiah's Reform," *JBL* 92 (1973): 11–22.

ever mandated exclusive worship at one site, such as Shechem (§24.2.b). In any case, by making centralization of worship at Jerusalem the cornerstone of the reforms, Josiah masterfully strengthened the administrative and religious power of Jerusalem. What price Josiah actually paid in accepting "constitutional limits" on the monarchy (e.g., Deut. 17:14–20) is far from clear since we do not know the extent to which he implemented the non-cultic aspects of Deuteronomic law.

Deuteronomy as preface to DH is concerned with land-getting, land-keeping, and land-recovering. The laws within the book provide the funda-mental conditions for Israel's *retention* of the land (seen from the viewpoint of Josiah and the first edition of DH) and, failing that, for Israel's eventual *recovery* of the land (seen from the viewpoint of stateless Jews and the DH exilic revision). The sonorous, almost mesmerizing, liturgical style of Deu-teronomy and DH interpretive passages sets forth a solemn coherent message about the indivisible unity of *one God* for *one people* in *one land* observing *one cult*.

37.4 Prophets of the International Power Shift

Apart from the abundantly documented work of Jeremiah, three other prophets from the last half of the seventh century are known to us from books credited to them: Zephaniah, Nahum, and Habakkuk. They re-sponded to the decline and fall of Assyria and the rise of Neo-Babylonia in terms of Yahwistic theology and with reference to the import of world events for the people of Judah. Very little is known about these prophets, however.

Zephaniah is given an extended genealogy (1:1), which may either intend to show that he was a great-great-grandson of king Hezekiah or that his father Cushi ("Egyptian/Ethiopian"?) was after all a full Israelite and not a foreigner. Dated in the reign of Josiah, Zephaniah's sharp criticism of religious irregularities and foreign attire strongly implies that he preached in Judah prior to the Deuteronomic Reform. Concerning Nahum the text tells us only that he was from Elkosh, an unknown place. He is situated between 663 and 612 because he refers to the Assyrian destruction of Thebes in the former year and anticipates (or perhaps celebrates) the fall of Nineveh in the latter year. Habakkuk is completely undescribed in his book, but is to be dated in conjunction with the rise of the Neo-Babylo-nians ("Chaldeans" of 1:6) who gained hegemony over Palestine by defeat-ing the Egyptians at Carchemish in 605. Indications within the book of an extended experience of Neo-Babylonian oppression may mean that Habakkuk continued his activity over some years, perhaps down to the fall of Jerusalem in 586.

The divine governance of the world in the face of cruel imperial powers and in the light of extensive unfaithfulness in Judah forms the conceptual matrix of the prophetic Books of Zephaniah, Nahum, and Habakkuk. The problematic of the justice of God is worked out with selective reference to particular political events and regimes and by means of thematic devices that pull together the original words of the prophets into larger entities that represent the work of redactors. Clearly this issue of divine justice in the unjust world of the ancient Near East continued to perplex and demoralize Jews far beyond the lifetimes of these prophets. Around the core of the original words of the three prophets larger literary structures were built that extended and prolonged their reflections in a way that made them useful and compelling for later generations who continued to face foreign domination and domestic injustice and religious disloyalty.

37.4.a Nahum

The construction of the Book of Nahum is relatively straightforward. Two vivid and impassioned prophecies of the destruction of Nineveh in chaps. 2 and 3 are prefaced by a psalmic introduction concerning divine power in creation and justice in history. Underlying the psalm in vv. 1–8(9) was an acrostic in which each line began with a successive letter of the Hebrew alphabet. As it stands, the acrostic has been disordered and broken off. In vv. 9–15, the persons referred to or addressed switch abruptly between Judahites and foreigners. This probably represents a redactional ploy to make the specific event of the fall of Nineveh into a paradigm of God's judgment on foreign nations that would be broad enough to accommodate Babylon or Persia as well as Assyria. The emphatic echo of the rhetoric of Isaiah of the Exile in v. 15 points to at least late exilic times as the date of redaction. Also, the fourfold reassurance of "no more" affliction on Judah from the oppressor (1:12, 14–15; 2:14) indicates a marked heightening of eschatological effect, pointing to a decisive deliverance in which Jews will no longer be troubled by *any* foreign nation.

The habit of earlier biblical critics to depreciate Nahum as a "nationalistic" prophet, or even a "false" prophet, because he does not summon Judah to repentance and merely condemns Assyria out of hatred and vengeance, was oddly insensitive to the nature of this literature. It is true that the Nineveh prophecies are largely given to descriptions of the city's military destruction rather than to justifications for its fall. Nonetheless, the terse allusion to "the bloody city, all full of lies and booty" (3:1) and the concluding rhetorical question, "For upon whom has not come your unceasing evil?" (3:19), constitute clear evidence of a moral judgment on the Assyrians.

Crucial to an understanding of Nahum is a grasp of the logic of prophetic criticism of foreign nations, attested already in Amos and Isaiah. The basic point was that nations stood under the judgment of Yahweh *irrespective* of the attitude or conduct of other nations. It would thus be immaterial, even intrusive, to the genre and conceptual format of the triumph songs over Nineveh to expect them to introduce a condition for the fall of that city that in some way hinged on Judah's repentance. As for whether Nahum derived any moral warning for Judah from the fall of Assyria, we cannot say because only the triumph songs of chaps. 2—3 are the work of Nahum.

The redactional psalm and its expansion in chap. 1 "generalizes" the principle of God's dependable judgment on the nations and is more explicit in warning that "Yahweh will by no means clear the guilty" (1:3). The perspective of this redacted introduction to Nahum does not raise questions of internal Jewish loyalty except indirectly in the reference to Yahweh's knowledge of "those who take refuge in him" (1:7). The good news of Judah's deliverance is expressed in the terms of Isaiah of the Exile (cf. 1:15 with Isa. 40:9; 52:7). In the writings of that prophet the deliverance of Israel occurs in full awareness of its former sinfulness which has been paid for and its present sinfulness which must be constantly fought and overcome (§50.2). It seems, then, that the overriding redactional and canonical framework of the prophecy does not warrant an amoral chauvinist reading of Nahum. Interpreters who have thought so were moralizing in defiance of the history of prophetic literary forms and prophetic theology about the nations.[19]

Zephaniah and Habakkuk are more complex books than Nahum. The former is constructed thematically around the day of Yahweh as a time of judgment and salvation. The latter is constructed around the threat to faith in the holy God in the face of wave after wave of foreign nations who, though they do God's work of judgment in the world, foment and multiply evil by their excesses. In these respects Zephaniah extends the concern of Amos with the day of Yahweh and Habakkuk plumbs the enigma of Isaiah concerning Yahweh's use of evil nations.

37.4.b Zephaniah

The articulation of the Book of Zephaniah is in the classic pattern of oracles against Judah (1:1—2:3), oracles against the nations (2:4—3:8), and

19. Brevard S. Childs, "Nahum," in *IOTS,* 441–46.

oracles of salvation to Judah (3:9–20). In the first section, two poems have been spliced together, one treating specific iniquities in Judah (1:2–6, 8–13) and the other depicting the grim day of Yahweh (1:7, 14–18). The opening of the first poem (1:2–3) and the closing of the second poem (1:17–18) form an inclusio on the motif of cosmic destruction, which is probably a redactional enlargement of the lesser scope of Zephaniah's original perception.

A distinctive note is struck by the imperative that culminates the opening section of judgment oracles. Addressed to "all you humble of the land, who do his commands," they are implored to seek Yahweh, righteousness, and humility in order to escape the coming wrath (2:3). This admonition is translated into a promissory proclamation in 3:11–13 when it is declared that Judah will be saved by a purgation of its prideful impenitents, leaving "a people humble and lowly" who "seek refuge in the name of Yahweh" and who "do no wrong and utter no lies." Thus, a body of "the humble" who take steps to reform themselves morally and religiously will be the historical vehicle for the renewal of Judah after the terrible judgment of the day of Yahweh. This appears to have been the kernel of the work of the prophet named Zephaniah.

Further complexities, however, are added toward the close of the oracles against the nations. They proceed in customary fashion until the introduction of judgment on Jerusalem in 3:1–5. This arrangement may be influenced by the inclusion of oracles against Judah and Israel among the foreign oracles of Amos 1—2 (§34.3), the point being that Judah along with all nations stands under judgment. The distinctive "twists" of Zeph. 3:6–10 are that judgment of other nations ought to serve Judah as a basis for self-correction, as well as to create new opportunities for the chastised nations to repent and worship Yahweh.

The book closes with an ecstatic paean of deliverance in the manner of Isaiah of the Exile in which the accent is on the defeat of oppressors and the ingathering of the exiles (3:14–20). If this is difficult to reconcile with the promised salvation of the nations, the very same "difficulty" inheres in the words of Isaiah of the Exile. Probably we have to do here with the final redactional level in the book that fell within late exilic or early postexilic horizons. Zephaniah's day of Yahweh has been universalized to all the earth, and, while this is to be a thoroughgoing judgment on all nations, it also contains the possibility (certainty?) of the conversion of the nations. The proud and impenitent in Judah and among the nations will be destroyed and the humble and lowly in Judah and among the nations will be saved.

Lurid and rhapsodic as the hopes may be, they do not envision the end of the world nor do they picture a dissolution of the familiar political framework of the nations. Like Isaiah of the Exile, this final redaction seems to picture purged nations worshiping Yahweh and returning the Jewish exiles to Palestine. A single dominant nation, such as Persia, is not pictured, however; we see rather a struggling community of "humble and lowly" Jewish exiles or returnees to Palestine.

37.4.c Habakkuk

The Book of Habakkuk is eccentrically constructed for a prophetic book, although the divisions are clear enough. The prophet opens with a complaint about injustice in Judah (1:1–4), to which a divine response assures him that the Neo-Babylonians are arising, presumably to bring punishment on Judah (1:5–11). Instead of Yahweh's "answer" settling the matter, the prophet lodges a further complaint that the Neo-Babylonians are merciless predators who compound wickedness (1:12–17), to which Yahweh's response is a "vision" consisting of some brief words that the prophet is to placard for all to read: "Behold, the one who is not upright in his very being shall fail [or "be puffed up"], but the righteous shall live by his faithfulness" (2:4). In context it appears that the Neo-Babylonian king is the one who is "not upright in his very being" and whose greed will destroy him and his empire (2:5, reading "wealth" for "wine" in the first line). There follows a series of woes constructed as second-person singular addresses to the Neo-Babylonian king. The composition closes with a psalm (chap. 3) possessing its own separate title and colophon, hymning the power and justice of God, and apparently modified at the beginning and end to first-person speech as though Habakkuk here gives personal testimony in response to the "vision" of 2:4.

The leaps in the form and line of argument in the book are sufficiently atypical and puzzling to have prompted several competing views of the identity of the oppressing nation. Some interpreters have doubted that Neo-Babylonia is the wicked nation, preferring to identify it as Assyria or Macedonia under Alexander the Great, while yet another view is that a preexilic oracle praiseworthy of the Neo-Babylonians has been built into a late exilic work that reflects on the bitter experience of Babylonian captivity. None of these proposals is an improvement on the view outlined above. Unknowingly, however, these alternative identifications of the wicked nation point to the force of the redactional framework of the book which pulls the specific instance of the Neo-Babylonians in the direction of a general paradigm about wicked oppressing nations. No doubt "Chaldea"/"Babylon" became a cipher for ruthless conquerors and overlords in later times, as regularly expressed in the conventions of apocalyptic literature where earlier classical empires became codewords for contemporary oppressors (§55).

The impressive combination of prophetic and psalmic forms in the Book of Habakkuk has stimulated much speculation about its relation to the cult ("But Yahweh is in his holy temple," 2:20). It has been argued that Habakkuk was a cultic prophet who recited some version of the text in temple worship. Others have located the cultic context of the book at a later redactional stage when the self-contained psalm was appended. Although clearly borrowing, as many prophetic writings do, from forms of speech shaped in the cult (§28), the resultant shape of Habakkuk 1—2 lacks conclusive liturgical signs. The appended psalm may imply a later cultic usage for the book, but even this is not certain since the psalm may simply be a rhetorical embellishment to reinforce confidence in the prophet by appeal to cultic traditions. If either in the prophet's time or in subsequent generations the prophecy was read in open-air laments or in temple festivities, the command to write 2:4 on a tablet may have been symbolically enacted.

Habakkuk shared with Zephaniah a sense of faithful waiting upon Yahweh in the face of prevailing arrogance and disillusionment. A difference is that Habakkuk internalizes the problem of abiding faithfulness by speaking in the first person at the moment of the vision (2:1) and in the psalmic conclusion (3:1, 16–19). Yet this "autobiographical" confidence in Yahweh, as with Jeremiah, is not solipsistic for it speaks against the backdrop of the whole people's plight (1:1–4) and looks to the vindication of faithfulness in a future salvation of the community (chap. 3). Habakkuk would have been recognizable among the humble and lowly bearers of the faith of whom Zephaniah spoke.

37.5 Jeremiah

Jeremiah is said to have prophesied from 626 to a time some few months or years following the destruction of Jerusalem in 586. Since the prophet's book contains no oracles concretely linked to Josiah's reign nor any certain indication that Jeremiah took a stand on the Deuteronomic Reformation, the prophet either experienced a long "silent period" (626–609), which is difficult to make plausible, or else the date in the superscription is in error or should be interpreted to refer to the date of his birth. The latter interpretation makes a measure of sense given the prophet's consciousness of having been predestined at birth to a prophetic task (1:4).[20] In any case, as far as the record goes, the public activity of Jeremiah began in 609 in connection with the death of Josiah which precipitated a wrenching change in political leadership in Judah. Jehoahaz, choice of "the people of the land" to succeed his father, ruled for a mere three months before the Egyptians replaced him as king with his brother, Jehoiakim.

Jeremiah's work presupposes the failure of the Deuteronomic Reformation and the shift of power in the ancient Near East from Assyria to Neo-Babylonia. Josiah's attempt at a cultic and sociopolitical renewal of Judah and the establishment of a neo-Davidic empire to fill the vacuum left by Assyria's precipitous decline had raised high hopes that went unrealized. Jehoiakim, first the vassal of Egypt and then of Neo-Babylonia, lacked the freedom and will to sustain reforms. Uncritical reliance on the protective sanctity of the Jerusalem temple to ward off difficulties for Judah seems to have been the main legacy of Josiah's reforms (7:4), while his efforts at meeting the social grievances of his people lapsed with his death (22:13–19). Jehoiakim remained compliant to Egypt and Neo-Babylonia for some years but opted to rebel against the latter in 601, a maneuver that initiated a fifteen-year-long chain of events issuing in the dissolution of the state of Judah (§36.4).

The burden of Jeremiah's message was that Judah's internal order was so corrupt that it would be swept away by Neo-Babylonia, unless the leadership repented and practiced the social justice that had been so long violated. In his view, the covenant traditions and the cult of Jerusalem provided no basis for security in the absence of social justice, nor did reliance on Egypt to spare Judah from Neo-Babylonia provide an external way of escape. In hinging so much of his reading of events on a summons to repentance or "turning," Jeremiah called for a fundamental realignment of the nation in keeping with its covenantal laws based on true change of values and allegiances. This suggests that he was committed to demanding aggressive implementation of the social reform rhetoric that had stirred the government of Judah under Josiah. That his public labors were met with hostility and rejection by the leading circles of Judah meant that in his judgment the scales of probability were increasingly tipped toward the imminent collapse of Judah.

Jeremiah believed that an adequate reformation of Judah could occur within the framework of its formal submission to Neo-Babylonia. By the

20. J. Philip Hyatt, "The Beginning of Jeremiah's Prophecy," *ZAW* 78 (1966): 204–14.

time Jehoiakim and Zedekiah had rebelled, and as Neo-Babylonia moved to crush the second rebellion as it had the first, Jeremiah perceived that there was no more "breathing space" for internal reform. He took the next logical step of calling on Zedekiah to surrender to the besiegers. Jeremiah was convinced that the ensuing stage of the people's life would have to be lived without king or temple cult. That Jeremiah fully intended such a reduced and altered program for his people is shown by his decision to stay in Judah and to participate in the Neo-Babylonian regime of reconstruction (§43) established at Mizpah under the direction of Gedaliah, the native governor appointed by the conquerors and an erstwhile supporter of the prophet (40:1–6).

Jeremiah thus not only drew the radical conclusion that his people's future was detachable from institutions of monarchy and cult, but he actually lived to take part in one political venture to realize new options (40:7–12). It was to be sure a short-lived venture, lasting no more than four years and perhaps a much briefer period, cut short when nationalists who aspired to revive a Judahite state assassinated Gedaliah and many of his associates (40:13—41:18). The upshot was that a large party of fearful survivors fled to Egypt to escape the expected Neo-Babylonian reprisals, carrying Jeremiah with them against his will (42:1—43:7). The last we hear of the prophet is a symbolically enacted threat against Egypt and against the fugitive Judahites who trusted in Egypt for asylum (43:8–13).

The exact balance and interaction of judgment threats and calls to repentance in the message of Jeremiah must be assessed in terms of the way his book came into existence. Earlier scholarship stressed the role of Jeremiah in writing down or dictating his own poetic oracles and the role of his secretary Baruch in penning the fairly extensive narrative passages about the career of the prophet (often called a "biography"). It was further concluded that to these poems and incidents were added prose sermons that reported the prophet's message in a very different style with marked affinities to DH prose.[21]

Nowadays there is much more emphasis upon a Jeremianic stream of tradition that included the prophet's own poetry, narratives about how his words were received by his contemporaries, together with prose "reactualizations" of words and themes from the prophet developed as preaching and teaching materials to apply to the situation of exiles or of politically deprived Palestinian Jews.[22] No doubt we meet the authentic Jeremiah

21. J. Philip Hyatt, "Jeremiah," in *IB* 5: 788; John Bright, ed., *Jeremiah*, AB 24 (Garden City, N.Y.: Doubleday & Co., 1965).

22. E. W. Nicholson, *Preaching to the Exiles: A Study of the Prose Traditions in the Book of Jeremiah* (New York: Schocken Books, 1971); Robert P. Carroll, *From Chaos to Covenant. Prophecy in the Book of Jeremiah* (New York: Crossroad, 1981).

within his book, but all the materials were preserved and put together by survivors of Jerusalem's fall who were constantly reading, assessing, and elaborating the prophet's words and deeds as one who could instruct them in their present wholly altered conditions of life (§43).

Jeremiah 36 tells how in 604/603 the prophet, debarred from the temple because of his critical preaching, dictated his words of judgment to Baruch who prepared a scroll that was publicly read by the secretary to a temple audience. When Jehoiakim heard the scroll read for his scrutiny, he contemptuously destroyed it, whereupon Jeremiah instructed Baruch to rewrite the scroll—but with further words added (36:32). Scholars have generally sought the contents of the original scroll in the poetic oracles of chaps. 1—25. Many of these oracles, however, are just as likely to have been formulated after 604 as before, so that conflicting opinions on the contents of the scroll have been advanced without consensus. One present view is that the first writing of the scroll included chaps. 1—6, comprising the prophet's call and his poems summoning to repentance and threatening "a foe from the north" (Neo-Babylonia), whereas chaps. 8—10 were added to 1—6 when Baruch prepared the "second edition" of Jeremiah's words.[23]

Theories of the composition of Jeremiah were long dominated by the assumption that the three types of material (poetic oracles, narratives, and prose sermons) were separately originated and then combined in stages to form the completed book. Subsequently there has developed among some scholars a strong preference for the view that all three types of material developed side by side in a number of "tradition complexes" generally identified as follows:

1. Jeremiah's words of judgment against Judah and Jerusalem (chaps. 1—24);
2. Jeremiah's words of judgment against the nations (chaps. 25; 46—51);
3. Narratives about the reception of Jeremiah's words by those in authority (chaps. 26—35, [36]);
4. A relatively cohesive extended narrative about Jeremiah and the last years of Judah's independence ([35], 36—45).

All these tradition complexes were probably developed and preserved in Deuteronomistic circles and eventually were assembled as a book by joining the complexes in a final redaction. There is considerable difference of judgment as to how extensively the redactor fixed a pattern on the whole book both by additions and by regrouping of materials within the separate complexes. In arguing for the predominance of a single literary hand in

23. William L. Holladay, *The Architecture of Jeremiah 1–20* (Lewisburg, Pa.: Bucknell University Press, 1976), 169–74.

bringing the book together, one redaction critic points out how the call account in chap. 1 foreshadows the entirety of the book in its mixture of poetry and prose and in its allusions to the major themes of the tradition complexes that follow: words of judgment and upbuilding directed to Judah and to the nations and a determined domestic opposition which the prophet must and will resist by the empowerment of Yahweh's presence with him.[24]

The previous assumption that Baruch, confidant of Jeremiah and copyist of the prophet's scroll, was likewise his "biographer" in the narratives of chaps. 26—45 is no longer so evident a conclusion. For one thing, Baruch was carried into Egypt along with Jeremiah (43:5–7), and an Egyptian setting for the compilation of the Book of Jeremiah is less likely than a Palestinian or Babylonian setting. More significant is the lack of true biography in the Book of Jeremiah, since the narratives do not give us a proportioned "life of the prophet" so much as they clarify the character of the domestic opposition to his preaching and validate the fulfillment of his words of doom in the final collapse of Jerusalem. The suggestion that they constitute a kind of "passion narrative" of the sufferings of Jeremiah is hardly appropriate to the narratives as a whole.

It is likely that the narratives in the complexes of 26—36 and 37—45 have been clustered for the purpose of showing how the word of Yahweh through Jeremiah overcame enormous resistance and misunderstanding to bring about a judgment on Judah that was fully explained *in advance* by Jeremiah and thus *avoidable* had the leadership of Judah heeded him. The lessons of this judgment, underscored by the narratives, were appropriated by exiles oriented to the DH outlook and/or "people of the land" left in Judah who have included sermonic prose among the narratives just as they have distributed sermonic prose among the poetic materials of 1—24 and 25; 46—51.

The appendix of chap. 52 is drawn from 2 Kings 24, except for vv. 28–30 that give independently derived information on the number of captives taken to Babylon. Since 39:1–10 already gave an abridged version of the fall of Jerusalem, chap. 52 is somewhat redundant but may have been added to attest the vindication of Jeremiah's prophecy of destruction in a final reprise of events. The insertion of chap. 52 produces the effect that both DH (in 2 Kings) and Jeremiah close with the same incident: the release of Jehoiachin from prison and his reception at the table of the king, thus giving him the status of "most favored royal prisoner." Some interpreters, however, claim to see in the addition of "until the day of his [Jehoiachin's]

---

24. Ibid., 27–29, 164–65.

death" a corroboration of Jeremiah's prediction in 22:26 and thus a denial or dampening of hope in a monarchic restitution in Judah.

The tradition complex of Jeremiah 26—35, as well as the earlier chap. 24, contain several expressions of chastened hope concerning Yahweh's future for his people beyond destruction.

1. *The Exiles of 597 as "Good Figs."* In a visionary report dated sometime after the deportation of 597, Jeremiah likens Jehoiachin and the deportees of that year to a basket of "good figs" and Zedekiah and the deportees of 586 to a basket of "bad figs" (chap. 24). Only the first group will be restored repentant from exile. The passage has obviously been shaped by an exilic traditionist with "axes to grind" in distinguishing "good" and "bad" exilic factions. The Jeremianic core of the passage was probably a severe warning to the Zedekiah faction that their hopes of rebellion, undeterred by the failure of the first rebellion, were as untimely as spoiled fruit. By comparison, those already in captivity stood to learn obedience to Yahweh and could rightfully expect to one day return to Palestine.

2. *Letter to the Exiles of 597.* Apparently in 594, when envoys from various Palestinian states came to Jerusalem to plot rebellion with Zedekiah and when prophets among the exiles were seeking to foment rebellion in Judah, Jeremiah sent a letter to the exiles of 597 counseling them to settle into a normal life in Babylonia in anticipation of a long exile (29:1–14). Here and elsewhere in the book he speaks of a seventy-year dominion of Neo-Babylonia over the nations before the exiles can expect release. If the beginning of Neo-Babylonian dominion in the ancient Near East was reckoned as the Assyrian defeat at Haran in 609, then it was exactly seventy years until Cyrus conquered Babylon in 539, but it is more likely that Jeremiah perceived Babylon's dominion as beginning with the defeat of Egypt at Carchemish in 605. Apparently the prophet intended to project a long period of time for Judah's subjection and exile, perhaps the typical full life span (Ps. 90:10), and the seventy years may have carried overtones of a fixed world period as implied in a text of the Assyrian king Esarhaddon who remarked that his predecessor Sennacherib's destruction of Babylon was to last seventy years according to a decree of the god Marduk.[25]

3. *Redemption of Family Property.* During the final siege of Jerusalem, Jeremiah exercised his "right of redemption" by purchasing a field located in his hometown of Anathoth from his cousin Hanamel (chap. 32). The dubious logic and credibility of such a purchase when invasion and siege had interrupted normal life, and when Jeremiah was announcing the cap-

25. Gottwald, *AKE,* 265–66; Carroll, *From Chaos to Covenant,* 203–4.

ture of the city, prompted the prophet to interpret the purchase as a sign of the future renewal of socioeconomic life in Judah: "Houses and fields and vineyards shall again be bought in this land!" (32:15). Although 32:36–41 embellishes the action with reference to a return of exiles, the central reference of the symbolically interpreted purchase appears to have been to renewed life in Judah among those who would stay in the land, pointing to a regime of reconstruction to be launched by the Neo-Babylonians.

4. *"The Little Book of Comfort" and the New Covenant.* Collected in chaps. 30—31 are prophecies of salvation to follow disaster, forming what has been called "a little book of comfort." Which, if any, of these prophecies stem from the prophet is a matter of dispute. Those who attribute them at least partially to Jeremiah have usually situated them either toward the beginning of the prophet's career in the reign of Josiah or at the end during the reconstruction regime of Gedaliah. In either case, the theme of the reunion of north and south struck in these oracles would have a possible context in hopeful political circumstances. Most likely they are a potpourri of promissory pieces from the exilic Jeremianic traditionists who reworked units from Jeremiah and developed more encouraging words of their own.

This collection contains the famous "new covenant" passage which foresees a fresh relationship between Israel/Judah and Yahweh that is internally grounded and motivated, no longer requiring external admonition and teaching, yet thoroughly communal. Christian readings of this passage as an anticipation of the new covenant in Jesus Christ (cf. Luke 22:20; 1 Cor. 11:25; Heb. 8:8–13; 10:16) have frequently distorted it into a highly individualized and spiritualized expectation. While the promise may very well presuppose the end of cult, it nonetheless envisions the realization of the old laws in a corporate body continuous with old Israel. It reads like the work of an exilic Jeremianic preacher who has pulled together aspects of the prophet's thought into a bold formulation of radical renewal.

Jeremiah also produced a number of individual laments in which he speaks in the first person about his mission, his opponents, his frustrations, and his self-doubts, sometimes cast in the form of dialogue between himself and deity (11:18–23; 12:1–6; 15:10–12, 15–21; 17:14–18; 18:18–23; 20:7–18). In modern critical scholarship these have customarily been called Jeremiah's "Confessions," eagerly fastened on for their disclosures about the man's personal thoughts and feelings concerning his task, especially welcome since the Hebrew Bible gives us few such "introspections."[26] Form

---

26. John Skinner, *Prophecy and Religion. Studies in the Life of Jeremiah* (Cambridge: At the University Press, 1922), 201–30.

401

critics and tradition-historical critics, on the other hand, have countered this tendency toward romanticization of the prophet's anguish by underscoring that the language of the prophet is typical lament language and that the "I" of the prophet is vicarious in that he functions as the spokesman for the desolation and alienation of his people. They caution that his remarks should not be taken too autobiographically, and certainly not as though they were comparable to the confessional genre of an Augustine or a Rousseau.

There is much value in these reminders about the corporate context of Jeremiah's words and deeds.[27] Nonetheless, there are aspects of individual torment that cannot be expunged from the laments and that vividly highlight the human struggle Jeremiah waged to sustain his work in the face of opposition so great that at times he had to reassess the grounds, motives, and resources of his calling. We learn of his voluntary desistance from marriage, his withdrawal from feasts and funerals, the scoffing and plots on his life from friends and relatives, his accusations of desertion and deception against Yahweh, his conclusion to speak the truth he knew in spite of consequences, and the fortification of resolve that he received from his religious commitment. The "cultic" interpretation of the "confessions" does contain the valid proviso that all these sufferings of the prophet were experienced as a fate with and on behalf of his people, none of which would have made any sense to him apart from his role as an interpreter of communal traditions in a crisis period of national history.

Particularly striking is Jeremiah's head-on confrontation with prophets who first promised the invulnerability of Jerusalem and, after 597, the speedy return of the king and deported leaders. Jeremiah accuses these prophets of following visions of their own making and of stealing one another's words: they are glib triflers with the welfare of Judah who simply do not have a word from Yahweh. The crisis in prophetic credibility when prophets gave contradictory words from Yahweh is dramatized by the encounter of Hananiah and Jeremiah, the former predicting a return of Jehoiachin and the exiles within two years, while the latter insisted that there would be decades of bondage to Babylon (chap. 28).

It is evident, however, that this was not simply a narrow religious issue over who had the best foresight into coming events. Considerable sociopolitical information in the Book of Jeremiah reveals two opposed alignments of prophets, priests, and political leaders crystallized around

27. Carroll, *From Chaos to Covenant*, 107–30.

antagonistic political programs in the period 609–586.[28] The kings and a majority of bureaucrats, priests, and prophets formed an "autonomy" party that sought independence from Babylon with the aid of Egypt. The prophet Hananiah, with whom Jeremiah heatedly clashed over the expected length of exile (chap. 28), was of this persuasion.[29] A smaller group of court officials (including the family of Shaphan who had been active in the Deuteronomic Reformation), Jeremiah (and perhaps other prophets such as Uriah of Kiriath-jearim [26:20–23], possibly Habakkuk [?]), and perhaps some priests, formed a "coexistence" party which favored continued submission to Babylonia or, once revolt had broken out, capitulation to the besieging enemy.

There are also discernible differences in the domestic assessments and policies of these two parties. The anti-Babylonian "autonomists" equated "national survival" with the full independence of Judah under its present leadership, whereas the pro-Babylonian "coexisters" equated "national survival" with the socioeconomic and religiocultural preservation of the people of Judah. The "autonomists" saw the ruling class as faithful representatives of the people's interests and, therefore, its overthrow would mean the downfall of the people. The "coexisters," by contrast, viewed the internal socioeconomic policies of the ruling class as disastrous to the interests of the people, and saw any strengthening of that ruling class against Babylon as an indefensible promotion of social injustice that would only further harm the common people. On the other hand, submission to or cooperation with Babylon would offer openings for renewed reformation along the lines of Josiah's aborted efforts.

In short, autonomists saw the main clash or contradiction in the situation to be an interstate conflict between Judah and Babylon, whereas coexisters saw the main clash or contradiction to be an interclass conflict between the opposed interests of the ruling class and the majority populace of Judah. For autonomists it was the will of Yahweh, expressed through his prophets (Hananiah, etc.), to preserve Judah under its present regime and prevailing policies. For coexisters it was the will of Yahweh, expressed through his prophets (Jeremiah, etc.), to preserve the people of Judah by sweeping

28. Burke O. Long, "Social Dimensions of Prophetic Conflict," *Semeia* 21 (1981): 31–53, with response by Gottwald, 107–9. Carroll, *From Chaos to Covenant*, 136–97, collects and comments, often astutely, on texts that treat Jeremiah's conflicts with kings and prophets, but generally from the perspective of exilic redactors rather than in the direct terms of sociopolitical organization and conflict in the late Kingdom of Judah.

29. Henri Mottu, "Jeremiah vs. Hananiah: Ideology and Truth in Old Testament Prophecy," in *BL*, 235–51.

away the present leadership and policies through a purging Neo-Babylonian military and political action.

In all probability both parties were headed by socially prominent and powerful persons. There was a division in the ruling class, one segment seeing internal socioeconomic and cultural oppression as central to the determination of foreign policy, whereas the other segment either did not recognize oppression within Judah or merely dismissed it as exaggerated or trumped-up and, in any case, inconsequential in comparison to the threat of foreign domination. In terms of anthropological and sociological perspectives on prophecy, Jeremiah and his allies occupied the dangerous position of "peripheral" irritants who sought to become "central" influencers of powerholders. Jeremiah and allies were "outsiders" in the sense that the public policies they fought for lost out, but they were "insiders" in the sense that their point of view was vigorously represented within the establishment before it was finally vanquished and its advocates neutralized.

As in many instances in the Hebrew Bible, it is not clear how far or in which form the split in ruling circles extended into the general populace. We do not know the extent to which the disputing coalitions were directly linked to a base in the general populace, either through attempts of the disputants to mobilize people behind their positions or through sectors of the populace pressing the leaders to adopt one or another state policy. It is known from contemporary military correspondence, the Lachish letters (table 1: 4L), that opposition to the revolt against Babylon was a serious issue within the Jerusalem court and the army ranks. Jeremiah's opponents believed that he had great power to sway people to his treasonous views and thus to undercut national unity in the war effort.

It is sensible to expect that many of the long-suffering peasants of Judah sympathized with popular preaching that implied or advocated policies that would lighten their burdens and spare them more war and hardship. Nevertheless, neither mob actions nor organizing activities among them is reported. Also, as far as we can judge, Jeremiah and the other coexisters did not attempt a coup or uprising against Jerusalem leadership but depended on the impending intervention of Babylon to overturn a status quo they viewed as prejudicial to the real interests of the people and inimical to the known will of Yahweh (§36.5).

PART IV

HOME RULE UNDER GREAT EMPIRES: ISRAEL'S COLONIAL RECOVERY

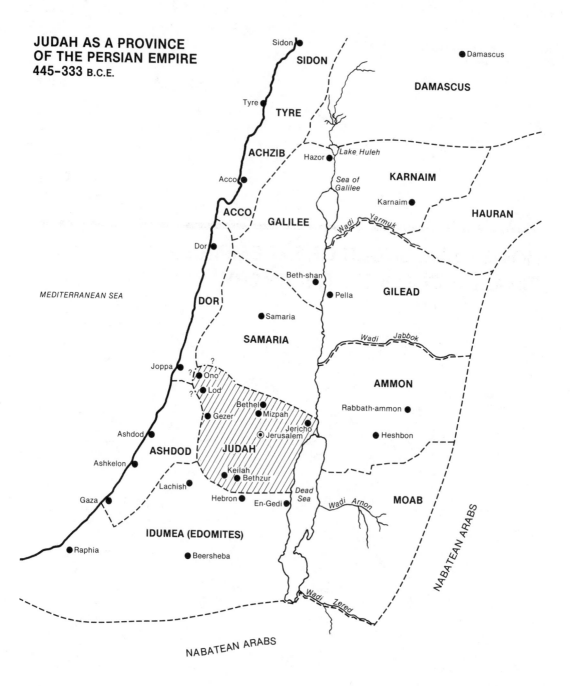

JUDAH AS A PROVINCE OF THE PERSIAN EMPIRE
445–333 B.C.E.

Sidon

SIDON

● Damascus

DAMASCUS

Tyre

TYRE

ACHZIB

Hazor ● *Lake Huleh*

Acco ●

ACCO

Sea of Galilee

KARNAIM

Karnaim ●

HAURAN

Dor ●

GALILEE

Wadi *Yarmuk*

MEDITERRANEAN SEA

DOR

Beth-shan ●

● Pella

GILEAD

● Samaria

SAMARIA

Wadi *Jabbok*

Joppa ●

?

? Ono ●

? Lod ●

Bethel ●

Gezer ● ● Mizpah

Jericho ●
◉ Jerusalem

AMMON

Rabbath-ammon ●

● Heshbon

Ashdod ●

ASHDOD

JUDAH

Ashkelon ●

Keilah ●
Bethzur ●

Lachish ●

Hebron ● ● En-Gedi

Dead Sea

Wadi *Arnon*

MOAB

Gaza ●

IDUMEA (EDOMITES)

Raphia ●

● Beersheba

Wadi *Zered*

NABATEAN ARABS

NABATEAN ARABS

| **SIDON** | Persian provinces in the satrapy "beyond the river" |

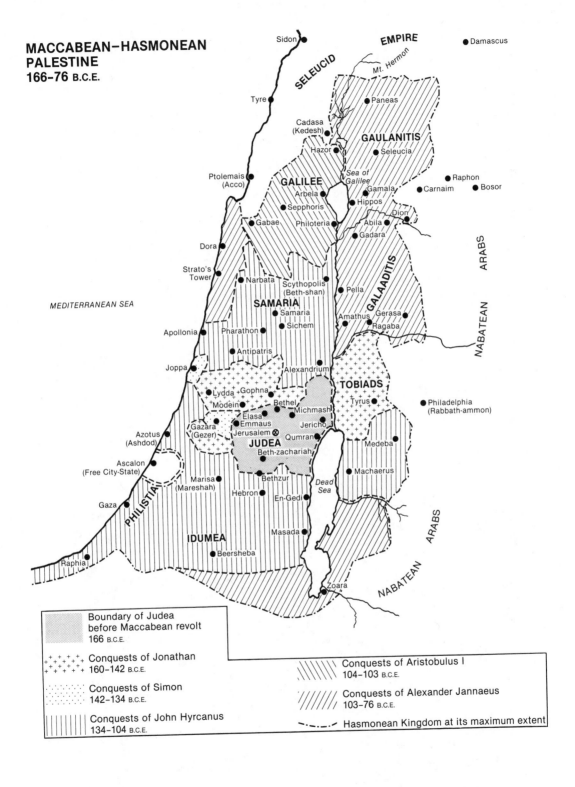

MACCABEAN–HASMONEAN PALESTINE 166–76 B.C.E.

SELEUCID EMPIRE

Sidon

Damascus

Mt. Hermon

Tyre

Paneas

GAULANITIS

Cadasa (Kedesh)

Hazor

Seleucia

Ptolemais (Acco)

GALILEE

Sea of Galilee

Raphon

Arbela

Gamala

Carnaim

Bosor

Sepphoris

Hippos

Gabae

Philoteria

Dion

Abila

Gadara

GALAADITIS

Dora

ARABS

Strato's Tower

Narbata

Scythopolis (Beth-shan)

Pella

MEDITERRANEAN SEA

SAMARIA

Samaria

Amathus

Gerasa

Ragaba

Sichem

NABATEAN

Apollonia

Pharathon

Antipatris

Joppa

Alexandrium

TOBIADS

Lydda

Gophna

Modein

Bethel

Tyrus

Philadelphia (Rabbath-ammon)

Elasa

Michmash

Emmaus

Jericho

Gazara (Gezer)

Jerusalem ⊗

Qumran

Azotus (Ashdod)

JUDEA

Medeba

Beth-zachariah

Ascalon (Free City-State)

Marisa (Mareshah)

Bethzur

Machaerus

Hebron

En-Gedi

Dead Sea

Gaza

PHILISTIA

Masada

IDUMEA

Beersheba

ARABS

Raphia

NABATEAN

Zoara

Boundary of Judea before Maccabean revolt 166 B.C.E.

+ + + + + Conquests of Jonathan 160–142 B.C.E.

Conquests of Simon 142–134 B.C.E.

Conquests of John Hyrcanus 134–104 B.C.E.

Conquests of Aristobulus I 104–103 B.C.E.

Conquests of Alexander Jannaeus 103–76 B.C.E.

Hasmonean Kingdom at its maximum extent

On the Sources for Israel's Colonial History in Dispersion and Restoration

38
DEMARCATION OF THE HISTORICAL PERIOD

We have been able to account for the oldest parts of the Hebrew Bible as the writings of a politically independent people who, from the thirteenth century B.C.E. on, lived in a relatively small region near the southernmost end of the Syro-Palestinian corridor that joined Mesopotamia and Egypt. Beginning with the sixth century, however, the former geographic and sociohistoric frameworks of ancient Israel shifted radically.

The people of Israel were increasingly scattered into foreign lands—by deportation, expulsion, and emigration—and they no longer ruled themselves at their own pleasure but were subjects of great imperial powers. In succession, their political overlords were Neo-Babylonia, Persia, Macedonia, Ptolemaic Egypt, and Seleucid Syria. These new conditions posed far-reaching challenges to the self-identity, ideology, and organizational life of the self-conscious descendants of old Israel. It is in this period that the name $y^e h\bar{u}d\bar{\imath}m$, formerly restricted to "Judahites" (inhabitants of Judah), came to mean "Jews" (adherents of the religion of Yahweh as interpreted in the Law and the Prophets).

The segment of this later history that we shall trace extends from the destruction of Jerusalem in 586 B.C.E. to Pompey's imposition of Roman rule on Palestine in 63 B.C.E. Our choice of the introduction of Roman dominion as a terminal date is shaped by the fact that this was the first major political breaking point following the completion of all the writings that were to be included in the Hebrew Bible. The cutoff date of 63 B.C.E. is arbitrary in the sense that, for a full accounting of why the Prophets and Writings came to stand alongside the Law as Scripture, it is necessary to take into account the triumph of the Pharisees as the shapers of Judaism following the unsuccessful War against Rome in 66–70 C.E. (§11.2.b). Nonetheless, the roots of some of the major ingredients in the emergence of Rabbinic Judaism can be identified prior to 63 B.C.E., since it was in the Maccabean-Hasmonean period (167–63 B.C.E.) that Jewish nationalism flared into political independence and the community was torn by internal strife among contending groups and strategies. These disputes and conflicts remained unresolved until the later war with Rome and the victory of Rabbinic Judaism over all rival ways of interpreting and living the Jewish religion.

39
BIBLICAL AND EXTRABIBLICAL SOURCES

There are major problems in reconstructing the exilic and postexilic history of the Jews, owing to meager and spotty biblical records that depend for their interpretation on supplementary extrabiblical information which is itself in rather short supply. Many key questions in this later biblical history must be answered by inference and conjecture. This does not mean that the later period was literarily inactive; in fact, the contrary was true. All three parts of the Hebrew Bible were edited in this period (§11.2.a). Moreover, there was abundant production of new writings that eventually found their way into the Law, the Prophets, or the Writings (§41), sometimes intertwined with or appended to preexilic writings and sometimes standing on their own. The difficulty is that hard historical data are scant except for the Maccabean-Hasmonean era. Some of this slack is taken up by Greco-Roman historians and by administrative documents from the great empires under which the Jews lived, and the archaeology of the Persian and Hellenistic periods in Palestine has been able to make important contributions.

It is instructive to compare the types and distributions of our historical sources for the earlier and later phases of biblical Israel. For the preexilic history of tribal and monarchic Israel we have fairly full, more or less continuous, data. This information appears in a body of literature that is either explicitly historical in interest (annalistic portions of DH), or at least history-like in its sequential organization of major themes and framed narratives (the structure of JE and DH), or contains episodic and thematic references to datable events or epochs (prophetic literature). In large measure, the preexilic history is given a biblical frame, however much it is necessary to modify the traditional views of editors who worked schematically and from hindsight.

For exilic and postexilic history there is nothing to equal the fullness and continuity of the historical and history-like materials of earlier Israel. The Priestly document of course gives a narrative but it covers the same era as the JE documents, ending with the conquest of the land, and thus has no direct bearing on late biblical history. The DH source extends only into the exile as far as 561 B.C.E. The last great history-like compilation within the Hebrew Bible is 1 and 2 Chronicles, Ezra, and Nehemiah (§51). Chronicles retraces the historical eras treated by JEP and DH, but omits telling us anything about the exile other than that Cyrus ended it. Ezra and Nehemiah clarify aspects of the reconstruction of Judah and give scattered clues to Jewish life in Babylonia and Persia, restricting themselves to a few high points beginning in 538 B.C.E. and ending in the period ca. 432–398 B.C.E. (depending on the date given to Ezra). Within this span of time, the period from 515 to ca. 458–445 B.C.E. (again depending on the Ezra date) is unreported by Ezra and Nehemiah.

The next great block of Jewish historiography is 1 and 2 Maccabees (in the Apocrypha) which treats the Maccabean revolt and the early Hasmonean dynasty from 186 to 135 B.C.E. Josephus, writing at the end of the first century C.E., drawing on traditional lore and the works of earlier Jewish Hellenistic historians as well as on the Bible, recounts the whole history from 586 to 63 B.C.E. in books X–XIV of his *Jewish Antiquities.* Josephus turns out to be our sole connected source for the more than two hundred years from 432–398 B.C.E. (end of Ezra-Nehemiah) to 186 B.C.E. (beginning of 1 and 2 Maccabees). Due to the limitations of Josephus's sources, even his recital of Jewish life under the late Persian kings, Alexander the Great, and the Ptolemaic rulers is sketchy over much of its course and confused at points.

Prophetic writings of Ezekiel and Isaiah of the Exile (Isaiah 40—55) obliquely provide valuable limited historical data on the Babylonian exile, as does Lamentations for exilic conditions in Palestine. The prophetic Books of Haggai and Zechariah 1—8 are important for documenting the rebuilding of the temple in 520–516 B.C.E., and Isaiah 56—66, Malachi, and Joel among the late prophetic writings throw light on communal conditions in restored Israel within the broad period 538–450 B.C.E. Daniel's propaganda piece for Jewish resistance, veiled as if written by a Jew in Neo-Babylonian captivity, actually dates from the Maccabean War against the Seleucids, 167–164 B.C.E., but may include older traditions of some historical value.

The remainder of the canonical writings are in literary genres that do not use historical modes of expression or attach obviously to particular historical milieus. They consist of cult lyrics (Psalms; Lamentations), love songs (Song of Songs), short stories (Ruth; Jonah; Esther), didactic wisdom (Proverbs; Job; Ecclesiastes), and symbolic prophecies with obscure references to historical events (Isaiah 24—27; Zechariah 9—14). In all these writings, the connections to particular historical contexts are highly problematic. Psalms and Proverbs are postexilic collections of originally separate songs and maxims, and those bearing the most substantial historical references are oriented to older monarchic institutions and happenings.

Since the biblical books and sections of books written after 586 B.C.E. are so meager in historical reference, it is difficult to construct a history of the literature in other than very general terms. The intriguing question of the social location of the various streams of tradition, such as law, prophecy, psalms, wisdom, and apocalyptic, and of their place in the conflict-ridden sociopolitical and religious history of the time, has proven just as difficult to answer (chart 12; Conclusion). Some progress in social scientific criticism can be expected as more attention is paid to the socioeconomic structural realities of subject peoples in the great empires of late antiquity.

Fortunately, there are extrabiblical Jewish writings in the Apocrypha and Pseudepigrapha (§10.2.a; tables 5–6) that illuminate the cultural and intellectual conditions of Jews in the Hellenistic Dispersion, especially in Egypt, and to a lesser extent aspects of Palestinian Jewry in Hellenistic times. The same sources, along with the Dead Sea Scrolls (§10.2.b; table 7) and early rabbinic traditions (§10.2.c), helpfully clarify the proliferation of traditions and parties in Palestine from 200 B.C.E. onward.

The recovery of occasional contemporary documents has enriched our knowledge of particular points in exilic and postexilic history: (1) the ration system of the Neo-Babylonians for royal captives (Weidner tablets [table 1: 5A]); (2) economic activities among Babylonian Jews in the fifth century (Murashu texts);[1] (3) cultic institutions among Egyptian Jews at the end of the fifth century (Elephantine papyri [table 1: 5D]); (4) political events in Samaria under Alexander the Great (Samaria or Wadi Dâliyeh papyri);[2] and (5) the political and economic administration of Ptolemaic Palestine (Zeno papyri).[3] Archaeology continues to illuminate trade and political administrative practices, and has assisted in fixing the third century B.C.E. as the likely time of the foundation of the Samaritan temple on Mt. Gerizim. A wealth of archaeological data on the earliest synagogues, all from Greco-Roman times, has yielded nothing to favor the long-popular view that the synagogue originated as early as the Babylonian exile. The earliest appearance of the synagogue seems to have been about 250 B.C.E.

40
DECLINE OF LATE BIBLICAL HISTORIOGRAPHY

Why do the later writings of the Hebrew Bible reflect such a diminished interest in large historical frameworks as compared with the older biblical writings? The answer to that question lies in a complex of factors, all of which have to do with the profound shock that Israel underwent in the transition from political independence to colonial servitude. Limited in their ability to determine their own destiny, the Jews experienced an incongruity between the promises of a great future in their older traditions and the narrowed material and political conditions experienced under foreign rule as a colonial people.

No historical or history-like overview of the entire span of Jewish colonial

1. On the Murashu tablets: D. Winton Thomas, ed., *Documents from Old Testament Times* (London: Thomas Nelson & Sons, 1958), 95–96.

2. On the Samaria or Dâliyeh papyri: Paul W. Lapp and Nancy Lapp, *Discoveries in the Wadi-ed-Dâliyeh* (AASOR 41, 1974).

3. On the Zeno(n) papyri: Victor A. Tcherikover and A. Fuks, *Corpus Papyrorum Judaicarum* (Cambridge: Harvard University Press, 1957), 1:1–47.

experience was attempted after the exile. The Priestly document (§11.2) reframed the sacred preconquest foundation period according to needs of the present. Structurally, the Chronicler (§12.1) imitated DH's project in Samuel-Kings. Ezra-Nehemiah (§10.3; 12.1), which did extend the history, limited its account to four short moments in the political and cultic reconstruction of Judah. As far as we know, no one wrote a history of the Neo-Babylonian exile or attempted to recount the succession of commissioners/governors and high priests in Judah, nor did anyone attend to what remains the "dark period" from 400 to 200 B.C.E. The Israelite sense of "making history" was attenuated. In just this climate the Law, and then the Prophets, stood out as collections of witnesses to a great past which was no longer matched in contemporary Jewish experience.

In Seleucid and Roman times, when major revolts shook Jewish Palestine—and when for about a century Jews were again politically independent—there was an outburst of historiography best surviving in 1 and 2 Maccabees and in Josephus. Interestingly, the Books of Maccabees did not enter the canon, in spite of their thrilling accounts of Jewish national revival, because they were written in Greek and celebrated political solutions which had become dubious, even counterproductive, to the rabbinic leaders who rounded out the Hebrew Bible after the disastrous War against Rome.

There were a considerable number both of Jewish historians, mostly from the Diaspora, and of Greek and Roman authors from the second century B.C.E. to the second century C.E. who provide us with limited information about Palestine in that period.[4] Unfortunately, their works are preserved only in partial or fragmentary form, sometimes incorporated into 2 Maccabees and Josephus. The Greco-Roman interest in contemporary historiography seems not to have motivated Palestinian Jews until the explosive Maccabean age. Thus, the phasing out of late biblical interest in historiography prior to 1 and 2 Maccabees seems to be a corollary of the move toward authoritative traditions about a more distant past whose interpretation set the norms for a community that felt marginated from the decisive currents of contemporary history. The diminishment of prophecy as a movement of critical interpreters of present history was also a facet of this sense of history being made "over the heads" of the Jews. Religiously, this sense of powerlessness was expressed in terms of faithful preservation of the glorious history of God's past deeds in Israel during a period of "marking time" and "making do" with cult, wisdom, and apocalyptic (§12.2; 12.4–5).

4. Peter Schäfer in *IJH*, 544–47.

41
ORGANIZING THE PRESENTATION OF LATE BIBLICAL LITERATURE

All in all, the paucity of historical sources in comparison with the fullness of "free-floating" religious writings in colonial Israel makes it difficult to organize the presentation of the later parts of the Hebrew Bible along the historical lines suitable to the preexilic traditions. Interpreters of postexilic times have sometimes attempted to present the literature in chronological order, but this approach makes central a temporal criterion that cannot be reasonably satisfied for many biblical books and only tends to draw attention away from the parallel development of bodies of tradition and their interaction in the community.

Sometimes syntheses of the period have been organized around central and peripheral institutions and bodies of tradition, characteristically placing *law* and *temple cult* at the center and treating *wisdom* and *apocalyptic* as eccentric departures from the norm. This approach tends to overstate the primacy of the "core" features, as though they were exclusive monopolies on religious interest and expression, and thus risks severing the various institutional and literary components from the start. Likewise, it leaves *prophecy* in limbo, since prophecy was "primary" as a body of accepted tradition but "peripheral" as a current institutional force.

The wisest procedure, especially in a treatment of literary traditions in their sociohistoric context, is to characterize the sociohistoric developments as precisely as possible and then to examine the late literature of the Hebrew Bible along a line of distinction between those exilic and postexilic writings that went into *the completion of the first two segments of the Hebrew Bible* (the Law and the Prophets), and those exilic and postexilic writings that eventually fell into a *third and entirely separate collection* (the Writings). The miscellaneous Writings developed as a collection of "other books" partly because some of them were written after the Law and Prophets were brought to completion as collections and partly because many of them exhibited literary genres and ideological outlooks that were either altogether absent from Law and Prophets or constituted minor aspects of the older narrative and prophetic writings.

In choosing this literary-canonical principle of division for treatment of the later biblical literature, we must be on our guard against an overly restrictive literary approach that neglects the literature as an expression of social reality and also against an overly rigid canonical outlook that retrojects the later decisions about canon into the earlier periods. In particular, we must put out of our minds any notion of a prejudgment that there was to be a canon composed of three parts and of so many books, and that writers, editors, and collectors labored at filling out the agreed prescriptions.

The whole of the Hebrew Bible, as we have stressed, grew by parts and in stages, and determinations of what was authoritative and what was not were made relative to existing interests and conflicts in the community. At no stage in our period is there any firm evidence that books were rejected from collections because a collection could be only so large or that there could be only so many books of a certain kind in a collection. When valued writings did not enter the Law or the Prophets, they did not cease to be valued in other contexts. On the other hand, they did not automatically become parts of a preestablished third collection that had to be filled out in a certain way. Only at the end of the first century C.E. was the canon of the Hebrew Bible rounded out as a whole, since prior to that time it had not seemed critical for Jews to fix the boundaries of authoritative writings more exactly.

Accordingly, chap. 10 will set forth the known history of late biblical times, observing the interactive dimensions of socioeconomic, political, cultural, and religious realities. The late biblical literary traditions that have direct or indirect bearing on this history will be commented on in context. Pertinent writings of the Apocrypha, Pseudepigrapha, and Dead Sea Scrolls will be alluded to.

In chap. 11 biblical traditions that completed the Law and the Prophets as collections will be considered in their own right. The later prophetic writings can be grouped in rough chronological succession since they yield a modest amount of historical data (table 24).

In chap. 12 we shall examine biblical traditions that extended beyond the literary types, primary interests, or time frames of the Law and the Prophets. These traditions became the eventual canonical collection of Writings, not clearly delineated until the Roman period. We shall group these traditions according to literary genres of historical narratives, songs, wisdom writings, and apocalypses, discussing both the separate books and the sociohistoric settings of the genres (table 25). Among these several genres, only the historical narratives provide significant clues for correlating them to specific postexilic historical events. We shall take occasional comparative note of extrabiblical Jewish writings that throw light on the late biblical works: Tobit, Susanna, Bel and the Dragon, and Judith as short stories; Ben Sira and the Wisdom of Solomon as wisdom writings; and *1 Enoch* as an apocalypse.

Priestly Document (P)   + JE + DH =   The Law and The Former Prophets

Ezekiel

Isaiah of the Exile (Isaiah 40—55)

Haggai

Zechariah 1—8

Obadiah

Isaiah of the Restoration (Isaiah 56—66)

Malachi

Joel

(Jonah)*

Zechariah 9—14

    +   earlier prophetic writings   =   The Latter Prophets

*Although the Book of Jonah is counted one of the Prophets, it is more convenient to treat it among the short stories in keeping with its genre (§53.3).

TABLE 25
Late Biblical Literature That Eventually Formed the Writings

Historical Narratives:
  1 and 2 Chronicles
  Ezra-Nehemiah

Songs:
  Psalms
  Lamentations
  Song of Songs

Short Stories/Novellas:
  Ruth
  Esther
  (Jonah)*

Wisdom Writings:
  Proverbs
  Job
  Ecclesiastes

Apocalypse:
  Daniel

= The Writings

*See note to table 24.

CHAPTER 10

Sociohistoric Horizons of Colonial Israel

Read the Biblical Text
Ezra-Nehemiah
1 and 2 Maccabees

Consult Maps in *MBA*
nos. 165–216

42

FROM INDEPENDENT ISRAELITES TO
COLONIZED JEWS

The customary way to periodize the history of late biblical Israel is to speak of the *exilic* and *postexilic* ages. This division focuses on the deportation of upper-class Judahites to Babylon and their extended captivity there until they were freed by the Persians and those who wished to do so returned to Palestine to repopulate a Jewish province under the Persian Empire. The well-worn exilic/postexilic categories tend, however, to slide over important aspects of the period and even to break apart the fundamental unity of the dispersion/reconstruction process.

For one thing, it is evident that only a fraction of the populace of the state of Judah was exiled to Babylonia. Moreover, many of those who were driven away or fled the land went to foreign lands nearer at hand than Babylonia, such as Transjordan, Phoenicia, Syria, and Egypt. For many, probably a majority of Jews who continued to live in Palestine, there never was an exile in the sense of a deportation or expulsion from the land. Correspondingly, the return of thousands of Jews to Palestine in the century following Cyrus's edict to reconstruct Judah was not a return of all Jews from abroad, probably not even a return of a majority of those in Babylonia and Persia, not to mention the Jews who had scattered to other lands.

"Exile," as commonly understood, suggests a temporary compulsory removal from the land that was completely reversed at the earliest opportunity, whereas increasingly "dispersion" became the reality for large numbers of Jews, and in many instances it was a self-confirmed condition of life preferable to the uncertainties or inequities of life in Palestine. Thus the Neo-Babylonian captivity of the sixth century was only one phase of a larger dispersion of Jews, begun as early as the Assyrian destruction of northern Israel in 722 B.C.E. and accelerated dramatically during the Persian and Hellenistic periods.

In time, the reconstructed community of Judah gave a vital impulse to the survival of Israel, as well as a critical institutional-ideological center and focus for Jewish communities elsewhere, but it could only do so by being in communication with the whole body of Dispersion Jews who during the period came to form a numerical majority spread widely over the Persian and Greco-Roman worlds. It is clear, therefore, that while the terminology of "exile" and "postexile" aptly characterizes the experiences of Jews carried to Babylon who returned under Persian aegis, it does not accurately describe the experience of multitudes of Jews who did not participate in that set of events. For Jewry as a whole, *dispersion* and *restoration* was a larger process in which Jews in Palestine and abroad participated in different ways and which involved the ongoing reciprocal influences of dispersed and restored communities on one another.[1]

In other words, at all times from 586 to 63 B.C.E., there was a Jewish community in Palestine organizing aspects of its own life, in however limited a way, although its renewal by groups of returned exiles in the late sixth and fifth centuries gave it new directions. By the same token, from 586 to 63 B.C.E. there were parallel communities of Jews widely spread abroad, steadily growing in size through emigration due to the push of socioeconomic and political pressures in Palestine and the pull of socioeconomic attractions in the wider world.

Given the dialectical unity of this Jewish dispersion/restoration process within the great empires of the time, it is appropriate to typify the condition and process of Israel's life in this period as "Jewish colonialism" in a twofold sense:

1. *Jewish colonialism as extensive settlement or colonization of Jews in foreign lands.* The old heirs of the tribal system and former subjects of the states of Israel and Judah were deported, scattered by force, or voluntarily emigrated in considerable numbers to form settlements in other lands. There they constituted minorities that nonetheless remained linked by tradition and sentiment to Jerusalem, and perhaps also to Samaria in some cases. After the reconstruction program of Nehemiah and Ezra, these foreign colonies increasingly looked to Jerusalem as the religiocultural center for shaping the essential forms of Jewish religious life while allowing for secondary adaptations dictated by foreign environments.

2. *Jewish colonialism as subservience of all Jews to the political dominion of great empires.* All Jews, whether restored to Judah or colonized abroad, were subject to the sovereign power of the great empires that successively ruled them. The sole exception to this rule was the period of the Jewish Hasmonean dynasty in Palestine from 140 to 63 B.C.E., made possible by structural weaknesses in the Seleucid Empire and ended by the incursion of more stable Roman power into Palestine. The Jewish colonies abroad were not only politically subject but dependent on the toleration of cultural and religious diversity for Jewish survival. The very revival and reconstitution of Judah proper was enabled by the sponsorship of the Persian government, and the main lines of the arrangements devised for limited home rule

---

1. On the chronological phasing and religiocultural conceptualization of "exile" and "restoration," see Peter R. Ackroyd, *Exile and Restoration*, OTL (Philadelphia: Westminster Press, 1968), chaps. I and XIII.

continued to be in effect throughout Persian, Macedonian, Ptolemaic, and early Seleucid times until the outbreak of civil war and open revolt in the Maccabean age. The home rule of Jews in Palestine, divided into political and religious jurisdictions, was a colonial form of rule over which the empire held ultimate veto power. This meant that it was difficult to launch or sustain any institutional changes in Judah that did not meet with the approval of imperial administrative policy.

In sum, "Jewish colonialism" meant that Jews, spread broadly in the ancient world while retaining Jerusalem as their religiocultural center, were subject to imperial rule both at the Palestinian center and in the peripheral colonies. This produced a complex structure of double loyalties and jurisdictions that tended to run at cross-purposes: whereas for Jews *Judah* was the metropolis and *Jewish settlements abroad* were the colonies, for the ancient political world as a whole the regnant great *empire* was the metropolis while Judah was one among a number of semiautonomous *homelands* and the dispersed Jewish settlements were *minority religiocultural communities* among others in the polyglot populace of the empire.

It is consistent with the epochal shift from Israelite autonomy to Israelite colonialism that we should henceforth speak of the Israelite people as Jews. Until 586 B.C.E., the name *yᵉhūdīm* had the restricted meaning of "Judahites" (or "Judeans" in later Latinized form) referring either to members of the tribe of Judah or to citizens of the state of Judah following the division of the united kingdom. This usage continued into the age of dispersion and restoration, but now with reference not to a state of Judah but to the province of Judah as a political subdivision of the great empires or to the region of Judah as the restored homeland and center of Jewish life. The captives from Judah, now settled in Babylonia, could also continue to be known as "Judahites." In time, however, *yᵉhūdīm* was also used in a wider sense to refer to all those who stood in the heritage of old Israel and who followed the religion of Yahweh that was given its definitive character more and more at the initiative of the restored community in Judah.

This broadened sense of *yᵉhūdīm* as "Jews" marked the people primarily with a religiocultural identity that on the one hand linked them to Palestine and its traditions, but on the other hand permitted a fully Israelite and Yahwistic identity in any land where the people happened to live. It is likely that the term "Jews" was first used in this extended sense by Gentiles in foreign lands where the Jews colonized. Indeed, it is common for religious minorities to receive a name from outsiders that eventually is taken up within the community—one such case being the name "Christians" for the early followers of Jesus. In any event, the term must have felt appropriate both to those who lived in Judah, the historic land of the Jews, and to those in Dispersion who looked to Judah to take the lead in religious matters.

43
JEWISH RESPONSE TO NEO-BABYLONIAN DOMINION (586–539 B.C.E.)

The destruction of Jerusalem and the infrastructure of the state of Judah in 586 B.C.E. signaled the decisive shift from "Israelite" autonomy to "Jewish" colonialism. The monarchic state of Judah ceased to exist, and the normal operation of the cult of Yahweh centered at the Jerusalem temple was disrupted. The leadership of the state and of the cult were killed or deported to Babylonia, except for a relatively small number assigned to the administration of the region as a part of the Neo-Babylonian Empire.

This political and religious institutional rupture was enormously consequential. Judah's full political independence was never again to be reestablished except for less than a century in late Hellenistic times and twice briefly during the revolts against Rome in the first two centuries C.E. A religious and cultural restoration did take place slowly and by increments, but only by means of a fundamental alteration of former arrangements. After 586 B.C.E. Jewish history proceeds on a tension-filled "double track" among *Palestinian Jews* and *Dispersion Jews*.

43.1 The Continuing Community in Palestine

Neo-Babylonian deportation and imperial administrative policies profoundly affected how Jewish life developed both in Palestine and abroad. One source reports that forty-six hundred citizens of Judah were deported in three waves (in 597, 586, and 582 B.C.E.), nearly two-thirds of them in the first wave (Jer. 52:28–30). An alternative claim that ten thousand were deported in 597 alone (2 Kings 25:14–17; no figures for the later dates) may include the families of the exiles in contrast to the smaller figures that tallied only the captive officials. In any event, we have to reckon with a forced removal of royalty, state officials, priests, army officers, and artisans who probably constituted no more than 5 percent of the total populace. This left a sizable Jewish settlement in Judah that was shorn of its high-level leadership.

A group of leaders who had been pro-Babylonian opponents of Judah's revolt, headed by Gedaliah, was installed in Mizpah as functionaries in a new unit of Neo-Babylonian administration over Judah. The new colonial administration was decimated by the assassination of Gedaliah. Fearing

Neo-Babylonian reprisals, a large party of survivors fled to Egypt. Other Jews scattered into Transjordanian lands, as well as into Syria and Phoenicia. Counting those who died in the revolt, those deported to Babylonia, and those who fled to other lands, there was a decided drop in the population of Judah. The infrastructure of the surviving Palestinian community was severely strained and had to rebuild its leadership from the ground up. Lamentations (§52.3), a series of public laments over the destruction of Jerusalem, provides brief vignettes of the disruption due to war-damaged agriculture and requisitions of crops and labor imposed by the conquerors.

While it is not clear how Neo-Babylonia administered Judah after the collapse of Gedaliah's regime, there were known aspects of Neo-Babylonian administration that contrast significantly with the policies followed earlier by the Assyrians in colonizing northern Israel after 722 B.C.E. The differences in Assyrian and Neo-Babylonian colonial policy may help to account for the contrasting outcomes of the Samarian and Judahite exiles. The Assyrians replaced deported Israelite leaders with colonists from other parts of the empire, thereby deliberately disturbing the previous social and cultural fabric of the region and making it difficult for a homogeneous Israelite culture and religion to flourish. By contrast, the Neo-Babylonians followed a less decisive policy with Judah. The leadership of Judah deported in 597 was replaced with a "second team" and, when the latter were deported in 586, yet another attempt was made to form a native administration under Gedaliah. The deportation of 582 may have followed in the wake of Gedaliah's assassination.

There is, in short, no indication that Nebuchadnezzar ever introduced foreign populations into Judah. On the other hand, neighboring people were enabled to encroach on the territory of Judah, most strikingly the Edomites who, crossing from Transjordan, settled northward into Judah to a point between Hebron and Bethzur. It is likely that Ammonites and Moabites reclaimed territories in Transjordan and perhaps even west of Jordan, while Samaritans probably pressed into Judah from the north to occupy deserted estates. Nonetheless, there remained a reduced heartland in Judah largely untouched by a residential infusion of foreigners.

Circumstances of life for the surviving Jewish populace must have been arduous. Even if some of those left in the land managed to take over large estates abandoned by deported officials, Neo-Babylonian authorities would have kept a close eye on taxable surpluses. In the DH accounts, the Jews who stayed in Palestine are called "the poor people of the land" (2 Kings 24:14; 25:12), whether with opprobrium, sympathy, or merely as a neutral description is unclear. Although they struggled in a scarcity economy and were inexperienced in state politics, these "poor of the land" tapped a wealth of local custom and were experienced participants and leaders in village cooperative networks. Thus the ancient village tribalism (§24.2.c), overlaid for centuries by monarchy, was able to reemerge as the dominant force in organizing and preserving Palestinian Jewish identity throughout the exile, no matter how much hampered by the imposition of Neo-Babylonian dominion.

Forms of cult continued. The ruined site of the old temple, with its large sacred rock, served as a place of worship, to which pilgrims came from as far as Samaria (Jer. 41:4–8). This worship may well have included animal sacrifices presided over by lower orders of priests who had escaped deportation. Compositions such as Lamentations and Psalms 79, 105—6 were publicly proclaimed on fast days commemorating the catastrophic events of Jerusalem's siege and destruction (Zech. 7:2–7; 8:18–19). A strong if inconclusive case can be made for Palestine as the locale for the final edition of the DH history, and it seems likely that Jeremianic and other prophetic traditions circulated there, although there is no certainty about whether the main literary activity in collecting pentateuchal and prophetic writings occurred in Palestine or in the exile, or was divided between them.

In fact, the prevailing assumption that most of the creative religious initiatives of this period arose among the Babylonian exiles is highly dubious. That assumption is especially questionable because the deported leaders of Judah had been antipathetic to the Deuteronomic reform circles and to the prophets who denounced their revolt against Babylonia. All in all, it seems likely that the Palestinian survivors would have been quicker than the Babylonian exiles to come to terms with the political and cultural debacle by adopting the Deuteronomistic and prophetic interpretations of its causes and lessons and to devote themselves to a Yahwist-oriented communal reconstruction. It is advisable, however, not to overstate the separate developments in Palestine and in the Dispersion, for we know that the two communities of Jews communicated with and influenced one another.

43.2 The Communities in Dispersion

The conditions in which the deported exofficials of Judah were detained are practically undocumented. From brief biblical notations (Ezra 2:59; 3:15) it has been judged that they were kept together in compact groups settled on deserted agricultural sites in Babylonia. It may have been Nebuchadnezzar's intention to hold them in detention until a propitious moment when he might reliably return them to Judah as a monarchist party loyal to him. Some have interpreted the improved conditions of detention for Jehoiachin in 561 (2 Kings 25:27–30) as part of a larger design by Amel-Marduk, Nebuchadnezzar's successor, to reestablish the monarchy in Judah (table 1: 5A). In any event, such a plan was never carried out, perhaps because the new king's reign was cut short after two years. As time went by and prospects of a return of the deportees to Palestine faded, a fair number may have been enlisted in Neo-Babylonian governmental service. Whether the detention camps were dissolved before Cyrus's capture of Babylon, allowing all the captives to find their own way in "open" society, we do not know. The poetry of Isaiah of the Exile, written toward the close of Neo-Babylonian rule, may imply that many Jews at least by then were a part of the cosmopolitan populace of Babylon and very much tempted by the allure of Babylonian religion and culture.

Improvised forms of religion doubtless flourished among Babylonian Jews who remained Yahwists just as they did among Palestinian Jews. Although we have no evidence, it is not impossible that animal sacrifice was observed in Babylon, at least for a while, since the program of Deuteronomic centralization of worship at Jerusalem did not necessarily carry full authority with all the exiles. Prayer and song were certainly practiced.

Two influential prophets worked among the Babylonian exiles, Ezekiel (§50.1) at the beginning of the exile and Isaiah of the Exile (§50.2) toward its end. Both sought to internalize in their audiences the lessons of national apostasy from Yahweh and to prepare them for the uprooting experiences of their forced transplantation. Ezekiel aimed at a consciousness and practice of moral and ceremonial law that would give cohesion to the exiles in line with their ancestral culture. Isaiah of the Exiles tried to alert the exiles to the favorable world conditions that Cyrus the Persian was bringing into being in his conquest of the Neo-Babylonian Empire, thereby unleashing opportunities for a restored Jewish community in Palestine and for Yahwism to become the professed religion of the dawning Persian Empire.

The Priestly document is often assigned an origin among the Babylonian Jews, mainly on the strength of its Babylonian orientation toward the creation and the flood and its equation with the Law of God that Ezra, a Babylonian Jew, brought with him to Palestine in the fifth century (§49). Actually, the Priestly writing may show no more Babylonian influence than appears in biblical traditions from Palestine, and it is far from certain that Ezra's law was the Priestly document. In fact, there are indications that P contains much ancient preexilic material. Granted that the priests who officiated at the Jerusalem temple were carried into exile, it is possible that P traditions had been gathered among priests outside of Jerusalem, or out of power in Jerusalem during the Deuteronomic reform, who were able to compile and expand their traditions in sixth-century Palestine.

Consequently, except for the localization of Ezekiel and Isaiah of the Exile in Babylonia and of Lamentations in Palestine, it is problematic how the other writings of this period should be assigned geographically. Since DH, Jeremiah, and P represent complex collections with preexilic Judean roots, whether brought to completion in their present forms in one place or the other, it is likely that some form of all these bodies of traditions would have been known before long among both Palestinian and Babylonian Jews.

Earlier scholarship was often confident in tracing the origin of the synagogue to Babylonian exile. The sudden cessation of the temple cult seemed a plausible milieu for elevating the written traditions in circles of study and prayer. In reality there is no documentary or archaeological evidence for the synagogue until centuries after the exile. Although the form of small-group study of valued writings during the exile looks superficially like a "synagogue" activity, the essential religious ingredients of the synagogue structure were lacking. There was as yet no canonical text. Not even the Law, much less the Prophets, was complete. Also, when the synagogue did arise it was as a supplement to the restored cult at Jerusalem. During the exile, the Jerusalem cult lay shattered and it was not evident that it could be restored. At most the conventicles of prayerful and studious Jews in exile, or in Palestine, were "proto-synagogal," that is, the protean forerunners of an institution whose preconditions of a canonical Law and an interpretive tradition practiced at a restored Jerusalem were not yet in force.

Our sketch of Jewish life in its Palestinian and Babylonian forms has focused on the communities we know best and presupposes a continuity of Jewish self-identity. In fact, numbers of Jews now lived elsewhere, in Egypt and in Syro-Phoenicia for example, but of whom we know nothing in detail in the sixth century. It is also evident that many Judahites did not make the transition from being Israelites to becoming Jews. They turned to other religions and ceased to be Yahwists. They become worshipers of Canaanite, Babylonian, Egyptian, or other cults. Sooner or later they became indistinguishable from the peoples among whom they lived and their descendants took no part in later Jewish life.

Even among those who remained Yahwists by deliberation there was no single authority to decide or interpret what their identity consisted of precisely. The recognized forms of Jewishness were variable from community to community. Even the centrality of the old homeland became questionable. Many Jews did not wish to return to Palestine when they were once again free to do so. It was not until the reforms of Nehemiah and Ezra in the last half of the fifth century that the outlines of a system of religious authority arose that could replace the shattered emblems and structures of the old religiopolitical unity of the states of Israel and Judah.

44
JEWISH RESPONSE TO PERSIAN DOMINION
(539–332 B.C.E.)

Neo-Babylonia declined rapidly under the internally divisive rule of its last king, Nabonidus (555–539; table 1: 5B), just as a fresh military power from the Iranian highlands was rising meteorically. In 550 B.C.E., Cyrus of Anshan, a petty prince of the Medes—a people who had helped Neo-Babylonia overthrow Assyria—seized the throne of Media and speedily became master of the whole region north and east of Babylonia. The new empire was known as Persia, from Pasargadae, one of the tribes of Cyrus's native Anshan. By 539 B.C.E., Persia had captured Babylon, apparently with the complicity of high Babylonian officials and Marduk priests who had become disaffected by Nabonidus's misrule. By adding the former Neo-Babylonian Empire to their vast holdings in Anatolia and Iran, the Persians suddenly ruled over a territory more than twice the size of any previous empire in the region. Their hegemony extended from the border of India to the Aegean Sea opposite Greece and southward through Egypt.

Cyrus inaugurated a Persian program of extending to certain subject peoples considerable local autonomy and respect for their indigenous cultural and religious life. Combined with an improved communication system and a tight espionage and police apparatus, he sought to integrate the vast empire into a viable political whole. Reversing the locally disruptive policies of the Assyrians and Neo-Babylonians, Cyrus selectively returned captive peoples to their homelands and restored their lapsed religious cults.[2] The edict of Cyrus to return Jewish exiles to Judah and to rebuild their temple could be pictured by Jews as a partisan Yahwist affirmation (1 Chron. 36:22–23; Ezra 1:1–4 [table 1: 5C]), but from the Persian viewpoint it was merely one instance of a wider policy of restoring colonial subjects when it seemed politically judicious, as evidenced in the more neutral and

---

2. A caution against overstating Persian tolerance and sponsorship of indigenous cultures and religions of the empire is expressed in Amélie Kuhrt, "The Cyrus Cylinder and the Achaemenid Imperial Policy," *JSOT* 25 (1983): 83–97.

matter-of-fact Aramaic version of the edict drawn from state archives (Ezra 6:1–5).

The fundamental features of Persian colonial restoration policy are known, but the exact stages by which Judah was reconstituted and the precise divisions of political jurisdiction are clouded in dispute. The major administrative subdivisions of the Persian Empire were immense entities called satrapies ("protectorates"), each being further divided into provinces. Judah fell within the satrapy "Beyond the River" (i.e., Trans-Euphrates) which included the whole of Syria and Palestine. Whether Judah had the status of a separate province from the start, or fell under the authority of the province of Samaria, at least until the time of Nehemiah, is unclear. In any event, the leadership within the restored Jewish community was split into civil and religious spheres of responsibility, respectively delegated to a governor and a chief priest.

It is uncertain whether the chief civil officer in Judah prior to the appointment of Nehemiah was in fact a full governor, since Sheshbazzar and Zerubbabel may actually have had circumscribed authority as deputies over delegations of returnees. This question is closely related to the issue of Judah's independence from or subordination to Samaria within the Persian imperial administration. The attempts of Samaritan authorities to intervene in the rebuilding of the Jerusalem temple may be construed either as the exercise of their legitimate authority or as extralegal meddling. Our difficulties in forming secure judgments on aspects of the Persian administration in Judah follows from the episodic and scrambled sources whose use of political terminology may be imprecise and, at times, anachronistic.[3]

It is evident that the colonial restoration of Judah proceeded slowly and by increments, partly because the Persians were involved in projects over a vast empire and partly because they relied on Jewish leadership for the restoration of the community. Although the Persians provided overall military security and physical resources in some quantity, it took a long while to rebuild the weakened socioeconomic fabric of Judah. Also, because the Jewish restoration required a reconciliation of the interests of Palestinian Jews and Jews repatriated from Babylon, the forging of a consensus—or, failing that, the achievement of sufficient power by one leading group to make its policies prevail—required many twists and turns of political maneuvering. Moreover, among the Palestinian Jews there were those who

3. Sean E. McEvenue, "The Political Structure in Judah from Cyrus to Nehemiah," *CBQ* 44 (1981): 353–64.

gave their allegiance to the Samaritan form of Jewish religion that had developed among the descendants of the former northern kingdom of Israel. The competing religiocultural alternatives of Samaritan and Judahite Yahwism were in turn intertwined with socioeconomic and political rivalries.

The restoration of colonial Judah is described as occurring in four stages, each connected with a Jewish leader from the exile sent to Judah under Persian authority. The status and sequence of these reformers, and the scope of the measures they enacted, is a matter of dispute since the confused sources permit of various interpretations.

44.1 Mission of Sheshbazzar in 538 B.C.E.

Shortly after the decree of Cyrus, a delegation of exilic Jews was sent by the Persian court to lay the groundwork for reestablishing the Judahite community (Ezra 1:5–11; 5:13–15). The head of the mission was Sheshbazzar, said to be a Judahite prince, and perhaps to be equated with Shenazzar reckoned to the Davidic line (1 Chron. 3:17–18). The size of the attempted resettlement of exilic Jews in Judah at this time is unreported, and there is considerable doubt whether the rebuilding of the temple was a part of the mission's assignment. Sheshbazzar may not have been sent as "governor" of a fully projected province but as head of an investigative team to gather information, possibly with limited charges to begin purification of the cult. No mention is made, however, of a chief priest sharing in Sheshbazzar's mission.

44.2 Mission of Zerubbabel and Joshua in 520 B.C.E.

With the death of Cyrus's successor Cambyses, a major uprising shook the Persian Empire. As part of an effort to pacify the empire, Darius decided to launch a more serious drive to recolonize Judah as a strategic military and political salient on the frontier with troublesome Egypt. In 520 B.C.E., Zerubbabel was made civil commissioner and Joshua high priest at the head of a large immigration of exilic Jews to Judah (Ezra 2:2b–70//Neh. 7:7b–73).

The returnees are detailed in subgroups ("descendants of x" or "inhabitants of x") verified as true descendants of the first exiles. They are pictured as resettling their former towns, while the provincial officials and primary temple personnel among them were placed in Jerusalem and vicinity, lesser temple attendants being assigned towns of their own.

The purpose of the genealogical list of returnees and the basis for calculating the numerical totals are problematic. The list has been variously interpreted as a Persian census of the province of Judah, as a list of returnees (and some non-exiled Palestinians?) with entitlements to land, as a compilation of lists of returnees between 538 and 520 B.C.E. (possibly extending to a later date), or as a legitimation of those who belonged to the true cult community of Yahweh distinguished from illegitimate Samaritans. According to which of these understandings of the document is favored, the numerical totals may refer to the entire population of Judah as of 520 B.C.E., or to the landed citizenry, or to a cumulative total of returnees from two or more migrations, or to the members of the cult community who were authorized to take part in the rebuilding and ceremony of the temple. Nearly fifty thousand people (are only males counted?) seems a large figure for any single movement of Jews from Babylon to Judah, whereas that figure is probably too small for the total population of Judah. It is likely that the fifty thousand refers to the privileged classes who controlled the colonial administration, the cult, and the best lands.

The temple was rebuilt under Zerubbabel and Joshua in the period 520–515 B.C.E. (Ezra 5:1–2; Hag. 1:1—2:9; Zech. 4:9). It is reported that the Samaritans, rebuffed from participation in rebuilding the temple, managed to interrupt work on the structure by bringing charges to the Persians that the reconstruction of the temple was part of a general Judahite scheme of insurrection (Ezra 4). After investigation of the charges demonstrated them to be groundless, the completion of the temple was permitted (Ezra 5—6). The civil head of the mission, Zerubbabel, is identified as of Davidic lineage (Ezra 3:2, 8; 5:2; Hag. 1:1, etc.). Prophetic references to Zerubbabel in an openly messianic vein (Hag. 2:20–23; Zech. 3:8; 4:6–7; 6:12), together with his unexplained disappearance from the scene, have been taken to point to a failed Judahite bid for independence which he initiated. In the absence of positive evidence, the notion of "Zerubbabel's revolt" remains conjectural. The same is true of claims for Judahite participation in uprisings against Persia on one or more occasions during the two centuries of Persian hegemony in the ancient Near East. It is evident that these revolts, customarily spearheaded by Egypt or Phoenicia and aided by Greece, were more recurrent and threatening to the stability of the empire than earlier biblical historians recognized. There are also archaeological indicators of considerable destruction to Palestinian cities in the fifth and fourth centuries. Lacking, however, is documentary evidence of Judah's participation in any of these revolts, while the Palestinian destruction that has been unearthed lies almost entirely outside of the province of Judah.[4]

4. Geo Widengren, in *IJH*, 500–503.

The periodic disturbances in the western part of the empire help to account for Persian commitment to strengthening reforms in Judah so as to secure the province as a bastion on the western frontier facing Egypt. By the same token, the reforming forces in Judah came to rely on Persian support against their Samaritan and internal Judahite opposition. Given the legitimate security fears of the Persians, it is understandable that the Jewish reestablishment in Palestine was consciously shaped by its leaders in politically neutral or collaborative directions in order to reassure the Persian lords that Jews were loyal subjects. No doubt there were periodic Judahite calculations of the feasibility of revolt, and the Samaritans nurtured hopes that the Judahites would be foolish enough to rebel. The Judahite leadership, however, had every reason to adhere closely to an imperial overlord whose support was crucial in implanting and enforcing the cult reformation they wanted.

44.3 Mission of Nehemiah in 445–430 B.C.E.

Whatever may have been the status of Jewish civil officials previously, Nehemiah clearly was sent to Judah as governor of the province with full powers to fortify Jerusalem and to reorganize the settlement patterns and provincial administration. Although the temple had been rebuilt, Jerusalem was unfortified and thinly populated. There were signs of slackness or abuse in political administration, cultic observances, and socioeconomic policies that were sapping the vitality of the province (see on Isaiah 56—66 and Malachi, §50.4.a–b).

From the Persian viewpoint this meant a weak point of defense in the west, and from the exilic Jewish point of view it meant a Judahite community not yet adequately reformed in religious practice. In 445 B.C.E., Nehemiah, a Jewish official in the Persian court, was sent at the head of a reforming delegation accompanied by military escort and empowered to call on Persian material and political resources to carry through a firm-handed reconstruction of the province. In 433 Nehemiah returned to Persia, perhaps upon culmination of his major reforms, only to come back to Judah for a further indeterminate period, in order to deal with unresolved communal difficulties.

At the heart of Nehemiah's measures was a form of *synoecism* ("binding together"), sometimes compared to the uniting of the whole of Attica under the central government of Athens but actually more closely paralleled by the forced resettlement of people for political purposes practiced by Greek tyrants. To appreciate the full impact of Nehemiah's alteration of power relations in Judah, we must view his celebrated refortification of Jerusalem together with his repopulation of the city with one-tenth of the Judahite populace selected by lot. A fortified and repopulated Jerusalem enhanced imperial administration and trade. The hand of Judah was thereby greatly strengthened against Sanballat of Samaria to the north, Tobiah of Ammon to the east, Geshem of the Arabs to the south, and the Ashdodites to the west, who separately or in alliance threatened to curtail the political status of Judah and, in line with the special interests of the Samaritans, to weaken the religious reform party in Judah that contested the legitimacy of the Samaritan Jewish cult.

As an advocate of the form of Jewish religion that had developed in the Babylonian and Persian exile, Nehemiah compelled strict Sabbath observance in the face of agricultural and commercial violations of the day of rest. Moreover, he adamantly opposed the marriage of Judahites to women from other lands, Samaritans included, which he viewed both as a dilution of the proper tendency in religion and as a "Trojan horse" through which enemies in adjacent provinces could weaken Judah politically. Doubtless these marriages were contracted largely by the upper class and Nehemiah's opposition to them may very well have been related to his efforts to alleviate socioeconomic hardship among the local populace which was proving an obstacle to effective provincial reconstruction.

A serious threat to stable rule in Judah sprang from the class division between the wealthy, who were largely returned exiles advantaged by Persian-backed privileges, and a more impoverished populace of small landholders who were sliding into debt and losing their properties by foreclosure and their children by debt servitude. Nehemiah moved firmly against these practices by arousing public opinion against the harsh creditors (Neh. 5:1–13). A kind of *seisachtheia* ("shaking off of debts"), comparable to that of Solon of Athens in 594–593 B.C.E., was implemented.[5] This one-time cancellation of debts provided temporary economic relief and solidified the control of the reformed party. Realistically, however, since the wealth of the abusive upper class was not confiscated, the combination of landed and commercial wealth probably worked toward the eventual undermining of the reforms in Judah, as proved to be the case in Athens after Solon's reforms.

Nehemiah's program provided that the Levites, now improverished temple assistants, were henceforth to receive a portion of offerings to subsidize their livelihood. Moreover, Nehemiah waived his own right to a food

---

5. Victor Ehrenberg, *From Solon to Socrates* (London: Methuen & Co., 1968), 54–73; Chester G. Starr, *The Economic and Social Growth of Early Greece, 800–500 B.C.* (New York: Oxford University Press, 1977), 181–87.

allowance in support of his local entourage and of visiting Persian officials, in order to set an example in alleviating the economic burdens of the general populace (Neh. 5:14–19). This forfeiture of rights of office strongly suggests that Nehemiah was independently wealthy or had friends of means willing to pay for the upkeep of several hundred officials and their dependents.

It has been plausibly argued that Nehemiah fits the model of the tyrants in contemporary Greek politics who rode to power on waves of popular socioeconomic discontent.[6] This discontent was generated among large numbers of people on the land who were greatly impoverished by the rise of commercial wealth that increasingly turned land into a salable commodity. Tyrants were resourceful leaders of the moment who often drew support from the lower classes and from reform or special-interest parties. They promised—and sometimes delivered—public works programs, debt release, confiscation of the property of rich opponents, redistribution of land, lowering or remission of taxes, and the like.

Various coalitions of the populace supported and opposed tyrants and their careers were typically stormy. They attempted to balance and "orchestrate" the conflicting forces of the landed aristocracy, the rising merchants, and the lower classes, and from one perspective they can be viewed as manipulative opportunists. From the point of view of the class conflicts being fought out, tyrants served as facilitators for politically realigning social forces and opening up the socioeconomic world to new *commercial* wealth by breaking the monopoly of *landed* wealth and regulating or alleviating some of the grossest inequities of both forms of wealth.[7] The measures of Nehemiah correspond to the policies of tyrants and probably had the overall intent of strengthening Persian-Jewish exilic reform control in Judah by tempering its hardships on the general populace. By appealing to the restiveness of the people at large, Nehemiah gained leverage to force policies and structural changes on the local elite that they resisted in the short run but that aided them in consolidating their hold on Judah in the long run.

44.4 Mission of Ezra in 458 B.C.E. or Later

The chronological order of the missions of Nehemiah and Ezra, and the substantive interconnection of their work, is a baffling, at present unre-

---

6. Morton Smith, *Palestinian Parties and Politics That Shaped the Old Testament* (New York: Columbia University Press, 1971), 136–47.

7. Starr, *Economic and Social Growth of Early Greece*, 178–80, minimizes the factors of class and economics in the rise of tyrants, whereas Ehrenberg, *From Solon to Socrates*, 22–25, and M. M. Austin and P. Vidal-Naquet, *Economic and Social History of Ancient Greece: An Introduction* (Berkeley and Los Angeles: University of California Press, 1977), 69–70, 142–44, 217–19, 352–57, underscore their prominence.

solvable, historical problem. A straightforward reading of the biblical text places Ezra's arrival in Judah in *458* B.C.E. for a public career of unspecified duration. Ezra is called both a priest (a Jewish title) and a scribe (probably understood as a secretary in Persian governmental service). The scope and powers of his commission are pertinent to determining his relationship to the mission of Nehemiah. Journeying to Judah with about five thousand returning exiles, Ezra bore a commission to investigate internal conditions in Judah in order to determine how they corresponded to the religious law which Ezra and his exilic Jewish community regarded as authoritative. Donations for the temple cult were sent by Ezra's hand and he was given power to call on state funds as needed to supplement the donations. Ezra was further empowered to appoint judges who would enforce the proper observance of the law, a measure presupposing that the religious law in the form brought by Ezra was decreed by the Persians as the civil law of the province of Judah.

According to the biblical account, Ezra thus preceded Nehemiah but was presumably still present in Judah in the time of Nehemiah's mission. It is striking, however, that neither man operates with any evident awareness of the work of the other. The Ezra traditions and the Nehemiah traditions are clearly two entirely separate literary blocks that have been fused together secondarily, with only the most superficial linkage of the two leaders (Nehemiah was inserted into an Ezra passage in Neh. 8:9 and Ezra was intruded into a Nehemiah passage in Neh. 12:26).

It has been widely doubted that two Persian appointees would have been assigned identical or closely related political, social, and religious responsibilities in the same time period, or, if they did have some overlapping jurisdictions, that they could have worked in such ignorance or deliberate disregard of one another. There are, moreover, indications that in fact Ezra *followed* Nehemiah. Nehemiah, in reviewing the populace of Judah, cites the repatriates under Zerubbabel but makes no mention of those who returned with Ezra. Nehemiah finds Jerusalem's defenses laid waste and the city sparsely populated, whereas Ezra discovers Jerusalem thriving within its walls. Nehemiah is the contemporary of the high priest Eliashib, while Ezra lives in the time of his grandson Jehohanan.

The most frequent resolution of this historical puzzle has been to conjecture that "the seventh year of Artaxerxes" for the date of Ezra's arrival in Judah refers, not to the reign of Artaxerxes I (465–424), but to the reign of Artaxerxes II (404–358), which would date Ezra's appearance in Judah in *398–397* B.C.E. Others have placed Ezra's visit in the period *433–432* between Nehemiah's two terms of office, or they have corrected "the seventh year" of Artaxerxes I to "the thirty-seventh year," thereby dating

Ezra in *428* B.C.E., after Nehemiah had completed both his terms of office in Judah.

By placing Ezra's mission *after* Nehemiah's mission, the work of Ezra in the religious sphere gains coherence as an accomplishment within the framework of the political consolidation achieved by Nehemiah. That the author-editor of Ezra-Nehemiah, widely thought to be writer of 1 and 2 Chronicles as well, could have made such a grievous chronological error accords with the limited sources available for the period. In historiography there is always a tendency to compress little-known periods and to conflate or misorder similar leaders and events. There may also have been motives of ecclesial politics that encouraged placing Ezra's work prior to Nehemiah's.

In recent years, on the other hand, there has been a trend toward defending the biblical order of Ezra's precedence over Nehemiah.[8] In part this springs from the argument that the apparent isolation of Ezra and Nehemiah from one another is a literary phenomenon that the author-editor has preserved by arbitrarily pasting their separate traditions together. This awkward literary happenstance does not necessarily reflect historical reality. In part the traditional sequence Ezra-Nehemiah is defended on the grounds that reform efforts in Judah probably did not follow a smooth incremental course, but experienced advances and setbacks, and that the two leaders may well have overlapped in office without policy conflict or violation of Persian directives since they shared much the same religiopolitical reform perspective. Consequently, it is imaginable that Ezra first attempted reforms that were impossible to realize in the realm of religious law until Nehemiah had effected his program of political centralization and debt release. On this hypothesis, the actual work of Ezra, launched before the coming of Nehemiah and spread over three decades, finally culminated only after the sum of Nehemiah's reforms bore fruit and the exilic reform party was in firm political control of Judah.

Ezra's introduction of a lawbook as the basis for civil and religious jurisprudence in Judah was an important moment in the movement toward canonization of the Law, the first section of the Hebrew Bible (§11.2; 48). The lawbook was read (in part or in whole) at a public assembly that subscribed to it as the law of the land (Nehemiah 8). Unfortunately, it is

---

8. Compare, for example, H. H. Rowley, "The Chronological Order of Ezra and Nehemiah," in *The Servant of the Lord and Other Essays on the Old Testament,* 2d rev. ed. (Oxford: Basil Blackwell & Mott, 1965), 135–68, who argues for placing Nehemiah before Ezra, with Shemaryahu Talmon, "Ezra and Nehemiah (Books and Men)," in IDBSup, 317–28, who upholds the biblical order of Ezra followed by Nehemiah.

impossible to determine the exact identity of Ezra's lawbook from the account of the public reading, beyond the apparent fact that it was composed of materials now found in Genesis through Deuteronomy. Whether Ezra's law was the finished Torah as we know it, or some part of it such as the Deuteronomic Code, Holiness Code, or Priestly document, or a topical selection of laws not corresponding to any of the pentateuchal sources or legal collections, cannot be conclusively determined.

What is clear is that at some point between 458 and 398 or shortly thereafter, probably toward the end of that period, the combined political authority of the Persians and the religious authority of the exilic Jewish reformers succeeded in establishing a body of traditional legal materials as *the binding law of the province of Judah*. Nehemiah 8 may describe the very moment when the Law as a totality was given its Persian-Judean "canonical" impress, or it may describe the endorsement of some section, or earlier edition, of the present Law which spurred further enlargements and revisions resulting in the final form of the Law after some years or decades. In either case, it is evident that the initial decisive impulse in this process was a confluence of Persian political edict and Jewish reforming zeal.

From the side of the reforming Jews the Law assured a well-defined and purified community and from the side of the Persians the Law guaranteed orderly and reliable colonial rule at the least cost to themselves. The general contours of the Persian policy in this regard are indicated by the Persian understanding of law as a continuum of religious and civil regulations in which no sharp distinctions were made between the two kinds of laws. Moreover, it was the Persian imperial habit, displayed for instance in Egypt, to encourage indigenous religious leaders to codify existing laws and customs and make them the basis of colonial law backed by Persian authority.[9] It can, therefore, be reasonably asserted, in spite of uncertainty of timing and detail, that the crucial initial move toward canonization of Jewish writings was a political act initiated and imposed upon the Palestinian Jewish community by the collaboration of Persian imperial authorities and a Jewish colonial elite imported from the exile to Judah.

Although our knowledge of reconstructed Judah in Persian times is chiefly restricted to the moments described above, some progress has been made toward reconstructing the chains of commissioners/governors and high priests who held office in Judah between 538 and 332 B.C.E. Evidence from seals and coins and from the Wadi Dâliyeh papyri has supplemented

9. Widengren, in *IJH*, 515; this point has also been urged and developed at some length in unpublished lectures by S. Dean McBride of Union Theological Seminary, Richmond, Virginia.

our limited information about the rosters of civil officials and high priests and has helped to clarify the chronology. While the sequence of civil officials remains incomplete, attempts have been made to provide a complete list of the high priests. Since names in the high priestly line tended to be repeated and absolute dates are in any case not available, these reconstructions are conjectural but nonetheless promising as a tentative basis for further historical inquiry.[10]

44.5 Developments Among Dispersion Jews

A striking feature of the protracted restoration of Judah throughout this period was the *repeated initiative for rebuilding and reshaping the Palestinian Jewish community that came from Jews of the Dispersion in Babylonia and Persia*. It is obvious that by the fifth century these Jewish communities in the eastern Dispersion had become securely and respectably lodged in their new environments. Composed originally of the highest leadership of the destroyed Kingdom of Judah, they came to provide officials in the Persian government, including Nehemiah who was "cupbearer" and Ezra who was "secretary." It was these circles who eventually "called the tune" in the colonial province of Judah and who provided the intellectual and religious energy for redefining Israelite-Jewish identity. That they were economically advantaged is shown by the donations they were able to send to the Jerusalem temple and also perhaps by the records of a Babylonian business firm headed by the Murashu family in the era of Nehemiah and Ezra which reveal that several clients of the firm were Jewish.

The western Jewish Dispersion is attested in the Persian period by the Elephantine papyri (table 1: 5D) which tell of a colony of Jewish mercenaries, perhaps totalling 350 people, who served as part of the Persian forces occupying Egypt. The documents are dated over much of the fifth century, but those of greatest interest are concentrated in the period 419–399 B.C.E. Intermarriage with Egyptians seems to have been practiced. A form of Passover was observed and a temple of Yahu (Yahweh) had been built. There are allusions to other deities, such as Ashambethel and Anathbethel, who were worshiped alongside Yahweh. Egyptian priests, opposed to the Jewish sacrifice of rams, stirred the local populace to destroy the temple in 410 B.C.E. The Elephantine colony appealed to authorities in Judah and Samaria for permission to rebuild the temple and were eventually allowed to do so, except that permission for animal sacrifices was omitted, perhaps in an effort to restrict Jewish sacrifice to Jerusalem or Gerizim or possibly

10. Ibid., 505–9.

to avoid inflaming Egyptian religious sensibilities. Shortly after 400 B.C.E., the colony was conquered in a general uprising of Egypt against Persia, at which point the Jewish mercenaries may have shifted their allegiance to Egyptian authorities.

Elephantine was in Upper Egypt near Aswan. It is likely that other groups of Jews settled in Lower Egypt, including descendants of the Judahites who fled to the Delta region after the assassination of Gedaliah in the early sixth century. We have no information on these communities from Persian times, but it is probable that they took firm root since it was in this region that Jewish colonization of Egypt experienced rapid growth in the Hellenistic period.

45
JEWISH RESPONSE TO MACEDONIAN AND PTOLEMAIC DOMINIONS (332–198 B.C.E.)

45.1 Impact of Alexander: The Meeting of Hellenism and Judaism

When Alexander the Great crossed from Greece into Asia and launched his conquests that toppled the Persian Empire, he opened a new epoch in the interaction of the ancient Near East and Hellenism. Alexander was committed somewhat contradictorily to a multiethnic cosmopolitan culture undergirded by the achievements and perspectives of Greek civilization. To the Jews it was a major shock to be faced with an assertive, and often militant, Gentile universalism. Judaism as a way of life was challenged with the prospect of cultural assimilation and religious syncretism or eclipse. The tide of Hellenism unleashed by Alexander and his successors had the eventual effect of confirming Judaism in its main features, but in the process it provoked heated internal Jewish conflict and shaped new developments institutionally, intellectually, and spiritually.

It is simplistic, however, to single out the cultural, philosophic, and religious aspects of the confrontation without recognizing that Hellenism came to the ancient Near East in the form of intrusive military and political power.[11] The confrontation was thus not solely a matter of the tastes and opinions of individual Jews toward Hellenism. In basic respects Jews faced

11. Mikhail I. Rostovtzev, *The Social and Economic History of the Hellenistic World,* 3 vols. (New York: Oxford University Press, 1941), details the brutish and vicious character of much Hellenistic politics with particular forcefulness, and Samuel K. Eddy, *The King Is Dead. Studies in the Near Eastern Resistance to Hellenism, 334–331 B.C.* (Lincoln: University of Nebraska Press, 1961), shows that philosophy and religion were the ideological counterpart of a fierce political contest between Near Eastern native rule and Hellenistic imperialism.

the same realities of foreign domination that they had experienced under Assyrians, Neo-Babylonians, and Persians, and with a heightened measure of cultural and intellectual imperialism. When Jews struggled with the allure of Hellenism, they were not merely making personal choices about life styles and mental outlooks. They were also inevitably taking a stance toward political powers that could not be avoided. Responses to Hellenism entailed decisions about how their own communities would be organized and how Judah and the various dispersed settlements of Jews would be related to the foreign powers espousing Hellenism. Although the imperial masters held the upper hand, many policy battles begun in imperial circles were fought out within the colonial communities of Jews who could not easily observe a strict neutrality in matters that affected them greatly and concerning which they were pressed to take positions.

Nor should "Hellenism vs. Judaism" be posed as an outright antagonism in which there were only two clear choices. Jews were exposed to Hellenism in different forms and situations and they found various dangers and attractions in it. Moreover, they adopted a wide variety of strategies for drawing on Greek thought and culture both to understand and express their faith and to commend it to potential converts or defend it against detractors. The "core" of uncompromised Jewishness and the permitted "periphery" of Greek adornment and articulation of that Jewishness were worked out differently in Jewish communities according to time and place.[12] Oftentimes the conflict within Jewish communities over proper demarcation of *Jewish core* and *Greek periphery* was bitter because it involved mutually exclusive immediate options that determined who would exercise the primary power in the community. Hellenism served to precipitate critical Jewish decisions about the canon of sacred writings and about the specification of authoritative leadership in interpreting and applying the old traditions.

Alexander, building on the initial accomplishments of his father, Philip of Macedon, resolved to invade Asia as Persia had invaded Greece more than a century before. At Granicus in Asia Minor in 334 and a year later at Issus on the frontier of Syria, the Persians were soundly defeated. Before turning to a climactic victory at Gaugamela in northern Mesopotamia in 331, Alexander swiftly secured his southern flank by conquering Syro-Palestine and Egypt. In most instances he was well received as a promising improvement over Persian rule. Samaria welcomed him profusely, and Judah ac-

---

12. Saul Lieberman, *Hellenism in Jewish Palestine* (New York: Jewish Theological Seminary of America, 1950); Martin Hengel, *Judaism and Hellenism. Studies in Their Encounter in Palestine During the Early Hellenistic Period,* 2 vols. (Philadelphia: Fortress Press, 1974).

knowledged Alexander's sovereignty through its high priest. Shortly thereafter, however, there was a Samaritan uprising which Alexander answered
by seizing the city of Samaria and turning it into a military colony. The
skeletons of leading citizens who fled this retaliation and were massacred in
a cave have been uncovered in the Wadi Dâliyeh, along with a considerable
group of fragmentary legal and administrative papyri which clarify aspects
of Samaritan history in the period 375–335 B.C.E. (see p. 413 n. 2).

In Palestine, as elsewhere, Alexander recognized local autonomy wherever possible, partly out of conviction and partly out of sheer inability of
several thousand Macedonians to administer a suddenly acquired empire
that stretched from Asia Minor to the borders of India. Occupied with
military reconnaissance and consolidation of empire, there was little opportunity to do more than accept the operative local forms of rule as long as
they conceded Macedonian sovereignty. Where occasional rebellion broke
out, as in Samaria, Alexander took quick repressive measures. Although
unable to introduce any new overall administrative framework, Alexander
did begin the establishment of Greek cities, replete with architectural,
cultural, and political forms of Hellenism, and peopled by Greek military
and commercial colonists. Other cities were founded or granted special
status by Alexander's successors, especially the Seleucids. While the influence of these Greek cities has been exaggerated at times, their wide
distribution and key role in trade and politics did serve to disseminate
Hellenism as a practical force in Asia.

45.2 Egyptian Hellenism Controls Palestine

Alexander's premature death in 323, without effective heir, triggered
more than twenty years of power struggles among his generals (the so-
called *diadochi*, "successors"). Antigonus strove to maintain the unity of
the Macedonian Empire, but after a long struggle the contrary program of
carving up the whole into a lesser number of still-sizable Hellenistic kingdoms prevailed. Ptolemy established himself in Egypt, while Seleucus
gained control in Syria and Mesopotamia. Together they opposed Antigonus and several military campaigns were waged in Palestine and the approaches to Egypt. Judah was drawn into these struggles, and Jerusalem
was conquered and damaged by Ptolemy. On one occasion a pro-Ptolemaic
Jewish high priest (or member of the high priestly family) took refuge in
Egypt, and Ptolemy is said to have deported many, presumably pro-Antigo-
nid, Jews to Egypt.

In 301, Antigonus was conclusively defeated at Ipsus and Ptolemaic
hegemony over Egypt, Palestine, and Phoenicia was consolidated. Judah

was to remain within the Ptolemaic imperial orbit for just over a century, until 198 B.C.E. The Ptolemies took over the theory of royal absolutism native to Egypt and gave it form in a tightly organized administrative system that extended into Palestine and Phoenicia in an effort to improve the economic contributions of the Asiatic colonies to the Nile heartland. The large Persian administrative units were broken down into smaller units supervised at every level by Egyptian civil, military, and financial officers and agents. A rigorously enforced system of taxes and leases materially increased the flow of wealth from the colonies to Egypt. The Zenon papyri tell of the tour in 260–258 B.C.E. of an Egyptian financial officer through large parts of Palestine. Zeno(n), accompanied by a large delegation, inspected and tightened up the financial administration of taxes and leases and also looked to better management of the royal estates in Palestine (see p. 413 n. 3).

On the other hand, the Ptolemies had to work with preexisting cultural and sociopolitical structures. Provided that the flow of taxes and goods was assured, considerable local autonomy was allowed. The old Persian system of a dual appointment of governor and high priest in Jerusalem seems to have been accommodated to Ptolemaic administrative practice by making the high priest titular head of Judah but appointing a civil officer (*prostasia*) who was the official representative of Judah to the Egyptian government and responsible for keeping a close watch on the high priestly management of the lucrative temple economy.

It appears that the tribute and tax burden on Judah was measurably heavier under the Ptolemies than it had been under the Persians who had been willing to absorb deficit spending in Judah for the sake of the military security investment. In the latter part of the third century, as the Seleucids increasingly contested Ptolemaic control of Palestine, there were signs of Judahite resistance to the Ptolemies. During the third Syrian war in 246–241, Onias II, the high priest, refused to pay the regular imperial tribute to Egypt. This led to the intervention of the Tobiads from Transjordan, a Jewish landed family that had challenged Nehemiah's reconstruction program in Judah and had more recently been installed by the Ptolemies as the head of a military colony of mixed peoples assigned to guard the desert frontier against the rising Nabatean Arabs. Joseph, one of these Tobiads, intervened in Jerusalem against the high priest and compelled him to pay the tribute. At the same time, Joseph was made general leaseholder of taxes for all of Palestine and Phoenicia.

No doubt this lucrative tax-farming position served to channel wealth toward Judah, but it certainly remained concentrated in upper-class hands.

The general intensity and rigor of Ptolemaic exploitation of Palestine, coupled with the maneuvers of a Jewish elite to prosper from farming out taxes and state trade monopolies on products such as wine and oil, sharpened the social differences that Nehemiah had tried to lessen by his reforms two centuries earlier. It is probable that improved cultivation of the soil in Judah under the Ptolemies led to increased productivity and population growth. Even so, much of the improvement had to do with specialized export products such as wine and oil. State monopolies on these exports, joined with heavy taxation farmed by self-serving local officials, created a debilitating pressure on the majority of the rural populace.

Emigration of Judahites to other parts of the world had been a factor since at least the seventh century. Jews had been in particular demand as military mercenaries, as the Persian-backed Jewish settlement at Elephantine in Egypt vividly illustrates. Emigration to Egypt quickened in pace as agricultural monopolies and population growth created pressures in Judah and the opportunities for mercenary service and work in the burgeoning trade centers such as Alexandria provided a foreign lure. Other parts of Palestine, particularly the coastal cities, received a share of these mobile Judahites.

Through its immersion in the life of rapidly growing Alexandria, the Dispersion Jewish community there soon became the chief center of Jews outside Palestine, eclipsing Babylonia in this respect. Alexandria, as the primary center of Greek learning and culture in this era, stimulated the Jewish residents to translate the sacred writings into Greek (cf. §12.1.a) and to produce further an extensive religious literature in Greek that served both to make Israelite/Jewish faith intelligible to Hellenistic Jews and to argue its intrinsic merits to the Greek world. Many of these writings have been preserved only because they found their way into Christian collections of the Apocrypha and Pseudepigrapha after they were renounced by Rabbinic Judaism (tables 5 and 6). It is clear that this Alexandrian literary, intellectual, and religious culture was a vibrant one at the forefront of Jewish-Greek contact.

46
JEWISH RESPONSE TO SELEUCID DOMINION: THE MACCABEES (198–140 B.C.E.)

46.1 Syrian Hellenism Controls Palestine

When dominion over Palestine passed from the Ptolemies to the Seleucids after Antiochus III's victory at Paneas in 198 B.C.E., there was widespread rejoicing among Judahites. Antiochus III had cultivated Jewish and other ethnic minority displeasures with the Ptolemies and, on taking Jerusalem, he decreed a general waiver of taxes for three years and permanently exempted priests and temple from taxation. It seems that Antiochus III fully intended to lighten the financial burden of empire that had made the Ptolemies so unpopular and to ingratiate himself with Judah by increasing support for the local cult. The Seleucid beginning in Judah was thus highly auspicious.

Within a very few years, however, there was a radical shift in Seleucid fortunes. The limits of Seleucid imperial advance were drawn decisively by the Romans who defeated Antiochus III at Magnesia in 190 B.C.E. and later blocked his plan to conquer Egypt. The Seleucid Empire lost Asia Minor and its eastern holdings were drastically reduced. A severe fiscal crisis struck the Seleucid government which thereupon resorted to plundering temples to replenish the dwindling state resources. Antiochus III himself died in one of these temple raids. As the crisis of rule deepened, a split opened in the royal family between the followers of Seleucus IV and the followers of Antiochus IV Epiphanes—the first of several dynastic rifts that plagued Seleucid rule in its efforts to subjugate the Jews of Palestine.

46.2 Enforced Hellenism and Civil War

The plans of Antiochus IV Epiphanes to consolidate his Seleucid Empire in the face of a rising Roman threat coincided well with the interests of Hellenizing Jewish leaders in Jerusalem. These leaders viewed rapprochement with Greek political and cultural forces as a way to enhance Judahite prosperity and to liberalize Jewish religion. They were attracted to the Seleucid program of equating Zeus Olympius with the Syro-Palestinian high god, and specifically with the Jewish deity, Yahweh.

To meet the critical shortage of state funds, Antiochus began to sell the office of Jewish high priest to the highest bidder among these Hellenizing Jews, first to Jason in 174 and then to Menelaus in 171. During their terms of office, steps were taken to create a Greek city-state, or polis, its citizens to be known as "Antiochians of Jerusalem." Toward that end, a gymnasium cultivated Greek athletics and culture among Jewish youth.

Meanwhile, Antiochus reached his acme of success by conquering all of Egypt outside of Alexandria. Returning from Egypt in 169, he intervened in Jerusalem in time to prevent an army headed by the ousted Jason from capturing the city. He also took the occasion to plunder the temple and to appoint a governor to facilitate the Jewish Hellenizing reform policies.

Unfortunately for him, on a second campaign to Egypt, Antiochus was compelled to obey a Roman ultimatum to abandon his Egyptian conquests.

The decision to replace the Jewish Law as the political constitution of Judah by making Jerusalem a Greek city was met with alarm by a majority of the populace. The resistance encountered by the Jewish Hellenists was so great that Antiochus sent a force to Jerusalem that killed and looted widely, pulled down the walls of the city, and established a citadel (Acra) garrisoned with Seleucid troops and settled with a mixed Gentile-Jewish populace loyal to the Hellenization program.

With the aid of Seleucid military force, the Jewish Hellenizers pushed through their radical religious reform measures which required the suppression of the traditional rites and the sacred literature of Judaism. Temple sacrifices, Sabbath observance, and circumcision were forbidden, and all copies of the Law were to be destroyed, on pain of death. The temple was turned into a syncretistic Syro-Hellenic shrine, cosmopolitan both in its modernized altar to Zeus and in its antique garden precincts harking back to Syro-Palestinian nature worship.

Open rebellion broke out in the countryside, led by the priest Mattathias and his hardy sons who came to be known as the Maccabees (after Judas nicknamed Maccabee, "the hammerer"). Those loyal to the Law, called Hasidim, rallied to the defense of the endangered ancestral religion and directed their arms both against Seleucid troops and the Jewish Hellenists. A religious and political civil war split the country.[13] Four times within the space of two years Syrian armies tried to crush the rebels but in each case they were hampered by military distractions elsewhere in the Seleucid Empire and roundly defeated by the cunning of Judas Maccabee's guerrilla tactics. By 164 Judas was able to recapture all of Jerusalem except for the Acra strong point. At this juncture, the Seleucids gave up trying to stamp out the Jewish religion and rescinded their proscriptive decrees, permitting Judas to cleanse and rededicate the temple for proper Jewish worship. The overt Jewish Hellenizing coup had been suppressed at the cost of deep divisions in Jewish society.

46.3 The Move from Religious Independence to Political Independence

With Seleucid concessions and the appointment of a moderate Hellenizing high priest Alcimus, it seemed for a time that peace might be restored.

---

13. Elias Bickerman, *From Ezra to the Last of the Maccabees. Foundations of Post-Biblical Judaism* (New York: Schocken Books, 1962), 54–135, gives a colorful account of the Maccabean struggle in terms of a Jewish civil war; Peter Schäfer, in *IJH*, 562–64, nuances Bickerman's original thesis in the light of later research and hypothesis.

Loyalties and passions among the factions in the three-year civil war had been so heightened and inflamed and the Seleucids had been by turn so heavy-handed and vacillating in their interventionist policies, that resolution of the conflict was not to be so easily achieved. Judas, in spite of diminished backing from the Jewish populace, chose to continue the movement of resistance with the goal of political independence from the Seleucids, toward which end he even entered into a treaty of defense with Rome. By now Antiochus was dead, but his successors took up the effort to suppress the prolonged Maccabean uprising, now explicitly political in its goals. Stronger Syrian armies were committed to pacification but, although the rebels were twice defeated and Judas killed, the Seleucids, thrown off balance by disorders in the empire and struggles for the throne, were unable to suppress the resistance movement and secure for their Jewish Hellenizing sympathizers a firm political hold on Judah.

Jonathan took up leadership from his fallen brother Judas; retreating to the countryside, he gradually extended control over Judah from a base at Michmash. Rival contenders for the Seleucid crown found themselves vying for support from Jonathan who managed thereby to parlay his appointment as high priest and civil and military commander of Judah in 152–150. Judah expanded its control far into the coastal plain and incorporated considerable regions of Samaria and Transjordan into its territory. So far had the fortunes of the rebels revived that in 150 Jonathan sent three thousand Jewish mercenaries to Antioch, the Seleucid capital, to assist Demetrius II in suppressing a revolt.

It is probable that Jonathan's acceptance of the office of high priest so offended sectors of pious Jews that a number of them withdrew into the countryside to form strict ascetic communities where they could practice the Law without compromise. These sectarians came to be known as Essenes. Apparently the expelled high priest led a small group (perhaps fifty or so sectarians) to found the Qumran community which over the next two hundred years wrote some, and collected the rest, of the voluminous Dead Sea Scrolls (§10.2.b; table 7). The Qumran scrolls refer to Jonathan (or possibly to Simon, his successor) as the Wicked Priest and to the unknown high priest he ousted as the Righteous Teacher (a more accurate translation than Teacher of Righteousness). Opinions differ as to whether the Essenes grew directly out of the Hasidim or were a sect of strict interpreters of the Law who returned from the Babylonian Diaspora at the start of the Maccabean War in order "to be in on the action."[14] In any case,

14. Jerome Murphy-O'Connor, "The Essenes and Their History," *RB* 81 (1974): 215–44.

the Essenes shared marked similarities with the Pharisees but were even stricter in their legalism and they chose a strategy of withdrawal from public life in contrast to the combative reformist and revolutionary spirit of those Hasidim who became the Pharisees.

47
A JEWISH STATE RISES AND FALLS:
THE HASMONEANS (140–63 B.C.E.)

47.1 Triumph and Hellenization of the Jewish State

When Jonathan was treacherously murdered in 142, his brother Simon stepped into leadership and within three years Judah had gained virtually full sovereignty over a region that was more than twice as large as at the start of the revolt. The hated Acra in Jerusalem was captured. Simon was granted full hereditary rights to the highest priestly, military, and civil offices by an assembly more or less representative of the Jewish elite, a bold action in which the weakened Seleucids agreed to acquiesce. The Hasmonean dynasty had begun, so named after Hashmon, an ancestor of Mattathias of the Maccabee family.

The succeeding Hasmonean rulers, John Hyrcanus (135–104), Aristobulus I (104–103), and Alexander Jannaeus (103–76), despite momentary setbacks, expanded Jewish conquests throughout Palestine and Transjordan in unremitting warfare against the Greek cities until, under Alexander Jannaeus, the Hasmonean kingdom approached the extent of the Davidic empire (minus the southern Negeb and Syria). The expansive Hasmoneans shrewdly maintained treaty connections with Rome in order to keep the Seleucids in check. They prosecuted a vigorous policy of forcibly converting conquered peoples to the Jewish religion, and it was in this way that Idumea (Latinized "Edom") and Galilee became Judaized. In 128 B.C.E., Hyrcanus leveled the city of Samaria and destroyed the Samaritan temple on Mt. Gerizim, suppressing the "heterodox" Jewish cult long practiced there in open defiance of the majority Jewish devotion to Jerusalem. In keeping with the rancorous and growing conflict between Samaritan and Judahite Jews since exilic times, the Samaritans had recently resisted both the Seleucids and the Hasmoneans. In settling old scores, Hyrcanus sealed an irreconcilable rupture between the two communities.

Increasingly, the administration of the Jewish state developed along Hellenistic political and military lines. John Hyrcanus gave his sons Greek names, and he began the practice of hiring Greek mercenaries to enhance his military strength and secure a power base independent of domestic support. He is even said to have plundered the tomb of David in order to pay for the mercenaries. The nationalistic fervor of the late Hasmonean kings was openly expressed through the Hellenistic notion of the personal honor and fortunes of the adventurous warrior-king, very much in the mold of Alexander the Great, Jannaeus's namesake.

Under John Hyrcanus, an internal conflict broke out between the ruling regime and devout Judahites, successors of the Hasidim who had backed the Maccabees so long as it was a question of religious freedom. These Hasidim were taking on the features of the later Pharisees, although we cannot be certain that they bore that name as yet. These opponents of the late Hasmoneans were troubled by Jewish rulers who so openly played the part of Hellenistic princes. For one thing, their conquests had tapped new wealth for a minority of enterprising Judahites in royal favor, but these benefits did not spread to the mass of people whose conditions of life only worsened. Certain Pharisees demanded that Hyrcanus give up the high priesthood, no doubt with the intent of denying him access to the lucrative temple economy and to the symbolic backing of the Jewish cult. In rejecting this effrontery, Hyrcanus countered by drawing closer to a group whom Josephus identifies as Sadducees, who at this time were probably largely composed of the newly enriched nobility spawned by the Hasmonean conquests.

During the reign of Alexander Jannaeus, the conflict flared into civil war that pitted a majority of the populace with the Pharisees against the king and his priestly and lay supporters. The internal political situation of Judah had shifted drastically in a few decades. Judas, the first Maccabee, had led a majority of Jews against a small but powerful group of Jewish Hellenizers and their Seleucid backers. In a turnabout, Alexander Jannaeus, a successor of the Maccabees, now led a small but powerful group of royal supporters in a desperate battle against a majority of countrymen who saw him as an embodiment of Hellenistic corruption and oppression. The anti-Hasmonean Jews called upon a Seleucid army to help them defeat the Jewish monarch in 88. It was an ironic moment in which a Seleucid army aided by Jewish troops overcame the Jewish king's army manned at its core by pagan mercenaries.

Although the Pharisees and the popular majority had victory in their grasp, the prospect of a Seleucid king once again taking control of Jerusalem prompted some of the people—putting nationalism ahead of class interests—to switch their loyalty back to Alexander Jannaeus. Returned to power, the king took his revenge by crucifying 800 of the rebel Pharisees and slaughtering their wives and children. One outcome of this traumatic rift in Judahite society was that 8000 rebels fled the population centers, some of them joining the Qumran sect whose original membership was quadrupled by the inclusion of another 150 or so adherents.

The next Hasmonean ruler, Queen Salome Alexandra, sought peace with the Pharisees and actually granted them majority power in domestic affairs, to the point that they began to take revenge on those who had encouraged Alexander Jannaeus in his butchery of the rebels. Her son Aristobulus II seized power and battled incessantly with his weaker brother Hyrcanus, who was supported by the Idumean leader Antipater, father of Herod. In 63, the rival contenders for the Hasmonean crown appealed for backing to Pompey, the Roman legate who had reached Damascus. Representatives of the Jewish people, doubtless including Pharisees, asked Pompey to refuse recognition to either of the discredited claimants. Pompey wished to postpone a decision until he had dealt with the Nabatean Arabs, but Aristobulus insisted on pressing his claim militarily, whereupon Pompey captured Jerusalem, deported Aristobulus to Rome, and appointed Hyrcanus II as high priest (but not as king), thereby honoring the request of the popular Jewish delegation and advancing the interests of Rome by bringing Judah under imperial administration. Judah was stripped of most of the Greek territories it had conquered, leaving only Galilee and a part of Transjordan.

Rome had come to stay in Palestine, in spite of some final spasms of Hasmonean power. Escaping from Rome, Aristobulus tried a comeback in Judah during 56–55 but failed. A final brief Hasmonean restoration occurred in 40–37 when the Parthians invaded Syro-Palestine and installed Antigonus as their puppet ruler in Judah. As soon as the Parthians were expelled from the area, Herod took up his position as dependent king of Judah under commission from Rome.

47.2 Factions and Parties in Hasmonean State and Society

The factions, parties, or sects called Sadducees, Pharisees, and Essenes originated in the Maccabean-Hasmonean period. Zealots, armed resisters against Rome, will be omitted from this account because they emerged as a break off from Pharisaic circles only in 6 B.C.E. under Judas the Galilean. Exactly when the Sadducees, Pharisees, and Essenes emerged in the second century, and under what precise circumstances, remain clouded issues. Nor is it certain how much their organizational and ideological features changed between Hasmonean times and the first Christian century when they are more fully documented. The names of these groups do not materially help us to pinpoint their origins or their religious and sociopolitical programs, since the most favored etymologies are simply broad adjectival designations of ethico-religious traits such as "the pious," "the purists," or "the separatists." The social classes or interests represented by these parties must mostly be inferred. Similarly, the degree to which party members were occupants of public offices is disputed, as is the extent of their active involvement in politics. Moreover, the appropriateness of the term "sect" for these factions is questionable, since "sect" in the parlance of sociology of religion and religious history usually refers to an isolated self-enclosed group that does not seek or achieve wider power or influence. Only the Essenes among these three groups might suitably be called a sect in this sense. The Sadducees and Pharisees contested and wielded power as they carried out public roles and mixed broadly in Jewish society.[15]

The national situation that generated sharply defined factions was the major realignment of socioeconomic, political, and religious forces set in unrelenting motion by the abortive attempt to Hellenize Judaism radically and by the reactive emergence of an independent Jewish state that ironically took on a decisive Hellenistic character in spite of its anti-Hellenistic beginnings. The radical minority coup to displace traditional Judaism by submerging it in a syncretistic Syro-Hellenistic cult failed totally. Thereafter, all sections of the populace stood firmly for maintenance of a Jewish religion based on the Law. Within that formal concurrence, however, there was a very wide latitude of understanding as to how the Law was to be practiced and exactly what fidelity to the Law implied for socioeconomic, political, and cultural structures and styles. With *Hellenistic religious syncretism* excluded by an overwhelming Jewish consensus, the key question now had to do with whether and how Jewish society and state should appropriate the internationally operative *Hellenistic socioeconomic and political structures and assumptions.*

Was Hellenism to be accepted or rejected as "a total package"? If not, by what criteria should Jews opt for one or another of its many aspects? If Hellenism was both "in the air" culturally and its presuppositions more or less "built into" politics and economics, what special efforts were necessary to become critically aware of its insidious detrimental effects on Jewish consciousness and activity? Practically speaking, what did it mean to live out a fully embodied Judaism in the Hellenistic world?

In going beyond the battle for religious freedom in order to reach for political independence and then for imperial expansion, the Maccabees and

---

15. Ellis Rivkin, *A Hidden Revolution* (Nashville: Abingdon Press, 1978), 316–18, sorts out some of the connotations of terms such as "sect," "school of thought," and "philosophy" used to describe what we here call "factions" and "parties" in late Hellenistic Judaism.

Hasmoneans increasingly adopted Hellenistic technology, political and military organization, and cultural styles. The Hasidim were reserved or hostile toward Hasmonean political and cultural ambitions. When Jonathan became high priest, the Hasmonean political rulers breached the separation of religious and civil offices that had been the official policy since the exile and, before that, the common practice under the old monarchies of Israel and Judah. It was probably this Maccabean ecclesial "power grab" that prompted some of the Hasidim to form disciplined associations of loyalists to the Law, forerunners of the Pharisees. These associations stressed the equality of Jews before the Law and they took a more and more active role in trying to limit the power and impact of the Hasmonean rulers on Jewish life. At about the same time disciplined groups of a similar but even stricter view decided to pull away from the corrupt society into rural communes where they could live out their religion uncompromisingly. These withdrawing conventicles were to become the Essenes.

One of the chief effects of the new opportunities for power and wealth spawned by the Maccabean War and the Hasmonean expansion was to catapult people into positions of power and leadership who had previously been insignificant in Jewish communal life. As a result, social cleavages in Judah deepened and spread. The old aristocracy had been heavily concentrated around the upper levels of the priesthood who controlled the lucrative temple economy. This hereditary priestly aristocracy was badly battered by the Jewish Hellenizers and it was soon preempted at the top by the Hasmonean assumption of high priestly office as a function of the royal line. At the same time the wars of expansion offered vast new commercial opportunities seized upon by Jewish entrepreneurs attached to the Hasmoneans who grew wealthy in trade and land purchases.

The rising commercial sectors formed an aristocracy of "new wealth" that openly vied with "old wealth" aristocrats for political and economic power, for instance, for control of seats on the national governing council, for influence on royal policies and appointments, and for control of the temple economy. It was this new aristocracy that came to be known as the Sadducees, stemming largely at first from lay circles, although in time they gained ascendency in the priesthood at the expense of the old aristocrats. By Herodian times it appears that "old" and "new" aristocracies reached an accommodation based in large part on their common need to block and counterbalance the rising influence of the "populist" Pharisees.

Governmental power in the now-independent Jewish state was vested primarily in the king and his officials who had replaced the Seleucid rulers. Alongside the royal establishment there existed an assembly of seventy (or

seventy-one?) representatives of the people which possessed extensive con-
sultative, legislative, and juridical powers. This body had been operative
since Persian times as the means for Jews to exercise local autonomy within
the framework of subservience to the foreign empires. This representative
body was known as the *Gerousia* before the Maccabean age, and as the
Sanhedrin afterward. The Hasmonean dynasty ruled in collaboration with
the Sanhedrin. When the Romans later took control in Judah, they honored the same basic arrangements for local autonomy by continuing to deal
with the Sanhedrin as "the voice of the people."

Sadducean and Pharisaic factions fought for control of the Sanhedrin,
representing two contradictory lines of public policy. The Sadducees promoted the Hellenization program of the Hasmoneans, now of course decisively shorn of any attempts at religious syncretism or construction of a
Greek polis in Jerusalem. The Pharisees resisted the growing sociopolitical
and cultural Hellenization process adopted by the native princes. It is
manifest that, whatever the case by New Testament times, in the Hasmonean age the Sadducees and Pharisees had explicit political aims and used
political methods, including taking leadership of factions in civil war.
Broadly speaking, the Sadducees were "aristocratic" and the Pharisees
"populist," but such labels must be qualified and nuanced by the particular
social dynamics of the Hasmonean age.

Because Sadducees and Pharisees appear prominently in Josephus, the
New Testament, and rabbinic writings, there is a tendency to exaggerate
their numbers and to picture them as operative in a religious vacuum apart
from social context. Josephus reports that there were upwards of six thousand Pharisees and four thousand Essenes in Herodian times. The number
of Sadducees is not given, but they would scarcely have been more numerous than the Pharisees. It is obvious that such relatively small numbers of
partisans, in a populace estimated at between one-half million and two
million, could not have been significant forces except as they spoke and
acted for and in collaboration with other sectors of the populace. In this
period, Sadducees spoke for the interests of the Hasmonean political
establishment, upper-order priests, and the expansionist commercial and
land-owning classes, while the Pharisees were in touch with the grievances
and aspirations of a wider peasant populace, lower-order priests, and small
shopkeepers and artisans. The "Sadducean" point of view, extravagant in
praise of the Hasmonean dynasty, is apparent in 1 Maccabees, while
"Pharisaic" acclaim for Judas Maccabee (but not for his successors) shows
up in 2 Maccabees. Judith, *1 Enoch* 92–105, and *Psalms of Solomon* may
also emanate from pro-Pharisaic circles.

The religious disputes between the parties were closely intertwined with socioeconomic and political issues of high moment. The Sadducees favored a narrow constructionist interpretation of the Law with the purity laws applicable primarily to priests when on duty in the temple. Their exclusion of all writings except the Law from authoritative religious status, combined with their double standards of purity for priest and laity, defined a narrow sphere of life as properly religious and allowed them great leeway in Hellenized power politics, culture, and personal conduct. By contrast, the Pharisees offered the innovation of "the twofold Law," an oral law paralleling and progressively interpreting the written Law. This position both mandated and enabled a flexible fulfillment of purity laws by all Jews over a wider range of life than was recognized by the Sadducees. Pharisaic inclusion of Prophets and at least some of the later Writings in the sacred literature, coupled with rejection of a double standard for laity and priesthood, paralleled their dim view of Hellenized politics and culture as lustily embraced by Hasmoneans and their Sadducean backers.

Essenes shared much of the basic Pharisaic outlook on religion and politics, although they were considerably stricter in their application of the Law. Their decision to opt out of state and society, however, removed them as working allies of the Pharisees and prompted them in practice to accuse the Pharisees of "selling out" to social and political evil which was tantamount to religious apostasy. The Essene community at Qumran is best known from sectarian writings that describe the history and organization of the group: Damascus Document (CD), Rule of the Community (1Qs), and commentaries on prophetic books, especially on Nahum (4QpNah). (See the fuller list of Qumran books in table 7.) Qumran Essenes viewed themselves as the only true Israelites who retained a correct cult that followed a solar calendar (as argued in a commentary on Genesis called the *Book of Jubilees*).

The Qumran library also included a versatile array of apocalyptic writings, including Enochian literature, which shows the sect's fondness for expectations of cosmic, political, and religious catastrophe and renovation through divine intervention in a dead-ended world history. It is by no means clear in all cases which documents originated at Qumran, or among the Essenes at large, and which came from non-Essene circles. Clearly, apocalyptic expectations and theories were not restricted to Essenes, as the canonical Book of Daniel and the *Testament of Moses* 1—5, 8—10, from early Maccabean Hasidic circles, demonstrate. Many Pharisees were apocalyptists of one sort or another until the Wars against Rome in 66–70 and

132–35 C.E. closed the door on such militant and speculative views (cf. §55.1)

It has been customary to equate Sadducees with priests and Pharisees with scribes, but this is an erroneous simplification. While the upper orders of priests became largely Sadducean, not all priests were Sadducees and many Sadducees—in the period we are studying, probably a majority—were lay. At least since the reform of Nehemiah and Ezra, interpretation and application to present practice of the text of the Law had been largely monopolized by priests, although lay wise men also became respected interpreters of the Law (§54.1). About 180 B.C.E., Ben Sira wrote a book of proverbial wisdom in which he shows himself to be a learned lay teacher of the Law who was also supportive of the priesthood just before it was to become the focal point of Hellenization. As confidence in the priesthood was shaken and popular forces were unleashed by the tumultuous Maccabean-Hasmonean age, priestly monopoly of the interpretation of the Law was sharply contested in pious lay circles. It appears that Hasids and Pharisees set up schools for training Law interpreters as scribes competent to make decisions on ritual and religious laws and to judge in civil and criminal cases. The scribal "graduates" of these training programs were largely laity.

Sadducean and Pharisaic schemes of interpretation contended fiercely for control of the scribal office and tradition, with the Pharisaic ideology gaining the ascendency, compelling the priestly establishment in Jerusalem to accommodate itself to many Pharisaic rulings in the practice of the Law. Pharisees proper were communities of believers mutually pledged to strict observance of purity laws and tithing. They included priests and laity, scribes and uneducated devout. While the Pharisaic leaders were scribes, not all Pharisees were trained as scribes, nor were all scribes Pharisees. The scribe, whether Sadducee or Pharisee or neither, occupied a professional office distinguished by special education and recognized experience in the performance of the vital role of rendering the old regulations of the Law into relevant and authoritative directions for contemporary daily conduct and for supplying the framework of a juridical system.

In sum, the Pharisee was a member of a sect who took on himself strictly "the yoke of the Law." The Pharisaic orientation and influence spread out from the core sect to permeate and link wider circles of Jews on varying religious and political issues. The Sadducee was a person of privilege in the priesthood or in the lay nobility who combined pro-Hasmonean sympathies with an elitist religious outlook. It is not known if the Sadducees formed separate associations apart from their strongholds in the priesthood, economy, and governmental services. The "Sadducean" orientation and influence, like the "Pharisaic," spread out from the commanding centers of Sadducean power closely allied with and buttressed by state authority. Owing to their elitism, however, the Sadducees failed to gain the loyalty and sympathy of the general populace with anything like the success of the Pharisaic faction.[16]

Modern-day evaluations of the Maccabean-Hasmonean course of events have tended to be simplistically polarized. Some analysts trace a single unbroken line of development in Jewish religion and politics combined as a harmonious triumph of the Law and of political freedom. Other interpreters posit a sharp break between the war for religious freedom up to 164 and the subsequent fight for political freedom which led to Hasmonean excesses of military conquest, court corruption, and domestic repression. These scholarly judgments are closely affected by initial assumptions either that any form of independent Jewish politics was justified by the divine promise of the land at the foundation of Jewish religion, or that secular politics was tabooed by the covenantal-prophetic brand of Jewish religion which forbade or sharply qualified the use of human power.

The reality is that the very same complex of issues that enthralls modern interpreters also tormented and divided Jewish society in the ideological struggle of Maccabean-Hasmonean times. The king, the new aristocracy, the higher order of priests, in short, the *Sadducean faction or tendency* understood their traditional religion to mandate messianic political action in terms of the prevailing blunt and cruel forms of international power politics. Small farmers, day laborers, shopkeepers, artisans, lower-order priests, many scribes and members of Pharisaic associations, even the withdrawn Essenes, in short, the *Pharisaic faction or tendency* understood their traditional religion to mandate messianic loyalty to domestic social equality and justice and to popular religious practice, while eschewing the conceits and excesses of power politics, even to the point of endangering political independence as long as religious purity and freedom of practice were assured. From issue to issue confronting the Jewish community in Maccabean-Hasmonean times, varying coalitions of population groupings coalesced around competing policies and programs of action, fostering a tumultuous domestic scene that twice broke into open civil war.

16. This reconstruction of the parties is indebted to Shmuel Safrai, "Jewish Self-Government," in *The Jewish People in the First Century. Historical Geography, Political History, Social, Cultural and Religious Life and Institutions,* ed. S. Safrai and M. Stern (Assen: Van Gorcum, 1974), 1:377–419; Menahem Stern, "Aspects of Jewish Society: the Priesthood and Other Classes," in *Jewish People* (1976), 2:561–630; and Rivkin, *Hidden Revolution.*

A crucial factor in how Jews of that age aligned themselves on these religio-political issues lay in their social class positions and perceived self-interests. It mattered greatly whether they were among those who prospered and wielded power in the Hasmonean revival of Jewish statehood or among those who suffered loss and decline of influence at the expense of the expansion of royalty and the newly enriched. The ambiguity and contradiction of the social class conflict that shadowed all the Mediterranean power struggles of that age likewise shadowed and shaped the power politics of the Hasmonean Jewish state.

When we assess the dubious balance of gains and losses in Hasmonean adventurism, we do no more than did the large majority of Jewish subjects of the Hasmoneans. The main difference is that we later students of that history need only make imaginative "as if" judgments rather than life-effecting decisions about a social conflict that, being past history, does not directly involve us. Nonetheless, though we strive not to distort the record of the past, how we assess Jewish statehood and social order in the second century B.C.E. will be greatly influenced by our own class interests and religious affiliations, as will also our views of international politics today, including the claims and policies of Israeli Zionism and of Palestinian and Arab nationalism.

CHAPTER 11

Traditions of Colonial Israel:
Completing the Law and the Prophets

Read the Biblical Text
Genesis 1
Ezekiel
Isaiah 40—55
Haggai
Zechariah 1—8
Isaiah 56—66
Malachi
Obadiah
Joel

48
HERMENEUTICAL POLITICS: THE INTERPLAY OF LAW AND PROPHETS

48.1 Traditions of Law and Prophecy Develop in Dialogue

Law and Prophets were to become two separate and firmly delimited collections of authoritative writings, constituting the first and second divisions of the three-part Hebrew Bible. Despite the division between the two collections, it is nonetheless evident that these two sets of traditions interacted intimately within the institutional life of Israel over approximately eight centuries from ca. 1050 to 250 B.C.E.

The history-like narratives and the covenantal and legal texts of the Law were solidly rooted in the premonarchic era, as evidenced in the old materials underlying J and E, and even discernible at points in D and P. From the time of Samuel onward, as centralized monarchic structures came into tension and conflict with the older tribal socioeconomic and religiocultural priorities, prophets appeared as ardent supporters or acid critics of public institutions, policies, and leaders.

Throughout the monarchy, extensive blocks of narratives and legal texts were committed to writing by J, E, D, DH, and the forerunners of P. During the entire time when these primal traditions were being successively published, prophets were likewise active in Israel. For example, J was probably written in the time of Nathan and Gad; E in the age of Elijah and Elisha; the earliest version of D, along with the redaction of JE, in the era of Hosea and Isaiah; a fuller form of D in the period of Zephaniah; and the first edition of DH in the time of Habakkuk and Jeremiah. The traditions of P, insofar as they are preexilic, are difficult to localize prior to Ezekiel, but at least the Holiness Code of Leviticus 17—26 was probably written at a time contemporary with the late seventh-century prophets.

The history of Israel and its social organizational forms presupposed in the traditions of J, E, D, DH, and P were part of the working environment of the prophets as of all other Israelite leaders. The precise familiarity of particular prophets with specific traditions of the Pentateuch is, however, difficult to determine. Ezekiel's close relation to P is an exceptional case, and Jeremiah's connection with Deuteronomy and DH is much debated, although in the latter instance it is much more likely that Deuteronomistic circles have edited the Book of Jeremiah than that the prophet himself shared closely in a Deuteronomistic perspective.

For the most part, the preexilic and exilic prophets demonstrate a broadly shared consensus with major presuppositions and contents of the

Pentateuchal traditions. The prophets often allude to major foundation events in early Israelite history. They presume a structured mutual relationship between Yahweh and the people of Israel. They concur that the will of Yahweh is knowable with respect to institutional and personal obligations. On the other hand, prophets did not in the main quote or closely adhere to Law traditions, while from prophet to prophet the points of possible contact with Law traditions are extremely varied. Some prophets are more concerned with the themes of the Davidic-Zion traditions than with the Pentateuchal events of exodus and conquest. The special relationship of Yahweh and people is not seen by most preexilic prophets as specifically "covenantal" but more often as a divine election or calling. The prophets do not cite legal texts but allude to infractions of the divine will in the public realm that seem to rest ultimately on laws of the general type gathered in the Pentateuch, but also on a general sense of what is humanly right, virtually in the manner of "natural law."[1]

In the other direction, the trenchant criticism of monarchy and stratified society introduced by prophecy had an impact on the written formulations of the Pentateuch. Possibly J, and certainly E, were affected by the prophetic critique of centralized government in offering their versions of the old traditions as a caution or corrective to forms of royal politics and societal oppression that endangered tribal society and religion. Deuteronomy even more obviously imbibed the prophetic judgments on society and proposed a program of reformation to avert the political catastrophe forewarned by prophets. DH, for which Deuteronomy was once the introduction, gave prominent place to a series of prophets throughout the monarchy who persistently though vainly sought national conversion and lasting reformation.

The historical-legal traditions that eventually became the Law and the judgment and salvation oracles that eventually became the Prophets, together with the advocates and bearers of those traditions, thus interacted and responded to one another more or less directly over centuries before final fixation of the traditions in two separate collections. We have earlier observed how the three major authoritative collections of the Hebrew Bible took shape (§11.2.a) as a result of a complex of sociohistoric and religious factors that fostered canonization (§11.2.b). With respect to the Law, we have seen that its authoritative form was reached after a major break in the production of history-like traditions occasioned by the exile (§40), and that

---

1. John Barton, "Natural Law and Poetic Justice in the Old Testament," *JTS* n.s. 30 (1979): 1–14, with application to Amos, Isaiah, and Ezekiel.

the formal commitment of the Jewish community to the Law as a fixed collection was a key element in the Jewish restoration program in Palestine fostered by Nehemiah and Ezra with the full concurrence of Persian imperial authority (§44.3–4). Regarding the Prophets, we indicated the overall process by which the individual oral and written messages were gathered into large collections that were edited according to several identifiable redactional techniques (§28). This redaction process gathered momentum during the exile and early restoration period as prophetic interpretations of events, rejected by a majority of their power-wielding contemporaries, at last won a more favorable hearing once the full course of events seemed in large measure to validate the prophets.

48.2 A Consensus Canon Elevates Law Tempered by Prophecy

The dominant scholarly view of the literary process by which the Law was given final form is that *Genesis-Numbers* (Tetrateuch, "four scrolls"), composed of JEP materials, was joined to *Deuteronomy,* transferred from its place at the beginning of DH, to form Genesis-Deuteronomy (Pentateuch, "five scrolls"). A persisting minority view argues, to the contrary, that *Genesis-Joshua* (Hexateuch, "six scrolls") was edited as one work (some think Genesis-Samuel or Genesis–1 Kings 12), with D revisions evident in parts of Genesis-Numbers and P materials present in Joshua. On this latter hypothesis, only subsequently was this longer composition shortened to Genesis-Deuteronomy to form the Law, while Joshua-Kings was eventually to become Former Prophets.

Whether the Pentateuch was built up from a shorter work of four books or cut down from a longer one of six or more books, it is recognized that Deuteronomy was unnaturally separated from its sequel in Joshua-Kings. The primary factor in this wrenching apart of the Deuteronomistic books was probably political: to play down the military and political features of Israel's history as a tribal confederation and state(s) so as not offend Persian sensibilities (§11.2.a). This arbitrary isolation of Genesis-Deuteronomy as a literary corpus was acceptable to the Jewish restoration leadership behind the formal publication of the Law because the Pentateuch contained all the basic religiously oriented regulations necessary for constituting Judah as a semiautonomous colonial sector of the Persian Empire.

A further factor in the delimitation of the Law underscores how Law and Prophets as authoritative collections continued to influence one another. Studies of the literary and theological streams of tradition advocated by different categories of leaders in the restored Jewish community strongly imply that the way in which Law and Prophets were put together and officially endorsed represents a *compromise among rival groups* who had to collaborate to a certain degree if efforts to pull the community together were to receive general consent among the Jewish populace and firm support from the Persians.[2] In order for there to be a functioning Jewish community in Palestine, there had to be civil order and legitimate cult. It was the *Law,* supplemented by *Persian imperial administration,* that provided the former, and it was the *sacrificial and ritual holiness system* centered on the temple and expounded in the Law that provided the latter. Priests were custodians of the cult system, and increasingly the promulgation of the Law required the training of interpreters of the Law who could apply it over the whole range of civil and cultic life. At first these scribal custodians of the Law were mainly priests, but in time lay experts in Law arose. By the second century, laity were strong enough to supersede the priests as the dominant interpreters of Law (§47.2).

Whoever succeeded in controlling the temple establishment in the restored Jewish community exercised significant political, economic, and ideological power. So many disturbances in the continuity of priestly leadership had occurred since the late seventh century that there was no community consensus as to which of the contesting priestly factions had the right to be custodians of the renewed cult. The Deuteronomic reform had cancelled out the exercise of priesthood in Judah apart from Jerusalem, but it failed in its hope of integrating the non-Jerusalemite priests into the newly centralized sanctuary. A few decades later most, if not all, of the Jerusalem priests in power were killed, deported, or scattered in 597 and 586 B.C.E. The reduced cult that continued on the site of the destroyed temple was officiated over by other priests, perhaps including some from northern Israelite communities (thus Samaritans). As waves of deported Jews returned to Judah in the late sixth and fifth centuries, descendants of the various priestly groups that at one time or another had presided over the cult now contended for the plum of ecclesial leadership in the rebuilt temple.

We do not know the actual historical line that linked the new postexilic priesthood with the older priesthoods. What is clear is that one group won out decisively over all the others, but that at least some of the losers were given secondary positions in cult administration. It is certain that this "battle of priestly pedigrees" was not simply a war of words since the winners depended on political and economic clout mustered among Jews

2. On "consensus canon," see Gerald T. Sheppard, "Canonization: Hearing the Voice of the Same God Through Historically Dissimilar Traditions," *Int* 37 (1982): 25–26.

and Persians to secure their hold in office. Nevertheless, the victors were in need of a plausible ecclesial ideology that would certify them as true successors of ancient priesthood. In this regard the new priesthood was amazingly resourceful in validating its claims.

The dominant view of the priesthood in early Israel is that nearly all priests were considered to be Levites and all Levites were equally legitimate priests. In restricting worship to the one temple at Jerusalem, the Deuteronomic reform sharply reduced the need for large numbers of priests and thus created an oversupply. The decisive change after the exile was to adjust to the oversupply of priests and to secure a commanding victory for one group of claimants by distinguishing between higher and lower orders of cultic personnel. The newly instituted gradations in cult personnel were impressively validated by tracing the greatly narrowed legitimate priestly line back to Aaron, the brother of Moses. All other priestly claimants were lumped together as Levites who were henceforth demoted to support roles as attendants of the priests. In this way, the Aaronid priests were lodged in firm control even as they granted limited recognition to rival priestly groups whose support activities could be closely monitored. The older office of chief priest was elevated in status and power owing in large part to the absence of Jewish political sovereignty which had formerly accorded the king great power of appointment and administration in cultic matters.

The postexilic political and religious lines of power are reflected in the arrangement of the Law and Prophets and in the ongoing interpretive interaction between the two collections. The Aaronid priests stood behind the P document (§49.3) and their decisive shaping of the Pentateuch showed forth in the rocklike stability of the cult revealed to Moses, whose detailed instructions and regulations form the single largest sweep of materials in the finished Pentateuch. The demoted Levitical attendants of the priests were not so clearly unified in purpose or program as the Aaronids, but it is likely that they shared with other non-elite groups of the Judahite populace in a more dynamic historical and moral view of the meaning and function of the cult, as expressed in Deuteronomy and DH, in aspects of Chronicles, and in certain of the late Prophets such as Trito-Isaiah, Malachi, and Joel. The Aaronids, in accepting Deuteronomy into the collection of the Law and conceding a subordinate role for Levitical interests, gambled on taming their opponents through cooptation.

The result was to combine, both within communal life and within the newly published Law, two rather different ways of looking upon law and cult and, at the same time, to set the stage for the eventual inclusion of prophecy as an authoritative voice of the community alongside law and cult.

The "Aaronid" establishment outlook, shared by a majority of the lay elite who had to cooperate with the Persians, viewed the cult as a virtually self-sufficient program for being a good Jew who at the same time had to be compliant with Persian authority. The P cult practice, and most of the P laws, were concerned with countering natural evils and contaminations (what has been called a "pollution system") [§49.2].[3] The view of history and social order in P and Chronicles largely lacks a sense of the contingency and ambiguity of events and institutions that evokes flexibility and humility of mind and calls for continuous critical assessment of oppressive or outmoded power. To the Aaronid mind history was a pageant that unfolded God's unshakeable institutional endowment "once and for all" to changeless Irael.

The "Levitical" critical outlook, probably less unified in its incorporation of various brands of dissent, tended to see the cult as deeply dependent on repentance and moral commitment, and on a finely tuned understanding of Israel's history, in order to live appropriately in each new set of altered conditions. The laws of Deuteronomy stressed social justice, were radically framed by hortatory appeals and motivations to obey them out of gratitude and love, and were to be read in constant interplay with the course of history and prophecy from Moses down to the exile as recounted in DH. To this way of viewing matters, law and cult were fundamentally involved in countering human evils and inequities both in individual deeds and in impersonal power structures (what has been called a "debt system") [§37.3].[4] Diverse as these protesters against the postexilic establishment were, we hear their many voices in late prophetic writings, in psalms of lament and thanksgiving, and in the bitter comments of skeptical wisdom literature. This very diversity meant that they probably formed no continuing organization or political party, but were scattered in various institutional niches. On occasion, however, as in the agrarian protest in Nehemiah's time or later on among the Hasids and Pharisees of Maccabean times, they might combine forces or in various ways cooperate to weaken or overthrow the momentarily vulnerable establishment.[5]

In the final form of the Law, P assured that the structures of the cult and law stood out as the central pillars of the collection, but at the same time, through the inclusion of JE and Deuteronomy, these structures were con-

3. Fernando Belo, "The Symbolic Order of Ancient Israel," in *A Materialist Reading of the Gospel of Mark* (Maryknoll, N.Y.: Orbis Books, 1981), 37–59, and see n. 14 below.

4. Belo, "Symbolic Order."

5. The groups I characterize as "Aaronid" and "Levitical" are described as "hierocratic" and "visionary" by Paul D. Hanson, *DA*, 70–76.

ceded to be mediated through the specificities of Israel's history and in close connection with Israel's social ethical priorities as a formerly tribal people. Prophecy left its mark upon the Law insofar as E and Deuteronomy, in particular, had been leavened by the impact of the prophets. More specifically, the Law referred to Moses as a prophet and more than a prophet and even made an effort to evaluate prophecy as a fresh voice from God, to the point of acknowledging the possible emergence of "a prophet like Moses" (probably meaning a succession of prophets). Also, by lifting Deuteronomy out of the larger DH composition, the authority of Law thus granted to it inevitably "rubbed off" on Joshua through Kings, enhancing their status and encouraging the feasibility and desirability of yet another collection of sacred writings that would carry the story beyond the death of Moses—where the Aaronid priests left to themselves would have been happy to let it end.

Although they saw rather different meanings in law and cult, all parties to the Judahite restoration did concur that the finished Law set forth essential foundational traditions to Israel. Yet that Law was neither a work of reasoned doctrine nor a rationally codified book of laws. The immense variety and somewhat arbitrary juxtaposition of traditions in the Law, together with the different interests and priorities of Judahite groups, meant that a very lively ongoing process of interpretation was urgent in order to determine how traditions from centuries past should be applied to present changed conditions. In plain fact, everyone had to come to terms with changed conditions, even the Aaronid priests who denied them in principle but struggled to minimize their harm in practice. In one direction, this "slippage" between the Law and ever-changing present circumstances of life led to the development of scribal traditions and eventually to Rabbinic Oral Law. In another direction, it forced the question of what other written traditions were necessary to supplement the Law in order that the full resources of Israelite experience and reflection might be marshaled for the guidance of restored and dispersed communities of Jews.

48.3 An Expanded Canon Incorporates
Prophecy Accommodated to Law

The steps in the process of collecting and editing the Prophets have not been as fully studied as the steps in the formation of the Law. It has been conjectured that at the time DH was last revised, shortly after 561 B.C.E., an accompanying collection of prophetic books was made under Deuteronomistic auspices.[6] DH itself had treated a series of prophets through-

---

6. Joseph Blenkinsopp, *Prophecy and Canon. A Contribution to the Study of Jewish Origins* (Notre Dame, Ind.: University of Notre Dame Press, 1977), 101–2.

out the course of its history of the monarchy in Samuel-Kings. With the exception of Jonah and Isaiah, however, DH did not allude to any of the prophets whose books now appear among the Latter Prophets. This oddity could be explained if the circles that produced DH intended it to be read in tandem with a supplementary collection of prophetic writings. In that event, DH deliberately mentioned only those prophets who lacked books in their names. Jonah, in fact, is no exception to this rule because the extant Book of Jonah was almost certainly written later than DH. The anomaly of Isaiah's mention in DH may be understandable as a cross-reference planted by the writer and carrying the coded message: Consult the collection of prophetic writings which begins with the prophet Isaiah. Interestingly, Isaiah 36—39 repeats the Isaianic material from 2 Kings and probably carries a similar message: Consult DH for stories of other prophets who did not leave books in their name. Moreover, the dating schemes and terminology of some of the superscriptions to prophetic books are decidedly Deuteronomistic.[7] The hypothetical sixth-century prophetic collection by the DH traditionists may have included Isaiah, Jeremiah, Hosea, Amos, Micah, Nahum, Habakkuk, and Zephaniah.

If the above conjecture is correct, then DH and prophetic writings traveled together in the same tradition circles. Once Deuteronomy was joined with Genesis-Numbers to constitute the authoritative Law, it was a logical extension of the same literary practice of combining related materials in a collection to regard Joshua-Kings (Former Prophets) plus a further expansion of the exilic DH collection of prophets (Latter Prophets) as two parts of a second authoritative block of writings. Estimation of the date when the Prophets corpus was rounded out to its completed form depends on how late one locates such sections as Isaiah 24—27 and Zechariah 9—14. Probably the final form was reached during the third century.

It appears that more than one principle of organization was followed in the collection of the Prophets. Size of the books determined that Isaiah, Jeremiah, and Ezekiel should be first, whereas all the other much-shorter works were joined together in a single Book of the Twelve (in Christian tradition, the Minor Prophets). Various Hebrew and Greek manuscript traditions put the first three books in different sequences, but the above chronological order—followed in printed Hebrew Bibles and in all modern translations—appears to be the oldest one. Within the Book of the Twelve,

---

7. Gene M. Tucker, "Prophetic Superscriptions and the Growth of the Canon," in *Canon and Authority. Essays in Old Testament Religion and Theology,* ed. George W. Coats and Burke O. Long (Philadelphia: Fortress Press, 1977), 56–70.

a rough chronological grouping is observed: (1) the period of Assyrian supremacy (Hosea, Joel, Amos, Obadiah, Jonah, and Micah); (2) the period of Assyrian downfall (Nahum, Habakkuk, Zephaniah); and (3) the period of Persian domination (Haggai, Zechariah, Malachi). It is also tempting to discern a catchword principle at work in common terms or phrases that link the endings of some books with the beginnings of others (e.g., "return to Yahweh your God," Hos. 14:1 and Joel 2:12; "Yahweh roars from Zion," Joel 4:16 and Amos 1:2; "Edom," Amos 9:12 and Obad. 1:1). That there are exactly twelve shorter prophetic books suggests an allusion to the twelve tribes of Israel.

Within the prophetic books certain broadly similar redactional conventions are at work. They are supplied with superscriptions or introductory notations that constitute a title together with information about the prophet, the book, and/or the date. There is a pronounced tendency to organize the contents of the prophecies in a threefold pattern: (1) words of judgment against Israel/Judah; (2) words of judgment against foreign nations; (3) words of salvation for Israel/Judah. This grouping is followed in Isaiah, Jeremiah, Ezekiel, and Zephaniah (LXX retains the original structure of Jeremiah by introducing the foreign oracles at the midpoint of the book following 25:13a instead of at the end as in MT and modern translations where they appear as chaps. 46—51). The Book of Amos artfully breaks with the customary pattern by placing foreign oracles at the opening of the book. This redactional exception scores a stunning point by leading up to similarly patterned oracles against Judah and Israel who, in their apostasy from Yahweh, are in effect stigmatized as "foreigners."

The obviously diverse and complicated redactions of the separate prophetic books, employing reuse, rearrangement, and amplification of older prophecies, means that the Prophets division of the Hebrew Bible is a collection of collections. As a consequence of this redactional process extending over generations, any given prophetic book is apt to contain reference to and comment on a whole series of turbulent events: the collapse of the northern kingdom, the reformation of Josiah, the fall of Judah, the exile, and the restoration. Increasingly after the exile, the past critical events and the prophetic reflections on them were read as pointers to exile and restoration. The double accent of judgment and salvation is prolonged from one critical event to another through the redactional reinterpretation and expansion process. This trend toward reading the Prophets for warning and consolation in the restoration era thematized the whole prophetic corpus as a message of judgment followed by salvation.[8] This

8. Roland E. Clements, *Old Testament Theology. A Fresh Approach* (Atlanta: John Knox Press, 1978), 131–54.

consciousness of a common prophetic message ending with an upbeat hope looked forward also toward an open future in which more blessing was expected than had so far been realized in the modest restoration program after the exile.

This larger literary context for reading individual prophetic books as parts of a collected whole that refers pointedly to the contemporary community entailed a significant measure of indeterminacy and ambiguity. It could readily be understood—especially by self-confident and proud secular and priestly leaders of the restoration—that the prophetic judgments referred largely or wholly to the past and that henceforth, the exile being past, only salvation lay in store. To the contrary, when read in the historical perspective of DH whose work in Joshua-Kings formed the preface to the prophetic writings, the individual prophecies hinted at, or openly affirmed, possibilities of judgment still hanging over the community insofar as it continued to exhibit the evils that the older prophets had condemned and that more recent prophets, such as Trito-Isaiah, Malachi, and Joel, were claiming to be rampant in the supposedly purified postexilic community. It was certainly in this latter way that the Prophets were appropriated by many circles in Judah, especially among Levites, recent prophets, and lay leaders who opposed the policies of the Judahite elite.

It is easy to imagine that the struggle over which of the latter books to include in the Prophets hinged in some measure on whether those disputed books were perceived as speaking judgmentally or only consolingly to the present. The last-dated prophecy in the collection is 515 B.C.E., although it is demonstrable that many undated prophecies and some entire books came from later periods, perhaps down to a time as late as 250 B.C.E. It is likely that the most ardent advocates of a Prophets collection read it through protesting "Levitical" lenses as combined judgment and salvation speech dialectically related to the present day. It is just as likely that those who reluctantly agreed to a Prophets collection were able to do so because they read it through establishment "Aaronid" lenses as containing judgment speech directed to the past and salvation speech referring to the "realized eschatology" of the restored community in which they served as a self-confident leadership.

Inevitably, as the Prophets collection expanded and took on more and more authority, it was read reflexively in the light of the already-authoritative Law. Within prophetic books, often among the speeches of the earliest prophets, there are references to *torah*, "law," in various senses such as "instruction," "prescription," or "custom" (e.g., Isa. 1:10; 2:3; 5:24; Jer. 2:8; 5:4; 7:19; 8:18; etc.). Once the collection of the Law (Torah) was given authoritative status, these varied citations of *torah* within the prophets were likely to be perceived increasingly as references to the now officially recognized *Torah*. In this way, prophets who had in fact seriously criticized aspects of law observance among their contemporaries were seen to be model preachers of fidelity to the Book of the Law. Such a "canonical consciousness" worked to assimilate elements of Law and Prophets to one another and to facilitate use of passages from any part of the two great collections to affirm a common message of adherence to law piety as read in conjunction with prophetic admonition and consolation.[9] It is obvious that such *interreadings of Law and Prophets* could operate either in the direction of self-critical "Levitical" interpretations or in the direction of triumphalist "Aaronid" interpretations.

The opening and closing Books of the Twelve have redactional conclusions that highlight this harmonizing and thematizing process by which all the parts of the Law and Prophets tended to be read as congruent and mutually expressive of the religious allegiance and practice incumbent on the restoration community, and could even be thematized by wisdom motifs. Hosea 14:9 declares that all who are "wise" can profit from reading "these things" that Hosea has spoken about because they are not simply past happenings but prototypes of present-day options for righteousness or for transgression.[10] Malachi 4:4 urges the critical centrality of law observance, while a further notation in 4:5–6 announces the return of Elijah as the restorer of peace through justice to the strife-torn Judahite community.

This anticipated return of Elijah, strategically placed at the close of the Latter Prophets, echoes his ascent into heaven in the Former Prophets at 2 Kings 2:1–11. It also stands in thematic connection and open tension with the close of the Law where it is said that no prophet like Moses has since risen (Deut. 34:10). On the one hand, this sets off the Mosaic office and law in a uniquely authoritative category; on the other hand, since a prophet is (or prophets are) anticipated who will be like Moses (Deut. 18:15–22), the Deuteronomic imprint on the Law has left open the probability that new prophetic revelations will occur, in which case they will not abrogate or

9. Technical terms for distinguishing types of "innerbiblical" exegesis are far from agreed upon. Michael Fishbane, "Revelation and Tradition: Aspects of Inner-Biblical Exegesis," *JBL* 99 (1980): 343–61, uses I. L. Seeligmann's term "canon conscious" exegesis for any kind of innerbiblical exegesis, whereas Sheppard, "Canonization," 22–23, 25, distinguishes three kinds of interpretation of scripture by scripture: (1) midrash which reemploys phrases anthologically; (2) canon-conscious redaction which relates one canonical book or a part of a book to some other canonical book or collection of books; and (3) thematization of historically disunified traditions under the canonical rubrics of Law, Prophets, and Wisdom.

10. Gerald T. Sheppard, *Wisdom as a Hermeneutical Construct. A Study in the Sapientializing of the Old Testament*, BZAW 151 (Berlin and New York: Walter de Gruyter, 1980), 129–36.

contradict the foundation laid by Moses. When Law and Prophets are placed together, these Deuteronomistic allusions to prophets yet to come serve as a signal to readers that the collection of Prophets was "prophetically" foreseen by Moses the Lawgiver. Likewise, the final words of the Latter Prophets tell us that, although the *collection* is closed, the *work* of prophets in the world is not finished. Insofar as the prophet yet to come in Mal. 4:4–5 is actually one of the old prophets returned, namely Elijah, the limits of the prophetic genre have been reached and we are close to the threshold of apocalyptic.[11]

Thus, in countless literary and conceptual details which redaction criticism has only barely begun to grasp, the process of collecting, redacting, and authorizing Law and Prophets contributed to a sense of the unity of message in the two works and to their jointly reinforcing effects on exegetical tradition. By this juncture, within the time span 450–250 B.C.E., the Jewish people had taken decisive steps toward becoming a people of the Book whose self-understanding and self-organization was inextricably bound up in a complex and sophisticated literary tradition that demanded constant exegesis and application to the concrete circumstances of life.

49
ROUNDING OUT THE LAW:
THE PRIESTLY WRITER (P)

We have earlier introduced the P source of the Pentateuch (§13.4) and listed its contents in Genesis 12—50 (table 10C) and in Exodus-Numbers (table 11D). To complete the contents of the P document it is necessary to include passages in Genesis 1—11 (table 26).

49.1 Vocabulary, Style, and Structure

There is a wealth of distinctive vocabulary in P: "to be fruitful and multiply," "according to their families" (in enumerations), "throughout your generations," "to be gathered to one's people" (euphemism for death), "this selfsame day," "establish a covenant" (rather than "cut a covenant" as in JE), "eternal covenant," "this is the thing that Yahweh commanded," "congregation of the Israelites" (instead of "assembly" or "people" in JE), *nephesh* in the sense of "person" (rather than "life force" or "soul" in JE), *gulgoleth*, "skull/head," for people in numerical tallies (as

---

11. Blenkinsopp, *Prophecy and Canon*, 85–89, 120–23, argues that the last paragraphs of the Law (Deut. 34:10–12) and of the Prophets (Mal. 4:4–6) show an acute awareness of the balance between Torah observance and prophetic judgment and hope.

TABLE 26
Priestly (P) Traditions in Genesis 1—11

Creation of the Cosmos and of Humans	1:1—2:4a
Genealogy of Seth (From Adam to Noah)	5:1–28, 30–32
Destruction by Flood	
Preparation for Flood	6:9–22
Execution of Flood	7:6, 11, 13–16a, 18–21, 24; 8:1–2a, 3b–5, 7b, 13a, 14–19
Covenant with Noah	9:1–17, 28–29
Table of Nations	10:1–7, 20, 22–23, 31–32
Genealogy of Shem (From Noah to Abram)	11:10–27

when we say "so many 'head' of cattle," or when we "count noses"), *maṭṭeh* for "tribe" (in JE *shēveṭ*), *Kiriath-arba* for Hebron (the latter in JE), and *Paddan-aram* for the homeland of Laban (*Aram-Naharaim* in J). In cultic terms, P speaks of "the unauthorized encroacher or usurper (of priestly office)" and employs *'avōdāh* strictly for "manual labor" (rather than for temple cultic service as in other Pentateuchal sources). There is a considerable set of terms—perhaps legally defined—for property: *rᵉkūsh* for "movable goods, including animals," *'aḥuzzāh* for "landed property," and *miqnāh/qinyān* for "purchased/acquired land, produce, or slaves."

The measured style of the Priestly writer is stamped by a large number of fixed formulas extensively repeated, notably at the beginning and conclusion of units. Each subject tends to be developed by fullness of description and stereotyped reiteration, with a fondness for describing an object at length each time it is mentioned and for giving the substance of an action first as a command or direction and a second time when the act is executed. The methodical and precise P style is strongly evident in a preponderance of instructions and regulations (encompassing 1745 verses) and in a sizable number of tribal and topographical lists (amounting to another 333 verses). Even its narratives are set forth in a similarly measured and stately form (approximately 517 verses) featuring literary techniques and an iconic style intended for instruction (§15.3.d). Since P can produce marvelous effects with this style, as in the rhythmic unfolding of the creation story and in the sly negotiations between Abram and Ephron for purchase of the Cave of Machpelah, the drabness and spiritlessness felt by many readers probably has less to do with style than with P's preoccupation with ritual and its rather colorless and contrived theological reading of history.

In a work so stereotyped in language and style, we expect a clearly marked structure and in this we are not entirely disappointed, although the extent of secondary expansions in P and the process of combining it with JE has disturbed what may once have been a much-greater symmetry in the P document. We note first of all that the formula "these are the generations of X" has been used to mark off eleven phases in the history that runs from creation to the era of Moses: the heavens and the earth (Gen. 2:4a), Adam (5:1a), Noah (6:9a), Shem, Ham, and Japheth (10:1a), Shem (10:10a), Terah (11:27a), Ishmael (25:12), Isaac (25:19), Esau (36:1, 9), Jacob (37:2), and Aaron and Moses (Num. 3:1).

In addition, P sets forth *three perpetual covenants* that sharply periodize the sacred history:

1. A covenant with *Noah* in Gen. 9:1–17, sealed by rainbow, promising that the earth will never again be destroyed, and permitting the eating of meat as long as the blood has been drained (prior to this, humans were vegetarian, cf. Gen. 1:29–30);

2. A covenant with *Abraham* in Genesis 17, sealed by the rite of circumcision, and promising his descendants national and royal greatness, possession of the land, and the abiding divine presence;

3. A covenant with the *people of Israel* in Exod. 31:12–18, mediated by the revelation of law to Moses, and sealed by Sabbath observance which overtly echoes the theme of God resting on the seventh day after creating the world (Exod. 31:17; cf. Gen. 2:2–3).

The covenant of the Mosaic age occurs, however, in a literary joint between the command to make the tabernacle and the execution of the command, and it lacks the full thematic development of the Noachian and Abrahamic covenants, implying a secondary insertion. P also provides a "covenant of perpetual priesthood" with *Phinehas* (an etiology to anchor the Aaronid line) in connection with his zealous suppression of the cult of Baal of Peor (Num. 25:10–13). Of course as the framework of the Pentateuch, P embraces the covenant traditions in Exodus 19—24, but without comment, apparently because the most important aspect of the revelation at Sinai for P was the tabernacle cult which assured the continuing presence of God within Israel's collective life.

Another way of viewing the structure of P is to single out two kinds of formulas that flag the completion of successive stages in the "works" of history on the one hand, and that emphasize the attendant continuous fulfillment of commands of God on the other hand.[12] A *conclusion* or *completion formula* demarcates three important moments in the Priestly account:

1. *Creation of the world* (Gen. 2:1–2): "Thus the heavens and the earth were finished and all the host of them . . . so God finished his work which he had done."

2. *Construction of the tabernacle* in the wilderness (Exod. 39:32; 40:33): "Thus all the work of the tabernacle of the tent of meeting was finished . . . so Moses finished the work."

3. *Division of the land* after setting up tabernacle at Shiloh (Josh. 18:1; 19:51): "So they finished dividing the land."

This analysis assumes that elements of P survive in Joshua, even though P did not have a full "conquest" story because his emphasis on the divine gift of the land precluded description of military action in order to seize it. A more frequent *executionary formula,* occurring at forty-one places in P, runs as follows: "X did according to all that Yahweh [God] commanded him [or commanded Moses]," underscoring the various specifically mandated actions by which the divine plan was implemented for rounding out the major stages in the movement from creation to Israel's physical and cultic occupation of the land.

12. Joseph Blenkinsopp, "The Structure of P," *CBQ* 38 (1976): 275–92.

49.2 Everything in Its Place: A Stable Cult in a Stable Cosmos

An analysis of P by means of these conclusion and execution formulas brings out a definite structural correspondence between creation of the world and construction of the tabernacle and its successful establishment in the land. There is likewise a structural correspondence between the ark of Noah and the tabernacle.[13] Some interpreters detect schematizing midrashic tendencies in P toward pushing back the origins of the Israelite cult into the very intention of God in creation (God rested on the archetypal Sabbath day!) and toward viewing the law of Moses as having made explicit what was implicit in a prior covenant with all peoples. It is of interest that the Noachian covenant ambivalently permitted bloodless meat eating but did not yet mandate sacrifice, nor did it provide civil justice for punishing the murder of humans which it forbade.

The drift toward *midrash* in P combines with an old Mesopotamian priestly scribal interest in fusing *myth and cult* by recounting how sanctuaries and their cults and priesthoods derive from creation itself and are even based on cosmic models (cf. Exod. 25:9, 40). Just as God overcame chaos in creating the world, he again conquered chaos with Noah's ark, and finally decisively defeated the disorder and sin of the world by means of the tabernacle with its divinely ordained cult that would secure the perpetual purity and fidelity of Israel to Yahweh.

The mythically generated fascination with cosmos and chaos should be read as a *stabilizing strategy* in the struggle to preserve Jewish community in the midst of disorienting exilic and restoration conditions. Similarly, the passion to differentiate Israel as a distinct people with its own peculiar marks of circumcision, Sabbath, food laws, festivals, and sacrifices is a comprehensive effort to fashion a *self-perpetuating and self-correcting community* that would not be eroded by internal division and uncertainty or by external oppression and persuasion.

Among the covenantal divisions of the Priestly document, some interpreters have included an implicit covenant with the first humans, sealed by a foreshadowing of Sabbath observance, and giving plants to humans for food. No covenant terminology or close parallel with the other covenant passages in P is visible in Genesis 1, however.

The connection of Genesis 1 to the rest of P is better clarified by the conclusion and execution formulas. Strictly speaking, there is no execution formula in Genesis 1, since there is no higher power than God to direct the

13. Ibid., 280–86.

deity to undertake creative acts. On the other hand, the description of creation in six days interweaves two ways of depicting the accomplishment of creation that pivot on a distinction between God *speaking* the world into being (fiat and realization formulas) and God *crafting* the world into being (work formula). On the one hand, the coupling of the fiat formula ("And God said . . .") with the realization formula ("And it was so") conceptually parallels the execution of command formula that runs throughout the remainder of P, while the work formula ("God created/made/divided . . .") formally parallels the completion of work formula that sums up the acts of creation in Gen. 2:1–2 and likewise rounds out both the making of the tabernacle in the wilderness and its placement in Canaan.

It has long been recognized that the P writer, in the process of fitting *eight* creative acts into *six* days, accommodated older sources to his programmatic aim of having God rest on the seventh day. It is probable also that P deliberately interwove the fiat/realization and work formulas from different sources in order to embrace alternative ways of talking about God's "speaking" and "doing" in creation, which in turn anticipated the interplay of similar divine modes of initiating new phases of the human story. The distribution of creative acts over six days, the symmetry between the acts of days 1–3 and days 4–6, and the fusion of fiat/realization and work formulas in Genesis 1 may be shown graphically (chart 4).

The "world picture" of P is that of a flat disk earth topped by a solid and transparent semicircular firmament, with threatening but controlled waters beneath the earth and above the firmament (figure 1). This cosmos is an orderly rule-governed environment for humans which anticipates the ark of Noah and the tabernacle in the wilderness as further *God-given safe environments* to protect humankind, and eventually Israel, against natural and historical "chaos." The establishment of the tabernacle in Canaan, after long wandering, signals a kind of "second creation" in which Israel receives a secure home that will remain unshaken as long as the rule-governed cult for the worship of God is observed faithfully.

A fusion of *cosmic myth* and *cultic scrupulosity* in these priestly scribal traditions, stretched upon a frame of stylized "history," contributes to a highly differentiated world of thought and practice in which every object, person, and activity has its meaningful place and its proper/improper function. The Priestly narratives and laws develop an elaborate network of social significations that correspond to a social system with the hierarchic order of Aaronic priests, Levitical attendants, laity, resident aliens, slaves, and children. Every Israelite has an area of competency subject to subordination to those higher in the hierarchy of access to the divine. The world

CHART 4

"Fiat," "Realization," and "Work" Formulas in Genesis 1

(1st Day)	Light and Darkness ←——————→ (4th Day)		Heavenly Bodies
	F, R, W		F, R, W
(2d Day)	Firmament and Waters ←——————→ (5th Day)		Birds and Fishes
	F, W, R		F, W
(3d Day)	Land ←——————————→ (6th Day)		Land Animals
	F, R		F, R, W
	Vegetation ←————————————————→ Humans		
	F, R, W		F, W, R

Key:

F: Fiat Formula, "And God said . . ."
R: Realization Formula, "And it was so"
W: Work Formula, "God created/made/divided . . ."

has a unity in the creative and salvific purposes of God, but everything once created has its own distinctive character and its definite boundaries which must not be exceeded nor mixed with other created things, lest the order of the world be undone.

FIGURE 1
The Cosmos of Genesis 1

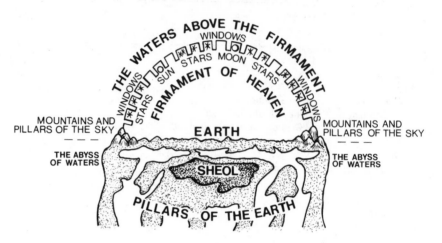

The greater part of P is devoted to clarifying the "cuts," that is, the *distinctions and differentiations,* appropriate to each stage of the primal history from creation to Moses: (1) the first humans are to make a "cut" between animals and plants, eating only the latter; (2) Noah is to make a "cut" between animal flesh and blood, eating only the former; (3) Abraham and his progeny are "to be cut" through circumcision, so that they will be separate from those uncircumcised; (4) Moses and his people are to make a complicated series of "cuts" between legitimate and illegitimate priests, sanctuaries, cultic appointments, festivals, foods, kinship ties, sexual relationships, and dispositions of property. The created world and the land of Canaan belong to the deity who sets the terms of distinction and differentiation for a prospering and enduring Israelite community.[14]

Arbitrary laws about clean and unclean foods—which in some details probably preseve hygienic origins—can be grasped as the outworking of the

14. Jean Soler, "The Dietary Prohibitions of the Hebrews," *The New York Review of Books* (June 14, 1979): 24–30; see also Mary Douglas, *Purity and Danger. An Analysis of Concepts of Pollution and Taboo* (Baltimore: Penguin Books, 1970), 54–72, and n. 3 above.

Priestly conviction about *orders of creation* that must be scrupulously respected by Israelites in their diet. P assumes three orders of living creatures, each with characteristic anatomical features and separate habitats, and which are intended never to encroach or prey upon one another: (1) *creatures of the earth* that walk on legs and are covered with skin; (2) *creatures of the air* that fly on wings and are covered with feathers; (3) *creatures of the water* that swim with fins and are covered with scales.

Any food seen to fall within these "proper" categories was considered clean and edible, while all of the numerous foods that violate the divinely decreed distinctions were forbidden. Since P's catalogue of "ideal creatures" was so circumscribed compared to the profusion of forms in nature, the list of unclean foods is long: carnivorous animals and birds, herbivorous animals who do not have the primary characteristic of a divided hoof, sea creatures that lack fins or have legs, birds that do not fly, winged insects, and land creatures that creep or slide because they have no legs.

Similarly, sexual practices must follow a strict heterosexual order according to *permitted sexual unions* that do not mix parents and children (incest), humans and animals (bestiality), and do not reverse or confuse sexual identities (homosexuality). In this connection, it is important to distinguish between the Priestly differentiated world view that "explains" these prohibitions and other possible explanations that may contain important elements of truth. In anthropological studies, prohibition of incest has sometimes been explained as a necessary measure to maintain internal family harmony and/or as a way of forcing human groups regularly into wider, peace-building community with other groups through obligatory out-group marriages. Biblical scholars have been inclined to think that homosexuality was stigmatized in ancient Israel because of its practice in Canaanite fertility religion; recently, however, doubts have been raised about whether cult prostitution was practiced as widely in Israel's environment as once thought. There is also the real possibility that male homosexuality (lesbianism is not mentioned in the Hebrew Bible) was abhorred in ancient Israel because it seemed to involve a prodigal waste of "male seed" which, according to ancient misunderstanding, was thought to be limited in quantity or potency. In that event, to be a homosexual was to be derelict in fathering the large families that were the cultural norm for the agricultural Israelites.

The Priestly conceptual and cultic world is highly rationalized and orderly, and yet precarious and endangered. At any moment one may knowingly or unknowingly breach the wonderfully balanced classificatory scheme in one direction or another and be plunged into the *disorder of uncleanness and impending death.* To abolish or ignore distinctions, not to make all the "cuts" ordered by God, is to subvert the order of the world, the very principle of self-identity, and to be exposed to the dissolution of death. Thus, every significant detail of life must be regulated according to the gracious revelation of the Priestly law through Moses.

Habitual and unavoidable exposure to uncleanness, such as menstruation and contact with corpses, must be rectified by proper ritual. It is likely, in this regard, that the *stigmatization of menstruation* as a "blemish" strengthened the *marginalization of women* in public and cultic roles which had long been underway in the move from tribal to monarchic social organization. Likewise, although P does not make a great deal of it, the postexilic prohibition of marriage to non-Jews was no doubt greatly reinforced by the P conception of not mixing like with unlike. Of course the practical social difficulties were that introducing foreigners into Jewish homes made for cultic confusion and, since it was mostly upper-class Jews who married foreigners, intermarriage introduced upwardly mobile social and economic striving that was divisive to the community.

49.3 Antecedents of P as the Charter of Postexilic Judaism

Older scholarship was emphatic in placing the P document in the exilic or postexilic periods, largely because its elaborate cultic provisions and its thought world do not show up in any of the preexilic literature which more or less covers the same subject matter, such as JE and D. It is only with Ezekiel during the exile and with Ezra and the Chronicler after the exile that the close affinities with P appear. More recent scholarship has made clear that the date and locus of P are no simple matter to determine. Even in fixing on the sixth or fifth century as the time of P composition, many scholars have long recognized that there is old material in P that may actually go back to premonarchic social and military organizational data and even to some form of migratory cult shrine underlying the lavish tabernacle.

It was also seen that there are sections of P that have their own character, once existed in independent form, and have only been secondarily drawn into the P framework of the Pentateuch through supplementation. Striking in this regard is the so-called Holiness Code of Leviticus 17—26 which is marked by the refrain, "You [Israel] shall be holy as I [Yahweh] am holy." The content of the Holiness Code includes generous sections of social legislation that show affinities with the older law codes of Exodus 20—23 and Deuteronomy 12—26. There is wide assent to the notion that the Holiness Code derives in written form from the late monarchy.

Characteristic of present research on the P document is the claim by many that it was written in large part before the fall of Jerusalem and perhaps even before Deuteronomy. P frequently uses vocabulary and describes cultic procedures that were *not* distinctive of the postexilic period according to other sources, and thus would have made little sense within a freshly created charter for the postexilic temple. On the other hand, how could a written monarchic version of such strikingly idiosyncratic priestly traditions have been ignored by all tradition circles of Israel prior to Ezekiel? A frequent resolution of this puzzle is to claim that the P traditions actually circulated and were compiled in priestly circles that lacked power to determine the cult practices of preexilic Israel. Some have identified Hebron or Shiloh as the tradition center of P, while others have argued for Jerusalem priests who were eclipsed both by priests who acculturated to foreign religious practices (e.g., under Manasseh and later under Jehoiakim and Zedekiah) and by the Deuteronomic reformers who had their own wide-ranging combined agenda of sociopolitical and cultic concerns. It is also argued that priestly regulations of the sort that make up so much of P are not customarily a matter of public knowledge but remain within the coterie of priestly experts as restricted professional lore.

We are confronted, it seems, with apparently conflicting evidence about the age and locale of P.[15] On the one hand, it is highly probable that P did not emerge in its present form until well into the exile at the earliest and that it was precisely the postexilic rebuilding of the temple that put such a high premium on P's hierarchic validation of the Aaronic priesthood and on P's passion for the cult as the distinguishing mark of Jewishness. It was this postexilic cultic coup that made P a suitable *charter for the reestablished temple* and won it an honored position as the framework for the final edition of the Law. By the same token, P served as *ideological justification for the power play of the Aaronic priests*.

On the other hand, P's multiple traditions reached back at certain points to ancient features of Israel's institutional life which were maintained and reshaped in accord with the practice of some relatively powerless priestly community in monarchic times. That a lawcode like Leviticus 17—26 could be affected by these priestly traditions suggests that P-type traditions were

---

15. Menahem Haran, "Behind the Scenes of History: Determining the Date of the Priestly Source," *JBL* 100 (1981): 321–33.

known in monarchic times. These traditions probably existed only in small collections and did not yet possess an extended narrative framework. They accompanied a voluntary priestly observance and a self-cultivated guild ethic which was not in a position to impose itself on the whole community, as eventually became possible in the postexilic Priestly editing of the Law and in the reforms of Ezra.

It was probably the fall of Judah and the publication of DH that precipitated a P-based narratized reading of the history from creation to Moses (or Joshua). This P "history" of Israelite beginnings both underlined the *primacy of cult as the true anchor of Israel* and in its treatment of ancient crises made veiled reference to the exilic discontinuities that would only be overcome through faithful adherence to the traditions published in P. Under exilic conditions, this P reading of the early history would have had a somewhat "utopian" ring, of the sort reflected in the related, but unrealized, vision of the rebuilt temple in Ezekiel 40—48. It was probably in connection with the postexilic restoration of the cult that the ritualistic sections of P were expanded and supplemented as it became germane to give directives on the specifics of cultic service. Yet even here it should be noted that the old *historicized utopian form* of P prevailed in that all the cultic instructions were attached to the wilderness tabernacle rather than to the Solomonic temple which would have been a more immediate and appropriate model for the rebuilt temple.

49.4 P as the Framework for the Law

The argument over whether P was an independent author or a traditionist redactor is not easy to formulate, much less decide. The fact is that we have P only as the redactional framework of the Pentateuch which encompasses J, E, and D. On the other hand, this P redaction is so sizable and complex, constituting in itself the largest of all the Pentateuchal sources, and it is so emphatic in its programmatic aims that it seems nit-picking to deny it "authorial integrity." Of course we do not know what shape P assumed before the Pentateuchal redaction or which of its supplements may have been added to fill out the redaction.

In any case, the chronologies, genealogies, itineraries, organizational lists, and cultic minutiae of P have placed a decisive stamp on the entire Pentateuch such that JE and D tend to be read within P's controlling structures and assumptions. In turn, the redaction has somewhat blunted the monolithic message of P and, particularly at the end of Exodus and in Numbers, has contributed to insertions, combinations, and rearrangements of materials that are highly confusing to the reader. We earlier noted how the insertion of Exodus 32—34 (JE) between the plan of the tabernacle (Exodus 25—31) and its construction (Exodus 35—40) has complicated the Sinai scenario (§17.2; 19.1). Even more chaotic is the intermixture of P narratives, laws, and lists with JE narratives and poems from Num. 10:29 to the end of that book. Unlike the larger blocks of P material prior to that point, it appears that the final edition of the Pentateuch has contributed to the fragmentation of P in this section.

When Deuteronomy was added as the last book of the Law and a P version of Moses' death was appended to it (32:48–52; 34:1, 4–8), an awkward separation in the narrative was opened up between the anticipation of Moses' death in Num. 27:12–14 and its realization in Deuteronomy 34. At the same time, by severing Deuteronomy from Joshua-Kings, the Pentateuch only anticipated the conquest through the appointment of Joshua without giving any account of the conquest beyond Transjordan. The result was to create a redactional "dumping ground" at the end of Numbers where a mélange of P traditions, and some J materials, were placed as a matter of convenience.

Two editorial "bracketings" of the Numbers traditions are distinguishable: two censuses of the tribes in Numbers 1 and 26 function as an inclusio for the traditions of chaps. 2—25, while the final miscellaneous additions to Numbers are marked off by an inclusio about women inheriting property in Num. 27:1–11 and 36:1–13. The intervening material moves from a commissioning of Joshua through assorted cultic and military laws to actual allotment of land in Transjordan and the anticipation of an eventual allotment in Cisjordan. A stage-by-stage itinerary of the movement of the people from Egypt to Moab interrupts the allotment traditions. The provision of Levitical cities and cities of refuge is detailed, but without giving their names in the manner of Joshua 20—21. The impression given by these anticipations of the uncompleted conquest is that, with the Book of Joshua excluded from the Law, the redactors wanted to include P-style "pointers" to the culmination of the conquest.

By means of its P-dominated redaction, the Law was brought to its definitive form probably in the fifth century. If it was the P-redacted Law that Ezra brought with him from the Persian Diaspora, it is likely that the redaction was done among Persian Jews. It is possible—and perhaps more in keeping with the "politics" of the redactional process—that Ezra brought a version of the P document that was prepared abroad and, in negotiation with Palestinian traditionists, among whom the Deuteronomistic circles were of special importance, facilitated a redaction that put the P-oriented version in the leading interpretive position but incorporated JE and gave the last word to the forceful admonitions and laws of the Book of Deuteronomy. The result was an amalgam of the "debt system" of the Deuteronomists with the "pollution system" of the Priestly partisans: the former stresses the *moral and historical precariousness* of Israel's status and future in a *socially unjust situation,* while the latter emphasizes the *orderliness of the world* as mediated by the *stabilizing mechanisms of the cult.* These two accents in the foundational Law, with all their affinities and contradictions intact, passed on to postexilic Jewish social actors and traditionists who went on to generate further definitive collections of the Scripture known as the Prophets and the Writings.

50
ROUNDING OUT THE PROPHETS

50.1 Ezekiel

The first prophet to speak out of Israel's exile reveals what a conceptually and emotionally wrenching experience removal from Palestine proved to be. The Book of Ezekiel is difficult and forbidding in large part because it throws us into the maelstrom of deep consternation and radical reorientation which the collapse of Judah forced upon one highly creative person who, despite his striking individuality, was a faithful barometer of the social world of Jewish exiles at large.

Ezekiel was a priest-prophet carried off to Babylonia in the deportation of 597 who preached the deserved final doom of Judah until its demise in 586. Afterward, however, he turned quickly to the task of laying a theoretical and pastoral basis for exiled Jews to assimilate the practical meanings of catastrophe and thus prepare themselves for the future rebuilding of Palestinian Jewry based upon a total conversion to Yahweh's will both in spirit and in practice. In this task the prophet labored until at least 570.

On the surface, Ezekiel presents the austere messages of a transcendent deity who had forthrightly abandoned his temple in Jerusalem but who would return there in good time with a people purified by shame, guilt, repentance, and radical reform. Behind the almost unfeeling exterior of the harsh imperious words of Yahweh, we encounter a prophet who is traumatized by events, struggles to a total identification with his message, ranges in vivid imagination over the symbols and themes of judgment and salvation, and bodily experiences the terror and shock of transforming cruel events into modes of thought and action that can "save" the exiles, not merely as physical survivors, but as a viable community with their traditional roots intact.

The Book of Ezekiel is so much a piece in its stylistic features, so historically oriented to the sixth-century Babylonian exile, and so apparently tight and logical in construction that doubts about the unity of the work were slow to arise among historical-critical scholars. When traditional assumptions were at last questioned, contradictory aspects of this prophet began to stream forth in a virtual torrent. How could a prophet with a moral and social vision also be a priest with ritual scruples and designs for a rebuilt temple? How could a prophet so soon after Jeremiah turn to wild and bewildering visions and allegories and even develop concepts of world calamity and of an earth-renewing temple, thus venturing to the threshold of apocalyptic thought in a single leap? How could a prophet called to preach judgment on Jerusalem do so when far removed in Babylonia? How could a priest-prophet, articulate and pedantic in the presentation of his message, have been tormented by haunting visions and bodily symptoms that have all the appearance of some form of mental illness? How could one and the same person write elegant poetry and turgid prose?

In an effort to resolve these contradictions which cut to the heart of a coherent understanding of the prophet, it was necessary to examine the book for signs of its origin and process of composition. The initial tendency was to cut away sizable parts of the book as "secondary" in the interests of minimizing or eliminating the inconsistencies in the portrait of the prophet. Ezekiel remained soberly anchored as a prophetic moralist by conjecturing that the Gog of Magog apocalypse and the restored temple, and perhaps even his pastoral consolation of the exiles, were elements contributed by someone after the exile. He could also be given a proper audience for his message of judgment before 586 by assigning him an actual ministry in Judah for all or part of his career which was deliberately obscured by a later revision of the book that located him solely in the exile. The prophet appeared less "crazy" when his weird visions and odd behavior were judged largely or entirely to be the additions of a later writer or editor. He became a consistent stylist by theorizing that his own words were in poetic form that was rewritten or expanded by prosaic hands.

Various attempts to reconstruct a credible Ezekiel within a radically reduced core of the book were not satisfactory. The literary analyses were arbitrary, disregarding the distinctive stylistic cohesion of the work, and frequently dictated in advance by the expurgated version of Ezekiel favored by the analyst. Moreover, there was a singular failure to account for how such a "trimmed down" prophet could have given rise to a multifaceted and contradictory, or at least tension-filled, stream of tradition. It awaited form-critical, tradition-historical, and redaction-critical inquiries to make progress in recovering a complex prophetic figure who had launched a fertile process of tradition formation that finally issued in the present Book of Ezekiel. The key to the book and to the prophet lies then somewhere between the simplistic notion of the book's unity and a splintering dissection that bypasses the nature of the traditions and the subtleties of Ezekiel's synthesis of judgment and salvation.[16]

The arrangement of the contents of the Book of Ezekiel shows a clear plan. Following a vividly detailed account of a theophany of Yahweh leading to a cataclysmic call to prophesy (1—3), the book divides into oracles of judgment against Judah/Jerusalem (4—24), oracles against foreign nations (25—32), and oracles of salvation directed to the exiles (33—48). Chronological and visionary schemes, as well as historical-theological thematizing devices, variously interconnect these topical subdivisions.

Placed throughout the work is a series of dates by year, month, and day reckoned from the first deportation in 597 (1:1–2; 8:1; 20:1; 24:1; 26:1; 29:1, 17; 30:20; 31:1; 32:1, 17; 33:21; 40:1). The initial date places Ezekiel's vision and call in 592 and the others proceed in chronological order down to 570, disturbed only by a redactional decision to keep all the Egyptian oracles together (29:17 gives a date of 570, and 40:1 a date of 572). These dates are important clues to the work of the prophet and the formation of the book, with the proviso that they apply only with some certainty to the immediate subunit they preface and not ipso facto to all the subunits that follow before the appearance of the next chronological note. There is considerable concurrence that these dates reflect the prophet's own work in putting at least some of his words in written form.

Three of the dates attach to the awesome and fantastic vision of Yahweh's glory, as it first broke upon the prophet at his call (1:1), as it recurred a year later when it transported him to Jerusalem to observe Yahweh's judgment on the city proleptically and then returned him to Babylonia to declare the fateful news to his compatriots (8:1), and as it recurred twenty years after his call to transport the prophet once again to Jerusalem for a tour of the restored temple to which the glory of Yahweh could now appropriately return (40:1; cf. 43:3–5). The mechanism of the *vision of God's glory* is vividly objectified as a pictorial and narratized statement of the concept that Yahweh, unlimited by his temple or worshipers, has deserted the holy place so that it will be destroyed, hovers over his people in exile—threateningly for sinners and protectively for the righteous—and will at the proper time of purification inhabit a rebuilt temple on the same site. This

16. Brevard S. Childs, "Ezekiel," in *IOTS*, 355–72.

schematization reflects the jolt and leap in consciousness called forth in a priest who is able to conceive God's complete freedom to reject his own place of worship until his corrupt worshipers are punished and purified.

A further linking of subdivisions in the book is accomplished by skillful employment of a historical-theological thematization of the fall of Jerusalem. The entire Book of Ezekiel pivots on the destruction of Jerusalem, anticipated and realized during the course of a full reading of the text, thereby setting the stage for the eventual purgative reconstruction of the city. The oracles against Jerusalem and Judah open with symbolic actions in which the prophet pictures the siege of Jerusalem with clay models and an iron plate (4:1–3), lies immobile on his side to picture a lengthy exile (4:4–6), eats the rations of an exile (4:9–17), and shaves his head and beard in order to dispose of the cuttings in ways that illustrate the delivery of the inhabitants of Jerusalem to famine, sword, and deportation (5:1–4). The recurring vision of God reveals the practice of foreign cults in the very temple precincts and the prophet watches as a scribe singles out the few inhabitants of the city who are repentant while six executioners kill all the rest (8—9).

In further symbolic actions, the prophet digs through a wall with baggage on his back to mime the flight of defenders during siege (12:1–7), eats bread and water, the rations of prisoners of war (12:17–20), dances menacingly with a sword that threatens the city (21:11–17), plays out Nebuchadnezzar's use of divination to ascertain whether to attack Jerusalem or the Ammonites first (21:18–20), and refuses to mourn for his dead wife as a sign to the people that they will be unable to mourn for the city's fall (24:15–27). The oracles of judgment against Jerusalem end with the revelation that the siege of Jerusalem has begun on 15 January 588, and that the prophet will be dumb until a fugitive shall arrive to announce the city's fall (24:25–27). On that note of suspense the oracles against the nations introduce a long digression. Only in the prologue to the concluding oracles of salvation are we informed of the fugitive's arrival with bad tidings on 8 January 585, and immediately Ezekiel's mouth is opened (33:21–22).

The ending of 1—24 and the beginning of 33—48 are thus directly linked by anticipation and confirmation of Jerusalem's fall, while the two subdivisions are consciously linked by additional motif repetitions. An early judgment against "the mountains of Israel" is reversed with a promise of salvation to the same figurative entity (6; 36). Two motifs that emerge with prominence in chaps. 24 and 33, the prophet's dumbness and his appointment as a watchman over the exiles, are also lodged in the early commission report where they function appropriately as redactional pointers toward the book's crux (3:26–27, cf. 24:27 and 33:22; 3:17–22, cf. 33:1–20). It is difficult to accept that the prophet was actually silent for the three years 588–585, since at least four of the dates attached to oracles fall in that period, much less to believe that he did not preach at all from the moment of his call in 592 until 585. Either scenario would cast Yahweh as a supreme "double binder" who commands the prophet to speak messages that he is physically prevented from delivering. Nonetheless, it is probable that Ezekiel experienced periodic and recurrent difficulties in bringing himself to speak his grim message, which may help to explain his frequent resort to symbolic action and strong physical gestures.

The watchman role of the prophet, fully developed in 33:1–20 (and redactionally anticipated in 3:17–22), has generally been construed by interpreters as possible only after 586. Absorbed in concentrating his energies to proclaim the fall of Jerusalem in the face of a facile optimism among the exiles (cf. 12:21–28), it has been doubted that he could have been a willing or convincing "consoler" of the repentant. Yet his closely intertwined "watchman" warnings to "wicked" and "righteous" were probably aspects of his mission throughout, fully as appropriate, if not more so, before the fall of Jerusalem as after, "whether they [the rebellious house of Israel] hear or refuse to hear" (2:5). Thus the very judgment declamations of Ezekiel contained the prospect that some hearers would repent and some hearers, about to sin, would refrain from wrongdoing. While none of these conversions would halt the inexorable destruction of Jerusalem, they did form the nucleus of the prophet's work as a pastoral moralist who guided responsive exiles beyond arrogance or despair to recognition of their shame and guilt, and finally to repentance, all the while instructing them in the content of Yahweh's teaching about the morally just and ritually proper life.[17]

In a speech form cast as a disputation that argues with vacillating over-confidence and complaint among the exiles about Yahweh's justice or injustice, and that also draws on an instructional legal style from priestly traditions,[18] Ezekiel summoned to repentance and advised practical changes of conduct (3:17–21; 14:1–11; 18; 22:1–16; 33:1–9). The alleged major shift of Ezekiel from "collective retribution" to "individual retribution" is a misunderstanding of the situation and of his counsel. The new

17. Moshe Greenberg, *Ezekiel 1–20,* AB (Garden City, N.Y.: Doubleday & Co., 1983).
18. Walter Zimmerli has enhanced our understanding of the priestly oriented instructional style of Ezekiel which gives his speech both an emphatic force and an abstractness of form, cf. Zimmerli, "Ezekiel," in IDBSup, 314–17; idem, *Ezekiel,* Hermeneia (Philadelphia: Fortress Press, 1979), 1:21–40.

teaching role of the prophet was precisely to rebuild the collective identity and accountability of Israel by converting and disciplining exiles, one by one, as trustworthy members of a new community. While old Jerusalem's sin had grown so massive that righteous individuals could not possibly avert its punishment, the new Jerusalem would be composed precisely of those who took their loyalty to Yahweh completely to heart and thus would never again contribute their share to an accumulation of sins that could undermine the foundations of the community.

Beginning with the majestic vision of Yahweh that draws on old traditions of *Yahweh's cultic and cosmic enthronement,* as well as on iconic details of Assyro-Babylonian myth and ritual, Ezekiel asserts the holiness and honor of Israel's God that require him to destroy the political and religious establishment of Judah but also impel him to vindicate his real presence in history by purifying and restoring a Judahite community. Again and again the final aim of Yahweh's doings with Israel is declared to be "that you/they [Israel/the nations] may know that I am Yahweh."

Ezekiel recites the history of Israel, either straightforwardly (chap. 20), or in elaborate metaphors with allegorical elements (16; 23), so as to underscore relentlessly the waywardness of the people from their very origins. Not only in the wilderness, which Hosea and Jeremiah had at least thought of as a "honeymoon" period between Yahweh and Israel, but even during the bondage in Egypt, Israel clung to idols (20:4–9). The metaphorical recitals concerning Yahweh's orphan wife Jerusalem (16) and his sister wives Samaria and Jerusalem (23) are intricately constructed enlargements and explorations of the husband-wife imagery which Hosea and Jeremiah had used for the ties between Yahweh and his people. Interestingly, Ezekiel brings together in these extended metaphors the two main Israelite tradition complexes that had previously remained isolated from one another in prophecy. The orphan wife Jerusalem has her origins in that ancient city, with an Amorite mother and a Hittite father, in keeping with the Zion traditions, whereas the sister wives Samaria and Jerusalem emerged from Egypt, in keeping with the exodus-settlement traditions.

Apparently one of the effects of the exile was to press Ezekiel to long and deep reflection on earlier prophetic traditions to the point of embracing previously separate elements in a larger complex of prophetic traditions. Ezekiel shows many signs of creative dependence on Jeremiah, Isaiah, Hosea, and Amos, as also on aspects of still-earlier prophecy (e.g., the prominence of the Spirit as a divine communicator to humans in continuity with the Elijah-Elisha traditions). Nevertheless, he transmutes all that he touches into his own *exotic twists and combinations of thought* and into his own *pedantic modes of exposition*. As with the P writer, this often plodding means of expression can on occasion attain a sparse and awesome grandeur, as in his vision of the valley of dry bones (37:1–14).

That there has been addition to and expansion of the words of Ezekiel is abundantly clear. In fact, in 570 the prophet himself revised one of his own earlier oracles (29:17–20), conceding that the promise of 586 that Nebuchadnezzar would capture Tyre was mistaken (26:1–14). Instead, he now insists, Yahweh will give Nebuchadnezzar Egypt in place of Tyre. (As a matter of fact, Ezekiel and Yahweh were wrong the second time since Neo-Babylonia was never able to capture Egypt!) But the impulse to "correct," "amplify," and "update" the original words of Ezekiel did not stop with the prophet himself. Like Isaiah, Ezekiel gave rise to, perhaps deliberately founded, a faithful and literate following.

The literary labor of the prophet's followers shows up frequently. In chap. 10 an attempt has been made to clarify aspects of the eccentric vision in chap. 1: the "wheels within wheels" are given more eyes and said to be "whirling," and the four-faced living creatures are equated with cherubim, the ox face of each replaced with a cherub face. Various of the symbolic actions and metaphorical discourses or allegories have been worked over or added to retrospectively with a view to giving them increased precision or closer correspondence to historical details. The vision of the restored temple shaped by Ezekiel probably was restricted to 40—43, with possible brief kernels in 44—48, to which later traditionists have added descriptions of the cultic personnel and rituals, layouts of the tribes in the land and of the secular parts of Jerusalem, and a description of the fructification of the wilderness of Judah by life-giving waters that flow from the temple. Ezekiel viewed the nations in their historical particularity (cf. 25—32), but in chaps. 38—39 a certain Gog of Magog (identity unknown, unless it be a mocking play on Gyges of Lydia) leads a host of nations in an attack on Judah, following its restoration to Palestine, where the entire army is destroyed by Yahweh's direct intervention, thereby clearing the way for undisturbed development of repristinated Jerusalem. It has been noted that 39:25–29 forms an appropriate summary after the vision of the valley of dry bones, the symbolic joining of staffs to represent the reunion of Ephraim and Judah, and the installation of David as king in chap. 37. It is probable that an early edition of the prophet's writings closed in this way, minus Gog of Magog and the restored temple.

Rhetorical and redactional studies of Ezekiel have revealed intricately constructed units that imply stages in the growth of the traditions. One study, for example, identifies a "whitewashed wall" metaphor that has been cleverly inserted (13:10b–15) between an oracle against false prophets (13:2–10a, 16) and an oracle against false prophetesses (13:17–23), which are themselves skillfully linked by permutations of a "delusive vision/lying divination" motif. The whole unit stands in turn within a larger cluster of oracles on aspects of prophecy that shows topical progression (12:21—14:11).[19]

The same study contends that the descriptive architectural plan of the restored temple in 40:5b—42:19 has been framed by a prescriptive inclusio arranged in a chiastic pattern (chart 5).

Breaking into the concluding chiastic series is the insertion of a vision of the return of Yahweh's glory to the temple which functions clearly to bracket the whole book by an overt connection with the visions of chaps. 1—3 and 8—11. It is evident that the insertion of 43:1–9 belongs to a late, if not the latest, stage in redaction that spans the entire book. What remains unclear is whether the prior or more restricted structural arrangements in chaps. 13 and 40—43 are parts of more extensive redactions and whether it is determinable which structures belong to the earliest stratum, or strata, whether the work of Ezekiel or a compiler.

What can be said of the supranormal powers of perception and the bizarre modes of behavior which the book when read literally attributes to the prophet? Ezekiel has been dubbed ecstatic, visionary, mystical, neurotic, psychotic, schizophrenic, and more—terms which label his unusualness without providing any certain understanding of it. He seems to have been susceptible to visions, trances, muteness, levitation, and possibly catatonic seizures. Attempts to diagnose his symptoms or read his garish symbolism in a psychoanalytic framework have not been very productive. Explorations of mystical and parapsychic phenomena, such as clairvoyance or premonitory foresight, have broadened our options for understanding the prophet without specifying a sound analytic strategy, if only because every attempt to decode the "extraordinary" or "pathological" behavior of the prophet depends upon some prior understanding (or misunderstanding) of his language in its sociocultural grounding. Recent progress in the literary analysis of the vision form discounts the common interpretation that Ezekiel claimed physical transport from Babylonia to Jerusalem and back (8:1–3; 11:24–25), and that he alleged clairvoyance about the death of Pelatiah (11:1, 13).[20]

19. Shemaryahu Talmon and Michael Fishbane, "The Structuring of Biblical Books: Studies in the Book of Ezekiel," *ASTI* 10 (1976): 129–53.
20. Greenberg, *Ezekiel 1–20;* Keith Carley, *Ezekiel Among the Prophets,* SBT, 2d ser., 31 (London: SCM Press, 1975).

CHART 5
Literary Inclusios in the Temple Plan of Ezekiel 40—43

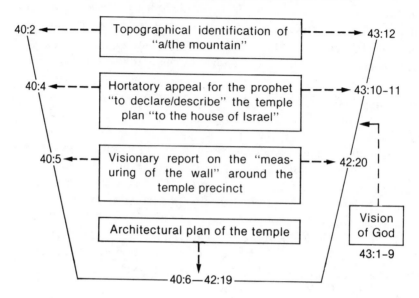

40:2 ◄──── Topographical identification of "a/the mountain" ────► 43:12

40:4 ◄──── Hortatory appeal for the prophet "to declare/describe" the temple plan "to the house of Israel" ────► 43:10–11

40:5 ◄──── Visionary report on the "measuring of the wall" around the temple precinct ────► 42:20

Architectural plan of the temple

Vision of God
43:1–9

40:6 — 42:19

It is possible that an existentialist psychological reading comes closest to interpreting Ezekiel's psychophysical symptoms.[21] Catatonic schizophrenia may roughly characterize the paralysis of will, and thus of body, that threatens a prophet who does not wish to carry so severe a message and yet cannot refuse to stand forth and try to speak. Depending on how his dumbness is to be dated (and this can scarcely be known as the book is now arranged), it is possible that at times Ezekiel, preacher of unmitigated disaster, found it difficult to assume his role. When he does speak, he asserts the words of Yahweh with a severity of exaggerated "overcompensation." It is only after 586, when circumstances give him an audience more amenable to his message, that his tongue is dependably and fully loosened. On this reading, there was a severe conflict in the prophet over acceptance of Yahweh's terrible decree and over having to convince his people of its inevitability.

Seen in this manner, the reluctance of Ezekiel to perform publicly is not merely a private quirk but a vivid expression of the difficulty many exiles had in reconciling their pride of tradition and lost privilege of office with the traumatic shift in personal fortunes and communal conditions of life forced on them willy-nilly. It became an enormous intellectual and emotional labor to master the deep prophetic lesson that Yahweh was at work both in smashing their past and in holding open their future, provided they had the insight and courage to move forward trustfully with the available resources.[22]

Adding to the enormity of the problem for the Babylonian exiles was the social reality that they had been the upper class of Judahite society. As a "declassed" elite who had once known excessive privilege, and who for the most part had not attended to prophetic or Deuteronomic warnings of Yahweh's judgment, it would have been a painful and protracted process for them even to begin to understand Ezekiel's words to them. In the prophet's wildness of demeanor and thought we may thus see a compressed distillation of that agony of renunciation and rebirth through which the deported Judahites passed—necessarily one by one even though in mutual support—in order to reach social stability and religious confidence.

The impression given by the form of the book that Ezekiel evoked a continuing interest in preserving, collecting, commenting on, and adding to

21. Thomas Alan Parry, "Crisis in Responsibility: Existential Psychology and the Prophet Ezekiel" (B.D. thesis, University of Alberta, 1964).
22. The devastating conceptual, ethical, and emotional shock of exile to people *and* prophet is analyzed with acute insight by Thomas M. Raitt, *A Theology of Exile. Judgment/Deliverance in Jeremiah and Ezekiel* (Philadelphia: Fortress Press, 1977).

his oracles is complemented by indications that his contemporaries consulted and dialogued with him. Elders are said to have come to Ezekiel at his house "to sit before him" and "to inquire" of Yahweh (8:1; 14:1; 20:1). Assuming that in the absence of normal political leadership these elders were the acting heads of the exilic community where the prophet resided, this implies their recognition of the authoritative calling of the prophet. Ezekiel is of course very abrupt and impatient with their "inquiry" because it seems to deny the impending fall of Jerusalem and thus to be premised on a quick resolution of the colonial plight of the Jews.

Aside from the elders, "the house of Israel" (12:9) or "the people" (24:19) ask him to explain his symbolic actions, and he once cries out in exasperation, "Ah, Lord Yahweh, they are saying of me, 'Is he not a spinner of *m^eshālīm* (aphorisms, parables, allegories, riddles)?'!" (20:49). This irritated outburst is further illuminated by a report that people come to Ezekiel to be entertained as with love songs but have no intention of doing what he says (33:30–33). All of the explicit consultations with the prophet seem to precede the fall of Jerusalem. The fact, however, that in the disputatious instructions about individual moral responsibility (18:2, 19, 25, 30; 33:10, 17, 20) and in the vision of the resurrection of "the bones of the house of Israel" (37:11) the prophet speaks to the quoted complaints of the people suggests that he received a renewed, possibly more serious, hearing once the gravity of a prolonged colonial fate was fully confirmed.

It is apparent that Ezekiel's oddity of personality and fantastic imagination did not cut him off from the people who struggled with him over the temporariness or finality of exile, over the meaning to be placed upon their circumscribed life conditions, and over a communal strategy for living through and beyond those conditions. For this reason alone it is myopic to place too much emphasis on the prophet's "mental illness" since that only obscures the social weight he carried as a person to be reckoned with even when his interpretations and recommendations were disputed and rejected as often as they were affirmed and embraced.

50.2 Isaiah of the Exile (Deutero-Isaiah)

Chapters 40—66 of the Book of Isaiah are composed in a "high" formal style in which traditional psalmic and polemical speech forms are fused and transformed into a vehicle of excited proclamation and urgent summons. Presupposed throughout is the impact of the sixth-century exile as a decisive rupture in the life of Israel. Characteristic of chaps. 40—55 is a relative tightness of thematic presentation and an anticipation of imminent release from captivity and return to Palestine. By contrast, chaps. 56—66 appear to be composed of originally disconnected literary blocks that largely reflect the conditions of Jews in Palestine after the return from exile (§50.4.a).

On the assumption that each of these segments forms a unity, the author of 40—55 has been called Deutero-Isaiah (Second Isaiah), while the author of 56—66 has been dubbed Trito-Isaiah (Third Isaiah). The relationship between these two is often conceived as master and disciple. The unmistakable continuities of style and theme between the two sections imply that the originating mind behind this emotive and elevated way of speaking about exile and return initiated a "school" or "stream of tradition" responsible for the shaping of 40—66. It is sometimes proposed that Trito-Isaiah was the redactor of 40—55 as well as the author of all or parts of 56—66. The meager signs of redaction in 40—55, however, do not favor this view. It has also been argued that the author of 40—55 returned to Palestine and, under later conditions, wrote at least parts of 56—66. It seems, however, that the evidence for Deutero-Isaianic materials in 56—66 is more readily explained as citations of words of the master which are amplified and reappropriated for later conditions. The subtle combination of similarity and difference in literary articulation and theological assertion in differing situations is difficult to formulate in any theory of authorship.

Between fifty and seventy-five literary units are customarily identified in chaps. 40—55, although some interpreters claim that these smaller units are actually strophes in a series of longer poems. Form-critical analysis has been moderately successful in showing many of these units to be recognizable specimens of fixed forms of speech that emerged out of traditional life situations in monarchic Israel.

The *oracle of salvation* (41:8–13, 14–16; 43:1–7; 44:1–5; 54:4–6) addresses Israel in a personified singular, silences fear, and promises deliverance in general terms of comfort, welfare, prosperity, and victory (for Assyrian parallels, see table 1: 6C). It presupposes an individual lament that precipitates an assurance of deliverance to the supplicant voiced by a priest. By applying this form to the collectivity of Israel, the prophet imbues his message of God's concern for Israel with intense personal intimacy. The *proclamation of salvation* (41:17–20; 42:14–17; 43:16–21; 49:7–12; 51:1–8; 54:11–17; 55:1–5), in contrast to the oracle of salvation, for the most part addresses Israelites distributively in the plural and promises deliverance in somewhat greater sociopolitical specificity: release from exile, return to Palestine, rebuilding of the temple, material abundance. It presupposes a collective lament voiced by the people. The *hymn of praise*, or *eschatological hymn* (42:10–13; 44:23; 45:8; 48:20–21; 49:13; 52:7–10;

54:1–3), calls on Israel, the peoples of the earth, and all nature to praise Yahweh who is about to deliver Israel from exile. It reproduces a familiar psalmic structure and idiom but with a decided skewing toward events of deliverance in the near future in contrast to the usual hymnic orientation toward God's wonderful deeds in the past (thus the term "eschatological hymn"). Hymnic language lauding Yahweh as creator and redeemer is scattered generously throughout other speech types (e.g., 40:12–31).

Alongside these affirmative speech forms stand two negating or polemical genres. The *trial speech* in its most complete form is addressed to the nations and their gods (41:1–5, 21–29; 43:8–13; 44:6–8) within a juridical scenario that exposes the ineffectuality of all "gods" except Yahweh God. In some cases the trial speech is turned against Israel (42:18–25; 43:22–28; 50:1–3) to lay bare the groundlessness of its complaints against Yahweh and the objective reality of its sinfulness, but in these instances the expected judgment due Israel is waived in favor of Yahweh's salvific purposes. The aim of this form so employed is to silence Israel's self-justification and set the people in readiness for the coming salvation. The *disputation* or *controversy* form is a rebuking and admonitory rebuttal of Israel's allegations of divine injustice. Instead of a legal proceeding that calls on witnesses for proofs, as in the trial speech, the disputation has the didactic tone of a "lecture" or "dressing down" in which, starting from presumably agreed first principles and clear "facts," Yahweh dismisses the ill-founded accusations of his people and urges their trusting adherence to him. The original life settings of the trial speech and disputation are far from clear. No civil court competent to judge nations and their gods or to assess complaints against deity is conceivable, but some have thought that trial scenes against the nations and/or Israel were enacted in the cult in connection with renewal of the covenant or in a festival of Yahweh's enthronement. The disputation, with its chiding and rather belittling tone, may reflect a wisdom school setting where the master sage instilled enlightenment and discipline in his pupils by overwhelming them with questions that demonstrated his knowledge and their ignorance (cf. a similar tone and genre in Job, §54.3).

The precise bearing of the diverse formal origins of the literary types employed in 40—55 on the particular shape and setting of the chapters as a whole is as yet unresolved. Many form critics insist that the units are so tradition-bound and self-contained that the "unity" of 40—55 is merely the aggregation of separate literary specimens strung together arbitrarily, often by catchwords, with no more connection to one another than some redactor's superficial notion of how they should be arranged. Others insist that the separate pieces have been carefully ordered with a larger plan in mind, whether by prophet or disciple. Yet others argue that a conscious whole was constructed from the start by a skillful juxtaposing and interweaving of genre structure and idiom. Certainly, apart from a relatively few "pure" specimens of each of the major genres, the traditional speech forms in 40—55 have been treated very freely, with elements of two or more genres fusing in varied permutations. In that sense those who opt for some version of "a shapely, orderly document" have the stronger case. On the other hand, the limits to the development and overt linkage of themes set by the strictures of traditional genre speech accounts for the difficulty in identifying what the shape and order of 40—55 actually consists of.[23]

Germane to the discernment of diversity and unity in 40—55 is the problem of identifying the setting in which these chapters were spoken or written. Unlike earlier prophetic writings, Isaiah 40—55 preserves no narrative information about the prophet's work, even lacking a superscription. All theories of the arena of communication for these prophecies are based on inferences from the text coupled with a few scraps of information about Jewish life in the Babylonian exile. It is generally assumed that the exiles gathered for worship and discussion of community issues, concerning which they may have had limited self-rule, and it is often posited that the prophet delivered his message to these gatherings, either orally or in writing.

Those who favor oral delivery point to the short formal units and to the stylistic repetitiveness and rhetorical devices such as imperatives and rhetorical questions. Those who favor written communication stress the elaborate, even overrefined, style. Some have argued that the prophet's politically seditious advocacy of Cyrus simply could not have been openly urged under the watchful eye of the Babylonian authorities. On the latter point, however, we do not know how closely the exilic communities were kept under surveillance. Moreover, although Cyrus and Babylon are openly written in the final form of the text, much of the message could have been proclaimed as a cryptic anticipation of and preparation for events readily recognizable to the audience. In fact, the fluid images and high incidence of enigma and ambiguity in 40—55 may have been in part a deliberately contrived "obfuscation" for outsiders and a "come-on" for knowing insiders.

The arguments for oral versus written original are in fact very inconclusive. Writing of this type in antiquity was generally intended to be

23. Carroll Stuhlmueller, "Deutero-Isaiah: Major Transitions in the Prophet's Theology and in Contemporary Scholarship," *CBQ* 42 (1980): 1–29.

read aloud and thus was couched in oral style and idiom. Nor can we be confident that orally delivered short units were always expanded into longer written compositions, since there is reason to believe that orally delivered units were of variable length and, on occasion, the written versions of such speech might be abridgments or condensations of longer oral originals. Likewise, a supposed public preaching or reading aloud of the prophecies does not obviously link up with any particular view of the diversity or unity of 40—55. The curious mixture of a limited repertory of repeated themes that falls short of advancing a well-marked line of argument need not imply a random collection of small units. It may as well be explained by successive occasions on which the prophet announced his prophecies, reassembling the themes and elaborating their connections and nuances as he proceeded, according to the interests and responses of his audience. In that event, 40—55 will have developed out of a sort of running proclamation and disputation extended over some period of time.[24]

The prophet who formulated the argumentation and rhetoric of 40—55 managed to concentrate a remarkable number of themes and imaginative figures within a brief compass, to combine and recombine them, to space and accent them variously, and to build and relax tension so that a satisfying forward movement and resolution of the whole is felt. The whole has a cohesive effect owing to the way key terms, concepts, and figures are repeated and variously developed so that reverberations are set off between units and the listener-reader is lured into tracing the cross-referential pathways that these interwoven associations open up.

In spite of the enormous amount of study invested in these chapters, the focus of inquiry has been relatively narrow and atomized, revolving around questions that tend to miss the distinctive qualities of the work: Does Deutero-Isaiah give the first biblical statement of monotheism? Does the prophet anticipate the conversion of the nations to Jewish faith? Has he been influenced by Zoroastrianism or by the Babylonian New Year Festival? Can we trace historical references within the poems to successive phases of the career of Cyrus? Who is the servant of Yahweh? Not that these questions are pointless or unimportant. Pursued in relative isolation from one another and out of the context of the special idiom of the book within Israelite tradition history, however, they can be given quite forced answers that do not throw much light on the work as literature or as a programmatic statement about how Jews should respond to their forthcoming freedom.

24. Yehoshua Gitay, "Deutero-Isaiah: Oral or Written?" *JBL* 99 (1980): 185–97.

Damaging above all to a grasp of the work as a whole has been the hypothesis that the four extended reflections on the servant figure, known as the Servant Songs (42:1–6; 49:1–6; 50:4–9; 52:13—53:12), are independent compositions secondarily inserted into their present contexts, so that the Servant of the songs and the servant of the remainder of the work have two different identities that a redactor unsuccessfully tried to harmonize. The claim that the work reads more smoothly and continuously without these "Servant Songs" is dubious, since much the same argument can be made for the excision of other figures such as Cyrus and the mother/wife Zion. Granted that these elaborated descriptions of the servant set up an inner tension and ambiguity of meaning, but this is only the strongest epitomization of a number of enigmas and ambiguities which the work artfully stages and plays upon: Cyrus who does not know Yahweh will know him, the nations will be conquered and saved, a blind and deaf servant will lead forth a blind and deaf people, a God who regards nations as nothing will save them, the same God who has been wearied by his people's sins will deliver them from their deserved bondage, and a deliverance from exile should be celebrated before it has occurred! These are but some of the astonishing "breaks in logic" with which the prophet regales his hearers.

The most promising heuristic question about the servant is probably not *Who* is the servant? but rather *What* does the servant do in relation to all that is to occur in the deliverance of Israel? or *How* does the servant function in relation to the other imaginatively developed figures? or even *Which* of the things that God and Israel and the nations are about to do are to be done by the servant?[25] When the problem of the servant is approached in this manner it becomes clear that the servant is one of a number of ways of speaking of Israel, in this instance with respect to Israel's self-conscious aspects as typified by representatives from the past and also now by someone at work in the present, probably the prophet himself.

In the first half of the work (chaps. 40—45), the prophet sets forth a wealth of historical entities and actors in individualized and personified dress. In the order of their appearance they are Zion/Jerusalem, the nations and their gods, Jacob/Israel, Cyrus, the servant of Yahweh, and Babylon/Chaldea. The interaction among and the destinies of these protagonists are emphatically grounded in Yahweh as creator and lord of history who, having announced beforehand through prophets "the former

25. Claus Westermann, *Isaiah 40–66*, OTL (Philadelphia: Westminster Press, 1969), 93. For a literary reading of the elusiveness of the servant figure, see David J. A. Clines, *I, He, We and They: A Literary Approach to Isaiah 53*, JSOTSup 1 (Sheffield: JSOT Press, 1976).

things" already done, now announces through a new prophet (who called himself "Isaiah"?) "the new/latter things" he is about to do.

The Jewish people, alternatively viewed as Zion/Jerusalem and Jacob/Israel are to be delivered and restored to Palestine after long but largely deserved suffering that borders on the excessive. Having discredited the gods as totally effete, Yahweh will disempower the nations who wrongly trusted in them, and he will accomplish this by equipping Cyrus to overthrow Babylon and assume world empire. In this "world-turning" crisis, the servant of Yahweh, rising from weakness to strength, will bring the justice of Yahweh to all the nations. Yahweh, creator and liberator, will see to it that these prophecies are accomplished.

In chaps. 46—47, all the chief actors having been presented and the basic scenario outlined, there is a slackening in the tempo of presentation. The downfall of the Babylonian gods (46) and of the Babylonian Empire (47) are celebrated in a prolongation of imagery about idols that worshipers have to carry to safety and about a city like an aristocratic widow now stripped of her oppressive powers and her inflated illusions.

In the last third of the composition (49—55), the dramatis personae of the earlier chapters are sharply reduced. Babylon/Chaldea is named no more, although obviously present as "oppressors" and "tormenters." The discredited idols have vanished. Cyrus gives way before Yahweh as the ultimate source of deliverance. Even Jacob/Israel ceases as a designation for the people of God and, in its place, the male figure of the servant and the female figure of Zion/Jerusalem come to the center in extended portraitures studded by a marked increase in historical analogies between past and present: the rock/quarry Abraham and Sarah (51:1–3), the Rahab monster defeated at the exodus (51:9–11), the days/waters of Noah that will not return (54:9–10), and the witness, prince, and command-giver David (55:3–5). The images of the oppressed servant, finally victorious as a multiplier of righteousness to "many," and the bereft mother and wife Zion/Jerusalem, abandoned but shortly to be delivered and consoled, are alternately developed toward an ecstatic climax amid declamations of the enduring character of Yahweh's accomplishment. The "lasting God" (40:28) and his word that "stands lastingly" (40:8) will produce "lasting salvation" (45:17), "lasting joy" (51:11), "lasting love" (54:8), "lasting covenant" (55:3), and a "lasting sign" (55:12).

A close structuralist analysis of the work might well reveal the fundamental binary oppositions of futility and efficacy, or of impotence and potency. Apparent strength and success in history collapse into weakness and failure; apparent powerlessness and wasted effort issue in productivity that turns the course of ancient Near Eastern history. At this deep level of the ironic reversal of apparent strength and weakness into their actual opposites, there is a decided affinity between the structure of thought in Isaiah of Jerusalem and the structure of thought in Isaiah of the Exile, notwithstanding their different vocabularies and thematic arsenals.

Because the servant figure is "Israel in the remaking," it is a slow and painful process of reeducation and transformation and the figure ranges in its reference between the collective destiny of Israel and the greater commitment and teachability of some Israelites compared to others not yet enlightened or obedient. The portraiture draws on "servant" features of Moses, of prophets such as Jeremiah, and even of the ideology of righteous kingship. It is also saturated with direct experience of controversy and persecution in exile. The confessing, lamenting, and thanksgiving language of 49:1–6 and 50:4–9, in which the servant speaks, and of 52:13—53:12, in which the servant is spoken of both by Yahweh and by deeply affected onlookers, draws liberally on traditional speech of the thanksgiving and lament genres, including the latter's "expression of confidence" in which the sufferer affirms with certainty that Yahweh will hear and vindicate. Because the language is formally derived, it is not clear that the text of 53:8–9, 12 attests to the servant's actual death, since it may, in accordance with customary genre idiom, refer rather to his last-minute rescue from the nearly triumphant clutches of death. In any event, the oppression and vindication of the servant are described with such compressed emotion and deliberate understatement that actual firsthand experience seems to inform the imagery.

It has been argued of late, in large part on the form-critical grounds that 53:1–12 is best understood as a straightforward third-person thanksgiving song of a type paralleled in Psalms, that the servant figure is the prophet himself, arrested and imprisoned by the Babylonians with the help of Jewish informers, and who was rescued on the verge of death, possibly by the Persian conquerors or by a pro-Persian party of Babylonians prior to the conquest of the city.[26] The way in which the servant figure is enmeshed with references to innercommunal conflict, involving entrenched resistance to the prophet's message, suggests that the imprisoned prophet may have been put there with the help of Jewish opponents who regarded him as a false prophet whose reckless words invited Babylonian punitive actions

26. R. N. Whybray, *Thanksgiving for a Liberated Prophet: An Interpretation of Isaiah Chapter 53*, JSOTSup 4 (Sheffield: JSOT Press, 1978).

against the exilic Jewish community.[27] Moreover, the central informational message of the writing that Cyrus will overthrow Babylon aligns with the sentiments and plans of groups within Babylon who were working to deliver the city to Cyrus because of the unpopularity of the policies of the Babylonian king Nabonidus.

Because 40—55 trades in a compressed and allusive image-filled style, one must move cautiously in translating the servant figure directly into the terms of innercommunal Jewish response to the shift of power from Babylon to Persia as precipitated by this most outspoken prophet. Nonetheless, a strong odor of political conflict surrounds the acclamation of Cyrus and the hostile treatment of the servant. Given the individual thanksgiving form of chap. 53, there is good reason to hypothesize that the actual imprisonment, persecution, and deliverance of a historical contemporary, most likely the prophet himself, has been employed as a microcosm of the macrocosm of Israel's fate insofar as the people's suffering has exceeded its deserved punishment. And that some of this suffering was inflicted on Jews by fellow Jews is not at all surprising in context.

In betraying the prophet to Babylonian authorities, his opponents would have thought themselves to be sparing the Jewish community still-greater suffering. Furthermore, since these Jewish exiles in Babylon had once been Judahite government officials and the appointment of Jewish exiles as Babylonian courtiers is attested in old traditions behind the later stories of the Book of Daniel, it is highly likely that some prominent members of the exilic community had been taken into the very Babylonian government that Isaiah of the Exile declared would be shortly destroyed. In moving to neutralize the prophet, these privileged Jews would have been fighting for their own stake in the survival of the Babylonian regime. That some Jews were profiting from supporting Babylonian hegemony while other Jews were active in a pro-Persian underground preparing for Cyrus's seizure of Babylon would be one more instance of the structurally embedded conflicts of interest in which prophets and other leaders had been involved from the very origins of prophecy. In this respect Jeremiah and his supporters and opponents give us an analogy to Deutero-Isaiah as here reconstructed within his field of sociopolitical and religious conflict (§37.5).

A rich array of covenant, law, and justice/righteousness language is used to assure Israel of its security in the hands of Yahweh amid the catastrophic events of transfer of imperial power in the ancient Near East (51:7–8; 54:9–

---

27. John W. Miller, "Prophetic Conflict in Second Isaiah. The Servant Songs in the Light of Their Context," in *Wort, Gebet, Glaube. Walter Eichrodt zum 80. Geburtstag,* ed. J. J. Stamm, ATANT 59 (1970), 77–85.

17). Of further moment is the striking way that these very themes of assurance to Israel are set within both cosmic-historical and textual inclusios that extend the operations and effects of covenant, law, and justice/righteousness among all the nations (42:1–7; 49:5–6; 51:4–5; 55:3–5). Recent scholarship has been right to deflate the imagined "missionary" program of the prophet, as though he called on Israel to propagandize and convert foreigners.[28] The anticipated "conversion" of the nations is set alongside contradictory images of the destruction and subjugation of the nations. When the nations do eventually "come to their senses" and confess Yahweh, it will be mainly through their own enlightenment about the efficacy of Yahweh's work in and through Israel.

Some of the "confusion" in this cluster of images about the nations may be reduced if we assume that the prophet envisions Cyrus as the destroyer and subjugator of the nations and Israel as the future "priestly prophetic enclave" within the Persian Empire to which more and more of the peoples of the earth will gather at their own initiative to confess Yahweh.[29] While we cannot be certain how the prophet structured all the elements of his understanding of Israel as the enigmatic "peoples' covenant" (42:6; 49:8) and "nations' light" (42:6; 49:6; 51:4), it is interesting that his later disciples speak of "foreigners" who "joined themselves" to the restored Jewish community in Palestine, worshiping at the rebuilt temple as "a house of prayer of all peoples" (56:3, 6–8). This means that in some measure his anticipation of Gentile conversions to Yahweh was realized, even if on a modest scale, and even if his followers also continued to speak of the subjugation and subordination of foreigners (60:10–14; cf. 61:5–6, which is more ambiguous regarding the status of the foreigners within the community). Later prophecy also envisions whole nations who "join themselves" to Yahweh (Zech. 2:10–12), and the survivors of "the families of the earth," including Egypt, who will be obligated "to go up to Jerusalem to keep the feast of booths" (Zech. 14:16–19).

Significant form-critical, tradition-historical, and historical research has contributed greatly to our understanding of Isaiah 40—55. Yet the overall fabric and tenor of the work has fared poorly at the hands of interpreters insufficiently sensitive to the work as literature and as an adroitly mediated aesthetic expression of the conflicting attitudes and responses among the Babylonian exiles to the radical new sociohistoric situation opening up in the years leading up to Babylon's fall. Fresh literary and sociohistoric

28. D. E. Hollenberg, "Nationalism and 'the Nations' in Isaiah XL–LV," *VT* 19 (1969): 23–36.
29. Norman K. Gottwald, *AKE,* 341–46.

inquiries, informing one another and not neglecting the contributions of earlier methods of study, promise to increase our comprehension of this energetic document of "controlled hysteria" which arrests and taxes us with its emotional intensity and its intellectual breadth.

50.3 Prophets of the Rebuilt Temple

Haggai and Zechariah were the last prophets connected with known historical events, as they were also the first prophets whose immediate aims were carried out by communal leaders. They summoned Zerubbabel and Joshua to make haste in rebuilding the temple that still lay in ruins eighteen years after the edict of Cyrus authorizing the reconstruction of Judah (§44.2). From dates formulated in the pattern of Ezekiel's chronological notations, we learn that Haggai prophesied during August-December 520 (1:1; 1:15a; 1:15b—2:1; 2:10; 2:18; 2:20) and that Zechariah prophesied from November 520 to as late as December 518 (1:1; 1:7; 7:1). Whereas virtually the entire stress of Haggai fell on initiating rebuilding of the temple and persevering in that project, Zechariah enlarged on the necessary cleansing and confirmation of leaders and people to accompany the new temple, as well as on disturbances among the nations that would facilitate the renovation of Jerusalem.

50.3.a Haggai

The present Book of Haggai is divided between words of the prophet urging rebuilding of the temple (1:2–11) and words of the prophet urging endurance in that enterprise (2:2–9, 11–19). These oracles are separated by a report on the beginning of reconstruction in September 520 (1:12–15a) and they culminate in a promise that Zerubbabel will become the neo-Davidic ruler of an independent Judah (2:20–23, where the condemnatory use of the "signet ring" image in Jer. 22:24–27 is reversed). Haggai stoutly addresses the reluctance of Zerubbabel and Joshua to lead in rebuilding the temple in the face of adverse economic conditions that are strangling the community. The prophet remonstrates that only as the temple is rebuilt will prosperity spring forth from the land of Palestine and from the largesse of the nations who will be drawn to the splendor of Yahweh's worship in Jerusalem. Using a highly disputatious style, Haggai comes to grips with the doubts and evasions of the community by calling them to "consider" the meager fortunes of the people to date and motivating them to risk the cost of temple reconstruction as the one and only course of action that will secure Yahweh's blessing.

The structure of the literary units and the prophet's line of argument, particularly in 2:10–19, are difficult to follow. On the assumption that the book is a collection of originally separate oracles serially arranged by date, there appear to be disorders and non sequiturs in argument. The chiding call to rebuild the temple falls into two parts (vv. 2–6 and 7–11) linked by similarity of theme and style, but in which the expected form would put vv. 7–8 after v. 11. The prophet's inquiry of priests for a ruling as to whether contact with holiness is as "contagious" as contact with uncleanness— answered by the priests in the negative—is taken to demonstrate that the community and its offerings are "unclean" (vv. 11–14). The connection of this emphatic judgment to the remainder of the dated unit in vv. 15–19 is tenuous and clouded. The most probable meaning from context requires a considerable stretching of the prophet's analogy: the contaminating "uncleanness" of the people is their willful delay in rebuilding the temple.

Given the ill fit of vv. 11–14 in their present setting, it has been proposed that these verses constitute a separate oracle directed against ritual defilement of the restored community resulting from the admission of Samaritans. Noting the date fragment oddly appended to the report of rebuilding, some critics have treated 1:15a as the original chronological heading for 2:11–14 and thus transfer the oracle to a position at the close of the first chapter. This is a very strained solution, especially since a prophetic condemnation of the inclusion of Samaritans in the Judahite cult runs against the evidence that the request of Samaritans to participate in rebuilding the temple was roundly rejected by the Judahites (Ezra 4:1–5).

Rather than a collection of separate oracles, the Book of Haggai may be more productively viewed as a redaction of prophetic speeches and chronological notes and a report of temple rebuilding cast in the third person. This redaction has taken once-separate oracles and worked them together into longer speeches in 1:2–11 and 2:11–19.[30] Since the prophet's words seem not to have been in verse to begin with, the redactor could all the more easily reshape his material for nuance and emphasis by cutting, rearranging, repeating, and juxtaposing elements without strict regard for the dating of oracles. The "fused oracles" emphasize the hesitancy and reluctance of the Jews to start the rebuilding and, once begun, to continue with it, both because the structure did not seem as glorious as Solomon's temple and because the expected economic improvement had not occurred as speedily as they had hoped.

In vv. 15–19 the redactor has Haggai underscoring the miserable plight of the Jews *before* they started to rebuild in an act of repentance and urging

30. Childs, *IOTS,* 467–70.

them forcefully now, *after* the laying of the foundation, to apply themselves to work on the temple in the assurance that prosperity is forthcoming (cf. "take courage" in 2:4). In a simple chronological series of separate oracles, this unit with reference to laying the foundation more logically belongs with the report of the beginning of reconstruction (1:11–15a). As now redacted, the stress falls on the precariousness of the community's position in failing to move the rebuilding with speed and alacrity. The tour de force by which the redactor awkwardly joins vv. 11–14 with vv. 15–19, apparently to link right ritual in the former with repentance and proper cult restoration in the latter, shows up in a repetition of date in 2:10 and 2:18 (as if to say, "Yes, this really is *one* speech given on a *single* day!") and also in the phrase "work of their/your hands" in 2:14 and 2:17 which Yahweh both rejects as an offering and denies to them as a food source.[31]

Finally, Haggai boldly insists that the risky and courageous act of rebuilding the temple will evoke the cooperation of the nations in provisioning the cult (2:6–9) and likewise trigger the political decline of the nations so that Zerubbabel can advance from his present role as a Persian-appointed petty official to the restored office of Davidic king (2:20–23). The Judahite community must do its part in readying the cult while Yahweh does his part in blessing the ground and "shaking heavens and earth."

50.3.b Zechariah 1—8

Zechariah 1—8 is organized around two foci: a set of eight nocturnal visions in chaps. 1—6 and answers to an inquiry in chaps. 7—8 as to whether fast days commemorating the fall of Jerusalem in 586 should be observed now that the temple is rising anew.

The visions are rife with bizarre imagery explained by an interpreting messenger in the manner of Ezekiel's visions. Owing to textual corruption and interpolations, and possibly some deletions, certain of the visions are very resistant to interpretation (especially the first, fifth, and eighth visions). They are grouped in a loose thematic "ring" or chiastic structure that situates the work of *Joshua and Zerubbabel* at the center (visions 4 [3:1–7] and 5 [4:1–5, 10b–14]) surrounded by an immediate paired concentric frame of *Jerusalem/Judah defended from the nations* (visions 2 [1:18–21] and 3 [2:1–5]) and *purged of evil* (visions 6 [5:1–4] and 7 [5:5–11]) and encompassed further by the outside frame of *patrolling horsemen/chariots* that at first find the earth quiet and at the end go forth "to assuage Yahweh's spirit [anger?]" on the nations (visions 1 [1:7–15] and 8 [6:1–8]).

31. Ibid., 467–68.

The vision sequence is prefaced by a call to repentance motivated by a reflection on Israel's stubbornness toward Yahweh in the past (1:2–6) and concluded by an oracle commanding the crowning of Zerubbabel as king and Joshua as high priest (6:9–15). Each of the three passages treating the leaders is defective or obscure in some regard, but when they are read together it is clear that the branch of 3:8 and of 6:12 is none other than Zerubbabel who shall build the temple (4:7–9; 6:12–13) and who, as king of Judah, will collaborate harmoniously with Joshua, the high priest. The reference to "crowns" in 6:11 makes it virtually certain that the name of Zerubbabel once stood in this passage alongside that of Joshua. The great confusion in these Zerubbabel-Joshua texts is probably due to the fact that the exuberant confidence of Zechariah about the reestablishment of the Davidic line did not come to fruition. The Persian Empire held firm and Zerubbabel disappeared from the scene without leaving a revived Davidic dynasty (§44.2).

When men from Bethel inquired of priests and prophets as to whether they should continue the fast days in memory of Jerusalem's downfall (7:1–3), Zechariah seized the opportunity to upbraid them for selfish motives both when they fasted and when they feasted. His "reply" is expanded into a long speech that weaves together the social ethical rigor of prophecy with the obligation to build up the cult, firmly asserting that in this age Yahweh purposes good for the people and thus they are to live justly with one another. At long last the petitioners' pointed question is directly answered: No, the fast days are no longer to be observed; instead, they are to become feast days and occasions to live justly (8:18–19). A closing oracle celebrates an insistent, even clamorous, turning of the nations to Yahweh at Jerusalem (8:20–23).

Zechariah 1—8 is an intricately redacted work that skillfully plays on the events of 520–518 in a wider paradigm of Jewish faithfulness and expectation that would serve later postexilic generations well. The redaction takes a large view of "the fathers" and "the former prophets" (1:4–6; 7:7, 12), the "seventy years" of exile (1:12; 7:5), the ingathering of the exiles (2:6–7; 8:7–8), rebuilding the temple (1:16; 4:7–9; 6:12–15; 8:9), the prosperity of Jerusalem/Judah (1:17; 2:1–4; 12; 3:10; 8:4–5, 12–13), and disturbances among the nations (1:15; 2:8–9; 6:1–8) that portend the exaltation of Jerusalem and the turning of nations to Yahweh (2:11; 8:20–23). The temporal standpoint within the redaction shifts between exile and restoration. The references and appeals to Israel's experience over the preceding century are not only citations of *past events* but depictions of *processes* of "exile," "repentance," "restoration," "doing justice," and "conversion of nations" which are far from having run their course. Thus, even the failure of the prophecy about Zerubbabel as Davidic ruler, which seems only halfheartedly concealed, is seen as one of the many twists and turns through which Judah must go in its struggle to become ever-anew Yahweh's people.[32]

50.4 Prophets of Conflicted Restoration

The last prophetic writings to be composed fell within the Persian period, following the rebuilding of the temple, possibly all appearing prior to the reforms of Ezra and Nehemiah in the latter half of the fifth century. Excluded from treatment here are the short story about the prophet Jonah (§53.3) and Isaiah 24—27 and Zechariah 9—14 which exhibit a more developed apocalyptic eschatology (§55.1.b).

50.4.a Isaiah 56—66 (Trito-Isaiah)

There is no mistaking the stylistic and conceptual influence of Isaiah of the Exile on these chapters, but it is equally evident that Isaiah 56—66 presupposes the return to Palestine and the rebuilding of the temple. Furthermore, the shifts in style, situation, topic, and mood within 56—66 do not lend credence to the view that these chapters are a structural unity created by a single author.[33]

If we speak at all of a "Third Isaiah," the term should apply to the author of the central poems in chaps. 60—62 which are closest to the style and thought of chaps. 40—55 in setting forth an ecstatic announcement of the pending, but still delayed, redemption of Zion when more exiles are to be gathered, the nations will contribute to the cult of Yahweh, and peace and righteousness will flourish without limit. The servant figure in 63:1–3 may speak of the mission of this prophet to serve his community. To this programmatic core of the work may be added the related passages in 57:14–20; 65:17–25; and 66:10–14. Sharply at variance with the words of salvation are laments and indictments concerning tensions and splits within Judah attributable to those who monopolize and abuse power by wronging fellow Jews on whose behalf the prophetic voice is raised.

Attempts to discern a literary, topical, or chronological arrangement in chaps. 56—66 have not been convincing. It is likely that our best clue to the articulation of the contents is the central placement of the visionary restoration scenario of chaps. 60—62 around which are balanced roughly matching

32. Ibid., 467–70.
33. Westermann, *Isaiah 40–66*, 296–308.

panels in chiastic arrangement. The symmetrically balanced panels that create a widening "ripple" effect from the center toward the outer limits are as follows: core proclamation of restoration + theophany of judgment + lament + indictment of corrupt worship + promise of salvation to Jerusalem/Judah + indictment of evil leaders + promise of salvation to foreigners (chart 6.) By opening and closing chaps. 56—66 with words of salvation and by awarding the fullest scope to salvation at the center, the redactor clearly gives priority to the authorial voice of salvation. In the middle panels of this ring arrangement, however, indictments and laments underscore the dire impediments to communal salvation which call for the severest judgment.

The symmetry of the chiastic structure carries only so far, since there are many details and idiosyncrasies in each of the matching members that do not "correspond." It is probable that a redactor worked with already-finished pieces that he collated and arranged without attempting to rewrite them extensively or even to provide transitional links or headings. "Asymmetry" of a purposeful sort occurs by intensification in the last four panels in chaps. 65—66. "The stakes are raised" decisively by a deepening in the communal conflict, an extension in the severity of judgment, and a widening in the scope of salvation. Wicked leaders will be replaced by the faithful "servants of Yahweh" (65:1–16), who have been excommunicated from the cult and who in turn reject the temple worship as apostate (66:1–17), which ushers in the re-creation of Jerusalem amid "new heavens and a new earth" (65:17–25), and issues not only in the ingathering of Jewish exiles and foreigners to Jerusalem but also in the dispatch of Gentile survivors to declare the glory of Yahweh among the nations (66:10–24). This articulation of the interaction of sin, judgment, and salvation traces a trajectory of deepening communal crisis.

What struggles within the restored community are referred to under these colorful, sometimes lurid, outbursts? The consistent viewpoint of the laments and indictments in Isaiah 56—66 is that those who control the temple establishment, and who are most ardent in observing cultic practices, are guilty of socioeconomic oppression and outright bloodshed, while they exercise a stranglehold on the cult that marginates and finally excludes others from leadership and participation. As we have noted (§48.2), the composition of the postexilic priesthood was "up for grabs," with various claimants contending for office, and eventually the prize went to the Aaronid group advocated in the Priestly Code, to the detriment of the "inferior" Levites. It is likely then that the "prophetic/priestly" voices speaking in Isaiah 56—66 are proponents of a more widely shared (or

CHART 6

Chiastic Arrangement of Isaiah 56—66 with
Terminal Intensification of "Message" Content

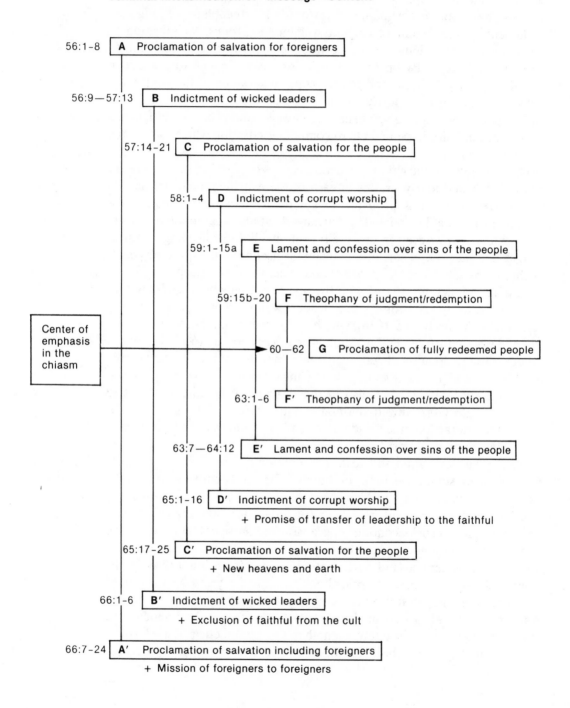

56:1–8   **A**   Proclamation of salvation for foreigners

56:9—57:13   **B**   Indictment of wicked leaders

57:14–21   **C**   Proclamation of salvation for the people

58:1–4   **D**   Indictment of corrupt worship

59:1–15a   **E**   Lament and confession over sins of the people

59:15b–20   **F**   Theophany of judgment/redemption

Center of emphasis in the chiasm

60—62   **G**   Proclamation of fully redeemed people

63:1–6   **F′**   Theophany of judgment/redemption

63:7—64:12   **E′**   Lament and confession over sins of the people

65:1–16   **D′**   Indictment of corrupt worship
+ Promise of transfer of leadership to the faithful

65:17–25   **C′**   Proclamation of salvation for the people
+ New heavens and earth

66:1–6   **B′**   Indictment of wicked leaders
+ Exclusion of faithful from the cult

66:7–24   **A′**   Proclamation of salvation including foreigners
+ Mission of foreigners to foreigners

alternative?) exercise of priestly office by ethically upright and communally accountable religious leaders backed by the same caliber of political leaders.

The impression given by these chapters is that some group (Aaronids?) has consolidated its hold on priestly office and has pushed other claimants (Levites?) and their prophetic partisans out of the cult altogether.[34] Ironically, a prophetic critic anticipates that among the Gentile survivors who will propagandize for Yahweh thoughout the nations there will be some whom Yahweh "will take for priests and for Levites" (66:21), an action that will circumvent Aaronid—or indeed any Israelite—attempt to dictate Yahweh's priesthood.

Because of the redactional ring composition of the work and its lack of historical details, it is impossible to know over what period of time the conflict raged and with what exact results and repercussions. It may well be that Darius's authorization of work to start (or resume?) the temple reconstruction carried with it certification of the Aaronids as sole legitimate priests, so that from 520 onward the priestly leadership narrowed, monopolizing power and corrupting itself to a point of irreconcilable conflict with other Judahite groups. This may have been the background of the reforms of Nehemiah who took steps to redress imbalances of ecclesial and socioeconomic power through a program of limited "democratization" (§44.4).

50.4.b Malachi

The Book of Malachi throws further light on severe tensions within the postexilic community over the laxity of leadership. The work is constructed of six oracles in the form of disputations with priests and people, and what is said of the latter implies that the socioeconomic and political elite are in view. The prophet establishes the following points:

1. Yahweh loves Israel in contrast to Edom which he has destroyed and will not restore, probably referring to pressure on Edom by the Nabatean Arabs (1:1–5);
2. Yahweh detests the inferior animals that priests and people are offering in a betrayal of the "covenant with Levi" which mandates a faithful priesthood (1:6—2:9);
3. Yahweh rebukes Jewish husbands who break covenant with their wives by divorcing them in order to take foreign wives (2:10–16);
4. Yahweh promises to send soon his "covenant messenger" to purify the faithless

---

34. Hanson, *DA*, 32–208, 380–401.

priests, after which Yahweh will judge the socially unjust laity as well (2:17—3:5);

5. Yahweh condemns widespread withholding of tithes and offerings which has brought on bad harvests (3:6–12);

6. Yahweh assures that he remembers the nucleus of righteous Jews and will soon come to vindicate them against the wicked Jews (3:13—4:3).

The disputation form is well marked with an opening statement of a principle or norm by the prophet, followed by a demurrer or protest from priests or people, and concluding with substantiation of the original statement accompanied by rebuke and threat of judgment.[35] The "substantiations" are loose in structure and variously expanded, with asides (e.g., 1:11; 2:4–9) and resumptions of argument (e.g., 2:1; 2:13) that suggest protracted and involved disputes. The prophet faced a communal leadership suffering deep doubts about Yahweh's commitment to Judah and Yahweh's readiness to enforce justice. The social injustice condemned (3:5) has its systemic counterpart in laxity of cult and abuses of marriage and divorce. To further their economic position, well-provided worshipers are "cutting corners" by withholding offerings or bringing inferior offerings. The taking of foreign wives by Jewish leaders and social climbers was a ploy to enhance their status by giving them protective and entrepreneurial connections with leading families in surrounding territories.

It is widely, but inconclusively, argued that the name Malachi, which means "my messenger," was supplied to an originally anonymous prophecy on the basis of "the messenger of the covenant" in 3:1. The book presents a fascinating play on "messenger" who appears in the guise of the prophet (1:1), the model of a true priest (2:7), the forerunner of Yahweh who will purify the priesthood (3:1–4), while the colophon added to the completed Book of the Twelve identifies this forerunner-messenger as Elijah who will reconcile fathers and children (4:5–6). One commentator offers the hypothesis that the forerunner-messenger of Yahweh in 3:1 is a cryptic reference to Ezra whose reform mission is thereby anticipated.

The horizons of Malachi fit well with the fifth century prior to the reforms of Nehemiah and Ezra. Disillusionment with ecclesial and sociopolitical establishments so tartly expressed in Isaiah 56—66 suffuses Malachi as well and points toward grave confrontations between factions in the community. Malachi shows affinities with the Deuteronomic traditions, but whether the reference to Yahweh's covenant with Levi (2:4) is an explicit counter to Aaronid claims is not certain. Nonetheless, it is evident that the prophet

---

35. Georg Fohrer, *IOT,* 469–70; James A. Fischer, "Notes on the Literary Form and Message of Malachi," *CBQ* 34 (1972): 315–20.

regards the incumbent priesthood as totally corrupt and soon to be replaced or radically reformed.

50.4.c Obadiah and Joel

The Books of Obadiah and Joel use occasions in the historical experience of Edom and Judah to introduce and enlarge on the coming day of Yahweh when the nations will be judged.

Obadiah 1—15 is an oracle of judgment against Edom because of its failure to aid Judah against the Neo-Babylonians in 586 and its actual participation in looting the land and seizing fugitive Judahites. Whether the closely parallel Jer. 49:7–22 is the source of Obadiah 1—15, or vice versa, or whether both depend on a third source, is indeterminable. It appears that Obadiah 1—15 could have been written at any time after 586. The core oracle has been expanded in two stages: vv. 16–18, addressed to Israelites, promises the destruction of Edom and the elevation of Zion, while vv. 19–21 affirms Mt. Zion's coming vindication through its possession of Mt. Esau. The geopolitical scenario in vv. 19–21 seems to envision returning Jews who repopulate Judah and subsequently expand into all the surrounding regions, notably into the Negeb and "Mt. Esau." At least vv. 19–21 belongs to restoration times.

Joel has long been a puzzling work because it presents contradictory facets which look back toward preexilic prophecy and forward toward postexilic prophecy.[36] It begins with a call to fasting and repentance in response to a devastating locust plague and drought (or is an invading army portrayed as locusts?) and it ends with a judgment of the nations in the Valley of Jehoshaphat (wordplay on "Yahweh judges," 3:12 = "Valley of [judicial] decision," 3:14). The unifying motif throughout the book is the day of Yahweh (1:15; 2:1, 11, 29; 3:1, 14, 18).

The collective lament over what most interpreters take to be a locust plague is vivid in its description of the catastrophe and excitatory in its repeated calls to elders, priests, and people to join in fasting, prayer, and repentance to avert the wrath of Yahweh, closing with a firm assurance that Yahweh will lift the plague (2:17–27). There then follows a series of "eschatological" oracles about the last days. The promise of a pouring out of Yahweh's spirit on the community (or the whole earth? cf. "all flesh") does not link concretely to anything in the preceding lament, but at the same time it differs from the destructive judgment oracles that follow. Chapter 3 is a pastiche of oracles about the judgment of the nations and the

36. Childs, *IOTS*, 386–93.

deliverance of Zion. Most of the allusions are very general, but a condemnation of Phoenicians for selling Judahites to the Greeks as slaves is intelligible within the context of fifth/fourth-century international politics when Phoenician and Greek cities were allied in uprisings and wars against Persia (3:4–8).

There is as yet no generally recognized explanation for the dual character of the Book of Joel. Some argue that a preexilic lament over locusts was expanded in postexilic times by means of the day of Yahweh rubric to include a judgment on nations. Others believe that the work in its entirety is postexilic, perhaps building on old traditions about a prophet Joel and a locust plague. It is possible to detect a redactional development in the lament that has put together two different locust plagues, the first of them described more "naturally" and the second more "symbolically," with the locusts assuming the shape of a foreign army. This upgrading of the eschatological dimension in the lament prepares for the final judgment on the nations.

Others have thought to explain peculiarities of form and content by assuming the book to be a liturgy that went through stages of growth over time, at first restricted to fasting over locusts and then broadened and redirected to a celebration of coming judgment on the nations. Whether the entirety of the book can be accounted for liturgically is problematic. A liturgical origin for chaps. 1—2, however, does help to account for the remarkable cohesion and movement of the lament and its textual preservation without major disturbance. Liturgical convention may also explain why no particular sins are mentioned in spite of the strong appeal to "return to me [Yahweh] with all your heart" (2:12).

Yet another approach is to see all the "locust" references as symbolic of an invading enemy which is variously understood as Assyria, Neo-Babylonia, or Macedonia. One version of this "foreign invaders as locusts" hypothesis regards chap. 1 as descriptive of the Neo-Babylonians who invaded Judah to subdue it at the start of the exile and chap. 2 as descriptive of the Persians who invaded Palestine/Egypt under Cambyses in 526–525 in a friendly intervention on behalf of the Judahites.

CHAPTER 12

Traditions of Colonial Israel:
The Writings

Read the Biblical Text
1 and 2 Chronicles
Psalms
Lamentations
Song of Songs

Ruth
Jonah
Esther

Proverbs
Job
Ecclesiastes

Isaiah 24—27
Zechariah 9—14
Daniel

The Writings, as its vagueness of title hints, is a less-cohesive literary ensemble than either the Law or the Prophets. Yet the variety of the Writings is no mere miscellany nor are its contents totally unrelated to the Law and the Prophets. The third division of the Hebrew Bible contains blocks of historical writings, songs, short stories, wisdom writings, and apocalyptic writings, which we shall examine in that order. Each of these types of literature, together with their subgenres—which are especially plentiful among the songs and the wisdom writings—have analogues or forerunners in the first two divisions of the Hebrew Bible. It is also evident at a number of points, as in the Chronicler's reuse of Samuel-Kings and in Daniel's reflections on the written prophets, that these works demonstrate explicit and implicit knowledge of the older divisions of the Hebrew Bible. The Hagiographa (Greek: "sacred writings") as a title for the third division of the Hebrew Bible has been widely used among Roman Catholics and some Protestants.

51
LATE HISTORICAL WORKS: 1 AND 2 CHRONICLES AND EZRA-NEHEMIAH

In addition to the two redacted histories of Israel, the JEP version in Genesis-Numbers and the DH version in Deuteronomy-Kings, a third redacted history of Israel was added following the exile. The JEP history, expanded to include the DH introduction in Deuteronomy, formed the Torah or first division of the Hebrew Bible. The remainder of the DH work formed the first half of the Prophets or second division of the Hebrew Bible. The final biblical history, composed of 1 and 2 Chronicles and Ezra-Nehemiah, formed the conclusion to the Writings or third division of the Hebrew Bible.

51.1 Relation Between 1 and 2 Chronicles and Ezra-Nehemiah

Oddly, Ezra-Nehemiah *precedes* 1 and 2 Chronicles in the Hebrew Bible, in plain violation of the historical order of their contents. A conjectured rationale for this jarring transposition is that Ezra-Nehemiah was first accorded canonical status, since it covered new historical ground, whereas Chronicles was initially viewed as a mere supplement to Samuel-Kings and was only later "tacked on" to the end of the Writings. It was probably in conjunction with this disturbance in the order of the books that the edict of Cyrus in Ezra 1:1–4 was repeated at 2 Chron. 36:22–23, both providing an upbeat ending to the Writings and directing the reader of Chronicles to "go back" to Ezra-Nehemiah for the continuation or repeat of the history. First and Second Chronicles and Ezra-Nehemiah are counted as only two books in the total of twenty-four books in the Hebrew Bible.

The contents of this late historical work retrace the entire history of Israel treated in JEP and DH combined, that is, from creation to the exile, and go on to extend the story into postexilic times as far as the work of Ezra and Nehemiah (table 27). The treatment, however, is often skeletal, cursory, or compressed, and so proportioned that it could be said to be a history of David, Solomon, the kings of Judah, Ezra, and Nehemiah, or, more topically, *a history of the temple and cult community of Jerusalem.* The kings of Judah, the Persian overlords, and political affairs in general, acquire meaning only insofar as they contribute to the founding, upbuilding, and rebuilding of the cult community centered on temple and law.

Scholarly convention speaks of the author of 1 and 2 Chronicles and Ezra-Nehemiah as the Chronicler and of his work as the Chronicler's History (CH). Until recently it was generally assumed that one hand was responsible for the entire composition. Nowadays the matter is heatedly debated. It is widely thought, for instance, that the genealogies in 1 Chronicles 1—9 and the lists of David's officials in 1 Chronicles 23—27 are secondary additions. Moreover, considerable differences in style and viewpoint separate Chronicles from Ezra-Nehemiah, to the extent that many critics judge them to have been written by different authors in different streams of tradition. Characteristic thematic interests of Chronicles, such as the faithful house of David, the dual assignment of prophetic functions to familiar public figures of the past and to cult singers of the present, and divine retribution on Judah's leaders, are absent or meager in Ezra-Nehemiah, while the openness of Chronicles toward including northerners in the Judahite cult is explicitly checked by the restrictive policies of Ezra and Nehemiah. Those who claim separate authorship are likely to date Chronicles toward the end of the sixth century, shortly after the rebuilding of the temple, and in the opinion of some Ezra 1—6 is to be included in the Chronicler's work. In their view, Ezra-Nehemiah (in toto or excepting Ezra 1—6) would necessarily have been written a century or more later, depending on one's notion of the correct dating for Ezra.

Defenders of the unity of Chronicles and Ezra-Nehemiah are now more likely to recognize a "Chronicler's school," to allow for secondary insertions such as the lists in 1 Chronicles and possibly for two or more editions of the whole, and even to speak of a "Deutero-Chronicler." Stylistic considerations are judged either to point to unity or to be neutral with respect to common or separate authorship. The conceptual incongruities in the two

TABLE 27
Divisions and Sources in Chronicles and Ezra-Nehemiah

---

1 Chronicles 1—9:   *Adam to Saul*

Here the "story" is told exclusively by means of extended genealogies, in part drawn from Torah and Prophets and in part independently supplied by the author.

---

1 Chronicles 10—29:   *David Prepares for Building and Staffing the Temple*

2 Chronicles 1—9:   *Solomon Builds the Temple*

2 Chronicles 10—36:   *Kings of Judah from Rehoboam to Zedekiah*

In these three sections the account is an interweaving of narratives from Samuel-Kings with new materials supplied by the author who cites as many as five historical works and twelve prophetic writings, some or all of which may in fact be merely ornate ways of referring to the extant books of Samuel-Kings.

Ezra 1—6:   *Return of the Exiles and Rebuilding of Temple*

Ezra 7—10:   *Ezra's Reforms*

Nehemiah 1—7:   *Nehemiah's Reforms*

Nehemiah 8—9:   *Ezra's Reforms Continued*

Nehemiah 10—13:   *Nehemiah's Reforms Continued*

In these five sections there are sizable accounts of the work of Ezra and Nehemiah, each shifting between first-person (so-called Ezra Memoirs and Nehemiah Memoirs) and third-person reporting. These once-independent accounts of the two reformers have been rearranged so that their careers are told in a "dischronologized" or "staggered" pattern. In addition, there are lists and documents, some in Aramaic, the diplomatic language of the Persian Empire (Ezra 4:6—6:18), including a list of the returnees from exile (Ezra 2, and repeated in Nehemiah 7).

---

parts of CH may be explained by the diversity of sources and by shifts in the sociohistoric circumstances from sixth to fifth centuries. The Chronicler, in giving relatively free rein to the Ezra and Nehemiah reports, showed how an earlier liberality toward Samaritans had lost ground amid the harsh struggles climaxing in the reforms of Ezra and Nehemiah. The Chronicler's praise for past prophets and commendation of temple singers as "prophets" (1 Chron. 25:1–8; 2 Chron. 20:13–17, 20; 29:25–30; 35:15) need not be inconsistent with the virtual absence of prophets and prophetic citations in the reformers' communities (only in the prayers, Ezra 9:11; Neh. 9:26, 30, 32, and negatively in Neh. 6:10–14). In any event, the more that differences of emphasis and outright tensions and contradictions between Chronicles and Ezra-Nehemiah have been highlighted, the more customary it has become to recognize two or more editions of the Chronicler's work.

51.2 Restored Jerusalem as True Successor to David's Kingdom

Assessment of CH has tended to revolve around the issue of how "good" or how "bad" its history is. Omission of the darker aspects of David, complete neglect of the northern kings, insertion of liturgical and homiletical materials to the neglect of political and military data—all such features of the Chronicler have been read as marks of dogmatic distortion of history. There has been an inclination to conceive all of CH's independent material as fanciful fabrication, and to see biases at work in the smallest departure of CH when excerpting from the text of Samuel-Kings. Further textual studies, controlled by the Dead Sea Scrolls, and expanded knowledge of biblical history have sharply qualified the older critical assessment of CH, as has an altered understanding of how the author viewed the work in relation to earlier histories of Israel.

It is now clear that CH used a version of Samuel-Kings more closely aligned to the Hebrew text underlying the Septuagint than to proto-MT (§11.3.a).[1] Many of CH's presumed "alterations" of Samuel-Kings are apparently faithful renderings of the Hebrew text at hand. Furthermore, there are a number of points where the Chronicler provides fresh information about Judah's monarchic history that may be reliable on balance, supplementing Samuel-Kings, or even on occasion correcting them.

The reigns of Manasseh and Josiah are illustrative. To the Kings account of Manasseh's excessive idolatries and bloodshed (2 Kings 21:1–18), Chron-

---

1. Werner E. Lemke, "The Synoptic Problem in the Chronicler's History," *HTR* 58 (1968): 350–63.

icles adds that the king was taken prisoner to Babylon by the Assyrians and returned repentant and faithful to Yahweh (2 Chron. 33:10–19). Although the claimed conversion and reforms of this king are dubious in the extreme, it is possible that Manasseh was summoned to Mesopotamia and detained in connection with Babylonian uprisings against the Assyrians. Whereas Kings knows only of Josiah's reformation beginning with the discovery of the law scroll in the temple in 622 (2 Kings 22:3–10), Chronicles refers to earlier reform activities in 632 and 628 (2 Chron. 34:3–7), implying that the king's program of military conquests and domestic reforms went "hand in glove" by incremental stages. Also, whereas Kings speaks cryptically of Josiah being killed by Pharaoh Neco when the Judean king "went to meet him" (2 Kings 23:29), Chronicles states outright that Josiah "went out against him [Neco] . . . to fight with him" (2 Chron. 35:20–22). Not all biblical historians are impressed with the validity of much of this special information in CH, since the author had ample biases for misconstruing or fabricating evidence. Nevertheless, historians do take CH's potential contributions to filling out the monarchic history with cautious respect. Whether the special sources of CH lay in oral tradition, written sources now lost, or possibly even in an expanded Samuel-Kings that has not survived remains uncertain.

Recent study of CH has focused on the purpose in preparing a work that deliberately chose to go over historical ground long since surveyed by JEP and especially by DH. There is little doubt that the Chronicler was fully aware that the older histories were established as recognized, even authoritative, versions of Israel's past. There could be no serious thought of replacing them. And, in fact, CH sometimes writes in a manner that presupposes or even necessitates familiarity with parts of Samuel-Kings not excerpted.

So why did CH "retell" the story of the southern monarchy? The basic intention was to make clear that the postexilic community devoted to Law and temple was the true continuator of the Davidic monarchy. Whether or not Chronicles anticipates a revived Davidic monarchy, it does insist that the substantial and lasting contribution of David and his successors was to bequeath a temple and priestly establishment to Judah, so that when the temple and its cult were reconstituted after the exile *all* the essential elements of monarchic life were recovered.[2] By repeated references to Law and Prophets (not necessarily yet canonized), CH shows that David and

2. Peter R. Ackroyd, "History and Theology in the Writings of the Chronicler," *CTM* 38 (1967): 501–15.

Solomon combined to found an enduring cult in accord with the revelation and admonition of Moses and the prophets. For all the differences in their sources, the analogous collaboration of Ezra and Nehemiah is set up as the reforming and repristinating counterpart to the obedient initiating labors of David and Solomon.

Looked at in terms of the major streams of traditions that were shaping the leaders and the led in the restored community, CH reflects and advances "the historic compromise" in which the Priestly and Deuteronomic traditions and practices were blended, under the hegemony of the former but with generous inclusions of the latter. The Aaronid priestly priority is asserted in CH, and at the same time the Levites are plentifully represented, inserted into many contexts where they are absent from Kings. The dedication of the temple is made to echo P's dedication of the tabernacle, and ritual procedures according to Samuel-Kings are here and there supplemented from P directives.

DH is of course prominent because of CH's decision to excerpt extensively from Samuel-Kings. In addition, the so-called Levitical sermons in Chronicles place calls to faith and obedience in the mouths of *kings* and *prophets,* and even one Levite (1 Chron. 28:2–10; 2 Chron. 15:2–7; 16:7–9; 19:6; 20:15–17, 20; 25:7; 30:6–9; 32:7–8a). These speeches have been called "Levitical sermons" because they exhibit the hortatory style and the concepts of DH speeches which are widely thought to have been declaimed by *Levites.*[3] It is significant that political and religious leaders of Judah deliver these sermons in Chronicles, and, at the same time, psalms are sung by the *Levitical singers* (1 Chron. 16:4–36; 2 Chron. 5:11–13; 20:19, 21–22; 29:25–30; 31:2) who are in turn conceived as *prophets and seers.* In short, all the major categories of leadership tend to "run together" in their sharing of similar, perhaps even interchangeable functions, in the conduct of a cult whose effects "spill out" of the temple and into the domain of political and military affairs. DH elements are also frequent in Ezra-Nehemiah where Deuteronomistic sanctions and provisions undergird the debt, marriage, and cult reforms quite as much as P provisions, perhaps even more, and where Deuteronomistic phraseology permeates the prayers of Ezra 9:6–15 and Neh. 9:6–37.

If the Chronicler was an establishment supporter of the Aaronid priestly leadership. as is generally thought, he at any rate leaned a long way to incorporate Deuteronomistic viewpoints and to see to it that the lower

---

3. Gerhard von Rad, "The Levitical Sermons in I and II Chronicles," in *The Problem of the Hexateuch and Other Essays* (Edinburgh and London: Oliver & Boyd, 1966), 267–80.

orders of Levitical priests were both honored and provisioned in their posts. CH also cites many of the prophetic writings approvingly and was probably a strong supporter of their adoption as authoritative communal books. Even so, it may be that the attempt of CH to restrict prophecy in his own day (late sixth or late fifth/early fourth centuries?) to temple singers greatly disturbed the deutero-prophetic circles and may have contributed, as one scholar has suggested, to clashes over who could be called a "prophet" and eventually to a discrediting of the term for living persons even among inheritors of the prophetic tradition (cf. Jer. 23:34–40; Zech. 13:2–6).[4]

51.3 Redactional Disorder in the Books of Ezra and Nehemiah

We have previously reviewed the difficulties in establishing the order of appearance of Ezra and Nehemiah in Jerusalem and the relationship between their respective reforms (§44.3–4). On balance, the hypothesis that Nehemiah preceded Ezra, and that they worked separately, Nehemiah having returned to the Persian court before Ezra arrived, makes the most satisfactory reconstruction of a situation greatly muddled by the way the sources have been redacted. Several factors may be at work in the recalcitrance of the sources to a totally plausible reconstruction.

For one thing, the sources were originally independent and their proper chronological placement may not always have been evident to the redactor(s). Because aspects of the work of Sheshbazzar, Zerubbabel, Nehemiah, and Ezra were similar, there was a danger of confusing and blurring the distinctiveness of their works and of misassigning particular traditions to one or another of them. The dating of events in the reigns of Persian kings could contribute to mistaken chronology since royal names were repeated. Thus, whether an Artaxerxes was I or II is not distinguished in the biblical text (e.g., Ezra 7:7; Neh. 2:1; 13:6). It has also been conjectured that a copyist's error may account for the separation of Ezra material in Neh. 7:73b—9:37 from its original connection with Ezra 7—10. It is distinctly possible, however, that a redactor deliberately devised this "dischronologizing" because he wished to associate Nehemiah and Ezra closely—highest political and religious authorities!—in both of the major reforms.[5] In that event, Nehemiah 8—9 will have been deliberately broken away from the Ezra report and "planted" within the Nehemiah material in order to give the two reformers the appearance of colaborers, their work now recounted

---

4. David L. Petersen, *Late Israelite Prophecy. Studies in Deutero-Prophetic Literature and in Chronicles,* SBLMS 23 (Missoula, Mont.: Scholars Press, 1977), 55–104.
5. Brevard S. Childs, *IOTS,* 626–37.

in a synchronous $E^1 + N^1 + E^2 + N^2$ pattern (E^1 and E^2 being the two phases of Ezra's reforms, and N^1 and N^2 being the two phases of Nehemiah's reforms). The effect was clinched by inserting Nehemiah at the reading of the Law (Neh. 8:9) and Ezra at the dedication of the walls (Neh. 12:26, 36).

What literary and sociohistoric sense can we make out of the Ezra-Nehemiah traditions? The Ezra materials are found in Ezra 7—10; Neh. 7:73b—9:37, and the Nehemiah materials in Neh. 1:1—7:73a; 9:38—13:31. Within both strands, the earlier portions are the most coherent and contain sustained "I" passages that suggest the presence of a Nehemiah Memoir and possibly an Ezra Memoir. The Nehemiah Memoir is clearly visible in Neh. 1:1—7:73a; 12:31–43; 13:4–31. At least the narrative frame of 11:1, 20, 36 may also be from the Memoir, and possibly also 12:27–30; 12:44—13:3; and 9:38—10:39 (which fits best in the account after Neh. 13:27). The first-person Ezra Memoir is in Ezra 7:27—9:15, and some have thought that Ezra 7:1–26 and Ezra 10 were once a part of the Memoir. Why first-person passages should have been changed to third person has not been satisfactorily explained. "Memoir" as a genre name for Nehemiah's document is a misnomer since in it the reformer is offering political self-justification against his enemies and commends himself to God that he should be "remembered" (is he childless and without heir?). Similarities between Nehemiah's Report and Memorials of ancient Near Eastern kings and Israelite Psalms of Lament, especially of persons falsely accused, have been noted.

To get a near approximation of the course of events in the reforms, for *the work of Nehemiah* one should read in order *Neh. 1:1—7:73a; 11:1—13:27; 9:38—10:39;* and *13:28–31;* and for *the work of Ezra* one should read in order *Ezra 7—10; Neh. 9:1–37; 7:73b—8:18.* This necessitates deleting the redactional references to Ezra in Neh. 12:26, 36, and to Nehemiah in Neh. 8:9. There may have been two stages in the rearrangement and conflation of these traditions. In a first stage the Ezra traditions would have been placed first in an effort to underscore the religious priorities in the series of reforms. In a second step, either due to copyist's error or by design, the final stages of Ezra's reforms would have been interpolated into the Nehemiah records, thereby clumsily affirming the collaboration of the two reformers. If this blending of the two reformers' activities correctly retained a historical reminiscence as some scholars think, then it depended entirely on other evidence than is preserved in the present literary records.

By drawing so straight and unerring a line from Moses through David to the restored and freshly reformed postexilic community, CH validates a vigorous recovery of national traditions and communal practices that was both a form of accommodation to the colonial status under Persia and also an act of national resistance by marking off a religiocultural identity for Jews that was drawn so tightly that in the end it excluded fellow Jews, such as the Samaritans, who did not fully succumb to the reform leadership in Judah.

52
SONGS

52.1 What Is Biblical Poetry?

We have noted the presence of verse structure in many parts of the Hebrew Bible and briefly discussed some of its features in connection with the Song of Deborah in Judges 5 (§23.1). It has been recognized since the work of Robert Lowth in 1753 that Hebrew songs are composed of sentences or lines that divide into two (sometimes three) "members" or clauses. The clauses are separated by a slight pause, and the sentence concludes with a full pause, forming the pattern

$$A \underline{\hspace{2cm}}/ + B \underline{\hspace{2cm}}//$$

or, on occasion

$$A \underline{\hspace{2cm}}/ + B \underline{\hspace{2cm}}/ + C \underline{\hspace{2cm}}//$$

Often the component clauses of the song sentence have a commonality or correspondence which has been described as "parallelism of members (= clauses)." This habit of forming a poetic sentence out of two or three clauses, with attending pauses and parallels, may be schematically illustrated by Ps. 24:1–3:

v. 1　A　The earth is Yahweh's and the fullness thereof /
　　　B　the world and those who dwell therein //

v. 2　A　For he has founded it upon the seas /
　　　B　and established it upon the rivers //

v. 3　A　Who shall ascend the hill of Yahweh? /
　　　B　and who shall stand in his holy place? //

Psalm 24:1–3 thus exhibits close parallelism (called "synonymous"), but there are practically as many lines in Hebrew verse where the correspondence between clauses is slight or absent altogether:

A   The angel of Yahweh encamps around those who fear him /
B   and he delivers them //
(Ps. 34:7)

A   Blessed be Yahweh /
B   who has not given us as prey to their teeth //
(Ps. 124:6)

A   Mark this, then, you who forget God /
B   lest I rend, and there be none to deliver //
(Ps. 50:22)

In Hebrew verse, lines *with* correspondence and lines *without* correspondence typically intermix, as in Ps. 2:1–6:

v. 1   A   Why do the nations conspire? /
       B   and the peoples plot in vain? //

v. 2   A   The kings of the earth set themselves /
       B   and the rulers take counsel together /
       C   against Yahweh and his anointed //

v. 3   A   Saying, "Let us burst their bonds asunder /
       B   and cast their cords from us" //

v. 4   A   He who sits in the heavens laughs /
       B   Yahweh holds them in derision //

v. 5   A   Then he will speak to them in his wrath /
       B   and terrify them in his fury //

v. 6   A   Saying, "I have set my king /
       B   on Zion, my holy hill" //

It is obvious that the close correspondence between clauses in vv. 1, 3, 4, and 5 in Psalm 2 is not present in vv. 2 and 6. In standard descriptions of parallel clauses it is customary to refer to such departures from strict correspondence as "synthetic" or "formal" parallelism.

More elusive has been the quest for poetic meter. Based on syllable counts and conjectured accenting schemes, it has been usual to identify lines with 3 + 3, 3 + 2, and 2 + 2 meters, as well as other less-frequent patterns. Often it has been assumed that a single meter prevailed throughout any one composition, and the biblical text has been generously emended on "metrical grounds." Although associated lines tend to be similar in length, there are so many exceptions and our ignorance of how the spoken language was stressed so total, that no convincing metrical analysis has yet been offered.

Our understanding of biblical poetics has been vastly enriched on the one side by the recovery of examples of ancient Near Eastern poetry, particularly Canaanite, which clarify the many ways of constructing sentences of parallel clauses and of employing rhetorical devices that Israel shared with its neighbors. On the other side more sophisticated attempts have been made to formulate precisely what it is that gives Hebrew poetry its specific character. The challenge is substantial, since meter has not been demonstrable and the paralleling of clauses has not been formulated with enough precision to cover the great variety of forms it takes. The two most ambitious recent inquiries have tried to penetrate below the generalities and assumptions about Hebrew poetry which derive heavily from the canons of Western literature.

One study finds that the lengths and interconnections of clauses A and B are not at all governed by metrical enumeration but by a matrix of syntactical constraints that specifies a range in the number of words of particular syntactic types that will occur together in the clause constructions. At the same time the ordering force of parallelism is described in a series of constant syntactic phenomena ("tropes" of repetition, coloration, matching, gapping, dependency, and mixing) that generate parallels at the word level, the line level, and the supralinear level.[6]

Another study, while respecting the analytic precision and synthesizing conclusions of the former work, finds the gist of Hebrew poetics not in syntax alone but in a subtle conjunction of syntactic, semantic, and phonological factors.[7] The basic difficulty, it claims, has been a misconception about the relations of similarity and dissimilarity between the A and B clauses. The essence is not that B *repeats* A, but that B, while *continuing* A, *goes beyond* it. The semantic connection is this: "A is so, and *what's more,* B is so," a meaning shaped by context that can produce such nuances, for example, as "Not only A, but *even* B" or "You know A, *now* understand B."

According to this latter understanding, we do not really have parallelism of members in the sense that one clause repeats the other or is in simple alignment with it. We have rather an emphatic "seconding sequence" of clauses in which "B typically *supports* A, carries it further, backs it up,

---

6. M. P. O'Connor, *Hebrew Verse Structure* (Winona Lake, Ind.: Eisenbrauns, 1980).

7. James L. Kugel, *The Idea of Biblical Poetry. Parallelism and Its History* (New Haven, Conn., and London: Yale University Press, 1981), chaps. 1–2. Appendix B, 315–23, comments on O'Connor's study.

completes it, goes beyond it." Moreover, biblical speakers/writers did not divide speech genres into "prose" and "poetry" as we do in Western literature. Biblical speech is more or less elevated ("poetic") to the degree that it exhibits "seconding" clauses, terseness, and ellipsis in style. To remind ourselves to lay aside Western literary notions when we examine the elevated biblical "seconding style," we should perhaps speak of so-called biblical poetry.

52.2 Psalms

The canonical Book of Psalms is an anthology of 150 "poetic prayers" composed in the "seconding sequence" style of paired A + B (or A + B + C) clauses. Similar compositions are found throughout the three divisions of the Hebrew Bible, with Jeremiah, Isaiah 40—66, and Job making especially abundant use of Psalm forms. The Psalms are by and large addressed *to* Israel's God, but the prayer medium here is broad enough to allow for speech *about* the attributes and deeds of God and for citation of oracles *from* God, as well as for appeals and instructions to worshipers and readers. The speech conventions of these prayers, in their vocabulary and genres, were shaped within the framework of Israel's "cult," that is, its formal worship centered on the temple at Jerusalem. The subject matter of these psalms is overwhelmingly the distress and deliverance of the people of Israel as a whole and of individual Israelites.

While the speech forms presuppose stated occasions of worship, the present grouping of the Psalms and the assorted titles attached to 115 of them do not fully or systematically reflect the actual occasions of worship or the exact manner in which they were used. The "time line" of these prayers extends in fact over centuries of cultic history, beginning with the first temple built by Solomon, and including its forerunners and competing shrines, continuing through the templeless exilic period, and reaching on into the era of the second temple built by Zerubbabel. The Book of Psalms is often called "the Hymnbook of the Second Temple," and this is apt in the sense that during the second temple era the compilation and redaction of the psalms was completed, perhaps approximately 325–250 B.C.E. As a deposit of cultic texts appropriated for study and reflection, Psalms thus gives us a compressed sampling of texts from the first and second temple programs of worship, but with a somewhat fuller sense of the postexilic uses of the psalms than of their preexilic uses.

The move from live cultic performance of psalms to their collection as literature was a major one, in which much of the actual cultic functioning of the psalms, both early and late, has been lost or obscured. It is evident that factors other than stated worship have had a part in the shaping of the Book of Psalms. In a measure, they reflect a tendency toward private "devotional" or "study" use apart from, or in between, times of temple worship. Originally separately composed, the psalms were gathered in lesser collections that were finally combined to produce the present book. As written compilations, the psalms became available for "meditation" and "study," by comparing one with another and with other biblical passages, and by "thematizing" them as expressions of loyalty to divine law (linking Psalms with Torah) and of prophetic revelations (linking Psalms with Prophets).

One entire category of psalms, called wisdom or didactic psalms, focuses proper prayer and worship on wholehearted adherence to the divine law (in many, if not all, instances this law is probably already the canonical Law). Psalms 1 and 2, which form a complementary introduction to the whole collection, epitomize this manner of praying and pondering the texts, for the Psalms have become testimonies to the proven power of fidelity to God's Law in shaping righteous and happy lives in a just community. And even though the Davidic monarch heralded in Psalm 2, and elsewhere throughout the Psalms, was no longer reigning when Psalms was finally shaped, he was remembered and anticipated as the executor of justice in Jewish society so that the divine law might be embodied on earth. In fact, the division of the Book of Psalms into *five* parts marked by summary refrains or colophons seems to have been intended to show a homology between Psalms and the five books of Torah:

Book I: Psalms 1—41, cf. 41:13
Book II: Psalms 42—72, cf. 72:18–20
Book III: Psalms 73—89, cf. 89:52
Book IV: Psalms 90—106, cf. 106:48
Book V: Psalms 107—50, cf. 150

Modern study of the Psalms has evolved through several stages in progressively clarifying psalmic literature and in narrowing and sharpening the still-unresolved questions. Breaking through the traditional religious assumption that David and singers of his generation wrote the Psalms, nineteenth-century (C.E.) scholars emphasized the postexilic origin of the anthology and claimed even to identify a large number of psalms from as late as Maccabean times. Nowadays it is judged that many of the psalms, while scarcely written by David, are preexilic, and that, among the many postexilic psalms, probably all of them were composed before Maccabean times (although Maccabean use of psalms may have affected the text at points).

52.2.a Literary Genres

In the early twentieth century C.E., Hermann Gunkel began "to crack the code" of psalm idiom, formal structure, and function. In addition to the five predominant types of *hymns, individual laments, individual thanksgiving songs, communal laments,* and *royal psalms,* Gunkel isolated several less common or more formally elusive types: *communal thanksgiving songs, songs of pilgrimage, blessings and curses, wisdom poetry, liturgies* (pieces from different literary types deliberately joined in a single unit for worship), and *mixed types* (fusion and free composition of psalms disconnected from cult).[8]

The main lines of Gunkel's form-critical analysis have held up remarkably well in the half century since he proposed them. Modifications and rearrangements within his basic system, and some new nomenclature, have been argued, but no encompassing reclassification of types has gained a consensus to replace the somewhat arbitrary manner in which Gunkel arranged the types according to "major" and "minor" groupings. It is perhaps helpful to show the array of genres in broad groupings according to their types or modes of speech, so as to emphasize the logical interconnections of genres. The genres may be grouped under four types or modes of speech:

I. Lamenting and Entreating Genres
II. Praising and Thanking Genres
III. Performing and Enacting Genres
IV. Instructing and Meditating Genres

I. Lamenting and Entreating Genres

A. Anonymous Individual Laments (44)

An unnamed person (excluding the data in the titles), suffering physical ills, psychological torment, and/or sociopolitical oppression and exclusion, describes the distress in harsh terms, sometimes protests innocence or confesses sin, pleads with Yahweh to remove the distress, and often passes over into an affirmation of certainty that the cry for help will be heard and deliverance is forthcoming. Other nomenclature is sometimes used for subdivisions of this genre. Laments expressing innocence are described as "prayers of the falsely accused," those confessing sins as "penitential

8. Hermann Gunkel, *The Psalms. A Form-Critical Introduction,* Facet Books 19 (Philadelphia: Fortress Press, 1967).

psalms," and those hinting at impending distress rather than present suffering as "protective psalms." The line between individual and communal laments is not agreed upon in all cases, since the "I" in some psalms may be a speaker for the community and it may be that some originally individual laments have been modified over time into communal laments. Similarly, there is dispute over whether certain of the individual psalms are laments or thanksgiving songs. This is because the lament typically anticipates deliverance with such confidence that it engages in virtual "thanksgiving in advance," while the thanksgiving song normally contains a report on the past distress.

Psalms 3, 5, 6, 7, 9—10, 13, 17, 22, 25, 26, 28, 31, 35, 36, 38, 39, 40, 42—43, 51, 54, 55, 56, 57, 59, 61, 63, 64, 69, 70, 71, 77, 86, 88, 94, 102, 109, 120, 130, 140, 141, 142, 143

B. Anonymous Individual Psalms of Confidence (8)

The section of the lament that Gunkel called "the certainty of a hearing" on occasion becomes the content of an entire psalm, with only the merest reference to the psalmist's difficulty. The anticipated deliverance from Yahweh is declared with utter confidence, such that these are sometimes called *Trust Psalms*.

Psalms 4, 11, 16, 23, 27, 62, 121, 131

C. Royal Individual Laments

The preexilic Davidic king is the subject of at least ten psalms and is alluded to in others. No entire psalm is given over to the lament of a king, but royal lamenting speech is contained in at least three psalms, one to be classified as a royal thanksgiving song (18:4–6) and the others as communal laments (89:46–51; 144:1–11).

D. Communal Laments (16)

Afflicted by famine, plague, socioeconomic oppression, or military disaster, the community gathers to fast, lament, and sacrifice. The communal lament follows the same basic structure as the individual lament, although it is at times more explicit about the calamity referred to. The complaints are usually in "we" form, with an occasional "I" speaker representing the community. It is possible that individual laments were also voiced during the public fast days that featured communal laments.

Psalms 12, 44, 58, 60, 74, 79, 80, 83, 85, 89, 90, 108, 123, 126, 137, 144

E. Communal Psalms of Confidence (3)

These are the communal counterparts of the individual psalms of confidence (see IB above).

Psalms 115, 125, 129

II. Praising and Thanking Genres

A. Hymns or Descriptive Praises (20)

Praises of God, or hymns, begin and end with calls to laud or bless the divine majesty. The body of the hymn is a description of Yahweh's attributes or deeds in nature and in the history of Israel. Hymns have much in common with thanksgiving songs, except that they cite general and long-standing aspects of God's goodness and power whereas the thanksgiving songs speak of recent deliverances from specific distress. In order to stress that "praise" is the common discourse of both types, C. Westermann has proposed that hymns be called "descriptive praises" and thanksgiving songs "declarative praises."[9] In addition to two important subclasses of hymns cited below, others have been classified as *victory hymns* for recitation after battle, *pilgrimage songs* for worshipers on their way to Jerusalem, and hymns judged to be connected with one of the *stated festivals* such as Passover or Tabernacles.

Psalms 8; 19:1–6; 29; 33; 95:1–7c; 98; 100; 103; 104; 111; 113; 114; 117; 135; 145; 146; 147; 148; 149; 150

1. Hymns of Zion (6)

Certain hymns picture Yahweh as dwelling at Jerusalem on invincible Mt. Zion which is attacked or threatened by enemies whom Yahweh overpowers. Gunkel took these to be eschatological references to a future day of salvation. Mowinckel understood that in the cultic drama Yahweh's present resecuring of the foundations of the community was affirmed. Both scholars recognized that these hymns of Zion drew on old Canaanite mythology about an impregnable holy mountain as the seat of deity.

Psalms 46, 48, 76, 84, 87, 122

2. Hymns Celebrating the Kingship of Yahweh (5)

A handful of hymns assert Yahweh's rule over the nations and contain the cultic exclamation, "Yahweh has become king!" As with the hymns of Zion,

---

9. Claus Westermann, "Psalms, Book of," in IDBSup, 705–10; idem, *Praise and Lament in the Psalms* (Atlanta: John Knox Press, 1981), 15–35, 81–90, 102–30 (see charts on pp. 85–86, 103–4).

Gunkel saw in them a noncultic hope influenced by prophets and projected into the future, while Mowinckel asserted that this "hope" was a cultically experienced present reality enacted at the annual fall New Year's Festival connected with the Feast of Tabernacles.

Psalms 47, 93, 96, 97, 99

B. Anonymous Individual Thanksgiving Songs or Declarative Praises (9)

The structure of this genre includes a call to give thanks, an account of past distress, declaration that Yahweh has delivered the sufferer, sometimes announcements of a sacrifice in payment of vows, and it may contain blessings and hymnic elements of general praise. There are indications that the ceremonies of individual thanksgiving where the songs were recited were attended by family and friends and a larger congregation.

Psalms 30, 32, 34, 41, 52, 66, 92, 116, 138

C. Royal Thanksgiving Song or Declarative Praise (1)

In one psalm, the king gives thanks for deliverance from a military foe. This psalm exhibits the fine line between descriptive and declarative praises, since it appears to be formulated in general enough terms (no particular enemy named) that it could be used by a king after any military victory. In one communal thanksgiving song, the king gives individual thanks (118:5–21).

Psalm 18 (= 2 Samuel 22)

D. Communal Thanksgiving Songs or Declarative Praises (6)

When the communal distress was lifted, a public thanksgiving day was observed, on which occasion communal thanksgiving songs were recited, very likely in company with the thanksgiving songs of individuals as a fitting aspect of national celebration.

Psalms 65, 67, 107, 118, 124, 136

III. Performing and Enacting Genres

It seems that a number of Gunkel's minor genres and some of his royal psalms can be grouped under the category of genres that describe or give the contents of acts performed within the cult. The peculiar details of many of these performing psalms, which make it awkward to classify them, have to do with the distinctive rites that the psalms either directly allude to, accompany as a program piece, or are imitatively modeled on.

A. Royal Ceremonial Songs (8)

Several of these psalms are connected either with the *coronation* of the king or the annual celebration of his *accession*. It is characteristic of them that the people (or their representative) and deity speak of the king in the third person. Psalm 45 is a royal *marriage song*, and Psalm 101 is a *royal promise* of fidelity to Yahweh and the community, perhaps a pledge on taking office.

Psalms 2, 20, 21, 45, 72, 101, 110, 132:11–18

B. Entrance and Processional Liturgies (5)

Psalms 15 and 24 contain queries and responses concerning who is entitled to enter Yahweh's temple, probably *spoken antiphonally* between worshipers approaching the temple and priests replying from the temple precincts. Four of these psalms presuppose or allude to *processions* in such a manner as to suggest that they were constructed for singing during liturgical processions or are imitative of processional songs.

Psalms 15, 24, 68, 118, 132

C. Prophetic Oracles of Judgment or Admonition (7)

In several psalms prominent place is given to condemnation or chiding which takes on the structure and idiom of prophetic speech. Gunkel assumed that they were noncultic texts influenced by prophetic ideals, whereas Mowinckel regarded them as *liturgies* in which cultic prophets spoke directly to the congregation as a stated part of the ceremony.

Psalms 14, 50, 53, 75, 81, 82, 95:7d–11

D. Blessings (3)

Blessings sometimes appear in hymns and thanksgiving songs. In addition, there are psalms that consist entirely of blessing, or, in the case of Psalm 134, a blessing on the worshiper is attached to an appeal for priests on temple duty to bless Yahweh.

Psalms 128, 133, 134

IV. Instructing and Meditating Genres

A. Wisdom and Law Psalms (10)

There is a considerable number of psalms that do not show any significant marks of the above genres but do display familiar features of wisdom writings: (1) key words such as "wisdom," "fear of Yahweh," addressees as "sons"; (2) rhetorical devices such as question and answer techniques, numerical sayings, beatitudes ("happy the one who . . ."); (3) a pronounced tone of teaching and warning; (4) preoccupation with unjust suffering, the wicked rich, divine guidance and protection of the pious, and the two ways of obedience that leads to life and of disobedience that leads to death. Furthermore, among these Psalms 1; 19:7–14; and 119 profusely praise the Law as the very embodiment of wisdom and faithful observance of the Law as the essence of wise thought and deed (Psalms 37 and 112 make this same equation in a more muted way). The mood of all these psalms is reflective and didactic, and the *law psalms* in particular presuppose concentrated study and meditation on texts (probably both the canonical text of Torah and other writings, including the Psalms themselves). It is also striking that wisdom elements are scattered widely among psalms that belong to other genres (e.g., 32:1–2, 6–7, 10; 34:11–22; 36:1–4; 78:1–4; 90:3–12; 92:5–15; 94:8–15; 111:10). Commentators have tended to view these as noncultic compositions, but that should not be so readily assumed nor should it be thought that the "wise" writers of these psalms were disinterested in or opposed to participation in cultic worship.

Psalms 1; 19:7–14; 37; 49; 73; 91; 112; 119; 127; 139

B. Historical Psalms (3)

Three long psalms review aspects of Israel's early history for purposes of reassurance, admonition, and legitimation of God's present dealings with Judah to the exclusion of the northern kingdom. Psalm 78 is introduced as a wisdom instruction, while the other two instances of the historical psalm form are hymns.

Psalms 78, 105, 106

52.2.b Life Settings

With respect to the life setting and function of the psalm genres, Gunkel stressed a threefold development:

1. All the primary *psalm genres* had their origin in the *preexilic cult,* but only a

relatively small number of the extant psalms actually derive directly from the corporate worship of the first temple.

2. From the eighth century on, under the influence of the prophetic critique of the cult, psalm forms of speech were increasingly detached from the cult and used to express a more *private and spiritual type of piety,* and to point to a *deferred ideal future* for the nation.

3. When the second temple was built after the exile, older cultic and noncultic psalms were joined with new psalms to provide a *temple hymnbook.* The interests of temple musicians and of law interpreters contributed in different ways to the final compilation of the work.[10]

Sigmund Mowinckel, star pupil of Gunkel, reconstructed a very different scenario for the setting and function of psalm genres:

1. Not only did all the primary psalm genres originate in the preexilic cult, as Gunkel discerned, but it is equally true that the great majority of *extant psalms* were directly generated in the *cult of the first temple.*

2. The *individualized spirituality* of many psalms is not a sign of withdrawal from the cult, but an integral aspect of Israelite worship. Prophecy also belonged to the temple worship insofar as *cultic prophets* took part in preexilic temple ceremonies. The "enthronement" of Yahweh was an act and affirmation of cultic drama that rested on *mythic actualization.* The central unifying festival that lay behind the main psalm genres was a fall *New Year Festival* in which Yahweh's lordship over nature and history was mythically reconfirmed.

3. When Israel's institutions for affirming Yahweh's kingship collapsed in defeat and exile, the frustrated cultic-mythological "hope" of Israel was projected toward the future and *eschatology* was born. Learned collectors, informed by law and wisdom, shaped the present Book of Psalms for study and reflection.[11]

The merits of these two reconstructions of the origins and uses of the psalms are still vigorously debated without consensus.[12] It is probable that a modified form of the cult-dramatic theory (one that does not too sharply sever myth from sociohistoric setting) will in the end prove more consistent with the textual evidence than the alternative of draining the cultic sphere of its contributions to and connections with personal spirituality, prophecy, and eschatological hope. Gunkel's sharp split between spirituality and cult so sunders the specific uses of psalms from cultic activity that it is difficult to see how spiritualists and ritualists could have used the same collection of texts in the second temple period. His proper insistence on an important

---

10. Gunkel, *Psalms.*

11. Sigmund Mowinckel, *The Psalms in Israel's Worship* (New York and Nashville: Abingdon Press, 1962), vol. 1, chaps. 1–2.

12. Inclining toward Gunkel's views is Aubrey R. Johnson, "The Psalms," in *OTMS,* 162–209. Favoring Mowinckel's cult theory is John H. Eaton, "The Psalms and Israelite Worship," in *TI,* 238–73.

dimension of individual spirituality can be accommodated by recognizing that the first temple cult made room for concrete expressions of personal faith and actually generated them, with or without the encouragement of the temple leadership.

Mowinckel's grasp of the living cult as the matrix for the experience of the immediate presence of Yahweh accords with what we know of ritual from anthropological studies and is critical for appreciating the psalm types, especially the intimate interplay between lamenting and praising genres. He is almost certainly correct in believing that a first temple festival celebrating the reactualization of Yahweh's kingship over nature and history lies behind the Hymns Celebrating Yahweh's Kingship and probably also behind other hymns, including the Hymns of Zion. It is also likely that this celebration of Yahweh's reconfirmed kingship coincided with celebration of the accession of the Israelite king.

Rituals for the renewal of divine and human kingship in Israel, broadly indebted to ancient Near Eastern culture, are by no means inconsistent with Israel's strong covenantal and historical traditions. Much depends, of course, on how the "mythic" frames or dressings of Yahweh's kingship are conceived and qualified. The cult drama had to be closely enough related to and expressive of Israel's sociohistorical realities and aspirations for meaningful "disillusionment" to occur when Judah fell, even on Mowinckel's theory. It is likely that the sphere of myth in the cultic drama was a bone of interpretive contention between status quo establishmentarians and restive critics of preexilic society and government. Efforts to deny or minimize "mythic" and "natural" aspects of divine kingship before the exile by redefining the central preexilic festival as a "covenant festival" (A. Weiser) or as a "covenant-renewal festival" turned into a "Zion festival" in Judah to celebrate Yahweh's election of Jerusalem and David (H.-J. Kraus) seem unnecessarily restrictive. It also seems reasonable that the prophetic judgment oracles in the psalms belong to cultic celebration, whatever the exact status of "cult prophets" may have been.

On the other hand, Mowinckel and other advocates of cult drama have asserted knowledge of a central festival program that remains a hypothetical reconstruction. We continue to be largely in the dark as to how the central celebrative acts of ancient Israel were distributed among the stated festivals of Passover, Weeks, and Tabernacles, although it is likely that the divine kingship/human kingship syndrome was especially prominent at Tabernacles, the beginning of the new year. Complicating and prejudicing the whole inquiry has been the repeated emergence of two claims about the cult drama (claims which in fact Mowinckel and most of his followers have not made) concerning which there is not the slightest shred of supporting evidence: (1) *that Yahweh "died and rose" as a fertility deity*; and (2) *that Israel's king played the part of Yahweh* in the festival drama.

52.2.c Redaction of the Book

Past scholarship emphasized the unprincipled, even random, manner in which the Book of Psalms was formed. It was observed that the psalms are not consistently grouped by theme, literary type, apparent date, or according to authorship/dedication or musical directions provided in the headings. Nevertheless, redaction critics have lately taken a renewed interest in the long-neglected question of the formation of the Psalter. While no theory of compilation and redaction yet accounts for all the curious complexities of the subcollections within the complete anthology, certain regularities little attended to in the past are now drawing attention.[13]

There are, for example, some gross patterns in the distribution of psalm genres. Individual genres are concentrated in the first half of the anthology by a ratio of about 3 to 1, so that more than half of the texts in Psalms 1—75 are devoted to individual genres, with laments predominating over a smaller number of Psalms of Confidence and Thanksgiving Songs by a similar ratio of 3 to 1. In sharp contrast, communal genres are concentrated in the last half of the book by a ratio of about 3 to 1, so that more than half of the texts in Psalms 76—150 are communal genres, with Hymns and Thanksgiving Songs predominating over laments by about 2 to 1. On the other hand, psalms featuring a king, prophetic judgments and admonitions, and the wisdom and law psalms are distributed practically evenhandedly between the two halves of the book, tending moreover to be scattered rather than bunched together.

In terms of the tone these distribution patterns give to the whole collection, there is *a dramatic shift from the lamenting individual to the praising community* and this shift is leavened or stabilized by the *common denominators of royalty, prophecy, law, wisdom, and history* (allowing that elements of Israel's history show up in Psalms 1—75 in genres other than the full-fledged Historical Psalms).

Examination of the five divisions of Psalms provides considerable, if not completely convergent, evidence of the process of compilation. Book I (Psalms 1—41) stands apart as a collection assigned to David and making overwhelming use of the divine name Yahweh (as do also Books IV–V). Books II (42—72) and III (73—89) stand together in two respects: (1)

13. Childs, *IOTS*, 508–23.

Psalms 42—83 overwhelmingly prefer the divine name Elohim, and (2) authorship or dedicatory headings are arranged so that the Davidic psalms are surrounded by psalms connected with temple musicians, forming something of a chiastic arrangement:

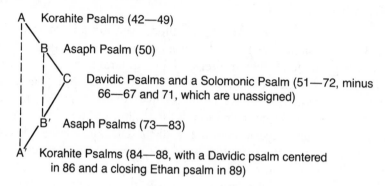

A   Korahite Psalms (42—49)

     B   Asaph Psalm (50)

        C   Davidic Psalms and a Solomonic Psalm (51—72, minus
            66—67 and 71, which are unassigned)

     B′ Asaph Psalms (73—83)

A′ Korahite Psalms (84—88, with a Davidic psalm centered
    in 86 and a closing Ethan psalm in 89)

That the Davidic psalms were once in a separate collection is clear from the note in 72:20, "the prayers of David . . . are ended," since another eighteen Davidic psalms appear after that note. The references to the Levitical musicians Korah and Asaph (as also to Jeduthun, Heman, and Ethan) most likely mean that the psalms connected with them were a part of the repertory of musical guilds in second temple renditions of the psalms.

It is likely that Book I and Books II–III were combined to produce a first edition of the Book of Psalms. Psalms 2 and 89 may have introduced and concluded that edition, the former with its stark assertion of the "world rule" of the Davidic monarchy and the latter with its faith-threatening bewilderment at the fall of the Davidic monarchy. By contrast with Books I–III, the large number of psalms in Books IV–V that are untitled altogether, or lack a notation of authorship or dedication, suggests that they were more miscellaneous in origin and were grouped as addenda to Books I–III.

Similarities in redactional method are detectable throughout the anthology, as well as apparent marks of anthological "rounding out" toward the end of Book V. There are "runs" of *individual laments* in Psalms 3—7, 25—28, 54—57, 61—64, and 140—43, and there are "runs" of *hymns* in Psalms 46—48, 96—100, 103—6, and 145—50. Psalms 120—34, largely laments, are all titled "songs of ascents" and may have been associated in pilgrim rites, although as a whole they are scarcely suitable as traveling songs. The close of Book V shows several redactional features aimed at a grand finale to the entire book. Eight Davidic psalms are joined in Psalms

138—45, the only such extended "run" in Books IV–V: the first two strike the note of trust, the next five lament, and the last breaks into hymnic praise which introduces the five concluding *Hallelujah* ("Praise Yahweh!") *hymns* to climax the work. The last of these Davidic psalms is called a *tᵉhillāh,* "psalm," which is the singular of the title of the book, *tᵉhillīm,* "Psalms." It is the sole usage of the term in a psalm superscription and seems intended as a concluding echo of the title given the entire collection.

To what extent changes were made in 1—89 at the stage of final redaction is unclear. Psalm 1, balancing well with the royal universalism of Psalm 2, was probably inserted to strike a thematic note of Law = wisdom as the hermeneutical key for reading all the psalms. It is interesting that Books I and V each contain four acrostic psalms, while there are none in the intervening divisions. This may indicate that the final redactor consciously provided the early acrostics with balancing counterparts toward the end of the anthology.

52.2.d Sociohistoric Horizons of the Psalms

Who are the sufferers and the oppressors that so richly populate the psalms? How did the psalms function within the social transactions and power relations of the community? A clear starting point is that the psalms celebrate an order of life created by God which is badly shaken by crises of public and private life and is only recoverable at a new level after passing through limit experiences of severe disorder. One way of stating the functions of these psalms groups them into the categories of: (1) *psalms of orientation,* celebrating creation, wisdom, retribution, and blessing; (2) *psalms of disorientation or dislocation,* pouring out laments and appeals of sufferers for whom the orderly world has fallen apart; and (3) *psalms of reorientation or relocation,* in which thanksgiving and praise affirm a reconstructed order that is no longer taken for granted because it has been won in pain and struggle and must be constantly rewon. The psalms of orientation may be said to correspond to a *hermeneutics of convention* (secure meaning), the psalms of disorientation to a *hermeneutics of suspicion* (radically doubted meaning), and the psalms of reorientation to a *hermeneutics of representation* (a new level and depth of meaning that does not forget the doubt).[14]

Conceptualizing the psalm functions in terms of a dynamic passage through "moments" of orientation, disorientation, and reorientation has so

---

14. Walter Brueggemann, "Psalms and the Life of Faith: A Suggested Typology of Function," *JSOT* 17 (1980): 3–32; idem, *Praying the Psalms* (Winona Lake, Ind.: Saint Mary's Press, 1982).

far been developed more in its psychological facets than in its societal dimensions. This is understandable, since the personal pain of the lamenting psalms bulks so large and since the Psalms have typically had their fullest use in private devotions and in pastoral care. It is evident, however, that the "disorientation" expressed in the Psalms is not a matter of individual physical or psychic breakdown in a neutral social situation. We meet *tensions, crises, and ruptures in the social order* that, while coming to very sharp expression in the lives of individual psalmists, nevertheless wrack the whole community.

Individualizing and psychologizing interpretations of the Psalms have been encouraged by the *historical notes* attached to several psalms that connect them to particular incidents in the life of David (Psalms 3, 7, 18, 34, 51, 52, 54, 56, 57, 59, 60, 63, and 142). It is very doubtful, however, that these postexilic exegetical notes were intended as an "individualizing" maneuver, since David stood for the righteous leader of the community. Interestingly, one historical note speaks anonymously of "a prayer of one afflicted when he is weak and pours out his complaint before Yahweh" (102:1). The righteousness of David and the psalmists is presented in the psalms less as a personal achievement than as a resource and power that undergirds and permeates community, or, when lacking, undermines and destroys community.

The exact identity of the sufferers and their oppressors has been difficult to agree upon because of the *conventionality of the psalm language.* Owing to its extravagance and pluriformity, often describing the plight variously in the same psalm, this language can hardly be taken as simple narrative reporting on the psalmist's condition. The sufferer sinks down into the cosmic waters or descends into the pit of the underworld, is set upon by wild beasts or fierce warriors, is pursued relentlessly and trapped like wild game, burns or melts or wastes away in body.

Since descriptions of physical distress are particularly prominent, it has been argued that the oppressors are *practitioners of witchcraft* and the sufferers are their victims who approach Yahweh through the cult in search of protection and cancellation of the curses unleashed on them. Likewise, since accounts of false accusation and social ostracism are frequent, it has been claimed that they reflect an *oath of clearance or ordeal* procedure in the temple, or perhaps in wider community settings, where the accused, lacking legal witnesses and social supporters, seeks vindication and release from the charges. In the Covenant Code there are laws about borrowed property, perhaps extended by analogy to apply to debt loans, in which disputes over failure to return or make repayment of the property are settled by "coming near or before God," presumably by means of priestly adjudication in the cult (Exod. 22:7–13). It may be that the origin of at least some of the psalms of lament was in such a cultic function and that this recourse became especially popular when the secular courts were progressively corrupted by the influence of big landholders and prosperous merchants.

Even allowing for hyperbole and the indirectness of cultic speech, the corpus of language about sufferers and oppressors is bluntly evocative of *a world of socioeconomic oppression*. The accused and beleaguered sufferer has been charged with crimes and cruelly slandered in order to deprive him of rights, means of subsistence, good standing in the community, and even of health and freedom of movement. (All the psalm sufferers seem to be men. Did women not have the same access to cultic protection? Were their rights protected through the male rights of the family unit to which they belonged? Did they have their own cultic procedures that were ignored in compiling Psalms?) These accusations and deprivations are carried out by fellow Israelites who are in a superior social position and can wield their power to get what they want. "Rich" and "wicked" are often spoken of in the same breath. The oppressors spill innocent blood in their greed for gain, seize the poor in village ambushes, speak deceitfully and bring false testimony, bribe judges shamelessly, all the while trusting and boasting in their wealth and virtue while they scorn and mock the sufferer. Oppression and fraud dominate the marketplace, the innocent are brought to trial with evil schemes, creditors seize property.

When this wealth of language about socioeconomic conflict is compared with and illuminated by speeches of the prophets and proverbs of the wise, there can be little doubt that an enormous part of the suffering which psalmists protest is the *pauperization of the populace* through the manipulation of debt and confiscation procedures in such a way that even the traditional courts of Israel can be used to amass wealth in defiance of the explicit laws of the community. In fact, because the oppressors so flagrantly violate the laws attributed to deity, their conduct and attitude loudly declare, "There is no God!"—no matter how piously they may dress up their appearance.

If indeed there was such a large-scale psalmic protest against the evils of the political economy, we may well wonder what social power the priesthood and cultic institutions actually had to alleviate the long slide of preexilic Israel and Judah into the impoverishment of the majority through land expropriation. In the first place, the law codes of Israel contained measures that, had they been strictly observed, would have prevented the loss of freeholdings among the Israelite peasants. These provisions are attested in the "cultic" and "priestly" layers of laws as well as in more ostensibly "secular" layers. The Deuteronomic Reform tried to couple a renewal of the cult with a renewal of land and debt laws which would at least have arrested the pauperization process if not reversed it. The priests in Jerusalem, as in the northern royal cult centers, were naturally in a difficult spot to champion the cause of the plundered freeholders because they served at the pleasure of the royal establishment that permitted, if it did not actively advance, the abusive domination of newly enriched classes.

Nonetheless, insofar as the royal ideology asserted social justice as its obligation, priests had some elbowroom to ameliorate the worst abuses by giving cultic support to the wronged even when the courts failed and by helping to build and disseminate a community climate for the defense of traditional rights. Because the socially powerful had a big stake in the cult, it is likely that they contested priestly sympathy for their victims but could not totally repress accepted cultic procedures. This may be one reason for the vagueness of language in the laments, since to have been more explicit might have brought further recriminations and penalties on the worshipers and priests alike. And the fact that there are individual thanksgiving songs, even though not so many as there are laments, implies that sometimes the actions of oppressors were blocked and frustrated, even though over the long run they largely prevailed in their determination to smash the tribal landholding system. One consequence of this reading of the psalms is to warn against drawing too sharp a line between prophets and priests and assuming that the priesthood contributed nothing to resistance against the socioeconomic imbalances that accumulated to the detriment of the general populace.

We have seen then that the rhythms of orientation, disorientation, and reorientation, which the psalms express on a psychic level, have their close inner connections with like patterns of *orientation to a just social order* (traditional tribalism and benevolent monarchy), *disorientation and de-stabilization of community through mass injustice* (state-empowered entrepreneurs crush the independent tribal order and foreign conquerors smash the state and dislocate its people), and *reorientation of community through new efforts at justice* (reform efforts under the monarchy, survival in and return from exile, restored colonial Jewish community).

Even the occurrences of physical illness lamented in the psalms are not to be dissociated from societal structures, since it is well known that the incidence of some diseases is closely related to poor diet, harsh working conditions, ecological abuse, social belittlement and disempowerment, and demoralization in the face of unrelenting injustice. If witchcraft is perhaps attested in some psalms, that too would probably signal extreme social conflicts in the community, for anthropological studies reveal that charges of witchcraft, entailing death or expulsion, are resorted to only as an extreme measure because witchcraft disputes may split the community beyond healing and boomerang on those who make the initial charges.[15]

All in all, to interpret the settings and functions of psalms it becomes necessary to consider the cultic traditions and institutions of ancient Israel as they intersected with major social and psychic dislocations in the lives of the people precipitated by conflicts and ruptures in the political economy over the long course of Israel's tribal-monarchic, exilic, and restoration history.

52.3 Lamentations

Lamentations consists of five verse compositions that are alphabetically structured. The first four are acrostics, that is, the twenty-two letters of the Hebrew alphabet appear in succession at the beginning of each strophe (three-line strophes in chaps. 1, 2, and 3, and two-line strophes in chap. 4) or at the beginning of each line (in chap. 3, three 'aleph lines, three beth lines, etc.). The fifth lament is alphabetic in that it has the same number of lines as there are letters in the Hebrew alphabet.

The acrostic form in Lamentations has been explained in several ways: as an instance of belief in the magical power of letters; as a memory aide in public recitation; as a display of compositional craft; as a format for giving a fully rounded statement on its subject matter, that is, from A to Z; and as a way of imposing economy of expression on otherwise boundless grief. Only the first explanation seems ruled out as a conscious factor for the writer, whatever the ultimate magical roots of the acrostic form. It may also be doubted that the acrostic is enough of a memory aide to have alone merited the compositional effort required. The combined conceptual-aesthetic intent of making a complete statement in sharply controlled form is the most likely motive behind the acrostic structure in Lamentations.[16]

Similarities of form and content suggest that possibly the first four poems have a single author; their commonalities, however, may simply reflect the development of a kind of lament liturgy that various writers of similar mind and tradition had a hand in producing. Since each section is a complete

15. Robert R. Wilson, *Prophecy and Society in Ancient Israel* (Philadelphia: Fortress Press, 1980), 73–76.
16. Norman K. Gottwald, *Studies in the Book of Lamentations*, SBT, 1st ser., 14, rev. ed. (London: SCM Press, 1962), 23–32.

acrostic or alphabetic poem, covering more or less the same subject matter from varying angles and with differing fusions of genres, it is not likely that they were composed as parts of a whole but rather have been collected around the common theme and the public occasion of lamentation over the fall of Jerusalem. There is evidence that lamentation at the site of the destroyed temple began soon after the city's destruction (Jer. 41:5) and that annual fast days commemorating the city's fall—possibly as many as four times a year—were observed throughout the exile and at least until the rebuilding of the temple (Zech. 7:1–7; 8:19).

The compilation of the five laments follows a chiastic principle in arrangement. Chapters 1 and 5 are generalizing summaries that show a greater psychic distance from events than the grim and pitiable scenes of death and destruction that are vividly drawn in chaps. 2 and 4. Chapter 3, with its intensified acrostic form, complexly splices the lamenting voices of a number of "I" speakers alongside the national "we," in order to build a subtle but powerful theological statement about the need for Israel to wait patiently on God's eventual decision to show mercy to the community. Chapter 5 was specially composed (or adjusted in its line count) in order to echo the form of the preceding acrostics. As a consistent communal lament, it avoids the splicing of individual and communal speech found in the acrostics and it also provides a more cohesive picture of life in Palestine under ongoing Babylonian rule in contrast to the episodic glimpses of Jerusalem's downfall and immediate aftermath presented in chaps. 2 and 4.

The dominant genre speech conventions are laments, both individual and communal, but the individual funeral dirge applied here to a sociopolitical entity has made an imprint on chaps. 1, 2, and 4. The afflicted city is personified as the woman "Fair Zion" ("daughter of Zion"), said to be "like a widow" (1:1, although her "husband" Yahweh is not dead!), but more often lamented and lamenting as a bereaved mother whose children (the populace and leadership of the city) have been killed, starved, driven away, or humiliated. The idioms of the wisdom psalm (3:25–39) and of the thanksgiving song (3:19–24, 52–58) occur in chap. 3. Prophetic speech appears at the end of chap. 4 (vv. 21–22), and hymnic speech at the close of chap. 5 (v. 19). The first four compositions, while drawing skillfully on varied genres, were deliberately constructed as complex liturgies of lament. The deliberation is apparent in the acrostic construction which required that the writer(s) work within formal strictures in choice of words, ordering of genre and conceptual elements, and scope of treatment. The patent liturgical structure shows up in the shifts of speakers throughout chaps. 1—4. It is very likely that different voices took part in the public recitation, which means that identity of the speakers—problematic for readers at points—was made naturally by the changes of voice in the oral renditions. The "we" parts may have been taken by a chorus or by the whole assembly of people.

Several voices are clearly heard throughout the laments. In chap. 1, the poet laments the fate of Fair Zion (vv. 1–11, 17) who in turn laments her own condition (12–16, 18–22, as well as being quoted by the poet in 9c and 11c). In chap. 2, the poet laments over the city (1–12), addresses consoling instruction to Fair Zion (13–17), and summons her to lament (18–19), which she promptly does (20–22). In chap. 4, the poet laments over the city (1–16), there is a "we" lament of the Jerusalemites (17–20), and the poet speaks a prophetic oracle of punishment on Edom and salvation for Fair Zion (21–22). In chap. 5, the "we" of the community is the one identified voice throughout the description of distress, but the opening and closing cries for deliverance (1, 19–22) may have been given to another speaker in public delivery.

By contrast to the other four laments, the discernment of the genre components and the number and identity of speakers in chap. 3 is a vexing problem that scholars have been unable to resolve. In the third lament, an unnamed exemplary "man" (some have thought Jeremiah, but possibly the poet?) tells of his immense suffering at the hands of Yahweh (1–18), gives a muted meditation on his hoped for deliverance (19–24), and offers didactic generalizations about how a sufferer should trust and hope in Yahweh who is just and compassionate (25–39). Thereupon, a communal "we" breaks into lament (40–47). The remainder of the unit is given to three "I" speakers: the poet laments Fair Zion's plight (48–51), an individual thanksgiving song celebrates Yahweh's just deliverance (52–58), and possibly Fair Zion or a speaker for the community prays for deliverance from assailants and for their punishment (59–66). Some interpreters read all the "I" passages of chap. 3 as individualizing personifications of the community. The actual public multivoiced recitation would have made the identity of the speakers completely clear; in the absence of that information, divergent readings of the "I/we" voices of chap. 3 seem inescapable.

There have been inconclusive proposals about the ideological components and institutional setting of these laments.[17] By drawing out the

17. Ibid., 47–62; Bertil Albrektson, *Studies in the Text and Theology of the Book of Lamentations*, Studia Theologica Ludensia 21 (Lund: C. W. K. Gleerup, 1963), 214–39; Delbert R. Hillers, *Lamentations*, AB 7A (Garden City, N.Y.: Doubleday & Co., 1972), xxiii, 22–23, 105; and cf. reviews by Gottwald of Albrektson in *JBL* 83 (1964); 204–7, and of Hillers in JAARSup 43/2 (1975): 311–13.

conceptual matrix of the poems we may be able to identify the streams of traditions and institutions where the laments were anchored.

In the first place, the destruction of Jerusalem is seen as a horrible but deserved punishment because of Israel's enormous sins (1:5, 8, 14, 15, 18, 20, 22; 3:42; 4:5; 5:7, 16). In one revealing detail it is charged that the prophets—who ought to have been Israel's "early warning system"—only envisioned what was false instead of disclosing iniquity. What's more, prophets and priests themselves joined in spilling "the blood of the righteous" (2:14; 4:13). This assertion of the moral culpability of false religious leaders corresponds to the critique of prophecy and priesthood in major prophets such as Jeremiah and Ezekiel.

Even so, the emotional shock at loss of state and temple and at the carnage and destruction was so severe that the initiator of these laments aims to lead the people step by step in giving vent to grief, in expressing guilt, and in attaining modest hope. He finds, however, that there are conceptual shocks and blockages that make it difficult for the people to appeal to Yahweh with trust and confidence. In two of the laments, he cites notions about the world significance and impregnability of Zion which imply that many of the mourners—in keeping with the Zion traditions of Psalms 46, 48, and 76—had believed that Yahweh would miraculously protect his holy city (2:15c; 4:12). Likewise, the people lament over the capture of King Zedekiah in fond and ceremonious language that tells of their confidence in his power to protect them against enemy attack (4:20). Given these shattered expectations, the writer of the laments underscores the reality that the sins of Judah had decisively overridden any apparently unconditional promises in the Zion and royal Davidic traditions. While no explicit covenant-breaking references are made, the destruction is described in terms shared by Deuteronomy 28 in its announcement of the curses that will fall on a disobedient Israel.

Yet another complication emerges in the lamenting community. The excesses of enemies in punishing Israel are felt to have been so enormous that grave injustice has been done to Judah. On the one hand, this makes the people reluctant to admit their own sins, and, at the same time, it provokes serious doubt about Yahweh's justice and love. The poet agrees that the enemy has "overdone it," and so he has the people calling for punishment on the enemies just as Judah has been punished; moreover, he actually delivers a prophetic promise of salvation that Judah's guilt has been requited and that it will never again be sent into exile. It should be noted, however, how carefully the words about judgment on enemies/deliverance for Zion are preceded in each poem by full acknowledgment of Zion's own sins. The move to deliverance and requital for excess suffering is only valid for the poet(s) when coupled with a deep-going prior confession of Judah's sins.

Since the situation, as viewed by the poet, includes *adversity that is deserved* and *adversity that is undeserved*, its very complexity poses a delicate pastoral and theological problem. With what attitude should Judah view this contradictory situation while awaiting deliverance? Chapter 3 makes a special effort to communicate an appropriate communal attitudinal shift beyond one-sided forms of self-righteousness or despair. The sins of sufferers, like the model "man," are held in tension with their valid rights to vindication (sufferers may both sin and be sinned against). That the "I" speaker of vv. 52–58 has suffered "without cause" (v. 52) means that he can rejoice that "Yahweh pleads my cause" (v. 58). The nation personified in vv. 59–66 can also cry out for a similar judgment with respect to "the wrong done to me" by assailants (v. 59).

What this comes down to is that the poet does not know the way in which Yahweh will weigh the deserved punishment against the gratuitous suffering—and especially *when* and *how* Yahweh will act to deliver Judah from the latter without negating the former. Thus, the suffering "man" is reflected on as a paragon of the wise and patient individual or group sufferer who confidently trusts and hopes in Yahweh, bearing adversity without complaint or despair because he knows that God "does not afflict from his heart" (v. 33) and that the deity's sovereign movements among the peoples will eventually vindicate everyone who "waits" on and "hopes" in him (cf. 3:21, 24–26, 29).

Lamentations thus reflects a *broadly prophetic and Deuteronomistic* grasp of Judah's sins against Yahweh as the primary category for understanding the catastrophe, and this starting point inexorably sets aside the *illusory protection of the Zion and royal Davidic traditions* taken in isolation. Also in prophetic manner (and implicitly in DH as well), the compilation of laments anticipates an ongoing punishment of nations that have "overdone" their attacks, together with a recovery of fortune for Judah once it has confessed its sins. The proper attitude in the interim between punishment and restoration, inculcated with *wisdomlike didacticism,* is to wait patiently for Yahweh. In the poet's view, this patient waiting is perfectly consistent with agonized cries for help!

As for its ideological setting, we can at least identify those from whom Lamentations could *not* have originated. It could not possibly have been written by anyone holding to a rigid prophetic or Deuteronomistic standpoint that Yahweh's severe judgment of his people was a total principled rejection of them for all time. Of course the major exemplars of prophetism and Deuteronomistic thought after 587 did not draw that dire conclusion but held out one or another form of sober hope (cf. discussions of Jeremiah [§37.5], Ezekiel [§50.1], and Isaiah of the Exile [§50.2], and the "critical traditionalism" in DH that seems to win out over "authoritarian dogmatism"). Lamentations belongs, therefore, to a pluriform exilic neo-prophetic and neo-Deuteronomistic outlook of chastened hope.

It is equally clear that Lamentations could not possibly have been written by anyone who thought that the destruction of Jerusalem was unmerited, either because of Judah's intrinsic righteousness before God (those who denied the prophetic critique as entirely misplaced or grossly exaggerated, relying on the sufficient moral qualities implied by the Zion and royal Davidic promises) or because of an unbreakable divine promise (in spite of Judah's sins, even great sins, a divine promise is a divine promise). We do not hear much from such folk, although they appear in the Book of Jeremiah and perhaps here and there in Psalms (e.g., Psalm 144?). A few scholars have contended that someone from the extreme nationalist party in the anti-Babylonian uprising, and thus opposed to Jeremiah and Gedaliah, wrote Lamentations. Apart from the nebulous evidence, such an attribution of authorship is absolutely ruled out by the ideological content of the book!

All that we can really say about institutional setting is that these laments were written and compiled by one or more people who had access to and interest in the cult that managed to carry on in attenuated form on the site of the destroyed temple. The writer(s) could have been a prophet, a priest, or a governmental or private lay figure. In any case this writer developed an *amalgam of prophetic, Deuteronomistic, and wisdom notions* that radically *subordinated and neutralized the Zion and royal Davidic promises,* and found a *liturgical-pastoral* way of expressing them in the cult. We may take this book's deft "eclecticism" of traditions, interconnecting a range of concepts with verve and originality, as an indication of how Jewish religious thinking in the populace of postdestruction Palestine adapted traditions in order to cope with the intellectual and cultural dislocations of the national catastrophe.

52.4 Song of Songs

This eloquent love verse is variously understood either as a loose collection of individual poems, possibly twenty-five to thirty-five in number, or as a unified composition consisting of perhaps five to eight longer poems that show thematic integrity or some degree of unity of action. In defense of the latter view, a unitary intent is often seen in the considerable refrains and repetitions (chart 7).

Some of the cited repetitions are verbally exact, while others are highly variable. At points the repetitions follow the same sequence (e.g., embrace wish leading to charge to let love take its course) and give the impression of refrains; more often, there is no discernible patterning in the recurrences. The imagery of lilies, apples and apple trees, vineyards, gardens, and the like, is used pliably with reference to shifting aspects of the lovers and their interactions. It is noteworthy that the links are most frequent between chaps. 1—2 and 8; closer examination shows, however, that the repeated features are distributed erratically and combined with other elements that diffuse the rhetorical and conceptual effects of the connections. If indeed chaps. 1—2 and 8 have been placed as a kind of inclusion to the work, it is not evident that the bonded structure points any more conclusively to a unified composition than to an artfully redacted anthology.

Form criticism has differentiated the love poetry of the Song into several genres on the basis of similar Egyptian poems (table 1: 11A). Among the now commonly recognized genres are *songs of yearning, admiration songs, boasts, teases, descriptions of a love experience,* and *descriptive songs (waṣfs)* depicting the physical charms of the loved one. There are also so-called *travesties,* or literary fictions, in which the lover is portrayed in a role deliberately outside—often above but sometimes below—the social class or occupational status to which he belongs (e.g., the roles of "king," "shepherd," "servant," "doorkeeper," etc.). This is part of the "make-believe" language of love. The genres are rather freely mixed and even interwoven in the Song of Songs. The resulting anthological fusion can be contrasted with Egyptian long songs collected as a chain of entirely separate works, often with their own headings.

For long centuries the Song was understood allegorically in the Jewish and Christian communities. For Jews the lovers represented God and Israel, while for Christians they stood for God or Christ and the church or soul of the believer, or even the Virgin Mary. Nothing in the Song itself or in the extrabiblical counterparts supports this line of interpretation. Some scholars have argued for a cultic-mythological interpretation in which the lovers originally described were male and female deities joined in sacred marriage, for example, the divine pair Tammuz and Ishtar. The presumed expurgation and revision required to make the poem "safe" for Jews is difficult to imagine and in fact unnecessary to account for possible traces of cultic idiom in the Song. Over the centuries, the erotic language of human love and of the cults of divine marriage mutually influenced one another, so

CHART 7
Refrains and Repetitions in Song of Songs

Chapter ⟶	1	2	3	4	5	6	7	8
Daughters of Jerusalem	1:5	2:7	3:5, 10		5:8			8:4
Maidens	1:3	2:1				6:8–9		
Male companions	1:7							8:13
Charge to daughters of Jerusalem to let love take its course		2:7	3:5					8:4
Embrace wish		2:6						8:3
Mutual possession		2:16				6:3	7:10	
Love better than wine	1:2, 4			4:10				
The woman brings the man to her house			3:4					8:2
Woman seeks/does not find the man but is found by watchmen			3:1–3		5:6–7			
Day breathes/ shadows flee		2:17	3:6					
Pasture/feed among lilies		2:16		4:5		6:2–3		
Apple tree		2:3						8:5
Coming up from wilderness			3:6					8:5
King	1:4, 12		3:9, 11			[Prince, 6:12?]	7:5	
Behold, you are beautiful, my love	1:15–16			4:1				
Voice of the beloved		2:8, 14						8:13
Man as gazelle/stag leaping on mountains		2:9, 17						8:14
Woman's breasts like twin gazelles				4:5			7:3	
Hair, teeth, cheeks of woman				4:1–3		6:5–7		
Woman as vineyard	1:6	[2:15?]			5:1			8:11–12
Woman as garden				4:12, 15–16		6:2		[8:13?]

that Jewish erotic language could readily have picked up the resonances of cult-derived speech.

From the start, then, the poems spoke of human love. Once-popular dramatic theories that saw plot and characterization in the book have virtually disappeared. Taking differing forms, they all assumed a movement from awakening love through the posing and overcoming of obstacles to a triumphant union of the lovers. The lovers might be anonymous, or Solomon and a rustic maiden called the Shulammite (6:13), or a triangle of lovers, with a country suitor winning back his maiden after she is futilely wooed by Solomon. The voices of the lovers were thought to be interspersed with choruses by the maidens (daughters of Jerusalem) and by the male companions. The groundlessness of the dramatic theory is exposed by the inability of its advocates to agree on division of the speeches and outline of plot. The modicum of truth to which the theory points is the presence of dialogical elements in the text.

As for the setting of the Song, it is widely held that these are marriage songs accompanying elaborate ceremonies in which bride and groom were feted in the fanciful roles of king and queen, shepherd and shepherdess, and the like. Only 3:6–11 mentions marriage, with reference to a Solomon travesty. The many comparable songs from Egypt, and a lesser number from Mesopotamia, are not connected with marriage. The imagery and sensibilities of the Song simply do not treat of the social structures of marriage and family; nothing is said about children or the duties of the man and woman toward one another or their families of origin. The lovers speak of longing, passion, seduction, coquetry, evasion, separation, and re-union—all with a clear destination of physical togetherness and sexual union. Sexual consummation is adroitly described through double-entendres that work metaphorically with physical features, flora, and fauna of the landscape—both wild and cultivated—which serves as the sensuous medium for the interplay of lovers. Significantly, the man and woman are "toe to toe" in their assertive acts and expressive words, a sexual equality which might equally bespeak the *comradeship of peasant lovers* not yet encumbered by children or the *companionship of upper-class lovers* whose affluence and education encourage feminist consciousness.

The extent to which this poetry, originating from the world of courtship, may have been appropriated for the formalizing of marriages is paralleled by a question about the class origins of the work, whether "popular" or "high culture." The parallels from Egypt suggest an aristocratic milieu of leisure and cultivated erotic self-consciousness. On the other hand, the travesty genre deliberately contrives strange, often higher, class roles and contexts. This may mean that, even if first written and polished by courtesans and literati, the idioms and genres may have been generated—and in part borrowed—from the everyday language of love. It is precisely this *"fictiveness" of the love genres,* both among common people and upper strata, which makes it so uncertain how to fix a single social setting or to indicate the date of composition.[18]

The Song of Songs is said to be Solomon's (1:1). This seems to have been taken as an attribution of authorship, certainly so by the time of the canonical discussion about the book. Earlier, however, it could very well have meant a song of the sort that Solomon wrote (1 Kings 4:32) or a song "to/concerning" Solomon in the sense that the lovers were cast in fictive roles of Solomon and one of his maidens (1 Kings 11:3; Ps. 45:6–17; cf. Song of Songs 3:11; 6:8). The references to Solomon in the body of the poems (1:5; 3:7, 9, 11; 8:11–12) gave support to the Solomonic connection. It is likely, however, that the strongest reason for the Solomonic claim was the publishing of the collection within a wisdom circle with the intention of illustrating what one saying calls "the way of a man with a maiden" (Prov. 30:19).

If that is the case, the poems would probably have been read by the wisdom collectors as affirming a monogamous relationship understood as issuing in an enduring marriage (Prov. 5:15–23, cf. "the wife of your youth"). Of course Solomon himself was far from monogamous (1 Kings 11:1–13)! As king, however, he may have been seen to possess a measure of "royal privilege" for his polygamy and, moreover, the wise probably felt that their patron figure had been appropriately rebuffed for his follies. Indeed it is possible that 8:6–8 is the signature of the wise collector of the Song, since it offers a generalizing proverblike reflection on the lovers, forming a moral for the reader to carry away:

> Set me as a seal on your heart,
>   as a seal on your arm;
> for love is strong as death,
>   passion as relentless as the grave.
> Its flashes are flashes of fire,
>   a most vehement flame.
> Many waters cannot quench love,
>   neither can floods drown it.
> If a man offered for love
>   all the wealth of his house,
>   it would be utterly scorned.

The *juxtaposition of love and death* is interestingly paralleled in the Egyp-

18. Roland E. Murphy, "Canticles (Songs of Songs)," FOTL vol. 13, 101–3.

tian Papyrus Harris 500 where a chain of love songs is "interrupted" by the Song of the Harper with a dour meditation on relentless death in the face of which one should "follow your heart as long as you live . . . Moral: Make celebration!" (table 1: 11A).

It is altogether likely that the trajectory of this poetry has moved through more than one social-class location, from the generation of idioms and scenes, and possibly whole surviving specimens, among the peasantry (wherein the *lowly folk fantasize themselves highborn*), through the conceits and aesthetic opulence of court culture (wherein the *sophisticates fantasize themselves bucolic primitives*), to the learned and moralizing circles of the wise (who harness both the "low" and "high" aesthetics to *monogamous counsel that fuses passion and fidelity* in praise of love that cannot be bought). Even after its publication as "the best of songs about the wisest of loves," its older aesthetic zones and forms of usage probably persisted. It may even have become popular at weddings. Eventually allegorical readings were given it, both to counter its secularity and to serve the cause of religious devotion.

53
SHORT STORIES

53.1 The Biblical Short Story: A New Literary Genre?

The three biblical short stories that form independent books in the Hebrew Bible must be viewed in the wider context of many other instances of the same genre. Some short stories are incorporated into larger biblical books (e.g., Genesis 24; 38; 37 + 39—50; Judges 3:12–30; 4; episodes in 2 Samuel 9—20 and 1 Kings 1—2; Job 1—2; 42:7–17; Daniel 1—6). Others appear in the Apocrypha, either as free-standing works (Tobit; Judith) or as parts of or additions to other books (The Three Guardsmen in 1 Esdras 3—4:42; Additions to Daniel in the LXX, known as Susanna and Bel and the Dragon).

This short story genre, also called novella ("novelette") or romance, is thus a frequent biblical genre that appears in all periods of Israelite literary history. Its genre features are multiple episodes within fairly brief compass, an elevated and ceremonious style, and skillful literary techniques for shaping full-bodied character in a suspenseful plot that communicates lifelikeness in important respects, even when the story exaggerates or caricatures to make its points.[19]

Typically the short story combines fairy tale, legendary, heroic, or mythic

19. Edward F. Campbell, Jr., *Ruth,* AB 7 (Garden City, N.Y.: Doubleday & Co., 1975), 5–6, 9–10.

elements with a history-like orientation to daily affairs in some recognizable sphere of life within a smaller community or in high politics. Historical vagueness and irregularities in the temporal settings of the stories, symmetries and extremities of plot, and stark reversals of fortune for the characters attest that the genre is not documentary history but believable fiction with general sociocultural lifelikeness, what the older commentators called "verisimilitude."

The historical settings of the short stories are problematic: Ruth in the time of the Judges, Jonah in the Assyrian period, and Esther in the Persian age. While traditions from the assigned age may be retained in the story, and in some cases an older version of the story may underlie the present text, the choice of an archaic setting for the story is also clearly a literary convention that aims to give its message a venerable "classical" aura. Furthermore, linguistic criteria for dating these short stories are notoriously inconclusive. Scholars differ widely in the dates they assign to the finished books, and frequently grant that oral or preceding written versions may have been much older. The tendency at present is to view Ruth as preexilic, possibly as early as the tenth to ninth centuries, to locate Jonah in the sixth to fifth centuries, and to assign Esther to the fourth to second centuries.

Earlier scholarly generations inclined to identify the purpose of the short stories as pointedly polemical and propagandistic. Ruth and Jonah in particular were often construed as narrative tracts aimed at rebutting the nationalist reforms and mind-set of Ezra and Nehemiah, the former by commending Ruth as a model Israelite of Moabite stock and the latter by showing that even hated Assyrians were capable of repentance and salvation, even to the extent that Jews should actively seek to convert them. Without denying that polemics played a part, even if not demonstrably against Ezra and Nehemiah, it is nowadays claimed that combined purposes are at work in the short story, including entertainment, moral instruction and formation, inspiration, and even a low-key theologizing that stresses the work of an unobtrusive God within the mundane activities of humans. The subdued religiosity in some, but not all, of the stories has been connected with Solomonic "enlightenment" which purportedly opened up a secular world to human scrutiny and adventure, and yet the most extreme "secularity" appears in the late short story of Esther.

Since many fine instances of the short story are premonarchic in milieu and perspective, it is probable that the short story was a new form introduced by the Yahwistic revolution at the beginning of Israel's intertribal egalitarian social and religious movement, "designed to portray the radical effect of a new and great commitment upon the part of a new people who were once not a people. . . . The literary form was new, the people were new, the purpose was new."[20] Starting from the form and content of the earliest short stories we can thus enter by another route into the sociohistoric horizons of the traditions about patriarchs, Moses, and the Judges (§16; 21; 24). The "new purpose" of the Israelite short story seems to have been to stress the active participation of people in the common life as precisely the sphere where Yahweh works without restriction to the realm of formal religious practices. The "new agenda" of these stories concerns the making of marriages, the birthing of children, the procurement of food, the securing of stable and just self-rule, the repelling of dangerous military threats, and the long-term survival of the new people of Yahweh amid the nations.

With the monarchy and later experiences of dispersion and restoration, new themes and variations on older themes develop in the short story repertory. Already evident in the preexilic Joseph story, the crucible of exile forges an urgent concern with how Jews in the service of foreign governments or impacted by their policies can keep their identity and conscience. The imperial-colonial theme of Jews in foreign service was of concern to Jews in Palestine, as in the Dispersion, since the lives of all were significantly affected by what their political overlords did. The absorption of many stories with foreigners, however, is broader than the theme of Jews in foreign service, for it includes how foreigners join Israel (Ruth), how an Israelite might, even unwillingly, convert foreigners (Jonah), and how dispersed Jews can cultivate a full and rich religious life amidst a foreign culture (Tobit).

It is further striking that many of these stories feature women who combine cunning and boldness to achieve ends of importance to the community: Deborah arouses Israel to victory over Canaanites, Jael slays a Canaanite general, Ruth saves a perishing family in Bethlehem, Judith and Esther deliver Jews from annihilation. Susanna is more passive than the other women, but her very persistence in marital fidelity is rewarded when Daniel is able to expose the falsehoods of her spiteful accusers. Despite the grossly fictitious casting of Judith and Esther, it is probable that one of the lifelike features of their stories is that they celebrate the active part that at least some women took in the Maccabean-Hasmonean conflicts.

Is it possible to identify the narrators and life settings of this versatile Israelite short story genre? So artful are the tales that it is logical to believe that a class of storytellers specialized in them, perhaps performing at

20. Ibid., 8–9.

religious festivals but also wherever people gathered publicly, at town gate, market, or watering place. It has been proposed that the early Levites, distributed among the tribes as ardent devotees of Yahweh, formed a storytelling cadre as part of their teaching function, and that possibly wise women also engaged in storytelling.[21] The stories evolved in ever-fresh live performances around a basic plot with formulas and stock themes. In this manner we can envisage stories generated in various public contexts that eventually entered the central cultic programs and that continued to be told both at the great festivals and in secular settings. The later short stories tend to be modeled on earlier literary examples in the Law and Prophets and no longer imply oral performance or cultivation by a class of storytellers. Nonetheless, among the Megilloth, scrolls for reading at Jewish festivals, Ruth found its place for reading at the Feast of Weeks and Esther was specifically composed for, or adapted to, recitation at the Feast of Purim.

53.2 Ruth

Ruth is easily the most charming and exquisite of the three independent biblical short stories, sharing as it does with the much later and apocryphal Book of Tobit a poignant and gracious evocation of family feelings and mores. It tells how two women, Naomi and Ruth, the one a Judahite from Bethlehem and the other her Moabite daughter-in-law, having lost their husbands, cleverly worked out their survival and happiness and at the same time secured the perpetuation of the family name of the dead through the practice of levirate marriage. To crown it all, it turns out that these women, acting on their own behalf, have contributed to the family line of none other than King David (4:17–21). The story in final form need be no later than the united monarchy, although it likely had a precursor form that lacked the Davidic genealogy.

Much of the pleasure of the story lies in the way all difficulties and chance events conspire to produce a happy ending, a lovely "human comedy." All the worst forebodings of solitariness, starvation, and childlessness are quieted by the steady progress of the plot toward community, abundance, and fertility. Almost everyone gains; the only loser is the unnamed kinsman who declines to marry Ruth and is publicly shamed, but this only heightens the gain of the others since it clears the way for Boaz to marry Ruth.

The "little whole" of Ruth is a thoroughly credible folk tale.[22] It deals

21. Ibid., 18–23.
22. Jack M. Sasson, *Ruth. A New Translation with a Philological Commentary and a Formalist-Folklorist Interpretation* (Baltimore and London: John Hopkins University Press, 1979), esp. 196–252.

with the stuff of everyday life, with the round of birth and death, with love and marriage, and with work as the necessity of life on the thin line between scarcity and abundance. Constructed out of the fabric of early tribal Israelite solidarity communities, it presents crises and complications which are resolved to the satisfaction of everyone involved. The movements of plot and functions of character flow together so harmoniously that we are left with few unanswered questions and no uneasy feelings.

Ruth has been much analyzed by new literary critics and structuralists to the enhancement of our understanding of why the story "works" so effectively.[23] The plot moves through six episodes (chart 8) in which the first two (Flight to Moab; On the road back to Bethlehem) balance the last two (At the city gate of Bethlehem; A son is born to restore Naomi). A deep structure of "emptiness" in the opening scenes shifts to a deep structure of "fullness" in the closing scenes. The two inner episodes (In the field of Boaz; On the threshing floor of Boaz) describe the activation and execution of the means for transforming emptiness into fullness for Naomi and Ruth, also enriching Boaz's life. The similarities of structure and the progressions in negotiations during the two meetings of Ruth and Boaz (the first meeting unknown to Naomi and the second orchestrated by her) deftly disclose the humane and resourceful way in which the principals cooperate to make the transformations possible. The hallmarks of Israel's artistry in short stories stand out: a terse setting of the *mise en scène,* effortless transitions between episodes that often signal what is to come, a lingering over actions in a manner both ceremonious and suspense-building, fluent dialogue, and repetitions of key terms and nuanced wordplays that link episodes.

The assertive deeds of Naomi and Ruth are the driving force of the story.[24] Ruth insists on returning with Naomi to Bethlehem. Once there, she goes boldly into the fields to get food, where she talks toe to toe with the influential Boaz, even before she knows that he is her kinsman. Naomi instructs her to go by night to the fields both to allure and to challenge Boaz to play the kinsman role and marry her. Ruth does so and keeps the initiative in a delicate situation, even when Boaz is so astonished by her forwardness that he hardly knows what to do. Threat of death is turned to promise of life solely because these women do not wait passively for men to solve their problems but take the lead to make things happen.

---

23. Stephen Bertram, "Symmetrical Design in the Book of Ruth," *JBL* 84 (1965): 165–68; D. F. Rauber, "Literary Values in the Bible: The Book of Ruth," *JBL* 89 (1970): 27–37; Phyllis Trible, "A Human Comedy," in *God and the Rhetoric of Sexuality*, OBT 2 (Philadelphia: Fortress Press, 1978), 166–99; Harold Fisch, "Ruth and the Structure of Covenant History," *VT* 32 (1982): 425–37.

24. Trible, "Human Comedy."

CHART 8
Structure in the Book of Ruth

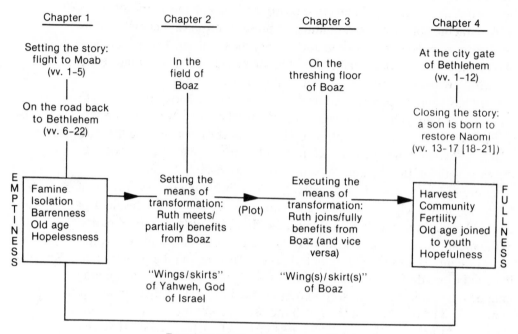

| Chapter 1 | Chapter 2 | Chapter 3 | Chapter 4 |

Setting the story: flight to Moab (vv. 1–5)

In the field of Boaz

On the threshing floor of Boaz

At the city gate of Bethlehem (vv. 1–12)

On the road back to Bethlehem (vv. 6–22)

Closing the story: a son is born to restore Naomi (vv. 13–17 [18–21])

E M P T I N E S S

Famine
Isolation
Barrenness
Old age
Hopelessness

Setting the means of transformation: Ruth meets/ partially benefits from Boaz

(Plot)

Executing the means of transformation: Ruth joins/fully benefits from Boaz (and vice versa)

Harvest
Community
Fertility
Old age joined to youth
Hopefulness

F U L L N E S S

"Wings/skirts" of Yahweh, God of Israel

"Wing(s)/skirt(s)" of Boaz

Transformations of binary oppositions
(deep structure)

Throughout the story, the women operate out of their own culture with their own values in mind. The dominant male value expressed is to perpetuate the family name. It is the "male" institution of levirate marriage, by which the relative of a dead man marries his widow, that becomes the instrument of salvation for Naomi and Ruth. Yet the women do not simply identify with the male values. Naomi's first concern is not that her daughters-in-law should help her acquire male heirs for her dead husband but that they return to their family of origin and eventually find husbands for their own good, since in that world the single woman had no social or economic security. Ruth makes her insistent claim on Boaz not primarily for the sake of the dead but because she wants life and wholeness for herself and for Naomi. From the overtones of the warm and lively exchanges she has with Boaz, we gather that the two of them develop respect and deepening feelings for one another.

At the close of the story, the difference between the male culture and the female culture emerges in two vignettes. The male elders celebrate Boaz's good fortune in finding Ruth because she will give him children. By contrast, the village women who gather around Naomi at the birth of Ruth's child rejoice in the boy who will bring consolation and pleasure to the aging grandmother. They go on to exclaim that the quality of Naomi's and Ruth's love for one another counts for more than bearing seven sons! It is precisely the happy coincidence of the story that the women are able to find joyful fulfillment within the male-headed social structures in such a way that both sexes profit. It is not difficult to imagine that this story was framed by a woman confidently at home in her social world.

God appears in the story largely in conventional idioms of speech, as when Naomi says to Ruth and Orpah, "May Yahweh deal kindly with you, as you have dealt with the dead and with me. Yahweh grant that you may find a home, each of you in the house of her husband!" (1:8–9), or when Boaz says to Ruth, "Yahweh recompense you for what you have done, and a full reward be given you by Yahweh, the God of Israel, under whose wings you have come to take refuge!" (2:12). Significantly, it is "the wings [skirt]" of Boaz's robe spread over Ruth (3:9) that signals the realization of this religiously expressed wish.

Only at two points in the narrative is deity noted as a direct participant in the story, once at the beginning when Naomi in Moab learns "that Yahweh had visited his people and given them food" (1:6) and again at the end when it is said that "Yahweh gave her [Ruth] conception, and she bore a son" (4:14). The parenthetical placement of these references to Yahweh's doings that set the story in motion and bring it to climax is presumably the narrator's adaptation of the folk tale form with its recital of the commonplace to the encompassing faith of Israel in the providence of Yahweh. The net effect, gentle but telling in its very understatement, is to attest to the guiding presence of Yahweh in the extraordinary deeds of these ordinary people.

53.3 Jonah

The Book of Jonah is placed among the Prophets because of its formal topic but, unlike all the other writings in that collection, it is entirely composed of a short story about a prophet. Jonah tries to escape his calling and, when compelled to fulfill it, resents and protests against the results. Its "antihero" is identified as Jonah ben Amittai who announced the territorial expansion of the Kingdom of Jeroboam II in the eighth century (2 Kings 14:25). Memory of an actual mission by that eighth-century prophet to Assyria is highly doubtful, for the story is filled with improbabilities and is of obvious didactic tenor in its stylization.

The plot (chart 9) is set forth in two parts that treat of Jonah's failed flight from his call to preach doom on Nineveh (chaps. 1—2) and of his shocked anger when, finally forced to deliver the message, the city unexpectedly repents and is spared (chaps. 3—4). Yahweh first uses a fierce storm and a great fish to intervene in Jonah's headlong flight from his prophetic duty, and later he uses a shade plant, a worm, and a sultry wind to confront the prophet with the utter incongruity of his anger and peevishness. The psalm of thanksgiving recited by Jonah (2:2–9) is widely thought to be a secondary insertion. Yet it may be altogether in place for the author, with tongue in cheek, to have the prophet sing a psalm from the belly of the fish, especially when viewed as a satiric comment on the forced and hypocritical "conversion" of Jonah to accept his mission—now that he has very little choice in the matter.[25]

That Jonah remains the reluctant and uncomprehending prophet quickly emerges when he responds with embitterment and personal pique to the mercy of Yahweh toward repentant Nineveh. He cares passionately about a shade plant that brings him comfort and is outraged when it withers, while he yearns for the death of more than one hundred thousand Ninevites! In fact, Jonah would rather die himself than see those Assyrians live! Or is it simply that he does not envision the people of Nineveh at all, but is consumed by the professional embarrassment of having delivered a proph-

25. John C. Holbert, "'Deliverance Belongs to Yahweh!': Satire in the Book of Jonah," *JSOT* 21 (1981): 59–81.

CHART 9
Structure in the Book of Jonah

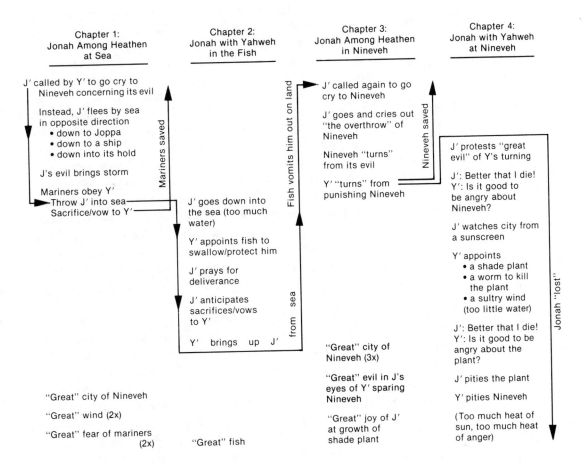

Chapter 1:
Jonah Among Heathen at Sea

Chapter 2:
Jonah with Yahweh in the Fish

Chapter 3:
Jonah Among Heathen in Nineveh

Chapter 4:
Jonah with Yahweh at Nineveh

J' called by Y' to go cry to Nineveh concerning its evil

Instead, J' flees by sea in opposite direction
• down to Joppa
• down to a ship
• down into its hold

J's evil brings storm

Mariners obey Y'
Throw J' into sea
Sacrifice/vow to Y'

Mariners saved

J' goes down into the sea (too much water)

Y' appoints fish to swallow/protect him

J' prays for deliverance

J' anticipates sacrifices/vows to Y'

Y' brings up J'

Fish vomits him out on land

from sea

J' called again to go cry to Nineveh

J' goes and cries out "the overthrow" of Nineveh

Nineveh "turns" from its evil

Y' "turns" from punishing Nineveh

Nineveh saved

J' protests "great evil" of Y's turning

J': Better that I die!
Y': Is it good to be angry about Nineveh?

J' watches city from a sunscreen

Y' appoints
• a shade plant
• a worm to kill the plant
• a sultry wind (too little water)

J': Better that I die!
Y': Is it good to be angry about the plant?

J' pities the plant

Y' pities Nineveh

(Too much heat of sun, too much heat of anger)

Jonah "lost"

"Great" city of Nineveh

"Great" wind (2x)

"Great" fear of mariners
(2x)

"Great" fish

"Great" city of Nineveh (3x)

"Great" evil in J's eyes of Y' sparing Nineveh

"Great" joy of J' at growth of shade plant

ecy that proved to be wrong? The book closes by accenting the ironic disproportion between Jonah's pity for the *plant,* really for himself, and Yahweh's pity for the *people* of Nineveh. The storyteller breaks off without telling us if Jonah ever "got the point" of Yahweh's dispute with him. The abrupt ending on the rhetorical question "And should not I [Yahweh] pity Nineveh?" forces questions on the reader: Am I (or is my group) like Jonah? If so, what do I (or we) make of Yahweh's rebuke?

The story adroitly opposes the straightforward heathens to the devious Jonah. The piety of the Gentile mariners saves them from the storm, whereas Jonah has to go into the sea and to the gates of death before he is ready to do his duty. The people of Nineveh (their animals included!) repent and are delivered, whereas Jonah wraps himself in anger and resentment toward Nineveh and toward Yahweh until he loathes his own life. The Gentiles are carried to swift and unproblematic salvation, while the "progress" of Jonah is downward, downward toward and into the sea in flight from his commission and downward into the depths of self-pity and isolation from his fellow humans, heathen though they be, and even from the God whose message he bore formally but could not bear to live with in its actual consequences.

The book is a satirical short story with parabolic force. It is an "example story" in that it presents "paradigmatic types of conduct or ways of thinking."[26] That it is not straight parable is clear from its direct caricature of a prophet instead of an account of someone who could be compared to a prophet. Nor is it an allegory of Israel coming through exile but failing to have compassion on the nations. The author must have known of a prophet, or group of prophets or other religious leaders, who exhibited the narrow outlook and petty hatefulness of Jonah. Since there are no firm grounds for dating the book more precisely than the sixth or fifth century, or even somewhat later, it is idle to speculate about which groups or situations prompted the author to write his devastating lampoon.

The choice of Assyria as the classic criminal nation that "repented," at least for a period of time, presupposes that the Assyrian Empire has fallen. Readers would understand at once that the story was scaffolding for a reflection on prophetic mission and prophetic self-understanding. Whoever has a call from Yahweh to warn of evil must do it obediently and with an understanding of Yahweh's intent to save all who will hear and repent (cf. Jer. 18:7–8). The one who carries Yahweh's message must not only be able

26. George M. Landes, "Jonah: A *Māšāl?*" in *Israelite Wisdom: Theological and Literary Essays in Honor of Samuel Terrien,* ed. John G. Gammie et al. (Missoula, Mont.: Scholars Press, 1979), 148.

to mouth traditional sayings about Yahweh's mercy (4:1–2), but must fully grasp and identify with the divine mercy. That the story concerns a foreign nation seems not to be intended prescriptively but illustratively, as an extreme test case of whether the human bearer of the divine message is rightly in accord with its sender. There is no indication that the book enjoins a mission to convert foreign nations or that it addresses the issue of whether proselytes should be incorporated in Israel if they come voluntarily. Nonetheless, because those who make the unexpectedly positive response to Yahweh are foreigners, the force of the book is to caution against prejudging and stereotyping Gentiles.

53.4 Esther

The Book of Esther locates the origin of the Feast of Purim in a spectacular last-minute deliverance of all the Jews within the Persian Empire from a plot to annihilate them. The plot is hatched in high government circles and it is Jews serving in those very circles who become the agents of Jewish salvation. Esther, the Jewish queen of Ahasuerus = Xerxes (486–465 B.C.E.), helped by her cousin and one-time guardian Mordecai, frustrates the designs of Haman to kill Mordecai and then to slaughter the entire Jewish populace. Instead, in perfect poetic justice, Haman is hanged on the gallows he prepared for Mordecai and the enemies of the Jews who would have killed them are themselves killed by the Jews.

The plot is replete with dramatic reversals: the Persian Vashti is replaced as queen by the Jewish Esther; newly promoted Haman, who cannot stand Mordecai's lack of deference toward him, in scheming to kill his rival loses his own life and his position is granted to Mordecai; an imperial decree to slaughter the Jews concocted by Haman is superseded by an imperial decree to slaughter the enemies of the Jews dictated by Mordecai. The action is framed by court banquet scenes and audiences with the king. The driving tension in the plot is whether the anti-Jewish or the pro-Jewish forces in the court will receive the blessing of the king who appears as a manipulable power figure without decided judgments of his own.

The turning point in the story is debated. Is it when Esther resolves to use her influence to save her people (4:16), or when the king is troubled by sleeplessness that prompts him to investigate whether Mordecai has been properly rewarded for warning him of a plot on his life (6:1), or when Haman, thinking that he is giving advice to the king concerning honors for himself, counsels the king to reward Mordecai handsomely (6:7–9)? At this midpoint in the plot, banquet and audience scenes are employed to slow down the action so that the reader, sensing the imminent failure of the anti-

Jewish plots (cf. 6:13), is kept waiting to see exactly by what twists and turns those plots will be exposed and avenged.[27]

The archaic placement of the story in the Persian court is accomplished with considerable knowledge of its inner workings and customs, but there are so many historical inaccuracies and improbabilities that the work cannot be taken at face value. The story may draw on memories of conflicts over Persian policies toward the Jews in which Jews serving in the imperial court were involved, but the actual setting of the narrator is in the Maccabean-Hasmonean era. This is indicated by several lines of evidence: the intensity and bitterness of the Jewish-Gentile conflicts in the book which are pictured as "fights to the finish," the lack of external references to the book until late Hellenistic times, and the very late appearance of Purim as a recognized Jewish festival.

Purim is first mentioned in the period 100–50 B.C.E. in 2 Macc. 15:36 where it is called "Mordecai's Day" (14 Adar) and associated with "Nicanor's Day" (13 Adar), when Jews celebrated a Maccabean victory over the Syrians. The colophon to the Book of Esther in LXX claims that a certain Dositheus brought the translation of Esther from Jerusalem to Egypt in 114–113 or 78–77 B.C.E., depending on which Egyptian ruler is referred to in the text. These references point to 150–100 B.C.E. as the likely date of composition for Esther. It was in this period that relations between Jews and Hellenistic Gentiles were especially strained and the Hasmonean rulers fought strenuous wars against surrounding Gentile nations (§47.1). The references in Esther to Gentile conversions to Judaism out of fear (8:17; 9:27) accord with the Hasmonean policy of forceably Judaizing certain Gentiles such as the Idumeans. In short, the intemperance and savagery of the anti-Semitic and anti-Gentile feelings in Esther, as well as the demonstrated capacity of Jews to defend themselves, are most intelligible in this Hasmonean context.[28] Similar bitterness in Jewish-Gentile relations and extremities of attack and defense emerge in the apocryphal Book of Judith which was written ca. 150 B.C.E.[29]

Noteworthy is Esther's studied avoidance of the name of God or of specific religious motivations or meanings. The deliberation of this reticence about religion is clear from the use of "place" as a circumlocution for

27. Sandra B. Berg, *The Book of Esther: Motifs, Themes, and Structure*, SBLDS 44 (Missoula, Mont.: Scholars Press, 1979).

28. Robert H. Pfeiffer, *Introduction to the Old Testament* (New York and London: Harper & Bros., 1941), 740–47.

29. Robert H. Pfeiffer, *History of New Testament Times with an Introduction to the Apocrypha* (New York: Harper & Bros., 1949), 291–97, shows convincingly that, although the Book of Judith confusedly telescopes events spanning centuries, its self-evident setting is the mid–second century B.C.E.

God ("relief and deliverance will rise for the Jews from another place [quarter]," 4:14). This refusal to speak of God and piety may have been dictated by the Mardi gras–style revelries at Purim, or it may have been a literary device to accent the importance of the Jews acting in their own behalf in order to secure divine deliverance. Some have thought that the author favored a secularized understanding of Jewish identity from which he expunged religion as irrelevant or obfuscating. The Additions to Esther in the Greek translation of the book show that the lack of religious reference was felt by many as a deficiency to be corrected. If the colophon to the LXX is believed, this religious expansion of the book was undertaken in Jerusalem by one named Lysimachus not many years, or decades at most, after the original composition.

The origins of the Feast of Purim remain conjectural. It is possible that a festival of that name had been observed by Jews in the Mesopotamian Dispersion, even as early as Persian times. It may have included emphasis on overcoming opposition from Gentiles among whom they lived, and it may have been arranged to coincide in date and possibly in some of its features with a Babylonian, Persian, or Hellenistic festival. As such, Purim would have held little attraction for Jews living in the western Dispersion and in Palestine. It was, on the other hand, the association of this older festival with deliverance from anti-Semitic pogroms in Maccabean-Hasmonean times that catapulted the Purim rites into prominence in Palestine and occasioned the Book of Esther.

In spite of the secular conception of Judaism in the book, giving it a very different tone from the explicit law piety of the otherwise related Book of Judith, Esther does specify the distinctiveness of the Jews as follows: "their laws are different from those of every other people, and they do not keep the king's laws, so that it is not for the king's profit to tolerate them" (3:8). In showing the vindication of the observers of those Jewish laws, the book makes at least an implicit religious affirmation. There is certainly no sign that its author would have favored the syncretistic religious program of the Hellenizing Jews of Maccabean times. On the other side, the alacrity and ease with which Esther and Mordecai fit into the Persian court and advance the royal interests give a ringing answer to the charge that Jewish laws contravene good citizenship or service in foreign empires. Stated in the extreme, one can be both a good Persian queen and a good Jew.

54
WISDOM WRITINGS

54.1 What Is Wisdom?

The clearest beginning point for defining wisdom in biblical tradition is to say that it consists of those literary genres and themes found in the canonical Books of Proverbs, Job, and Ecclesiastes, and in the apocryphal Books of Ben Sira and Wisdom of Solomon. The dominant literary forms are the proverb and the admonition—whether simple or elaborated—and the overriding theme is how to accommodate one's life to the fundamental orderliness of the world, or what to do when the anticipated order fails. In this literature the traditional pursuit of wisdom is traced back to Solomon, the archetypal wise king, who is viewed as the author of Proverbs, Ecclesiastes, and Wisdom of Solomon. Similar ideas and forms of expression in related documents from Egypt and Mesopotamia happily provide a wealth of comparative data. Thus, the way to an understanding of wisdom is open and wide.

In practice, however, the characterization of wisdom has turned out to be increasingly complicated and vexed. There are actually a considerable number of genres in the wisdom writings (table 28) and a host of rhetorical devices that turn up over a wide swath of historical, prophetic, and psalmic texts. Wisdom themes such as creation, reward and punishment, and innocent suffering likewise appear in nonwisdom books, often dressed out in the literary features of wisdom writings. Either the writers of the core wisdom books have written or edited many nonwisdom books or a "wisdom influence" has reached into most of the nooks and crannies of the canon. It has become a scholarly fashion to pursue this elusive wisdom influence throughout large parts of the Hebrew Bible, but, given our lack of basic controls on the evidence, it has proven difficult to know exactly what kind of "influence" was operative. A major difficulty is that the wisdom writings, sparse in historical references, are not easy to date, and the setting(s) for the production of wisdom traditions is highly disputed.

54.1.a Literary Genres and Mind-set

Each of the canonical wisdom books has its own peculiar mix of genres (table 28).[30] In Proverbs, the basic building materials are the artistic proverbs and the admonitions which are often clustered by form or topic. In the instructions, hymns, confessions, and example stories, the thought is often sustained over several poetic lines and something like "strophes" or "miniature essays" result. When the headings to the six subcollections of Proverbs are considered, the resulting anthology is much more complex and nuanced in its effects than a mere chain of single proverbs would be. In Job, proverbs and admonitions in some quantity are employed in subordination to the dialogue structure of a disputation in which there are prominent

---

30. Roland E. Murphy, FOTL vol. 13, 3–6, 9–12, 172–85.

TABLE 28
Genres in Wisdom Literature

I. *Saying* or *Proverb,* a pithy aphorism distilling human experience in an apt and memorable form
  A. *Folk Proverb,* generally in prose form (e.g., 1 Sam. 24:14; 1 Kings 20:11; Jer. 23:28)
  B. *Artistic Proverb,* structured in the A_____/ B_____// pattern of Hebrew verse
    1. *Observational* or *Experiential Proverb,* noting a feature of life without evaluation (e.g., Prov. 11:24; 17:27–28; 18:16)
    2. *Didactic* or *Learned Proverb,* inculcating values or lines of conduct (e.g., Prov. 10:7; 14:31; 15:33)

II. *Admonition,* generally structured in the A_____/ B_____// verse form, either appearing in isolation among proverbs or grouped as an *Instruction* delivered by an authoritative teacher to a learner (e.g., Proverbs 1—9; 22:17—24:22)
  A. *Command* (e.g., Prov. 8:33; 16:3; 31:6–9)
  B. *Prohibition* (e.g., Prov. 22:22–23; 30:10)

III. *Riddle,* a "tricky" question whose answer or solution is ambiguous (the only complete biblical example, Judges 4:10–18; referred to in Prov. 1:6; Ps. 49:4; etc.)

IV. *Fable,* a short story with plants or animals as characters (Judges 9:8–15; 2 Kings 14:9)

V. *Allegory,* an extended metaphor (Prov. 5:15–23, wife as "cistern"; Eccl. 12:1–6, aging person as a "falling house")

VI. *Hymn,* a praise of personified wisdom (Job 28; Prov. 1:20–33; 8; Sir. 24:1–22; Wisd. of Sol. 6:12–20; 7:22—8:21)

VII. *Controversy Speech* or *Disputation,* characteristic of the dialogue of Job with his friends, mixed with lament and lawsuit genres (Job 4—31)

VIII. *Example Story,* concrete illustration of point made by sage (Prov. 7:6–23; 24:30–34; Eccl. 4:13–16)

IX. *Confession, Autobiographical Narrative,* or *Reflection,* in which a sage shares his rich experience with pupils or readers (Prov. 4:3–9; Eccl. 1:12—2:26; Sir. 33:16–18)

X. *Name List* or *Onomasticon* of geographical, cosmological, meteorological phenomena (Job 28; 36:27–37; 38:4—39:30; 40:15—41:34; Ben Sira 43; Wisd. of Sol. 7:17–20, 22–23; 14:25–26)

lament, hymn, and lawsuit features held together in an edifying narrative frame that has the ring of an example story. In Ecclesiastes, strings of proverbs and admonitions form almost half of the book but are embedded in a "confession" or "reflection" form whose reading as prose or poetry is much disputed. The overall structures of Job and Ecclesiastes are so uniquely developed that they do not conveniently fit into known genre categories.

The plentiful ancient Near Eastern wisdom literature offers many illuminative contact points with Israelite wisdom writings. Proverbs, admonitions, instructions, and name lists are amply attested from Egypt and Mesopotamia (table 1: 8A–C). The hymn personifying wisdom is probably derived from an Egyptian prototype. Job and Ecclesiastes are less paralleled from abroad in their genres than in their thematic preoccupations with injustice, undeserved suffering, and death (table 1: 9). Riddles and fables occur in the ancient Near Eastern wisdom texts and are mentioned in the Hebrew Bible, although the intact biblical examples fall outside the wisdom books. The author of Prov. 22:17—24:22 has made free use of the Egyptian Instruction of Amen-em-opet in writing his "thirty sayings" (table 1: 8B).

What exactly is wisdom thought or the wisdom mind-set? "Wisdom" typifies a way of viewing the world based on close observation and careful reflection in an effort to discern the substantial harmony and order that is sensed to be constitutive of it. The characteristic wisdom style does not, however, stop with observation and reflection, since its goal is to develop life strategies that will *integrate the individual's existence with the perceived order of the world*. Wisdom aims for a practical and comprehensive ethic and behavioral style adequate to the situations in which its followers live, labor, and interact with one another and with others who are less attentive to wisdom.

For wisdom the sphere of the "world" is as broad as everything that may be encountered in the natural environment, historical events, social relations, political order, family affairs, daily work, and religious belief and practice. Wisdom's center is the teachable human observer and social actor. Religion is looked at as one of the many areas and resources of life, but its value to the wisdom outlook is learned through experience rather than by authoritative fiat. This means that the stance of wisdom toward religion is "nonrevelatory," and for this reason wisdom's approach to religion appears somewhat relaxed and optional, running "against the grain" of other religious domains in Israel which start off from confidence in Yahweh as the authoritative revealer.

It is not that Israel's wise were antireligious, or even nonreligious, in any programmatic way. From all that we can tell they participated in the cult. It was simply that anyone adopting the mode of wisdom treated the religion of Yahweh as something whose value and meaning for life had to be tested and determined and integrated with all the rest of knowledge and truth. Because religion was so major a factor in ancient Israel, Israelite sages early on came to considered conclusions about the place of "the fear of Yahweh" in their wisdom schemes. For the most part, however, the allegiance they gave Yahweh was not a bowing to divine revelation so much as an assenting to truth they had established through human reflection. As Torah gained ascendency during and after the exile, the wisdom affirmation of an orderly world that undergirded right practice was focused on Torah as the signal accessible source of wisdom.

When wisdom is defined in this descriptive manner, it is easy to see that, while distinct at its core, its interests and perspectives shaded off into many, possibly all, the other aspects of Israel's life. If, for example, we leave aside explicitly literary criteria and simply think of wisdom as *a nonrevelatory mode of thought that focuses on individual consciousness of truth and right conduct,* displaying *a humanistic orientation* and *a didactic drive* to pass on its understandings to others, it is easy to see "wisdom" almost everywhere in the Hebrew Bible where there is no direct speech of God. The truth in this "confusion of categories" is that Israel's sages were of the temper of mind to make them congenial, if somewhat reserved, participants in many aspects of Israel's religious life. By the same token, they were oriented to bring their observations and reflections to bear on rulers, elders, prophets, priests, legislators, and whoever showed interest in their learning. "Wisdom influence" probably did reach far and wide.

54.1.b Sociohistoric Horizons of Wisdom

The main point, however, is to find the base from which all this wisdom influence emanated. Who were the generators and propagators of wisdom teaching and its genres? Where were they situated historically and socially within the body of ancient Israel?[31] Three primary proposals about the identity and setting of the wise have been advanced. On one view the wise were parents in families or elders and counselors in clans and tribes. On a second view they were government officials, scribes and possibly priests, who kept records of state, counseled kings, and trained future political cadres. On a third view they were nonpriestly authorities in the collected

31. Ibid., 6–9; Robert Gordis, "The Social Background of Wisdom Literature," *HUCA* 18 (1943/44): 77–118.

and venerated Law of Moses who interpreted its meaning and present application and who passed on their skills in legal-scribal schools. A frequent scenario is to picture secular wisdom as starting in government circles around Solomon and, after the fall of the state, transmuting into religious wisdom focused on the Torah in scribal circles of interpreters and transmitters of the Law. Fewer interpreters think that family or tribal contexts had much to do with the canonical wisdom traditions.

How shall we assess the evidence about wisdom's sociohistoric setting? We are dealing with a temporal and institutional grid of factors, representable in a simplified way (chart 10). In which of these institutional matrices was "wisdom" generated and propagated during which periods?

Family and tribe were certainly spheres for the passing on of "collective wisdom" by parents and elders, not only before there was a state, but through all later periods, even when the public dimensions of familial and tribal power were drastically reduced. But is the wisdom of Proverbs, Job, and Ecclesiastes familial and tribal wisdom? Only, it seems, in the sense that some details of form (e.g., "father/son" metaphor for "teacher/pupil" relationship) and certain major topical interests reflect familial/tribal concerns. Yet this "familial/tribal" topical interest in wisdom writings does have significance for a proper locating of wisdom.

Torah religion really did not emerge in Israel in any sense that would have required scholars of legal texts prior to the Deuteronomic reformation. Before that time *torah* was "instruction" that included laws to be interpreted and applied by wise elders and probably by state-appointed judges. The full Torah religion developed only after the exile. Nothing in the form or content of the wisdom writings shows the sages to have been such elders or judges. Nevertheless, the presupposed concern of the wise for an orderly society implies their interest in the upholding of legal traditions.

State scribalism, as the biblical tradition clearly reports, began with Solomon (1 Kings 4:29–34) and continued unbroken to the exile (cf. Prov. 25:1). This was the scribalism of educated state officials who kept public records, advised kings, and taught scribal skills and political craft to their successors and colleagues. Wherever they touch on authorship or setting, the evidence of wisdom writings in Israel and in the ancient Near East pinpoints their origins in royal court schools. The contention that wisdom writings were intellectual fare and entertainment for a wider readership probably carries some truth, but in antiquity "the educated reading public" would have been small, probably not extending very far beyond the royal establishment and the upper-class urban circles. A royal court provenance for wisdom does not, of course, give us the whole story, if only because

CHART 10
Institutional Settings of Israelite Wisdom

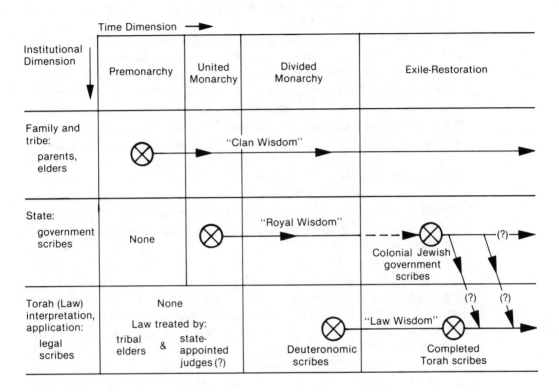

Proverbs, Job, and Ecclesiastes came to completion *after* the government scribalism of Judah had collapsed and *before* the new religious scribalism of Torah was fully developed.

As in other respects, the hiatus of the exile and the obscurities of the early restoration period create serious obstacles to discerning the course that wisdom took in this later period. Among the exiles to Babylonia there were numbers of Israelite government scribes who preserved and continued to enlarge the wisdom traditions. At the same time, Deuteronomists committed to the Law of Moses were viewing it in part through the medium of wisdom teaching (and in fact particular Deuteronomists were likely also to be governmental scribes). Thus, we have no problem seeing how the wisdom traditions survived the exile.

More problematic is how the institutional matrix for wisdom was reconstituted after the exile. We can posit on principle that a Judean province of the Persian Empire would have had scribal officials to conduct business and that these would have been Jewish natives. It is easily conceivable that proverbial and admonitory sayings (as in Proverbs) and skeptical reflections (as in Job and Ecclesiastes) were both preserved from the past and freshly composed in these colonial administrative scribal circles. The Deuteronomistic wing of the DH/P entente that produced the finished Torah was sympathetic to wisdom and probably was a factor in encouraging the shift toward equating wisdom with Torah which eventually transferred most of the wisdom activities from the political scribal context to the religious scribal-legal context. We can see the fuller development of this process in the Torah-oriented scribe Ben Sira who composed his own version of "Proverbs" in 180 B.C.E. The earlier phases of this "taming" of wisdom by Torah can be inferred from the redaction of later biblical books that thematizes them under wisdom and Torah rubrics.

Surveying the whole course of wisdom traditioning in Israel we can see a firm anchorage of wisdom in the royal court, both in its genres and in its particular way of formulating ethical and theological concerns. Some of the wisdom literature for this reason has a very limited topical range, focused, for example, on the cultivation of a pedestrian ethic of obedience to superiors and the refinement of proper court manners which were highly self-protective of the precarious position of lesser officials under arbitrary rulers. On the other hand, the wise officials had family and tribal ties, as well as wider socioreligious concerns, and their literature also reflects a pronounced concern to preserve the integrity of rural communities against predatory wealth and suborned legal institutions. In the sense that wisdom topics include a major regard for family and tribe it can be said that those spheres are represented in the wisdom traditions. That means also that the laws of Israel in the tribal milieu, before there was a full-blown Torah religion, were also of concern to wisdom writers—even though they had no duties in the discharge of justice. By the same token we can account for the partial "overlap" of wisdom and prophecy in terms of a shared concern for just social order.

The much-discussed *wisdom influence* was thus not merely *literary* and *intellectual* but also *ethical-social*. Some wise officials cared not only about their careers but also about a wise and just social order, which brought them into contact with prophets, priests, and elders who had similar concerns. The Deuteronomic reformation almost certainly brought together a coalition of just such interested Israelite functionaries from various institutions. In this manner it is possible to provide a general interpretive framework for explaining both the narrow specificity of wisdom's institutional base and the broad range of its interests and of the influences that flowed from it and into it.

54.2 Proverbs

This anthology of several hundred proverbs and admonitions was composed out of at least six subcollections (see headings in 1:1; 10:1; 22:17; 25:1; 30:1; 31:1). Further subdivisions in the materials are evident: differences of form and content set off chaps. 10—15 from 16:1—22:16 and chaps. 25—27 from 28—29. In 24:23–34 there is a supplement to the preceding "sayings of the wise."

It is generally thought that the second, third, and fourth subcollections derive largely from preexilic times, since they allude regularly to kingship and an operative state structure. The first, fifth, and sixth subcollections are more often regarded as postexilic. The older argument that the extended "thought runs" and theologizing of wisdom in chaps. 1—9 mark it as a late postexilic composition is no longer so compelling since the elaboration of admonitions into an instruction genre has been identified as an ancient Egyptian literary practice, as has also the sacralizing and personifying of Lady Wisdom as a goddess. Possibly more indicative of postexilic origin for chaps. 1—9 is its preoccupation with adultery as a threat to the nuclear family and to the integrity of the learned man. The last two subcollections are oddly attributed to the unknown Agur and Lemuel, possibly north Arabian sages, but the proper reading of these corrupt texts is problematic. Early and late features appear to be combined in these chapters, with 30:5–6 pointing toward veneration of a canonical text. The acrostic praise of a good wife in 31:10–31 might aptly apply to an upper-class woman of either preexilic or postexilic times.

An anthologizing fascination with the words of the wise has brought the whole collection together under an introduction that connects a lavish wisdom vocabulary with Yahweh piety (1:1–7). The redactional structure of the book, probably to be dated 450–350 B.C.E., is very deliberate in its refinements. One theory has it that the book is put together as "a house of wisdom" (cf. 9:1; 14:1), analogous to the tripartite Solomonic temple: the "front" is chaps. 1–9; the "nave" is 10:1—22:16; the "inner sanctuary" is 22:17—31:31.[32] The "seven pillars" (9:1) are found in seven columns of text of twenty-two or twenty-three lines each (alphabetizing practice) constituting chaps. 2—7. Moreover, it is contended that the exact number of proverbs and lines is consciously contrived according to the numerical values of the letters in the names of Solomon, David, Israel, and Hezekiah in the subcollection headings. There are, for instance, exactly 375 proverbs in 10:1—22:16, which is the numerical equivalent of the Hebrew letters in the name of Solomon, the claimed author (cf. 10:1). It is also possible to see the midpoint of these 375 proverbs as the "seam" made by the compiler when joining chaps. 10—15 to 16:1—22:16. This architectonic theory of the construction of Proverbs depends upon the elegance of its interlocking parts, but is thrown into question by recourse to textual deletions and rearrangements. Few scholars have endorsed the scheme in toto, but it advances a productive heuristic position in the current redactional inquiry.

It has been common to stress the strictly limited prudential character of the teaching in Proverbs, even its superficiality and opportunism as a manual for survival in royal politics. There is no doubt that such *is* the horizon of parts of the book. It is interesting, however, that a much larger portion of the content is devoted to familial and economic affairs. It is likewise commonplace to assume for the outlook of Proverbs a rigid dogma of reward for virtue and punishment for vice, virtually correspondent to a like Deuteronomistic dogmatism of reward and punishment. On this view, the survivalist mentality of the recommended court etiquette and mores is somewhat of an embarrassment. Generally this sensed misfit of theory and application is explained by a middle-term formula of "right attitudes issue in right consequences" (cf. the "righteous" and "wicked" antinomies of chaps. 10—15). In other words, those who by definition were now "wise" and "righteous" in their inner beings would be blameless when they

32. Patrick W. Skehan, *Studies in Israelite Poetry and Wisdom*, CBQMS 1 (Washington, D.C.: Catholic Biblical Association of America, 1971), 9–45.

adopted chameleonlike conduct required by royal establishments, their opportunism being justified by their preestablished status as "wise."

It becomes increasingly clear, however, that Proverbs, like DH, is not monolithic in its ideology. There were among the wise, as among the Deuteronomists, "critical traditionalists" as well as "authoritarian dogmatists (§23.2). Much of the proverbial and instructional discourse of Proverbs stays close to actual life conditions and tries to discern the best choices in ambiguous situations where the basic order of things is not completely obvious and must be searched out. The attitudes and directives, for example, with respect to production, distribution, exchange, and consumption of goods illustrate a variety of viewpoints, which may at times represent side-by-side competing outlooks and at other times the changing emphases of differing historical settings.

The truism about wisdom's dogmatic reading of virtue and vice and their consequences construes Proverbs to be teaching that the righteous will be wealthy and the wicked will be poor. To be sure, a vision of the world as an ordered place that combines justice, power, and wealth is strongly articulated, for instance in the speech of Lady Wisdom (8:15–21). It is evident, however, that much of the commentary in the book is on the prevailing imperfect conditions that the sages are observing and making decisions about. Many remarks on wealth and poverty are more or less neutral observations, e.g., that the rich are praised and sought after while the poor are despised and shunned, that wealth is fickle, etc. When it comes to assessing the causes or occasions of wealth and poverty and to passing ethical judgment on the wealthy and the poor, there is an array of criteria and angles of approach and, in the end, a dissonance in emphasis and explanatory frameworks.

It is something of a surprise that, generously reckoned, no more than one-third of the evaluative proverbs and admonitions about wealth and poverty support the alleged wisdom dogma that the rich and the poor deserve their fortunes. In the minority of cases where poverty is morally condemned, the plight of the poor is most often laid to idleness, which smacks rather more of class conceit than of Yahwistic theological judgment. Also, among the occasions of poverty, especially among those who were formerly rich or aspired to riches, mention is made of hastiness in amassing wealth and stinginess in refusing to share it. By contrast, the largest single category of "socioeconomic appraisals" attributes existing wealth and poverty to the oppression and dishonesty by which riches are in effect stolen from the poor. This process of transferring wealth from the many to the few is noted in richly detailed references to exorbitant interest on loans, moving the boundary markers of fields, judicial perjury and bribery, violent confiscations and killings of rightful owners, and the permissiveness and complicity of the king in this planned impoverishment of most of the populace. A very similar bill of particulars about riches as the product of plunder and murder on a societywide basis is given in Job and Ecclesiastes.

What practical advice follows from these evaluations? Corresponding to the assumption that poverty and wealth are distributed according to what people morally deserve, some texts warn against standing surety on loans to debtors, since the good-hearted backer of the debtor is likely to lose his pledge. There is also counsel to harbor rather than squander one's wealth, a particular danger for gluttons and drunkards. On the one hand, corresponding to the exposés of the mechanisms of enrichment and impoverishment, and of their dreadful human costs, many texts emphasize God's immediacy to the poor in creation and in potential redemption, and there are repeated injunctions for the wise to show their kindness by giving to the poor. It is difficult to determine the extent to which these counsels call for a shoring up of the *solidarity system of mutual help* among families, protective associations, and tribes, or, alternatively, for measures of *charity to individuals* now that the solidarity system is in collapse (especially in urban settings). Apparently both social situations and strategies are implicit here and there in the sum total of the wisdom teaching about economics.

In short, the *bearers of wisdom are caught in class contradiction.*[33] They enjoy a measure of class privilege through their vocational status and education. On the one hand, their class advantage and tendency to universalize their privileged position prompt them to endorse the operative socioeconomic order as an instance of wise cosmic order. On the other hand, their acute observations of how the life of the rich and the poor violates cosmic order inclines them to "preach" amelioration and reformation of such gross "disorder" = "folly" = "injustice" = "sin against Yahweh." Precisely these sages, torn by contrary interests and perceptions, were in the thick of the great debates that took place in governmental circles over what policies Judah should adopt. In themselves, the wise had little direct political power but their "winged words" might temper politics with "moral influence" based on accumulated wisdom that had survived previous fallen regimes.[34]

33. John Pairman Brown, "Proverb-Book, Gold-Economy, Alphabet," *JBL* 100 (1981): 169–91, connects contradictory attitudes toward wealth and power both in Theognis of Megara and biblical Proverbs with their origins in a rising commercial class attached to a gold-economy and to the alphabet as a facilitator of trade.

34. Brian W. Kovacs, "Is There a Class-Ethic in Proverbs?" in *Essays in Old Testament Ethics. J. P. Hyatt, In Memoriam,* ed. James L. Crenshaw and John T. Willis (New York: Ktav Publishing, 1974), 171–89.

Even though many voices speak in Proverbs, the one that grew loudest over time was the dogmatic authoritarian voice that ripped wisdom out of its particular sociohistoric contexts and robbed it of its careful observational and inquiring mode of reasoning. *Contextless wisdom dogmatism* had the advantage of being easy to grasp. Moreover, those with the communal power to encourage some ideas and discount others found that wisdom dogmatism was a most effective justification of their own exercise of power. It was tempting to convert the search for a situational approximation to wisdom and righteousness into an assertion of automatic possession of wisdom and righteousness as evidenced by one's prosperity and success. Messy details of having "achieved" prosperity and success by opportunism and violence could be overlooked. We know that this dogmatic voice was loud and insistent, perhaps far more so than the text of Proverbs indicates, because two sages wrote works that openly challenged and rebutted the easy self-confidence that it voiced. The remarkable pluriformity and flexibility of wisdom traditions show up in the way that the authors of Job and Ecclesiastes used wisdom genres, rhetoric, values, and methods of reasoning to renounce a simplistic, and ultimately immoral and impious, appeal to order that demeaned human life and caricatured God.

54.3 Job

Sometime during the exile or within a century or so after the first return to Palestine, a sage wrote the Book of Job in order to break the grip of a moralism and dogmatism that was reducing wisdom to canards and formulas about the surface appearances of human life. Insofar as a book can help to change minds as it combines with other forces, Job was a provocative tour de force that could not be easily disregarded. Those who search in the book for a clear explanation of innocent suffering have trouble finding it, probably because none was intended. The author is content to establish that there really is *innocent* suffering, something that wisdom dogmatics could not allow. For the writer "innocent" does not mean that the sufferer is sinless but simply that suffering happens again and again for which we cannot assign any formulaic reason. A meaning to that suffering, either as a cause or as a consequence, may or may not emerge in time. It is vital to our integrity as humans and to our belief in God that we not parrot conventional meanings about particular sufferings and successes, either beforehand, in the midst of them, or afterward.

As the springboard for his argument, the writer has used an old popular tale about a righteous man who widely benefited his community and who patiently suffered extreme adversity. This tradition takes the form of a sagalike story, in its flavor reminiscent of patriarchal times. It is also a quasi-mythological story insofar as it entails a member of the divine court, an accuser (*satan* is not yet a proper name), who tests out the piety of believers in Yahweh. In this story Job was unmoved from his faith by the worst sufferings and was restored to a good life after testing. It looks as though the author of Job chose this contrived "limit situation" to give readers a necessary viewpoint "above" the awareness of Job and his friends, none of whom ever comes to learn the "real" reason for the suffering they argue over. Probably the author was not troubled by this potentially demonic view of deity. With the *satan*-accuser he seems to have wanted to make only one point: sometimes there is suffering totally beyond our ability to understand it and we should at least spare ourselves and others the stupidity and cruelty of imposing meanings that will not fit. Those false explanations may keep us from doing what can be done if we treat it as a piece of reality to be directly and freshly coped with.

The old folk story, perhaps modified by the author, was used as an inclusio around a long verse composition which included: (1) an opening complaint of Job; (2) three rounds of speeches with three of his friends (the third round is disrupted accidently or intentionally); (3) a summary demand from Job for God to speak; and (4) a culminating speech of Yahweh to Job. A poem on wisdom and a long brace of speeches by a fourth friend who appears from nowhere have been widely regarded as late additions which disturb the symmetrical structure. This may be so, but the "intrusions" are intelligible as part of the original composition, especially when we grant this writer the novelty of a work which is so evident that we cannot even give a convincing genre label to the whole (to have a genre there must be at least two specimens of it). The poem on wisdom (chap. 28) rounds out the cycles of speeches between Job and his friends, underscoring the superficiality of the friends' "explanations" of Job's plight by showing how difficult it is to come by true wisdom. The speeches of the fourth friend, Elihu (32—39), add little in content (perhaps a greater stress on the purgative value of suffering), but his angry intrusion into the conversation, his self-confident academicism, and his long-windedness deliciously illustrate the flaws of the very formulaic and sloganeering dogmatism which he hopes to resuscitate where others have failed.

The genre ingredients in the Book of Job are numerous and artfully employed to bring several streams of Israelite tradition to bear upon the problem posed.[35] The *individual lament* form is common as the vehicle for

---

35. Murphy, FOTL vol. 13, 15–20.

Job to pour out his distress and to appeal for deliverance. As the argument proceeds, Job widens his citations of human suffering so that he laments political catastrophe and social injustice that would normally be the subject of communal laments. The same speeches are fraught with legal language which picks up from the charge of the friends that God must be justly punishing Job for something he will not admit. Job turns the *lawsuit* around and charges God with injustice in tormenting him. The idiom of juridical process in ancient Israel is extensively mined so that images of litigation, tense with accusation and defense, are conjured, and the final speech of Job includes an oath of innocence, as it were "swearing on the Bible." It is instructive, however, that the closest ancient Near Eastern parallel to this speech is a "negative confession" that was not used in a courtroom but in the religious cult (table 1: 9F). In fact, Job concedes that there is no third-party adjudicator who can stand between him and God. Specific legal genres are thus indeterminable in spite of the legal conceptuality and idiom.

The most apt encompassing genre description for the dialogue between Job and friends is *disputation speech*, in the course of which Job not only disputes with friends but with deity. When Yahweh finally breaks the silence in which wisdom genres customarily enshroud deity, his "answer" to Job has the character of a disputation speech intended to overwhelm an opponent. A reasonably close analogue to the combination of rhetorical questions and lists of natural phenomena with which Yahweh accosts Job in biting dispute has been found in an Egyptian satirical letter in which a master scribe berates his pupils for their naive presumption to knowledge (table 1: 9E). Some lesser genre forms that have recently been claimed in the Book of Job are an *appeal to ancient tradition* (8:8–13; 12:7–12; 15:17–35; 20:4–29) and a *summary-appraisal formula* (8:13; 18:21; 20:29).

The exterior form of the speeches in Job has been recognized as normally alphabetizing (twenty-two or twenty-three lines per speech), with the replies of Job to his friends tending to be always a few lines longer than their statements. It is further claimed that there is a three-line grouping in Job's speeches in chaps. 9—10 and 12—14 that anticipates a three-part division in Job's challenge to God (chaps. 29—31) and which the deity in turn answers by a three-part speech. Moreover, the divine reply exceeds the length of Job's speech to deity in the same ratio as Job's speeches exceed his friends' speeches. The argument is elaborate and not totally convincing because the evidence cited is somewhat selective; nonetheless, it does suggest self-conscious compositional techniques that had become "second nature" to the scribal author, their rhetorical flourishes lying ready at hand for driving home his stunning challenge to complacent orthodoxy.[36]

Is there not, after all, some "answer" or "message" in the book concerning theories of suffering? Job at first tries to counter Yahweh's disputation speech, but then he relents from trying to argue with God. Job does not repent of what he has earlier argued, for in that respect Yahweh confirms Job (cf. 42:7, 9). It might be said that Yahweh accepts the content of Job's rebuttal of dogmatism but reprimands Job for toying with a dogmatism of his own, that is, that any one person, even a righteous Job, can explain everything. The book may be saying that only God, the all-wise, is entitled to be a dogmatist, but that God is *not* a dogmatist can be plainly seen by looking at the irony, ludicrousness, and absurdity of what God has created. Behind the sharp satire of Yahweh's speech there seems to lurk the idea that God does not have evil and suffering totally under control and thus God also suffers.

Clearly, even at this high point of the book, the author will not allow any theological propositions or interpretive frames to enter in from some other aspect of Israelite religion in order to "explain" things. The only explanation is further happenings: after Job sees God and relents from arguing, Job intercedes with God for his friends' folly and the sufferer's fortunes are restored. It can of course be objected that the latter two points are not the author's "authentic self" speaking because they belong to the old folk story about Job. Nonetheless, rather than end the book with a theological interpretation or speech, the author tells the rest of the traditional story and this almost-pedestrian "everyday" manner of concluding so sophisticated a work (life goes on!) must be judged a conscious choice. As new literary critics have observed, this "happy ending" makes even of the tormented Book of Job not a tragedy but a comedy since the central figure is brought back into community with other humans and with God after extreme isolation and alienation (§20.2).[37]

The Book of Job is so eccentric and intensely "psychological" in its probing of the impact of physical, mental, sociocultural, and intellectual suffering that it is difficult to know what consequences the author intended to be drawn from it. It is after all a narrative as it stands, and thus does not ask the reader to do anything in particular. Some have taken it to be a kind of treatment in microcosm of the macrocosm of Israel's suffering in exile.

---

36. Skehan, *Studies in Israelite Poetry and Wisdom*, 96–123.
37. J. William Whedbee, "The Comedy of Job," *Semeia* 7 (1977): 1–39; Robert M. Polzin, *Biblical Structuralism. Method and Subjectivity in the Study of Ancient Texts*, Semeia Studies (Philadelphia: Fortress Press; Missoula, Mont.: Scholars Press, 1977), 54–125.

Job, however, does not parabolically "represent" or "model" the whole people. To be sure, Job's sketches of mass social suffering could certainly evoke memories of communal hardships but the effect would be subtly associational rather than to cast Job as a veiled representation of Israel at large. Probably the author would have been satisfied if his "whistle blowing" on moralism and dogmatism managed to alert the custodians of wisdom to the perils of cheapening and betraying its critical powers of observation and reflection.

54.4 Ecclesiastes

This last and bleakest of the canonical wisdom books is a unique fusion of genre elements in an extended reflection by a sage who speaks in the first person throughout, until in 12:9–14 a third party comments on the author's wisdom activities and sums up the import of his teaching. This reflection has the thematic discursive character of an "essay" or "treatise" but without the expected form of expository development. Among the genre elements incorporated are *experiential and didactic sayings, comparative sayings* (often in the form "better is x than y"), *observations* ("I applied myself to know, . . . I saw . . ."), *self-discourses* ("I said in my heart"), *admonitions, parables, allegory*, and an extended piece of *royal fiction* in which the sage strikes the pose of Solomon, the exemplary sage jaded with wisdom (1:12—2:11). Most commentators agree that the collected sayings have a verse structure, but there is disagreement as to whether the total work can be scanned as poetry, demonstrating the difficulty in ascertaining the criteria of Hebrew "elevated speech."

The varied genre elements, including strings of sayings, taken together with the explicit editorial notation of 12:9–10, make it clear that the writer gathered diverse materials for his sustained and penetrating reflections. At the same time, similarity of language and recurrence of themes, and the use of numbers, give to the work a pronounced unity of thought—albeit paradoxical thought—that has a cumulative impact on the reader.[38] Attempts, however, to describe a progressive development of thought, whether by identifying a succession of topics and their subdevelopments or by citing the placement of key refrains, have not been convincing.

Likewise, the assumption of literary strata, some laid down by pious commentators on the book, does not convincingly restore an original kernel to the book and has glaringly failed to take adequate account of the

---

38. Murphy, FOTL vol. 13, 127–31; Addison G. Wright, "The Riddle of the Sphinx: The Structure of the Book of Qoheleth," in *SAIW*, 245–66; idem, "The Riddle of the Sphinx Revisited: Numerical Patterns in the Book of Qoheleth," *CBQ* 42 (1980): 38–51.

curious dialectic of the author's mind. With the exception of the third-person postscript (12:9–14), there is no certain later interpolation in the book. Possibly 11:9—12:8 is a secondary reapplication of the sage's pessimistic teaching with a view to encouraging conventional piety in spite of all philosophic doubts, but even here the admonitions are conformable to the general structure of the sage's line of reasoning which does not flatly negate conventional behaviors but radically qualifies and relativizes their value and meaning.

The book begins and ends with exclamations that everything in human life is *hevel*, "vanity" in the older English translations, but better understood as "emptiness, senselessness, futility" (1:2; 12:8, plus thirty times throughout). The unity of the work consists of a relentless working up of this theme by illustrations, rebuttals of contrary indications, and attendant admonitions. The sage works with polar thought structures of life and death, the gains and losses in labor, love, wealth, and wisdom, political power and powerlessness, security and insecurity, and so forth. In each case he comes down heavily on the negative pole, but without totally surrendering a continuing tension with the positive pole.[39]

In each of the realms of human experience, whether work, pleasure, family, property, religious cult—even wisdom itself—there are proximate values, but none of these confers an absolute "profit" or "gain" that cannot be snatched away in this life, while all are subject to loss at death. The result is an uneasy amalgam of contentions: there is a God; we do not know God's ways; all the experiences given to us—or chosen by us—may have some relative profit; we should live the uncertain relativities of our life joyously without any confidence in punishment or reward. Wisdom is plainly better than folly, but true wisdom enlightens and empowers best by showing us that wisdom confers only modest insight into and power over a world that constantly eludes rational or moral mastery.

How are we to understand the socioreligious setting of this astonishingly blunt writer? There is a solid consensus among scholars that Ecclesiastes belongs to the third century B.C.E., that is, to Ptolemaic Palestine. The author uses the royal fiction of Solomon early on in his book, but later so speaks that he obviously distinguishes himself from kings. The Solomonic attribution of the book belongs to a later stage (1:1), later even than the notation of 12:9–14 which does not view the author as Solomon. In the text the writer is simply identified as *qōheleth*, which most translations have

---

39. John A. Loader, *Polar Structures in the Book of Qoheleth*, BZAW 152 (Berlin: Walter de Gruyter, 1979).

rendered inappropriately as "the Preacher." The term rather means "the Assembler or Gatherer," that is, either of audiences or of sayings. The postscript tells of his studious efforts at "weighing, studying, and arranging [or composing?] sayings." This he did in an effort both to be aesthetically pleasing and to speak the truth. Such sayings, remarks the redactor, are "like goads and nails firmly fixed," presumably meaning to say that they both stimulate thinking and connect ideas. It is possible that this redactional commentary refers both to the Book of Proverbs and the Book of Ecclesiastes,[40] and that the warning against additional books was meant to exclude further wisdom writings (possibly some that carried Ecclesiastes' pessimism to even more extreme practical conclusions?). The Neo-Babylonian Dialogue between Master and Servant ends with contemplation of suicide or euthanasia, but in a somewhat mocking and jocular way (table 1: 9D).

The use of the Solomonic royal fiction, the parables drawn from political life, and the counsel about obeying kings, suggests that, like preexilic wise men, this sage was in government service, although the redactional comment that he "also taught the people knowledge" implies that his instruction extended outside the limited sphere of officialdom. Whether he formed anything like an independent house of instruction with a student following, as did Ben Sira in the following century (Sir. 51:23), is not determinable. Speculations about specific historical references in the political parables of 4:13–16 and 9:14–15 have cancelled one another out by their arbitrariness in ignoring the way parables refract historical reality. The remarks about injustice, agriculture, and high officialdom in 5:8–9 correspond well with what we know of the Ptolemaic administration in Palestine, however.

If you see oppression of the poor and denial of justice in the state, don't be surprised at the situation.
The high one [official?] is watched by a higher, and there are yet higher ones over them.
But the gain of a country in such circumstances would be a king who serves fields [agriculture].

The Ptolemies introduced layers of colonial administration into Judah, with attending rivalry and corruption, and the intensification of agriculture which resulted was chiefly for export products such as wine and oil rather than for grain and vegetable production for the native populace (§45.2).

40. Gerald T. Sheppard, "The Epilogue to Qoheleth as Theological Commentary," *CBQ* 39 (1977): 182–89.

Qoheleth sympathizes deeply with the oppressed poor (cf. his plaintive observation in 4:1–3), but he only obliquely condemns crimes against them—to speak more openly would put him in conflict with his warning to obey kings who have absolute power (8:2–9). The sage's class-privileged position is at stake in what he chooses to say and not to say about governments and the condition of the poor landed populace. It would be best, he opines, if the king's absolute power were used to upbuild agriculture to the benefit of the impoverished cultivators of the soil.

The socioreligious situation of this astute sage is a setting where *God and government are distanced from the people.* He presupposes the reality and absolute power of God and state, though the former is vaster than the latter. Both the divine and secular authorities work in unfathomable ways that cannot be contested. Their decisions and deeds are consequential for human life, but they are not approachable or swayable in their doings, except perhaps through what modest voice the sage might have in his writings and in the counsels of state when he is consulted for his views. This personal powerlessness, over against a God who is remote and a colonial apparatus of domination that milks the province of Judah for Egypt's gain and for the profit of Jewish elites, has its counterpart in the sage's strategy for keeping his own sanity by doing his work well, enjoying his family, observing the cult correctly, and spreading to all who can appreciate it his caution that life is by no means as rational or moral as inherited wisdom would have it. Job undermined the dogma of retribution by affirming amoral suffering, while Ecclesiastes undermines the dogma throughout the gamut of human experience and especially with respect to all human endeavors after success or profit.

55
APOCALYPTIC WRITINGS

55.1 What Is Apocalyptic?

The term "apocalypse," from Greek for "revelation," "disclosure," or "unveiling," is conventionally used for a type of revelatory literature of which there are scores of Jewish, Christian, Gnostic, Greco-Roman, and Persian examples from the period 200 B.C.E.–300 C.E. The only full-fledged apocalypse to be accepted into the Hebrew Bible was the Book of Daniel, although a number of biblical prophetic texts display sufficient anticipatory marks of the genre to give us a sense of how apocalyptic arose in Jewish circles. Just as "wisdom" may refer to wisdom literature, wisdom thought, or wisdom movement, so "apocalyptic" may refer to *apocalyptic literature, apocalyptic thought,* or *apocalyptic movement.* Discussions of this phenomenon, complicated from the start by strangeness of form and content, have often failed to distinguish adequately among the literary, ideological, and sociological aspects of the inquiry. As a result, discussants using different definitions, different literary repertories of apocalyptic, and different notions of its origins and social base have frequently talked past one another.

55.1.a Literary Genre and Mind-set

Since our solidest evidence is textual, a literary clarification of apocalyptic is the place to begin. Form-critical analysis identifies a number of elements that are constitutive of the apocalyptic genre.[41] These elements concern both the form of the revelation and the content of the revelation. The revelation may be delivered by sight *(vision)* or by a spoken statement *(audition),* or by both together, and may be additionally contained in a written document. The vision may expand into an *otherworldly journey.* In all cases an *otherworldly mediator,* normally conceived as an angelic being, either delivers or explains the revelation or serves as guide in the visionary tours. The human recipient of the revelation is usually identified as a venerable figure from the past. In Jewish apocalypses, favorite *pseudonyms* are drawn from the primeval period (Enoch, Abraham) and especially from the era of exile and early restoration (Baruch, Daniel, Ezra).

What is revealed in an apocalypse? The content of revelation runs along either a "temporal" or a "spatial" axis.

The *temporal revelation* discloses an impending crisis of persecution and other world upheavals that will lead rapidly to the end of the present world order in judgment and salvation. This end may involve world transformation, but always includes personal salvation for the faithful believer in some form of afterlife, often bodily resurrection. In order to set the stage for the end time, there is often a "revelation" about past history in the form of prophecy-after-the-event (so-called *vaticinia ex eventu*) related from the standpoint of the ancient recipient (e.g., "Daniel" from his vantage point in the exile is shown the course of events as far as 165 B.C.E. when the Book of Daniel was in fact written). Sometimes there is also a disclosure about origins (e.g., the creation of the world, sin of Adam, fallen angels, etc.).

The *spatial revelation* introduces the human recipient of the revelation to "the geography and demography of heaven and hell," usually in the vehicle of a guided journey through cosmic regions where the angelic and demonic beings are encountered, and the throne of God is approached. Some

---

41. John J. Collins, ed., *Apocalyptic: The Morphology of a Genre, Semeia* 14 (1979).

apocalypses have only a temporal revelation and some only a spatial revelation, while others include both. In any case, it appears that the apocalyptic world view of Jews embraced both axes as a matter of principle, even where only one aspect is articulated explicitly in texts. On the other hand, Gnosticism—giving up all interest in historical life—knew nothing of revelations about the end of history but only of revelations about the heavenly or spiritual realm of higher beings. For apocalyptic Jews, history moves toward an end time under the pressure of a sovereign heavenly realm that "calls the shots" about what happens *in* and *to* history.

An apocalypse customarily rounds out with *instructions to the recipient* to "stand fast" or "await the end," and frequently to conceal the revelation until the end time. Given the pseudonymous form, this instruction had the effect of a command to publish since, for example, "Daniel" of the exile was to hide his book *until 165 B.C.E.* when its contents would be divulged (by divine instruction to the custodians of the book?).

This kind of close literary formulation of apocalyptic yields a middle-range definition that is not so narrow as to require any particular way of picturing the end of history, whether by prophecy after the event or by cosmic transformation, but which is also not so broad as to include all kinds of revelations in the category, such as those that do not have any end of history or personal afterlife. It also means that a functional apocalypse may be only one part of a larger composition (e.g., the visions of Daniel 7—11 distinguishable from the "nonapocalyptic" supportive stories of Daniel 1—6), or, for that matter, several apocalypses may be included in one composition *(1 Enoch)*. For a full view of apocalyptic books one needs to look at the form resulting from combining other genre materials with apocalypses as strictly defined. It also means that an apocalypse may itself include other kinds of material which are not strictly a part of the genre (e.g., the prayer in Daniel 9, and it might also be argued that Daniel as a whole is an apocalypse that subtends the stories of chaps. 1—6 as necessary forerunners and foils to the genre-specific apocalyptic visions of chaps. 7—12). Furthermore, the apocalyptic scenario or paradigm may be repeated one or more times in the same book as when visions go over the same set of events, or parts of them, in differing ways in a circular or spiral technique called "recapitulation."

On the basis of the above literary characterization of apocalyptic we may say that *the apocalyptic genre is a type of revelatory literature with a narrative framework in which a revelation about end-time judgment and salvation and/or about the heavenly realms is given to a human being by an otherworldly messenger.* With these literary criteria for defining apocalyptic literature, one may designate a corpus of approximately fourteen Jewish apocalypses up to the second century C.E. (table 29).

In spite of the neatness of the preceding typology, there does not exist a clear consensus about an appropriate definition of apocalyptic and the exact scope of the apocalyptic corpus of writings. Starting from a phenomenological description of the apocalyptic thought-world, one can come to a different specification of "true" apocalyptic writings distinguishable from those that have merely been affected by literary mannerisms or isolated ideas.[42] In a phenomenological description, the heart of apocalyptic thought is a radically new *summing up and evaluation of history as having run its course.* The one remaining value of historical time is that in it individual believers prepare themselves for salvation in the dawning kingdom of God that negates degenerate history. *Radical pessimism* about the meaning of history fuses with *radical optimism* that history is about to pass away before the divine kingdom. Paradoxically, also, this worthless predetermined time is precious time for the believer to take a firm stand and to receive a share in the world beyond. Thus, this time at the end of time is without any parallel in previous human experience.

In the light of this radically disjunctive conceptual definition of apocalyptic, the list of apocalyptic writings becomes shorter than the one proposed above on literary grounds (table 29). It includes Daniel, *1 Enoch,* 2 Esdras (= 4 Esdras), *2 Baruch,* and adds portions of the *Sibylline Oracles* and the *Testament* or *Assumption of Moses.* It is denied, however, that *2 Enoch, 3 Baruch, Jubilees,* or *Testament of Levi* are genuinely apocalyptic,[43] since, while employing apocalyptic literary devices and concepts, they do not on this understanding envision a decisive end to history but only a continued, though perhaps sectarian, existence within history. The influence of apocalyptic is acknowledged over a wide front, including employment of some of its features, minus its central claim, in very unlikely contexts: as material for the Jewish Diaspora mission and propaganda (the *Sibylline Oracles*) and as a way to envision afterlife in rabbinic theology (elements of eschatology in the Talmudic literature).

55.1.b Sociohistoric Horizons of Apocalyptic

Lastly, various attempts have been made to work backward from the apocalyptic literature to the several communities or larger movement that

---

42. Walter Schmithals, *The Apocalyptic Movement. Introduction and Interpretation* (New York and Nashville: Abingdon Press, 1975).

43. Ibid., 188–212, details the arguments for judging each of these documents to be apocalyptic or nonapocalyptic.

TABLE 29
Jewish Apocalypses, 250 B.C.E.–150 C.E., According to Literary Criteria*

Book of Heavenly Luminaries (1 Enoch 72—82)	ca. 250 B.C.E.
1 (Ethiopic) Enoch 1—36	before 175 B.C.E.
Daniel 7—12	164 B.C.E.
Dream Visions or Animal Apocalypse (1 Enoch 83—90)	164–160 B.C.E.
Jubilees 23	167–140 B.C.E.
Testament of Levi (in Testaments of the Twelve Patriarchs)	137–107 B.C.E.
Apocalypse of Zephaniah	100 B.C.E.–70 C.E.
Similitudes of Enoch (1 Enoch 37—71)	50 B.C.E.–50 C.E.
2 (Slavonic) Enoch	1–100 C.E.
2 Esdras (= 4 Esdras or Ezra Apocalypse)	100–120 C.E.
2 (Syriac) Baruch	100–120 C.E.
Testament of Abraham 10—15 (form A) and 8—12 (form B)	75–125 C.E.
Apocalypse of Abraham	70–150 C.E.
3 (Greek) Baruch	70–150 C.E.

*This is the list of J. J. Collins (see n. 41). Except for the biblical Daniel 7—12, all are translated in Charlesworth, *OTP,* and a majority are translated in Charles, *APOT.* The approximate dates are based on the discussions in *OTP* and in Nickelsberg, *JLBBM.* See also table 6 for early Jewish Pseudepigrapha, including nonapocalyptic writings.

produced them.[44] This inquiry, while soundly based in principle, is handicapped by the limited historical and social data at our disposal. One form of this inquiry works from the apparent continuities and transformations of ideas from postexilic prophecy into full-blown apocalyptic, with due attention to transitional expressions of "proto-apocalyptic" in works such as Isaiah 56—66, Isaiah 24—27, and Zechariah 9—14. These writings from postexilic prophetic circles show the growth of assumptions and themes that were fundamental in later apocalyptic: the increasing conflict between good and evil, the universalizing of judgment, the transformation of cosmos and history, etc. In stressing these texts, the contribution of prophecy to apocalyptic is seen to be mainly *eschatological*, that is, with respect to notions of the end time. In another group of late prophetic writings, Ezekiel and Zechariah 1—8, specific features popular in apocalyptic are already employed, such as bizarre symbolism, visions, and an interpreting angel. In stressing these texts, the contribution of prophecy to apocalyptic is seen to be mainly *visionary*, that is, with respect to direct revelation of divine mysteries by grant of visions.

In all instances prior to Daniel (or the earliest sections of *1 Enoch* which may predate Daniel), these patently apocalyptic elements fail to congeal into the integrated literary-conceptual pattern outlined above that articulates the heavenly world or announces the imminent end of history. It seems then that scattered *proto-apocalyptic* forms and contents stemming from prophecy had a life of some four centuries within Israel before fusing in the critical mass of radical end-time revelations. Much the same extended development is presupposed if one stresses the wisdom contribution to apocalyptic in terms of wisdom's fascination with cosmic order, determinism, theodicy, and dream interpretations. Wisdom associations with apocalyptic are apparent, but they largely concern the form of apocalyptic rather than the content which is much more heavily indebted to prophetic eschatology and perhaps also to prophetic visionary experience. The alleged influence of Persian Zoroastrian eschatology on Jewish apocalyptic is questionable, in part because the dating of Zoroastrian eschatological texts is even more problematic than the dating of the Jewish texts, and also because Zoroastrian ethical dualism was world-affirming and triumphalist about life in history in contrast to the world-breaking Jewish apocalyptic outlook.

The facets of sociohistoric experience that precipitated apocalyptic com-

44. Robert R. Wilson, "From Prophecy to Apocalyptic: Reflections on the Shape of Israelite Religion," *Semeia* 21 (1981): 79–95, with response by N. K. Gottwald, 109–11.

munities in Hellenistic times had to do with the contact, interchange, and conflict between Jews and Gentiles over a broad cultural, political, and religious front. Jews lived widely in the Gentile world, often shared its culture, and in instances rose to power and influence as government officials in Persian and Hellenistic regimes. At the same time, Jews were subject to foreign rule even in Palestine and the Hellenistic culture penetrated the elites of Judah so extensively that by Maccabean times the entire construct of Jewish religion was open to question. Jewish-Gentile stress and conflict points over culture, political dominion, and religious identity were internalized by Jewish factions that struggled for hegemony in the community.

In the Maccabean and Hasmonean struggles, the "Jewish-Gentile" bifurcation was projected as civil strife among Jews as to how "Jewish" or how "Hellenistic" their politics, culture, and religion should be. The cosmopolitan universalizing and individualizing effects of the Greco-Roman world challenged all branches of Jewish life and thought. In the apocalyptic movement these conflicts came to expression as a radical option for the Jewish God and his righteous rule in which all the universal and individualistic impulses of the time were "stood on their head," negated by and transformed into the kingdom of God as the end point of history.

Who were these apocalyptists? By assuming a one-to-one correlation between the tradition elements in apocalyptic, they may be seen as *alienated prophets* or as *disillusioned wise men*. By noting the prominence of apocalyptic thought in the Dead Sea community in association with priestly concerns, they may be seen as *priests disaffected* from the Jerusalem cult. Because the apocalyptic literature is such a compound of genre and conceptual elements, and because it is now recognized as having been produced both in Palestine and the Dispersion, it is questionable whether apocalyptic circles were ever closed homogeneous groups of prophets, wise men, or priests. Some groups may have been singular in composition, but others were likely of mixed membership, including people with no previous socioreligious role or status. The extreme sociopolitical conditions of the time would have tended to trigger realignments of traditional lines of thought and new coalitions of people working for particular interests.

The producers of the Book of Daniel are frequently said to have been the *Hasidic* "party" that backed the Maccabean wars as long as they were struggles for religious survival. This is a reasonable hypothesis, but unfortunately we know very little about the origins or membership of the Hasidim. In their Maccabean form they were probably less a long-defined "party" than a coalition of anti-Hellenistic traditionalists whom the pressure of circumstances threw together. In that coalition there were probably many points of view represented, among them the apocalyptic. The Book of Daniel shows affinities with wisdom tradition in that it begins with stories about Jews in foreign government service and identifies the righteous who will live or be resurrected to see the kingdom of God as "the wise." It has been suggested that those responsible for the book may have included Jews from the Dispersion who returned to Palestine during the Maccabean crisis. Possibly the flash point for the ignition of end time–thinking arose among those who once had favorable experiences with foreign governments but who now experienced the Seleucid regime joining with Jewish Hellenizing elites to destroy the distinctive Jewish cult and tradition. In this situation, all human government, including apostate Jewish government, was thrown into fundamental question and God alone was seen to provide a way out of the terrible impasse. The totalizing calm and calculated resignation of the sage in Ecclesiastes was a way to respond to a precarious world as long as a Jewish survival space remained intact within it. Once that Jewish space was seen to be corrupted and jeopardized in its very existence, one can understand the opposite totalizing dynamic of world despair and radical reorientation toward the only imaginable resolution. To the apocalyptists, the end of Jewish world space meant the end of history.

Relative deprivation theory in the study of nativist and millenarian movements provides a helpful intellectual framework for thinking about Jewish apocalyptic communities. Anthropological studies of cult movements that attempt to revitalize society or that prepare for a break in social order (whether actively or passively) emphasize a *perceived discrepancy between expectation and actuality* with respect to goods, status, behavioral possibilities, and/or self-worth.[45] The discrepancies may be between past and present experience, or between the present and the projected future, or between the experiences of two contemporary groups. The deprivation is "relative" in that it is a matter of "how it looks and feels" to the group, and it is "relative" in that it may involve any one or more of the types of possible deprivation. (In the Hellenization crisis of 167–164 B.C.E. it appears that *all* the possible kinds of deprivation were experienced.) The formulation of ideology and program to cope with deprivation is coincident with a new group formation. While this literature on cult movements and relative deprivation has been fairly widely used to illuminate Jewish prophecy and apocalyptic, the choices of examples have been somewhat random and it remains to be seen whether the anthropological studies present results in

45. David Aberle, "A Note on Relative Deprivation Theory as Applied to Millenarian and Other Cult Movements," in *Millennial Dreams in Action*, ed. Sylvia L. Thrupp (New York: Schocken Books, 1970), 209–14.

such a way that a more discriminating use of them can be made to delineate the probable conditions under which Jewish apocalyptic arose.

Even allowing for the limited comparisons made so far from anthropological studies of cults, we may form some reasonable conclusions about the Jewish apocalyptic communities. We should expect that there were *various apocalyptic communities*, even if the Maccabean Hasidic context provided the first identifiable instance. We should also expect that the *membership* of apocalyptic groups would be *diverse in class and status*. The frequent assumption that only very impoverished people would be apocalyptists is undercut by the clear evidence from relative deprivation theory. People suffering any kind of serious disadvantage, such as Jewish courtiers in foreign governments or in Judean government who were expelled from office or who were losers in major policy battles, might be ready candidates for membership in an apocalyptic group. Thus, if the Book of Daniel gives the impression of a community with members influenced by prophecy and wisdom, it is not at all surprising that the Testament of Moses, coming from nearly the same time, indicates a marked priestly interest, as do also the members of the Dead Sea sect several decades later. The "right" combination of general conditions converging on the "right" experience of deprivation could have turned virtually any Jew into an apocalyptist, precipitating an eclectic use of old traditions within the fresh apocalyptic complex.

55.2 Daniel

It can be solidly concluded that the present form of the Book of Daniel was composed in the year 165 B.C.E. because of "the final events" which it announces as revelations to the seer Daniel. The author knows of the profanation of the temple by cessation of daily sacrifices and setting up of an image of Zeus Olympius in 167 ("the abomination that desolates," 11:31; 12:11), of the severe proscriptions against the practice of Judaism (7:25; 11:28, 30), and of the deaths of many righteous in the war of defense led by Judas Maccabee (11:33–35). The career of Antiochus Epiphanes is sketched more or less accurately down to the beginning of 165. The author, however, expects a third—this time totally victorious—Seleucid invasion of Egypt, and this did *not* occur (11:42–43). He is also unaware of Antiochus's campaign in the east during which the ruler died. Also, the profaned temple still awaits rededication.

One vision sees the temple lying under profanation for 1150 days, that is, about the actual three-year period between its desecration in December 167 and its reconsecration in December 164 (8:14). Interestingly, two recalculations of that figure have been appended to the book, extending the time of profanation to 1290 and 1385 days respectively (12:11–12). It is difficult to make any sense of these figures except as modifications made in the text when the rededication of the temple did *not* trigger the expected "end." This suggests that the book was closely followed, at least for some months, as a manual of predictions about the approaching end.

The apocalyptic structure of the book is achieved by combining a series of stories about Daniel and his companions in Babylonian-Median government service with a series of visions reviewing ancient Near Eastern history from the exile to 165 B.C.E. The interplay between stories and visions is intricate. The stories provide a narrative setting in royal courts some four centuries earlier than Maccabean times where the Jewish exile Daniel functioned as a wise interpreter of dreams. This same Daniel is the recipient of the visions that culminate the book. At the same time, the Daniel of the stories serves foreign monarchs and exegetes their dreams in a manner that lays out the chief dynamics and ingredients of the conflictual situation that will emerge in the visions. The relations of Daniel to Nebuchadnezzar, Belshazzar (= Nabonidus), and Darius are on the whole cordial and positive, but we are given glimpses of the persecutorial rage and overweening arrogance of kings which prepare us for the sharpening of the conflict in the visions.

The dream of the human statue that represents four kingdoms sets forth the notion of the periodization of world history (chap. 2). Its bodily parts made of metals that range from precious to common signify the successive degeneration of the world empires. This adumbrates the same scheme worked out in greater detail in the first vision on chap. 7 where the four kingdoms are represented by separate beasts and are named as Babylonia, Media, Persia, and Greece (i.e., Alexander and his successors, the Ptolemies, and the Seleucids). The "fifth kingdom," left somewhat obscure in the dream (2:44), is clarified in the vision as the rule of the saints of the Most High (7:18, 21, 27). The dire threats to Daniel and his companions in the lion's den (chap. 6) and in the fiery furnace (chap. 3), from which they are miraculously saved, adumbrate the murder of the saints in the visions, which are not prevented by miracles but which will be abrogated by the great final miracle: their bodily resurrection at the appointed end time (12:1–3). The effect then of the association of the stories and the visions is to create a series of interchanges between ancient foreign rulers and faithful Jews that operate as foils and foreshadowings of the contemporary relations between the Seleucids and pious Jews which have sharpened into hostility and warfare, bringing world events swiftly toward their end.

Why Daniel should have been chosen as the recipient of this revelation of the end in 165 B.C.E. and how the "nonapocalyptic" stories could have been included in the book have been much discussed. Apparently the stories had an extensive prehistory. From Ezek. 14:14 we learn of a righteous Daniel, named alongside Noah and Job, who may be the same as the Daniel of a Canaanite myth and who may also have become the prototype of Jews in foreign service. Similar stories of Jews in foreign governmental service are told in the Joseph narrative (Genesis 37—50) and in the Book of Esther. Babylon as the archetypal world power that threw Judah into a form of permanent exile may have come to stand *negatively* for political oppression at large and *positively* for cultural opportunity open to those Jews wise enough to avail themselves of the new vocational possibilities of the Dispersion.

Some scholars trace the core of the Daniel stories back to Babylonian or Persian times. The single human image with its four "kingdom parts" once referred to members of a single dynasty within one kingdom. Some have argued that the specifics of this image are much more appropriate to the Ptolemaic dynasty in Egypt in the third century than they are to the Babylonian dynasty of the sixth century.[46] It is possible that a cryptic message once dealing with Ptolemaic rule has been reworked to fit with a decision to cast the book as the revelations of Daniel under Babylonian rule concerning the four successive world empires. If the actual referents of the stories, however, were the Egyptian Ptolemies, the association of the Ptolemaic stories and the Seleucid visions would be understandable as the work of an apocalyptic community that wished to emphasize the gathering storm under the successors of Alexander.

The visions of the end are four in number (7; 8; 9; 10:1—12:4), although technically the third is more accurately a spoken revelation concerning a prophecy of Jeremiah. The *vision of the four beasts* (chap. 7) giving way to the kingdom of the saints (persecuted faithful Jews) also pictures God as the Ancient of Days = Source of Time and equates the saints with "one like a son of man" who descends from the heavens. The precise force of this equation is far from clear. It may be a collective individualization of the community of saints as "human" in its bearing, as against the beastly kingdoms headed by kings who are "animalistic." It may also be that "one like a son of man" is an angelic messenger who serves as the guardian or titular head of the community of saints. The *Similitudes of Enoch* (*1 Enoch* 37—71), written perhaps more than a century later, pictures Enoch, who

46. John G. Gammie, "The Classification, Stages of Growth, and Changing Intentions in the Book of Daniel," *JBL* 95 (1976): 191–204.

had been taken directly to heaven without dying (Gen. 5:24), as one who will return at the end time as "son of man" to establish God's rule on earth. Whether this is at all the sense of Daniel 7 is questionable, since no name is given to the cryptic Danielic "son of man."

The *vision of the ram and he-goat* (chap. 8) focuses on Alexander and his successors, particularly "the little horn" Antiochus Epiphanes, and looks toward the imminent reconsecration of the profaned Jerusalem temple. The angelic interpreter of this vision is called Gabriel. In chap. 9, Daniel's query about Jeremiah's prophecy of seventy years of exile is reinterpreted by Gabriel as *seventy weeks of years* (= 490 years), thereby opening up the several century time span between the exile and the Maccabean War. The reinterpretation, which refers to the murder of the high priest Onias III in 170 (9:26a), is interrupted by a long confessional prayer of Daniel.

In the final vision, more disparate than the others, an unnamed messenger encourages Daniel by informing him that the earthly battles between nations and with the faithful are accompanied—and ultimately determined—by *battles between heavenly beings* ("prince of the kingdom of Persia," 10:13; and "Michael, your [Israel's] prince," 10:21; cf. 10:13; 12:1). The relations of the Ptolemies and Seleucids—their diplomacy, wars, and intermarriages—are then recited prophetically in a somewhat clumsy and veiled manner, issuing in a bombastic account of the career of Antiochus Epiphanes down to the beginning of 165 B.C.E.

The "end" of history is described tersely and obliquely in terms of the agency of Michael who will see that "your people" (the faithful Jews) are delivered. Deliverance here includes bodily resurrection of "many" (not all), including the righteous (martyred sectarians?) and the wicked (apostate Hellenizing Jews?). This compressed scenario leaves much unanswered about "the appointed end." Since the heavenly realms are only indirectly treated in the book (Daniel does not get a tour of the heavens), it is not surprising that the site of the gathering of the surviving and resurrected saints and apostates is this earth, without any reference to cosmic transformation. Since an aspect of the book's expectation is that the temple will be reconsecrated, the author's understanding may be that the redeemed saints will enjoy a purified cult at Jerusalem, unhindered by alien political powers that have perished, and uncontaminated by wicked Jews who have also perished, or, in the case of apostates who are "alive" in resurrected form, will know only shame and contempt. Now this is certainly so radical a break with history that it can legitimately be called an "end" to countless injustices and frustrations, but it seems rather more "a heaven and hell on earth" than is foreseen by some of the more explicitly otherworldly apocalypses.

The question of what stance the apocalyptists of Daniel took toward events in their day has been inconclusively discussed.[47] It is often said that they were *pacifists*, since Judas Maccabee's contribution is called only "a little help" (11:34), and the great image is brought down by "a stone cut from a mountain with no human hand" (2:45). If they were Hasids, however, it is likely that they did join in the defensive wars against the Seleucids and took part in the political infighting among Jews. The supposed "pacifism" of the book (passivity?) may be a misimpression derived from the apocalyptic view that even the utmost that humans can do is minimal compared to the decisive act of God. Nevertheless, "the people who know their God shall stand firm and take action" (11:32).

A realistic estimate of the apocalyptic devotees as activists, probably combatants, within the limits of their situation accords with the interesting fact that they did not discard or repudiate their apocalypse when it turned out that Daniel's visions were wrong about the time of the end. Apparently, like other apocalyptists who have been studied in terms of social psychological cognitive dissonance theory, they reinterpreted events and carried on the struggle. They may, along with other Hasids, have withdrawn their support from Judas Maccabeus after religious freedom was secured. The book, which in fact does not *name* Antiochus Epiphanes as the last world oppressor, could be reread with a new hermeneutic of the prolongation of the times, as in fact early Christians and Rabbinic Jews read it. Interestingly, however, the Danielic group did *not* redact the book to explain the delay of the end, nor did anyone else so redact it. The seemingly discredited work was taken into the canon of Rabbinic Judaism untouched because it spoke so powerfully of God's rule over history amid the memorable Maccabean struggle to keep open the Jewish world space.

47. John J. Collins, *The Apocalyptic Vision of the Book of Daniel,* HSM 16 (Missoula, Mont.: Scholars Press, 1977), 191–218.

THE INTERPLAY OF TEXT, CONCEPT, AND SETTING IN THE HEBREW BIBLE

A common complaint about critical study of the Bible is that it dissects and analyzes the Bible without resynthesizing it. Can the Hebrew Bible be "put back together" as a living whole? It certainly cannot be reunified precritically by setting aside the methods of inquiry we have studied. Alternatively, are there ways to reconceive the Bible postcritically that will ensure its integrity and active contribution to the cultural, intellectual, and religious life of today? There are strong indications that the Hebrew Bible, critically understood, can and will be revisioned as a complex unity of enduring significance and relevance.

Study of the Hebrew Bible is first and foremost study of a text. The biblical text, however, is not an isolated datum pure and simple. Precisely as literature, each text in the Hebrew Bible expresses a point of view and reflects a social setting. By focusing now on the text in itself, then on its conceptual world, and again on its social placement, different methods in biblical studies have contributed valuable understandings to the interpretation of the text as a whole. As they deepen and ramify, these literary, conceptual, and social understandings, which at first glance appear discrete, press toward convergence and mutual interaction.

Text, concept, and setting display distinctive features, each with its own network of connections (text related to texts, concept to concepts, and setting to settings) and each with its own history. The history of the literary growth of the Hebrew Bible is matched by a history of the development of biblical concepts (whether seen as theology or ideology), and further paralleled by a history of biblical social contexts that include political and religious settings. A geometric growth of literary genres and compositions, of concepts and patterns of thought, and of sociopolitical structures and processes produces a cumulative "snowballing" effect through the course of biblical history.

More and more literary, conceptual, and sociopolitical options, few of which drop completely from sight, offer ever more complex ways of combining texts, concepts, and settings. We have observed that virtually all of the literary genres developed in the earlier literature reappear in the later writings. We have also noted that concepts from before, during, and after the monarchy compete or associate with one another in varying ways in the restored postexilic community. Likewise, we have seen that the social dynamics of tribalism, state rule, colonial dispersion and subordination to great powers flow one into the other, overlap in part, and create institutional settings where new literature and concepts are generated and where old literature and concepts thrive with modifications in function and meaning.

In spite of difficulties in dating many parts of the Hebrew Bible, it is now widely recognized that the literature and concepts of ancient Israel and early Judaism developed in "families" or "clusters" of genres and composite tradition complexes stamped with distinctive theological perspectives. These firmly centered groupings of texts and concepts, elaborated and intertwined over centuries and yet open to influence on one another, have been called "streams of tradition" or "trajectories."[1]

Corresponding to these literary-conceptual groupings there are sets of sociopolitical events, structures, and processes. These social groupings, treated under "sociohistoric horizons" in the foregoing chapters, generated texts and concepts and are directly or indirectly reflected in these texts and concepts. It is important to illuminate these social settings because the biblical writers were also actors in concrete social formations under particular modes of production and political regimes. This general consideration applies all the more forcefully to ancient Israel because of the explicit orientation of much of its literature and thought toward sociopolitical life sectors. By topic and stance, the literature of the Hebrew Bible is highly historical and communal in the sense that it is concerned with human life in community under concrete conditions subject to change.

The task of conceiving and fruitfully studying the correlations and interplay among texts, concepts, and sociohistoric settings is both exciting and tricky to carry out satisfactorily. Our "everyday" or "common-sense" way of thinking tends to treat these sectors separately. Scientific inquiry is also structured to look at the phenomena one sector at a time, and not many investigators have equal scientific skill in two or more sectors. Sometimes it is objected that to relate the sectors too closely "contaminates" or "confuses" the inquiry. As a plea for purism in scholarship, this is a futile complaint, but it does raise a proper caution against doing speculative interdisciplinary work without solid knowledge of the sectors under examination.

Granted that "one sector at a time" procedures will always be necessary in biblical studies, we are now at a point where regular and disciplined correlation or "interreading" of the literary, conceptual, and sociohistoric sectors is possible and urgent in order to make the fullest sense of the knowledge we already have. It is time to rethink the field of biblical studies and to restructure our approaches to the Hebrew Bible to encourage systemic study of the literary, conceptual, and sociohistoric sectors as

1. Odil H. Steck, "Theological Streams of Tradition," in *Tradition and Theology in the Old Testament,* ed. Douglas A. Knight (Philadelphia: Fortress Press, 1977), 183–214; Walter Brueggemann, "Trajectories in Old Testament Literature and the Sociology of Ancient Israel," in *BL,* 307–33.

integral elements of ancient Israelite/Jewish life. This is to recognize that these sectors are internally related in such a way that to know any one of them adequately we must also know as much as possible about the others.

We can make a start on rethinking and restructuring biblical studies by trying to identify the basic components of a unified socio-literary-theological grid of the Hebrew Bible. This requires that we consciously bring together all the major elements of each sector that we have uncovered in the preceding study. While acknowledging that our knowledge is rudimentary in certain regards, enough is known that we can sketch a grid of key components arranged along domain, sectoral, and geographical axes.

1. The *domain axis* corresponds to the historical experience of Israel that we have followed through its successive stages of socioeconomic, political, and religious organization and ideology. In this instance we are identifying the broadest determinative level of social and political organization operative in each temporal phase. The following sociopolitical "domains" or "force fields" are distinguished as of primary significance for literary and theological production:

a. The socioreligious revolution of confederated Yahweh-worshiping tribes in Canaan.
b. The sociopolitical counterrevolution of united Israel under monarchic state rule.
c. The internal division of the united monarchy into the two weaker states of Judah and Israel.
d. The destruction of both states by imperial conquest and the subjection of their populaces to deportation and colonial rule.
e. The restoration of Judah to colonial home-rule status subject to a long succession of foreign powers, broken by eighty years of Jewish independence under the Hasmonean state.

2. The *sectoral axis* links to the domain axis by assessing within each of the above sociopolitical frames how specific social contexts produced particular literary forms with their distinctive theological expressions. The "unpacking" of the internally related sectors proceeds in this way:

a. Identify and characterize the relevant sociopolitical domain (one of the five listed above).
b. Identify and characterize the specific sociopolitical sectors that generate texts and concepts. What social institutions, offices, or roles singularly or in combination produce what texts and concepts? Care must be taken to distinguish between societal sectors that originate genres and societal sectors that "recycle" genres and fuse them in larger tradition complexes.
c. Identify and characterize the genres, tradition complexes, sources, and books that constitute the literary sector. What is the repertory of single and associated literary genres? How are the genres built into larger tradition complexes that

form biblical books in part or whole? Care must be taken to distinguish how the genres function at successive stages in the growth of the literature.

d. Identify and characterize the concepts and patterns of thought that constitute the theological or ideological sector. As theology, these concepts are "talk about God," "talk to God," or "talk from God." As ideology, the religious ideas are connected to the larger sociopolitical domain which tends to be legitimated or criticized by these concepts when they are wielded by various social actors. Care must be taken to distinguish concepts closely connected with particular literary genres and tradition complexes and concepts that "float free" and "cross over" into other genres and tradition complexes as social groups interact and as traditions clash or combine to "cross-fertilize" one another.

3. A *geographical axis* is involved chiefly at two points:

a. During the divided monarchy when developments in the northern and southern kingdoms are to be distinguished;

b. During the exile when the literary, social organizational, and theological situations of Palestinian Jews and deported Jews likewise require separate considerations.

These intersecting domain, sectoral, and geographical axes, or categories of analysis, have been traced in some detail throughout the Hebrew Bible in the preceding chapters of this book. It remains here to sum them up in chart form. Two charts will be presented: one on the operative social and political organizational domains in historical succession (chart 11), and another on the literary and conceptual developments as they unfold within the framework of the sociopolitical domains (chart 12). A word is in order concerning certain graphic features of the charts.

1. The *sociopolitical organizational domain* (chart 11) condenses the history presented in this text, distinguishing the periods of Israelite *political independence* or *dependence*—the periods of *tribal* or *state dominance* and the *succession of foreign empires* to which Jews were subject throughout the later biblical era.

a. Slanting broken lines on either side of the chart from the united monarchy onward represent the endurance of tribal social organization and culture in northern and southern Israel which, although diminishing overall in their vitality and scope, continued to shape the thought and practice of Israelites and Jews both politically and religiously throughout the biblical era. The lines are broken to emphasize that state and tribal spheres interpenetrated, often involving the same people in different roles or functions and the same or related institutions in cooperation or conflict (e.g., tribal draftees in a state army professionally staffed).

b. Arrows drawn on the chart mark the direction of political dominance. In the periods of Israelite political independence, the arrows thrust *outward* to sym-

CHART 11
Sociopolitical Organizational Domains in Biblical Israel

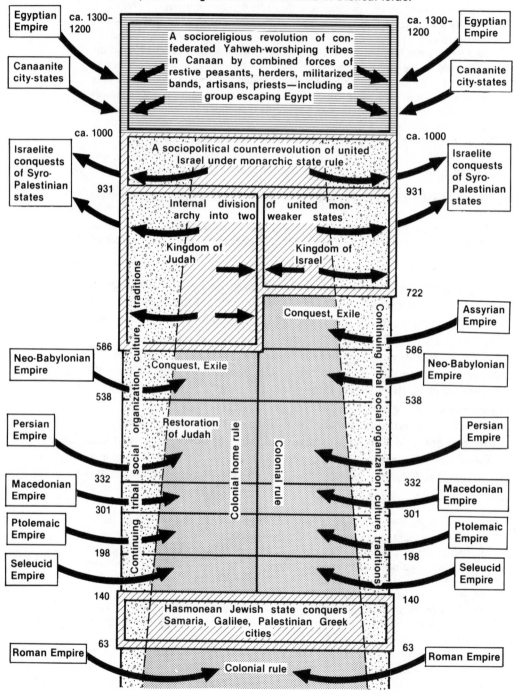

Egyptian Empire — ca. 1300–1200

Canaanite city-states

A socioreligious revolution of confederated Yahweh-worshiping tribes in Canaan by combined forces of restive peasants, herders, militarized bands, artisans, priests—including a group escaping Egypt

Egyptian Empire — ca. 1300–1200

Canaanite city-states

ca. 1000

A sociopolitical counterrevolution of united Israel under monarchic state rule

Israelite conquests of Syro-Palestinian states

931

Internal division of united monarchy into two weaker states

Israelite conquests of Syro-Palestinian states

931

Kingdom of Judah

Kingdom of Israel

722

Conquest, Exile

Assyrian Empire

586

Neo-Babylonian Empire

Conquest, Exile

586

Neo-Babylonian Empire

538

538

Persian Empire

Restoration of Judah

Persian Empire

Colonial home rule

Colonial rule

332

Macedonian Empire

332

Macedonian Empire

301

Ptolemaic Empire

301

Ptolemaic Empire

198

Seleucid Empire

198

Seleucid Empire

Continuing tribal social organization, culture, traditions

Continuing tribal social organization, culture, traditions

140

Hasmonean Jewish state conquers Samaria, Galilee, Palestinian Greek cities

140

63

Roman Empire

Colonial rule

63

Roman Empire

bolize the boundary maintenance asserted by sovereign tribes or sovereign states. In the case of the monarchy, the arrows extend *beyond* Israel to denote the foreign conquests undertaken by Israelite rulers. In the periods of Israelite political dependence from the exile onward, the arrows thrust *into* Israel *from without* to symbolize that Israel has been "boundary breached" and thus subjected to the colonial rule of empires. Except for the premonarchic era when Israel was intertribally sovereign, these arrows are drawn so as to "pass over" the level of tribal organization because they represent the claims and acts of sovereign states to whom "tribalism" is strictly a cultural or internal administrative matter.

2. The chart of *socio-literary-theological sectors* (chart 12) is much more complex than the chart of sociopolitical organizational domains because it is both multidimensional and intersectoral. In it I attempt to show the *integral relations* between the literary and theological sectors of the Hebrew Bible and the immediate social sites that generated them as they were overarched by the determinative domains of general social and political organization.

    a. The "clusters," "families," "streams of traditions," or "trajectories" of the literary sector, together with their respective social and theological sectors, are placed in more or less synchronized chronological order within vertical parallel columns.

    b. Broken lines and arrows indicate three forms of "movement" within and between the tradition sectors: (1) appropriation of north Israelite lines of tradition by Judahite circles after the fall of Israel in 722 B.C.E.; (2) introduction of tradition elements from the exile into the restored Judahite community; and (3) "lateral" appropriation of literary materials from one socio-literary-theological complex by another (e.g., when the royalist J epic takes over and elaborates tribal traditions).

    c. It appears that the originative tribal social revolution of Israel spawned a considerable unity and harmony of traditions that was fractured by the subsequent impact of monarchic and imperial-colonial structures and processes. Inset boxes on the chart contain information on two later sociohistoric "moments" when several socio-literary-theological sectors converged to support major restructuring of the total communal life that attempted to recover the unity and harmony of the originative era: the Deuteronomic Reformation and the Restoration of the Judahite community following exile. Each of these catalytic moments, particularly the postexilic restoration around temple and Law, contributed enduring features to ongoing Jewish life. Nonetheless, these stabilizing reforms did not simplify or homogenize the literary traditions nor did they put an end to social and intellectual struggle because *who* was to hold power in the community and *how* the texts were to be interpreted remained disputed points throughout biblical times.

This initial attempt to show the coexistence and correlation of traditions

CHART 12

Socio-Literary-Theological Sectors Within the Frame of Sociopolitical Organizational Domains

1250–1000 B.C.E.

General sociopolitical domain

1250–1000 B.C.E. — A socioreligious revolution of confederated Yahweh-worshiping tribes in Canaan

SOCIOLOGICAL

Tribal assemblies/festivals: covenant inclusions of new groups/covenant renewals	Village/tribal courts of justice
	Family/village/tribal formal and informal instructional activities

LITERARY

Narratives of deliverance	Case laws
Theophanies	
Covenants = treaties	
Categorical laws	
Songs of deliverance	Wisdom sayings and admonitions

THEOLOGICAL

Yahweh as Deliverer from political oppression and want, Founder and Guarantor of Israel's communal order = tribes of Yahweh	Yahweh as Sanctioner of concrete breaches of communal order
Yahweh as Covenant Maker/Keeper	God of justice and righteousness
	Yahweh as Giver and Backer of a "rational," humanly supportive, natural-cultural social-ethicoreligious world order

1000–930 B.C.E.

General sociopolitical domain

1000–930 B.C.E. — A sociopolitical counterrevolution of united Israel under monarchic state rule

SOCIOLOGICAL

Continuing tribal cult, courts of justice, teaching functions	Jerusalem royal "historian-scribes"	Jerusalem royal "wisdom-scribes"	Jerusalem royal cult

LITERARY SECTOR

Narratives
Theophanies
Songs

Wisdom sayings
Admonitions

Songs

J Epic (major use of tribal cult traditions)

Apology of David (1 Samuel 16—2 Samuel 5)

Court History of David (2 Samuel 9—1 Kings 2)

Artistic wisdom sayings, admonitions, instructions, hymns (limited use of tribal instructional traditions)

Songs:
Laments
Hymns
Thanksgiving songs
Songs of Zion (limited use of tribal songs)

Priestly laws (?)

THEOLOGICAL SECTOR

Continuing tribal theological conceptions

Yahweh as Creator and guiding Lord of Israel—at first as tribes, now as preeminent monarchic state

God as Creator

Wisdom as norm of personal and social ethics

Professional ethics of royal bureaucracy

Yahweh as Creator with Jerusalem as center of world order, secure under Davidic dynasty

General socio-political domain

Internal division of the united monarchy

930–586 B.C.E.

General socio-political domain

930–586 B.C.E.

State of Judah

State of Israel

SOCIAL SECTOR

Continuing southern tribal cult, courts of justice, teaching

Continuing Jerusalem royal "historian-scribes"

Continuing Jerusalem royal "wisdom-scribes"

Continuing Jerusalem royal cult

Continuing northern tribal cult, courts of justice, teaching

Proto-Deuteronomic preaching, teaching of covenant laws

Northern prophetic circles

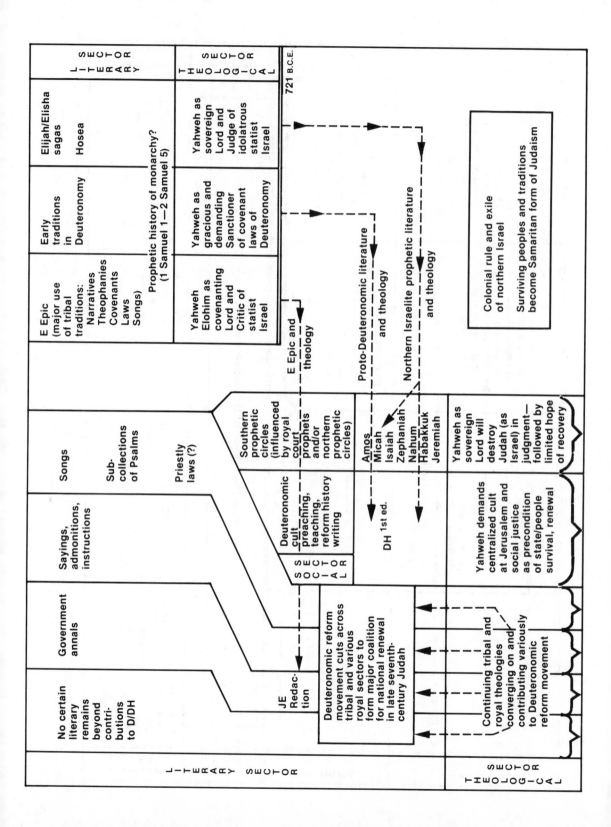

Destruction of Judah: subjection to colonial rule and exile

General socio-political domain	Colonial rule in Judah			Exile, Dispersion in Babylonia, Persia, Egypt, etc.		
	Surviving Jerusalem cult on temple ruins	Deuteronomistic circles	Prophetic circles	Prophetic circles	Priestly circles (probably beginning in seventh-century Judah)	Wisdom circles
SOCIAL	(Surviving elements of tribal social organization in rural Judah)			(Tradition circles in exilic communities with surviving elements of tribal social organization renewed selectively for organizing internal communal affairs)		
LITERARY	Lamentations Some Psalms: Laments	DH 2d ed. D edition of Jeremiah (other prophets?)	Further collections and editions by prophet disciples and sympathizers	Ezekiel Isaiah of the Exile	Holiness Code Early edition of P (?)	Sayings, admonitions, instructions
THEOLOGICAL	Hope in Yahweh as righteous Lord of judgment who will eventually be merciful	Yahweh has brought nation to deserved end but there is modest hope for repentant survivors	A future Jewish king appears in some versions of the new age	Yahweh, the righteous but gracious Judge of Israel, will restore Judah and Jerusalem	Yahweh's demands for moral/ritual purity met by scrupulous observance of P laws	Yahweh's goodness as Creator and Governor of life thrown into question by excessive suffering and despair

586–538 B.C.E.

Restoration of Judah: colonial home rule subject to imperial dominion

| | General socio-political domain | 538–63 B.C.E. | | | | 538–63 B.C.E. | General socio-political domain |

Top row labels: General socio-political domain | 538–63 B.C.E. | (title) | 538–63 B.C.E. | General socio-political domain

	Restored temple cult, scribes of Law of Moses, Aaronic priests	Deuteronomistic circles (Levites)	Prophetic circles	Wisdom circles	Prophetic writings: Ezekiel, Deutero-Isaiah
SOCIAL HISTORY	P writing — JEP Redaction — Chronicles, Ezra-Neh — Songs: redaction of Psalms	Deut joined to JEP (Law of Moses) — Josh-Kings (DH²) = "Former Prophets"	Haggai, Zech 1—8, Isa 56—66, Malachi, Joel, Isa 24—27, Zech 9—14, plus earlier prophetic writings = "Latter Prophets"	Proverbs, Job, Ecclesiastes, Ben Sira	Proto-P writings / Wisdom writings
THEOLOGY	Yahweh approves restored cult and promises life to his people as they keep Mosaic Law. Zion-David traditions applied to colonial Jerusalem in "realized eschatology"	Failed history of preexilic Israel/Judah is dire warning to keep Yahweh's Law with a cautious and critical eye on "cultic triumphalism"	Yahweh accepts or rejects cult and community leaders/policies (varying from prophet to prophet). Heightened hope in eschatological judgment/salvation	Critique of complacent moralistic wisdom. Yahweh, Creator and Governor, is beyond all human knowledge. Wisdom = Law	

Central box: Restoration of community and cult based on temple and Law, headed by returned exiles, supported by coalitions of Palestinian socioreligious groups—but with reservations and ongoing criticisms and conflicts only partly moderated by reforms of Ezra-Neh

Upper box: Exilic literary traditions and theologies brought to Palestine by repatriated exiles

Right box: Majority of Jews abroad remain in Dispersion by choice and develop communities that look to restored Palestinian center for religious direction

After 250 B.C.E.

SOCIAL HISTORY	**LITERARY**	**THEOLOGY**
Apocalyptic circles prompted by extreme sociopolitical/religious crisis (influence from prophetic, wisdom, priestly, extra-Jewish sources)	Daniel, *1 Enoch, *Testament of Moses (* in part)	End of human kingdoms in earthly or cosmic rule of God

and theologies in their social contexts over time is limited to components discussed in the body of this text and further limited by the intent to avoid "visual overload" on the chart. It should serve, however, to encourage students and scholars in the habits and skills of "interreading" texts, theologies, and social settings.

A final word is appropriate about how the socio-literary pluriformity of the Hebrew Bible compels Jews and Christians to rethink all forms of confession of faith and of reflective theology that base themselves on these writings as scripture.[2]

It is abundantly clear that the Hebrew Bible, far from presenting a body of fixed religious ideas or doctrines, gives us theological reflections embedded in historically changing social situations and articulated in concrete literary genres and genre complexes. The theology of the Hebrew Bible is thus both "theology of social struggle" and "theology of literary imagination."[3] There is no "message" of the Hebrew Bible that can be lifted out of its social contexts and literary forms without irreparable loss both of its original meaning and of its potency to speak meaningfully to us.

Likewise it is evident that the theological expressions of the Hebrew Bible do not speak into a present vacuum of "pure faith." We Jews and Christians experience God in our own historically evolving social situations through concrete forms of speech and imaging which are not simply repetitions of biblical speech but are the complex product of postbiblical religious and secular culture as these realities are presently embodied in ourselves. In employing the Hebrew Bible as a *mediator* of religious faith and theological reflection, we must at one and the same time interpret both the social situations and the literary idioms of the *biblical texts* and the social situations and literary idioms of *ourselves as interpreters/actors*. This is the multidimensioned interpretative task now widely called either the hermeneutical "fusion of horizons" (the horizon of the text *and* the horizon of the interpreter)[4] or "the hermeneutical circle" (or the process of "hermeneutical circulation"),[5] perhaps even better described as "the hermeneutical spiral" in that each phase of the hermeneutical movement brings a refinement, advance, or clarification of understanding. As Jews and Christians, when we exegete the Bible we are also exegeting ourselves in our own socio-literary worlds.

2. Norman K. Gottwald, "The Theological Task After *The Tribes of Yahweh*," in *BL*, 190–200.

3. John Dominic Crossan, "Waking the Bible. Biblical Hermeneutic and Literary Imagination," *Int* 32 (1978): 281–83.

4. Hans-Georg Gadamer, *Truth and Method* (New York: Seabury Press, 1975), esp. 258, 333–41.

5. Juan Luis Segundo, *The Liberation of Theology* (Maryknoll, N.Y.: Orbis Books, 1976), where the term is treated throughout (see p. 8 for definition).

Certain strands of Jewish and Christian "orthodoxy" try to circumvent the radical sociohistoric process of contemporary believing. They attempt "to protect" God and the Bible by raising them above and beyond qualification by historical circumstances or reduction to the psychosocial sphere of writers and readers. This defensive ploy fails, even when adopted by oppressed peoples who have good reason to seek a fixed point of reference amidst their historic experience of injustice and dehumanization. It fails because it disembowels the Hebrew Bible of its socio-literary specificity and lobotomizes its religious bite and thrust. This "spiritualizing" and "abstracting" theology is in itself the most severe and destructive form of "reductionism," for it flattens and denatures the powerful individualities of style and content that play throughout the rich texture of the Hebrew Bible. The lively biblical voices that speak concretely of, for, and to God become a boring and pretentious monotone as out of place in the biblical milieu as in our own.

Every method of knowing involves a reduction of what is studied to regularities in phenomena and to abstractions about relationships among the phenomena. Historical criticism reduces *events*. Literary criticism reduces *texts*. Sociological criticism reduces *societal structures and processes*. Theological criticism reduces *religious beliefs and practices*. Accordingly, the Hebrew Bible may be looked at entirely as historical, entirely as literary, entirely as social, entirely as theological, but in such a way that none of these ways of looking is able to exclude the others. Thus, an adequate theology will take into account that it has no monopoly on the Bible and that, in fact, it has in itself no capacity to reflect faithfully and intelligibly on the Bible without the assistance of historical, literary, and social scientific methods of biblical inquiry.

The mandate of theology is continually to reexamine its status and ground in relation both to faith and to all the data it alleges to explain. Theology is an inevitable trafficker in reductionist currencies, since it must take into account whatever is plausibly validated by other ways of knowing. It wrongly "reduces" only when it ignores relevant results from other disciplines or when it seeks to establish historical, literary, or societal truths at its own dictate. This is of supreme import when theology is referring to data which form part of its own prime evidence, as in the case of biblical traditions. We have seen one such significant prime datum to be the growing disclosure that ancient Israel's religion—and thus the beginning of our own as Jews and Christians—was an integral aspect of a long conflictual social history that had revolutionary origins and for which it provided a wealth of symbols and ritual practices.

Insofar as theology is an arm of synagogue and church, Jewish and Christian communities are called upon to grapple with the conflictual social origins and content of their own Bible and to ponder deeply what all this means for their placement amid contemporary social conflict and for their social mission within an arena of conflict that cannot be escaped.

A. Books and Articles
Arranged by Divisions of the Text

PART I: THE TEXT IN ITS CONTEXTS

Chapter 1: Angles of Vision on the Hebrew Bible

1. A Wealth of Methods in Biblical Studies

Avishur, Issac. "Exegesis Among Jews in the Modern Period." In *EJ* 4 (1971): cols. 899–903.

The Cambridge History of the Bible. 3 vols. New York and Cambridge: Cambridge University Press, 1963–70.

Grant, Robert M., John T. McNeill, and Samuel Terrien. "History of the Interpretation of the Bible." In *IB* 1: 106–41.

Hayes, John H., and Carl Holladay. *Biblical Exegesis.* Atlanta: John Knox Press, 1981.

Hummel, Horace D. "Bible: Bible Research and Criticism." In *EJ* 4 (1971): cols. 903–15.

Soulen, Richard N. *Handbook of Biblical Criticism.* 2d ed. Atlanta: John Knox Press, 1981.

2. The Confessional Religious Approach to the Hebrew Bible (*see also* 4)

Alonso-Schökel, Luis. *The Inspired Word. Scripture in the Light of Language and Literature.* New York: Sheed & Ward, 1965.

Payne, J. Barton. *The Theology of the Older Testament.* Grand Rapids: Wm. B. Eerdmans, 1962.

Reid, John K. S. *The Authority of Scripture: A Study of the Reformation and Post-Reformation Understanding of the Bible.* London: Methuen & Co., 1957.

Smith, Richard F. "Inspiration and Inerrancy," In *JBC* 2: 499–514.

3. The Historical-Critical Approach to the Hebrew Bible (*see also* 4; 11.1)

General

De Vries, Simon J. "Biblical Criticism, History of." In *IDB* 1: 413–18.
Grobel, Kendrick. "Biblical Criticism." In *IDB* 1: 407–13.

Historical Criticism

Hayes, John H., and J. Maxwell Miller, eds. *Israelite and Judaean History.* Philadelphia: Westminster Press, 1977. [Hereafter *IJH.*]

Miller, J. Maxwell. *The Old Testament and the Historian.* GBS. Philadelphia: Fortress Press, 1976.

Source (Older Literary) Criticism

Fretheim, Terence E. "Source Criticism, OT." In IDBSup, 838–39.

Habel, Norman C. *Literary Criticism of the Old Testament.* GBS. Philadelphia: Fortress Press, 1971.

Form Criticism

Hayes, John H. *Old Testament Form Criticism.* San Antonio: Trinity University Press, 1974. [Hereafter *OTFC.*]

Knierim, Rolf, and Gene M. Tucker, eds. The Forms of the Old Testament Literature. 24 vols. projected. Grand Rapids: Wm. B. Eerdmans, 1981–. [Hereafter FOTL.]

Koch, Klaus, *The Growth of the Biblical Tradition. The Form-Critical Method.* New York: Charles Scribner's Sons, 1971.

Tucker, Gene M. "Form Criticism, OT." In IDBSup, 342–45.

———. *Form Criticism of the Old Testament.* GBS. Philadelphia: Fortress Press, 1971.

Oral Tradition

Coote, Robert B. "Tradition, Oral, OT." In IDBSup, 914–16.

Finnegan, Ruth. *Oral Poetry. Its Nature, Significance, and Social Context.* New York and Cambridge: Cambridge University Press, 1977.

Tradition (Tradition-Historical) Criticism

Coats, George W. "Tradition Criticism, OT." In IDBSup, 912–14.

Knight, Douglas A. *Rediscovering the Traditions of Israel.* Rev. ed. SBLDS 9. Missoula, Mont.: Scholars Press, 1975.

Rast, Walter E. *Tradition History and the Old Testament.* GBS. Philadelphia: Fortress Press, 1972.

Redaction Criticism

March, W. Eugene. "Redaction Criticism and the Formation of Prophetic Books." In SBLSP 11 (1977): 87–101.

Wharton, James A. "Redaction Criticism, OT." In IDBSup, 729–32.

Willis, John T. "Redaction Criticism and Historical Reconstruction." In *Encounter with the Text,* ed. M. J. Buss, 83–89. Semeia Studies. Philadelphia: Fortress Press, 1979.

4. Interaction Between Religious and Historical-Critical Approaches to Biblical Studies

Barr, James. "Biblical Theology." In IDBSup, 104–11.

———. "Revelation in History." In IDBSup, 746–49.

Betz, Otto. "Biblical Theology, History of." In *IDB* 1: 432–37.

Brown, Raymond E. "Hermeneutics." In *JBC* 2: 605–23.

Childs, Brevard S. *Biblical Theology in Crisis.* Philadelphia: Westminster Press, 1970.

Collins, Thomas A., and Raymond E. Brown. "Church Pronouncements." In *JBC* 2: 624–32.

Hahn, Herbert H. "The Theological Approach to the Old Testament." In *The Old Testament in Modern Research.* Rev. ed., 226–49. Philadelphia: Fortress Press, 1966.

Hasel, Gerhard. *Old Testament Theology: Basic Issues in the Current Debate.* 2d ed. Grand Rapids: Wm. B. Eerdmans, 1975.

Hoffman, Thomas A. "Inspiration, Normativeness, Canonicity, and the Unique Character of Scripture." *CBQ* 44 (1982): 447–69.

Stendahl, Krister. "Biblical Theology, Contemporary." In *IDB* 1: 418–32.

Stuhlmacher, Peter. *Historical Criticism and Theological Interpretation of Scripture.* Philadelphia: Fortress Press, 1977.

5.2.a The Bible as Literature and New Literary Criticism
(*see also* **15; 20; 23; 29**)

New Literary Criticism

Frye, Northrop. *The Great Code: The Bible and Literature.* New York and London: Harcourt Brace Jovanovich, 1982.

Lentricchia, Frank. *After the New Criticism*. Chicago and London: University of Chicago Press, 1980.

Richards, Ivor A. *Principles of Literary Criticism*. London: Routledge & Kegan Paul, 1924.

Wellek, Rene, and Austin A. Warren. *Theory of Literature*. 3d ed. New York: Harcourt Brace and World, 1962.

Bible as Literature

Alter, Robert. *The Art of Biblical Narrative*. New York: Basic Books, 1981.

Auerbach, Erich. *Mimesis: The Representation of Reality in Western Literature*. Garden City, N.Y.: Doubleday & Co., 1957.

Cromack, Robert E. "Discourse, Direct and Indirect." In IDBSup, 236–37.

Licht, Jacob. *Storytelling in the Bible*. Jerusalem: Magnes Press, 1978.

Newman, Barclay M., Jr. "Discourse Structure." In IDBSup, 237–41.

Robertson, David. "Literature, The Bible as." In IDBSup, 547–51.

———. *The Old Testament and the Literary Critic*. GBS. Philadelphia: Fortress Press, 1977.

Rhetorical Criticism

Bitzer, Lloyd F., and Edwin Black, eds. *The Prospect of Rhetoric*. Englewood Cliffs, N.J.: Prentice-Hall, 1971.

Greenwood, David. "Rhetorical Criticism and Formgeschichte: Some Methodological Considerations." *JBL* 89 (1970): 418–26.

Jackson, Jared, and Martin Kessler, eds. *Rhetorical Criticism*. PTMS 1. Pittsburgh: Pickwick Press, 1974.

Muilenburg, James. "Form Criticism and Beyond." *JBL* 88 (1969): 1–18.

Trible, Phyllis. *God and the Rhetoric of Sexuality*. OBT 2. Philadelphia: Fortress Press, 1978.

Canonical Criticism (see also *11.2*)

Blenkinsopp, Joseph. *Prophecy and Canon*. Notre Dame, Ind.: Notre Dame University Press, 1977.

Brueggemann, Walter. *The Creative Word. Canon as a Model for Biblical Education*. Philadelphia: Fortress Press, 1982.

Childs, Brevard S. *Introduction to the Old Testament as Scripture*. Philadelphia: Fortress Press, 1979. [Hereafter *IOTS*.]

Sanders, James A. *Canon and Community: A Guide to Canonical Criticism*. GBS. Philadelphia: Fortress Press, 1984.

———. "Hermeneutics." In IDBSup, 402–7.

———. *Torah and Canon*. Philadelphia: Fortress Press, 1972.

Sheppard, Gerald T. "Canonization: Hearing the Voice of the Same God Through Historically Dissimilar Traditions." *Int* 37 (1982): 21–33.

5.2.b Structural Criticism (*see also* 15; 20; 23; 29)

General

Piaget, Jean. *Structuralism*. New York: Basic Books, 1970.

Scholes, Robert. *Structuralism in Literature: An Introduction.* New Haven, Conn., and London: Yale University Press, 1974.

Biblical

Detweiler, Robert. *Story, Sign, and Self.* Semeia Studies. Missoula, Mont.: Scholars Press, 1978.

Jobling, David. *The Sense of Biblical Narrative: Three Structural Analyses in the Old Testament.* JSOTSup 7. Sheffield: Department of Biblical Studies, 1978.

Johnson, Alfred M., Jr., ed. *Structuralism and Biblical Hermeneutics.* PTMS 22. Pittsburgh: Pickwick Press, 1979.

Polzin, Robert. *Biblical Structuralism.* Semeia Studies. Missoula, Mont.: Scholars Press, 1977.

_____. *Moses and the Deuteronomist,* esp. chap. 1. New York: Seabury Press, 1980.

Robertson, David. "Literature, The Bible as (4a)." In IDBSup, 549–50.

Spivey, Robert A. et al. Articles in Structuralism and Biblical Studies issue of *Int* 28 (1974): 131–200.

Taber, Charles R. "Semantics." In IDBSup, 800–807.

5.3 Social Science Methods (*see also* 16; 21; 24; 28; 30.5; 52.2; 54.2)

General

Carney, T. F. *The Shape of the Past: Models and Antiquity.* Lawrence, Kans.: Coronado Press, 1975.

Gottwald, Norman K. "Israel, Social and Economic Development of." In IDBSup, 465–68.

_____. "Sociological Method in the Study of Ancient Israel." In *Encounter with the Text,* ed. M. J. Buss, 69–81. Semeia Studies. Philadelphia: Fortress Press, 1979.

_____, ed. *The Bible and Liberation: Political and Social Hermeneutics.* Rev. ed. Maryknoll, N.Y.: Orbis Books, 1983. [Hereafter *BL.*]

Long, Burke O. "The Social World of Ancient Israel." *Int* 37 (1982): 243–55.

de Vaux, Roland. *Ancient Israel. Its Life and Institutions.* New York: McGraw-Hill, 1961.

Wilson, Robert R. *Sociological Approaches to the Old Testament.* GBS. Philadelphia: Fortress Press, 1984.

Wolff, Hans Walter. "The World of Man. Sociological Anthropology." In *Anthropology of the Old Testament,* 157–229. Philadelphia: Fortress Press, 1974.

Special Studies

Carroll, Robert P. *When Prophecy Failed: Cognitive Dissonance and the Prophetic Traditions of the Old Testament.* New York: Seabury Press, 1979.

Chaney, Marvin L. "Ancient Palestinian Peasant Movements and the Formation of Premonarchic Israel." In *Palestine in Transition: The Emergence of Ancient Israel,* ed. D. N. Freedman and D. F. Graf, 39–90. SWBAS 2. Sheffield: Almond Press, 1983.

Culley, Robert C., and Thomas W. Overholt, eds. *Anthropological Perspectives on Old Testament Prophecy. Semeia* 21 (1982).

Gottwald, Norman K. *The Tribes of Yahweh: A Sociology of the Religion of Liberated*

Israel, 1250–1050 B.C.E. Maryknoll, N.Y.: Orbis Books, 1979 (corrected 2d printing, 1981). [Hereafter *TY.*]

Hanson, Paul D. *The Dawn of Apocalyptic: The Historical and Sociological Roots of Jewish Apocalyptic Eschatology.* 2d ed. Philadelphia: Fortress Press, 1979. [Hereafter *DA.*]

Mendenhall, George E. "The Hebrew Conquest of Palestine." *BA* 25 (1962): 66–87 = *BAR* 3 (1970): 100–120.

———. *The Tenth Generation: The Origins of the Biblical Tradition.* Baltimore: Johns Hopkins University Press, 1973.

Rogerson, John. *Anthropology and the Old Testament.* Atlanta: John Knox Press, 1979.

Weber, Max. *Ancient Judaism.* Glencoe, Ill.: Free Press, 1952 (Eng. trans. of German original, 1921).

Wilson, Robert R. *Prophecy and Society in Ancient Israel.* Philadelphia: Fortress, 1980.

Zeitlin, Irving. *Ancient Judaism.* Cambridge: Polity Press, 1984.

Chapter 2: The World of the Hebrew Bible

7. Physical and Economic Geography

Atlases

Aharoni, Yohanan, and Michael Avi-Yonah. *The Macmillan Bible Atlas.* Rev. ed. New York: Macmillan Co., 1977. [Hereafter *MBA.*]

Amiran, David H. K. et al., eds. *Atlas of Israel.* 2d ed. Jerusalem: Bialik Press, 1970.

Baly, Denis, and A. D. Tushingham. *Atlas of the Biblical World.* New York: World Publishing, 1971.

Beek, Martin A. *Atlas of Mesopotamia.* New York: Thomas Nelson & Sons, 1962.

Grollenberg, L. H. *Atlas of the Bible,* ed. J. M. H. Reid and H. H. Rowley. New York: Thomas Nelson & Sons, 1956.

Kraeling, Emil G. *Rand McNally Bible Atlas.* Chicago: Rand McNally, 1956.

May, Herbert G., ed. *Oxford Bible Atlas.* 3d ed. New York and London: Oxford University Press, 1984.

Monson, J., general consultant. *Student Map Manual: Historical Geography of the Bible Lands.* Grand Rapids: Zondervan, 1979.

Negenman, Jan H. *New Atlas of the Bible,* ed. H. H. Rowley. Garden City, N.Y.: Doubleday & Co., 1969.

Wright, George E., and Floyd V. Filson, eds. *The Westminster Historical Atlas to the Bible.* Rev. ed. Philadelphia: Westminster Press, 1956.

Geography, Culture, and Daily Life

Aharoni, Yohanan. *The Land of the Bible: A Historical Geography,* ed. A. F. Rainey. Rev. ed. Philadelphia: Westminster Press, 1979. [Hereafter *LB.*]

Avi-Yonah, Michael. *The Holy Land from the Persian to the Arab Conquests (536 B.C. to A.D. 640): A Historical Geography.* Grand Rapids: Baker Book House, 1966.

Baly, Denis. *Geographical Companion to the Bible.* New York: McGraw-Hill, 1963.

———. *The Geography of the Bible.* Rev. ed. New York: Harper & Row, 1974.

Bodenheimer, F. S. *Animal and Man in Bible Lands.* Leiden: E. J. Brill, 1960.

Brice, William C. *South-West Asia: A Systematic Regional Geography.* London: University of London Press, 1966.

Cornfeld, Gaalyah, ed. *Pictorial Biblical Encyclopedia.* New York: Macmillan Co., 1964.

Corswant, W. *A Dictionary of Life in Bible Times.* London: Hodder & Stoughton, 1960.

Frank, Harry Thomas. *Discovering the Biblical World.* New York: Harper & Row, 1975.

Heaton, Eric W. *Everyday Life in Old Testament Times.* New York: Charles Scribner's Sons, 1968.

Noth, Martin. *The Old Testament World.* Philadelphia: Fortress Press, 1966.

Orni, Efraim, and Elisha Efrat. *Geography of Israel.* 3d ed. New York: American Heritage, 1971.

Pedersen, Johannes. *Israel. Its Life and Culture.* 4 vols. published in 2. London: Oxford University Press, 1926, 1940.

Pfeiffer, Charles F. *The Biblical World.* Grand Rapids: Baker Book House, 1966.

Reifenberg, A. *The Struggle Between the Desert and the Sown: Rise and Fall of Agriculture in the Levant.* Jerusalem: The Jewish Agency, 1955.

Zohari, M. *Plant Life of Palestine: Israel and Jordan.* New York: Ronald Press, 1962.

8. Archaeology: Material and Written Remains (*see also* 10.1; 27)

Aharoni, Yohanan. *The Archaeology of the Land of Israel,* ed. M. Aharoni. Philadelphia: Westminster Press, 1978. [Hereafter *ALI.*]

Albright, William F. *The Archaeology of Palestine.* Rev. ed. Baltimore: Penquin Books, 1960.

Avi-Yonah, Michael. "Archaeology." In *EJ* 3 (1971): cols. 303–31.

Avi-Yonah, Michael, and Ephraim Stern, eds. *Encyclopedia of Archaeological Excavations in the Holy Land.* 4 vols. Englewood Cliffs, N.J.: Prentice-Hall, 1975–78.

Blaiklock, Edward M., and R. K. Harrison, eds. *The New International Dictionary of Biblical Archaeology.* Grand Rapids: Zondervan, 1983.

Cornfeld, Gaalyah. *Archaeology of the Bible: Book by Book.* New York: Harper & Row, 1976.

Dever, William G. "Archaeology." In IDBSup, 44–52.

Gibson, J. C. L. "Inscriptions, Semitic." In IDBSup, 429–36.

Hestrin, Ruth, et al., eds. *Inscriptions Reveal: Documents from the Time of the Bible, the Mishnah, and the Talmud.* 2d ed. Jerusalem: Israel Museum, 1972.

Kenyon, Kathleen M. *Archaeology of the Holy Land.* 4th ed. New York: W. W. Norton, 1979.

Lance, H. Darrell. *The Old Testament and the Archaeologist.* GBS. Philadelphia: Fortress Press, 1981.

McCullough, W. S. "Inscriptions." In *IDB* 2: 706–13.

Schoville, Keith N. *Biblical Archaeology in Focus.* Grand Rapids: Baker Book House, 1978.

Thomas, D. Winton, ed. *Archaeology and Old Testament Study.* New York and London: Oxford University Press, 1967.

Van Beek, G. W. "Archaeology." In *IDB* 1: 195–207.

Wright, George E. *Biblical Archaeology.* 2d ed. Philadelphia: Westminster Press, 1962.

9. Political, Cultural, and Social History of the Ancient Near East

Braidwood, Robert J. *Prehistoric Men.* 8th ed. Glenview, Ill.: Scott, Foresman, 1975.

Contenau, George. *Everyday Life in Babylonia and Assyria.* New York: St. Martin's Press, 1954.

Diakonoff, I. M., ed. *Ancient Mesopotamia: Socio-Economic History. A Collection of Studies by Soviet Scholars.* Moscow: Nauka, 1969.

Frankfort, H., and H. A. Frankfort. *Before Philosophy.* Harmondsworth: Penguin Books, 1949 = *The Intellectual Adventure of Ancient Man.* Chicago: University of Chicago Press, 1946.

Gray, John. *The Canaanites.* New York: Frederick A. Praeger, 1964.

Grosvenor, Gilbert, ed. *Everyday Life in Ancient Times,* 5–167. Washington, D.C.: National Geographic Society, 1951.

Gurney, O. R. *The Hittites.* Harmondsworth: Penguin Books, 1961.

Hallo, William W., and William K. Simpson. *The Ancient Near East.* New York: Harcourt Brace Jovanovich, 1971.

Harden, Donald B. *The Phoenicians.* New York: Frederick A. Praeger, 1962.

Jacobsen, Thorkild. *Toward the Image of Tammuz and Other Essays on Mesopotamian History and Culture,* ed. W. Moran. Cambridge: Harvard University Press, 1970.

Kees, Hermann. *Ancient Egypt: A Cultural Topography.* London: Faber & Faber, 1961.

Kramer, Samuel N. *The Sumerians: Their History, Culture, and Character.* Chicago: University of Chicago Press, 1963.

Olmstead, A. T. *History of Assyria.* Chicago: University of Chicago Press, 1923.

_____. *History of the Persian Empire.* Chicago: University of Chicago Press, 1948.

Oppenheim, A. Leo. *Ancient Mesopotamia: Portrait of a Dead Civilization.* Chicago: University of Chicago Press, 1964.

Ringgren, Helmer. *Religions of the Ancient Near East.* Philadelphia: Westminster Press, 1973.

Rostovtzeff, M. I. *Social and Economic History of the Hellenistic Period.* 3 vols. London: Oxford University Press, 1941.

Roux, Georges. *Ancient Iraq.* Harmondsworth: Penguin Books, 1964.

Sandars, Nancy K. *The Sea Peoples. Warriors of the Ancient Mediterranean.* London: Thames & Hudson, 1978.

Steindorff, George, and Kurt C. Seele. *When Egypt Ruled the East.* 2d ed. Chicago: University of Chicago Press, 1963.

Wilson, John A. *The Culture of Ancient Egypt.* 2d ed. Chicago: University of Chicago Press, 1956.

Wiseman, D. J., ed. *Peoples of Old Testament Times.* New York and London: Oxford University Press, 1973.

Chapter 3: The Literary History of the Hebrew Bible

10.1 Independent National Literatures: The Ancient Near Eastern Texts (*see also* chap. 4 n. 8)

Bermant, Chaim, and Michael Weitzman. *Ebla: A Revelation in Archaeology.* New York: The New York Times Book Co., 1979.

Beyerlin, Walter, ed. *Near Eastern Religious Texts Relating to the Old Testament.* Philadelphia: Westminster Press, 1978. [Hereafter *NERT.*]

Heidel, Alexander. *The Babylonian Genesis: The Story of Creation.* 2d ed. Chicago: University of Chicago Press, 1963.

_____. *The Gilgamesh Epic and Old Testament Parallels*. 2d ed. Chicago: University of Chicago Press, 1963.

Maloney, Paul C. "Assessing Ebla." *BARev* 41/1 (1978): 4–10.

Pritchard, James B., ed. *Ancient Near Eastern Texts Relating to the Old Testament*. 3d ed. Princeton, N.J.: Princeton University Press, 1969. [Hereafter *ANET*.]

_____, ed. *The Ancient Near East in Pictures Relating to the Old Testament*. 2d ed. Princeton, N.J.: Princeton University Press, 1969.

Thomas, D. Winton, ed. *Documents from Old Testament Times*. London: Thomas Nelson & Sons, 1958.

10.2.a Apocrypha and Pseudepigrapha

Brown, Raymond E. "Apocrypha; Dead Sea Scrolls; Other Jewish Literature." *JBC* 2: 535–60.

Charles. *APOT*.

Charlesworth, James H., ed. *The Old Testament Pseudepigrapha: Vol. I, Apocalyptic Literature and Testaments*. Garden City, N.Y.: Doubleday & Co., 1983. Vol. II forthcoming. [Hereafter *OTP*.]

_____. *The Pseudepigrapha and Modern Research*. Missoula, Mont.: Scholars Press, 1976.

Fritsch, Charles T. "Apocrypha." In *IDB* 1: 161–66.

_____. "Pseudepigrapha." In *IDB* 3: 960–64.

Metzger, Bruce M. *An Introduction to the Apocrypha*. London: Oxford University Press, 1957.

Nickelsburg, George W. E. *Jewish Literature Between the Bible and the Mishnah*. Philadelphia: Fortress Press, 1981. [Hereafter *JLBBM*.]

Pfeiffer, Robert H. *History of New Testament Times with an Introduction to the Apocrypha*. New York: Harper & Bros., 1949.

Rost, Leonhard. *Judaism Outside the Hebrew Canon. An Introduction to the Documents*. Nashville: Abingdon Press, 1976.

Stone, Michael E. "Pseudepigrapha." In IDBSup, 710–12.

10.2.b Dead Sea Scrolls

Betz, Otto. "Dead Sea Scrolls." In *IDB* 1: 790–802.

Bruce, F. F., and Jacob Licht. "Dead Sea Scrolls." In *EJ* 5 (1971): cols. 1396–1408.

Cross, Frank M. *The Ancient Library of Qumran and Modern Biblical Study*. 2d ed. Garden City, N.Y.: Doubleday & Co., 1958.

Cross, Frank M., and Shemaryahu Talmon, eds. *Qumran and the History of the Biblical Text*. Cambridge and London: Harvard University Press, 1975.

Fitzmyer, Joseph A. *The Dead Sea Scrolls. Major Publications and Tools for Study*. Missoula, Mont.: Scholars Press, 1975; with an addendum January 1977.

Gaster, Theodor. *The Dead Sea Scriptures in English Translation with Introduction and Notes*. 3d ed. Garden City, N.Y.: Doubleday & Co., 1976.

Ringgren, Helmer. *The Faith of Qumran. Theology of the Dead Sea Scrolls*. Philadelphia: Fortress Press, 1963.

Vermes, Geza. "Dead Sea Scrolls." In IDBSup, 210–19.

_____. *The Dead Sea Scrolls in English*. Rev. ed. Baltimore: Penguin Books, 1970.

10.2.c Talmud and Rabbinic Literature (*see also* below)

Berkovits, Eliezer. "Talmud, Babylonian." In *EJ* 15 (1971): cols. 755–68.

Danby, Herbert. *The Mishnah Translated from the Hebrew with Introduction and Brief Explanatory Notes.* Oxford: At the Clarendon Press, 1933.

Epstein, Isadore. "Talmud." In *IDB* 4: 511–15.

———. "Midrash," In *IDB* 3: 376–77.

———, ed. *Babylonian Talmud in English.* 36 vols. London: Soncino Press, 1935–48.

Green, William S. "Reading the Writing of Rabbinism: Toward an Interpretation of Rabbinic Literature." *JAAR* 51 (1983): 191–206.

Handelman, Susan A. *The Slayers of Moses. The Emergence of Rabbinic Interpretation in Modern Literary Theory.* Albany: State University of New York Press, 1982.

Herr, Moshe D. "Midrash." In *EJ* 11 (1971): cols. 1507–14.

Miller, Merrill P. "Midrash." In *IDBSup*, 593–97.

Moore, George Foot. *Judaism in the First Centuries of the Christian Era. The Age of the Tannaim.* 3 vols. Cambridge: Harvard University Press, 1927.

Neusner, Jacob. *Method and Meaning in Ancient Judaism.* Missoula, Mont.: Scholars Press, 1979.

———. *The Rabbinic Traditions About the Pharisees Before 70 A.D.* 3 vols. Leiden: E. J. Brill, 1971.

———, ed. *The Talmud of the Land of Israel: A Preliminary Translation and Explanation.* Vol. 34. Chicago Studies in the History of Judaism. Chicago: University of Chicago Press, 1982.

Rabinowitz, Louis I. "Talmud, Jerusalem." In *EJ* 15 (1971): cols. 772–79.

Strack, Hermann L. *Introduction to the Talmud and Midrash.* New York: Atheneum, 1969.

Urbach, Ephraim E. "Mishnah." In *EJ* 12 (1971): cols. 93–109.

Weingreen, Jacob. *From Bible to Mishna: The Continuity of Tradition.* New York: Holmes & Meier, 1976.

10.2.c New Testament and Early Christian Literature (*see also* above)

Bauer, Walter. *Orthodoxy and Heresy in Earliest Christianity,* ed. R. A. Kraft and G. Krodel. Philadelphia: Fortress Press, 1971.

Bultmann, Rudolf. *The History of the Synoptic Tradition.* New York: Harper & Row, 1963.

———. *Theology of the New Testament.* 2 vols. New York: Charles Scribner's Sons, 1951, 1955.

Cameron, Ron, ed. *The Other Gospels: Non-Canonical Gospel Texts.* Philadelphia: Westminster Press, 1982.

Conzelmann, Hans. *History of Primitive Christianity.* Nashville and New York: Abingdon Press, 1973.

Fiorenza, Elisabeth Schüssler. *In Memory of Her. A Feminist Theological Reconstruction of Christian Origins.* New York: Crossroad, 1984.

Goppelt, Leonhard. *Theology of the New Testament,* ed. J. Roloff. 2 vols. Grand Rapids: Wm. B. Eerdmans, 1981–82.

Koester, Helmut. *Introduction to the New Testament.* 2 vols. Philadelphia: Fortress Press, 1982.

Perrin, Norman, and Dennis C. Duling. *The New Testament: An Introduction. Procla-*

mation and Parenesis; Myth and History. 2d ed. New York: Harcourt Brace Jovanovich, 1982.

Sanders, E. P. *Paul and Palestinian Judaism.* Philadelphia: Fortress Press, 1977.

11.1 Formation of the Separate Literary Units

This list of critical introductions to the Hebrew Bible/Old Testament is annotated as follows:

    1 = organized principally by canonical order
    2 = organized principally by literary genre and historical development
    * = treats the books of the Apocrypha
    ** = treats the books of the Apocrypha and Pseudepigrapha

Anderson, Bernhard W. *Understanding the Old Testament.*[2] 3d ed. Englewood Cliffs, N.J.: Prentice-Hall, 1975.

Bentzen, Aage. *Introduction to the Old Testament, I[2]–II[1]***. 2 vols. bound as 1. 2d ed. Copenhagen: G. E. C. Gad, 1952.

Bewer, Julius. *The Literature of the Old Testament.*[2] Rev. by Emil G. Kraeling. 3d ed. New York: Columbia University Press, 1962.

Buck, Harry M. *People of the Lord. The History, Scriptures, and Faith of Ancient Israel.*[2] New York: Macmillan Co., 1966.

Childs, Brevard S. *IOTS.*[1]

Driver, Samuel R. *Introduction to the Literature of the Old Testament.*[1] 9th ed. Edinburgh: T. & T. Clark, 1913.

Eissfeldt, Otto. *The Old Testament: An Introduction.*[1]** New York: Harper & Row, 1965. [Hereafter *TOT.*]

Ellis, Peter F. *The Men and the Message of the Old Testament.*[2]* Collegeville, Minn.: Liturgical Press, 1963.

Fohrer, Georg (revision of Ernst Sellin). *Introduction to the Old Testament.*[1] Nashville: Abingdon Press, 1968. [Hereafter *IOT.*]

Harrelson, Walter. *Interpreting the Old Testament.*[1]* New York: Holt, Rinehart & Winston, 1964.

Harrison, R. K. *Introduction to the Old Testament.*[1]* Grand Rapids: Wm. B. Eerdmans, 1969.

Hayes, John H. *An Introduction to Old Testament Study.*[2] Nashville: Abingdon Press, 1979.

Humphreys, W. Lee. *Crisis and Story. Introduction to the Old Testament.*[2] Palo Alto, Calif.: Mayfield Publishing, 1979.

Jensen, Joseph. *God's Word to Israel.*[2]* Rev. ed. Wilmington, Del.: Michael Glazier, 1983.

Kaiser, Otto. *Introduction to the Old Testament: A Presentation of Its Results and Problems.*[1] Minneapolis: Augsburg Press, 1974.

Kuhl, Curt. *The Old Testament. Its Origin and Composition.*[1]* Richmond: John Knox Press, 1961.

Kuntz, J. Kenneth. *The People of Ancient Israel: An Introduction to Old Testament Literature, History, and Thought.*[2] New York: Harper & Row, 1974.

Larue, Gerald A. *Old Testament Life and Literature.*[2]* Boston: Allyn & Bacon, 1968.

LaSor, William S., David A. Hubbard, and Frederic W. Bush. *Old Testament Survey.*

The Message, Form, and Background of the Old Testament.[1] Grand Rapids: Wm. B. Eerdmans, 1982.

Napier, Davie. *Song of the Vineyard: A Guide Through the Old Testament.*[2] Rev. ed. Philadelphia: Fortress Press, 1981.

Pfeiffer, Robert H. *Introduction to the Old Testament.*[1] New York: Harper & Bros., 1941.

Robert, André, and André Feuillet, eds. *Introduction to the Old Testament.*[1*] New York: Desclee Co., 1968.

Rowley, H. H. *The Growth of the Old Testament.*[1] New York: Harper & Row, 1963.

Sandmel, Samuel. *The Hebrew Scriptures: An Introduction to their Literature and Religious Ideas.*[2] New York: Alfred A. Knopf, 1963.

Soggin, J. Alberto. *Introduction to the Old Testament from Its Origins to the Closing of the Alexandrian Canon.*[1*] Philadelphia: Westminster Press, 1976.

Thompson, Leonard L. *Introducing Biblical Literature: A More Fantastic Country.*[2] Parts I–III on Hebrew Bible. Englewood Cliffs, N.J.: Prentice-Hall, 1978.

Weiser, Artur. *The Old Testament: Its Formation and Development.*[1**] New York: Association Press, 1961.

West, James K. *Introduction to the Old Testament. "Hear, O Israel."*[2*] New York: Macmillan Co., 1971.

Wolff, Hans Walter. *The Old Testament. A Guide to Its Writings.*[2] Philadelphia: Fortress Press, 1973.

Young, Edward J. *An Introduction to the Old Testament.*[1] Rev. ed. Grand Rapids: Wm. B. Eerdmans, 1958.

11.2 Authoritative Collections and Canonical Closure
(*see also* 5.2.a: Canonical Criticism)

Blenkinsopp, Joseph. *Prophecy and Canon.* Notre Dame, Ind.: University of Notre Dame Press, 1977.

Childs, Brevard S. *IOTS.* Part I.

Coats, George W., and Burke O. Long, eds. *Canon and Authority. Essays in Old Testament Religion and Theology.* Philadelphia: Fortress Press, 1977.

Cohen, Shaye J. D. "Yavneh Revisited: Pharisees, Rabbis and the End of Jewish Sectarianism." SBLSP 21 (1982): 45–61.

Freedman, David N. "Canon of the Old Testament." In IDBSup, 130–36.

Jeffery, Arthur. "The Canon of the Old Testament." In *IB* 1: 32–45.

Leiman, Sid Z. *The Canonization of the Hebrew Scripture: The Talmudic and Midrashic Evidence.* Hamden, Conn.: Archon Books, 1976.

———, ed. *The Canon and Masorah of the Hebrew Bible.* New York: Ktav Publishing, 1974.

Murphy, Roland E., A. C. Sundberg, and S. Sandmel. "A Symposium on the Canon of Scripture." *CBQ* 28 (1966): 189–207.

Ostborn, Gunnar. *Cult and Canon: A Study in the Canonization of the Old Testament.* Uppsala: Lundeqvist, 1950.

Pfeiffer, Robert H. "Canon of the Old Testament." In *IDB* 1: 498–520.

Sanders, James A. *Torah and Canon.* Philadelphia: Fortress Press, 1972.

Sarna, Nahum M. "Bible: Canon." In *EJ* 4 (1971): cols. 816–32.

———. "The Order of the Books." In *Studies in Jewish Bibliography, History and*

Literature in Honor of I. Edward Kiev, ed. C. Berlin, 407–13. New York: Ktav Publishing, 1971.

Sundberg, Albert C., Jr. *The Old Testament of the Early Church.* HTS 20. Cambridge: Harvard University Press, 1964.

Turro, James C., and Raymond E. Brown. "Canonicity." In *JBC* 2: 515–34.

11.3 Preservation and Transmission of the Hebrew Bible

Ap-Thomas, D. R. *A Primer of Old Testament Text Criticism.* 2d ed. Oxford: Basil Blackwell & Mott, 1964.

Driver, Godfrey R. *Semitic Writing from Pictograph to Alphabet.* 3d ed. London: Oxford University Press, 1976.

Klein, Ralph W. *Textual Criticism of the Old Testament.* Philadelphia: Fortress Press, 1974.

Roberts, J. Bleddyn. *The Old Testament Text and Versions.* Cardiff: University of Wales Press, 1951.

———. "Text, OT." In *IDB* 4: 580–94.

Sarna, Nahum M. "Bible: Text." In *EJ* 4 (1971): cols. 832–36.

Thompson, J. A. "Textual Criticism, OT." In IDBSup, 886–91.

Würthwein, Ernst. *The Text of the Old Testament.* 4th ed. Grand Rapids: Wm. B. Eerdmans, 1979.

Yeivin, Israel. *Introduction to the Tiberian Masorah,* ed. E. J. Revell. Missoula, Mont.: Scholars Press, 1980.

12.1 Ancient Versions

Brock, S. P. "The Phenomena of the LXX." *OTS* 17 (1972): 11–36.

Gribomont, J. "Latin Versions." In IDBSup, 527–32.

Jellicoe, Sidney. *The Septuagint and Modern Study.* New York and Oxford: Oxford University Press, 1968.

Le Déaut, R. "The Current State of Targumic Studies." *BTB* 4 (1974): 3–32.

McNamara, M. "Targums." In IDBSup, 856–61.

Metzger, Bruce. "Versions, Ancient." In *IDB* 4: 749–60.

O'Connell, Kevin G. "Greek Versions (Minor)." In IDBSup, 377–81.

Skehan, Patrick W. "Texts and Versions." In *JBC* 2: 569–80.

Swete, Henry B. *An Introduction to the Old Testament in Greek.* Cambridge: At the University Press, 1914.

Tov, Emanuel, and Robert A. Kraft. "Septuagint," In IDBSup, 807–15.

Vööbus, A. "Syriac Versions." In IDBSup, 848–54.

Wevers, John W. "Septuagint." *IDB* 4: 273–78.

12.2 English Versions and Translations

Bailey, Lloyd R. *The Word of God: A Guide to English Versions of the Bible.* Atlanta: John Knox Press, 1982.

Branton, J. R. "Versions, English." In *IDB* 4: 760–71.

Bratcher, Robert G. "One Bible in Many Translations." *Int* 32 (1978): 115–29.

Brown, Raymond E. "Texts and Versions." In *JBC* 2: 586–89.

Bruce, F. F. *History of the Bible in English: From the Earliest Versions.* 3d ed. New York and London: Oxford University Press, 1978.

Crim, Keith R. "Old Testament Translations and Interpretations." *Int* 32 (1978): 144–57.

———. "Versions, English." In IDBSup, 933–38.

Kubo, Sakae, and Walter Specht. *So Many Versions? Twentieth Century English Versions of the Bible.* Grand Rapids: Zondervan, 1983.

MacGregor, Geddes. *A Literary History of the Bible from the Middle Ages to the Present Day.* Nashville and New York: Abingdon Press, 1968.

Taber, Charles R. "Translation as Interpretation." *Int* 32 (1978): 130–43.

PART II: INTERTRIBAL CONFEDERACY: ISRAEL'S REVOLUTIONARY BEGINNINGS

Prologue: On the Sources for Israel's Premonarchic History

Bright, John. *Early Israel in Recent History Writing. A Study in Method.* SBT, 1st ser., 19. London: SCM Press, 1956.

Brueggemann, Walter, and Hans Walter Wolff. *The Vitality of Old Testament Traditions.* 2d ed. Atlanta: John Knox Press, 1982.

Clements, Roland E. "Pentateuchal Problems." In *TI,* 96–124.

Freedman, David N. "Pentateuch." In *IDB* 3: 711–27. *See also* Freedman, "Documents." In *IDB* 1: 860–61.

Gottwald, Norman K. *TY.* Parts II–IV.

Knight, Douglas A. *Rediscovering the Traditions of Israel.* SBLDS 9. Missoula, Mont.: Scholars Press, 1975.

North, C. R. "Pentateuchal Criticism." In *OTMS,* 48–83.

Noth, Martin. *The Deuteronomistic History.* JSOTSup 15. Sheffield: JSOT Press, 1981. [Hereafter *TDH.*]

———. *A History of Pentateuchal Traditions,* with introduction by Bernhard W. Anderson. Englewood Cliffs, N.J.: Prentice-Hall, 1972. [Hereafter *HPT.*]

Porter, J. R. "Old Testament Historiography." In *TI,* 125–62.

von Rad, Gerhard. *The Problem of the Hexateuch and Other Essays,* 1–78. Edinburgh and London: Oliver & Boyd, 1966.

Snaith, N. H. "The Historical Books." In *OTMS,* 84–114.

Tigay, Jeffery. "An Empirical Basis for the Documentary Hypothesis." *JBL* 94 (1975): 329–42.

de Vaux, Roland. *The Early History of Israel.* Philadelphia: Westminster Press, 1978. [Hereafter *EHI.*]

Weinfeld, Moshe, and Louis I. Rabinowitz. "Pentateuch." In *EJ* 13 (1971): cols. 231–64.

Chapter 4: Traditions About the Fathers and Mothers of Israel

15. The Shape of the Traditions in Genesis 12—50
(*see also* **Part II, Prol.; 31.1; 34.1; 49**)

Alter, Robert. "Biblical Type-Scenes and the Uses of Convention." In *The Art of Biblical Narrative,* 47–62. New York: Basic Books, 1981.

_____. "Characterization and the Art of Reticence." In *The Art of Biblical Narrative,* 114–30.

Coats, George W. "Abraham's Sacrifice of Faith: A Form-Critical Study of Genesis 22." *Int* 27 (1973): 389–400.

_____. *From Canaan to Egypt. Structural and Theological Context for the Joseph Story.* CBQMS 4. Washington, D.C.: Catholic Biblical Association of America, 1976.

_____. *Genesis, with an Introduction to Narrative.* FOTL, vol. 1. Grand Rapids: Wm. B. Eerdmans, 1983.

Cross, Frank M. *Canaanite Myth and Hebrew Epic. Essays in the History of the Religion of Israel,* 1–75. Cambridge: Harvard University Press, 1973. [Hereafter *CMHE.*]

Ellis, Peter F. *The Yahwist: The Bible's First Theologian,* 87–111. Notre Dame, Ind.: Fides, 1968. [Hereafter *YBFT.*]

Fishbane, Michael. "Composition and Structure in the Jacob Cycle (Gen. 25:19—35:22)." *JJS* 26 (1975): 15–38.

Fokkelman, J. P. *Narrative Art in Genesis. Specimens of Stylistic and Structural Analysis.* Assen and Amsterdam: Van Gorcum, 1975.

Gunkel, Hermann. *The Legends of Genesis.* New York: Schocken Books, 1964.

Humphreys, W. Lee. "Joseph Story, The." In IDBSup, 491–93.

McEvenue, Sean E. "A Comparison of Styles in the Hagar Stories." *Semeia* 3 (1975): 64–80.

_____. *The Narrative Style of the Priestly Writer.* AnBib 50. Rome: Biblical Institute Press, 1971.

McKane, William. *Studies in the Patriarchal Narratives.* Edinburgh: The Handsel Press, 1979.

Polzin, Robert. "'The Ancestress in Danger' in Danger." *Semeia* 3 (1975): 81–98.

Roth, W. "The Wooing of Rebekah: A Tradition-Critical Study of Genesis 24." *CBQ* 34 (1972): 177–87.

Sarna, Nahum M. "Genesis, Book of." In *EJ* 7 (1971): cols. 386–98.

Van Seters, John. "Patriarchs." In IDBSup, 645–48.

Westermann, Claus. *The Promises to the Fathers: Studies on the Patriarchal Narratives.* Philadelphia: Fortress Press, 1980.

_____. "Promises to the Patriarchs." In IDBSup, 690–93.

Westermann, Claus, and Rainer Albertz. "Genesis." In IDBSup, 356–61.

Whybray, R. N. "The Joseph Story and Pentateuchal Criticism." *VT* 18 (1968): 522–28.

Wilcoxen, Jay A. "Narrative." In *OTFC,* 57–98.

Williams, James G. "The Beautiful and the Barren: Conventions in Biblical Type-Scenes." *JSOT* 17 (1980): 107–19.

16. Sociohistoric Horizons of the Ancestor Traditions

General

Archaeology and Geography

Aharoni. *ALI,* 9–112.

_____. *LB,* 133–81.

Dever, William G. "The Patriarchal Traditions, 1: Palestine in the Second Millennium BCE: The Archaeological Picture." In *IJH,* 70–120.

History and Society

Bright. *HI,* 45–103.

Clark, W. Malcolm. "The Patriarchal Traditions, 2: The Biblical Traditions." In *IJH,* 120–48.

Herrmann, Siegfried. *A History of Israel in Old Testament Times.* Rev. ed. Philadelphia: Fortress Press, 1981. [Hereafter *HIOTT.*]

Noth, Martin. *The History of Israel.* Rev. ed., 121–27. New York: Harper & Brothers, 1960. [Hereafter *THI.*]

Religion

Fohrer, Georg. *History of Israelite Religion.* Nashville: Abingdon Press, 1972. [Hereafter *HIR.*]

Ringgren, Helmer. *Israelite Religion.* Philadelphia: Fortress Press, 1966. [Hereafter *IR.*]

Vriezen, Theodorus C. *The Religion of Ancient Israel.* Philadelphia: Westminster Press, 1963. [Hereafter *RAI.*]

Special Studies

Alt, Albrecht. "The God of the Fathers." In *EOTHR,* 1–100.

Clements, Ronald. *Abraham and David. Genesis 15 and Its Meaning for Israelite Tradition.* SBT, 2d ser., 5. London: SCM Press, 1967.

Eichler, Barry L. "Nuzi." In IDBSup, 635–36.

Gordon, Cyrus H. "Biblical Customs and the Nuzu Tablets." *BA* 3 (1940): 1–12.

Haran, Menahem. "The Religion of the Patriarchs." *ASTI* 4 (1965): 30–55.

Holt, John M. *The Patriarchs of Israel.* Nashville: Vanderbilt University Press, 1964.

Mazar, Benjamin. "The Historical Background of the Book of Genesis." *JNES* 28 (1969): 73–83.

Redford, D. B. *A Study of the Biblical Story of Joseph (Genesis 37–50).* VTSup 20 (1970).

Speiser, E. A. "Nuzi." In *IDB* 3: 573–74.

Thompson, Thomas L. *The Historicity of the Patriarchal Narratives. The Quest for the Historical Abraham.* BZAW 133. Berlin: Walter de Gruyter, 1974.

Tucker, Gene M. "The Legal Background of Genesis 23." *JBL* 85 (1966): 77–84.

Van Seters, John. *Abraham in History and Tradition.* New Haven, Conn., and London: Yale University Press, 1975.

de Vaux. *EHI,* 161–287.

Vawter, Bruce. "The Canaanite Background of Genesis 49." *CBQ* 17 (1955): 1–18.

Chapter 5: Traditions About Moses: Exodus, Covenant, and Lawgiving

17. The Shape of the Traditions in Exodus, Leviticus, and Numbers (*see also* Part II, Prol.; 13; 14)

The Biblical Books

Exodus

Clements, R. E. "Exodus, Book of." In IDBSup, 310–12.

Greenberg, Moshe. "Exodus, Book of." In *EJ* 6 (1971): cols. 1050–67.

Wright, G. E. "Exodus, Book of." In *IDB* 2: 188–97.

Leviticus

Davies, G. Henton. "Leviticus." In *IDB* 3: 117–22.
Milgrom, Jacob. "Leviticus." In IDBSup, 541–45.
_____. "Leviticus, Book of." In *EJ* 11 (1971): cols. 138–47.

Numbers

Caine, Ivan. "Numbers, Book of." In *EJ* 12 (1971): cols. 1249–54.
Dentan, Robert C. "Numbers, Book of." *IDB* 3: 567–71.
Levine, Baruch. "Numbers, Book of." In IDBSup, 631–35.

Special Studies

Beyerlin, Walter. *Origins and History of the Oldest Sinaitic Traditions.* Oxford: Basil Blackwell & Mott, 1965.
Coats, George W. *Rebellion in the Wilderness. The Murmuring Motif in the Wilderness Traditions of the Old Testament.* Nashville: Abingdon Press, 1968.
Cross. *CMHE*, 121–215.
Cross, Frank M., and David N. Freedman. "The Song of Miriam." *JNES* 14 (1955): 237–50.
Newman, Murray L. *The People of the Covenant: A Study of Israel from Moses to the Monarchy.* Nashville and New York: Abingdon Press, 1962.
Nicholson, E. W. *Exodus and Sinai in History and Tradition.* Atlanta: John Knox Press, 1973.
Thompson, Thomas L. "The Joseph and Moses Narratives, 2: The Joseph-Moses Traditions and Pentateuchal Criticism." In *IJH*, 167–80.

18. Historical-Critical Approaches to the Moses Traditions

General: Archaeology, Geography, History

Aharoni. *ALI*, 112–52.
_____. *LB*, 181–209.
Bright. *HI*, 107–29, 144–62.
Herrmann. *HIOTT*, 56–85.
Noth, *THI*, 110–21, 127–38.

Special Studies

Batto, Bernard F. "The Reed Sea: Requiescat in Pace." *JBL* 102 (1983): 27–35.
Buber, Martin. *Moses.* Oxford and London: East and West Library, 1946.
Campbell, Edward F., Jr. "Moses and the Foundation of Israel." *Int* 29 (1975): 141–54.
Davies, G. I. *The Way of the Wilderness. A Geographical Study of the Wilderness Itineraries in the Old Testament.* Cambridge: At the University Press, 1979.
Haran, Menahem. "Exodus, The." In IDBSup, 304–10.
Hay, Lewis S. "What Really Happened at the Sea of Reeds?" *JBL* 83 (1964): 397–403.
Hermann, Siegfried. *Israel in Egypt.* SBT, 2d ser., 27. London: SCM Press, 1973.
Newman, Murray L., Jr. "Moses." In IDBSup, 604–5.
Oded, Bustanay. "Exodus (date and route of)." In *EJ* 6 (1971): cols. 1042–50.
Rowley, H. H. "Early Levite History and the Question of the Exodus." *JNES* 3 (1944): 73–78.

Thompson, Thomas L. "The Joseph and Moses Narratives, 1: Historical Reconstructions of the Narratives." In *IJH*, 149–66.

de Vaux. *EHI*, 291–472.

Widengren, Geo. "What Do We Know About Moses?" In *Proclamation and Presence. Old Testament Essays in Honor of G. H. Davies,* ed. J. I. Durham and J. R. Porter, 21–47. Richmond: John Knox Press, 1970.

19. Religion of Moses and the Exodus-Wilderness Israelites

Fohrer. *HIR*, 60–86.

Ringgren. *IR*, 28–40.

Vriezen. *RAI*, 124–53.

19.1 Covenant

Baltzer, Klaus. *The Covenant Formulary in Old Testament, Jewish, and Early Christian Writings.* Philadelphia: Fortress Press, 1971.

Hillers, Delbert R. *Covenant: The History of a Biblical Idea.* Baltimore: Johns Hopkins University Press, 1969.

McCarthy, Dennis J. *Old Testament Covenant: A Survey of Current Opinions.* Atlanta: John Knox Press, 1972.

_____. *Treaty and Covenant: A Study in Form in the Ancient Oriental Documents and in the Old Testament.* AnBib 21. Rome: Pontifical Biblical Institute, 1963.

Mendenhall, George E. "Covenant." In *IDB* 1: 714–23.

_____. *Law and Covenant in Israel and in the Ancient Near East.* Pittsburgh: Presbyterian Board of Colportage of Western Pennsylvania, 1955.

Riemann, Paul A. "Covenant, Mosaic." In IDBSup, 192–97.

Weinfeld, Moshe. "Covenant." In *EJ* 5 (1971): cols. 1011–22.

19.2 Covenant Stipulations: "Laws" (*see also* 37.3; 49)

Alt, Albrecht. "The Origins of Israelite Law." In *EOTHR*, 101–71.

Andreasen, Niels-Erik A. *The Old Testament Sabbath: A Tradition-Historical Investigation.* SBLDS 7. Missoula, Mont.: Scholars Press, 1972.

Boecker, Hans J. *Law and the Administration of Justice in the Old Testament and Ancient East.* Minneapolis: Augsburg Publishing House, 1980.

Clark, W. Malcolm. "Law." In *OTFC*, 99–139.

Cody, Aelred. *A History of Old Testament Priesthood.* AnBib 35. Rome: Pontifical Biblical Institute, 1969.

Falk, Zeev W. *Hebrew Law in Biblical Times. An Introduction.* Jerusalem: Wahrmann Books, 1964.

Greenberg, Moshe. "Crimes and Punishments." In *IDB* 1: 733–44.

Greengus, Samuel. "Law in the OT." In IDBSup, 532–37.

Harrelson, Walter J. "Law in the OT." In *IDB* 3: 77–89.

_____. *The Ten Commandments and Human Rights.* OBT 8. Philadelphia: Fortress Press, 1980.

Nielsen, Eduard. "Moses and the Law." *VT* 32 (1982): 87–98.

_____. *The Ten Commandments in New Perspective.* SBT, 2d ser., 7. London: SCM Press, 1968.

Noth, Martin. *The Laws in the Pentateuch and Other Essays,* 1–107. Philadelphia: Fortress Press, 1967.

Paul, Shalom M. *Studies in the Book of the Covenant in the Light of Cuneiform and Biblical Law.* VTSup 18 (1970).

Phillips, Anthony. *Ancient Israel's Criminal Law: A New Approach to the Decalogue.* Oxford: Basil Blackwell & Mott, 1970.

Pritchard, ed. *ANET,* 159–223, 542–49.

Stamm, J.-J., and M. E. Andrew. *The Ten Commandments in Recent Research.* SBT, 2d ser., 2. London: SCM Press, 1962.

19.3 The Divine Name

Anderson, Bernhard W. "God, Names of." In *IDB* 2: 407–17.

Brekelmans, C. H. W. "Exodus 18 and the Origins of Yahwism in Israel." *OTS* 10 (1954): 215–24.

Cross. *CMHE,* 65–71.

Eichrodt, Walther. "The Name of the Covenant God." In *Theology of the Old Testament,* 1: 178–205. Philadelphia: Westminster Press, 1961.

Frick, Frank S. "The Rechabites Reconsidered." *JBL* 90 (1971): 279–87.

Kuntz, J. Kenneth. *The Self-Revelation of God.* Philadelphia: Westminster Press, 1967.

Labuschagne, C. J. *The Incomparability of Yahweh in the Old Testament.* Leiden: E. J. Brill, 1966.

Murtonen, Aimo. *A Philological and Literary Treatise on the Divine Names El, Eloah, Elohim and Yahweh.* Helsinki: Societas Orientalis Fennica, 1952.

19.4 Cultic Rites and Objects (*see also* 49)

Davies, G. Henton. "Tabernacle." In *IDB* 4: 498–506.

Gaster, T. H. "Sacrifices and Offerings, OT." In *IDB* 4: 147–59.

Gray, George B. *Sacrifice in the Old Testament,* with a Prolegomenon by B. A. Levine. New York: Ktav Publishing, 1971 (reprint of 1925 edition).

Kraus, Hans-Joachim. *Worship in Ancient Israel. A Cultic History of the Old Testament,* 1–70, 76–88, 93–101, 112–34. Richmond: John Knox Press, 1966.

Levine, Baruch A. "Cult." In *EJ* 5 (1971): cols. 1155–62.

———. "Cult Places, Israelite." In *EJ* 5 (1971): cols. 1162–69.

Milgrom, Jacob. "Sacrifices and Offerings, OT." In IDBSup, 763–71.

Rainey, Anson. "Sacrifice." In *EJ* 14 (1971): cols. 599–607.

de Vaux, Roland. *Studies in Old Testament Sacrifice.* Cardiff: University of Wales Press, 1964.

20. Newer Literary Approaches to the Moses Traditions

Ackerman, James S. "The Literary Context of the Moses Birth Story (Exodus 1–2)." In *Literary Interpretations of Biblical Narratives,* vol. I, ed. K. R. R. Gros Louis, 74–119. Nashville and New York: Abingdon Press, 1974.

Barzel, Hillel. "Moses: Tragedy and Sublimity." In *Literary Interpretations of Biblical Narratives,* 120–40.

Exum, J. Cheryl. " 'You Shall Let Every Daughter Live': A Study of Exodus 1:8—2:10." *Semeia* 28 (1983): 63–82.

Irvin, Dorothy. "The Joseph and Moses Narratives, 3: The Joseph and Moses Stories as Narrative in the Light of Ancient Near Eastern Narrative." In *IJH*, 180–209.

Jobling, David. *The Sense of Biblical Narrative. Three Structural Analyses in the Old Testament (1 Sam. 13–31; Num. 11–12; 1 Kings 17–18),* 26–62. JSOTSup 7. Sheffield: JSOT Press, 1978.

Robertson, David. *The Old Testament and the Literary Critic,* 16–32. GBS. Philadelphia: Fortress Press, 1977.

Ryken, Leland. "The Epic of the Exodus." In *Perspectives on Old Testament Literature,* ed. W. Ohlsen, 41–52. New York: Harcourt Brace Jovanovich, 1978.

21. Sociohistoric Horizons of the Moses Traditions

Gottwald, Norman K. *TY,* 32–41, 57–59, 453–59, 577–80, 648–49, 688–90.

Irvin, Dorothy. "The Joseph and Moses Traditions, 4: The Narratives about the Origins of Israel." In *IJH,* 210–12.

Noth, Martin. "Final Outlook: Historical Implications." In *HPT,* 252–59.

Chapter 6: Traditions About Intertribal Israel's Rise to Power in Canaan

22. The Shape of the Traditions in Joshua and Judges (*see also* Part II, Prol.)

The Biblical Books

Joshua

Aharoni, Johanan. "Joshua, Book of." In *EJ* 10 (1971): cols. 271–77.

Good, Edwin M. "Joshua, Book of." In *IDB* 2: 988–95.

Miller, J. Maxwell. "Joshua, Book of." In IDBSup, 493–96.

Judges

Bacon, Gershon. "Judges, Book of." In *EJ* 10 (1971): cols. 442–50.

Kraft, Charles F. "Judges, Book of." In *IDB* 2: 1013–23.

Rogers, Max G. "Judges, Book of" In IDBSup, 509–14.

Special Studies

Auld, A. Graeme. *Joshua, Moses and the Land. Tetrateuch-Pentateuch-Hexateuch in a Generation Since 1938.* Greenwood, S.C.: The Attic Press, 1980.

———. "Judges 1 and History: A Reconsideration." *VT* 25 (1975): 261–85.

Childs, Brevard S. "A Study of the Formula 'Until This Day.' " *JBL* 82 (1963): 279–92.

Craigie, Peter C. "The Song of Deborah and the Epic of Tukulti-Ninurta." *JBL* 88 (1969): 253–65.

Cross. *CMHE,* 77–111.

Gurewicz, S. B. "The Bearing of Judges 1—2:5 on Authorship of the Book of Judges." *Australian Biblical Review* 7 (1959): 37–40.

McCarthy, Dennis J. "The Theology of Leadership in Joshua 1–9." *Bib* 52 (1971): 165–75.

Nelson, Richard D. "Josiah in the Book of Joshua." *JBL* 100 (1981): 531–40.

O'Doherty, Eamonn. "The Literary Problem of Judges 1:1—3:16." *CBQ* 18 (1956): 1–7.

Weinfeld, Moshe. "The Period of the Conquest and the Judges as Seen by the Earlier and Later Sources." *VT* 17 (1967): 93–113.

Wenham, Gordon J. "The Deuteronomic Theology of the Book of Joshua." *JBL* 90 (1971): 140–56.

Wilcoxen, Jay A. "Narrative Structure and Cult Legend: A Study of Joshua 1–6." In *Transitions in Biblical Scholarship*, ed. J. C. Rylaarsdam, 43–70. Chicago and London: University of Chicago Press, 1968.

Wright, George E. "The Literary and Historical Problem of Joshua X and Judges I." *JNES* 5 (1946): 105–14.

23. Newer Literary Approaches to Joshua and Judges

Crenshaw, James L. *Samson*. Atlanta: John Knox Press, 1978.

Exum, J. Cheryl. "Aspects of Symmetry and Balance in the Samson Saga." *JSOT* 19 (1981): 3–29.

_____. "Promise and Fulfillment. Narrative Art in Judges 13." *JBL* 99 (1980): 43–59.

_____. "The Theological Dimension of the Samson Saga." *VT* 33 (1983): 30–45.

Greenstein, Edward L. "The Riddle of Samson." *Prooftexts* 1 (1981): 237–60.

Gunn, David M. "Narrative Patterns and Oral Tradition in Judges and Samuel." *VT* 24 (1974): 286–317.

Hauser, Alan J. "Judges 5: Parataxis in Hebrew Poetry." *JBL* 99 (1980): 23–41.

Jobling, David. " 'The Jordan a Boundary': A Reading of Numbers 32 and Joshua 22." SBLSP 19 (1980): 183–207.

Murray, D. F. "Narrative Structure and Technique in the Deborah and Barak Story." VTSup 30 (1979): 155–89.

Polzin, Robert. *Moses and the Deuteronomist. A Literary Study of the Deuteronomic History*. New York: Seabury Press, 1980.

Taylor, J. Glen. "The Song of Deborah and Two Canaanite Goddesses." *JSOT* 23 (1982): 99–108.

24. Sociohistoric Horizons of Joshua and Judges

General

Archaeology, Geography, History

Aharoni. *ALI*, 153–91.

_____. *LB*, 209–85.

Bright. *HI*, 129–43, 162–82.

Herrmann. *HIOTT*, 86–127.

Mayes, A. D. H. "The Period of the Judges and the Rise of the Monarchy." In *IJH*, 285–93, 297–322.

Miller, J. Maxwell. "The Israelite Occupation of Canaan." In *IJH*, 213–84.

Noth. *THI*, 53–109, 141–63.

Religion

Fohrer. *HIR*, 42–60, 87–122.

Ringgren. *IR*, 41–54.

Vriezen. *RAI*, 154–78.

Special Studies

Ahlström, G. W. "Where Did the Israelites Live?" *JNES* 41 (1982): 133–38.

Alt, Albrecht. "The Settlement of the Israelites in Palestine." In *EOTHR,* 173–221.

Blenkinsopp, Joseph. *Gibeon and Israel.* Cambridge: At the University Press, 1972.

Buber, Martin. *Kingship of God.* 3d ed. New York: Harper & Row, 1967.

Chaney, Marvin L. "Ancient Palestinian Peasant Movements and the Formation of Premonarchic Israel." In *Palestine in Transition,* ed. D. N. Freedman and D. F. Graf, 39–90.

de Geus, C. H. J. *The Tribes of Israel: An Investigation into Some of the Presuppositions of Martin Noth's Amphictyony Hypothesis.* Amsterdam and Assen: Van Gorcum, 1976.

Gottwald, Norman K. "Early Israel and the Canaanite Socio-Economic System." In *Palestine in Transition,* ed. D. N. Freedman and D. F. Graf, 25–37.

————. "The Hypothesis of the Revolutionary Origins of Ancient Israel: A Response to Hauser and Thompson." *JSOT* 7 (May 1978): 37–52.

————. "Two Models for the Origins of Ancient Israel: Social Revolution or Frontier Development." In *The Quest for the Kingdom of God: Studies in Honor of George E. Mendenhall,* ed. H. B. Huffmon et al., 5–24. Winona Lake, Ind.: Eisenbrauns, 1983.

————. *TY.*

Greenberg, Moshe. *The Ḫab/piru.* American Oriental Series 39. New Haven, Conn.: Yale University Press, 1955.

Halpern, Baruch. *The Emergence of Israel in Canaan.* SBLMS. Chico, Calif.: Scholars Press, 1984.

Hauser, Alan J. "Israel's Conquest of Palestine: A Peasants' Rebellion?" *JSOT* 7 (May 1978): 2–19.

Hopkins, David C. *The Highlands of Canaan: Agricultural Life in the Early Iron Age.* SWBAS 3. Decatur, Ga.: Almond Press, 1985.

King, Philip J. "Contributions of Archaeology to Biblical Studies." *CBQ* 45 (1983): 1–16.

Lapp, Paul W. "The Conquest of Palestine in the Light of Archaeology." *CTM* 38 (1967): 283–300.

Malamat, Abraham. "Charismatic Leadership in the Book of Judges." In *Magnalia Dei: The Mighty Acts of God. Essays on the Bible and Archaeology in Memory of G. Ernest Wright,* ed. F. M. Cross et al., 152–69. Garden City, N.Y.: Doubleday & Co., 1976.

Mayes, A. D. H. *Israel in the Period of the Judges.* SBT, 2d ser., 29. London: SCM Press, 1974.

McKenzie, John L. *The World of the Judges.* Englewood Cliffs, N.J.: Prentice-Hall, 1966.

Mendenhall, George E. "The Hebrew Conquest of Palestine." *BA* 25 (1962): 66–87 = *BAR* 3 (1970): 100–120.

————. "Social Organization in Early Israel." In *Magnalia Dei,* ed. F. M. Cross et al., 132–51.

————. *The Tenth Generation. The Origins of the Biblical Tradition.* Baltimore: Johns Hopkins University Press, 1973.

Meyers, Carol L. "Procreation, Production, and Protection: Male-Female Balance in Early Israel." *JAAR* 51 (1983): 569–93.

————. "The Roots of Restriction: Women in Early Israel." In *BL,* 289–306.

Muhly, James D. "How Iron Technology Changed the Ancient World and Gave the Philistines a Military Edge." *BARev* 8/6 (November/December 1982): 42–54.

Mullen, E. Theodore, Jr. "The 'Minor Judges': Some Literary and Historical Considerations." *CBQ* 44 (1982): 185–201.

Ramsey, George W. *The Quest for the Historical Israel*. Atlanta: John Knox Press, 1973.

Smend, Rudolf, Jr. *Yahweh War and Tribal Confederation*. Nashville: Abingdon Press, 1970.

Thompson, Leonard L. "The Jordan Crossing: *Sidqot* Yahweh and World Building." *JBL* 100 (1981): 343–58.

Thompson, Thomas L. "Historical Notes on 'Israel's Conquest of Palestine: A Peasants' Rebellion?' " *JSOT* 7 (May 1978): 20–27.

de Vaux. *EHI*, 475–824.

von Waldow, Eberhard. "Social Responsibility and Social Structure in Early Israel." *CBQ* 32 (1970): 182–204.

Weippert, Manfred. *The Settlement of the Israelite Tribes in Palestine. A Critical Survey of Recent Scholarly Debate*. SBT, 2d ser., 21. London: SCM Press, 1971.

PART III: MONARCHY: ISRAEL'S COUNTERREVOLUTIONARY ESTABLISHMENT
Prologue: On the Sources for Israel's Monarchic History

25. Chronology of the Divided Kingdoms

Albright, William F. "The Chronology of the Divided Monarchy of Israel," *BASOR* 100 (1945): 16–22.

Childs, Brevard S. "The Problem of the Chronology in the Book of Kings." In *IOTS*, 294–300.

De Vries, Simon J. "Chronology, OT." In IDBSup, 161–66.

_____. "Chronology of the OT." In *IDB* 1: 580–99.

Hayes and Miller, eds. *IJH*, 678–83.

LaSor, William S. et al. "The Chronological Puzzle." In *Old Testament Survey*, 288–97.

Miller, J. Maxwell. "Establishing a Chronological Framework." In *The Old Testament and the Historian*, 70–87 and appendixes, 84–87.

Shenkel, James D. *Chronology and Recensional Development in the Greek Text of Kings*. HSM 1. Missoula, Mont.: Scholars Press, 1968.

Thiele, Edwin R. *A Chronology of the Hebrew Kings*. Grand Rapids: Zondervan, 1977.

_____. *The Mysterious Numbers of the Hebrew Kings*. 3d ed. Grand Rapids: Zondervan Publishing, 1983.

26. DH as a Source for Monarchic History (*see also* Part II, Prol.)

Cross. *CMHE*, 274–89.

Freedman, David N. "Deuteronomic History, The." In IDBSup, 226–28.

Fretheim, Terence E. *Deuteronomic History*. Nashville: Abingdon Press, 1983.

Friedman, Richard E. *The Exile and Biblical Narrative: The Formation of the Deuteronomistic and Priestly Works*, 1–43. HSM 22. Chico, Calif.: Scholars Press, 1981.

Gray, John. "The Composition of Kings." In *I & II Kings. A Commentary*, 1–43. 2d rev. ed. Philadelphia: Westminster Press, 1970.

Kenik, Helen A. *Design for Kingship: The Deuteronomistic Narrative Technique in 1 Kings 3:4–15*. SBLMS. Chico, Calif.: Scholars Press, 1983.

McCarter, P. Kyle, Jr. "The Deuteronomistic History." In *I Samuel,* 12–17. AB 8. Garden City, N.Y.: Doubleday & Co., 1980.

Miller, J. Maxwell. *The Old Testament and the Historian,* 1–4, 14–15, 20–39.

Nelson, Richard D. *The Double Redaction of the Deuteronomistic History.* JSOTSup 18. Sheffield: JSOT Press, 1981.

Noth, Martin. *TDH.*

Wolff, Hans Walter. "The Kerygma of the Deuteronomic Historical Work." In *The Vitality of Old Testament Traditions,* ed. W. Brueggemann and H. W. Wolff, 83–100.

27. Archaeology as a Source for Monarchic History
(*see also* 8)

Aharoni. *ALI,* 192–279.

Cornfeld, Gaalyah. *Archaeology of the Bible Book by Book.* New York: Harper & Row, 1977.

Frank, Harry Thomas. *Discovering the Biblical World,* 75–130. New York: Hammond, 1977.

Gray, John. "Recent Archaeological Discoveries and their Bearing on the Old Testament." In *TI,* 65–95.

Kenyon, Kathleen M. *Royal Cities of the Old Testament.* New York: Schocken Books, 1971.

Lance, H. Darrell. "The Archaeologist at Work: The Age of Solomon." In *The Old Testament and the Archaeologist,* 67–93.

Miller, J. Maxwell. *The Old Testament and the Historian,* 4–11, 40–48.

Thompson, John A. *The Bible and Archaeology.* 3d ed. Grand Rapids: Wm. B. Eerdmans, 1982.

Wright, G. Ernest. *Biblical Archaeology.* Rev. ed., 121–82.

28. Forms and Settings of Prophetic Speech
General

Buss, Martin J. "Prophecy in Ancient Israel." In IDBSup, 694–97.

Blenkinsopp, Joseph. *A History of Prophecy in Israel from the Settlement in the Land to the Hellenistic Period.* Philadelphia: Westminster Press, 1983.

Fohrer, Georg. "Remarks on Modern Interpretation of the Prophets." *JBL* 80 (1961): 309–19.

Huffmon, Herbert B. "Prophecy in the Ancient Near East." In IDBSup, 697–700.

Napier, Davie. "Prophet, Prophetism." In *IDB* 3: 896–920.

Paul, Shalom M. "Prophets and Prophecy." In *EJ* 13 (1971): cols. 1150–75.

Special Studies

Carroll, Robert P. *When Prophecy Failed: Cognitive Dissonance in the Prophetic Traditions of the Old Testament.* New York: Seabury Press, 1979.

Christensen, Duane L. *Transformations of the War Oracle in Old Testament Prophecy.* Harvard Dissertations in Religion 3. Missoula, Mont.: Scholars Press, 1975.

Clements, Ronald E. *Prophecy and Tradition.* Atlanta: John Knox Press, 1975.

Cohen, Martin A. "The Prophets as Revolutionaries: A Sociopolitical Analysis." *BARev* 5 (May/June 1979): 12–19.

Crenshaw, James L. *Prophetic Conflict. Its Effect Upon Israelite Religion.* BZAW 124. Berlin: Walter de Gruyter, 1971.

Culley, Robert, and Thomas Overholt, eds. *Anthropological Perspectives on Old Testament Prophecy. Semeia* 21 (1982).

Fohrer. *IOT*, 347–62.

Gottwald, Norman K. *All the Kingdoms of the Earth: Israelite Prophecy and International Relations in the Ancient Near East.* New York: Harper & Row, 1964. [Hereafter *AKE.*]

Long, Burke O. "Prophetic Authority as Social Reality." In *Canon and Authority,* ed. G. W. Coats and B. O. Long, 3–20.

March, W. Eugene. "Prophecy." In *OTFC,* 141–77.

_____. "Redaction Criticism and the Formation of Prophetic Books." SBLSP 11 (1977): 87–101.

McKane, William. *Prophets and Wise Men.* SBT, 1st ser., 44. London: SCM Press, 1965.

Mowinckel, Sigmund. *Prophecy and Tradition.* Oslo: Jacob Dybwad, 1946.

Petersen, David L. *The Roles of Israel's Prophets.* JSOTSup 17. Sheffield: JSOT Press, 1981.

Tucker, Gene M. "Prophetic Speech." *Int* 32 (1978): 31–45.

Westermann, Claus. *Basic Forms of Prophetic Speech.* Philadelphia: Fortress Press, 1967.

Wilson, Robert R. *Prophecy and Society in Ancient Israel.* Philadephia: Fortress Press, 1980.

Chapter 7: Traditions About the United Kingdom

29. The Shape of the Traditions in 1 and 2 Samuel and 1 Kings 1—11 (*see also* 26)

The Biblical Books

Samuel

Gottwald, Norman K. "Samuel, Book of." In *EJ* 14 (1971): cols. 788–97.

Szikszai, Stephen. "Samuel, I and II." In *IDB* 4: 202–9.

Tsevat, Matitiahu. "Samuel, I and II." In IDBSup, 777–81.

Kings

Ackroyd, Peter R. "Kings, I and II." In IDBSup, 516–19.

Gray, John. "Kings, Book of." In *EJ* 10 (1971): cols. 1021–31.

Szikszai, Stephen. "Kings, I and II." In *IDB* 3: 26–35.

Special Studies

Alter, Robert. *The Art of Biblical Narrative.* New York: Basic Books, 1981.

Birch, Bruce C. *The Rise of the Israelite Monarchy: The Growth and Development of 1 Samuel 7–15.* SBLDS 27. Missoula, Mont.: Scholars Press, 1976.

Campbell, Anthony F. *The Ark Narrative (1 Sam. 4–6; 2 Sam. 6): A Form-Critical and Traditio-Historical Study.* SBLDS 16. Missoula, Mont.: Scholars Press, 1975.

Carlson, R. A. *David, the Chosen King: A Traditio-Historical Approach to the Second Book of Samuel.* Stockholm: Almqvist & Wiksell, 1964.

Clements, Ronald E. "The Deuteronomistic Interpretation of the Founding of the Monarchy in I Sam. VIII." *VT* 24 (1974): 398–410.

Conroy, Charles. *Absalom, Absalom! Narrative and Language in 2 Sam. 13–20.* AnBib 81. Rome: Pontifical Biblical Institute, 1978.

Gunn, David M. *The Fate of King Saul. An Interpretation of a Biblical Story.* JSOTSup 14. Sheffield: JSOT Press, 1980.

―――. *The Story of King David. Genre and Interpretation.* JSOTSup 6. Sheffield: JSOT Press, 1978.

Kessler, Martin. "Narrative Technique in 1 Sam. 16:1–13." *CBQ* 32 (1972): 543–54.

Leach, Edmund. "The Legitimacy of Solomon: Some Structural Aspects of Old Testament History." In *Genesis as Myth and Other Essays,* 25–83. London: Jonathan Cape, 1969.

Liver, Jacob. "The Book of the Acts of Solomon." *Bib* 48 (1967): 75–101.

McCarter, P. Kyle, Jr. *I Samuel,* 12–30.

McCarthy, Dennis J. "The Inauguration of Monarchy in Israel: A Form-Critical Study of 1 Sam. 8–12." *Int* 27 (1973): 401–12.

Mettinger, T. N. D. "The Sources." In *King and Messiah: The Civil and Sacral Legitimation of the Israelite Kings,* 19–105. ConBOT 8. Lund: C. W. K. Gleerup, 1976.

Miller, Patrick D., Jr., and J. J. M. Roberts. *The Hand of the Lord: A Reassessment of the 'Ark Narrative' of 1 Samuel.* Baltimore: Johns Hopkins University Press, 1977.

Porten, Bezalel. "The Structure and Theme of the Solomon Narrative." *HUCA* 38 (1967): 93–128.

Rost, Leonhard. *The Succession to the Throne of David,* with Introduction by Edward Ball. Sheffield: Almond Press, 1982.

Segal, Moses H. "The Composition of the Books of Samuel." In *The Pentateuch. Its Composition and its Authorship and Other Biblical Studies,* 173–220. Jerusalem: Magnes Press, 1967.

Whybray, R. N. *The Succession Narrative: A Study of 2 Sam. 9–20 and 1 Kings 1 and 2.* SBT, 2d ser., 9. London: SCM Press, 1968.

30. The Rise and Triumph of Monarchy in Israel

General: Archaeology, Geography, History, State Politics

Aharoni. *ALI,* 192–239.

―――. *LB,* 286–320.

Bright. *HI,* 183–228.

Cohen, Ronald, and Elman R. Service, eds. *Origins of the State. The Anthropology of Political Evolution.* Philadelphia: ISHI Publications, 1978.

Fried, Morton. *The Evolution of Political Society. An Essay in Political Anthropology.* New York: Random House, 1967.

Herrmann. *HIOTT,* 131–86.

Noth. *THI,* 164–224.

Soggin, J. Alberto. "The Davidic-Solomonic Kingdom." In *IJH,* 332–80.

Special Studies

Alt, Albrecht. "The Formation of the Israelite State in Palestine." In *EOTHR,* 171–237.

Buccellati, Giorgio. *Cities and Nations of Ancient Syria. An Essay on Political Institu-*

tions with Special Reference to the Israelite Kingdoms. Studi Semitici 26. Rome: Istituto di Studi del Vicino Oriente, 1967.

Frick, Frank S. *The Formation of the State in Ancient Israel: A Survey of Models and Theories.* SWBAS 4. Decatur, Ga.: Almond Press, 1985.

Halpern, Baruch. *The Constitution of the Monarchy in Israel.* HSM 25. Chico, Calif.: Scholars Press, 1981.

Heaton, Eric W. *Solomon's New Men: The Emergence of Ancient Israel as a National State.* London: Thames & Hudson, 1974.

Ishida, Tomoo. *The Royal Dynasties in Ancient Israel. A Study on the Formation and Development of Royal-Dynastic Ideology.* BZAW 142. Berlin: Walter de Gruyter, 1977.

_____, ed. *Studies in the Period of David and Solomon and Other Essays.* Tokyo: Yamakawa-Shuppansha, 1982.

Malamat, Abraham. "Aspects of the Foreign Policy of David and Solomon." *JNES* 22 (1963): 1–17.

_____. "Organs of Statecraft in the Israelite Monarchy." *BA* 28 (1965): 34–65 = *BAR* 3 (1970): 163–98.

Maly, Eugene H. *The World of David and Solomon.* Englewood Cliffs, N.J.: Prentice-Hall, 1966.

Mendelsohn, Isaac. *Slavery in the Ancient Near East.* New York and London: Oxford University Press, 1949.

Mettinger, T. N. D. "The Civil Legitimation of the King." In *King and Messiah,* 107–50.

_____. *Solomonic State Officials: A Study of the Civil Government Officials of the Israelite Monarchy.* ConBOT 5. Lund: C. W. K. Gleerup, 1971.

Rainey, Anson F. "Compulsory Labor Gangs in Ancient Israel." *IEJ* 20 (1970): 191–202.

Stern, Ephraim. "Craft and Industry." In *World History of the Jewish People,* vol. 4/2, ed. A. Malamat, 237–64. Jerusalem: Jewish Historical Publications Ltd., 1979. [Hereafter *WHJP.*]

Tadmor, Hayim. "Traditional Institutions and the Monarchy: Social and Political Tensions in the Time of David and Solomon." In *Studies in the Period of David and Solomon,* ed. T. Ishida, 239–57.

Whitelam, Keith W. *The Just King: Monarchical Judicial Authority in Ancient Israel.* JSOTSup 12. Sheffield: JSOT Press, 1979.

Whybray, R. N. "Some Historical Limitations of Hebrew Kingship." *CQR* 163 (1962): 136–50.

Yeivin, Shmuel. "Administration." In *WHJP,* vol. 4/2, ed. Malamat, 147–71.

30.1 External and Internal Factors

Cundall, Arthur E. "Antecedents of the Monarchy in Ancient Israel." *VE* 3 (1964): 42–50.

Cohen, Martin A. "The Role of the Shilonite Priesthood in the United Monarchy of Ancient Israel." *HUCA* 36 (1965): 59–98.

Dothan, Trude. "What Do We Know About the Philistines?" *BARev* 8/4 (July/August 1982): 20–44.

Flanagan, James W. "Chiefs in Israel." *JSOT* 20 (1981): 47–73.

Mendelsohn, Isaac. "Samuel's Denunciation of Kingship in the Light of the Akkadian Documents from Ugarit." *BASOR* 143 (1956): 17–22.

30.2 Saul

Blenkinsopp, Joseph. "The Quest of the Historical Saul." In *No Famine in the Land. Studies in Honor of John L. McKenzie,* ed. J. W. Flanagan and A. W. Robinson, 75–99. Missoula, Mont.: Scholars Press, 1975.

Evans, William E. "An Historical Reconstruction of the Emergence of Israelite Kingship and the Reign of Saul." In *Scripture in Context II. More Essays in Comparative Method,* ed. William W. Hallo, James C. Moyer, and Leo G. Purdue, 61–77. Winona Lake, Ind.: Eisenbrauns, 1983. [Hereafter *SC 2.*]

Hauer, Chris E., Jr. "The Shape of Saulide Strategy." *CBQ* 31 (1969): 153–67.

Miller, J. Maxwell. "Saul's Rise to Power: Some Observations Concerning 1 Sam. 9:1—10:16; 10:26—11:15 and 13:2—14:46." *CBQ* 36 (1974): 157–74.

Weingreen, Jacob. "Saul and the Habiru." In *Fourth World Congress of Jewish Studies Papers,* 1: 53–66. Jerusalem: Magnes Press, 1967.

30.3 David

Cazelles, Henri. "David's Monarchy and the Gibeonite Claim." *PEQ* 87 (1955): 165–75.

Cohen, Martin A. "The Rebellions During the Reign of David. An Inquiry Into Social Dynamics in Ancient Israel." In *Studies in Jewish Bibliography, History and Literature in Honor of I. E. Kiev,* ed. C. Berlin, 91–112. New York: Ktav Publishing, 1971.

Flanagan, James W. "The Relocation of the Davidic Capital." *JAAR* 47 (1979): 233–44.

Hauer, Chris A., Jr. "David and the Levites." *JSOT* 23 (1982): 33–54.

Levenson, Jon D., and Baruch Halpern. "The Political Import of David's Marriages." *JBL* 99 (1980): 507–18.

Mazar, Benjamin. "The Military Elite of King David." *VT* 13 (1963): 310–20.

Olyan, S. "Zadok's Origins and the Tribal Politics of David." *JBL* 101 (1982): 177–93.

Weingreen, Jacob. "The Rebellion of Absalom." *VT* 19 (1969): 263–66.

30.4 Solomon

Gihon, M. C. "The Defenses of the Solomonic Kingdom." *PEQ* 95 (1963): 113–26.

Hauer, Chris E., Jr. "The Economics of National Security in Solomonic Israel." *JSOT* 18 (1980): 67–73.

Meyers, Carol L. "The Elusive Temple." *BA* 45 (1982): 33–41.

Parrot, André. *The Temple of Jerusalem.* SBA 5. London: SCM Press, 1957.

Redford, D. B. "Studies in Relations between Palestine and Egypt During the First Millennium BC: I. The Taxation System of Solomon." In *Studies on the Ancient Palestinian World,* ed. J. W. Wevers and D. B. Redford. Toronto: Toronto University Press, 1972.

Wright, G. Ernest. "The Provinces of Solomon (I K. 4:7–19)." *Eretz Israel* 8 (1967): 58*—68*.

30.5 Major Enduring Structural Effects of the Monarchy

Elat, Moshe. "The Monarchy and the Development of Trade in Ancient Israel." In *State and Temple Economy in the Ancient Near East,* vol. 2, ed. E. Lipinski, 527–46. Louvain: Dept. Orientalistiek, 1979.

Gottwald, Norman K. "Israel, Social and Economic Development of." In IDBSup, 465–68.

Hopkins, David C. "The Dynamics of Agriculture in Monarchical Israel." SBLSP 22 (1983): 177–202.

Neufeld, Eduard. "The Emergence of a Royal-Urban Society in Ancient Israel." *HUCA* 31 (1960): 31–53.

Otzen, Benedikt. "Israel Under the Assyrians. Reflections on Imperial Policy in Palestine." *ASTI* 11 (1977): 96–110.

Reviv, H. "The Structure of Society." In *WHJP*, vol. 4/2, ed. Malamat, 125–46.

Robinson, Theodore H. "Some Economic and Social Factors in the History of Israel." *ET* 45 (1933/34): 264–69, 294–300.

Rosenbloom, Joseph R. "Social Science Concepts of Modernization and Biblical History: The Development of the Israelite Monarchy." *JAAR* 40 (1972): 437–44.

Silver, Morris. *Prophets and Markets. The Political Economy of Ancient Israel.* Boston: Kluwer-Nijhoff, 1983.

31. Literary Culture: Religious Cult and Ideology

Ahlström, G. W. *Royal Administration and National Religion in Ancient Palestine.* SHANE 1. Leiden: E. J. Brill, 1982.

Engnell, Ivan. *Studies in Divine Kingship in the Ancient Near East.* 2d ed. Oxford: Basil Blackwell & Mott, 1967.

Fohrer. *HIR*, 123–222.

Greenberg, Moshe. "Religion: Stability and Ferment." In *WHJP*, vol. 4/2, ed. Malamat, 79–123.

Hooke, Samuel H., ed. *Myth, Ritual, and Kingship: Essays on the Theory and Practice of Kingship in the Ancient Near East and in Israel.* London: Oxford University Press, 1958.

North, C. R. "The Old Testament Estimate of the Monarchy." *AJSL* 48 (1931): 1–19.

Ringgren. *IR*, 57–247.

Talmon, Shemaryahu. "Kingship and Ideology of the State." In *WHJP*, vol. 4/2, ed. Malamat, 3–26.

Vriezen. *RAI*, 79–102.

31.1 The Yahwist

Brueggemann, Walter. "David and His Theologian." *CBQ* 30 (1968): 156–81.

_____. "Yahwist." In IDBSup, 971–75.

Clines, David J. A. "Theme in Genesis 1–11." *CBQ* 38 (1976): 483–507.

Ellis. *YBFT*.

Habel, Norman C. *Literary Criticism of the Old Testament,* 18–64. GBS. Philadelphia: Fortress Press, 1971.

Jobling, David. "The Myth Semantics of Genesis 2:4b—3:24." *Semeia* 18 (1980): 41–49.

Miller, Patrick D., Jr. *Genesis 1–11: Studies in Structure and Theme.* JSOTSup 8. Sheffield: JSOT Press, 1978.

North, Robert. "Can Geography Save J from Rendtorff?" *Bib* 63 (1982): 47–55.

von Rad. *OTT,* 1: 48–56, 121–87.

Rendtorff, Rolf. "The 'Yahwist' as Theologian? The Dilemma of Pentateuchal Criticism." *JSOT* 3 (1977): 2–10.

Rosenberg, Joel W. "The Garden Story Forward and Backward: The Non-narrative Dimension of Gen. 2–3." *Prooftexts* 1 (1981): 1–27.

Vriezen, Theodorus C. *An Outline of Old Testament Theology,* 54–59, 79–80. 2d rev. ed. Oxford: Basil Blackwell & Mott, 1970.

Wagner, Norman E. "Abraham and David?" In *Studies on the Ancient Palestinian World,* ed. J. Wevers and D. B. Redford, 117–40. Toronto: Toronto University Press, 1972.

Wolff, Hans Walter. "The Kerygma of the Yahwist." In *The Vitality of Old Testament Traditions,* ed. W. Brueggemann and H. W. Wolff, 41–66.

31.2 Psalms and Wisdom (*see also* 52.2; 54.1)

Bryce, Glendon E. *A Legacy of Wisdom.* Lewisburg, Pa.: Bucknell University Press, 1979.

Mowinckel, Sigmund. "The Psalmists." In *The Psalms in Israel's Worship,* 2: 85–103. Nashville: Abingdon Press, 1962.

Scott, R. B. Y. "Solomon and the Beginnings of Wisdom in Israel." In *SAIW,* 84–101 = VTSup 3 (1955): 262–79.

Weiser, Artur. "The Collection of the Psalms." In *The Psalms. A Commentary,* 95–101. Philadelphia: Westminster Press, 1962.

31.3 David and Zion Traditions

Clements, Ronald E. *God and Temple,* 40–78. Philadelphia: Fortress Press, 1965.

Cross, *CMHE,* 217–73.

Hayes, John H. "The Tradition of Zion's Inviolability." *JBL* 82 (1963): 419–62.

Johnson, Aubrey R. *Sacral Kingship in Ancient Israel.* 2d ed. Cardiff: University of Wales Press, 1967.

Kraus, Hans-Joachim. *Worship in Israel,* chap. 5. Atlanta: John Knox Press, 1966.

McCarthy, Dennis J. "II Samuel 7 and the Structure of the Deuteronomic History." *JBL* 84 (1965): 131–38.

Mettinger, T. N. D. "The Sacral Legitimation of the King." In *King and Messiah,* 151–297.

Noth, Martin. "God, King and Nation in the Old Testament." In *The Laws of the Pentateuch and Other Studies,* 145–78. Edinburgh and London: Oliver & Boyd, 1966.

Porteous, Norman W. "Jerusalem-Zion: The Growth of a Symbol." In *Verbannung und Heimkehr,* ed. A. Kuschke, 235–52. Tübingen: J. C. B. Mohr (Paul Siebeck), 1961.

Roberts, J. J. M. "The Davidic Origin of the Zion Tradition." *JBL* 92 (1973): 329–44.

———. "Zion Tradition." In IDBSup, 985–87.

Weinfeld, Moshe. "Covenant, Davidic." In IDBSup, 188–92.

———. "The Covenant of Grant in the Old Testament and in the Ancient Near East." *JAOS* 90 (1970): 184–203.

Chapter 8: Traditions About the Northern Kingdom

32. The Shape of the Traditions in 1 Kings 12—2 Kings 17
(*see also* 26; 34.2)

Cohn, Robert L. "Form and Perspective in 2 Kings 5." *VT* 33 (1983): 171–84.

———. "The Literary Logic of 1 Kings 17–19." *JBL* 101 (1982): 333–50.

Cross. *CMHE,* 223–29.

DeVries, Simon J. *Prophet Against Prophet. The Role of the Micaiah Narrative (1 Kings 22) in the Development of Early Prophetic Tradition.* Grand Rapids: Wm. B. Eerdmans, 1978.

Gray, John. *I & II Kings. A Commentary,* 25–33.

Jobling, David. *The Sense of Biblical Narrative: Three Structural Analyses in the Old Testament (1 Samuel 13–31; Numbers 11–12; 1 Kings 17–18).* JSOTSup 7. Sheffield: JSOT Press, 1978.

Koch, Klaus. *The Growth of the Biblical Tradition. The Form-Critical Method,* 183–200.

Long, Burke O. "The Social Setting for Prophetic Miracle Stories." *Semeia* 3 (1975): 46–63.

———. "2 Kings III and Genres of Prophetic Narrative." *VT* 23 (1973): 337–48.

Noth. *TDH,* 63–74.

von Rad, Gerhard. *Studies in Deuteronomy,* 74–91. SBT, 1st ser., 9. London: SCM Press, 1953.

Rofé, Alexander. "Classes in the Prophetic Stories: Didactic Legenda and Parable." VTSup 26 (1974): 143–64.

———. "The Classification of Prophetic Stories." *JBL* 89 (1970): 427–40

33. History of the Northern Kingdom and Its Relations with Judah

General: Archaeology, Geography, History, State Politics

Alt, Albrecht. "The Monarchy in the Kingdoms of Israel and Judah." In *EOTHR,* 311–35.

Aharoni. *ALI,* 239–53.

———. *LB,* 321–86.

Bright. *HI,* 229–66.

Donner, Herbert. "The Separate States of Israel and Judah." In *IJH,* 381–434.

Herrmann. *HIOTT,* 187–254.

Mazar, Benjamin. "The Aramean Empire and Its Relations with Israel." *BA* 25 (1962): 97–120 = *BAR* 2 (1964): 127–51.

Murphy, Roland E. "Israel and Moab in the 9th Cent. B.C." *CBQ* 15 (1953): 409–17.

Noth. *THI,* 225–50.

Tadmor, Hayim. "Assyria and the West: The Ninth Century and Its Aftermath." In *Unity and Diversity. Essays in the History, Literature and Religion of the Ancient Near East,* ed. H. Goedicke and J. J. M. Roberts, 36–48. Baltimore: Johns Hopkins University Press, 1975.

Yeivin, Shmuel. "The Divided Kingdom: Rehoboam to Ahaz/Jeroboam to Pekah." In *WHJP,* vol. 4/1, 126–78.

33.1–2 The Schism and the Jeroboam and Baasha Dynasties

Aberbach, Moses, and Leivy Smolar. "Jeroboam." In IDBSup, 473–75.

Evans, Carl D. "Naram-Sin and Jeroboam: The Archetypal *Unheilsherrscher* in Mesopotamian and Biblical Historiography." in *SC 2,* 97–125.

Halpern, Baruch. "Levitic Participation in the Reform Cult of Jeroboam I." *JBL* 95 (1976): 31–42.

———. "Sectionalism and the Schism." *JBL* 93 (1974): 519–32.

de Vaux, Roland. "The Religious Schism of Jeroboam I." In *The Bible and the Ancient Near East,* 97–110. Garden City, N.Y.: Doubleday & Co. 1971.

33.3 Omri Dynasty

Miller, J. Maxwell. "The Elisha Cycle and the Accounts of the Omride Wars." *JBL* 85 (1966): 441–54.

Napier, B. Davie. "The Omrides of Jezreel." *VT* 9 (1959): 366–78.

Parrot, André. *Samaria: The Capital of the Kingdom of Israel.* SBA 7. London: SCM Press, 1958.

Pienaar, D. N. "The Role of the Fortified Cities in the Northern Kingdom During the Reign of the Omride Dynasty." *JNSL* 9 (1981): 151–57.

Whitley, Charles F. "The Deuteronomic Presentation of the House of Omri." *VT* 2 (1952): 137–52.

33.4 Jehu Dynasty

Ahlström, G. W. "King Jehu—A Prophet's Mistake (2 Kings 9f.)." In *Scripture in History and Theology: Essays in Honor of J. Coert Rylaarsdam,* ed. A. L. Merrill and T. M. Overholt, 47–69. PTMS 17. Pittsburgh: Pickwick Press, 1977.

Haran, Menahem. "The Rise and Decline of the Empire of Jeroboam ben Joash." *VT* 17 (1967): 266–97.

Miller, J. Maxwell. "The Fall of the House of Ahab." *VT* 17 (1967): 307–24.

North, Robert. "Social Dynamics from Saul to Jehu." *BTB* 12 (1982): 109–19.

33.5 Collapse of the Northern Kingdom

Eph'al, Israel. "Israel: Fall and Exile." In *WHJP,* vol. 4/1, 180–91.

Oded, Bustenay. "The Historical Background to the Syro-Ephraimite War Reconsidered." *CBQ* 34 (1972): 153–65.

Tadmor, Hayim. "The Campaigns of Sargon II of Assur." *JCS* 12 (1958): 22–40.

33.6 Patterns of Development in the Two Kingdoms

Parker, Simon B. "Revolutions in Northern Israel." *SBLSP* 10 (1976): 311–21.

Thornton, T. C. G. "Charismatic Kingship: Israel and Judah." *JTS* 14 (1963): 1–11.

34. Literary Culture, Religion, and Prophetic Critique
(*see also* 28)

Fohrer. *HIR*, 223–51.

Hummel, Horace D. "The Influence of Archeological Evidence on the Reconstruction of Religion in Monarchical Israel." *CTM* 41 (1970): 542–57.

Ringgren. *IR*, 248–69.

Vriezen. *RAI*, 179–220.

34.1 The Elohist (E) (*see also* Part II, Prol.)

Craghan, J. F. "The Elohist in Recent Literature." *BTB* 7 (1977): 23–35.

Fohrer. *IOT,* 152–58.

Fretheim, Terence E. "Elohist." In IDBSup, 259–63.

Jenks, Alan W. *The Elohist and North Israelite Traditions.* SBLMS 22. Missoula, Mont.: Scholars Press, 1977.

Noth. *HPT,* 20–41.

Wolff, Hans Walter. "The Elohistic Fragments in the Pentateuch." In *Vitality of Old Testament Traditions,* ed. W. Brueggemann and H. W. Wolff, 67–82.

34.2 Elijah and Elisha

Andersen, Francis I. "The Socio-Juridical Background of the Naboth Incident." *JBL* 85 (1966): 46–57.

Blenkinsopp, Joseph. *A History of Prophecy in Israel,* 68–79.

Bronner, Leah. *The Stories of Elijah and Elisha as Polemics Against Baal Worship.* Leiden: E. J. Brill, 1968.

Carroll, Robert P. "The Elijah-Elisha Sagas: Some Remarks on Prophetic Succession in Ancient Israel." *VT* 19 (1969): 400–415.

Cohen, Martin A. "In All Fairness to Ahab: A Socio-political Consideration of the Ahab-Elijah Controversy." *Eretz Israel* 12 (1975): 87–94.

Gottwald. *AKE,* 57–85.

von Rad. *OTT,* 2: 6–32.

Rowley, H. H. "Elijah on Mt. Carmel." In *Men of God,* 37–65. London: Thomas Nelson & Sons, 1963.

Würthwein, Ernst. "Elijah at Horeb: Reflections on 1 Kings 19:9–18." In *Proclamation and Presence: Old Testament Essays in Honor of G. Henton Davies,* ed. J. Durham and J. R. Porter, 152–66. London: SCM Press, 1970.

34.3 Amos

Bentzen, Aage. "The Ritual Background of Amos 1:2—2:16." *OTS* 8 (1950): 85–99.

Coote, Robert B. *Amos Among the Prophets. Composition and Theology.* Philadelphia: Fortress Press, 1981.

Craghan, J. F. "The Prophet Amos in Recent Literature." *BTB* 2 (1972): 242–61.

Crenshaw, James L. *Hymnic Affirmations of Divine Justice: The Doxologies of Amos and Related Texts in the Old Testament.* SBLDS 24. Missoula, Mont.: Scholars Press, 1975.

Gitay, Yehoshua. "A Study of Amos's Art of Speech: A Rhetorical Analysis of Amos 3:1–15." *CBQ* 42 (1980): 293–309.

Kapelrud, Arvid S. *Central Ideas in Amos.* 2d ed. Oslo: Aschehoug & Co., 1956.

Melugin, Roy F. "The Formation of Amos: An Analysis of Exegetical Method." SBLSP 13 (1978): 369–91.

Overholt, Thomas W. "Commanding the Prophets: Amos and the Problem of Prophetic Authority." *CBQ* 41 (1979): 517–32.

Paul, Shalom M. "Amos 1:3—2:3: A Concatenous Literary Pattern." *JBL* 90 (1971): 397–403.

Tucker, Gene M. "Prophetic Authenticity: A Form-Critical Study of Amos 7:10–17." *Int* 27 (1973): 423–34.

de Waard, Jan. "The Chiastic Structure of Amos 5:1–17." *VT* 27 (1977): 170–77.

Ward, James M. *Amos and Isaiah: Prophets of the Word of God.* Nashville and New York: Abingdon Press, 1969.

Wolff, Hans Walter. *Amos the Prophet: The Man and His Background.* Philadelphia: Fortress Press, 1973.

34.4 Hosea

Ackroyd, Peter R. "Hosea and Jacob." *VT* 13 (1963): 245–59.

Brueggemann, Walter. *Tradition in Crisis: A Study in Hosea.* Richmond: John Knox Press, 1968.

Buss, Martin J. *The Prophetic Word of Hosea. A Morphological Study.* BZAW 111. Berlin: Walter de Gruyter, 1969.

Eichrodt, Walter. "The Holy One in Your Midst: The Theology of Hosea." *Int* 15 (1961): 259–73.

Farr, George. "The Concept of Grace in the Book of Hosea." *ZAW* 70 (1958): 98–107.

Gelston, A. "Kingship in the Book of Hosea." *OTS* 19 (1974): 71–85.

Good, Edwin M. "The Composition of Hosea." *SEÅ* 31 (1966): 21–63.

Janzen, J. Gerald. "Metaphor and Reality in Hosea 11." *Semeia* 24 (1982): 7–44.

Lundbom, Jack. "Poetic Structure and Prophetic Rhetoric in Hosea." *VT* 29 (1979): 300–308.

Ostborn, Gunnar. *Yahweh and Baal. Studies in the Book of Hosea and Related Documents.* Lund: C. W. K. Gleerup, 1956.

Rowley, H. H. "The Marriage of Hosea." In *Men of God,* 66–97. London: Thomas Nelson & Sons, 1963.

Tushingham, A. Douglas. "A Reconsideration of Hosea, Chapters 1–3." *JNES* 12 (1953): 150–59.

Wolff, Hans Walter. "Guilt and Salvation. A Study of the Prophecy of Hosea." *Int* 15 (1961): 274–85.

Chapter 9: Traditions About the Southern Kingdom

35. The Shape of the Traditions in 2 Kings 18—25 (*see also* 26; 37.2–3, 5)

Ackroyd, Peter R. "An Interpretation of the Babylonian Exile: A Study of 2 Kings 20, Isaiah 38–39." *SJT* (1974): 329–52.

Childs, Brevard S. *Isaiah and the Assyrian Crisis.* SBT, 2d ser., 3. London: SCM Press, 1967.

Gray, John. *I & II Kings.* OTL, 33–43, 657–775.

Montgomery, James A. "Archival Data in the Book of Kings." *JBL* 53 (1934): 46–52.

Orlinsky, Harry. "The Kings-Isaiah Recensions of the Hezekiah Story." *JQR* 30 (1939/1940): 33–49.

36. History of the Southern Kingdom

General: Archaeology, Geography, History, State Politics

Aharoni. *ALI,* 253–79.

———. *LB,* 387–423.

Alt, Albrecht. "The Monarchy in the Kingdoms of Israel and Judah." In *EOTHR,* 311–35.

Bright. *HI,* 269–339.

Cogan, Morton. *Imperialism and Religion: Assyria, Judah and Israel in the Eighth and Seventh Centuries* B.C.E. SBLMS 19. Missoula, Mont.: Scholars Press, 1974.

Eph'al, Israel. "Assyrian Dominion in Palestine After the Fall of Samaria." In *WHJP,* vol. 4/1, 276–89.

Evans, Carl D. "Judah's Foreign Policy from Hezekiah to Josiah." In *Scripture in Context: Essays on the Comparative Method,* ed. Carl D. Evans, William W. Hallo, and John B. White, 157–78. PTMS 34. Pittsburgh: Pickwick Press, 1980. [Hereafter *SC 1.*]

Ginsberg, Harold L. "Judah and the Transjordan States from 734 to 582." In *Alexander Marx Jubilee Volume*, 347–68. New York: Jewish Theological Seminary, 1950.

Gordis, Robert. "Sectional Rivalry in the Kingdom of Judah." *JQR* 25 (1934/1935): 237–59.

Herrmann. *HIOTT*, 255–86.

Malamat, A. "The Last Years of the Kingdom of Judah." In *WHJP*, vol. 4/1, 205–21.

McKay, John. *Religion in Judah Under the Assyrians, 732–609 B.C.* SBT, 2d ser., 26. London: SCM Press, 1973.

Noth. *THI*, 253–89.

Oded, Bustenay. "Judah and the Exile (parts 1–5)." In *IJH*, 435–76.

Reviv, H. "The History of Judah from Hezekiah to Josiah." In *WHJP*, vol. 4/1, 193–204.

Talmon, Shemaryahu. "The Judean *'am ha'ares* in Historical Perspective." In *Fourth World Congress of Jewish Studies*, 1: 71–76. Jerusalem: Magnes Press, 1967.

36.1 Ahaz and Hezekiah

Broshi, M. "The Expansion of Jerusalem in the Reigns of Hezekiah and Manasseh." *IEJ* 24 (1974): 21–26.

Rowley, H. H. "Hezekiah's Reform and Rebellion." In *Men of God*, 98–132. London: Thomas Nelson & Sons, 1963.

Stohlmann, Stephen. "The Judaean Exile after 701 B.C.E." In *SC 2*, 147–75.

36.2 Manasseh

Nelson, Richard. "*Realpolitik* in Judah (687–609 B.C.E.)." In *SC 2*, 177–89.

Nielsen, Eduard. "Political Conditions and Cultural Developments in Israel and Judah During the Reign of Manasseh." In *Fourth World Congress of Jewish Studies*, 1: 103–6. Jerusalem: Magnes Press, 1967.

36.3 Josiah (*see also* 37.3)

Claburn, W. Eugene. "The Fiscal Basis of Josiah's Reforms." *JBL* 92 (1973): 11–22.

Cross, Frank M., and David N. Freedman. "Josiah's Revolt Against Assyria." *JNES* 12 (1953): 56–59.

Frost, Stanley B. "The Death of Josiah: A Conspiracy of Silence." *JBL* 87 (1968): 369–82.

Malamat, Abraham. "Josiah's Bid for Armageddon." *JANES* 5 (1973): 267–78.

36.4 Jehoiakim, Jehoiachin, and Zedekiah

Albright, William F. "The Seal of Eliakim and the Last Pre-exilic History of Judah." *JBL* 51 (1932): 77–106.

David, Martin. "The Manumission of Slaves Under Zedekiah." *OTS* 5 (1948): 63–79.

Malamat, Abraham. "The Twilight of Judah: In the Egyptian-Babylonian Maelstrom." VTSup 28 (1975): 123–45.

Stern, Ephraim. "Israel at the Close of the Period of the Monarchy: An Archaeological Survey." *BA* 38 (1975): 26–54.

37. Literary Culture, Religion, and Prophetic Critique (*see also* 28)

Fohrer. *HIR*, 251–306.

Ringgren. *IR*, 269–94.

Vriezen. *RAI*, 220–39.

37.1 Micah

Brueggemann, Walter, "'Vine and Fig Tree': A Case Study in Imagination and Criticism." *CBQ* 43 (1981): 188–204.

Childs. *IOTS*, 428–39.

Gunkel, Herrman. "The Close of Micah: A Prophetical Liturgy." In *What Remains of the Old Testament*, 115–49. New York and London: Macmillan Co., 1928.

Jeppesen, K. "New Aspects of Micah Research." *JSOT* 8 (1978): 3–32.

Kapelrud, Arvid S. "Eschatology in the Book of Micah." *VT* 11 (1961): 392–405.

McFadden, W. Robert. "Micah and the Problem of Continuities and Discontinuities in Prophecy." In *SC 2*, 127–46.

Willis, John T. "The Structure of the Book of Micah." *SEÅ* 34 (1969): 5–42.

―――. "Thoughts on the Redactional Analysis of the Book of Micah." SBLSP 13 (1978): 87–107.

Wolff, Hans Walter. *Micah the Prophet*. Philadelphia: Fortress Press, 1981.

van der Woude, Adam S. "Micah in Dispute with the Pseudo-prophets." *VT* 19 (1969): 244–60.

37.2 Isaiah of Jerusalem (*see also* 50.2; 50.4.a; 55.2)

Isaianic Tradition, chaps. 1―66

Carroll, Robert P. *When Prophecy Failed*, 130–56.

Childs. *IOTS*, 311–38.

Holladay, William L. *Isaiah: Scroll of a Prophetic Heritage*. Grand Rapids: Wm. B. Eerdmans, 1978.

Isaiah 1―39

Ackroyd, Peter R. "Isaiah I–XII: Presentation of a Prophet." VTSup 29 (1978): 16–48.

Auld, A. Graeme. "Poetry, Prophecy, Hermeneutic: Recent Studies in Isaiah." *SJT* 33 (1980): 567–81.

Barton, John. "Ethics in Isaiah of Jerusalem." *JTS* 32 (1981): 1–18.

Blank, Sheldon H. *Prophetic Faith in Isaiah*. New York: Harper & Bros., 1958.

Childs, Brevard S. *Isaiah and the Assyrian Crisis*. SBT, 2d ser., 3. London: SCM Press, 1967.

Clements, Roland E. *Isaiah and the Deliverance of Jerusalem*. JSOTSup 13. Sheffield: JSOT Press, 1980.

―――. *Isaiah 1–39*, 1–23. NCBC. Grand Rapids: Wm. B. Eerdmans, 1980.

Engnell, Ivan. *The Call of Isaiah: An Exegetical and Comparative Study*. Uppsala: Lundeqvist, 1949.

Exum, J. Cheryl. "'Whom Will He Teach Knowledge?': A Literary Approach to Isaiah 28." In *Art and Meaning: Rhetoric in Biblical Literature*, ed. D. J. A. Clines et al., 108–39. JSOTSup 19. Sheffield: JSOT Press, 1982.

Fichtner, Johannes. "Isaiah Among the Wise." In *SAIW*, 429–38.

Gottwald, Norman K. "Immanuel as the Prophet's Son." *VT* 8 (1958): 36–47.

Hasel, Gerhard F. *The Remnant: The History and Theology of the Remnant Idea from Genesis to Isaiah*. Berrien Springs, Mich.: Andrews University Press, 1972.

Jones, D. R. "The Traditio of the Oracles of Isaiah of Jerusalem." *ZAW* 67 (1955): 226–46.

Knierem, Rolf. "The Vocation of Isaiah." *VT* 18 (1968): 47–68.

Melugin, Roy. "The Conventional and the Creative in Isaiah's Judgment Oracles." *CBQ* 36 (1974): 301–11.

von Rad. *OTT*, 2: 147–87.

Sheppard, Gerald T. "The Anti-Assyrian Redaction and the Canonical Context of Isaiah 1–39." *JBL* 104 (1985).

Whedbee, J. William. *Isaiah and Wisdom*. Nashville and New York: Abingdon Press, 1971.

37.3 Deuteronomy (*see also* 26)

Carmichael, Calum M. *The Laws of Deuteronomy*. Ithaca, N.Y., and London: Cornell University Press, 1974.

Childs. *IOTS*, 202–25.

Clements, Roland E. *God's Chosen People. A Theological Interpretation of the Book of Deuteronomy*. London: SCM Press, 1968.

Emerton, John A. "Priests and Levites in Deuteronomy." *VT* 12 (1962): 129–38.

Lohfink, Norbert. "Deuteronomy." In IDBSup, 229–32.

Mayes, A. D. H. *Deuteronomy*, 25–108. NCBC. Grand Rapids: Wm. B. Eerdmans, 1979.

Nicholson, E. W. *Deuteronomy and Tradition*. Philadelphia: Fortress Press; Oxford: Basil Blackwell & Mott, 1967.

Noth. *TDH*, 12–17, 26–35.

von Rad, Gerhard. *Studies in Deuteronomy*. SBT, 1st ser., 9. London: SCM Press, 1953.

Rofé, Alexander. "The Strata of the Law about the Centralization of Worship in Deuteronomy and the History of the Deuteronomic Movement." VTSup 22 (1972): 221–26.

Weinfeld, Moshe. *Deuteronomy and the Deuteronomic School*. Oxford: At the Clarendon Press, 1972.

_____. "The Origin of Humanism in Deuteronomy." *JBL* 80 (1961): 241–47.

Welch, Adam C. *The Code of Deuteronomy. A New Theory of Its Origin*. London: James Clark, 1924.

37.4.a Nahum

Childs. *IOTS*, 440–46.

Christensen, Duane L. "The Acrostic of Nahum Reconsidered." *ZAW* 87 (1975): 17–30.

Fohrer. *IOT*, 447–51.

Haldar, Alfred. *Studies in the Book of Nahum*. Uppsala: Lundeqvist, 1947.

Mihelic, Joseph L. "The Concept of God in the Book of Nahum." *Int* 2 (1948): 199–208.

37.4.b Zephaniah

Anderson, George W. "The Idea of the Remnant in the Book of Zephaniah." *ASTI* 11 (1977/1978): 11–14.

Childs. *IOTS,* 457–62.

Hyatt, J. Philip. "The Date and Background of Zephaniah." *JNES* 7 (1948): 25–29.

Kapelrud, Arvid S. *The Message of the Prophet Zephaniah: Morphology and Ideas.* Oslo: Universitetsforlaget, 1975.

Williams, Donald L. "The Date of Zephaniah." *JBL* 82 (1963): 77–88.

37.4.c Habakkuk

Albright, William F. "The Psalm of Habakkuk." In *Studies in Old Testament Prophecy Presented to T. H. Robinson,* ed. H. H. Rowley, 1–18. Edinburgh: T. & T. Clark, 1950.

Brownlee, William H. "The Placarded Revelation of Habakkuk." *JBL* 82 (1963): 319–25.

Childs. *IOTS,* 447–56.

Gowan, Donald E. *The Triumph of Faith in Habakkuk.* Atlanta: John Knox Press, 1976.

Grintz, Yehoshua M., and Dvora Briskin-Nadiv. "Habakkuk." In *EJ* 7 (1971): cols. 1014–17.

Gruenthauer, Michael J. "Chaldeans or Macedonians?" *Bib* 8 (1927): 129–60, 257–89.

Janzen, J. Gerald. "Eschatological Symbol and Existence in Habakkuk." *CBQ* 44 (1982): 394–414.

Nielsen, Eduard. "The Righteous and the Wicked in Habaqquq." *ST* 6 (1952): 54–78.

37.5 Jeremiah

Berridge, John. *Prophet, People and the Word of Yahweh.* Zurich: EVZ-Verlag, 1970.

Bright, John. "The Date of the Prose Sermons in Jeremiah." *JBL* 70 (1951): 15–35.

Carroll, Robert P. *From Chaos to Covenant: Prophecy in the Book of Jeremiah.* New York: Crossroad, 1981.

Childs, Brevard S. "The Enemy from the North and the Chaos Tradition." *JBL* 78 (1959): 187–98.

———. *IOTS,* 339–54.

Crenshaw, James L. "A Living Tradition: The Book of Jeremiah in Current Research." *Int* 37 (1983): 117–29.

Davidson, R. "Orthodoxy and the Prophetic Word: A Study in the Relationship Between Jeremiah and Deuteronomy." *VT* 14 (1964): 407–16.

Hobbs, T. R. "Some Remarks on the Composition and Structure of the Book of Jeremiah." *CBQ* 34 (1974): 257–75.

Holladay, William L. *The Architecture of Jeremiah 1–20.* Lewisburg, Pa.: Bucknell University Press; London: Associated University Presses, 1976.

———. *Jeremiah. Spokesman Out of Time.* Philadelphia: Pilgrim Press, 1974.

Lundbom, Jack R. *Jeremiah: A Study in Ancient Hebrew Rhetoric.* SBLDS 18. Missoula, Mont.: Scholars Press, 1975.

Mottu, Henri. "Jeremiah vs. Hananiah: Ideology and Truth in Old Testament Prophecy." In *BL,* 235–51.

Nicholson, E. W. *Preaching to the Exiles: A Study of the Prose Tradition in the Book of Jeremiah.* Oxford: Basil Blackwell & Mott, 1970.

Overholt, Thomas W. *The Threat of Falsehood: A Study in the Theology of the Book of Jeremiah.* SBT, 2d ser., 16. London: SCM Press, 1970.

Raitt, Thomas M., *A Theology of Exile. Judgment/Deliverance in Jeremiah and Ezekiel.* Philadelphia: Fortress Press, 1977.

Skinner, John. *Prophecy and Religion. Studies in the Life of Jeremiah.* Cambridge: At the University Press, 1922.

Weinfeld, Moshe. "Jeremiah and the Spiritual Metamorphosis of Israel." *ZAW* 88 (1976): 17–56.

Wilcoxen, Jay A. "The Political Background of Jeremiah's Temple Sermon." In *Scripture in History and Theology,* ed. A. L. Merrill and T. W. Overholt, 151–66.

PART IV: HOME RULE UNDER GREAT EMPIRES: ISRAEL'S COLONIAL RECOVERY

Prologue: On the Sources for Israel's Colonial History in Dispersion and Restoration

Biblical Sources, including Maccabees

1 and 2 Chronicles

Ackroyd, Peter R. "Chronicles, I and II." In IDBSup, 156–58.

Japhet, Sarah. "Chronicles, Book of." In *EJ* 5 (1971): cols. 517–34.

Pfeiffer, Robert H. "Chronicles, I and II." In *IDB* 1: 572–80.

Ezra-Nehemiah

Myers, Jacob M. "Ezra and Nehemiah, Book of." In *EJ* 6 (1971): cols. 1111–23.

Pfeiffer, Robert H. "Ezra and Nehemiah, Books of." In *IDB* 2: 215–19.

Talmon, Shemaryahu. "Ezra and Nehemiah (Books and Men)." In IDBSup, 317–28.

1 and 2 Maccabees

Brownlee, William H. "Maccabees, Books of." In *IDB* 3: 201–15.

Goldstein, Jonathan A. *1 and 2 Maccabees.* AB. Garden City, N.Y.: Doubleday & Co., 1976, 1983.

Zeitlin, Solomon, and Sidney Tedesche. *The First Book of Maccabees.* New York: Harper & Bros., 1950.

_____. *The Second Book of Maccabees.* New York: Harper & Bros., 1954.

Extrabiblical Literary Sources

Charles. *APOT.*

Charlesworth. *OTP.*

Cross, Frank M. "The Papyri and their Historical Implications." In *Discoveries in the Wâdî ed-Dâliyeh,* ed. P. W. Lapp and N. L. Lapp, 17–29. AASOR 41, 1974.

_____. "Papyri of the 4th Century B.C. from Dâliyeh." In *New Directions in Biblical Archaeology,* ed. J. C. Greenfield, 41–62. Garden City, N.Y.: Doubleday & Co., 1969.

Goldin, Judah. "Josephus, Flavius." In *IDB* 1: 987–88.

Nickelsburg. *JLBBM,* 1–193.

Porten, Bezalel. *Archives from Elephantine.* Berkeley and Los Angeles: University of California Press, 1968.

Schalit, Abraham. "Josephus Flavius." In *EJ* 10 (1971): cols. 251–63.

Thackeray, Henry St. John, and Ralph Marcus, eds. *Josephus,* vols. I–IX. Loeb Classical Library. Cambridge: Harvard University Press, 1926–65.

Archaeological Sources

Weinberg, Saul S. "Post Exilic Palestine: An Archaeological Report." In *Israel Academy of Sciences and Humanities,* vol. 4 (1971), 78–97.

Yamauchi, Edward M. "The Archaeological Background of Nehemiah." *BSac* 137 (1980): 291–309.

Chapter 10: Sociohistoric Horizons of Colonial Israel

42. From Independent Israelites to Colonized Jews

Avi-Yonah, Michael. *The Holy Land from the Persian to the Arab Conquests (536 B.C. to A.D. 640). A Historical Geography.* Grand Rapids: Baker Book House, 1966.

Bickermann, Elias. *From Ezra to the Last of the Maccabees: Foundations of Post-biblical Judaism.* New York: Schocken Books, 1962.

Bright. *HI,* 341–464.

Foerster, Werner. *From the Exile to Christ: A Historical Introduction to Palestinian Judaism.* Philadelphia: Fortress Press, 1964.

Herrmann. *HIOTT,* 289–392.

Noth. *THI,* 289–401.

Ringgren. *IR,* 297–348.

Smith, Morton. *Palestinian Parties and Politics That Shaped the Old Testament,* 57–201. New York and London: Columbia University Press, 1971.

43. Jewish Response to Neo-Babylonian Dominion

Aharoni. *LB,* 407–23.

Davison, Jean M. "The Oikumene in Ferment: A Cross-Cultural Study of the 6th Century." In *SC 1,* 197–219.

Fohrer. *HIR,* 307–29.

Klein, Ralph W. *Israel in Exile. A Theological Interpretation.* OBT 6. Philadelphia: Fortress Press, 1979.

Malamat, Abraham. "Exile, Assyrian." In *EJ* 6 (1971): cols. 1034–36.

Newsome, James D., Jr. *By the Waters of Babylon: An Introduction to the History and Theology of the Exile.* Atlanta: John Knox Press, 1979.

Oded, Bustenay. "Judah and the Exile (parts 6–7)." In *IJH,* 476–89.

Porten, Bezalel. "Exile, Babylonian." In *EJ* 6 (1971): cols. 1035–41.

Thomas, D. Winton. "The 6th Century B.C.: A Creative Epoch in the History of Israel." *JSS* 6 (1961): 33–46.

Vriezen. *RAI,* 240–51.

44. Jewish Response to Persian Dominion

Ackroyd, Peter R. *The Age of the Chronicler.* Auckland: Supp to *Colloquium,* 1970.

———. "Archaeology, Politics, and Religion: The Persian Period." *The Iliff Review* 39 (Spring 1982): 5–23.

Bossman, D. "Ezra's Marriage Reform: Israel Redefined." *BTB* 9 (1979): 32–38.

Cook, Stanley A. "The Age of Zerubbabel." In *Studies in Old Testament Prophecy Presented to T. H. Robinson,* ed. H. H. Rowley, 19–36.

Cross, Frank M. "A Reconstruction of the Judaean Restoration." *JBL* 94 (1975): 4–18.

Fohrer. *HIR,* 330–59.

Japhet, Sara. "Sheshbazzar and Zerubbabel—Against the Background of the Historical and Religious Tendencies of Ezra-Nehemiah." *ZAW* 94 (1982): 66–98.

Koch, Klaus. "Ezra and the Origins of Judaism." *JSS* 19 (1974): 173–97.

Kuhrt, Amélie. "The Cyrus Cylinder and the Achaemenid Imperial Policy." *JSOT* 25 (1983): 83–97.

Leeseberg, M. W. "Ezra and Nehemiah: A Review of the Return and Reform." *CTM* 33 (1962): 79–90.

McEvenue, Sean E. "The Political Structure in Judah from Cyrus to Nehemiah." *CBQ* 44 (1981): 353–64.

Rowley, H. H. "The Chronological Order of Ezra and Nehemiah." In *The Servant of the Lord and Other Essays on the Old Testament,* 135–68. 2d ed. Oxford: Basil Blackwell & Mott, 1965.

———. "Nehemiah's Mission and its Background." In *Men of God,* 211–45.

———. "Sanballat and the Samaritan Temple." In *Men of God,* 246–76.

Schultz, Carl. "The Political Tensions Reflected in Ezra-Nehemiah." In *SC 1,* 221–44.

Vriezen. *RAI,* 251–62.

Widengren, Geo. "The Persian Period." In *IJH,* 489–538.

45. Jewish Response to Macedonian and Ptolemaic Dominions

Coggins, Richard J. *Samaritans and Jews: The Origins of Samaritanism Reconsidered.* Oxford: Basil Blackwell & Mott, 1975.

Eddy, Samuel K. *The King Is Dead. Studies in the Near Eastern Resistance to Hellenism, 334–31 B.C.* Lincoln: University of Nebraska Press, 1961.

Fohrer. *HIR,* 359–90.

Hengel, Martin. *Judaism and Hellenism. Studies in Their Encounter in Palestine During the Early Hellenistic Period.* 2 vols. Philadelphia: Fortress Press, 1974.

MacDonald, John. "Samaritans." In *EJ* 14 (1971): cols. 725–32.

Purvis, James D. *The Samaritan Pentateuch and the Origin of the Samaritan Sect.* HSM 2. Missoula, Mont.: Scholars Press, 1968.

Rivkin, Ellis, "Ben Sira—The Bridge Between the Aaronide and Pharisaic Revolutions." *Eretz Israel* 12 (1975): 95*–103*.

Rowley, H. H. "The Samaritan Schism in Legend and History." In *Israel's Prophetic Heritage. Essays in Honor of James Muilenburg,* ed. B. W. Anderson and W. Harrelson, 208–22. New York: Harper & Bros., 1962.

Schäfer, Peter. "The Hellenistic and Maccabaean Periods." In *IJH,* 539–604.

Stone, Michael E. "The Book of Enoch and Judaism in the Third Century B.C.E." *CBQ* 40 (1978): 479–92.

Tcherikover, Victor. *Hellenistic Civilization and the Jews.* New York: Jewish Publication Society of America, 1961.

Vriezen. *RAI,* 263–78.

Zeitlin, Solomon. *The Rise and Fall of the Judaean State. A Political, Social and Religious History of the Second Commonwealth, Vol. I: 332–37 B.C.E.* Philadelphia: Jewish Publication Society of America, 1962.

46. Jewish Response to Seleucid Dominion: The Maccabees

Beckwith, Roger T. "The Pre-History and Relationships of the Pharisees, Sadducees and Essenes: A Tentative Reconstruction." *RevQ* 11 (1982): 3–46.

Doran, Robert. "Parties and Politics in Pre-Hasmonean Jerusalem: A Closer Look at 2 Macc. 3:11." SBLSP 21 (1982): 107–11.

Jones, Bruce W. "Antiochus Epiphanes and the Persecution of the Jews." In *SC 1*, 263–90.

Knibb, Michael A. "Exile in the Damascus Document." *JSOT* 25 (1983): 99–117.

Murphy-O'Connor, Jerome. "The Essenes and Their History." *RB* 81 (1974): 215–44.

47. A Jewish State Rises and Falls: The Hasmoneans

Buehler, William W. *The Pre-Herodian Civil War and Social Debate.* Basel: Friedrich Reinhardt Kommissionsverlag, 1974.

Finkelstein, Louis. *The Pharisees: The Sociological Background of Their Faith.* 3d ed. Philadelphia: Jewish Publication Society of America, 1946.

Rabin, Chayim. "Alexander Jannaeus and the Pharisees." *JJS* 7 (1956): 3–11.

Zeitlin, Solomon. *The Rise and Fall of the Judaean State,* 118–363.

Chapter 11: Traditions of Colonial Israel: Completing the Law and the Prophets

48. Hermeneutical Politics: The Interplay of Law and Prophets

Blenkinsopp, Joseph. *Prophecy and Canon.* Notre Dame, Ind.: Notre Dame University Press, 1977.

Childs. *IOTS,* 109–35, 229–38, 305–10.

Collins, John J. *Between Athens and Jerusalem. Jewish Identity in the Hellenistic Diaspora.* New York: Crossroad, 1983.

Mack, Burton. "Under the Shadow of Moses: Authorship and Authority in Hellenistic Judaism." SBLSP 21 (1982): 299–318.

Nickelsburg, George W. E., and Michael E. Stone. *Faith and Piety in Early Judaism: Texts and Documents.* Philadelphia: Fortress Press, 1983.

Patte, Daniel. *Early Jewish Hermeneutic in Palestine.* SBLDS 22. Missoula, Mont.: Scholars Press, 1975.

49. Rounding Out the Law: The Priestly Writer (P) (*see also* Part II, Prol.; 15; 17; 19.2; 19.4)

Abba, Raymond. "Priests and Levites." In *IDB* 3: 888–89.

Allan, Nigel. "The Jerusalem Priesthood During the Exile." *HeyJ* 23 (1982): 259–69.

Bailey, Lloyd R. *Where Is Noah's Ark? Mystery on Mt. Ararat.* Nashville: Abingdon Press, 1978.

Blenkinsopp, Joseph. "The Structure of P." *CBQ* 38 (1976): 275–92.

Brueggemann, Walter. "The Kerygma of the Priestly Writers." In *The Vitality of Old Testament Traditions,* 101–13.

Cody, Aelred. *A History of Old Testament Priesthood,* 146–92. AnBib 35. Rome: Pontifical Biblical Institute, 1969.

Douglas, Mary. "The Abominations of Leviticus." In *Purity and Danger. An Analysis of Concepts of Pollution and Taboo,* 54–72. Harmondsworth: Penguin Books, 1966.

Haran, Menahem. "Behind the Scenes of History: Determining the Date of the Priestly Source." *JBL* 100 (1981): 321–33.

_____. *Temples and Temple-Service in Ancient Israel—An Inquiry Into the Character of Cult Phenomena and the Historical Setting of the Priestly School.* Oxford: At the Clarendon Press, 1978.

Haran, Menahem, and Menaham Stern. "Priests and Priesthood." In *EJ* 13 (1971): cols. 1069–88.

Hurvitz, A. "The Evidence of Language in Dating the Priestly Code." *RB* 81 (1974): 24–56.

Levine, Baruch A. *In the Presence of the Lord, a Study of Cult and Some Cultic Terms in Ancient Israel.* Leiden: E. J. Brill, 1974.

_____. "Priestly Writers." In IDBSup, 683–87.

McEvenue, Sean. *The Narrative Style of the Priestly Writer.* AnBib 50. Rome: Pontifical Biblical Institute, 1971.

Milgrom, Jacob. *Cult and Conscience. The ASHAM and the Priestly Doctrine of Repentance.* Studies in Judaism in Late Antiquity 18. Leiden: E. J. Brill, 1976.

_____. *Studies in Levitical Terminology, I: The Encroacher and the Levite, the Term ʿAboda.* University of California Publications, Near Eastern Studies 14. Berkeley and Los Angeles: University of California Press, 1970.

Soler, Jean. "The Dietary Prohibitions of the Hebrews." *The New York Review of Books* (6/14/79): 24–30.

50. Rounding Out the Prophets (*see also* 28)

Blenkinsopp, Joseph. *A History of Prophecy in Israel,* 177–280.

Hammershaimb, E. "The Change in Prophecy During the Exile." In *Some Aspects of Old Testament Prophecy from Isaiah to Malachi,* 91–112. Aarhus: Rosenkilde og Bagger, 1966.

Petersen, David L. *Late Israelite Prophecy. Studies in Deutero-Prophetic Literature and in Chronicles,* 13–53, 97–104. SBLMS 23. Missoula, Mont.: Scholars Press, 1977.

50.1 Ezekiel

Aberbach, Moses. "Ezekiel." In *EJ* 6 (1971): cols. 1078–95.

Ackroyd, Peter R. *Exile and Restoration. A Study of Hebrew Thought of the 6th Century B.C.,* 103–17. Philadelphia: Westminster Press, 1968.

Carley, Keith W. *Ezekiel Among the Prophets.* SBT, 2d ser., 31. London: SCM Press, 1975.

Childs. *IOTS,* 355–72.

Greenberg, Moshe. "Ezekiel 17 and the Policy of Psammetichus II." *JBL* 76 (1957): 304–9.

Hammershaimb, E. "Ezekiel's View of the Monarchy." In *Studia Orientalia, Ioanni Pedersen Septuagenario,* 130–40. Copenhagen: Einar Munksgaard, 1953.

Howie, Carl G. *The Date and Composition of Ezekiel.* JBLMS 4. Philadelphia: Society of Biblical Literature, 1950.

Levenson, Jon D. *Theology of the Program of Restoration of Ezekiel 40–48.* HSM 10. Missoula, Mont.: Scholars Press, 1976.

Lindars, Barnabas. "Ezekiel and Individual Responsibility." *VT* 15 (1965): 452–67.

Parunak, H. Van Dyke. "The Literary Architecture of Ezekiel's *Mar'ôt 'Elōhîm*." *JBL* 99 (1980): 61–74.

Smith, Sydney. "The Ship Tyre." *PEQ* 85 (1953): 97–110.

Talmon, Shemaryahu, and Michael Fishbane. "The Structuring of Biblical Books: Studies in the Book of Ezekiel." *ASTI* 10 (1976): 129–53.

Tsevat, Matitiahu. "The Neo-Assyrian and Neo-Babylonian Vassal Oaths and the Prophet Ezekiel." *JBL* 78 (1959): 199–204.

Vogelstein, Max. "Nebuchadnezzar's Reconquest of Phoenicia and Palestine and the Oracle of Ezekiel." *HUCA* 23 (1950/1951): 197–220.

Zimmerli, Walther. *I Am Yahweh*. Atlanta: John Knox Press, 1982.

50.2 Isaiah of the Exile (Deutero-Isaiah)
(*see also* 37.2; 50.4.a; 55.2)

Avishur, Isaac. "Isaiah 40–66." In *EJ* 9 (1971): cols. 61–66.

Clines, David J. A. *I, He, We, and They: A Literary Approach to Isaiah 53*. JSOTSup 1. Sheffield: JSOT Press, 1976.

Gitay, Yehoshua. "Deutero-Isaiah: Oral or Written?" *JBL* 99 (1980): 185–97.

Harner, P. D. "The Salvation Oracle in Second Isaiah." *JBL* 88 (1969): 418–34.

Hollenberg, D. E. "Nationalism and 'the Nations' in Is. 40–55." *VT* 19 (1969): 23–36.

Hyatt, J. Philip. "The Sources of the Suffering Servant Idea." *JNES* 3 (1944): 79–86.

Kruse, Colin G. "The Servant Songs: Interpretive Trends Since C. R. North." *StudBT* 8 (1978): 3–27.

Lindblom, J. *The Servant Songs in Deutero-Isaiah*. Lund: C. W. K. Gleerup, 1951.

Lindhagen, Curt. *The Servant Motif in the Old Testament. A Preliminary Study to the Ebed-Yahweh Problem in Deutero-Isaiah*. Uppsala: Lundeqvist, 1950.

Melugin, Roy. *The Formation of Isaiah 40–55*. BZAW 141. Berlin: Walter de Gruyter, 1976.

North, C. R. *The Suffering Servant in Deutero-Isaiah: Historical and Critical Studies*. 2d ed. London: Oxford University Press, 1956.

Schoors, Anton. *I Am God Your Savior: A Form-Critical Study of the Main Genres in Isa. XL–LV*. VTSup 24 (1973).

Smith, Morton. "II Isaiah and the Persians." *JAOS* 83 (1963): 415–21.

Smith, Sydney. *Isaiah Chaps. XL–LV: Literary Criticism and History*. London: Oxford University Press, 1944.

Spykerboer, H. C. *The Structure and Composition of Deutero-Isaiah*. Franeker: T. Wever, 1976.

Stuhlmueller, Carroll. *Creative Redemption in Deutero-Isaiah*. AnBib 43. Rome: Pontifical Biblical Institute, 1970.

————. "Deutero-Isaiah (chaps. 40–55): Major Transitions in the Prophet's Theology and in Contemporary Scholarship." *CBQ* 42 (1980): 1–29.

Torrey, Charles C. *The Second Isaiah. A New Interpretation*. Edinburgh: T. & T. Clark, 1928.

Whybray, R. N. *Thanksgiving for a Liberated Prophet: An Interpretation of Isaiah 53*. JSOTSup 4. Sheffield: JSOT Press, 1978.

50.3 Prophets of the Rebuilt Temple

Ackroyd, Peter R. "The Book of Haggai and Zechariah 1–8." *JJS* 3 (1952): 151–56.

_____. "Two Old Testament Historical Problems of the Early Persian Period." *JNES* 17 (1958): 13–27.

Carroll, Robert P. *When Prophecy Failed*, 157–68.

Hanson. *DA*, 240–62.

James, Fleming. "Thoughts on Haggai and Zechariah." *JBL* 53 (1934): 229–35.

Siebeneck, Robert T. "The Messianism of Aggaeus and Proto-Zacharias." *CBQ* 19 (1957): 312–28.

50.3.a Haggai

Ackroyd, Peter R. *Exile and Restoration*, 153–70.

_____. "Studies in the Book of Haggai." *JJS* 2 (1951): 163–76; 3 (1952): 1–13.

Childs. *IOTS*, 463–71.

Fohrer. *IOT*, 458–60.

Mason, Rex A. "The Purpose of the 'Editorial Framework' of the Book of Haggai." *VT* 27 (1977): 415–21.

North, Francis S. "Critical Analysis of the Book of Haggai." *ZAW* 68 (1956): 25–46.

50.3.b Zechariah 1—8 (*see also* 55.2)

Ackroyd, Peter R. *Exile and Restoration*, 171–217.

Childs. *IOTS*, 472–87.

Fohrer. *IOT*, 460–64.

Halpern, Baruch. "The Ritual Background of Zechariah's Temple Song." *CBQ* 40 (1978): 167–90.

Le Bas, Edwin E. "Zechariah's Enigmatical Contribution to the Corner-Stone." *PEQ* 82 (1950): 102–22.

McHardy, W. D. "The Horses in Zechariah." In *In Memoriam Paul Kahle*, 174–79. BZAW 103. Berlin: Walter de Gruyter, 1968.

North, Robert. "Zechariah's Seven-Spout Lampstand." *Bib* 51 (1970): 183–206.

Waterman, Leroy. "The Camouflage Purge of Three Messianic Conspirators." *JNES* 13 (1954): 83–87.

50.4.a Isaiah 56—66 (Trito-Isaiah)
(*see also* 37.2; 50.2; 55.2)

Eissfeldt. *TOT*, 341–46.

Fohrer. *IOT*, 384–88.

Hanson. *DA*, 32–208, 380–401.

Kosmala, Hans. "Form and Structure of Isaiah 58." *ASTI* 5 (1967): 69–81.

McCullough, W. Stewart. "A Re-examination of Isaiah 56–66." *JBL* 67 (1948): 27–36.

Morgenstern, Julius. "Isaiah 63:7–14." *HUCA* 23 (1950/1951): 186–203.

Murtonen, Aimo. "Third Isaiah—Yes or No?" *AbrN* 19 (1980/1981): 20–42.

Odeberg, Hugo. *Trito-Isaiah (Isa 56–66). A Literary and Linguistic Analysis*. Uppsala: Lundeqvist, 1931.

Westermann, Claus. *Isaiah 40–66. A Commentary*, 296–308.

50.4.b Malachi

Braun, Roddy L. "Malachi—A Catechism for Times of Disappointment." *CurTM* 4 (1977): 297–303.

Childs. *IOTS*, 488–98.

Fischer, James A. "Notes on the Literary Form and Message of Malachi." *CBQ* 34 (1972): 315–20.

Fohrer. *IOT*, 469–70.

Lipinski, Edward. "Malachi, Book of." In *EJ* 11 (1971): cols. 812–16.

Swetnam, J. "Malachi 1:11: An Interpretation." *CBQ* 31 (1969): 200–209.

Torrey, Charles C. "The Prophecy of 'Malachi'." *JBL* 17 (1898): 1–15.

50.4.c Obadiah and Joel

Cannon, William W. "Israel and Edom: the Oracle of Obadiah." *Theology* 14 (1927): 129–40, 191–200.

Childs. *IOTS*, 385–94 (Joel), 411–16 (Obadiah).

Gray, John. "The Diaspora of Israel and Judah in Obadiah, v. 20." *ZAW* 65 (1953): 53–59.

Kapelrud, Arvid S. *Joel Studies*. Uppsala: Lundeqvist, 1948.

Lipinski, Edward. "Obadiah, Book of." In *EJ* 12 (1971): cols. 1304–6.

Myers, Jacob M. "Edom and Judah in the 6th–5th Cents. B.C." In *Near Eastern Studies in Honor of W. F. Albright*, 377–92. Baltimore: Johns Hopkins University Press, 1971.

———. "Some Considerations Bearing on the Date of Joel." *ZAW* (1962): 177–95.

Ploeger, Otto. *Theocracy and Eschatology*, 96–105. Richmond: John Knox Press, 1968.

Robinson, Theodore H. "The Structure of the Book of Obadiah." *JTS* 17 (1916): 402–8.

Treves, Marco. "The Date of Joel." *VT* 7 (1957): 149–56.

Wolff, Hans Walter. *Joel and Amos*, 3–15. Hermeneia. Philadelphia: Fortress Press, 1977.

Chapter 12: Traditions of Colonial Israel: The Writings

51. Late Historical Works: 1 and 2 Chronicles and Ezra-Nehemiah (*see also* Part IV, Prol.; 39; 44)

Ackroyd, Peter R. "The Chronicler as Exegete." *JSOT* 2 (1977): 2–32.

———. "History and Theology in the Writings of the Chronicler." *CTM* 38 (1967): 501–15.

———. "The Theology of the Chronicler." *LTQ* 8 (1973): 101–16.

Braun, Roddy L. "Chronicles, Ezra and Nehemiah: Theology and Literary History." VTSup 30 (1979): 52–64.

Childs. *IOTS*, 639–55 (Chronicles), 624–38 (Ezra-Nehemiah).

Freedman, David N. "The Chronicler's Purpose." *CBQ* 23 (1961): 436–42.

Japhet, Sara. "The Supposed Common Authorship of Chronicles and Ezra-Nehemiah Investigated Anew." *VT* 18 (1968): 330–71.

Petersen, David L. *Late Israelite Prophecy. Studies in Deutero-Prophetic Literature and in Chronicles*, 55–104.

von Rad, Gerhard. "The Levitical Sermon in I & II Chronicles." In *The Problem of the Hexateuch and Other Essays*, 267–80.

Williamson, H. G. M. *Israel in the Books of Chronicles*. Cambridge: At the University Press, 1977.

52.1 What Is Biblical Poetry?

Dahood, Mitchell. "Poetry, Hebrew." In IDBSup, 669–72.

Gottwald, Norman K. "Poetry, Hebrew." In *IDB* 3: 829–38.

Hrushovski, Benjamin. "Prosody, Hebrew." In *EJ* 13 (1971): cols. 1199–1203.

Kugel, James L. *The Idea of Biblical Poetry. Parallelism and Its History.* New Haven, Conn., and London: Yale University Press, 1981.

O'Connor, M. P. *Hebrew Verse Structure.* Winona Lake, Ind.: Eisenbrauns, 1980.

52.2 Psalms (*see also* 31.2)

General

Barth, Christoph. *Introduction to the Psalms.* New York: Charles Scribner's Sons, 1966.

Childs. *IOTS,* 504–25.

Eaton, John H. In *TI,* 238–73.

Gerstenberger, Erhard. In *OTFC,* 179–223.

Hempel, Johannes. "Psalms, Book of." In *IDB* 3: 942–58.

Johnson, Aubrey R. In *OTMS,* 162–209.

Kapelrud, Arvid S. "Scandinavian Research in the Psalms After Mowinckel." *ASTI* 4 (1965): 74–90.

Sabourin, Leopold. *The Psalms. Their Origin and Meaning.* New York: Alba House, 1970.

Sarna, Nahum M. "Psalms, Book of." In *EJ* 13 (1971): cols. 1303–22.

Westermann, Claus. "Psalms, Book of." In IDBSup, 705–10.

Special Studies

Braude, William G. *The Midrash on Psalms.* 2 vols. New Haven, Conn.: Yale University Press, 1959.

Brueggemann, Walter. "Psalms and the Life of Faith: A Suggested Typology of Function." *JSOT* 17 (1980): 3–32.

Childs, Brevard S. "Psalm Titles and Midrashic Exegesis." *JSS* 16 (1971): 137–50.

Drijvers, Pius. *The Psalms: Their Structure and Meaning.* New York and London: Herder & Herder, 1965.

Gunkel, Hermann. *The Psalms. A Form-Critical Introduction.* Facet Books 19. Philadelphia: Fortress Press, 1967.

Guthrie, Harvey H., Jr. *Israel's Sacred Songs. A Study of Dominant Themes.* New York: Seabury Press, 1978.

Johnson, Aubrey R. *The Cultic Prophet and Israel's Psalmody.* Cardiff: University of Wales Press, 1979.

Mowinckel, Sigmund. *The Psalms in Israel's Worship.* 2 vols. Nashville and New York: Abingdon Press, 1962.

Murphy, Roland E. "A Consideration of the Classification 'Wisdom Psalms.' " In *SAIW,* 456–67.

Rowley, H. H. "Psalmody and Music." In *Worship in Ancient Israel,* 176–212. London: SPCK, 1967.

Westermann, Claus. *Praise and Lament in the Psalms.* Atlanta: John Knox Press, 1981 (incorporates the author's previous work *The Praise of God in the Psalms,* 1965).

52.3 Lamentations

Albrektson, Bertil. *Studies in the Text and Theology of the Book of Lamentations.* Lund: C. W. K. Gleerup, 1963.

Childs. *IOTS,* 590–97.

Gordis, Robert. "A Commentary on the Text of Lamentations." *JQR,* 75th Anniv. Vol. (1967): 267–86.

———. "Commentary on the Text of Lamentations (II)." *JQR* 58 (1967/1968): 14–33.

Gottlieb, Hans. *A Study on the Text of Lamentations.* Aarhus: Acta Jutlandica, 1978.

Gottwald, Norman K. *Studies in the Book of Lamentations.* SBT, 1st ser., 14. 2d ed. London: SCM Press, 1962.

Gwaltney, W. C., Jr. "The Biblical Book of Lamentations in the Context of Near Eastern Lament Literature." In *SC 2,* 191–211.

Lanahan, W. F. "The Speaking Voice in the Book of Lamentations." *JBL* 93 (1974): 41–49.

Mintz, Alan. "The Rhetoric of Lamentations and the Representations of Catastrophe." *Prooftexts* 2 (1982): 1–17.

Shea, W. H. "The qinah Structure of the Book of Lamentations." *Bib* 60 (1979): 103–7.

Tigay, Jeffrey H. "Lamentations, Book of." In *EJ* 10 (1971): cols. 1368–75.

52.4 Song of Songs

Audet, Jean-Paul. "The Meaning of the Canticle of Canticles." *TD* 5 (1957): 88–92.

Childs. *IOTS,* 569–79.

Exum, J. Cheryl. "A Literary and Structural Analysis of the Song of Songs." *ZAW* 85 (1973): 47–79.

Gottwald, Norman K. "Song of Songs." In *IDB* 4: 420–26.

Landsberger, Franz. "Poetic Units Within the Song of Songs." *JBL* 73 (1954): 203–16.

Landy, F. "Beauty and the Enigma: An Inquiry Into Some Interrelated Episodes of the Song of Songs." *JSOT* 17 (1980): 55–100.

Murphy, Roland E. "Canticles (Song of Songs)." In FOTL vol. 13, 98–124.

———. "Song of Songs." In IDBSup, 836–38.

———. "The Unity of the Song of Songs." *VT* 29 (1979): 436–43.

Rowley, H. H. "The Interpretation of the Song of Songs." In *The Servant of the Lord and Other Essays on the Old Testament,* 197–245. 2d ed. Oxford: Basil Blackwell & Mott, 1965.

White, John B. *A Study of the Language of Love in the Song of Songs and Ancient Egyptian Poetry.* SBLDS 38. Missoula, Mont.: Scholars Press, 1978.

53.2 Ruth

Beattie, D. R. G. "The Book of Ruth as Evidence for Israelite Legal Practice." *VT* 24 (1974): 251–67.

Bertman, Stephen. "Symmetrical Design in the Book of Ruth." *JBL* 84 (1965): 165–68.

Childs. *IOTS,* 560–68.

Fisch, Harold. "Ruth and the Structure of Covenant History." *VT* 32 (1982): 425–37.

Hals, Ronald M. *The Theology of the Book of Ruth.* Philadelphia: Fortress Press, 1969.

Loretz, Oswald. "The Theme of the Ruth Story." *CBQ* 22 (1960): 391–99.

Murphy, Roland E. "Ruth." In FOTL vol. 13, 84–95.

Myers, Jacob M. *The Linguistic and Literary Form of the Book of Ruth*. Leiden: E. J. Brill, 1955.

Prinsloo, W. S. "The Theology of the Book of Ruth." *VT* 30 (1980): 330–41.

Rauber, D. F. "Literary Values in the Bible: The Book of Ruth." *JBL* 89 (1970): 27–37.

Rowley, H. H. "The Marriage of Ruth." In *The Servant of the Lord and Other Essays on the Old Testament*, 169–94.

Trible, Phyllis. *God and the Rhetoric of Sexuality*, 166–99. OBT. Philadelphia: Fortress Press, 1978.

53.3 Jonah

Burrows, Millar. "The Literary Category of the Book of Jonah." In *Translating and Understanding the Old Testament*, ed. H. T. Frank and W. L. Reed, 80–107. Nashville: Abingdon Press, 1970.

Childs. *IOTS*, 417–27.

Cohn, Gabriel H. "Jonah, Book of." In *EJ* 10 (1971): cols. 169–73.

Fretheim, Terence E. "Jonah and Theodicy." *ZAW* 90 (1978): 227–37.

Holbert, John C. "'Deliverance Belongs to Yahweh!': Satire in the Book of Jonah." *JSOT* 21 (1981): 59–81.

Johnson, Aubrey R. "Jonah 2, 3–10: A Study in Cultic Phantasy." In *Studies in Old Testament Prophecy Presented to T. H. Robinson*, ed. H. H. Rowley, 82–102.

Landes, George M. "Jonah: A Māšāl?" In *Israelite Wisdom: Theological and Literary Essays in Honor of Samuel Terrien*, ed. J. G. Gammie et al., 137–58. Missoula, Mont.: Scholars Press, 1978.

_____. "Jonah, Book of." In IDBSup, 488–91.

_____. "Linguistic Criteria and the Date of the Book of Jonah." *Eretz Israel* 16 (1982): 147*–70*.

Wolff, Hans Walter. *Jonah: Church in Revolt*. St. Louis: Clayton Publishing House, 1978.

53.4 Esther

Baumgarten, Albert I. "Scroll of Esther." In *EJ* 14 (1971): cols. 1047–57.

Berg, Sandra B. *The Book of Esther: Motifs, Themes, and Structures*. SBLDS 44. Missoula, Mont.: Scholars Press, 1979.

Childs. *IOTS*, 598–607.

Craghan, John F. "Esther, Judith, and Ruth: Paradigms for Human Liberation." *BTB* 12 (1982): 11–19.

Humphreys, W. Lee. "Esther, Book of." In IDBSup, 279–81.

_____. "A Life-Style for Diaspora: A Study of the Tales of Esther and Daniel." *JBL* 92 (1973): 211–23.

Jones, Bruce W. "Two Misconceptions About the Book of Esther." *CBQ* 39 (1977): 171–81.

Moore, Carey A., ed. *Studies in the Book of Esther*. New York: Ktav Publishing, 1982.

Murphy, Roland E. "Esther." In FOTL vol. 13, 152–70.

Talmon, Shemaryahu. "'Wisdom' in the Book of Esther." *VT* 13 (1963): 419–55.

54.1 What Is Wisdom?

General

Blank, Sheldon H. "Wisdom." In *IDB* 4: 852–61.

Crenshaw, James L. *Old Testament Wisdom. An Introduction.* Atlanta: John Knox Press, 1981.

————. "Wisdom." In *OTFC,* 225–64.

————. "Wisdom in the OT." In IDBSup, 952–56.

Murphy, Roland E. "Introduction to Wisdom Literature/Glossary." In FOTL vol. 13, 1–12, 172–85.

Scott, R. B. Y. "Wisdom/Wisdom Literature." In *EJ* 16 (1971): cols. 557–63.

Special Studies

Collins, John J. "Proverbial Wisdom and the Yahwist Vision." *Semeia* 17 (1980): 1–17.

Crenshaw. *SAIW.*

Fontaine, Carol. *Traditional Sayings in the Old Testament.* Sheffield: Almond Press, 1982.

Gammie, John G. et al., eds. *Israelite Wisdom: Theological and Literary Essays in Honor of Samuel Terrien.* Missoula, Mont.: Scholars Press, 1978.

Lambert, Wilfred G., ed. *Babylonian Wisdom Literature,* 21–91. Oxford: At the Clarendon Press, 1960.

McKane, William. *Prophets and Wise Men.* SBT, 1st ser., 44. London: SCM Press, 1965.

Morgan, Donn F. *Wisdom in Old Testament Traditions.* Atlanta: John Knox Press, 1981.

Murphy, Roland E. "Assumptions and Problems in Old Testament Wisdom Research." *CBQ* 29 (1967): 101–12.

von Rad, Gerhard. *Wisdom in Israel.* Nashville and New York: Abingdon Press, 1972.

Rankin, Oliver S. *Israel's Wisdom Literature. Its Bearing on Theology and the History of Religion.* Edinburgh: T. & T. Clark, 1936.

Rylaarsdam, J. Coert. *Revelation in Jewish Wisdom Literature.* Chicago: University of Chicago Press, 1946.

Scott, R. B. Y. *The Way of Wisdom in the Old Testament.* New York: Macmillan Co., 1971.

Sheppard, Gerald T., *Wisdom as a Hermeneutical Construct: A Study in the Sapientializing of the Old Testament.* BZAW 151. New York and Berlin: Walter de Gruyter, 1980.

Whybray, R. N. *The Intellectual Tradition in the Old Testament.* BZAW 135. New York and Berlin: Walter de Gruyter, 1974.

Williams, James G. *Those Who Ponder Proverbs: Aphoristic Thinking and Biblical Literature.* Sheffield: Almond Press, 1981.

54.2 Proverbs

Brown, John Pairman. "Proverb-Book, Gold-Economy, Alphabet." *JBL* 100 (1981): 169–91.

Childs. *IOTS,* 545–59.

Fox, Michael V. "Aspects of the Religion of the Book of Proverbs." *HUCA* 39 (1968): 55–69.

Gemser, Berend. "The Spiritual Structure of Biblical Aphoristic Wisdom." In *SAIW,* 208–19.

Gordis, Robert. "The Social Background of Wisdom Literature." *HUCA* 18 (1943/1944): 77–118.

Kovacs, Brian W. "Is There a Class-Ethic in Proverbs?" In *Essays in Old Testament*

Ethics: J. P. Hyatt, In Memoriam, ed. J. L. Crenshaw and J. T. Willis, 171–89. New York: Ktav Publishing, 1974.

Murphy, Roland E. "The Kerygma of the Book of Proverbs." *Int* 20 (1966): 3–14.

_____. "Proverbs." In FOTL vol. 13, 48–82.

Scott, R. B. Y. "Folk Proverbs of the Ancient Near East." In *SAIW,* 417–26.

Skehan, Patrick W. *Studies in Israelite Poetry and Wisdom,* 9–45. CBQMS 1. Washington, D.C.: Catholic Biblical Society of America, 1971.

Thompson, John M. *The Form and Function of Proverbs in Ancient Israel.* The Hague and Paris: Mouton Press, 1974.

Whybray, R. N. *Wisdom in Proverbs 1–9.* SBT, 1st ser., 45. London: SCM Press, 1965.

Williams, James G. "The Power of Form: A Study of Biblical Proverbs." *Semeia* 17 (1980): 35–58.

54.3 Job

Childs. *IOTS,* 526–44.

Dick, Michael B. "The Legal Metaphor in Job 31." *CBQ* 41 (1979): 37–50.

Ginsberg, Harold L. "Job, Book of." In *EJ* 10 (1971): cols. 111–21.

Glatzer, Nahum. "The Book of Job and Its Interpreters." In *Biblical Motifs,* ed. A. Altmann, 197–221. Cambridge: Harvard University Press, 1966.

_____. *The Dimensions of Job: A Study and Selected Readings.* New York: Schocken Books, 1969.

Good, Edwin M. "Job and the Literary Task: A Response." *Soundings* 56 (1973): 470–84 (a reply to Robertson, "The Book of Job," below).

Hurvitz, A. "The Date of the Prose-Tale of Job Linguistically Reconsidered." *HTR* 67 (1974): 17–34.

Murphy, Roland E. "Job." In FOTL vol. 13, 14–45.

Polzin, Robert. *Biblical Structuralism,* 54–125. Semeia Studies. Philadelphia: Fortress Press; Missoula, Mont.: Scholars Press, 1977.

Pope, Marvin H. "Job, Book of." In *IDB* 2: 911–25.

von Rad, Gerhard. "Job xxxviii and Ancient Egyptian Wisdom." In *The Problem of the Hexateuch and Other Essays,* 281–91.

_____. *Wisdom in Israel,* 206–26.

Robertson, David. "The Book of Job: A Literary Study." *Soundings* 56 (1973): 446–69.

Sanders, P. S. *Twentieth Century Interpretations of the Book of Job.* Englewood Cliffs, N.J.: Prentice-Hall, 1968.

Skehan, Patrick W. *Studies in Israelite Poetry and Wisdom,* 96–123.

Tsevat, Matitiahu. "The Meaning of the Book of Job." In *SAIW,* 341–74.

Whedbee, J. William. "The Comedy of Job." *Semeia* 7 (1977): 1–39.

Zuckerman, Bruce. "Job, Book of." In IDBSup, 479–81.

54.4 Ecclesiastes

Childs. *IOTS,* 580–89.

Crenshaw, James L. "The Eternal Gospel (Eccl. 3:11)." In *Essays in Old Testament Ethics,* ed. J. L. Crenshaw and J. T. Willis, 25–55.

Ginsberg, H. L. "The Quintessence of Koheleth." In *Biblical and Other Studies,* ed. A. Altmann, 47–59. Cambridge: Harvard University Press, 1963.

Good, Edwin M. *Irony in the Old Testament,* 168–95. Philadelphia: Westminster Press, 1965.

Horton, E., Jr. "Koheleth's Concept of Opposites." *Numen* 19 (1972): 1–21.

Loader, John A. *Polar Structures in the Book of Qoheleth.* BZAW 152. New York and Berlin: Walter de Gruyter, 1979.

Murphy, Roland E. "Ecclesiastes (Qoheleth)." In FOTL vol. 13, 126–49.

Ogden, Graham S. "The 'Better'-Proverb (Tob-Spruch), Rhetorical Criticism, and Qoheleth." *JBL* 96 (1977): 489–505.

———. "Qoheleth's Use of the 'Nothing Is Better' Form." *JBL* 98 (1979): 339–50.

Priest, John. "Humanism, Skepticism, and Pessimism in Israel." *JAAR* 36 (1968): 311–26.

Sheppard, Gerald T. "The Epilogue to Qoheleth as Theological Commentary." *CBQ* 39 (1977): 182–89.

Williams, James G. "What Does It Profit a Man?: The Wisdom of Koheleth." In *SAIW,* 375–89.

Wright, Addison. "The Riddle of the Sphinx: The Structure of the Book of Qoheleth." In *SAIW,* 245–66.

———. "The Riddle of the Sphinx Revisited: Numerical Patterns in the Book of Qoheleth." *CBQ* 42 (1980): 38–51.

55.1 What Is Apocalyptic?

Charlesworth. *OTP.*

Collins, John J., ed. *Apocalyptic: The Morphology of a Genre. Semeia* 14 (1979).

Flusser, David. "Apocalypse (genre)." In *EJ* 3 (1971): cols. 179–81.

Frost, Stanley B. *Old Testament Apocalyptic. Its Origin and Growth.* London: Epworth Press, 1952.

Funk, Robert W., ed. *Apocalypticism.* New York: Herder & Herder, 1969.

Hanson, Paul D. "Apocalypse, Genre." In IDBSup, 27–28.

———. "Apocalypticism." In IDBSup, 28–34.

Nicholson, E. W. "Apocalyptic." In *TI,* 189–213.

Oswalt, John N. "Recent Studies in Old Testament Eschatology and Apocalyptic." *JETS* 24 (1981): 289–301.

Rist, Martin. "Apocalypticism." In *IDB* 1: 157–61.

Rowland, Christopher. *The Open Heaven. A Study of Apocalyptic in Judaism and Early Christianity.* New York: Crossroad, 1982.

Russell, David S. *The Method and Message of Jewish Apocalyptic.* Philadelphia: Westminster Press, 1964.

Schmithals, Walter. *The Apocalyptic Movement. Introduction and Interpretation.* Nashville and New York: Abingdon Press, 1975.

Thomas, J. Douglas. "Jewish Apocalyptic and the Comparative Method." In *SC 1,* 245–62.

55.2 Daniel and Its Apocalyptic Forerunners

Isaiah 24—27

Anderson, George W. "Isaiah XXIV–XXVII Reconsidered." VTSup 9 (1963): 118–26.

Coggins, Richard J. "The Problem of Isaiah 24–27." *ET* 90 (1978/1979): 328–33.

Millar, William R. *Isaiah 24–27 and the Origin of Apocalyptic.* HSM 11. Missoula, Mont.: Scholars Press, 1976.

Otzen, Benedict. "Traditions and Structures of Isaiah XXIV–XXVII." *VT* 24 (1974): 196–211.

Ploeger, Otto. *Theocracy and Prophecy,* 53–78.

Zechariah 9—14

Fohrer. *IOT,* 464–68.

Hanson. *DA,* 280–401.

Jones, Douglas R. "A Fresh Interpretation of Zechariah IX–XI." *VT* 12 (1962): 241–59.

Ploeger, Otto. *Theocracy and Eschatology,* 78–96.

Treves, Marco. "Conjectures Concerning the Date and Authorship of Zechariah IX–XIV." *VT* 13 (1963): 196–207.

Daniel

Beasley-Murray, George R. "The Interpretation of Daniel 7." *CBQ* 45 (1983): 44–58.

Childs. *IOTS,* 608–23.

Collins, John J. *The Apocalyptic Vision of the Book of Daniel.* HSM 16. Missoula, Mont.: Scholars Press, 1977.

_____. "The Son of Man and the Saints of the Most High in the Book of Daniel." *JBL* 93 (1974): 50–66.

Davies, Philip R. "Eschatology in the Book of Daniel." *JSOT* 17 (1980): 33–53.

DiLella, Alexander A. "Daniel." In IDBSup, 205–7.

Frost, Stanley B. "Daniel." In *IDB* 1: 761–69.

Gammie, John G. "The Classification, Stages of Growth, and Changing Intentions in the Book of Daniel." *JBL* 95 (1976): 191–204.

Ginsberg, Harold L. "Daniel, Book of." In *EJ* 5 (1971): cols. 1277–89.

Jones, Bruce W. "The Prayer in Daniel 9." *VT* 18 (1968): 488–93.

Moore, Michael S. "Resurrection and Immortality: Two Motifs Navigating Confluent Theological Streams in the Old Testament." *TZ* 39 (1983): 17–34.

Noth, Martin. "The Holy Ones of the Most High." In *The Laws in the Pentateuch and Other Studies,* 215–28.

_____. "The Understanding of History in Old Testament Apocalyptic." In *The Laws in the Pentateuch and Other Studies,* 194–214.

Ploeger, Otto. *Theocracy and Eschatology,* 10–25.

Porter, Paul A. *Metaphors and Monsters. A Literary-Critical Study of Daniel 7 and 8.* ConBOT 20. Lund: C. W. K. Gleerup, 1983.

Rowley, H. H. *Darius the Mede and the Four World Empires in the Book of Daniel.* 2d ed. Cardiff: University of Wales Press, 1959.

Zevit, Zioni. "The Structure and Individual Elements of Daniel 7." *ZAW* 80 (1968): 385–96.

CONCLUSION: THE INTERPLAY OF TEXT, CONCEPT, AND SETTING IN THE HEBREW BIBLE

Ackroyd, Peter R. "Continuity and Discontinuity: Rehabilitation and Authentication." In *Tradition and Theology in the Old Testament,* ed. D. A. Knight, 215–34. Philadelphia: Fortress Press, 1977.

Albrektson, Bertil. *History and the Gods. An Essay on the Idea of Historical Events as Divine Manifestations in the Ancient Near East and in Israel.* ConBOT 1. Lund: C. W. K. Gleerup, 1967.

Altizer, Thomas J. *Total Presence: The Language of Jesus and the Language of Today.* New York: Seabury Press, 1980.

Barr, James. "The Multiplex Nature of the Old Testament Tradition." In *Old and New in Interpretation,* 15–33. London: SCM Press, 1966.

Barton, John. "Understanding Old Testament Ethics." *JSOT* 9 (1978): 44–64.

Belo, Fernando. "The Symbolic Order of Ancient Israel." In *A Materialist Reading of the Gospel of Mark,* 37–59. Maryknoll, N.Y.: Orbis Books, 1981.

Birch, Bruce C., and Larry L. Rasmussen. *Bible and Ethics in the Christian Life.* Minneapolis: Augsburg Publishing House, 1976.

Brandon, S. G. F. "The Propaganda Factor in Some Ancient Near Eastern Cosmogonies." In *Promise and Fulfillment. Essays Presented to Prof. S. H. Hooke,* ed. F. F. Bruce, 20–35. Edinburgh: T. & T. Clark, 1963.

Brueggemann, Walter. *The Prophetic Imagination.* Philadelphia: Fortress Press, 1978.

———. "Trajectories in Old Testament Literature and the Sociology of Ancient Israel." In *BL,* 307–33.

Childs. *IOTS.*

Cobb, John B., Jr. "Trajectories and Historic Routes." *Semeia* 24 (1982): 89–98.

Cross. *CMHE.*

Crossan, John Dominic. "Waking the Bible. Biblical Hermeneutic and Literary Imagination." *Int* 32 (1978): 269–85.

Eagleton, Terry. *Criticism and Ideology. A Study in Marxist Literary Theory.* London: Verso Editions, 1978; distributed in U.S.A. by Schocken Books.

Fierro, Alfredo. *The Militant Gospel: A Critical Introduction to Political Theologies.* Maryknoll, N.Y.: Orbis Books, 1977.

Fromm, Erich. *You Shall Be as Gods. A Radical Interpretation of the Old Testament and Its Tradition.* New York: Holt, Rinehart & Winston, 1966.

Gadamer, Hans-Georg. *Truth and Method.* New York: Seabury Press, 1975.

Gilkey, Langdon B. "Cosmology, Ontology, and the Travail of Biblical Language." *JR* 41 (1961): 194–205.

Gottwald, Norman K. "The Theological Task After *The Tribes of Yahweh.*" In *BL,* 190–200.

———. *TY,* parts X–XI.

Hanson, Paul D. *The Diversity of Scripture. A Theological Interpretation.* OBT 11. Philadelphia: Fortress Press, 1982.

———. *Dynamic Transcendence.* Philadelphia: Fortress Press, 1978.

Hartshorne, Charles. *Omnipotence and Other Theological Mistakes.* Albany: State University of New York Press, 1984.

Innis, Harold A. *The Bias of Communication,* with introduction by Marshall McLuhan, 3–131. Toronto: University of Toronto Press, 1968.

Jeppesen, Knud, and Benedikt Otzen, eds. *The Productions of Time: Tradition History in Old Testament Scholarship.* Sheffield: Almond Press, 1984.

McGovern, Arthur F. *Marxism: An American Christian Perspective.* Maryknoll, N.Y.: Orbis Books, 1980.

Miskotte, Kornelis H. *When the Gods Are Silent*. New York and Evanston: Harper & Row, 1967.

Ogletree, Thomas W. *The Use of the Bible in Christian Ethics*. Philadelphia: Westminster Press, 1983.

Palmer, Richard E. *Hermeneutics. Interpretation Theory in Schleiermacher, Dilthey, Heidegger, and Gadamer*. Evanston, Ill.: Northwestern University Press, 1969.

Parsons, Talcott. "Two 'Seed-Bed' Societies: Israel and Greece." In *Societies. Evolutionary and Comparative Perspectives*, 95–108. Englewood Cliffs, N.J.: Prentice-Hall, 1966.

Pellauer, David. "Paul Ricoeur on the Specificity of Religious Language." *JR* 61 (1981): 264–84.

Pixley, George V. *God's Kingdom. A Guide for Biblical Study*. Maryknoll, N.Y.: Orbis Books, 1981.

Rivkin, Ellis. *The Shaping of Jewish History. A Radical New Interpretation*, 1–83. New York: Charles Scribner's Sons, 1971.

Robinson, James M., and Helmut Koester. *Trajectories Through Early Christianity*. Philadelphia: Fortress Press, 1971.

Schneidau, Herbert N. *Sacred Discontent. The Bible and Western Tradition*. Berkeley and Los Angeles: University of California Press, 1976.

Segundo, Juan Luis. *Liberation of Theology*. Maryknoll, N.Y.: Orbis Books, 1976.

Sheppard, Gerald T. "Canonization: Hearing the Voice of the Same God Through Historically Dissimilar Traditions." *Int* 37 (1982): 21–33.

Smith, Morton. "The Common Theology of the Ancient Near East." *JBL* 71 (1952): 135–47.

_____. *Palestinian Parties and Politics That Shaped the Old Testament*. New York and London: Columbia University Press, 1971.

Steck, Odil H. "Theological Streams of Tradition." In *Tradition and Theology in the Old Testament*, ed. D. A. Knight, 183–214. Philadelphia: Fortress Press, 1977.

Weber, Max. *Ancient Judaism*. Glencoe, Ill.: The Free Press, 1952.

B. Commentaries on Biblical Books

This list of commentaries on the biblical books is arranged according to the order of the books in English Bibles. Under each biblical book the commentaries are placed in chronological order from the oldest to the most recent. A superscript number after a date indicates the edition. Publishing data are given for commentaries not in series. Consult the list of abbreviations for identification of the commentary series.

GENESIS

J. Skinner. ICC. 1930.[2]
U. Cassuto. *A Commentary on the Book of Genesis.* Part I: Genesis 1—6:8; Part II: Genesis 6:9—11:32. 2 vols. Jerusalem: Magnes Press, 1961, 1964.[2]
E. A. Speiser. AB. 1964.
G. von Rad. OTL. Rev. ed. 1972.
B. Vawter. *On Genesis: A New Reading.* Garden City, N.Y.: Doubleday & Co., 1977.
R. Davidson. CNEB. 2 vols. 1973, 1979.
W. G. Plaut. "Genesis." In *The Torah. A Modern Commentary,* 3–318. New York: Union of American Hebrew Congregations, 1981.
Westermann, Claus. *Genesis 1–11. A Commentary.* Minneapolis: Augsburg Publishing House, 1984.
G. W. Coats. FOTL. 1984.

EXODUS

J. C. Rylaarsdam. IB. 1952.
M. Noth. OTL. 1962.
U. Cassuto. *A Commentary on the Book of Exodus.* Jerusalem: Magnes Press, 1967.
J. P. Hyatt. NCBC. 1971.
R. E. Clements. CNEB. 1972.
B. S. Childs. OTL. 1974.
W. G. Plaut. "Exodus." In *The Torah. A Modern Commentary,* 363–94.

LEVITICUS

N. Micklem. IB. 1953.
M. Noth. OTL. 1965.
N. H. Snaith. NCBC. 1967.
J. R. Porter. CNEB. 1976.
G. Wenham. NICOT. 1979.
B. J. Bamberger. "Leviticus." In *The Torah. A Modern Commentary,* 733–96.

NUMBERS

G. B. Gray. ICC. 1903.
J. Marsh. IB. 1953.

N. H. Snaith. NCBC. 1967.
M. Noth. OTL. 1968.
J. Sturdy. CNEB. 1976.
W. G. Plaut. "Numbers." In *The Torah. A Modern Commentary,* 1011–1250.

DEUTERONOMY

S. R. Driver. ICC. 1902.[3]
G. E. Wright. IB. 1953.
G. von Rad. OTL. 1966.
A. Phillips. CNEB. 1973.
P. C. Craigie. NICOT. 1976.
A. D. H. Mayes. NCBC. 1979.
W. G. Plaut. "Deuteronomy." In *The Torah. A Modern Commentary,* 1289–1588.

JOSHUA

J. Bright. IB. 1953.
J. Gray. NCBC. 1967.
J. A. Soggin. OTL. 1972.
J. M. Miller, and G. M. Tucker. CNEB. 1974.
M. Woudstra. NICOT. 1981.
R. G. Boling. AB. 1982.
E. J. Hamlin. ITC. 1984.

JUDGES

G. F. Moore. ICC. 1898.[2]
C. F. Burney. *The Book of Judges with Introduction and Notes.* London: Rivingtons, 1920[2]; reprinted with introduction by W. F. Albright. New York: Ktav Publishing, 1970.
J. M. Myers. IB. 1953.
J. Gray. NCBC. 1967.
J. D. Martin. CNEB. 1975.
R. G. Boling. AB. 1975.
J. A. Soggin. OTL. 1981.

RUTH

J. Gray. NCBC. 1967.
W. J. Fuerst. CNEB. 1975.
E. F. Campbell, Jr. AB. 1975.
J. M. Sasson. *Ruth: A New Translation with a Philological Commentary and a Formalist-Folklorist Interpretation.* Baltimore: Johns Hopkins University Press, 1979.
R. E. Murphy. FOTL. 1981.

SAMUEL

G. B. Caird. IB. 1953.
H. W. Hertzberg. OTL. 1964.
P. Ackroyd. CNEB. 2 vols. 1971, 1977.
P. K. McCarter, Jr. AB. 2 vols. 1980, 1984.

KINGS

J. Montgomery, and H. S. Gehman. ICC. 1951.
N. H. Snaith. IB. 1954.
J. Gray. OTL. 1970.[2]
J. Robinson. CNEB. 2 vols. 1972, 1976.
B. O. Long. *1 Kings*. FOTL. 1984.

CHRONICLES

W. A. L. Elmslie. IB. 1954.
J. M. Myers. AB. 2 vols. 1965.
R. J. Coggins. CNEB. 1976.
H. G. M. Williamson. NCBC. 1982.

EZRA-NEHEMIAH

R. A. Bowman. IB. 1954.
J. M. Myers. AB. 1965.
R. J. Coggins. CNEB. 1976.
F. C. Fensham. NICOT. 1982.

ESTHER

L. B. Paton. ICC. 1908.
B. W. Anderson. IB. 1954.
C. A. Moore. AB. 1971.
W. J. Fuerst. CNEB. 1975.
R. E. Murphy. FOTL. 1981.

JOB

S. R. Driver, and G. B. Gray. ICC. 1921.
E. Dhorme. *A Commentary on the Book of Job.* London: Thomas Nelson & Sons, 1967 (orig., 1926).
S. Terrien. IB. 1954.
H. H. Rowley. NCBC. 1970.
M. H. Pope. AB. 1974.[3]
N. C. Habel. CNEB. 1975.

R. Gordis. *The Book of Job: Commentary, New Translation and Special Studies.* New York: Ktav Publishing, 1978.

R. E. Murphy. FOTL. 1981.

PSALMS

W. O. E. Oesterley. *The Psalms Translated with Textcritical and Exegetical Notes.* 2 vols. London: SPCK, 1939.

A. Weiser. OTL. 1962.

M. J. Dahood. AB. 3 vols. 1966–70.

A. A. Anderson. NCBC. 2 vols. 1972.

J. W. Rogerson, and J. W. McKay. CNEB. 3 vols. 1977.

PROVERBS

W. O. E. Oesterley. WC. 1929.

C. T. Fritsch. IB. 1955.

R. B. Y. Scott. AB. 1965.

W. McKane. OTL. 1970.

R. N. Whybray. CNEB. 1972.

R. E. Murphy. FOTL. 1981.

ECCLESIASTES

G. A. Barton. ICC. 1908.

H. Odeberg. *Qohaeleth. A Commentary on the Book of Ecclesiastes.* Uppsala: Almquist & Wiksell, 1929.

O. S. Rankin. IB. 1956.

R. B. Y. Scott. AB. 1965.

R. Gordis. *Koheleth—The Man and His World.* New York: Schocken Books, 1968.[3]

W. J. Fuerst. CNEB. 1975.

R. E. Murphy. FOTL. 1981.

SONG OF SONGS

T. J. Meek. IB. 1956.

R. Gordis. *The Song of Songs and Lamentations: A Study, Modern Translation and Commentary.* New York: Ktav Publishing, 1974.[2]

W. J. Fuerst. CNEB. 1975.

M. H. Pope. AB. 1977.

R. E. Murphy. FOTL. 1981.

ISAIAH

Chaps. 1—66

G. A. Smith. ExB. 2 vols. 1927.[2]

E. J. Kissane. *The Book of Isaiah Translated from a Critically Revised Hebrew Text with Commentary.* Vol. 1, 1960²; vol. 2, 1943. Dublin: Browne & Nolan.
E. J. Young. NICOT. 3 vols. 1965–72.

Chaps. 1—39

G. B. Gray. ICC. (Chaps. 1—27.) 1912.
R. B. Y. Scott. IB. 1956.
O. Kaiser. OTL. 2 vols. Vol. 1, 1983²; vol. 2, 1974.
R. E. Clements. NCBC. 1981.

Chaps. 40—66

J. Muilenburg. IB. 1956.
C. R. North. *The Second Isaiah. Introduction, Translation and Commentary to Chaps XL–LV.* Oxford: At the Clarendon Press, 1964.
J. D. Smart. *History and Theology in Second Isaiah. A Commentary on Isaiah 35, 40–66.* Philadelphia: Westminster Press, 1965.
J. L. McKenzie. AB. 1968.
C. Westermann. OTL. 1969.
R. N. Whybray. NCBC. 1975.

JEREMIAH

J. P. Hyatt. IB. 1956.
J. Bright. AB. 1965.
E. W. Nicholson. CNEB. 2 vols. 1973, 1975.
J. A. Thompson. NICOT. 1980.

LAMENTATIONS

T. J. Meek. IB. 1956.
D. R. Hillers. AB. 1972.
R. Gordis. *The Song of Songs and Lamentations: A Study, Modern Translation and Commentary.* New York: Ktav Publishing, 1974.²
W. J. Fuerst. CNEB. 1975.

EZEKIEL

G. A. Cooke. ICC. 1936.
H. G. May. IB. 1955.
J. W. Wevers. NCBC. 1969.
W. Eichrodt. OTL. 1970.
W. Zimmerli. Hermeneia. 2 vols. Philadelphia: Fortress Press, 1979, 1983.
M. Greenberg. AB. (Chaps. 1—20.) 1983.

DANIEL

J. A. Montgomery. ICC. 1927.

R. H. Charles. *A Critical and Exegetical Commentary on the Book of Daniel.* Oxford: At the Clarendon Press, 1929.
A. Jeffery. IB. 1956.
R. Hammer. CNEB. 1976.
L. F. Hartman, and A. A. Di Lella. AB. 1978.
A. Lacocque. *The Book of Daniel.* Atlanta: John Knox Press, 1979.
N. W. Porteous. OTL. 1979.[2]
R. A. Anderson. ITC. 1984.

HOSEA

W. R. Harper. ICC. 1905.
J. Mauchline. IB. 1956.
J. Ward. *Hosea: A Theological Commentary.* New York: Harper & Row, 1966.
J. L. Mays. OTL. 1969.
H. W. Wolff. Hermeneia. Philadelphia: Fortress Press, 1974.
F. I. Andersen, and D. N. Freedman. AB. 1980.

JOEL

J. Bewer. ICC. 1911.
J. A. Thompson. IB. 1956.
J. D. W. Watts. CNEB. 1975.
L. C. Allen. NICOT. 1976.
H. W. Wolff. Hermeneia. Philadelphia: Fortress Press, 1977.

AMOS

W. R. Harper. ICC. 1905.
R. S. Cripps. *A Critical and Exegetical Commentary on the Book of Amos.* London: SPCK, 1955.[2]
H. E. W. Fosbroke. IB. 1956.
J. L. Mays. OTL. 1969.
E. Hammershaimb. *The Book of Amos: A Commentary.* Oxford: At the Clarendon Press, 1970.
H. W. Wolff. Hermeneia. Philadelphia: Fortress Press, 1977.

OBADIAH

J. A. Bewer. ICC. 1911.
J. A. Thompson. IB. 1956.
J. D. W. Watts. *Obadiah: A Critical Exegetical Commentary.* Grand Rapids: Wm. B. Eerdmans, 1969.
L. C. Allen. NICOT. 1976.

JONAH

J. A. Bewer. ICC. 1911.
J. D. Smart. IB. 1956.
J. D. W. Watts. CNEB. 1975.
L. C. Allen. NICOT. 1976.

MICAH

J. M. P. Smith. ICC. 1911.
R. E. Wolfe. IB. 1956.
J. M. Mays. OTL. 1976.
L. C. Allen. NICOT. 1976.
D. R. Hillers. Hermeneia. Philadelphia: Fortress Press, 1984.

NAHUM

J. M. P. Smith. ICC. 1911.
W. A. Maier. *The Book of Nahum, A Commentary.* St. Louis: Concordia Publishing House, 1959.
J. D. W. Watts. CNEB. 1975.

HABAKKUK

W. H. Ward. ICC. 1911.
C. L. Taylor, Jr. IB. 1956.
J. D. W. Watts. CNEB. 1975.

ZEPHANIAH

J. M. P. Smith. ICC. 1911.
C. L. Taylor, Jr. IB. 1956.
J. D. W. Watts. CNEB. 1975.

HAGGAI

H. G. Mitchell. ICC. 1912.
D. Winton Thomas. IB. 1956.
R. A. Mason. CNEB. 1977.

ZECHARIAH

H. G. Mitchell. ICC. 1912.
D. Winton Thomas. IB. (Chaps. 1—8.) 1956.
R. C. Dentan. IB. (Chaps. 9—14.) 1956.
M. F. Unger. *Zechariah.* Grand Rapids: Zondervan, 1963.
R. A. Mason. CNEB. 1977.

MALACHI

J. M. P. Smith. ICC. 1912.
R. C. Dentan. IB. 1956.
R. A. Mason. CNEB. 1977.

INDEX

Page references to definitions or key explanations of terms appear in boldface type. Page references to maps, tables, and charts are indicated by italics. (There are two maps on p. 291. Therefore, *291L* refers to the left-hand map; *291R* to the right-hand map; and *291* to both maps.)

14